T0304315

This collection of essays is the first full account of the largest estate in early modern England, against which the fortunes of all other estates may be judged. Previous accounts have tended to regard the Crown lands as a resource to be plundered by successive monarchs in times of need: much of the monastic land confiscated by Henry VIII had been sold by the time of his death, and the estates had mostly been liquidated to meet the demands of expenditure by 1640.

It is not denied in these essays that the estates suffered from the attrition of periodic sale, but the estates are here seen as a continuing enterprise of complexity and sophistication. The volume looks sympathetically at the problems of administering estates quite different in scale to any others in England, and attempts to show how what has often been seen as weak management on the Elizabethan estates was a reasonable response to insurmountable difficulties. What emerges more generally is a sense not only of endeavour but also of failure. Each essay is concerned with the dialogue between the Exchequer and its local administrators and tenants. The success and failure of initiatives launched by the Exchequer is illustrated by examples drawn from many communities throughout England. The essays draw on a wide range of sources to explain why the estates could never satisfy the demands placed on them and how the problems of tenurial reform identified here were far from unique.

THE ESTATES OF THE ENGLISH CROWN,
1558–1640

THE ESTATES OF THE
ENGLISH CROWN, 1558–1640

EDITED BY

R. W. HOYLE

CAMBRIDGE
UNIVERSITY PRESS

CAMBRIDGE UNIVERSITY PRESS
Cambridge, New York, Melbourne, Madrid, Cape Town, Singapore, São Paulo

Cambridge University Press
The Edinburgh Building, Cambridge CB2 8RU, UK

Published in the United States of America by Cambridge University Press, New York

www.cambridge.org
Information on this title: www.cambridge.org/9780521360821

First published 1992
First paperback edition 2002

A catalogue record for this publication is available from the British Library

Library of Congress Cataloguing in Publication data
The Estates of the English Crown, 1558–1640 / edited by R. W. Hoyle.
p.   cm.
Includes bibliographical references and index.
ISBN 0 521 36082 X (hardback)
1. Crown lands – England – History.   I. Hoyle, R. W.
HD604.E88   1992
333.1′0942–dc20   91-34372   CIP

ISBN 978-0-521-36082-1 hardback
ISBN 978-0-521-52651-7 paperback

Transferred to digital printing 2008

Contents

Tables

Contributors

DR MADELEINE GRAY is a part-time tutor in the extra-mural department at the University of Wales College of Cardiff and a freelance lecturer and researcher.

DR GRAHAM HASLAM was formerly archivist to the Duchy of Cornwall and is now a member of the staff of the Yale Center for Parliamentary History

DR RICHARD HOYLE is a British Academy Research Fellow at Magdalen College, Oxford.

DR PETER LARGE is Managing Director of Corporate Finance at Swiss Bank Corporation Investment Banking.

DR JOAN THIRSK was Reader in Economic History at the University of Oxford until her retirement.

DR DAVID THOMAS is an assistant keeper at the Public Record Office.

Acknowledgements

The Crown lands have not been well served by historians. The lack of any study of the estates in the eighty or so years between the accession of Elizabeth I and the first meeting of the Long Parliament may seem to be an obvious gap in the literature on the period, but no more so than the absence of any account of the management of the medieval estates. Having come to the subject more or less by accident, I soon realised that it was too large a void to be filled by any single author working alone. The materials are not only scattered – I, for one, am resigned to discovering pertinent materials for the rest of my professional life – but also voluminous. The idea that a collective history of the estates might be the appropriate way to proceed only became practicable as the result of a chance meeting with Graham Haslam. I am deeply grateful to him and all the other contributors for making this volume the vehicle in which their researches might appear. And whilst I have learnt a considerable amount from my colleagues in this enterprise, it should be added that we do not in any sense constitute a school or party. The volume does not pretend to be comprehensive or to offer a final word on the subject; nor is it a local history of the estates (although it discusses the history of many places, sometimes at length, in order to generalise about the whole).

All the contributors would wish to thank many individuals, often unknown to us, for producing documents in the PRO and British Library. Amongst my own debts, I am grateful to Mr Donald Gibson at the Kent Archives Office for making Lionel Cranfield's papers available whilst under rearrangement. In Oxford, Susan Burdell and her staff in the History Faculty Library agreed to lend me everything I asked. Ruth Fisher, Maddy Gray and Marjorie McIntosh lent me copies of unpublished papers. Gerald Aylmer put me on to the minutes of the 1626 commissioners in London. An early version of chapter 12 was read to the Spring conference of the British Agricultural History Society in 1990: Bruce Campbell raised a point afterwards which served to clarify much of my thinking. The book was conceived whilst I was at Magdalen College, Oxford, put to one side during my two years at Bristol and finally completed, late (but the delay was perhaps beneficial), back at Magdalen. I am grateful to the British Academy for the award of a fellowship which made possible its completion. Other debts, of a more domestic nature, can be neither forgotten nor repaid, but Gill, like me, will be glad to see the end of the Crown lands.

RWH
March 1992

Abbreviations

Agrarian History, IV	J. Thirsk (ed.), *The Agrarian History of England and Wales*, IV, *1540–1640* (Cambridge, 1967)
APC	*Acts of the Privy Council*
BIHR	*Bulletin of the Institute of Historical Research*
BL	British Library, London
Bodl.	Bodleian Library, Oxford
CJ	*Journals of the House of Commons*
CPR	*Calendar of Patent Rolls*
CSPD	*Calendar of State Papers Domestic*
DCO	Duchy of Cornwall Office, 10 Buckingham Gate, London, SW1E 6LA
Dietz, *English Public Finance*	F. C. Dietz, *English Public Finance, 1559–1641* (New York, 1932)
Dietz, *Receipts and Issues*	F. C. Dietz, *The Receipts and Issues of the Exchequer during the Reigns of James I and Charles I* (Smith College Studies in History, Northampton, MA, XIII (4), 1928)
DNB	*Dictionary of National Biography*
EcHR	*Economic History Review* (second ser., 1948–)
EHR	*English Historical Review*
HJ	*Historical Journal*
HMC	Historical Manuscripts Commission reports
HP 1558–1603	P. W. Hasler (ed.), *The History of*

xiii

	Parliament. *The Commons, 1558–1603* (3 vols., London, 1982)
JBS	*Journal of British Studies*
Johnson, *Letter*	Letter of Sir Robert Johnson to James I on the condition of the Crown lands, 24 March 1602 (described below)
Kent AO, U269/1, OE (with number)	Kent Archives Office, Sackville MSS, official papers of Lionel Cranfield, earl of Middlesex, as Lord Treasurer
LJ	*Journals of the House of Lords*
NLW	National Library of Wales, Aberystwyth
Pettit, *Royal Forests*	P. A. J. Pettit, *The Royal Forests of Northamptonshire. A Study in their Economy* (Northamptonshire RS 23, 1968)
Prestwich, *Cranfield*	M. Prestwich, *Cranfield. Politics and Profits under the Early Stuarts* (Oxford, 1966)
Richardson, *1552 Report*	W. C. Richardson (ed.), *The Report of the Royal Commission of 1552* (Morgantown, WV, 1974)
RO	Record Office
RS	Record Series
St John, *Observations*	J. St John, *Observations on the Land Revenue* (London, 1787)
Sharp, *In Contempt*	Buchanan Sharp, *In Contempt of All Authority. Rural Artisans and Riot in the West of England, 1586–1660* (Berkeley, CA, 1980)
Somerville, *Duchy of Lancaster*	Sir Robert Somerville, *History of the Duchy of Lancaster* (2 vols., priv. pub., 1953, 1970)
Spedding, *Bacon*	J. Spedding (ed.), *The Letters and Life of Francis Bacon* (7 vols., London, 1861–74).
SR	*Statutes of the Realm*

Stuart Royal Procs.	*Stuart Royal Proclamations*, ed. P. L. Hughes and J. F. Larkin (2 vols., Oxford, 1973, 1983)
Tawney, *Business and Politics*	R. H. Tawney, *Business and Politics under James I. Lionel Cranfield as Merchant and Minister* (Cambridge, 1958)
Thomas, 'Administration of crown lands'	D. L. Thomas, 'The administration of crown lands in Lincolnshire under Elizabeth I' (University of London, PhD thesis, 1979)
TRHS	*Transactions of the Royal Historical Society*
VCH	Victoria County History
Vernon, *Considerations*	Christopher Vernon, *Considerations for Regulating the Exchequer* (London, 1642)
WHR	*Welsh Historical Review*

All documents are in the Public Record Office, London, unless otherwise stated. A list of the PRO classes cited follows.

The spelling of quotations from manuscript sources has been modernised.

Sir Robert Johnson's letter to James I of May 1603 conflated letters sent earlier to Sir Robert Cecil (later earl of Salisbury). One of these letters survives in autograph (SP12/283A, fols. 167r–72v). Johnson's draft of the whole letter survives amongst Caesar's papers (CRES40/18, fols. 158r–79v). Copies of the whole letter may also be found in BL, Add. MS 41613, fols. 92v–111v, and Bodl., MS Perrot 7, fols. 49r–86v. There are small variants between the various texts. R. W. Hoyle has an edition of the letter and Johnson's other writings in preparation. As the text to be published will be based on the Bodleian copy, references have been standardised to that source.

Public Record Office classes cited

Chancery
C2	Chancery Proceedings, series I
C54	Close Rolls
C65	Parliament Rolls
C66	Patent Rolls
C142	Inquisitions Post Mortem, series II
C205	Special Commissions (Petty Bag Office)

CRES40	Crown Estates Commissioners, Miscellaneous Books

Duchy of Lancaster
DL1	Equitable Pleadings
DL4	Depositions and Examinations
DL5	Entry Books of Decrees and Orders
DL6	Draft Decrees
DL28	Accounts (Various)
DL30	Court Rolls
DL41	Miscellanea
DL42	Miscellaneous Books
DL44	Special Commissions and Returns

Exchequer
E101	King's Remembrancer, Accounts (various)
E112	King's Remembrancer, Bills, answers
E123–5	King's Remembrancer, Entry Books of decrees and orders, series I–IV
E134	King's Remembrancer, Depositions Taken by Commission
E159	King's Remembrancer, Memoranda Rolls
E163	Miscellanea of the Exchequer

E164	Miscellaneous Books, series 1
E178	Special Commissions of Inquiry
E306	Augmentation Office, Duchy of Cornwall Records
E310	Augmentation Office, Particulars for Leases
E311	Augmentation Office, Counterparts and Transcripts of Leases
E315	Augmentation Office, Miscellaneous Books
E317	Augmentation Office, Parliamentary Surveys
E318	Augmentation Office, Particulars for Grants of Crown Lands
E351	Pipe Office Declared Accounts
E368	Lord Treasurer's Remembrancer, Memoranda Rolls
E401	Lord Treasurer's Remembrancer, Enrolments and Registers of Receipts
E403	Lord Treasurer's Remembrancer, Enrolments and Registers of Issues

Land Revenue

LR1	Enrolment Books
LR2	Miscellaneous Books
LR3	Court Rolls
LR9	Auditors' Memoranda
LR17	Surveyor-Generals of Land Revenue: Papers

PC2	Privy Council Registers
PRO30/24	Shaftesbury Papers
PROB11	Prerogative Court of Canterbury, Registered Copy Wills

Special Collections

SC2	Court Rolls
SC6	Ministers' and Receivers' Accounts
SC11	Rentals and Surveys (rolls)
SC12	Rentals and Surveys (in portfolios)

State Papers

SP12	State Papers Elizabeth
SP14	State Papers James I
SP16	State Papers Charles I

SP38   Docquets
SP46   State Papers Supplementary
SP59   Border Papers

STAC8   Star Chamber Pleadings, James I

CHAPTER I

Introduction: aspects of the Crown's estate, c. 1558–1640

Richard Hoyle

The Crown lands stand at the cross-roads where the study of estate management and the profitability of land meets that of public finance and the income and solvency of the state. Throughout the early modern period (and despite their progressive diminution) the Crown's estates were the biggest and most widely scattered of all English estates. Their management constitutes the standard against which all other estates ought to be judged. They were much more than a source of rental income, but formed an important part of the Crown's armoury of patronage and rewards. Given that they served to confer status on a considerable number of stewards and bailiffs whose activities were supervised by the Lord Treasurer and the itinerant auditors of the land revenue, the estates can be claimed to be another (to use an overworked notion) 'point of contact' between Westminster and the provinces.[1] There was, of course, a tension between the estates as a source of revenue and their role as a source of patronage. But because they served that patronage purpose, the management of the estates was not a private matter between the Crown and its tenants but a highly public one which concerned the society of provincial England as a whole. And the success with which the estates were run bears directly on the financial history of the English state. The estates still contributed a sizeable proportion of income; conversely, shortfalls in overall income were met by the progressive liquidation of the estates.

If a history of the Crown lands belongs to both fiscal and agrarian history, then it falls between two areas of scholarship which have not been well served in recent years. There are remarkably few recent studies of estates in the century following the dissolution of the monasteries (as opposed to studies of rural communities) and the

---

[1] The phrase is Professor Elton's; see his papers in *TRHS* fifth ser., 24–6 (1974–6).

most recent overviews of secular estate management, by Stone in his
Crisis of the Aristocracy and various hands in the fourth volume of the
Agrarian History, are now a quarter-century old.[2] Public finance has
fared even worse. For a comprehensive survey one needs to turn to
the monograph by Dietz, published as long ago as 1932.[3] Dr
Thomas's short essay is the only recent attempt to assess the financial
strength of the Crown and the problems of raising levels of income
and controlling expenditure.[4] Sixteenth-century financial history has
been diverted into the study of financial and accounting institutions
which, whilst valuable, is interesting only in so far as it edges us
towards a fuller understanding of how the Crown managed its
money.[5] Early seventeenth-century financial history has become an
adjunct to debates over the role of Parliament.

For previous accounts of the Crown lands, the historian must turn
to a short pamphlet by Professor Pugh, the relevant chapter of Dietz's
English Public Finance or the overview of developments on the Crown
estates by Professor Batho in the *Agrarian History*.[6] The particular
contribution of post-war historians to the study of the Crown lands
has been their elucidation of the work of the commissions of sale to
which the Crown resorted intermittently throughout the sixteenth
century and the consequences of sale upon landholding.[7] But this has

[2] L. Stone, *The Crisis of the Aristocracy, 1558–1641* (Oxford, 1965), ch. 6; G. Batho and
J. Youings, in *Agrarian History*, IV, ch. 5.   [3] Dietz, *English Public Finance*.
[4] D. L. Thomas, 'Financial and administrative developments', in H. Tomlinson (ed.), *Before
the English Civil War* (Basingstoke, 1983). But see now C. Russell, *The Causes of the English Civil
War* (Oxford, 1990), ch. 7.
[5] C. Coleman, 'Artifice or accident? The reorganization of the Exchequer of Receipt,
c. 1554–1572', in C. Coleman and D. Starkey (eds.), *Revolution Reassessed. Revisions in the
History of Tudor Government and Administration* (Oxford, 1986), can represent this school of
scholarship.
[6] R. B. Pugh, *The Crown Estates. An Historical Study* (London, 1960). Of Batho it was said in the
commentary which accompanied the republication of his article in 1990, 'Professor Batho's
treatment of the Crown Estate provides a survey which is not simply useful, but
indispensable in the absence of any comparable treatment elsewhere in the literature' (C.
Clay in C. Clay (ed.), *Rural Society. Landowners, Peasants and Labourers 1500–1750* (Cambridge,
1990)). It could not be claimed that the medieval estates have fared better. Professor
Wolffe's studies (*The Crown Lands, 1461–1536. An Aspect of Yorkist and Early Tudor Government*
(London, 1970) and *The Royal Demesne in English History. The Crown Estate in the Governance of
the Realm from the Conquest to 1509* (London, 1971)) are predominantly institutional. No one
has attempted to discuss such matters as the accumulation and dispersal of estates, the level
of rents and fines, the terms of the leases and the Crown's involvement in demesne agriculture. There is, though, C. R. Young, *The Royal Forest in Medieval England* (Leicester, 1979),
and R. C. Stacey, 'Agricultural investment and the management of the royal demesne
manors, 1236–1240', *Journal of Economic History* 46 (1986), shows what might be possible.
[7] H. J. Habakkuk, 'The market for monastic property, 1539–1603', *EcHR* 10 (1957–8);
R. B. Outhwaite, 'The price of crown land at the turn of the sixteenth century', *EcHR*
20 (1967); *idem*, 'Who bought crown lands? The pattern of purchases, 1589–1603', *BIHR* 44
(1971). Chantry lands are dealt with by C. J. Kitching, 'The disposal of monastic and

produced the less than desirable consequence that the Crown lands have come to be seen as an asset awaiting liquidation in times of emergency – a larger and less convenient equivalent of plate or bullion – rather than an estate with its own aims and momentum which sales served to interrupt. The assumption prevails in the literature that possession by the Crown was merely a period of waiting of longer or shorter duration before the manor was sold. It is in this spirit that the *Victoria County History* rarely indexes the fact that a manor belonged to the Crown either under the name of a monarch or some general heading (Crown lands, Exchequer). Some historians have produced studies of Crown manors without acknowledging the fact (or potential significance) of their ownership. The segmentation of the history of the Crown estates into the history of individual manors is unfortunate enough, but more regrettable still when local historians concerned with a Crown manor have failed to appreciate the documentary advantages which possession by the Crown brings.[8] In other respects, the existing literature on the estates is deficient. The houses of the Tudor and Stuart monarchs have been meticulously studied,[9] but no one has thought to place these in the context of the estates in which they stood, so we lack studies of the town and honour of Windsor and the enparking and remodelling of the landscape undertaken by Henry VIII and James I at such places as Nonsuch, Grafton and Theobalds.

The literature is not without its glories. Sir Robert Somerville's two-volume history of the Duchy of Lancaster is an enduring achievement of scholarship.[10] Dr Pettit's history of the Crown forests

chantry lands', in F. Heal and R. O'Day (eds.), *Church and Society in England, Henry VIII to James I* (London, 1977). For the local consequences of the sale of Crown lands, see the recent contributions to the genre by M. Zell, 'The mid-Tudor market in crown land in Kent', *Archaeologia Cantiana* 97 (1981); G. Woodward, 'The disposal of chantry lands in Somerset', *Southern History* 5 (1983); and M. Gray, 'Crown property and the land market in South-East Wales in the sixteenth century', *Agricultural History Review* 35 (1987). The seventeenth-century sale of Crown lands remains largely uninvestigated, but see below, pp. 23–9.

[8] VCH, *Cambridgeshire*, IX (1989) indexes 'Crown, ecclesiastical patronage of' but contains no index heading for the estates. Happily, no such criticism could be levied against VCH, *Oxfordshire*, XII (1990). Ravensdale tells us that his manor of Waterbeach cum Denny was a Crown manor only in mentioning that it was sold in 1614. J. R. Ravensdale, *Liable to Floods. Village Landscape on the Edge of the Fens, AD 450–1850* (Cambridge, 1974), p. 165. Margaret Spufford acknowledges the fact of Crown ownership of Orwell (Cambs.) throughout the sixteenth century until its sale in 1627 but draws no conclusions as to the significance of the fact. M. Spufford, *Contrasting Communities. English Villagers in the Sixteenth and Seventeenth Centuries* (Cambridge, 1974), pp. 94–5. For a regional study written in full consciousness of the potential importance of Crown ownership, J. T. Swain, *Industry before the Industrial Revolution. North-East Lancashire, c. 1500–1640* (Chetham Soc., third ser., 32, 1986), esp. ch. 4.

[9] H. M. Colvin (ed.), *The History of the King's Works*, III (London, 1975), IV (London, 1982).

[10] Somerville, *Duchy of Lancaster*.

of Northamptonshire, though ostensibly a local history, provides a thorough study of forest administration which may be read with Dr Hammersley's pioneering work on woodland management and exploitation.[11] But the serious study of the Crown lands in their own right can only be said to have begun with the doctoral theses of G. D. Haslam, D. L. Thomas and K. H. S. Wyndham undertaken in the 1970s.[12]

This volume will not deny that the Crown lands were a diminishing asset, reduced by financial exigency, but it will not make that fact the central feature of the work. Instead, it will consider the Crown lands as a continuing enterprise of fearsome complexity (but also administrative sophistication) to which men devoted their careers and which, like any other early modern estate, was managed to a range of ends of which fiscal profit was only one. There remain some areas of importance which are not the subject of chapters in the book. With the notable exception of Dr Gray's second contribution, there is little on the power and influence which office-holding on the estates conferred, nor on the Crown's parliamentary patronage. Neither is there a sustained account of the Duchy of Lancaster (although the existence of Somerville's work may offer an excuse for that particular omission). The book contains no study of the Crown as the owner of urban property, nor of its forests and parks, and most regrettably the chapters presented here stop short of considering the experience of the Crown lands during the dislocation of the Civil War.[13] It would not be our claim to have covered every aspect of the estates or to have solved every problem, but to have made and justified a bold claim for the interest of the Crown lands.

[11] Pettit, *Royal Forests*; G. Hammersley, 'The revival of forest laws under Charles I', *History* 45 (1960); *idem*, 'The crown woods and their exploitation in the sixteenth and seventeenth centuries', *BIHR* 30 (1957).

[12] G. D. Haslam, 'An administrative study of the Duchy of Cornwall, 1500–1650' (Louisiana State University, PhD thesis, 1975), and his contributions to C. Gill (ed.), *The Duchy of Cornwall* (Newton Abbot, 1987); Thomas, 'Administration of crown lands'; K. H. S. Wyndham, 'The redistribution of crown land in Somerset by gift, sale and lease, 1536–72' (University of London, PhD thesis, 1976), and her articles, 'The royal estate in mid-sixteenth-century Somerset', *BIHR* 52 (1979), and 'Crown land and royal patronage in mid-sixteenth century England', *JBS* 19 (1979–80).

[13] As a matter of deliberate policy the profits of the Crown's feudal rights of wardship are not treated in the present volume contrary to the practice of both Dietz and Batho.

I

As a landowner, the Crown possessed every sort and type of landed property known to sixteenth- and seventeenth-century society. Much of its estates consisted of unexceptional leaseholds and copyholds of rural and urban tenements. Like other conservative landowners, it still possessed serfs in the sixteenth century which it sought to manumise for profit.[14] It was a feudal landlord with the right to take wardship from its military tenants; but many private landlords did likewise. Like most other landlords of status, it devoted a proportion of its land to unproductive ends for recreation, maintaining parks and forests.

The Crown is to be distinguished from all other English landlords in three respects. The first is simply that of scale. No other estate was so large, scattered or unsystematic in its contents. Simple considerations of size made it impossible for it to be supervised by its owner and his senior administrators; scale forced delegation and this in turn permitted the possibility of peculation and corruption by local officers. Given the size of the estates, it was inevitable that the Crown should, through either administrative error or deliberate concealment, sometimes lose sight of lands which properly belonged to it. The steps taken to overcome these problems feature prominently in the following pages.

Secondly, the Crown's estate had a privileged legal position. It was managed by bodies constituted as courts which could act judicially to punish their officers or try cases concerning the possession of their lands. These judicial rights were used to the Crown's advantage to establish a claim over land which was 'empty' (such as fenland) or in which the Crown claimed a residual right of ownership, such as forests and assart lands. The use of judicial process to enlarge the Crown's lands by proving the deficiency of the occupier's title was a characteristic of the early seventeenth century and is considered at length below by Joan Thirsk.

The third respect in which the Crown differed from other landowners was in the wide range of other sources of income it possessed and the relative unimportance of estate revenue in the whole. At the turn of the sixteenth century the income drawn from the lands was about 39 per cent of the Crown's total income, about

---

[14] D. MacCulloch, 'Bondmen under the Tudors', in C. Cross, D. Loades and J. J. Scarisbrich (eds.), *Law and Government under the Tudors* (Cambridge, 1988), pp. 107–8.

14 per cent *c.* 1641.[15] Landed income was fairly reliable; it was not, for instance, prone to the sudden downturns from which customs revenue occasionally suffered, but it was also inflexible and incapable of rapid increase. It may be helpful to bear in mind the transformation in customs revenue brought about by the revision of the book of rates in 1607 with the rather pitiful achievements of the prolonged contemporaneous attempts to reform the Crown lands described in chapter 9 below. Lord Treasurers, Chancellors of the Exchequer and (later) Treasury Commissioners had responsibility for all founts of revenue and it would not be too surprising to find that the Crown lands were often overlooked by them in favour of more promising areas in which recurrent income could be more easily raised.

In a very real sense, it is mistaken to talk of the Crown lands or the Crown's estate as though it consisted of one unit. The lands were in fact under the control of a number of institutions, all with their own officers, courts and procedures, but not all of which had a continuity of existence. The first and most important was the Exchequer, headed by the Lord Treasurer. Its form throughout our period was the result of the merger into the Exchequer of the Court of Augmentations in 1554. From this date, the Exchequer had three historically distinct groups of estates under its supervision.

The oldest (and most obscure) were the lands under the charge of the sheriffs, the so-called custody lands. The income from these lands (which included the fee-farms of towns as well as the rents of lands) was paid to the Clerk of the Pipe and never passed through the hands of the Exchequer's auditors of land revenue. Even contemporaries were uncertain as to their nature. Sir Walter Cope, in his apology for Salisbury said that the late Lord Treasurer had found them to be 'a revenue which seemeth decayed by descent of time and worn out of all knowledge and remembrance'. As a good hagiographer, Cope naturally claimed that Salisbury had revived many of these revenues, but in 1642 the Exchequer man Christopher Vernon wrote that a good number of them were very hard to levy and were likely to be

---

[15] Figure for *c.* 1600 calculated from the table in W. R. Scott, *The Constitution and Finance of English, Scottish and Irish Joint-Stock Companies to 1720* (3 vols., Cambridge, 1910–12, repr. 1951), III, p. 517 (printing an abstract of BL, Cotton MS Titus B IV, fols. 285v–93v); that for *c.* 1641 calculated from C. Russell, 'Charles I's financial estimates for 1642', *BIHR* 58 (1985), pp. 109–20.

lost.[16] As table 1.1 shows, the income from these lands never exceeded £15,000 per annum.[17]

The second and third groups of estates were all lands which had been under the control of the Court of Augmentations and, in the phrase used by Elizabethan administrators, had been 'annexed' to the Exchequer. The revenue of these lands was collected by the county receivers under the supervision of the seven auditors of land revenue. The first of these groups of estates were those of private landlords, like the Duchy of York, which had accrued to the Crown over time by marriage or inheritance. These estates had no separate administrative existence except as units within the accounts of the Exchequer.[18] The second component was the remaining monastic and chantry lands which had augmented the core estate of the Crown during the decade or so after 1536.

The other landholding agency was the only noble estate which had become subsumed in the Crown and preserved its administrative identity, the Duchy of Lancaster. The Duchy had its own staff and officers under the Duchy Chancellor and despite the suggestions made in the 1550s and again in 1617 that it should be merged into the Exchequer as a cost cutting measure, the institutional continuity of the Duchy has been preserved through to the present day.[19]

No such claim can be made for the estates assigned to the Prince of Wales, the Duchy of Cornwall and the principality of Wales. In the absence of a prince, his estates were placed in the charge of the Exchequer. Whilst the Henrician arrangements for Wales were clearly designed to be unscrambled in the appropriate circumstances,[20] the lack of a figurehead gave neither politicians nor administrators cause to regard the interests of the Duchy and, as Dr Haslam describes, it was largely (and illegally) sold during the late Elizabethan land sales. Haslam goes on to show how the Duchy was reconstructed for Henry Prince of Wales in the first years of James's reign and then reestablished for Prince Charles. On his accession to

---

[16] Sir Walter Cope, 'An apology for the late Lord Treasurer, Sir Robert Cecil, earl of Salisbury', in J. Gutch (ed.), *Collectanea Curiosa* (2 vols., Oxford, 1781), I, p. 123; Vernon, *Considerations*, p. 58. I owe these to Dr Thomas.

[17] This is an exaggeration; the figures given there include the income from Ulnage (the tax on cloth) which cannot always be separated out from land income. Ulnage was worth £639 in 1560 and £1,407 in 1606.

[18] The lands were divided between the auditors and receivers along the usual territorial lines.

[19] For the abortive proposals of the 1550s, see below, pp. 36–8. *APC 1618–19*, p. 220, also *CSPD 1611–18*, p. 520; Somerville, *Duchy of Lancaster*, II, pp. 10–11. Cf. Prestwich, *Cranfield*, pp. 256–8.   [20] Dr Gray describes this subsequently, pp. 138–9.

the throne, Charles broke with precedent to maintain the Duchy as an independent entity with its own Council.[21]

The Crown's estate, like that of any other landlord, was also divided when the need arose to provide jointures for wives and estates for younger sons. Where the principality and Duchy formed discrete entities within the Crown lands, the jointure estates had only an *ad hoc* existence tied to the life of the Queen herself. On the accession of James there was a general ignorance of the proper arrangements for the endowment of both Queen and heir and in the case of the jointure it is clear that the precedent of Catherine Parr's jointure was consulted.[22] Each Queen possessed her own Council (based on that of the Duchy of Lancaster)[23] and officials but no body of estates can be identified as being invariably assigned to the Queen for her support. Anne of Denmark's jointure estate (or as much of it as was not granted away) was on her death absorbed back into the Exchequer and Duchy of Lancaster from whence it came; the jointure created for Henrietta Maria had no administrative continuity with that of her late mother in law, nor did it consist of the same lands. Anne of Denmark's jointure consisted of lands worth £4,310 and fee-farm rents of £16,547, Greenwax (a tax on sealings) leased for £10, the farm of sugars (£5,000) and an annuity of £500 out of the Exchequer, in all £26,367. Henrietta Maria had slightly more, with £28,190 in rents and Greenwax leased for £514 in 1632–3, but had no customs.[24]

These divisions need to be acknowledged because of the problems they bring in writing the history of the Crown lands. One problem is entirely practical. The documentation for each part of the Crown lands is uneven. It is not surprising that the jointure lands, where the administrative continuity was least, are the worst documented. The order books of the Queen's Council (which administered her estates and supervised her finances) are entirely lost until after 1660. But many other papers survive, absorbed back into the Exchequer archive in much the same way as the estates themselves were returned to the charge of the Exchequer's administrators. The other problem concerns the writing of the history of the estates. The historian of the Crown lands needs to keep his eye on several moving objects at once, rather like the targets in a shooting range.

[21] See below, pp. 110, 267–8, 284.   [22] LR9/11/48; SP14/3, no. 37.

[23] SP14/12, no. 7 (a reference I owe to Mrs Ruth Fisher).

[24] SP14/86, nos. 28, 29; BL, Stowe MS 322, fol. 52.

II

If the Crown lands were in administrative terms several estates and not merely one, they were equally not the same lands throughout the period. At some periods the Crown sold land heavily and from time to time made grants to subjects for reasons of patronage; but there was also a constant circulation of lands in and out of the Crown's hands which stands apart from the progressive reduction of the estates by sale.

Before considering the ways in which lands entered and left the estates it is helpful to turn to estimates of their overall value. It is remarkably difficult to prepare reliable estimates of income for pre-modern landowners and the Crown is no exception to this general rule. The most accessible sources are the contemporary estimates of revenue made intermittently throughout the period. These tend not to be consistent in their use of accounting categories. The problem in essence is that the Crown's income from land can be measured at two different points as it made its way into the Crown's coffers. Figures were produced for the charge placed on the receivers, in effect rental income. We have called this gross income in table 1.1. Figures were also produced for the net income available from the receivers after charges on their accounts (of officers' fees, repairs, monastic annuities, quit rents, expenses of manorial court dinners, etc.) had been satisfied. Some payments made by the receivers funded the local agencies of executive government including the fees of keepers of castles, the northern wardens, the garrison at Carlisle, the Northern and Welsh Councils and the Welsh Court of Great Sessions.[25] Clearly, these are not in any sense the costs of managing the estates or the collection of revenue but for the sake of compatibility they have been included in the figures in table 1.1. The distinction between gross and net income is extremely important. At an extreme, the figures for the year ending Michaelmas 1551 show that only two-fifths of the income charged on the Augmentation's receivers was paid into the central treasury, the remainder being expended locally in fees, pensions and other costs (table 1.4). By the end of Elizabeth's reign the local charges on the receivers had fallen to 13 per cent of gross revenue for reasons which are of themselves of the greatest interest.

[25] The Councils cost about £1,357 in 1572 and £3,600 in 1635.

Table 1.1. *Estimates of income from the Crown lands, 1551–1641*

	1551[a]		1560[b]		1572[c]		Mean of five years 38–42 Elizabeth[d]	
	(gross)	(net)	(gross)	(net)	(gross)	(net)	(gross)	(net)
Revenue in the Pipe	£7,495	£3,665	[NI]	£4,467	£11,432	[NI]	£14,168	£14,068
Exchequer	£134,515	£51,468	£90,423	£61,377	£99,002	£76,760	£106,523[j]	£91,089[j]
Duchy of Lancaster	£17,984	£8,972	£12,744[n]		£14,755[o]		£17,309	£14,461
Duchy of Cornwall	£4,496	£3,717	£3,500[p]		£3,701[q]		£4,066	£3,719
Jointure						[NI]		
Total	£164,490	£67,822	c. £115,000		c. £129,000		£142,066	£123,337

	1605[e]		1621[f]		Mean of five years to 1635[g]		1641[h]
	(gross)	(net)	(gross)	(net)	(gross)	(net)	(gross)
Revenue in the Pipe	£14,710	[NI]	£9,296	[NI]	£12,133	£11,851	£9,093
Exchequer	£90,927	£72,479	£81,656[k]	£66,774	£61,902[l]	£38,220	£55,170[m]
Duchy of Lancaster	£13,802	£12,372	£12,410	£11,176	£10,855	£8,635	£10,522
Duchy of Cornwall	£4,090[r]	£3,612	£12,000	[NI]	£14,880	£14,103	£19,435
Jointure		£20,851[s]			£28,190[t]	[NI]	£28,974[u]
Total	c. £145,000	c. £123,300	£115,362		£127,960[v]	c. £97,000	c. £123,194

Notes and sources: All sums have been rounded to the nearest pound. [NI] = no information. Totals marked '*c.*' are estimates.

[a] Calculated from Richardson, *1552 Report*: the figures given for the Exchequer are actually for Augmentations. All figures include casualties. See table 1.4 for a further breakdown of these figures.

[b] BL, Lansd. MS 4, fols. 57r–64v (giving income in the Exchequer only).

[c] BL, Lansd. MS 14, fols. 7r–14v (giving income in the Exchequer only).

[d] BL, Cotton MS Titus B IV, fols. 285r–94v.

[e] BL, Add. MS 36969, fols. 1r–10v.

[f] Kent AO, U269/1, OE 1373.

[g] E407/78/5.

[h] C. Russell, 'Charles I's financial estimates for 1642', *BIHR* 58 (1985), pp. 114–19 (printing BL, Egerton MS 2541, fols. 266–71).

[i] My calculation from the assignments and allowances listed without distinction.

[j] Including the palatinate of Chester (worth £771 gross, £282 net).

[k] Including £18,554 assigned to the Prince of Wales.

[l] MS gives £90,696 gross, £67,014 net with an assignment of £28,794 to the Queen for jointure (which is deducted here).

[m] MS gives £83,964 which appears to include the assignment for Queen's jointure (£28,974) as in the corresponding figure for 1635.

[n] Calculated as the charge on the Receiver-General's account for 3 Elizabeth less arrears, DL28/9/3.

[o] Calculated as the charge on the Receiver-General's account for 13 Elizabeth less arrears, DL28/9/13.

[p] Under the head of payments into the Pipe.

[q] Under the head of payments into the Exchequer.

[r] Includes £2,121 for coinage of tin.

[s] Figure from SP14/86, nos. 28, 29 (certificate of the Queen's income based on her receiver's account for 12 James I with allowances, etc., deducted).

[t] Figure for the rents of the Queen's manors in 1633 taken from BL, Stowe MS 322, fols. 54r–5v. The profits of courts amounted to an additional £943. The 1635 and 1641 estimates include this approximate sum as an assignment from the Exchequer.

[u] Sum assigned to the Queen.

[v] Including £25,000 for lands in the hands of the Queen.

The picture is further confused by the seventeenth-century practices of charging the income with assignments which were not properly distinguished from allowances in the abstracts of income and treating lands granted to the jointure and Prince of Wales as assignments on the revenue of the Exchequer.[26] This was simply to develop further the basis on which the provincial Councils had been funded. It was perfectly legitimate to lump together allowances and assignments in so far as the Exchequer wished to know its freedom of movement rather than its gross income (in 1641 only a little over £14,000 was available from the receivers, £70,000 being assigned out of a total charge of £84,000), but the burden is laid on the historian of trying to disentangle the two where it is possible.[27]

The figures presented in table 1.1 are additionally unsatisfactory in that they include the fines on copyhold lands (which were paid to the receivers) but not the fines on leases (which were paid directly into the Exchequer of Receipt). Fines on leases occasionally appear as a further head within the contemporary estimates, but not invariably and are ignored here.

It would be incautious to read too much into the figures contained in table 1.1. It is convenient to start with the very full abstract of income produced by the commission of 1552. Total gross income from lands, including casualties, then stood at about £165,000. The sales of Mary's reign and the first years of Elizabeth's reduced this somewhat, but each estimate of gross income from the whole estate from 1560 to 1641 falls in a band between £120,000 and £140,000. This seems paradoxical given the sales of land which punctuated the intervening century, but income was maintained at this approximate level by the flow of lands into the estates, the sale of lands in fee-farm and the successful exploitation of the preemption of tin by the Duchy of Cornwall.[28] If this seems a creditable performance, then it must be admitted that it makes no allowance for inflation; in real terms the value of the estates was progressively reduced.

During Elizabeth's reign the increase in net income brought about by the reduction of charges on the receivers more than compensated for inflation. The 1552 report shows how 29·8 per cent of the recurrent income charged to the receivers was paid out by them to ex-monastics as pensions or to monastic annuitants.[29] As these indi-

[26] In this context 'assignment is the regular earmarking of particular revenue to particular expenditure'. Russell, 'Financial estimates for 1642', p. 113.

[27] Ibid., p. 115. The assignments on the Duchy of Lancaster exceeded the income.

[28] See below, pp. 14–15, 28–9, 285–92.   [29] See table 1.4 below.

viduals were a charge on the Exchequer for their lives only, the normal process of ageing served to relieve the Exchequer of a sizeable burden. Other steps were taken to reduce the charges on the receiver's accounts with the result that where in 1552, 62 per cent of income was expended before it reached the Exchequer, in 1596–1601 the corresponding figure was only 15 per cent. The 1552 report also shows how a smaller sum, £12,744, was expected to return to the Crown's hands as reversionary grants fell in. From the vantage point of 1552, the Crown's administrators could look forward to a gradually rising level of receipts at the Exchequer but the Crown was to assist this with a policy of reducing the charges on the receivers by transferring the costs of repairs onto the tenants themselves.[30] Net receipts at the Exchequer were therefore 40 per cent greater in 1596–1601 than 1552 even though the gross income of the Exchequer had fallen by a quarter over this same period.[31]

As income was gradually rising of its own accord, it is understandable why the management of the Elizabethan estates tended to complacency. The possibility of benefiting from such savings was denied the Stuarts. Table 1.1 makes clear the damage done to the Crown's finances by the establishment of the jointure and the Prince of Wales's appanage (although the period when both were in existence was limited to a few months in 1616–18): in 1617–19 the Duchy of Cornwall and other lands granted to Charles were worth £35,000.[32]

On the evidence of the table, it would be wrong to equate the sale of lands with the reduction of recurrent income from land. The balance of sales and the countervailing movement of lands into the estates through attainder and exchange was not unfavourable to the Crown, as Dr Thomas's careful calculations for Lincolnshire show.[33] But even there three-quarters of the Crown's increase in net income came from the cessation of pensions rather than the improvement of landed income.

[30] See below, pp. 39–42, 175–6.
[31] 1552: gross £140,512, net £54,329 (table 1.4); 1596–1601: gross £105,752, net £90,807 (BL, Cotton MS Titus B IV, fol. 290v).
[32] See table 10.3 below. In Kent AO, U269/1, OE 1373 (1621) the Duchy of Cornwall is estimated to have been worth £12,000 (an underestimate) and the Prince of Wales was noted as having an assignment of £18,554 charged on the Exchequer's receivers.
[33] See below, pp. 60, 79–81, and table 2.2.

III

Since the publication of Dr Wyndham's article on the Crown estate in mid-sixteenth-century Somerset, we have come to appreciate the degree to which the acquisition and loss of land from the estate was a continuing process.[34] Except in scale, the monastic confiscations and seizure of chantry lands in the 1530s and 1540s were not unique moments in the history of the estates. The Crown gained extensive tracts of land from the attainder of the nobility, in the case of Somerset most notably the marquess of Exeter in 1538 and the duke of Somerset in 1552. The attainders of 1570–2 brought the Crown extensive lands in northern England, especially in Yorkshire and Durham, and, with the execution of the fourth duke of Norfolk, in East Anglia. Political misfortune later in the century made the Crown the owner of the estates of Sir John Perrot in West Wales and the earl of Essex. Some, but not all of this land, was finally returned to the family from whence it came. The Dudleys were highly successful in reversing the losses of the 1550s in the 1560s, but the Neville earls of Westmorland and a majority of the Yorkshire gentry who were attainted after the northern rising remained cast out and their lands were granted away.[35] Smaller estates also came to the Crown by attainder through felony.[36]

Escheat brought the Crown some windfalls of significance. This could happen in two circumstances: where a person died without heirs or where a man holding land from the monarch in tail male died without surviving male relations. While land occasionally came to the Crown by the former means, the later sixteenth century saw the escheat of some large estates, notably those of Matthew, earl of Lennox,[37] William Parr, marquis of Northampton and the Dudley brothers, the earls of Warwick and Leicester. The making of grants in tail male was elevated to a principle of Queen Elizabeth's policy by an unknown writer, claimed by some to be Burghley, but Lennox's grant dated from 1544 and Parr's 1554, and so such grants were less of an innovation than this commentator would have us believe.[38]

---

[34] Wyndham, 'Royal estate'.
[35] Ibid., pp. 132–3; Dietz, English Public Finance, pp. 295–6, gives a list of attainders. For the Dudleys, see the comments by S. L. Adams in Parliamentary History 8 (1989), p. 220. The whole subject needs further study.
[36] Wyndham offers the case of lord Stourton, 'Royal estate', p. 133.
[37] For Lennox, see CPR 1575–8, no. 3407.
[38] Dietz, English Public Finance, p. 84, citing SP12/255, no. 84. Grants in tail male must have made it difficult for the grantee to sell the land and it is noticeable that Leicester's lesser

Whether James I maintained this policy and made grants to his courtiers in this fashion remains to be ascertained.

Land also came to the Crown through exchange with noblemen or bishops, a means considered below by Dr Thomas, occasionally by purchase and more often by seizure for debt.[39] The result was that some manors entered and left the estates several times over the century and income rose and fell, especially at the local level, according to the ebb and flow of lands into and out of the estates.[40] Despite the heavy sales of mid-century, Dr Wyndham found that the Crown possessed more lands in Somerset in 1570 than before 1536.[41]

Wyndham's work, by revealing the dynamic expansion and contraction of the estates, reminds us that they were not shaped by sale alone. The objection to her work is perhaps that the mid-sixteenth century, with its successive changes of regime and willingness to plunder the resources of the bishops, is unrepresentative of the longer period. Much less land came to James in these various ways and over the century after 1558 the overall tendency was for the Crown lands to diminish, largely, but not exclusively, through sale.[42] Our understanding of the sales of Crown lands between 1558 and 1640 is by no means as complete or profound as the quantity of literature on the matter might suggest. The balance of interest has strongly favoured the Elizabethan sales, and the mechanisms and profits of the seventeenth-century sales are much less fully understood.

The Elizabethan practice can be briefly outlined. Throughout her reign Elizabeth made grants or sales of lands to reverse previous confiscations or as a sign of favour to petitioners.[43] This continuing process stands apart from the periods in which commissions for land sales were active. Commissions were issued in 1559, 1561 (apparently reactivated in 1563–5), 1571, 1573, 1589, 1599 and 1601. The value of the lands they sold is shown in table 1.2.[44]

grants, where he was purchasing land to sell on, were made in fee simple, for instance *CPR 1560–3*, pp. 189–91; *CPR 1563–5*, no. 414.

[39] We might also include the possession of bishops' temporalities and recusants' lands as further, temporary, enlargements of the estate.

[40] It might also be added that keeping track of the movement of land into and out of the Crown's hands was beyond the means of the Exchequer; for examples see below, pp. 70, 74.

[41] Wyndham, 'Royal estate', p. 137.

[42] There appears to be no study of the grant of lands to favourites by James I. One is badly needed.

[43] Caesar thought that Elizabeth 'gave away' lands worth £5,003 per annum in the first five years of her reign. BL, Lansd. MS 165, fol. 166. For such a request (albeit abortive) for a grant, W. J. Tighe, 'Herbert Croft's repulse', *BIHR* 58 (1985), p. 108.

[44] The following account is based on Outhwaite, 'Who bought crown lands?', esp. pp. 18–19, 31 n. 2.

Table 1.2. *Sales of Crown lands, 1559–1613*

Date of commission	Purchases in fee simple		Purchases in fee-farm		Advowsons		Total	
	value	consideration	value	consideration	value	consideration	value	consideration
1559	£3,828	£89,332	nil		£1,120	£1,419	£4,948	£90,751
1561	£1,564	£50,940	nil		£141	£479	£1,705	£51,419
1563–5	£4,190	£117,110	nil		£868	£1,861	£5,058	£118,971
1571, 1573	£225	£5,653	£30	£180	£59	£117	£314	£5,950
Lands sold by Hatton, 1572	£163	£4,615	nil		£73	£147	£238	£4,762
1589	£4,624	£141,186	£46	£1,082	£270	£1,295	£4,940	£143,563
1599	£6,202	£254,450	£482	£14,518	£434	£3,999	£7,117	£272,967
1601[a]	£3,442	£-27,359			£95	£697	£3,536	£128,056
Total, Elizabeth I	£24,238	£790,645	£558	£15,780	£3,060	£10,014	£27,856	£816,439
1603	nil		£940	£35,691			£940	£35,691
1609	£249	£10,139	£116	£5,027			£365	£15,166
1611	£595	£19,902	nil				£595	£19,902
1613 (12 Aug.)	£1,711	£67,839	£284	£8,688			£1,994	£76,527
1613 (20 Dec.)	£16	£787	£1,020	£32,424			£1,036	£33,211
Sales by contract 1607–13	£11,883	£320,811	£9,996	£180,645			£21,879	£501,456
Total, James I	£14,454	£419,475	£12,356	£262,475			£26,809	£681,953

Notes: All figures have been rounded to the nearest pound.

[a] The 1601 return does not distinguish between sales in fee-farm and fee simple.

Sources: figures for 1559–1601 calculated from SP14/47, fols. 202r–44v; those for 1603–13 from BI, Lansd. MS 169, fols. 139r–40v ('A brief of all the sales in fee simple and fee-farm since the king's majesty's coming to the Crown with the money made for the same'). The Jacobean synopsis does not separately itemise the sales of advowsons.

The commissions for the sale of lands were issued to the Lord Chancellor, Lord Treasurer, Chancellor of the Exchequer and other senior officials by letters patent under the Great Seal. The commissioners operated with the guidance of articles of instruction.[45] These laid down the tenures on which lands were to be held when sold and the later articles included a note of the price to be secured, but overall the commissioners enjoyed a wide discretion to sell lands on terms agreed between themselves and the purchaser. Whilst the articles were redrafted for each sale, certain types of land were customarily withheld from sale. Only smaller manors were offered, the 1600 articles (for instance) forbidding the sale of any manor worth more than £30 per annum. The Elizabethan articles forbad the sale of lands belonging to the 'ancient inheritance of the Crown', the Duchies of Lancaster and Cornwall and the earldom of Chester and properties lying near the Queen's houses. Lands in strategically sensitive areas were also withheld; by the end of the century they included Portsmouth, the Isles of Wight, Scilly, Sheppey and the Anglo-Scottish marches. This last restraint was progressively lifted in the early seventeenth century although the prohibition on sales of lands in the Isle of Wight was reinstated in 1626.[46]

Beyond this, all was available for purchase. The procedures leading to a sale were initiated by individual purchasers making their interest in a particular property known to the commissioners.[47] Once appraised of this, the commissioners would issue a warrant for the auditor to draw up a parchment particular (description) of the lands requested which the purchaser then would carry back to a sitting of the commissioners. There the purchaser would negotiate the price and other terms of sale which, once agreed, would be endorsed on the particular and the whole registered in the commission's 'book of rates'. After the making of bonds for the separate purchase of woods and the payment of the purchase price, the sale proceeded to the issue of letters patent; but we now understand that many purchasers saw

---

[45] The articles were apparently not enrolled. Those known to me are 1556, BL, Harl. MS 606, fol. 3r–v; 1558, BL, Harl. MS 608, fol. 3*r–v; (undated but 1559), BL, Lansd. MS 114, no. 45; (undated but 1561), CRES40/19A; 1589, SP12/228, no. 3; 1599, J. P. Collier (ed.), *The Egerton Papers* (Camden Soc., 12, 1840), pp. 285–7, 302–3. A draft of those for 1604 is *CSPD Add. 1580–1625*, p. 440.

[46] *CSPD Add. 1625–49*, p. 174. The Marian articles are more permissive and make no reservation of larger manors or lands in militarily sensitive areas.

[47] The following account is based on Outhwaite, 'Who bought crown lands?', pp. 18–20.

Table 1.3. *Purchase price of lands bought in fee simple, by number of years' value*

	1559	1561	1563–5	1571–3	Hatton sale 1572	1589–90	1599	1601
< 20	6·6		5·6	11·3	13·2			3·4
20	14·4	0·6	3·5	3·2	1·5			0·1
21	2·9		0·5					
22	6·7		0·1					
23	5·6	0·7		22·7				
24	31·0	0·1	< 0·1					
25	9·0	0·4	1·1					
26	9·4	2·2	0·9	32·1	0·2			
27	1·4		1·8					
28	2·4	0·1	8·8		0·8			
29	0·6	12·8	1·5					
30	8·3	11·3	69·1	30·6	84·2	47·8		8·4
31	0·6	25·7	4·5			0·3		
32	< 0·1	7·9	0·9			1·1		
33		2·7	0·4			3·2		1·2
34	< 0·1	6·5	0·6			2·3		
35		6·1	< 0·1			34·4	0·4	16·7
36		9·1	0·3			1·3	1·0	11·9
37		1·5					5·0	10·7
38	< 0·1	2·6				2·9	8·4	17·4
39		1·5					3·0	2·5
40	< 0·1	5·3	0·3			5·1	49·6	23·6
41		1·9					2·0	2·5
42		0·5					4·5	0·7
43							2·2	
44							2·2	
45		0·2				1·0	7·3	0·8
46		0·2					2·2	
47							0·9	
48							1·4	
49							0·6	
50		0·2				0·5	5·4	
> 50							3·7	< 0·1
Total	100·0	100·1	100·0	99·9	99·9	99·9	99·8	99·9

Sources: calculated from the schedules in SP14/47, fols. 202r–44v, except for 1601 which is calculated from Outhwaite, 'Price of crown land', table 4.

the process only so far and once the agreement had been concluded, they placed responsibility for seeing the process completed in the hands of agents. In this event, the letters patent would be made in the name of the nominee and so in each sale a small number of individuals had the grant of many scattered properties, not to speculative ends, but for immediate reassignment.[48]

It needs to be borne in mind that in its sales of lands the Crown sold into a buyers' market. Whilst it is easy to believe that the sale of lands offered great opportunities for estate building and speculation, the truth is that the price of land remained low and business was hard to stimulate. In Elizabeth's reign the Crown only sold at times of urgent need, usually warfare, and as these periods coincided with moments of taxation and compulsory borrowing through forced loans, the Crown offered its lands for sale when the liquidity of potential purchasers was at its lowest. However, it must also be recalled that the Crown was a victim of its own success. In the 1530s and 1540s it was the obvious source of land for an investor or landowner wishing to enlarge his estates. As time passed such people could increasingly purchase in the secondary market ex-Crown lands as the Crown's virtual monopoly of supply was broken.

In the 1540s the usual sale price for Crown land was twenty times its annual value.[49] This rose over the period of Elizabeth's reign to the point where the instructions offered to the commissioners in 1589 ordered them to try and secure forty years' value for grants in fee simple or thirty years' for the lands of attainted persons. In 1599 the guide price reached sixty years' value 'if the same by industry may be so sold'.[50] Table 1.3 shows the range of prices achieved for land sold in fee simple in the Elizabethan sales. The wide distribution of values revealed partly arises from the fact that the figures include a small proportion of assets, cottages for instance, which sold more cheaply than manors and messuages, but also because the commissioners did not unbendingly apply the guide price but weighed other factors and bargained with potential purchasers.

It is the case though that in each sale a high proportion of the land granted was sold at a single value. When these modal values are examined, it can be seen how the price of land crept up, from twenty-

---

[48] Some purchasers favoured the use of agents because they thought they could buy lands more cheaply if their identities were concealed. HMC, *Rutland*, 1, p. 277.

[49] Habakkuk, 'The market for monastic property', p. 362.

[50] HMC, *Rutland*, 1, p. 277; Collier (ed.), *Egerton Papers*, p. 286.

four years' in 1559 to thirty-one years' (or perhaps more generally in
the range twenty-nine to thirty-two years') in 1561 to thirty years'
purchase in the late 1590s. In 1571–3, slightly more land was sold at
twenty-six years' purchase than thirty years'; in 1591–2, no land was
sold for under thirty years' and a third of all land achieved a price of
thirty-five years'. In 1599, less than a fifth of the land sold fetched
under forty years', although this happy state of affairs was not
maintained in the sale of 1601.

The justification for raising the rate at which land was retailed was
not to profit from an eager market but to make some allowance for
the improved value of the land. Throughout the period, a return of
5 per cent was expected from a landed investment; the normal price
for land was twenty times its annual profit. The valuation available
to the Crown was a relatively fresh one in the 1540s but by the end of
the century the evidence was often a half-century out of date. The use
of a forty years' purchase rule of thumb was an admission that the
Crown only drew from its property half the rack-rented value; but it
also assumed that revenue produced by the property was capable of
improvement. Of course, and the surveyor Ralph Agas testifies to
this, some was, but much, especially where the tenants held by
copyholds of inheritance, was not.[51] Purchasers had every incentive
to cream off the most readily improvable land.

Although the Crown managed to compensate for the inadequacy
of its records in this way, it failed to secure the price it sought for its
lands. As table 1.3 shows, only a small proportion of land was sold at
forty years' purchase in the sale commenced in 1589, thirty-five or
even thirty years' being the prevailing price commanded. No land
was sold at sixty years' purchase in 1599; the commissioners were
forced to accept lower offers in mid-sale to reach their revenue
targets. In 1599, 88 per cent of the ratings made before June were at
forty-one years' purchase or more, but from July to the end of the
year a much larger proportion were rated at forty years'.[52] Table 1.3
shows how the sale of 1601 was even less successful. Where in 1599,
forty years' value was practically the minimum price accepted, in
1601, 72.3 per cent of the land sold passed for less than this.

These were wartime sales, but the rather scanty Jacobean evidence
does not suggest that the price of Crown land rose in peacetime to

---

[51] For Agas's observations, see below, p. 205.
[52] Outhwaite, 'The price of crown land', pp. 237–9.

anything near the sixty years' thought reasonable in 1599. As late as 1628, the City of London had the Royal Contract estates for twenty-eight years' purchase although the fact that much of this was unimprovable copyhold land served to drag down the price.[53] All the indications are that the Crown actually found it quite hard to sell its lands and, as the occasion to do so came at moments when money was urgently needed, it may be all the more readily understood why it turned to contractors in the reign of James I. And it is in this light that we must view the Crown's willingness to allow the clerks of the Exchequer's auditors to deal in lands. In the first of her chapters, Dr Gray shows how the auditors and their clerks, many of whom held manorial stewardships and other local offices, took a leading role in spreading word of the Crown's willingness to sell lands and acted on behalf of purchasers. This was not so much corrupt as a practical means of advancing the larger objective of releasing capital quickly in the most expeditious fashion.

Alarm at the dissipation of the estate had been expressed by Sir Walter Mildmay as early as 1576. Making the case in the Commons for the grant of a subsidy, Mildmay declared the Crown's un-willingness to draw upon the sources of extraordinary revenue which had sustained Edward and Mary. Debasement was too damaging, the borrowing of money too burdensome and land sales were rejected, 'seeing that by the same the revenues of the Crown are greatly diminished which it can no more bear'.[54] This determination to preserve the estate held until circumstances forced the establishment of a commission for sale in 1589.

The need to conserve and reorganise the Crown lands was recognised by the end of Elizabeth's reign. In 1604, an attempt was made to restrain the King from making further gifts by annexing selected estates to the Crown.[55] These arrangements were announced to be unsatisfactory (it was said that the lands annexed were of poor quality and in some cases had been sold) and an attempt to give the

[53] R. Ashton, *The Crown and the Money Market, 1603–40* (Oxford, 1960), p. 135; for the price of land sold to the contractors, see pp. 25–6 below.

[54] T. E. Hartley (ed.), *Proceedings in the Parliaments of Elizabeth I*, I, *1558–1581* (Leicester, 1981), pp. 443–4.

[55] This was not an original idea; an 'annexation' of lands to the Crown, to remain 'inviolable, untouched and undismembered for ever' was proposed by the 1552 commission, Richardson, *1552 Report*, pp. 227–8. The annexation was announced by proclamation, *Stuart Royal Procs.*, I, no. 43.

arrangement statutory confirmation failed in the Commons.[56] A new
annexation, signed on 9 May 1609, took the form of an indenture
made between the King and his Privy Council by which the lands
named in a schedule were declared to be inalienable except (and here
the good intentions of the annexation were completely undermined)
'in case of wars, increase of issue or such like considerations of state
(wherein the benefit or utility of private men is not the motive or
end)' when they could be disannexed with the written approval of
eight privy councillors.[57] The indenture was sufficiently widely
drawn to be easily overturned when need arose; indeed, a reading of
the section just quoted and the final clause (in which the councillors
promised not to advance suits for lands contained in the entail but to
'dissuade and hinder' those who sought to violate the annexation)
suggests that its real motive was to protect the core of the estates from
James's predatory clients.

The indenture of annexation not only conferred a special inalienable status on a part of the estates but announced the intention
of selling a proportion of the remainder and a commission of sale to
do so was established on 10 May. This was justified in terms of
James's great costs in paying off the debts of the late Queen, in his
and Anne of Denmark's attire for the coronation, the increase of the
navy, the entertainment of ambassadors and the costs of warfare in
Ireland (estimated to be £1 million).[58] On the other hand, the lands
to be sold were mills and rectories, the least profitable areas of the
estates and, as will appear, the sales were to be in fee-farm which
served to protect the Crown's financial interest. The redrafted
annexation appears to have attempted to separate out a core estate of
valuable property from a residue of quillets, mills, rectories and other
low yielding assets which could be sold for the settlement of the
King's debts. In fact the sale of the entailed lands started in 1613.[59]
As late as the mid-1620s, lip-service was still being paid to it, with
declarations of the King's decision to break the annexation on the

---

[56] Dietz, *English Public Finance*, p. 106; P. Croft (ed.), 'A collection of several speeches and
treatises of the late Lord Treasurer Cecil...', *Camden Miscellany* 29 (Camden fourth ser., 34,
1987), p. 274 n. 69.

[57] The text of the annexation is printed in St John, *Observations*, App. iv. The indenture and
schedules may be found most conveniently in SP14/46. The lands annexed were manors
worth £50,088 drawn from the Exchequer and Duchy of Lancaster and fee-farm rents of
£16,782 from the Exchequer.

[58] St John, *Observations*, App. iv (pp. 17–18). The commission is SP14/50, fols. 110v–15v.

[59] Dietz, *English Public Finance*, p. 157.

recommendation of his Council being prepared, doubtless to free purchasers from the imputation that their purchase was illegal.[60]

Commissions for sale came thick and fast in the early years of James's reign with their issue in 1603 (still active in 1606), 1609, 1610 and twice in 1613. These sales are much less well known than Elizabeth's because the documentation is poorer, for neither the books of rates kept by the commissioners nor the parchment particulars have generally survived.[61] The characteristic mechanism for sale in these years was not the commission but the contract.[62] This cannot be seen as wholly an innovation of the early seventeenth century. Consciously or not, it developed the idea behind the sales of concealments in Elizabeth's reign where lands were purchased by speculators for retail to their occupiers.[63] The chosen method in the Jacobean contracts was for an agreement to be made by the commissioners for sales with a syndicate of London merchants. They undertook to purchase Crown property of a certain value and character at a specified rate for which more or less immediate payment was promised. To take the contract made in June 1609 with the syndicate headed by John Eldred, the King agreed to sell to the contractors lands excluded from the annexation to the value of £500 per annum (above reprises) at forty-six years' purchase.[64] (Exceptionally, the same contract gave the syndicate the right to make leases of lands in the annexation worth £2,000 per annum at a rate of twenty-two years' value.) The bargain was worth £67,000 to the Crown, of which £30,000 was to be paid promptly and the balance in quarterly payments of £9,500.[65] Whilst we are largely ignorant of the procedure followed in the contractors' sales, it seems that books of available property were supplied by the Exchequer and from these the contractors made their choice. They then requested a particular

---

[60] See, for instance, *CSPD Add. 1625–49*, p. 169 (1626).

[61] LR2/65–74 are books of rates, mostly for Elizabethan sales. E164/52 is a book of rates for three contractors' sales, 1611–13, but this seems to be the only extant Jacobean book. Bodl., Rawlinson MS B253, is a contractor's private record of land purchased and assigned, 1609–11.

[62] See Dietz, *English Public Finance*, pp. 124–5, 147, 157–8. A. F. Upton, *Sir Arthur Ingram c. 1565–1642. A Study in the Origins of an English Landed Family* (Oxford, 1961), pp. 24–6, 39, 41–3; Tawney, *Business and Politics*, pp. 109–13, give the fullest accounts of the syndicates.

[63] C. J. Kitching, 'The quest for concealed lands in the reign of Elizabeth I', *TRHS* fifth ser., 24 (1974).

[64] In this context value means rent rather than rack-rented value. For the contractors' leases see below, p. 258.

[65] SP14/45, no. 159. The earlier agreement with the syndicate led by Cope is printed in *CSPD Add. 1580–1625*, p. 497.

from the appropriate auditor which was passed before the commissioners in the usual way. The contractors were permitted to return land to the Crown and choose afresh if they so wished.[66]

In all, seventeen contracts were made in the years 1607–13 and lands worth £470,000 passed through the contractors' hands (table 1.2).[67] The single largest contract, made in July 1609 with the syndicate headed by William Garway, was for lands worth £2,541 per annum, in fee simple, selling at thirty-eight or forty years' value. Syndicates were assembled as the need arose and interest could be raised, Sir Arthur Ingram being particularly prominent as an intermediary between the commission and the London mercantile community. Within the syndicates themselves, land was bought and sold between the partners.

The contractors' sales started as the way of implementing the laudable objective of sifting the least profitable lands from the estates. Four of the five early contractors' sales (in November 1607–January 1609) were almost all sales of mills, rectories, tithes or chantry lands in fee-farm. In the case of mills the decision was taken to sell after it was discovered by Salisbury how the costs of repair ate into income; in a letter to Caesar of August 1608 Salisbury outlined his vision of using the rod of the contractors as the way to persuade the tenants of mills to bid for their freeholds.[68] It was only after the signing of the annexation in the summer of 1609 that the contractors were employed to dismantle the estate by selling the excluded lands. From this moment, the majority of sales were made in fee simple and not fee-farm.

The contracts were a means of expediting the release of capital in a slack market by placing the burden of finding purchasers on entrepreneurs whilst ensuring that the proceeds were promptly paid into the Exchequer. The contractors carried the risk of having a considerable investment tied up in land which might not be readily saleable. As at least some of the contractors undertook to sell land to recover loans made to the Crown, they may not have set about the task with the greatest enthusiasm.[69]

---

[66] Bodl., Rawlinson MS B253, fols. 49r, 56r, 137r, 138r (for instance) and 167v. For orders to the auditors detailing the procedures to be followed in the contractors' sales, see LR9/9/1280/1 (24 Dec. 1608), LR9/11/15 (24 Oct. 1609), LR9/61/pt 1, unnumbered Yorkshire auditor's book (Feb. 1610), LR9/9/1253 (4 May 1610), LR9/9/1264 (19 June 1610).

[67] The contracts themselves are listed with the value of the lands sold, the rates and receipts in BL, Lansd. MS 69, no. 110, and this is the basic source for what follows.

[68] BL, Add. MS 36767, fol. 196r.   [69] Prestwich, Cranfield, pp. 78–9.

The workings of the secondary market and the ultimate destination of much of this land remains mysterious, but whilst some contractors acquired lands for themselves, there is no sign that they were generally buying to the order of interested purchasers. Instead they were buying the plums from the lands offered them. The surviving evidence suggests that they often had to work hard to dispose of their investment, some of which remained in the hands of individual contractors for long periods. On several occasions Eldred and Whitmore commenced suits against the tenants of the lands they had purchased, perhaps as a means of encouraging them to take their tenancies off the contractors' hands.[70] Cranfield only managed to liquidate his share of a contract of 1610 in 1618; one of the groups with which Ingram was associated bought lands for £6,652 in 1612 but still had lands and debts worth £5,825 in 1616.[71] In at least one case a partnership was formed to sell the lands on. Justinian Povey, the deputy to Auditor Spencer (and soon-to-be auditor) purchased lands in Yorkshire from Eldred and Whitmore at the prompting of one Thomas Sandwith of York. The intention was to sell the lands jointly for a shared profit, but within two years Povey was claiming in the Exchequer that Sandwith was selling the lands without his consent or knowledge and failing to pay Povey his share of the receipts.[72] Whether all those who partook in the contracts made a profit may be doubted. Certainly, many chanced borrowed money in the adventure and may have found themselves in difficulty if the land could not be sold on quickly. Cranfield entered the field with borrowed money but could still claim a profit of 16 per cent on his investment.[73] Nonetheless, it was claimed in the Parliament of 1614 that excessive profits had been made by the contractors and this may have served to discourage further ventures in the sale of land through agents.

But by 1613, the unannexed Crown lands were largely worked out and the quality of the land available for purchase declined. The price of land sold in fee simple to the earliest contractors had been in line with the rate paid on sales by commissions, but it fell from forty-five or so years' in the contracts of December 1608 and June 1609 to forty years' in the Garway contract of July 1609, thirty years' in October 1610 and the low twenties or high teens in the contracts of 1612–13.

[70] E112/138/1368, 1369.
[71] Tawney, *Business and Politics*, p. 113; Upton, *Ingram*, p. 43.
[72] E112/138/1308. Bodl., Rawlinson MS B253, fols. 67r, 68r, etc., shows purchases by Povey and Sandwith.   [73] Tawney, *Business and Politics*, p. 111–12.

It could be argued that the market was sated, but when the decision was taken to sell the lands of the duke of York after the death of Prince Henry in 1613, Ingram put together a syndicate to bid (unsuccessfully as it happened) for these new lands at forty years' value.[74]

Whilst the Exchequer continued to receive small sums from the sale of lands in the decade after 1614, no formally constituted commission was in operation and the grants were made by the Elizabethan practice of securing the royal assent to a petition. No new commission was established until October 1626 when the financial crisis which followed the failure of the 1626 Parliament prompted desperate attempts to increase income and retrench on revenue.[75] It would be true to say that the decisions taken in late 1626 mark the end of the Crown as a major landholding corporation. The commissioners sold land in the orthodox fashion and uniquely, the survival of some of their minute books allows us to view the process of bargaining and negotiation between them and potential purchasers.[76] When the commission was terminated it has been impossible to discover, but land sales continued (though at a slower pace) throughout the first ten years of the reign of Charles I. There was also a return to contractors' sales during 1630, but one contractor asked to resign his contract as a 'hard and unprofitable bargain'.[77]

The commission was also charged with negotiating the Royal Contract with the City of London.[78] In a sense, this was a further adaptation of the contract system of selling although with the important difference of the 'unexpressed trust' to which we shall return. The essential background to the negotiations was that at the end of 1626 the Crown had outstanding loans from the City community (but raised through the Corporation) of £96,500 and £60,000 dating from 1617 and 1625 respectively, some of which was charged on mortgaged lands.[79] It was recognised that the repayment of sums of this size was beyond the government's means and from late 1626 proposals were made to satisfy the debt by advancing land to

---

[74] Upton, *Ingram*, pp. 39–40.

[75] C66/2385, dorse, no. 10. For the commissions for retrenchment and sale in 1626–7, see ch. 12 below.

[76] The minutes of their earlier sessions are in University of London Library, MS 195, pt i, continued in Cheshire RO DCH/X/15/5 (sessions 7 Nov.–2 Dec. [1626]) and SP16/69 (sessions 2 Dec.–16 June 1627).   [77] Bodl., Rawlinson MS C451, fols. 39v–40v, 50r.

[78] Ashton, *Crown and the Money Market*, ch. 6, considers the Royal Contract at length from the financial point of view. The process of disposal of the estates and their management by the City remains entirely unstudied.

[79] By late 1627 the total debt with interest stood at £229,897. Ashton, *Crown and the Money Market*, p. 135.

trustees for the City, the initial hope being that the City would take forests in settlement.[80] The agreement which emerged in December 1627 was for trustees for the City (in effect the contractors) to receive lands in fee-farm to the value of £12,496 which, at twenty-eight years' purchase, would be worth a little under £350,000. These lands were to be sold to satisfy the principal and interest on the loans. The City was to pay £120,000 to complete the transaction and volunteered a further £5,000 to have the lands granted in socage.[81]

It is not clear how great a choice (if any) the City had in the lands it received, but their disposal was a protracted process, continuing into the 1650s and beyond. The early sales were made at a rate in advance of the Crown's selling price (about thirty-three years' purchase); by 1632, the City was expressing its fear that the remainder of the lands (about a half of the whole) would not sell for more than twenty years' purchase.[82] Where the Royal Contract came to differ from the Jacobean contractors' sales was in the fact that the Crown expected to be refunded whatever surplus remained after the satisfaction of its debts. The City rejected this requirement, the so-called 'unexpressed trust' (which was omitted from the final contract), and in 1632, the government instituted a thorough and critical investigation of the City's dealings. Whilst the Crown had some right to complain about the City's malpractices, it sought to overturn the basis on which the earlier contracts had been founded.

In retrospect, it may be suggested that the City secured a most disadvantageous bargain. The lenders of 1617 and 1625 had an unreasonably long wait to be repaid and few if any of them are likely to have welcomed the City's acceptance of a role as a land contractor as a means to recover their loans. From the point of view of a Crown forced by circumstance to liquidate most of its remaining lands, the Royal Contract transferred not only the lands themselves but also the considerable difficulty of achieving a sale.

The liquidation of the remaining estate was a trick which could never be repeated. The outbreak of the first Bishop's War with Scotland was the first for a century which was not accompanied by land sales although the suggestion of selling some of the remaining forests and chases was investigated in 1642.[83] The years 1626–8 mark the end of a period in English history. Since 1542, selling land to

---

[80] Cheshire RO, DCH/X/15/5, fols. 1r, 2v.
[81] Ashton, *Crown and the Money Market*, pp. 132–5. The City refused to accept lands in double fee-farm, SP16/69, fols. 67v, 86r.
[82] Ashton, *Crown and the Money Market*, pp. 144, 147.   [83] *CSPD 1641–3*, pp. 334, 365.

finance war had given the Crown a degree of independence from parliamentary scrutiny; in 1640, without assets to realise (or upon which to secure loans), the advantage lay with Parliament.

This account of the mechanisms of sale has served to show how the decade and a half after 1598 was the decisive period in the dispersal of the Crown lands. But we must now attempt to quantify the sales over the whole period. It is possible to produce figures for the receipts from sales from the records of payments into the Exchequer (making allowance for those sales in which the purchase money was paid into the hands of a special receiver). Dietz's abstracts of the Exchequer records can be used to this end, but the material for 1572–1603 has been reworked with greater care by Dr Outhwaite. His best figure for receipts from sales over this period is £559,176 7s 9½d.[84] A Jacobean estimate for the whole of Elizabeth's reign gives sales of lands totalling £817,472 at an average rate of thirty-one years' purchase.[85]

Our immediate concern is not with the revenue raised by sale but the part sales played in the diminution of recurrent revenue. The requirement is for estimates of the rental value of lands sold which make the all important distinction between lands sold in fee simple and fee-farm. In grants in fee simple no rent (or at most a small quit rent) was reserved to the Crown. The sale of lands on these terms immediately diminished the Crown's revenue. Grants in fee-farm prohibited the Crown from taking fines on leases in the future but maintained its rental income. Indeed, fee-farming was a means by which the Crown could have its capital and keep its income whilst shedding its responsibility for repairs. The sale of mills illustrates this well. It offered the cheery prospect of jam, jam and more jam, so much so that some commentators in the early seventeenth century saw it as the way to solve all the Crown's financial problems. Bacon suggested fee-farming all the Crown's lands at double or treble the ancient rent.[86]

Sales in fee-farm and fee simple are distinguished in a series of tabulations of the rates at which land was sold by Elizabeth, drawn up for Caesar in 1609, and in a digest of the commissions and

---

[84] For the methods used, problems encountered and full year by year figures, see R. B. Outhwaite, 'Studies in Elizabethan government finance; royal borrowing and the sale of crown lands, 1572–1603' (University of Nottingham, PhD thesis, 1964), App. 2.

[85] BL, Lansd. MS 165, fol. 166 (notes by Caesar).

[86] Spedding, *Bacon*, IV, pp. 327–36. For projects to grant customary lands in fee-farm, see below pp. 233–56 *passim*.

contracts of James's reign. This material is drawn together in table 1.2. For Charles's reign there survives a digest of sales made for the Treasury Commissioners in 1635 although this is deficient in some of the information one would like.[87] The Elizabethan sales were overwhelmingly sales of fee simples and it was not until the last years of the century that a market for sales in fee-farm appeared. The signs are that the original policy of the Jacobean regime was to make extensive sales with the reservation of rents. The 1603 commission for sales sold entirely in fee-farm; there is evidence that hopes were harboured for a sale of customary lands in fee-farm and the original contractors' sales were made (mostly) in fee-farm.[88] The later contractors' sales (which must be understood to have been virtually bankruptcy sales) were normally in fee simple probably because sales on those terms produced a better price, possibly because it made land more attractive to the purchaser. The commission of 1626 only made sales in double fee-farm, thus allowing it to tell the King of its apparently contradictory achievements of selling lands with a rental value of £845 for £30,600 whilst raising his rents by £876.[89] The disadvantage with fee-farming was that the purchase price had to be discounted to allow for the continuing financial obligation of freeholder to landlord. To take the two commissions of 1613, lands in fee-farm sold at thirty and thirty-two years' purchase where lands in fee simple sold at forty-six and forty-eight years'.

For all its imperfections, table 1.2 allows us to refine further the chronology and impact of sales on Crown finance before 1625. Whilst the sales of 1559–65 were heavy enough (selling land worth £11,711), the middle part of the reign was marked by the cessation of sales until the needs of war finance in the early 1590s made inevitable the recourse to sale. Lands worth £15,593 were sold in this decade. But this was a mere aperitif to the sales made in the first decade of James's reign when he sold nearly as much land as Elizabeth had throughout her entire reign. This may be found all the more surprising given that James was not fighting a war in the European theatre at this time. Charles received in the first ten years of his reign £339,599 for lands

---

[87] SP14/47, no. 100. The schedule for the 1599 sale is printed by Outhwaite, 'The price of crown land', table 1. BL, Add. MS 18795, fols. 1r–22v (also BL, Harl. MS 3796, fol. 21r–v).

[88] In the five contracts made up to January 1609, lands worth £9,683 were sold in fee-farm and only £1,000 in fee simple. BL, Lansd. MS 69, no. 110.

[89] University of London Library, MS 195, pt ii, fol. 34r.

sold to the City of London (largely for debts contracted in the previous reign) and £241,058 for lands sold to individuals, in all £580,657. Most of this was sold in fee-farm, but it also includes disafforested land. Without further information, it is hard to be certain what its rental value was, but it must have been in the range of £20,000.[90]

Yet it is easy to be mesmerised by the figures and fail to place them in perspective. During her life Elizabeth sold land worth approximately a fifth of the gross value of the entire estate *c.* 1600, but these sales had not prevented the gross revenue increasing by £20,000 between *c.* 1560 and *c.* 1600. One could argue that the sales were in part funded by the influx of estates into her hands by escheat and attainder. (The commission of 1571 was only empowered to sell the lands of the attainted rebels of the northern rebellion.)

Elizabeth's sales certainly had a deleterious effect on income but must be viewed in the context of an otherwise buoyant state of affairs. The impact of James's sales can only be understood if we acknowledge that whilst he sold lands with a rental of approximately £27,000, because about half of those sales were made in fee-farm, the cost to the Crown was only £14,500 in lost revenue. This was far less damaging to the financial interests of the Crown than the assignment of the jointure in 1604 (a cost of £20,000), the granting of livery to the Prince of Wales in 1610 (£31,000) or the establishment of Henrietta Maria's jointure after 1626 (£30,000).[91] In comparison, the sale of lands with a capital value of nearly £700,000, a rental value of £27,000 but at an annual cost to the Crown of £14,450 was a minor matter and one which could be pursued as an acceptable and necessary course. It is in this light that the sales after 1625 should be seen. All were made in fee-farm (including those to the City of London), and so did nothing to diminish the recurrent (as opposed to the casual) revenue of the Crown.

In this light, it can be appreciated that the sale of lands did much less damage to the Crown's landed income than might at first be assumed. Seventeenth-century Lord Treasurers knew this and behaved accordingly. In this context we might recall Mrs Prestwich's maxim that successful Lord Treasurers were those who sold land. And as Dr Thomas observes later in the book, they were right to do

[90] BL, Harl. MS 3796, fols. 35r–7v.
[91] For the financial consequences of the Prince of Wales's grant of livery, Croft (ed.), 'A collection of several speeches', pp. 258–9.

so.[92] But fee-farming altered the character of the estates. The land ceased to be the King's, tenants owed him no obligation besides their rent and this would often be paid through an intermediate landlord, vested with the Crown's seigneurial rights. The Crown ceased to be a landowner and became, in the purest sense, a *rentier*, unable to effect further improvements in its revenue. As these fixed rents depreciated in value and became a nuisance to collect, even they were in time sold, ending the Crown's interest in its landed revenues.[93]

IV

In reading the chapters which follow, it might be thought helpful to bear in mind a schematic division of the history of the estates into two sections, admittedly with many continuities between them but with a reassessment of the means of management in *c.* 1598–1605. The first period can be dated from the commission of 1552, the absorption of the Court of Augmentations by the Exchequer in 1554 and the debate over the management of the estates in 1555.[94] The lack of discussion of the estates in Elizabeth's reign can be explained as reflecting the belief that the major issues had been settled before her accession. During this period, the management of the estates was designed to produce a stable recurrent income with as many of the running costs of the estates as possible passed onto the tenants. There was a preference for leasing manors in gross to tenants who paid a flat rent for the liberty of subletting the land and collecting the fines and other casualties of the manorial courts. Customary tenants were offered confirmations of their customs or preferential leasehold arrangements for taking upon themselves the expense of repairing river banks and coastal defences or undertaking border service against the Scots without wages. The Elizabethan administrators were not blind to the possibility of increasing rental income through the recovery of decayed medieval rents and in some cases made the renewed payment of such rents a condition of confirmations of custom.[95] There was always an anxiety to recover lost or concealed lands although this was often farmed out to private individuals on generous terms to encourage their investment of time and energy. But the Elizabethans

---

[92] Prestwich, *Cranfield*, pp. 373–4; see below pp. 86–7.

[93] C. D. Chandaman, *The English Public Revenue, 1660–88* (Oxford, 1975), pp. 112–15.

[94] Discussed below, pp. 33–8.

[95] As at Bromfield and Yale (Denb.), see below, p. 202, and Hatfield (Yorks.), E123/1A, fol. 69r–v.

never took advantage of the possibility of raising rents and placed a small premium on fines on leases and copies which remained low or nominal.

This was logical enough behaviour if viewed in the context of its own times. The previous 200 years of agricultural depression had taught estate administrators that income should be maximised by ensuring that every tenement had a tenant rather than appropriating the maximum rental income from each and risking the vacancy of a proportion. The analogy of the options open to a theatre manager might not be inappropriate. Faced with the need to fill a large theatre, an impresario with a production of limited appeal might well choose to maximise his income by selling every seat at £10 with a free programme. Given the same theatre and a play which people were eager to view, income could be maximised by charging £30 for the stalls, £10 for the upper balcony and doubling the price of gin and tonic at the crush bar. Whether rightly or wrongly, the administrators of the 1550s thought in the medieval terms of the first impresario; but by the end of the sixteenth century, rising population had considerably increased the demand for land and made the Crown lands a bargain for the tenants.

To the generation which grew up in the much altered circumstances of the late sixteenth century, this policy of fixed renders was incomprehensible: they saw it not in the light of its historical origins but for the opportunities it gave the ticket touts outside the hall. Certainly the proportion of its tenants' income which the Crown took in rent must have fallen quite severely over the sixteenth century (if only because of inflation); but the rising value of land gave stewards and other officers the opportunity to fleece the tenants at the Crown's expense. The response to this were attempts to increase income by estimating the real market value of lands through surveying, raising the fines on leases and copyholds and the closer supervision of local officers, taken to its extreme on the Duchy of Cornwall estates where the manorial steward was reduced to a functionary of the Duchy Council.[96] A vocal lobby argued for the agricultural improvement of wastes, fens and forests.

The Crown's ability to trade on its awareness of improved economic and social conditions was limited by a variety of constraints. It was no longer possible (if it ever had been) to alter significantly the terms and conditions by which customary tenants held their lands. In

[96] See the observations of Haslam, below, pp. 282–3.

some cases copyhold had been confirmed by the previous generation of administrators; in others an unimpeachable prescriptive right had developed. Moreover, ideological restraints served to limit the burden which might be placed on the tenants. In addition, the inability of the Crown from the 1590s onwards to balance its budget forced the adoption of a policy of sale or the implementation of other devices to raise ready capital. The desperate need for immediate revenue negated hopes of reconstructing the estates along modern lines and even the disafforestation of woodland turned out to be a device for making saleable the undesirable residue of the Crown's landed assets.

v

What from the vantage point of the last years of the sixteenth century appears to be a lack of policy was in fact a deliberate system of management instituted in the years after 1552 which had, in changed conditions, outlived its usefulness.

The occasion for a review of government finance was the reestablishment of peace in 1551–2. Of the various commissions established in 1552, the most important was that charged with the investigation of the revenue courts. Appointed in March, its report of December stands as the fullest attempt to produce a comprehensive assessment of the state of the Crown's income and to evaluate the reforms necessary for its future management.[97] It is here and with the decisions taken in the years immediately following that the history of the Elizabethan estates may be said to begin.

The 1552 report falls into three sections. The first is a thorough and detailed abstract of the income and expenditure of the major departments of government in the year ending at Michaelmas 1551. The second contains the commissioners' recommendations on the areas where reform was necessary and in the third section (which was apparently not circulated and may have been suppressed), they urged the amalgamation of the Crown's revenue-gathering functions into either a pair of courts or (preferably) a single court. The reforms which took place in early 1554 were not those advocated by the commissioners and this has prompted one recent commentator to suggest that the commission made no significant contribution to the formulation of policy. This is perhaps so; yet the real significance of

---

[97] The report is printed by Richardson, *1552 Report.* J. D. Alsop attempts to rubbish it in 'The Revenue Commission of 1552', *HJ* 22 (1979), pp. 511–33, and in doing so seems to misunderstand many aspects of the report.

the report of 1552 lies not in the degree to which its proposals were exactly implemented but the cast of mind it reveals. The preoccupations of the report reappear in the limited evidence of a debate within the Council about the management of the lands in 1555, in notes made by Winchester in late 1561 of the additional reforms he desired and the practical administration of the estate in the following decade and more.[98]

The state of the Crown lands found by the report can be quickly summarised. The estates were divided between three authorities; the Clerk of the Pipe, the lands in whose charge were fairly negligible, the Court of Augmentations (which had absorbed the Court of General Surveyors in 1547) and the Duchy of Lancaster. Augmentations had a gross income of £133,076 from rent and farms in 1551 and £7,436 from casualties (mainly fines on copyholds and woodsales).[99] The Duchy of Lancaster had £16,498 in rents and farms and £1,486 in casualties. In all, landed income came to a little short of £160,000 with the promise of a further £12,816 as reversions fell in. But charges on the income amounted to 60 per cent of the whole (table 1.4).[100]

Many of the proposals, for instance that regular surveys should be made, that leases ought to be registered with the auditors and that duplicate court rolls should be deposited in a central muniment room, were entirely laudable but fiscally neutral.[101] The basic assumption which lay behind the report was that gross income was fixed and incapable of improvement except at the margins. Proposals were made to increase income by letting lands by copy rather than lease, by leasing casualties and raising the fines taken on sealing leases, worthy suggestions but hardly likely to increase revenue

---

[98] The 1555 debate consists of the report of a sub-committee charged with examining (lost) articles and the Council's rejoinder to this report, copies of which can be found in BL, Cotton MS Titus B iv, fols. 129r–31v, and Add. MS 12505, fols. 164–7. They were also known to Christopher Vernon and partly printed by him; *Considerations*, pp. 67–71. There is little evidence as to the context of this debate. Winchester's articles are BL, Harl. MS 6850, fols. 103r–6v. Dietz accepted the date endorsed on the manuscript in an eighteenth-century hand, January 1561, *English Public Finance*, p. 20. Internal evidence suggests that it must be assigned to the autumn of that year for the articles refer to the commission for the sale of castles, issued in March 1561 (*CPR 1560–3*, p. 169) and propose the initiative over tenant right which resulted in the commission of July 1562 (*ibid.*, pp. 92–3), but they also look forward to the following Hilary term.

[99] These figures include the Duchy of Cornwall.

[100] In the report, these lands are both charged as income and then deducted (together with monastic pensions) from the net income after the payment of costs and expenses charged on the receiver. Alsop criticises the report for this 'manipulation' ('Revenue Commission', p. 524) but the commissioners themselves wanted the reversions to be included in the receiver's accounts to ensure that they were kept in sight. Richardson, *1552 Report*, p. 183.

[101] Richardson, *1552 Report*, pp. 169, 181, 190, 192.

substantially. Elsewhere, it was suggested that a better return could be obtained from woods and that assiduous surveyors could recover 'decayed' (i.e. lost) rents.[102] The only idea likely to offer large returns was the recommendation that distant forests and parks should be disafforested and leased as cultivable lands, but here the emphasis was as much on cost cutting as revenue advancing.[103] This typified the general approach of the commission. The report followed the usual pattern of early modern investigations of income and expenditure of looking to the reduction of costs so as to permit the increase of net revenue. The charges on income identified by the report are shown in table 1.4. Rents and perpetual charges were obviously largely immutable. Monastic pensions and annuities would decline over time as their recipients passed away although the commission did recommend the sifting out of corrupt or collusive grants. At best, this was capable of producing only a minor reduction in costs.[104] The only means by which the commission could effect any immediate reduction was by reducing the staff costs and expenditure on repairs.

In its general observations the report suggested the wholesale decimation of the local staff of the Court of Augmentations. It recommended that consideration be given to the abolition of the two masterships of woods, the two surveyors of woods, the forty-four county surveyors and the twenty-six woodwards, proposals which, if implemented, would have saved £1,172. The keeperships of castles and parks which were decayed or never used by the King were also to be discontinued. Thought should be given to reducing the number of stewards and their fees. The same strictures were applied to the Duchy (where the commission also remarked that there were too many receivers).[105]

But the real savings came in the radical restructuring proposed in the third section of the report. Here two options were floated. The first was for the amalgamation of the revenue-gathering agencies into two new bodies, the second of which (to be called the Court of the King's Revenue) would have charge of all the Crown lands then under the Augmentations and Duchy. As a streamlined organisation, it would have ten auditors and ten receivers with a total staff cost of £4,393, a saving over the existing arrangements of £8,905. The second option offered (and the one preferred by the commission) was

---

[102] *Ibid.*, pp. 189, 222, 225.
[103] *Ibid.*, p. 227 (the idea appears in the uncirculated section of the report).
[104] *Ibid.*, p. 186.   [105] *Ibid.*, pp. 185–6, 195.

Table 1.4. *Charges on the income of the Duchy of Lancaster and Court of Augmentations, 1551*

	Duchy	Augmentations[a]
Total receipts from rents and fines in possession	£16,498	£133,076
Receipts from Casualties	£1,486	£7,436
Total	£17,984	£140,512
Senior officers of Augmentations[b]		£2,357
Charges on receivers' accounts:		
Fees	£5,701	£15,290
Expenses of audit and steward's costs	£268	£2,716
Rents and perpetual charges	£774	£6,817
Decayed rents	£1,217	£5,555
Repairs	£573	£5,458
Monastic pensions, annuities, etc.		£38,870
Other charges	£479	£9,120
Total	£9,012	£86,183
Balance	£8,972	£54,329

Notes: All figures have been rounded to the nearest pound.
[a] Including the Duchy of Cornwall.
[b] The equivalent costs for the Duchy are included under fees.
Source: calculated from Richardson, *1552 Report*, pp. 40–66, 75–7, 102–7.

for the amalgamation of all the existing agencies into a single revenue-gathering body to be called the Exchequer. This would have ten auditors again, but the responsibility for revenue collection would be placed with the sheriffs of each county 'for their travail may very well serve that which the receivers do now'. The supervision of the estates would be placed in the hands of two assistants to the Lord Treasurer who would fulfil the sort of role taken by the General Surveyors some forty years before. This option would also have revived the Chamber as a disbursing department. The savings were greater than in the previous option, £10,242, even though the scheme allowed for the increase of the fees of officers whose responsibilities were enlarged and the payment of £600 to the sheriffs for their costs.

In fact neither proposal was implemented and it has been suggested that the decision was taken some weeks before the commission reported to opt for a third scheme.[106] This may not be so; the statutory authority for dissolving the courts sought in Edward VI's

[106] Alsop, 'Revenue Commission', p. 532.

last Parliament and then again in Mary's first (because the sanction had only been granted for the late King's life) allowed the uniting of *all* the revenue courts into one or two new bodies in a most unspecific manner suggesting that no firm decisions had been taken. The reform of 1554 effectively grafted the structures of Augmentations onto the existing Exchequer organisation whilst preserving the Duchy and the Court of Wards as independent units. The number of local officers was not reduced in line with the 1552 proposals and inevitably the savings promised there failed to materialise. The 1555 debate still looked to a reduction in the number of officers.

This has allowed some commentators to regard the 1552 report as having contributed nothing to the reforms of 1554.[107] There are reasons to suppose that these were less final than might appear in retrospect. Even if the new Exchequer retained the receivers inherited from Augmentations' practice, the first article of its standing orders stated that revenue from lands was to be paid into the Exchequer by the sheriff of the county where the land lay or by such other persons as the Lord Treasurer appointed.[108] In the following year, the debate over the use of sheriffs in place of receivers was still continuing and it is far from clear when (or indeed if) a positive decision was taken to continue with the collection of land revenue by salaried officials rather than unpaid sheriffs. In one respect, the choice between the two became immaterial; the enabling statutes of 1552 and 1553 both provided that feed officials should continue to receive their stipends even if their offices were abolished.[109] Moreover, the fate of the Duchy had not been settled in the autumn of 1552, otherwise why should both the Edwardian and Marian enabling statutes provide for its abolition? The question of its future was still being debated in 1555 when a strong body of opinion clearly saw no justification for its continuance, but the matter was doubtless settled before (or by) the Parliament of that year when a statute reunited with the Duchy lands severed from it since 1547 and annexed to it additional lands worth

---

[107] *Ibid.*, p. 532.

[108] The 1554 articles are annexed to the enrolled patent abolishing Augmentations and establishing the Exchequer, C54/500, mm. 4–5. They are printed in paraphrase in F. S. Thomas, *Notes of Materials for the History of Public Departments* (London, 1846), pp. 98–101.

[109] 7 Edw. VI c. 2, 1 Mary. c. 10 (and note especially the proviso to this statute). Alsop fails to realise this and sneers at the way in which a Duchy office marked for abolition continued to be filled until 1574 which was, of course, the year when the last incumbent (appointed in 1553!) died. The most the government could do was decline to make further appointments to an office, which it did.

up to £2,000.[110] The Duchy might owe its survival to the fact that it was not simply a land-managing agency but provided the entire judicial system in Lancashire. Its courts did not simply correspond to those of Augmentations; they were qualitatively quite different and there is no reason to suppose that the Exchequer could successfully have taken on its responsibilities.[111]

The aim of streamlining the administration of the estates as a means of saving salaries remained only partially achieved. But the ambition to reduce expenditure in this area was still a motivating force in the early 1560s. Winchester's proposals of late 1561 include the radical suggestion that the Queen should dispense with all her bailiffs and make the receivers responsible for the collection of rent, an alteration which would save £2,500 per annum.[112] The Council can be seen at work in December 1562 weeding out redundant offices on the estates.[113]

It is possible to offer other instances where the ideas of the commission were adopted as policy in the years following. Both sides of the 1555 debate were agreed on the desirability of making a full survey; in January 1557 a commission to survey the whole of the estates (and which was also to enforce a range of 'commonwealth' legislation) was issued.[114] Likewise, the idea of disafforestation and disparking was further approved in 1555 and a commission to set this in hand was issued in December 1557.[115] The desire to abandon decayed or otherwise redundant castles appears in the 1555 debate and in 1561 a commission was issued to identify such property and dispose of it as seemed appropriate.[116]

A further area in which there was a continuing debate about the possibility of making savings was repairs. Although they were only a minor charge on income, this was a matter which the Exchequer could control and even pass on to the tenants themselves. The 1552 report had seen advantage in the grant of copyholds in place of leases

---

[110] Somerville, *Duchy of Lancaster*, I, pp. 302–3. The lands annexed were mostly in southern England and were worth £1,176 in 1558–9. For the local dimensions of this, Diarmaid MacCulloch, *Suffolk and the Tudors. Politics and Religion in an English County, 1500–1600* (Oxford, 1986), pp. 237–8.

[111] G. R. Elton, *The Tudor Revolution in Government* (Cambridge, 1953), pp. 242–3, prints the relevant materials and offers an alternative explanation.

[112] BL, Harl. MS 6850, fol. 104r.   [113] BL, Lansd. MS 1215, fols. 2r–6v.

[114] 1555 debate cl. 1; *CPR Philip and Mary*, III, p. 313.

[115] 1555 debate cl. 14; *CPR Philip and Mary*, IV, p. 73.

[116] 1555 debate cl. 13; Colvin (ed.), *History of the King's Works*, III, pp. 231–2. For the implementation of this commission by one auditor, E163/15/35 (second document at this reference).

because it discharged the King of the burden of repairs. Elsewhere, it advocated tightening up the means by which repairs were costed.[117]

The policy of having the tenants shoulder the cost of repairs may firstly be looked at in the context of urban property. The connection between urban decay, the problems faced by corporations in raising fee-farms and the very poor state of the Crown's urban property has not previously been made. The Crown's tenements and burgages in Scarborough *c.* 1565 were said to be

> marvellously decayed, so as thereby the town is much defaced, the Queen's majesty loseth much rent... and the corporation is not answered of such rent thereof as they ought to have towards the payment of the fee farm to the Queen's majesty, whereby they answer the Queen of an unleviable rent in that part.[118]

The need for repairs to the Crown's urban property was a recognised problem: as far as possible, it was an obligation which the Exchequer sought to evade. In the 1555 debate it was agreed that the Crown's urban property should be let in fee-farm or in some other way to relieve the Crown of its responsibilities for repairs. In 1561, Winchester recommended the granting of urban property by copy.[119] The only place where this was obviously done during Mary's reign was at Abingdon, where the town was incorporated and granted the Crown's urban tenements in fee-farm in November 1556.[120] When Beaumaris was granted a new charter in 1562, it had (in consideration, the patent said, of the damage done to the tenements and walls of the town by the sea) the fee-farm of the Crown's tenements in the borough, but it was charged with the upkeep of the fortifications and sea walls.[121] The same policy was put into effect a generation later at Leicester. Here, a Duchy commission of 1587 found widespread decays in its urban property, the necessary repairs to which were costed at £5,123. On the town's petition, Leicester was incorporated and granted the property in fee-farm. It is plausible to assume that the whole process was initiated by the town itself.[122] Fee-farming urban property served more purposes than simply endowing urban corporations.

In a similar fashion, the Crown also pursued a policy in the 1560s

[117] Richardson, *1552 Report*, pp. 181, 189–90. For policy in the early 1560s towards the Crown's customary tenants, see below, ch. 8.

[118] SP12/36, no. 52. See also the report on the Crown's property in Stanford in 1600, cited by Thomas, below, p. 63. [119] BL, Harl. MS 6850, fol. 103v.

[120] *CPR Philip and Mary*, III, pp. 380–6. [121] *CPR 1560–3*, pp. 349–50.

[122] James Thompson, *The History of Leicester* (Leicester, 1849), p. 282.

of shifting the burden of repair and maintenance on to its lessees in return for leases of an unusually long term, often forty years but sometimes sixty years. The commission for leases issued in 1557 made no provision for this, but that of 1560 gave the commissioners authority to make leases of decayed mills, marshes and houses for terms of up to sixty years without the reservation of rent.[123] A few instances can be seen in which this provision was applied to urban tenements. In 1563, the Exchequer leased extensive but ruinous urban property in Northampton for sixty years, the patent explaining that the lands had been rented at £50 but that because of the poor state of the property no one would offer more than £30 in rent until the lessee agreed to give £40 and undertake repairs, doubtless in return for the concession of a longer estate.[124] Two decades later, the city of York had a lease for sixty years of extensive ex-monastic and chantry tenements in York at a rent of £56 16s 6d, apparently without fine, the Council agreeing to bear the costs of putting the tenements into good repair.[125]

The Crown's most determined attempt to reduce the cost of repairs was to pass the charges of sea defences and harbours on to its tenants.[126] David Thomas shows how from 1563, leasehold tenants in Lincolnshire normally undertook such repairs to sea defences as were necessary.[127] This was but one means by which such obligations were transferred. The decree made with the tenants of Low Furness in 1564 (a package which included the confirmation of tenant right and the definition of their border service obligation) also transferred to them the responsibility for the repair of the sea walls of the island of Walney, the Queen contributing no more than great timber when required. If any of the lands were lost to the sea, the tenants were to make up the rent; conversely, any thrown up by the sea were to be rented separately.[128] This may have been a confirmation of a customary arrangement, but the decree for the maintenance of the banks of the River Severn made with the tenants of Longley (Gloucestershire) in 1569 has the appearance of a new arrangement conjured into existence. The tenants accepted responsibility for the maintenance of the river banks, but to assist with the expected

---

[123] *CPR 1560–3*, pp. 444–5.   [124] *Ibid.*, pp. 433–4.
[125] *Draft Calendar of Patent Rolls, 27 Elizabeth I* (List and Index Soc., 241, 1990), pp. 249–51.
[126] Or even by their sale; the 1561 commission for the sale of Crown lands authorised the sale of marshlands if the Queen was charged with their defence, even if the commission was barred from the sale of the manor in which they lay. Thomas, 'Administration of crown lands', pp. 215–16.   [127] See below pp. 175–6.   [128] DL6/12.

expenditure the Exchequer gave them a half-share of the fines on copyhold grants and amercements and the tenants also secured valuable concessions over the way in which future copyhold demises would be made. A precedent for this grant might well be the assignment of the Hull Blockhouse to the city authorities in 1552 with an endowment for its upkeep; the city lost heavily on this arrangement and the Longley arrangement was dissolved at the end of Elizabeth's reign.[129] At Barrow on Humber (Lincolnshire), where the Crown had spent heavily on refurbishing the manorial piers and other sea defences, the tenants of the manor (who held by copies for lives) agreed in 1563 to accept responsibility for the future upkeep of the works and a covenant binding them to do so was inserted in future copies.[130]

A similar problem arose at Bridlington (Yorkshire) where after the dissolution of Bridlington Priory in 1537 the Crown found itself charged with the costs of maintaining the harbour and its pier. In 1562, Winchester wrote to the Queen informing her that despite a heavy investment, both the pier here and that further up the coast at Robin Hood's Bay were in decay and that the best provision that could be made for future repairs would be to let the manor of Bridlington and adjoining lands without fine but charging the lessee with responsibility for maintenance.[131] The proposal was finally accepted and in 1566 the manor and rectory of Bridlington was leased to twelve inhabitants of the town on behalf of the whole community for a term of forty years.[132] The subsequent history of the lease seems chequered. Although the tenants spent heavily on the works (an expenditure of £960 was mentioned in 1581), the lease was called in in 1585 and a new lease to the tenants granted in 1595. The task of rebuilding and maintaining the pier was clearly beyond their means (and one only needs to recall the history of the Crown's improvements at Dover to appreciate the failings of even the best

[129] E123/4, fols. 21r–2r; E123/28, fol. 228r. Colvin (ed.), *History of the King's Works*, IV, p. 475. VCH, *East Riding*, I, p. 415.

[130] SC2/183/119. A similar arrangement was arrived at with the tenants of the manor of Goxhill (Lincs.) in 1579, Thomas, 'Administration of crown lands', pp. 215–16, citing E123/1A, fols. 195v–6r.

[131] SP12/25, no. 56, printed by J. S. Purvis, *Bridlington Charters, Court Rolls and Papers, XVIth–XIXth Century* (London, 1926), pp. 167–8. Most of the sources referred to in this section are printed by Purvis with the exception of the 1566 lease, *CPR 1563–6*, no. 2558.

[132] In SP12/36, no. 52, Sir William Strickland claims the credit for this idea. He also suggested that the way to maintain the pier at Scarborough was to lease the rectory and the Crown's urban property there to the Corporation and to bind them with its upkeep.

sixteenth-century engineering when faced with a truculent sea). The scale of the task can be seen from the self-interested proposal of a local gentleman that he should take responsibility for the upkeep of the pier in return for a grant of the manor of Bridlington and additional lands worth £100.[133]

The final instance of the Crown assigning the upkeep of sea defences to tenants comes from the Yorkshire manors of Whitgift and Airmyn on the Humber. Here in 1563, the tenants were induced to surrender their copyhold estates to take a forty-year lease of their manors, having the duty placed upon them of maintaining the banks of the Humber and other drainage works.[134]

There are enough cases from within a short period to suggest that the Crown was following a deliberate policy of trading the costs of repairs against other concessions, normally extended leases. In that this increased net revenue, it can be seen to be very much in the retrenchment spirit of the 1550s.

Whilst the Duchy of Lancaster survived attempts to incorporate it into the Exchequer, it was by no means placed above scrutiny. The survey of the Duchy's manors in Staffordshire, Leicestershire and Derbyshire authorised in May 1557 may be seen as rising from the general commission for surveys issued the previous January. Whilst the instructions for these surveys required the collection of an almost unparalleled level of detail, there is no sign that they were extended to the Duchy's other estates.[135] The Duchy's Chancellor, Sir Ambrose Cave, was instructed to make a fuller examination of the possibilities for retrenching on expenditure and increasing income in July 1561. (It may not be unreasonable to see Winchester's hand behind this.) Cave was to investigate the state of castles and the sums allowed for their repairs in the previous four years, report on the keeping of the Queen's houses, view the forests, the state of the game and woods, audit the records of recent woodsales and (most significantly) consider the quantity and *fertility* of the soil of forests. He was to view mills and milldams and calculate recent expenditure on their

---

[133] Purvis, *Bridlington Charters*, pp. 173–5. Nearby Flamborough was leased in January 1562 to a group of its inhabitants who accepted similar obligations for the upkeep of the port and harbour; they had the lease without fine but it was only for twenty-one years. It was renewed for a further twenty-one years in 1570. *CPR 1560–3*, pp. 321–2; *CPR 1569–72*, no. 558.   [134] *CPR 1560–3*, pp. 572–3, 579; also SP14/35, no. 37; SP14/51, no. 22.

[135] *CPR Philip and Mary*, III, p. 313; DL42/96, fol. 197r–v (commission for survey); Leeds Archives Dept, Ingleby MS 3097 (articles for surveyors). The completed surveys are DL42/109–11.

maintenance. He was given a shopping list of waste lands and parks which might be improved 'to our honour and profit and for the benefit of the commonwealth where they be'. All forests, parks and chases more than 7 miles from any of the Queen's houses or castles were to be ordered for her best advantage.[136] The spirit of the report of 1552 can clearly be seen at work in these articles with their concentration on the reduction of costs and the improvement of parks and forests. Cave apparently took this commission as his cue to make a personal inspection of the Duchy's property in Yorkshire and the north Midland counties in the summer of 1561. He certainly made some sort of return of his findings which appears not to have survived, but by April 1562 Winchester had seen his surveys, plots and other observations and these were considered at a conference of councillors in July 1562. Here, a number of reforms were identified. Whilst some castles were to be kept for military or other reasons, others were to be abandoned. Various offices attached to castles were to be allowed to lapse when their incumbents died. The parks attached to castles, as at Sandal, were to be converted to herbage and leased to the constable of the castle; in turn he was to be responsible for repairs. A number of mills in the Honour of Pontefract which had required heavy repairs were to be abandoned and replaced by wind or horse mills if the tenants would not accept responsibility for their maintenance. In the case of Ripon minster, it was suggested that the parishioners be made responsible for repairs to the nave. The purpose of all these proposals was to reduce costs (and so increase net income) by transferring them to tenants or officers.[137]

Writing for his son in 1570, the Chancellor of the Exchequer and councillor Sir Walter Mildmay offered the aphorisms that one should 'consider thy revenue and frame thy charge thereafter' and 'grieve not thy tenants with exactions'.[138] Such thinking guided the administration of the estates after 1553. Gross income was pretty much fixed (although the improvement of lands by exchange could offer some increase). Net income could be increased by cost cutting.

---

[136] DL5/13, unnumbered pages between pp. 108–9.

[137] DL41/12/33 (Winchester's opinion, 7 April 1562), DL44/75 (report of the conference of 4 July 1562 which merely adopts many of the proposals in the previous). The episode has previously been discussed by Somerville, *Duchy of Lancaster*, I, pp. 320–1 (although he introduces a confusion of dates) and see also Colvin (ed.), *History of the King's Works*, III, pp. 179–81.

[138] Quoted by S. E. Lehmberg, *Sir Walter Mildmay and Tudor Government* (Austin, TX, 1964), p. 78.

Casualties, fines and woodsales were but a marginal element; the Crown's preference was for a reliable recurrent revenue. The appropriate course to be taken when expenditure exceeded revenue was for expenditure to be cut; it was morally incorrect to burden one's tenants. This remained the perspective of administrators throughout the later sixteenth century. But where Winchester actively worked to increase net income, his successor, Burghley, appears to have simply accepted the principles of this policy without attempting to maintain his predecessor's policy of making marginal improvements in revenue when and where he could. The issues were settled in the 1550s and early 1560s. By the 1590s, economic conditions had changed so much as to force their reassessment, and the policy of masterful inactivity pursued by Burghley had to end.

VI

Earlier, it was suggested that the sheer scale of the lands and their unsystematic character forced a degree of delegation and produced problems of supervision on a scale found on no other English estate. The anxiety in the mid-sixteenth century to reduce costs by cutting the administrative staff of the estates can only have compounded the problem. As the Crown's primary concern was to secure the receipt of fixed renders, it had little occasion to look too closely at the activities of its local officers. Stewards and bailiffs may well have sought, even occasionally competed for, office; but when we see Lord Keeper Bacon amassing stewardships in Suffolk, we must acknowledge that his first concern was to advance his own esteem and local authority rather than to serve the Crown's purposes.[139] This tendency was particularly marked in Wales, where, as Dr Gray shows, Crown offices had an importance far in excess of that in England. Where in England the possession of an office seems to have conferred relatively little status in itself, in Wales it was valued for the status and possibilities for profit it brought in a society where the Crown remained the predominant landowner. Here, and at many other points in this volume, we shall encounter local agents of the Crown whose behaviour was directly contrary to their employer's best interest.

The consequence of possessing a small central staff whilst dele-

---

[139] Part of his motive may have been to use the Crown's tenants as a voting bloc in shire elections; MacCulloch, *Suffolk and the Tudors*, pp. 33, 87–8.

gating extensive responsibilities to local officers was a considerable confusion between the public and the private in the management of the estates. This raises a number of questions about the circulation of information between the central agencies of the estates and their local officials. How was the central administration informed about developments on the estates? How did it communicate with its tenants when it needed to do so? Could it take the lead in encouraging innovation or did it merely respond to a process of innovation driven from below?

At the top of the administrative structure stood the Lord Treasurer. Reporting to him (or at periods when the office was vacant, the Treasury Commissioners) were the auditors of the land revenue, below them the receiver and surveyor for each county and at the very local level, the steward and bailiff of each manor and the woodwards. The auditors were the linchpin of the whole administration and are, should this book have any, its heroes.

The auditors were a body of seven men whose office was grafted on to the Exchequer after the abolition of the Court of Augmentations.[140] As *parvenu* within the organisation whose status and duties were never quite thought through or regulated by statute, they were the objects of some hostility from the older officers for reasons of professional jealousy as well as principled doubts over working practices.[141] Each of the seven had responsibility for a circuit of counties varying from three (the north-eastern circuit) to eleven (the Midland–north-western circuit).

As with all early modern Exchequer offices, much of the work was done by clerks appointed and employed by the auditors themselves. The qualification for appointment to an auditorship was experience acquired as an auditor's clerk. When Justinian Povey petitioned for the reversion of an auditorship in 1606, he claimed sixteen years' experience in the Court of the Exchequer including twelve in the office of Sir William Spencer (auditor 1579–1609).[142] Robert

---

[140] For a list of auditors, their dates of appointment and period in office, see J. C. Sainty, *Officers of the Exchequer* (List and Index Soc. special ser., 18, 1983), pp. 105–34. My understanding of the auditors' role owes much to a forthcoming paper by Dr Gray which she kindly allowed me to read.   [141] See, for instance, Vernon, *Considerations*, pp. 60–2, 96–8.

[142] *CSPD 1580–1625*, pp. 476–7. Povey had his grant but had to wait until 1619 to enter office. He was more fortunate in securing the Queen's auditorship after the death of Ralph Ewens (who was also Clerk of the Commons) in 1610. A notable pluralist, he was appointed receiver in Suffolk and Huntingdonshire in 1615 (*CSPD 1610–18*, p. 277).

Paddon's undated petition (but of the 1630s) traced his career over the previous twenty-seven years as first a clerk to his father, an auditor of land revenue (d. 1613), then deputy to Auditor Hockmore of the Duchy of Cornwall and finally clerk to Sir William Uvedale, Treasurer of the Chamber.[143] A few sons followed their fathers in the post, but the system of making grants in reversion to the first post that came free tended to ensure that sons rarely inherited their fathers' circuit. This was quite right; the auditor's claim to professional status came not from long familiarity and acquaintance with a specific circuit, its lands and personalities, but from an understanding of methods and procedures. (It is not without significance that the office of auditor, unlike that of receiver, was never sold.)

The fact that the auditors had a range of technical skills also meant that they were employed on an *ad hoc* basis on other tasks. Auditor Neale was charged with preparing an inventory of the Queen's wardrobe in 1601.[144] In 1638, Auditors Sawyer and Philips examined household accounts from 1526 onwards to report on irregularities in accounting which had developed since that date.[145] In 1660, the restored auditors complained that the new branches of revenue had appointed their own auditors, surplanting them, when they could do the task as well and more cheaply.[146] These occasional employments should not disguise the fact that their major responsibility was the auditing of estate accounts prepared by receivers and other junior officers.

If anyone was employed to know about the Crown lands, it was the auditors. When Lord Treasurers sought information about the state of the land revenue, or had some query about the estates (as, for instance, in the drawing up of a particular for the lease or sale of lands), it was to the auditors that they turned. So long as the Crown lands were organised to run mechanically to ensure the regular payment by bailiffs to receivers of a calculated and fixed rental and a small fluctuating income drawn from fines on copyholds, heriots, amercements and woodsales, the quality of information required by the central administration was very slight. When in late 1614 the new Lord Treasurer asked the auditors for a certificate of the manors under their charge, including the names of individual tenants, the

---

[143] *CSPD 1634–5*, p. 608. Paddon's appointment is not noticed by Sainty.
[144] E403/2723, fol. 89r; Neale was paid £30. The inventory he prepared may perhaps be BL, Stowe MS 57, printed by J. Arnold, *Queen Elizabeth's Wardrobe Unlock'd* (Leeds, 1988), ch. 10 (although Neale is not there named as its author).
[145] *CSPD 1637–8*, pp. 148, 312.   [146] PRO30/24/4/96.

auditor Thomas Neale made a return saying that the task 'cannot be done by any records remaining with the said auditor but your lordship may receive the best satisfaction from the stewards of every manor'.[147] This was doubtless equally true for all his colleagues.

At this distance, it is hard to be certain exactly what materials the auditors had available to them in their offices. The surviving surveys and rentals in the Public Record Office have been swept into a number of classes without regard for their archival origins or the purposes they were expected to fulfil in contemporary administration. The study of these documents as a body of records rather than as evidence of local circumstances has barely begun. They are but the remnants of what once survived in the Exchequer's hands. Surveys, rentals, court rolls and other papers were removed from the archives of the Crown when the estates themselves were sold and this loss makes it excruciatingly hard to reconstruct what once existed. But it needs to be conceded that the auditors were often ignorant, as Neale admits, of circumstances on individual estates. There had been a total failure to implement the various proposals for record-keeping made in the 1550s. The commission of 1552 thought that rentals should be renewed every ten, twelve or twenty years. The standing orders of 1554 looked to the yearly return of court rolls.[148] Of course, historians would have cause to applaud such a far-sighted system of record-keeping had it been implemented and maintained, but the recurrent collection of nearly identical sums from the estates year upon year made up-to-date surveys and rentals, the regular return of court rolls or even a familiarity with the lie of the land of the individual estates otiose. Nonetheless, the fact that such records were unavailable was taken by a vocal surveyors' lobby in the early seventeenth century as evidence of the inadequacies of the Crown's administration.[149]

It was the auditors who acted as the Crown's first line of communication with the estates through the mechanism of their annual autumn audit when they made a circuit of the counties under their charge. It is possible to find them spreading the word of land sales as early as 1563. In 1608 they were instructed to warn the tenants of mills of the Crown's intention to sell. A year later, they were to test the acceptability of altering the forfeiture clause in leases. An undated (Jacobean) proposal that the Crown's tenants should

---

[147] E101/524/3 (unfoliated).
[148] Richardson, *1552 Report*, pp. 169, 181; Thomas, *Notes of Materials*, p. 100 (cl. 26).
[149] See below, pp. 208, 216.

offer a year's rent as a loan stressed that the project needed to be accepted or rejected quickly as the auditors and receivers were about to embark on their circuits.[150] The auditors did not have a monopoly on this. Salisbury in particular tended to announce policy by writing directly to stewards. In 1611 he wrote to the bailiffs and stewards telling them to 'give general and public notice' of the King's intention to sell land to the tenants within their charge and to all others 'such as are likeliest either to divulge the same or become purchasers'.[151]

The reverse flow of information was certainly much greater in volume and came to the central administration by a variety of routes. The auditors had a part to play in this although it is hard to pin down what they actually did. Correspondence between auditors and the Lord Treasurer describing circumstances on the estates is scarce although it can be found. A number of draft letters from Auditor King to Burghley bear on King's work in absorbing the Dacre estates into the Crown lands in 1589–90,[152] but the exhaustive archives of Salisbury and Cranfield appear to contain no letters from auditors. Officers in the counties occasionally wrote directly to Burghley. In 1575, the surveyor of the North Riding, Sir William Fairfax of Gilling, wrote telling him of disputes between the tenants of Staingrave, Cawton and Hovingham over common grazings, some of the protagonists in which had been murdered, and asking him to issue a commission for the division of the common. This was done.[153] A few years later, Thomas Lovell, the surveyor in Huntingdonshire, sent Chancellor Mildmay a long list of complaints against Sir Henry Williams alias Cromwell, the Queen's lessee of the manors of Hartford and Kings Ripton. These had been brought to his notice by 'a great number of Her Majesty's poor tenants wronged in diverse places who do very often repair unto me for my counsel and advice in many of these causes'.[154] As with the auditors, it is possible to say that a

---

[150] Outhwaite, 'Who bought crown lands?', p. 18 n. 4; SP46/68, fol. 246; BL, Add. MS 36767, fol. 196r; LR9/1/102; SP14/75, no. 43.

[151] For examples of Salisbury's letters to stewards, see below, p. 228; Bodl., Rawlinson MS D908, fol. 7; Bodl., Clarendon MS 1, no. 59. Instances can be offered from slightly later of the auditors being asked to write circular letters to stewards (e.g. LR1/195, fols. 228v–9r).

[152] Scattered through the auditors' miscellanea, LR9 (a large part of which comes from the office of King and his successors).   [153] HMC, *Various Collections*, II, p. 94.

[154] E163/16/5 (of 1582). See E123/7, fol. 263v. A more institutionalised system may have operated in mid-century. There are extant two books of queries about the administration

channel of communications ran directly from local officers to Burghley; it is less certain how often it was utilised.

In asking Burghley to look favourably upon the tenants, Lovell held out the prospect that '[the tenants] are minded if the said Sir Henry do not cease from his oppressions to become humble suitors unto your honour [Mildmay] and my said Lord [Burghley] for their aid'. This leads us to consider the means by which the central administration normally became aware of events on the estates: through the tenants taking the initiative to complain. Here we must distinguish between two types of documents which, although superficially similar and to a degree interchangeable, sought to activate two different forms of proceeding.

The petition was ubiquitous in both medieval and early modern society. Petitions were received not only by the monarch but by all officers of state. Unlike the letter, the petition was not directed between equals; petitions flowed upwards in the graduation of social status. This was reflected in the understood form of the petition. It employed a formal address, was never signed and was usually written, landscape fashion, on paper. As ephemeral documents, petitions were never systematically preserved, enrolled or regis-tered.[155] The petitions which concern us, most of which were directed to the Lord Treasurer or the Chancellor, asked for executive action. Petitioners sought the granting of leases to themselves or the withholding of leases from third parties,[156] they asked for letters to be written advancing the petitioner's case. Sometimes they requested the expedition of litigation or the issuing of commissions. In short, they petitioned for a concession which lay in the hands of a single officer of the Exchequer.

Perhaps surprisingly, the evidence of the endorsements on the surviving Elizabethan petitions shows that they were taken seriously and the allegations they made investigated. Burghley's normal practice seems to have been to refer petitions to the senior baron of the Exchequer and the Queen's Remembrancer for confirmation of

---

of the estates for the Lord Treasurer's attention, raising such matters as the need to make leases, undertake repairs and (a sign of the times) sell church goods. E163/15/29, 35; also E315/478, fols. 31–2, 57.

[155] Petitions to the Lord Treasurer may be found scattered throughout the Exchequer archive, but especially in the early volumes of SP46 (amongst both the 'private' and 'Exchequer' papers in that class.) Petitions to Salisbury are printed in HMC, *Salisbury*, xxiii–iv and those to Cranfield survive in his papers at Kent AO.

[156] SP46/29, fol. 50 (1571), *CSPD 1640*, p. 94.

the facts of the matter and their opinion as to the appropriate action.
This may be illustrated by two petitions from late in Burghley's life.
In the summer of 1590, the tenants of the manor of Monk Bretton in
Yorkshire, who were engaged in a long-running enclosure dispute
with a neighbouring landlord, Richard Wortley, sent Burghley a
petition complaining of Wortley's breach of the spirit of orders made
in the Exchequer the previous year. The tenants sought an injunction
against Wortley and the issuing of a commission to Christopher
Saxton and others to make a plan of the manor and the lands in
contention. Burghley forwarded the petition to Baron Sotherton and
the Remembrancer, Fanshawe, with instructions to speak with
Wortley. They returned the petition with a note that Wortley had left
London before they received the petition and were in his absence
reluctant to proceed with an injunction against him, but that they
approved the making of a plan. The petition was then endorsed with
a further note of Burghley's request that Fanshawe should issue a
commission to Saxton and others for the survey. When the tenants of
Compton Magna (Somerset) complained that the inhabitants of
Axholme were enclosing their common and engaging in a campaign
of intimidation against them, the petition was passed for comment to
the auditor who recommended the issuing of a commission; this was
then approved by Burghley and the petition sent on to Fanshawe.
Dozens of other instances of petitions being circulated in this way
could be offered.[157]

Burghley was also prepared to test the truth of a petition by asking
local figures to investigate informally. In 1591 he asked the mayor of
York and the receiver of Yorkshire to view some houses in Castlegate
in York, the tenants of which had petitioned him claiming that the
Crown's lessee was not only failing to carry out repairs but trying to
expel them. Burghley was informed that the tenants' claims were
unfounded.[158]

The equitable bill was a special form of petition, directed not to an
individual officer of the Exchequer but to the Lord Treasurer,
Chancellor, Chief Baron and the other barons in their judicial
capacity.[159] The bill was written on parchment and signed by

---

[157] These examples come from SP46/18, fol. 222; SP46/39, fols. 244–5. SP46/30, fol. 276, is
a reference to the Solicitor-General by Burghley (1576). For a similar case, SP46/39, fols.
219–20, where the county surveyor was asked to report.

[158] York City Archives, B30, fols. 280v–2r.

[159] The fullest account of the history, procedures and records of the equitable jurisdiction of the
Exchequer is W. H. Bryson, *The Equity Side of the Exchequer* (Cambridge, 1975). For the
titles to bills, see p. 97.

counsel. It possessed a clear structure which reflects the use of exemplars; it normally concluded by asking for the court to issue a subpoena to oblige a third party to answer the allegations made against him. The bill in the Exchequer was a subspecies of the English bill employed by the other equity courts including (before its abolition) Augmentations and the procedures employed were broadly common to all. A bill having been lodged with the court, the defendant presented his countercase in an answer, the plaintiff replied with a replication and the defendant with a rejoinder. When the matters in contention were deemed to have been defined ('at issue'), the court would proceed to take evidence. Bills submitted by the Attorney-General and other royal officials were technically not petitions but informations in that they did not ask the court's favour but directed the court to hear the case.[160]

The origins of the Exchequer's equitable jurisdiction are obscure. Bryson has pointed to bills predating the reign of Mary (although no decree and order books survive from before 1557) and suggested that the jurisdiction was in existence during the reign of Edward and perhaps earlier. It is hard to see that the pre-Marian arrangements were anything but rudimentary or that before the merger with Augmentations (with its established jurisdiction and responsibility for the management of land) the Exchequer had much call for an equitable court. It was only later in Elizabeth's reign that the Exchequer started to attract large numbers of bills. Bryson has shown that on average 84 bills per annum were filed in 1558–87 but 334 per annum in 1588–1603, a figure roughly comparable with the levels pertaining in the reigns of James I and Charles I.[161] A large part of this litigation took the form of pleadings over the inheritance and possession of Crown tenements and whilst this business was doubtless dull and burdensome, it was an area in which the Exchequer was monopolistic.[162] The court also dealt with a wide range of disputes

---

[160] The pleadings of the court are contained in the PRO class E112 to which there are no modern indexes (except for Welsh cases before 1625; E. G. Jones (ed.), *Exchequer Proceedings (Equity) Concerning Wales, Henry VIII–Elizabeth* (Board of Celtic Studies, History and Law ser., 4, Cardiff, 1939), and T. I. Jeffreys Jones (ed.), *Exchequer Proceedings Concerning Wales in tempore James I* (Board of Celtic Studies, History and Law ser., 15, Cardiff, 1955). The ESRC has funded the preparation of a calendar of the early Yorkshire pleadings which will appear in the *List and Index Series*, but the lack of convenient finding aids had led to a wholesale ignorance of the riches of the material.

[161] Bryson, *Equity Side*, pp. 15, 168.

[162] As early as 1561 the earl of Rutland as President of the Council of the North was asked not to try cases concerning the Queen's tenants, HMC, *Rutland*, i, p. 77. For an enclosure case sent by the Council to be tried in the Exchequer, SP46/30, fols. 298–300 (1576). A tenant

concerning tenure on the estates including the maintenance of copyhold customs against lessees. The court was the natural location for litigation brought by or against officials and accountants in the Exchequer or concerning such matters as the sale of lands and alienation of leases. But a small (though for our purposes significant) proportion concerned the defence of the Queen's title.[163] Exactly the same types of business arising from the estates of the Duchy of Lancaster were tried before its own court with the result that in boundary disputes the tenants of the Exchequer could sue Duchy tenants in the Exchequer and the latter countersue in the Duchy.[164] By the time of the jointure creations of the early seventeenth century, the existence of such a jurisdiction could not be assumed, but was granted by patent to both Stuart Queens.[165] The Duchy of Cornwall, on the other hand, never acquired a judicial character and conducted its litigation elsewhere.

In fact, the distinction between petitions and bills is not as clear as might be assumed. It is possible to point to instances in Elizabeth's reign when paper petitions addressed to the Lord Treasurer alone were treated by the court as equitable bills. Occasionally, these were rewritten to conform to the normal Exchequer pattern when copies were made for dispatch to the putative defendant.[166] There are signs that the ability to use a petition as the basis for litigation was lost as time progressed. In c. 1588, a number of Yorkshire tenants who submitted a petition to Burghley describing the enclosure of their commons were instructed to reformulate their grievances and resubmit them as an English bill.[167] Injunctions could be issued by

right case was sent to the Council in 1586 'because they were best acquainted in what places of the country the custom of tenant right [was] allowed'; the Council's decree was then ratified. BL, Lansd. MS 171, fol. 448r, v. Other courts acknowledged the supremacy of the Exchequer in cases concerning its tenants, see for instance E123/7, fol. 253v (a case sent from the Court of Requests in 1582). Letters asking that the Court of Requests should not involve itself with Duchy and Exchequer tenants can be found at CSPD Add. 1580–1625, pp. 319, 329 (1590, 1591).

[163] Bryson overlooks 'A brief collection of the decrees, judgements and other principal matters in the Exchequer and Exchequer Chamber from the end of Queen Mary to the end of Trinity Term, 40 Elizabeth', BL, Lansd. MS 171, fols. 437r–56r, an indispensable collection of leading cases made for Caesar (similar to his collection of Requests cases) and which deserves publication.

[164] For instance, E112/52/373 (tenants of the Exchequer's manor of Sawley, Yorks. v. tenants of the Duchy's manor of Slaidburn, 1598); E112/53/409 (tenants of the Exchequer's manor of Raskelf v. the tenants of the Duchy's manor of Easingwold, 1590).

[165] Our knowledge of these jurisdictions is much increased by an excellent paper by Mrs Ruth Fisher which I hope will soon appear in print.

[166] Bryson, Equity Side, pp. 95–6 (although it will be noticed that I find it impossible to accept the explanation for this he offers there).   [167] SP46/35, fol. 163.

the Exchequer on the strength of a petition, as in petitions of 1596 and 1618 which complained of the felling of timber.[168] But petitions could also form the basis of an informal bill procedure. In a mid-Elizabethan case, the countess of Lennox answered allegations made against her in a petition to Burghley by the tenants of Middleham with a submission which, whilst on parchment and unsigned, was written in an informal style wholly inappropriate to an equitable answer.[169] In other instances, Burghley satisfied himself of the truth of the allegations by having the libelled party offer him their version of events.[170]

In the later part of Elizabeth's reign, it was normal for the defence of the Queen's title to be made by interested individuals or groups of tenants acting primarily with the aim of protecting their own profits as Crown tenants. A familiar case in the pleadings is that of the Crown lessee of a mill attempting to maintain his exclusive monopoly in the face of rival water or horse mills. Other Crown tenants complained of the enclosure of their commons by neighbouring landowners, especially where townships intercommoned. The lessees of rectories complained of refusals to pay tithes, or, in a few cases, the loss of tithe income or glebe lands as part and parcel of enclosure and agricultural change. In all these cases, the Crown harnessed the private interests of lessees and tenants to the larger interest of maintaining its title. The costs of such cases fell on the tenants and not on the Crown. In protracted litigation, these could be considerable. A tenant of a parcel of heath land worth only 10s per annum over the Queen's rent in the Bedfordshire manor of Clophill claimed to have spent 200 marks in defending the Queen's title. A Yorkshire tenant was £700 out of pocket.[171]

The Crown's own officers occasionally commenced suits. They could do so either in their own name or by relation to the Attorney-General.[172] Neither sort of suit was common. Of the 877 Elizabethan Exchequer cases for Yorkshire, 16 were brought by the Attorney-General, 8 by stewards, 5 by the county surveyors and 9 by the surveyor of woods north of the Trent.[173] Nor were these suits always

---

[168] SP46/40, fol. 104; SP46/70, fols. 162–3. Injunctions could also be granted on the application of officers, e.g. SP46/30 fol. 1 (1574). [169] SP46/16, fols. 71–2.
[170] *Ibid.*, fols. 237–43. [171] SP46/39, fol. 295. HMC, *Salisbury*, xxiv, p. 214.
[172] Bryson, *Equity Side*, pp. 94–5.
[173] Calculated from the forthcoming calendar of Yorkshire cases.

prosecuted with enthusiasm. Sir Richard Shirburn of Stonyhirst (Lancashire), Master Forester of the Forest of Bowland, regularly submitted bills to the Duchy court either in his name or that of the Duchy's Attorney-General reporting hunting and the spoiling of timber in the forest, but few of his bills are associated with an answer or show signs of being acted upon.[174]

Local officers were doubtless discouraged from commencing prosecutions by the fact that they had to bear the costs of their litigation although they could petition for a reward or allowance.[175] The lack of any regular procedure for their reimbursement is reflected in the strange arrangements that the Exchequer entered into with its surveyors of woods. In 1570, Roger Taverner, surveyor of woods south of the Trent, had a decree in the Exchequer which, in acknowledgement of his past and future service and the fact that he claimed no allowances for his work, promised him a third of all the arrears of woodsales he could claim for the Queen and a third of all fines in the Court of the Exchequer which arose from informations he laid there against the spoilers of the Queen's woods. In 1578, a new decree increased his share of the arrears and fines to a half and later that year this same arrangement was extended to his colleague, Thomas Compton, the surveyor of woods north of the Trent.[176] Some twenty years later, when the office was held by Taverner's son John, these arrangements were the subject of some unfavourable comment. The Queen's Remembrancer, Fanshawe, described to Burghley the way in which the younger Taverner exhibited bills in the Exchequer in his own name (when Fanshawe believed they ought to be moved by the Attorney-General) and then conferred with the defendant, drawing his answer for him and agreeing with him for his fine. Taverner then drew up an order which he had the Chancellor decree, so circumventing the judicial workings of the Exchequer. Elsewhere, Fanshawe expressed his doubts as to whether these arrangements had served to protect the Crown's woodlands.[177]

The remuneration of surveyors of woods was not purely an Elizabethan problem. When Robert Treswell was making a presentation about the state of the King's woods to the commissioners for

---

[174] For instance, DL1/133, S7 (1585); DL1/135, A50 (1586); DL1/138, A21 and A46 (1587); DL1/149, A11 and A16 (1590).

[175] The agreement of 1604 that the Exchequer would take over the expenses of a privately commenced suit against woodstealers in Needwood Forest is unusual. CSPD Add. 1580–1625, p. 451.   [176] E123/4, fol. 115r–v; E123/5, fol. 383v; E123/7, fol. 9r–v.

[177] SP46/40, fols. 31, 146 (1596). The moiety of the fines was still being paid to the Taverner in 1605–6, e.g. E403/2725, fols. 51r, 142v; E403/2736, fols. 28v, 49v, 200v, etc.

retrenchment in 1626, the Chancellor of the Duchy of Lancaster remarked on the deliberate damage done to the King's trees by the keepers where they had the right to take dotard (decayed or misshaped) trees. Treswell told the commission that he had fifty suits for damaging timber in hand but that he bore the charges of prosecution, and asked to have the privilege granted to Taverner extended to him. The commissioners agreed to grant him a moiety of the fines arising from his litigation but not the damages, an offer which Treswell stated would not cover his costs. The commissioners then conceded that the Lord Treasurer should make him *ad hoc* payments and that he should be entitled to sue in the Exchequer without paying fees.[178]

The inevitable consequence of associating the defence of the Crown's interests with the profit of private individuals was that it encouraged strangers to lay claim to premises on the Crown's behalf for their own private profit. The Elizabethan practice of leasing concealed lands to speculators is discussed by Dr Thomas. In the early seventeenth century, the search for lands which the Crown could claim came to encompass not only the detritus of the monastic and chantry lands but also assart lands and lands thrown up by the sea. The specialised standing commissions which concerned themselves with the recovery of this land for the Crown are described by Dr Thirsk elsewhere in this volume, but it might be noticed that the assart lands scheme appears to have started as a private venture before being placed on a semi-public basis.[179] But all tenants ran the risk of having their titles probed by nuisance-makers. An example of this may be briefly given. In 1582, John Brograve (later the Duchy of Lancaster's Attorney-General) had a Duchy lease of the provision rents (of foodstuffs) which had been paid by the tenants of the monastic house of Furness and which the dissolution commissioners had commuted into money payments. Brograve's attempts to collect them forced the tenants to sue him in the Duchy Chamber and in 1583 they had a decree confirming the existing arrangement and cancelling Brograve's lease.[180] This neatly illustrates the confusion between the Crown's need to establish its rights (were the rents concealed?) and the private profit of its agent (the provisions were

---

[178] University of London Library, MS 195, pt i, fol. 21r–v. Other Crown officers worked on a percentage basis including Otto Nicholson, the receiver of assart lands, whose patent in 1606 gave him a fifth of all receipts. Pettit, *Royal Forests*, p. 73.

[179] Pettit, *Royal Forests*, p. 73.

[180] T. West, *The Antiquities of Furness* (1774 edn, repr. Beckermet, 1977), pp. 99–108, 124–9, App. 8 (unpaginated).

doubtless worth a great deal more than the rents established in 1537).
But did the Duchy take the initiative and make a lease to a willing
party or was Brograve the originator of a speculation for his own
profit? We cannot tell.

In a rather later case the association between private profit and
public sanction can be examined more closely. In December 1626,
the commissioners for retrenchment received a petition from one
John Melville describing how he had discovered an area of waste or
common in Kent called Swingfield Minnis (about 4 miles north of
Folkestone) which brought the King no profit. He sought a lease for
fifty-one years on such terms as the commissioners felt reasonable.
The common was the subject of an inquisition into its ownership in
the spring of 1627. This found that it was a common of over 500 acres
not belonging to any of the neighbouring parishes and so, by default,
the King's. The commissioners for retrenchment were informed of
this outcome by a further petition of Melville's and heard a report
from the Surveyor-General and the auditor for Kent that it was in
fact the common of the royal manor of Swingfield. The presumption
was that it was indeed the King's land but before the commissioners
would make a lease to Melville, the Attorney-General was to try the
King's title further by bringing a suit against the neighbouring
landowners.[181] Melville had his lease in 1630 at a rent of £14 5s 6d,
but he seems never to have had possession and the land remained in
contest between the Crown's lessee and the lord paramount who had
traditionally taken a rent from the commoners.[182]

Other instances will be found in this volume of individuals taking
for their own profit leases of lands or rights of which the Crown had
lost sight. Coupled with the need, in the absence of any other aid, for
tenants to take the initiative in the defence of their rights, we can
appreciate the way in which the Crown relied on the determination
of private individuals for the advancement of its interests. This shifted
the financial burden of litigation from the Crown to the tenants, but
it also served to make the Crown reactive rather than proactive.
There was, for instance, no mechanism whereby the Crown could
initiate the enclosure of either open field or common land, and if it
became aware of such alterations in the landscape (and profitability)

---

[181] University of London Library, MS 195, pt ii, fols. 19r, 64–5; E178/5355. The procedure
of bringing an English bill against neighbouring landowners to find the King's title was
used at Sedgemoor, see below, p. 378.

[182] E317/18/41. For additional material (which I have not used), Kent AO, U270 (Radnor
MSS).

of its estates, it was probably because of the lodging of equitable bills claiming that the process had been unjustly implemented or was actually detrimental to the interests of its tenants. It is hard to imagine any private landlord remaining so ignorant of, or incapable of taking advantage from, agricultural change on its estates.

CHAPTER 2

The Elizabethan Crown lands: their purposes and problems

David Thomas

What were the Crown lands for? The most obvious answer is that they were a source of revenue. Indeed, they were regarded by some contemporary observers as having the potential to solve the Crown's financial problems. Sir Julius Caesar was

> not ignorant that they be the surest and best livelihood of the Crown, and that the realm is then most happy when they be so great as that by them the King's state and honour may be maintained, and his expenses, both ordinary and extraordinary, sufficiently defrayed; but this may be wished and hoped for.[1]

When Sir Robert Johnson was asked how much the true value of certain manors was above its rent, he replied:

> I see such a chaos of losses, sustained for want of true knowledge in that point, that I stand almost in fear to think of them, much less dare I delate upon them, for so in my poor judgement should I fall into account of greater masses than all the subjects have yielded in subsidies these forty years, being flatly of this mind, that Her Majesty's own estate, if it were so husbanded, would yield and discharge more than it doth almost the whole burden to which many thousands have dutifully contributed.[2]

The history of the Crown lands as a source of revenue cannot be summarised easily. The nightmarish complexity of the methods of accounting used in the Elizabethan Exchequer (where statements of income and expenditure were rarely produced and even more rarely mean what they appear to mean) makes it difficult to be completely confident about the precision of any figures. However, a reasonable view of the situation is that at the start of Elizabeth's reign, her total land revenue (including Duchy lands) was about £86,000 a year;

---

[1] S. R. Gardiner (ed.), *Parliamentary Debates in 1610* (Camden Soc., 81, 1862), p. 171.
[2] Johnson, *Letter*, BL, Add. MS 41613, fol. 97v (Bodl., MS Perrot 7, fol. 59v).

approximately 30 per cent of the Crown's total ordinary income. By the end of the Queen's reign, her landed income had increased to about £111,000 or about 34 per cent of her total income. By the early 1630s, the position had radically changed. Although the income from the Crown lands had risen to about £116,000 this represented only about 19 per cent of the Crown's total income; because of the Crown's policy of assigning its revenues directly to debtors or suppliers of services, the net cash value to the Crown of the land revenues was only £38,000.[3]

During Elizabeth's reign, the income from the Crown lands rose (although more slowly than the rate of inflation) and the royal estates maintained their position as one of the twin bases of government finance. What is more, this increase in revenue was achieved during a period when large amounts of land were being sold to pay for war. However, no credit can be given to Elizabeth's government for this increase in revenue. The Crown lands were not managed solely for their revenue-producing capacity. Instead, they were used as a source of patronage, a means of rewarding royal servants and clients and as a capital asset which could be converted into ready money when times became tight. The possession of land was also bound up with status, lifestyle and pleasure. Elizabeth and her successors acquired splendid houses set in vast estates and devoted considerable resources and much land to the development of parks for hunting. The increase in the Crown's landed revenue occurred despite, rather than because of, the management policies which the government pursued.

Where had they come from? At the start of Elizabeth's reign, four separate bodies, the Exchequer auditors of land revenue, the Duchies of Cornwall and Lancaster, and the sheriffs, were responsible for administering parts of the royal estate. The Exchequer was the major land management department and its auditors of land revenue ran the lands which had come to the Crown on the dissolution of the monasteries, as well as various miscellaneous properties which had been acquired by attainder, purchase or exchange, or which had

---

[3] This is based on the financial statements given in W. R. Scott, *The Constitution and Finance of English, Scottish and Irish Joint-Stock Companies to 1720* (3 vols., Cambridge, 1910–12, repr. 1951), III, pp. 512, 517. For the Crown lands, I have included revenues of land, fines of leases, sales of woods and the income from the two Duchies. For the Crown's ordinary income, I have taken the net figure without including the income from subsidies. For the 1630s, see E407/78/5.

Table 2.1. *Types of revenue from the Lincolnshire Crown lands,*
1559–60

	%	%
Capable of improvement:		
Farms of manors	9	
Farms of lands, etc.	25	
Rent of land held at will	2	
Fines for leases	3	
Total		39
Capable of improvement with difficulty:		
Copyhold and customary rents	6	
Profits of courts	2	
Farms of rectories	13	
Farms of tithes	2	
Farms of ferries and tolls	1	
Total		24
Incapable of improvement:		
Fee-farms and reserved rents	18	
Pensions and portions of tithes	2	
Free rents and rents of free tenants	5	
Total		25
Unspecified		12
TOTAL		100

Source: Thomas, 'Administration of crown lands', pp. 87–90.

been used to provide jointures for the Tudor queens. Even after
twenty years of sales, the monasteries remained the major source of
the royal estate as it existed in mid-century. In Somerset, Elizabeth
inherited 37 per cent of the monastic land which had been seized by
her father.[4] Attainder was the second major source of lands and the
royal estates were continually enriched with the properties of the
many traitors, rebels and unfortunates who fell foul of the Tudor
monarchs. The lands came from a wide variety of sources; in
Lincolnshire, they had been acquired from forty-two religious houses,
seventy-eight chantries and thirty-seven individuals as well as various
friaries, guilds and free chapels.[5]

[4] K. H. S. Wyndham, 'Crown land and royal patronage in mid-sixteenth century England',
JBS 19 (1979–80), p. 32.   [5] Thomas, 'Administration of crown lands', p. 78.

The Duchies of Cornwall and Lancaster were separately administered units which together accounted for about 15 per cent of the Crown's landed revenue. Both formed part of the ancient endowment of the Crown. The management of the estates of the Duchy of Lancaster has not been studied in much detail, but the main picture which seems to emerge is of neglect and indifference by the Crown over a long period. The Duchy's income – which was derived from its ancient lands, some ex-monastic land in Lancashire and profits of judicial administration – was normally within the range £11,000 to £13,000 a year from 1558 to 1642.[6] The Crown's income from this source failed to rise in a period of inflation and rising rents. Writing in 1642, Christopher Vernon claimed that the Crown's failure to transfer the administration of the Duchy to the Exchequer had cost £200,000 since Mary's reign.[7]

The most obscure area of the royal estate was the old Crown lands which had always been administered by the sheriffs and which had not been placed under the control of the Exchequer land revenue auditors during the reforms of the mid-sixteenth century.[8] These lands yielded between £10,000 and £15,000 a year at the start of Elizabeth's reign. Even contemporaries appear to have been unsure about their nature; perhaps the best comment on them was given by Sir Walter Cope in his apology for Sir Robert Cecil, where he said that Salisbury had found them to be 'a revenue which seemeth decayed by descent of time, and worn out of all knowledge and remembrance'.[9]

The most important question for any landlord in a period of inflation was the extent to which its income could be increased. Table 2.1 is an attempt to show what proportion of the Crown's landed revenue in Lincolnshire in 1559–60 could be improved. The revenues which could be increased consisted of the rents and entry fines from lands which were leased or held at will; there were no legal or economic reasons why such properties should not have been let for market rents. The situation was slightly more complex in the case of manors. In the sixteenth century, owners of manors were entitled to various different types of revenue, including rents from the demesne lands

[6] Dietz, *English Public Finance*, p. 302. For a general history of the Duchy, Somerville, *Duchy of Lancaster*.
[7] Vernon, *Considerations*, p. 58.   [8] For these, see above pp. 6–7.
[9] Sir Walter Cope, 'An apology for the late Lord Treasurer, Sir Robert Cecil, earl of Salisbury', in J. Gutch (ed.), *Collectanea Curiosa* (2 vols., Oxford, 1781), I, p. 123.

and from copyhold tenants, profits of the manorial courts and fixed rents paid by free tenants. The Crown's ability to increase its revenues from its manors was determined by the proportion of demesne to copyhold (rents from the demesne lands could be increased more easily) and by the precise types of tenure by which the copyhold lands were held. Profits of court could be increased on those manors where the fines were arbitrable at the will of the lord, although Chancery was ready to insist that fines had to be reasonable. On other manors, the income from copyholders could not be increased without the complex process of enfranchisement. Even this would only have increased income in the very short term by releasing capital – it would not have increased income in the longer term and might have diminished it if some projects recommending enfranchisement for quit rents rather than fee-farms had been implemented.

Of the seventy-two manors held by the Crown in Lincolnshire, twenty-seven were leased to lords farmers, while forty-five were directly administered, the Crown appointing bailiffs to collect the rents and stewards to run the manorial courts. In table 2.1 it has been assumed that the rents from manors leased to lords farmers could be easily increased, as could the rents from demesne land on manors directly administered by the Crown. Copyhold rents and profits of court on the directly administered manors have been assigned to the category of income 'capable of improvement with difficulty', while the rents from free tenants were fixed.

The revenue from tithes and rectories was inflexible, although tithe income should have risen at a time of rising agricultural prices and output. The problem was that if the Crown increased the rent it charged for tithes, the lessees would have been forced to attempt to increase the quantity of tithes actually collected. This could have led to expensive and tedious litigation. Similarly, market tolls were difficult to raise without provoking local opposition, while the rents from the ferries on the Humber were restricted because the service was not very profitable: the boats would sink from time to time.

Some of the revenues consisted of payments which could not be improved. These included fixed rents or pensions which had been payable to monasteries or chantries, as well as rent charges which arose as a result of the policy of reserving an annual rent of a tenth of the value of property sold between 1536 and 1548.

Table 2.1 shows quite clearly how the Crown lands were not a sort of magic box which could be easily unlocked to provide sufficient wealth to solve the monarchy's financial problems. A quarter of its revenues in Lincolnshire were in the form of copyhold rents, profits of manorial courts and farms of rectories and tithes which could only be improved with great difficulty, while a further quarter could not be increased at all.

Moreover, because the Crown lands had come from so many sources they presented an additional problem to anyone seeking to increase their yield. On the whole, they consisted of small scattered properties which were costly and hard to administer. The Exchequer received £6,700 from its lands in Lincolnshire in 1559–60. This revenue was collected by 134 bailiffs in units which ranged in size from the manors of East and West Deeping (rented to Sir William Cecil for £157 a year) to small parcels of land let at 4d each. Most properties were small; there were only three manors worth more than £100 a year.[10]

A further problem was that many of the buildings on the estate appear to have been in a poor state of repair. The evidence on this point is necessarily impressionistic; no complete survey of the Crown lands was conducted in this period. It is certainly true that the level of expenditure on repairs seems quite low to a modern householder: in some years, the Crown spent less than 1 per cent of its landed income on maintenance. Surveys of Crown property often show that buildings were dilapidated; an investigation of the state of royal property in Stamford in 1600 reported that 'all Her Majesty's buildings through long continuance without repair are now fallen into great decay'.[11] Robert Cecil found that the cost of repairing the King's mills cost more in timber than they produced in rents.[12]

This point can be overstressed. A survey of the fabric of churches in Lincolnshire of 1602 revealed that 10 of the 132 churches of which the Crown was patron were in decay. This was a poor record, but not as bad as that of the bishop of Lincoln, 7 of whose 40 churches were in disrepair.[13] However, it may be that the possibility of increasing rents on the royal lands was limited because of the poor condition of buildings and the lack of investment.

As well as being in a poor state of repair, the Crown lands in the mid-sixteenth century were heavily burdened with out-payments,

---

[10] Thomas, 'Administration of crown lands', pp. 78–80.   [11] E178/1337.
[12] Cope, 'Apology', p. 129.
[13] C. W. Foster (ed.), *The State of the Church in the Reigns of Elizabeth and James I, as Illustrated by Documents Relating to the Diocese of Lincoln*, I (Lincolnshire RS, 23, 1926), pp. lvi, 221–35.

pensions, etc., which had been inherited from the former owners of the lands. At the start of Elizabeth's reign, a sum equivalent to about 4 per cent of the Crown's net income from its lands was going to provide stipends for schoolmasters and curates, perpetual pensions and other continuing payments. Over £17,000 a year, equivalent to approximately 20 per cent of the Crown's net landed revenue was being spent on pensions to former monks and nuns and annuities which had been granted by the monasteries.[14] The great advantage of these pensions was that they died with the recipients. By 1572, spending on pensions had fallen by half and it had all but disappeared by the end of the reign.

The apparent increase in the yield of the Crown's lands under Elizabeth can be accounted for by three factors. First, there was this remarkable decline in spending on payments to the ex-religious which created the appearance that its landed income was rising. Secondly, the Crown acquired a great deal of property, including the lands of rebels, lands accepted in payment of debts and rediscovered concealed property. Finally, the Crown increased its revenue because of its practice of exchanging land with the nobility; it normally imposed a rent charge on the land it granted in these exchanges. The impact of these changes in the Crown's landholding in Lincolnshire are shown in table 2.2.

The one theme which was constantly stressed by contemporary commentators was the need for a comprehensive survey and improved record-keeping. The 1552 revenue commission suggested that a perfect survey should be made of all the royal lands and manors. In 1602, Sir Robert Johnson wrote to Cecil of 'the chief foundation of mischiefs, nay, rather, heaps of inconveniences that have grown through the want of authentical surveys'.[15] The records which did exist were regarded by the auditors of the land revenue as their own property and were kept by them in their offices in their own houses. Contemporaries painted a picture of sorry confusion in the Crown's record-keeping. A writer in 1612 said the records of the King's lands were 'lying disorderly upon confused heaps'; another commentator said that 'a great part of the evidences of abbeys, etc., are sold, stolen and lost'. Sir Robert Johnson claimed that scarcely

[14] Scott, *Joint-Stock Companies*, III, p. 490.
[15] Richardson, *1552 Report*, p. 181; Johnson, *Letter*, SP12/283A, no. 80, fol. 168 (Bodl., MS Perrot 7, fol. 69v).

Table 2.2. *Changes in the Crown's landholding in Lincolnshire, 1558–1603*

Lands acquired		
By attainder:		
Duke of Norfolk	£220	
Francis Norton	£130	
Earl of Arundel	£132	
	£482	
Lands acquired by Exchange	£1,004	
Lands acquired for debt	£250	
Concealed land	£50	
Miscellaneous	£42	
		£1,828
Less, lands granted		
In exchange	£624	
Sold	£888	
Gift	£42	
		£1,554
Surplus of lands acquired over lands granted		£274
Decline in pensions paid		£809
Net increase		£1,083

Source: Thomas, 'Administration of crown lands', pp. 94–102.

one court roll in a hundred could be found and wanted to set up a special office to house manorial documents and surveys. Forty years later, in 1642, Christopher Vernon complained of the 'many great losses to the Crown and inconveniences to the subject' caused by the lack of court rolls and rentals of manors.[16]

In these circumstances, lands were simply overlooked. Monastic lands had been valued before the dissolution in the *Valor Ecclesiasticus*, but this was a valuation, not a survey, and it provided little information about the size, nature or location of particular pieces of property. Even less was known about the chantry lands; the commissioners undertaking their confiscation did not have time to visit every parish and relied on reports from local laymen and clerics.[17] Subsequently, lands were surveyed when they were

[16] Edwin Green, 'The management of Exchequer records in the 1560s', *Journal of the Society of Archivists* 5 (1974–7), pp. 28–9; BL, Add. MS 12504, fols. 189v–90; SP14/40, no. 30; BL, Cotton MS Titus B IV, fol. 375; Johnson, *Letter*, BL, Add. MS 41613, fol. 102 (Bodl., MS Perrot 7, fol. 70r–v); Vernon, *Considerations*, p. 98.

[17] J. Caley and J. Hunter (eds.), *Valor Ecclesiasticus temp Henrici VIII auctoritate regia institutus* (6 vols., 1810–34); C. J. Kitching, 'The quest for concealed lands in the reign of Elizabeth I', *TRHS* fifth ser., 24 (1974), p. 64.

acquired, but there is little evidence that Elizabeth's government undertook surveys of existing properties for the purpose of good estate management. A lot of surveys of Crown property do survive from this period, but most appear to have been produced as evidence in litigation or in an effort to discover concealed lands.

To some extent, this was simply the result of an inadequate administrative structure. The Crown employed men called 'surveyors' in every county, but their main task was to certify the cost of repairing Crown buildings. The post of surveyor in Lincolnshire was held successively by Sir William Cecil and his son Thomas, both of whom exercised the office through a deputy and neither of whom was ever employed by the Crown on commissions of survey. Sir Robert Johnson complained that the Queen paid 'so many yearly fees to idle, skill-less surveyors'.[18]

There may also have been a technical problem, because the science of surveying was only just being developed. Johnson's complaints were directed against surveys made by holding inquests before a manorial jury. Measured surveys and plans were an innovation of the Elizabethan period and began to be produced from the 1570s. The initiative for mapping estates seems to have come from the need to provide evidence for, or to take precautions against, lawsuits. By the 1590s, it was fashionable for landowners to employ map makers. From 1586, the Walkers produced maps of estates in Essex, while Christopher Saxton was surveying the lands of St Thomas's Hospital and Thomas Clerke and Thomas Langdon were performing a similar function for All Souls.[19]

What is surprising is the role of Burghley, Lord Treasurer from 1572 to his death in 1597, who has been seen as an influence on the development of mapping. He had his own collection of maps, and, in 1582, Edward Worsop's book on surveying was dedicated to him.[20] Yet Burghley did not extend his personal interests to the management of the Crown's lands; Saxton and his contemporaries were not

---

[18] For the office of the surveyor, see below, pp. 212–13.
[19] On the development of surveying, see H. C. Darby, 'The agrarian contribution to surveying in England', *Geographical Journal* 82 (1933); H. H. Lockwood, 'Those greedy hunters after concealed lands', in K. Neale (ed.), *An Essex Tribute. Essays Presented to Frederick G. Emmison* (London, 1987), pp. 155–6; S. Tyacke and J. Huddy, *Christopher Saxton and Tudor Map-Making* (London, 1980), pp. 16–23 and 47–60; and Peter Eden, 'Three Elizabethan estate surveyors, Peter Kempe, Thomas Clerke and Thomas Langdon', in S. Tyacke (ed.), *English Map-Making 1500–1650* (London, 1983).
[20] Eden, 'Three Elizabethan estate surveyors', p. 69; Tyacke and Huddy, *Saxton*, p. 52.

employed to map the royal estate. Perhaps Burghley felt that the science of surveying was too new to be of value to the Crown. After all, Worsop's book was called *A discovery of sundry errors and faults daily committed by landmeeters*. And, in 1597, Ralph Agas wrote to Burghley of the 'dangerous abuses in land measure... because through the insufficiency of practitioners and diversity of instruments applied thereunto, almost so many errors are committed as there are operations undertaken'.[21]

The inevitable result was that the Crown was ignorant about its lands. This led to much confusion, mismanagement and harm to Crown tenants. Crown leases were imprecise and some tenants had to go to court to defend their interest in the land they had leased. In other cases, the Crown appeared to have made leases which were against the interests of other tenants.

In 1588, there was a lawsuit between the inhabitants of Crowle (Lincolnshire) and one Thomas Tildesley arising from leases the Crown had made to Tildesley of certain woods in Crowle. Unfortunately, the woods were vital to the local economy because the tenants kept a vast herd of cattle there during the winter when Crowle common was flooded; Tildesley was trying to stop them from doing this. Ultimately, the Exchequer was forced to admit that the lease to Tildesley had been a mistake.[22]

From the Crown's point of view, one of the worst effects of its ignorance about its lands was that they were greatly undervalued and consequently it lost vast amounts of money when it came to lease or sell them. Sir Robert Johnson believed that when Crown land was being sold, the value of the property was seldom known and 'by the corruption, negligence or skill of this age, there was sold the pig in the panier (as the proverb is)'.[23] In 1606, Henry Woodhouse claimed that the Crown had lost £100,000 since 1583 because it had sold land at valuations far below the ancient rent.[24]

The inadequacies of management and supervision are particularly clearly exposed in the management of the Crown's woods. Under Elizabeth, the Crown's policy was to derive revenue from its woods, but also to try to ensure that they were managed in an ecologically sound way in order to relieve the perceived shortage of timber. The fear of this was a constant worry to contemporaries and four acts

---

[21] BL, Lansd. MS 84, fol. 69.   [22] E112/24/135; E123/14, fol. 120v.
[23] Johnson, *Letter*, SP12/283A, no. 80, fol. 167 (Bodl., MS Perrot 7, fol. 67v).
[24] BL, Lansd. MS 165, fol. 205.

relating to the conservation of woods were passed between 1540 and 1590.[25] On the Crown lands, the sale of timber and fuel and the prevention of waste was the responsibility of the county woodwards. In Lincolnshire, these officials seem to have been remarkably inactive. The total revenue from the sale of wood in Elizabeth's reign was only £86 or slightly less than half the fees paid to the woodwards. Only two detailed surveys of woods in Lincolnshire survive; both were drawn up when the woods were being leased and contain recommendations for their management, but there are many more examples of woods being leased without any surveys being made. Contemporaries were invariably critical of the Crown's management of its woods; the Marian commissioners for leases were accused of allowing house-bote and great timbers to the farmers of Crown lands 'by reason whereof Her [Majesty's] great timber is greatly consumed and where no timber was near, money was continually allowed to the farmers in recompense which hath been a great charge to Her Majesty'.[26] In 1598, fearing 'such scarcity of timber is already or in short time may grow, as may tend to a general mischief and inconvenience to the whole realm', the Exchequer ordered the sheriffs to assume responsibility for the prevention of illegal felling and waste of royal timber.[27] John Norden, writing in 1613, complained that because lops and tops of trees in forests, parks, chases and woods had been leased 'there is not left in any wood thus granted a branch of a tree bigger than a walking staff'.[28]

Salisbury made great efforts to reform the administration of the woods, making surveys and even numbering individual trees. A copy of a survey of trees made in 1608 and 1609 shows the incredibly detailed nature of his work. Fifteen manors in Lincolnshire were surveyed, the number of timber and decayed trees were recorded, as well as the number and types of trees sold. Instructions for new planting were also given.[29] There is nothing comparable for the Elizabethan period.

In managing its woods, the Elizabethan government had two aims: to raise revenue and to preserve its supply of timber. It appears to have failed on both counts; not all woods were surveyed before

[25] G. Hammersley, 'The crown woods and their exploitation in the sixteenth and seventeenth centuries', *BIHR* 30 (1957), pp. 149–50.
[26] BL, Lansd. MS 105, fol. 141.
[27] Thomas, 'Administration of crown lands', p. 23; E123/25, fol. 129.
[28] BL, Lansd. MS 165, fol. 238. [29] BL, Add. MS 38444, p. 27.

they were let and Crown leases appear to have allowed tenants to damage its woods. At the same time, its income from sales of timber was minimal, while almost all woodland in England was let at below the economic rent. Writing some years ago, Dr Hammersley argued that the whole of this policy was misguided; except for a few local shortages, the demand for wood was very uneven and the Crown might have done better had it not attempted to preserve the woods, but, instead, sold them for agricultural use.[30]

The worst characteristic of the Crown's administrative weakness and ignorance was that many lands and rights were concealed and revenues lost. In some cases, monastic lands which were clearly identified in the *Valor Ecclesiasticus* were concealed, no rent being paid until they were subsequently rediscovered by Elizabethan concealment hunters.[31] There were two methods for discovering concealed lands in Elizabeth's reign; in a number of cases, the Queen licensed courtiers to hunt for such lands and they would obtain grants or fee-farms of the lands they discovered. In other cases, the Crown would grant speculative leases to men who undertook to prove that the land in question was concealed.[32]

It was not only lands which were concealed. On the dissolution of the monasteries the Crown became entitled to herds of cattle on the monastic lands. These were leased out, but no arrangements were made to recover them at the end of the leases; so in the 1580s, Thomas Crooke was given a licence to hunt for concealed herds of cows.[33]

Concealment hunting was the Crown's private enterprise solution to the problem of its ignorance about its lands. Unfortunately, the methods of the concealment hunters did much to harm the relationship between the Crown and its subjects. Elizabeth was forced to restrict the activities of her concealment hunters as a result of complaints in Parliament and in 1600 set up a public body, the Commissioners to Compound for Defective Titles, to allow landowners to insure against problems with the titles to their properties. James reverted to private enterprise and granted a licence to Sir Giles Mompesson, the most notorious concealment hunter of the age. The

[30] Hammersley, 'Crown woods', pp. 148, 158–9.
[31] K. H. S. Wyndham, 'The royal estate in mid-sixteenth-century Somerset', *BIHR* 52 (1979), p. 135.
[32] Kitching, 'Concealed lands', *passim*; Lockwood, 'Those greedy hunters', *passim*. For other examples of speculative leases, see below, pp. 179–81.
[33] SP46/16, fol. 258.

Commons' charges against Mompesson are a catalogue of the problems caused by this method of discovering concealed lands. It was alleged that he had undervalued properties, claimed that land was concealed when rent was being paid to the Crown, attacked people who had spent vast sums draining land or embanking it against the sea and had pretended to discover concealed land by the simple process of copying out the records of the Elizabethan concealment hunters.[34]

The lands identified by the concealment hunters consisted of many small, scattered properties; not just farmland, but buildings too, as in Lincoln, where the tailors' and shoemakers' halls and chapel on the High Bridge were discovered by an Exchequer commission in 1584.[35] This profusion of small properties added to the administrative burden on the Exchequer which had to keep track of hundreds of new tenants. The problem was compounded by the failure to decide which arm of the government machine was responsible and the auditors of land revenue, the Pipe Office and the Duchy of Lancaster all managed lands which had been concealed and rediscovered. As a result, not all the rents due were collected.

Francis Neale, one of the auditors of land revenue, and Peter Osborne, Lord Treasurer's Remembrancer, drew this problem to the attention of the government in the 1590s. Neale claimed that since 1571, the Crown had granted out concealed lands with a total annual value of £1,632, but that £600 of this was not being collected. In some cases, this was because the land from which the rents were due had not been proved to belong to the Queen, but about £200 a year was certainly due to the Crown and was being overlooked. Burghley was willing to pursue the matter but was dissuaded from doing so by Lord Chief Baron Periam who said that 'the parties passed their lands from the concealers not willingly but for fear and therefore it were hard to charge them with the rents'.[36]

As a result of this opposition nothing was done and the pursuit of these missing revenues was left to future generations; Peter Osborne's son raised the issue again in 1608, as did Thomas Neale in 1612. Thomas Neale's memorandum is an expression of the frustration of a

---

[34] C65/185; House of Lords RO, main papers, 23 March 1620–16. And see below, pp. 327–8.
[35] E178/3050. These properties were subsequently 'rediscovered' by Sir Giles Mompesson. House of Lords RO, main papers, 9 July 1620.
[36] BL, Lansd. MS 34, fols. 131–2; BL, Lansd. MS 66, fol. 217; BL, Harl. MS 4807, fols. 49–50; also SP14/35, no. 51.

go-ahead official faced with Exchequer inertia; he wrote 'these rents will be paid when they are demanded and there is nothing wanting to this service but some pains'.[37]

Yet it might seem perverse to suggest that the problem of concealments arose from the Crown having too many officers rather than too few. The lands were organised on a county basis under the control of a Receiver-General. Within the counties they remained in the same administrative units as had been used by their former owners. The lands formerly belonging to Spalding monastery or to the duke of Norfolk continued to be accounted for separately; there was no attempt to rationalise or merge estates. To some extent, this was a practical recognition of the sixteenth-century realities. Maintaining the lands in their historical units served to protect the Crown's title. By keeping the Duchy of York's lands together, it was easy to recreate the Duchy if required; similarly, the lands of attainted persons were kept together because their heirs might be restored.

The retention of the former administrative structure complicated the management of the lands. Rent collectors moved straight from private employment into the Crown's service when properties changed hands. The Elizabethan government appears to have taken no steps to reduce the number of officials it employed. To some extent, its hands were tied as many bailiffs and stewards held their appointments for life or during good behaviour and could not easily be dismissed. When the Crown tried to transfer the responsibility for paying bailiffs or other officials to lessees, it was forced to sacrifice rents or entry fines.[38] Moreover, the post of steward was a minor form of patronage and the Crown could not afford to abandon a way of rewarding its officials. The office of manorial steward was popular as it conveyed local prestige and influence and could be exercised by deputy. In Lincolnshire, the Cecils held stewardships on three royal manors close to their house at Burghley, while the earls of Rutland were stewards of Grantham. The office of bailiff was slightly less popular with senior officials, although a number of clients and relatives of courtiers and officials held such posts. The use of offices as a source of patronage was quite incompatible with the exploitation of the Crown lands as a source of revenue because it meant that the

---

[37] BL, Harl. MS 4807, fols. 49–50; BL, Add. MS 36767, fol. 27.
[38] See below, pp. 178–9.

Crown had to employ a large number of unskilled part-time officers whose only qualification was that they were part of the patronage network. The use of stewardships as a source of patronage was only possible if the Crown continued to administer its manors direct and did not farm them out or to convert copyhold tenures to leasehold. The result was that there was an excessively large number of officials. At the start of Elizabeth's reign, there were 134 posts of bailiff and 35 stewards in Lincolnshire.

Although Elizabeth did not attempt to cut down on the number of officials, the problem was well known to the Jacobean government. In 1612, a sub-commission appointed by the Treasury Commissioners to investigate the King's revenues reported that in the first forty years of the Queen's reign, the total profits of her manorial courts (excepting those in western England) had amounted to £34,575, but that the fees and allowances of officers had exceeded this by £25,504.[39] In 1620, a commission was issued to Bacon, Pembroke, Arundel, Digby, Naunton, Greville, Caesar and Cranfield to investigate the problem that a great proportion of the King's revenues passed through a 'needless circumference and circuit through the hand and by the oversight of a multitude of surveyors, collectors, bailiffs, particular receivers, messengers' and other officers. This was expensive and it increased the possibility of fraud and the danger of loss through the insolvency of minor officers.[40] By the 1630s, the number of bailiffs on the Crown lands in Lincolnshire had been reduced from over 130 to less than 60, 18 of which were held by one man.[41]

The central administration was also not well equipped to maximise income. In 1554, the Court of Augmentations was merged with the Exchequer which then became responsible for administering the Crown lands. The merger had created a rigid and poorly structured body which was incapable of effective estate management. Unlike the Court of Augmentations (which was a specialised land management agency), the Exchequer had much wider financial responsibilities and failed to develop the appropriate means to manage the Crown lands. The main problem was that there was no intermediate layer of management between the auditors of land revenue, who were primarily responsible for drawing up accounts, and the senior

[39] BL, Add. MS 10038, fol. 9v, printed in Spedding, *Bacon*, IV, p. 322.
[40] T. Rymer, *Foedera, Conventiones, Litterae etc.* (1727, ed. Robert Sanderson), XVIII, p. 227.
[41] SC6/Chas. I/542.

officials, the Lord Treasurer and Chancellor. The result was that decisions were taken at an inappropriate level.

Under the Court of Augmentations, leases had been granted by the senior officials of the court, the Chancellor and general surveyors.[42] Under Elizabeth, the details of all leases of land (and about 13,000 were granted during her reign) were decided by the Lord Treasurer and Chancellor. This was no empty formal task. Every particular for a lease was signed by the commissioners for leases and, in many cases, they endorsed the particular with the terms and conditions of the lease. How could Burghley with his many offices and enormous political responsibilities be in a position to determine the conditions of a lease of tithes in Hereford?[43]

If such decisions were taken at too high a level, then there is also some evidence that the auditors of land revenue were too junior to be really effective. The auditors seem to have found it hard to compel reluctant members of the nobility to pay their rents and at the end of Elizabeth's reign, 37 per cent of the arrears of rent from the Crown lands in Lincolnshire were owed by peers.[44]

The worst effect of the 1554 merger was that it created jealousies between the officials of the older sections of the Exchequer and the auditors whom they regarded as upstart newcomers. The auditors were condemned for failing to account by the Ancient Course of the Exchequer and receiving excessively large fees.[45] The Exchequer was riven by internal feuds and divisions which affected the collection of the Crown's revenues. The worst examples of this come from attempts to collect arrears of rents. Technically, the position was that the auditors and Receiver-Generals were responsible for collecting rents. If tenants failed to pay, then responsibility for collection passed to the Lord Treasurer's Remembrancer, who had various powers to collect debts. The problem arose that because of administrative confusion laced with professional jealousy, the auditors and the Remembrancer failed to communicate. The auditors were apparently slow in telling the Remembrancer about debts that were due, with the result that

---

[42] G. R. Elton, *The Tudor Revolution in Government* (Cambridge, 1953), p. 226.

[43] For a fuller discussion of this point, see Thomas, 'Administration of crown lands', pp. 158–63.

[44] SC6/Eliz./1350, mm. 10–16.

[45] On the administrative problems of the Elizabethan Exchequer, see J. D. Alsop, 'Government, finance and the community of the Exchequer', in C. Haigh (ed.), *The Reign of Elizabeth I* (Basingstoke, 1984), pp. 101–24.

the process for levying them was often not initiated for many years; consequently, money was not collected and when the Exchequer eventually got round to acting, some debtors were dead and their lands sold. Conversely, when the older sections of the Exchequer did manage to collect debts, they seemed to have failed to tell the auditors, so that debts continued to be recorded as being outstanding when they had long since been paid. In 1610, Salisbury claimed that when James came to the throne, £900,000 was owed to the Crown. It is likely that a high proportion of these 'debts' had long since been satisfied or exonerated and that nobody had told the auditors. In 1571, the Exchequer conducted an investigation into debts and discovered that in Lincolnshire 68 per cent of the debts which appeared on the auditor's books had either been paid off or forgiven.[46]

Supporters of the Ancient Course of the Exchequer claimed that there was insufficient control over the auditors and that they abused their positions. One objection was that they were responsible both for determining how much money was owed and for ensuring that it was collected. Although their accounts were judicially controlled and declared before the senior Exchequer officials, there was no attempt to check them against subsidiary vouchers and it was suspected that they gave excessive allowances for fees, diets and repairs. When Thomas Lichfield tried to investigate these abuses under Elizabeth, he found that the auditors held all the relevant records in their own hands.[47] It was believed that the auditors abused their position when drawing up particulars for the sale or exchange of Crown lands. The earl of Essex appears to have had close contacts with them; it was claimed that in 1588 he had been granted land worth £300 in fee-farm, but that in reality he had been given lands worth three times as much, 'the benefit whereof was divided amongst the auditors and managers of the deceit'.[48] In 1590, Essex conveyed the manor of Keiston to the Crown. No rent was charged by the Crown to the tenant of the manor until 1601 when John Hill, auditor for Huntingdonshire, claimed it was the first he had heard of the matter

---

[46] Thomas, 'Administration of crown lands', pp. 167–74. Evidence of the 1571 investigation into debts can be found in the accounts of the Receiver-Generals, e.g. SC6/Eliz./1319, mm. 14d–17d.

[47] BL, Lansd. MS 806, fol. 136v; BL, Cotton MS Titus B IV, fols. 269v–70r; BL, Add. MS 12504, fols. 81–188; Elton, *Tudor Revolution*, pp. 254–5.

[48] BL, Lansd. MS 169, fol. 125v.

although the manor had been surveyed by Hill's predecessor just before the exchange in 1589.[49]

The other major abuse practised by estate officials was one which affected most Crown revenue departments in this period. Because there was a time-lag between the collection of revenue from Crown tenants and the moment when it had to be paid to the Exchequer, the receivers were able to make use of the cash balances on their accounts. In 1637, Wentworth calculated that as receiver of the northern recusant revenues he ought to have the constant use of £4,000 to £5,000 in hand, which he felt was the chief benefit of the place.[50] This practice was not officially sanctioned, but was not outlawed, and provided a useful supplement to the income of officials. Unfortunately, the receivers were not always fortunate in their investments and several of them were unable to meet their obligations to the Crown. To some extent, the Crown was protected against these financial collapses because all revenue-collecting officers on its lands had to provide sureties who would be responsible for their debts in the event of bankruptcy, and this prevented the sort of scandals which affected the tellers of the Exchequer under Elizabeth.[51] The use of sureties was an effective safeguard against default; in 1561, the Receiver-General for Lincolnshire, Nicholas Girlington, failed to pay the rent he had collected into the Exchequer. The Exchequer acted with remarkable efficiency, the sheriff was instructed to collect the outstanding balance (about £1,900) from the lands of Girlington's sureties and about £1,400 was recovered.[52]

Considerable work was needed if the Crown lands were to help to increase the Crown's income in a period of inflation. In particular, strenuous efforts would be needed to improve their quality, through the consolidation of small, scattered parcels and the repair or disposal of decayed buildings. Attempts would have to be made to push up rents, and in particular to increase the revenue from the copyhold lands. The central and local administrations would have to be

---

[49] *Ibid.*, MS 156, fols. 45–52; C66/1349, mm. 11–15; C66/1390, mm. 22–34; E178/1068.

[50] G. E. Aylmer, *The King's Servants, the Civil Service of Charles I, 1625–42* (London, 1961), pp. 167–8.

[51] Statute 7 Edw. VI c. 1 (*SR*, IV, pp. 161–4); J. Guy, *Tudor England* (Oxford, 1988) pp. 393–5; C. Coleman, 'Artifice or accident? The reorganization of the Exchequer of Receipt c. 1554–1572', in C. Coleman and D. R. Starkey (eds.), *Revolution Reassessed. Revisions in the History of Tudor Government and Administration* (Oxford, 1986), pp. 163–98.

[52] E159/346, recorda, Easter, mm. 167–201; E159/347, recognisances, Hilary, m. 241d.

streamlined. Above all, there was a vital need for a comprehensive survey of the estates.

What is so surprising is that Elizabeth, who was noted for her parsimony and had to finance major wars towards the end of her reign, failed to take any steps to improve the revenue from her lands. Indeed, Elizabeth's administration appears as a hiatus between the reforms of her siblings and the enormous attempts to increase the revenues which were initiated by Salisbury. The chronology of the exploitation of the estates was sketched out by Sir John Habakkuk in the 1950s. He argued that in the 1530s the rent charged for the Crown lands equalled their market worth. By the 1550s, rising prices meant that the rents charged had fallen behind the real value of property and the Crown began to use entry fines to compensate for its lost income. In the 1560s, the entry fines charged were generally an exact multiple (usually four or five times) of the rents; this implied that the real values of the lands were 40–50 per cent more than the rents. Using entry fines was a convenient way to increase royal revenues without going to the enormous trouble of surveying and revaluing the lands.[53]

Unfortunately, the situation remained as it was in the 1560s for the rest of Elizabeth's reign: in Lincolnshire, rents were not revalued and fines remained at four times the annual rent until the Queen died.[54] On the Duchy of Lancaster estates, there was no increase in income over the reign. Nor did rents rise on the lands which Elizabeth acquired from the bishops in the 1559 Act of Exchange.[55] Apart from a few sensible reforms, such as making tenants responsible for repairing properties and for their defence against the sea, the Elizabethan government took no steps to improve the management of its lands.[56]

This failure to push up rents was at a time when some lay landlords were successfully exploiting their estates. The earl of Sussex, for example, secured some dramatic increases in his rental income between 1559 and 1583.[57] In Northamptonshire, Sir Thomas Tresham was improving his landed income from about 1575 onwards,

[53] H. J. Habakkuk, 'The market for monastic property, 1539–1603', *EcHR* 10 (1957–8), pp. 370–1.
[54] See below, pp. 172–3.
[55] Felicity Heal, 'The bishops and the Act of Exchange', *HJ* 17 (1974), p. 243.
[56] See below, pp. 190, 418–22.
[57] Susan Doran, 'The finances of an Elizabethan nobleman and royal servant: a case study of Thomas Radcliffe, 3rd earl of Sussex', *BIHR* 61 (1988), p. 291.

while in Lincolnshire, lord Clinton was pushing up the value of former Crown property in the 1550s.[58] In general, historians appear to believe that the move to increase income from land only really gathered pace towards the end of the century. This view was held by Stone and appears to have been reinforced by Cliffe's work on the Yorkshire gentry and Coward's on the Stanleys, earls of Derby.[59] Thomas Wilson's view in 1600 was that exploitation of landed estates was a comparatively recent phenomenon.[60]

One factor which may be thought to have influenced the Crown's rental policy was its perception of the need to maintain good relations with its tenants. Tudor moralists stressed the virtues of good landlords. Burghley's contemporary biographer described approvingly how 'He did never raise his own rents, nor displace his tenants. But as the rent went when he bought the lands, so the tenants still held them. And, as I know, some of his tenants paid him but twenty pounds for a thing worth two hundred.'[61] On the estates of leading noblemen, such as the Stanleys, earls of Derby, the military relationship between lord and tenant continued into the sixteenth century and the elite corps which was formed to defend the Queen at the time of the Armada consisted of the servants and tenants of the leading gentry of England.[62] The relationship between the Crown and its tenants was regarded as particularly special by Lionel Cranfield, who felt that it was 'A greater tie of obedience to be a tenant to the king than to be his subject: for as a subject he did only obey him according to his laws, but as a tenant he was ready upon all occasions to serve him and drew others on by his example.'[63] Writing in the early 1950s, Dr Kerridge argued that Salisbury, by increasing rents on the Crown lands, may have sacrificed a measure of support.[64] In reality, it is doubtful whether considerations such as these carried much weight with the Crown, simply because, apart from the two Duchies, the Crown lands were not a coherent estate which had been

[58] M. E. Finch, *The Wealth of Five Northamptonshire Families, 1540–1640* (Northamptonshire RS, 19, 1956), pp. 72–3, 149–63, and see below, pp. 80. 173.

[59] L. Stone, *The Crisis of the Aristocracy, 1558–1641* (Oxford, 1965), pp. 326–7; J. T. Cliffe, *The Yorkshire Gentry from the Reformation to the Civil War* (London, 1969), pp. 43–8; B. Coward, *The Stanleys, Lords Stanley and Earls of Derby, 1385–1672* (Chetham Soc., third ser. 30, 1983), pp. 56, 93.

[60] Thomas Wilson, 'The state of England, anno Dom. 1600', ed. F. J. Fisher, *Camden Miscellany* 16 (Camden Soc., third ser., 52, 1936), p. 39.

[61] F. Peck (ed.), *Desiderata Curiosa* (2 vols., London, 1732), I, p. 43.

[62] Coward, *The Stanleys*, pp. 96–7, 155.   [63] Prestwich, *Cranfield*, p. 339.

[64] E. Kerridge, 'The movement of rent, 1540–1640', *EcHR* 6 (1953), p. 33.

built up over a long time and on which generations of the same
families had lived and died as tenants of the monarch. At the start of
her reign, Elizabeth held lands in Lincolnshire with a net annual
value of £4,646. By 1603, she had disposed of about a quarter of these
by gift, sale or exchange and had acquired by exchange, attainder
and seizures for debt property worth slightly more than the lands she
had disposed of.[65] In 1558, the lands administered by the Exchequer
were worth about £66,000 a year; during her lifetime, the Queen
sold properties worth about £25,000 a year and granted others worth
at least £8,600 a year in exchange, as well as acquiring large estates
by attainder, escheat, etc.[66]

Hence, with the exception of the Duchy of Lancaster, it would be
difficult to identify a group of tenants who could have had the sort of
relationship with the Crown which Lionel Cranfield described.
Instead, the lands were a miscellaneous collection of properties and
rights which had been acquired in a random fashion in the sixteenth
century and which the Crown would happily sell, exchange, dispose
of or reacquire in response to the importunities of its servants or its
own financial situation. The need to cultivate the loyalty of its
tenants played no role in its calculations.

The Elizabethan management of the Crown lands was influenced by
the general state of Crown finances. For most of her reign, Elizabeth
had a surplus on her ordinary income and by 1576 had paid off most
of the debts she had inherited. In the 1580s she was very successful
with her investments in privateering, and it was only the wars of the
1590s which upset the financial equilibrium. In the years of peace,
Elizabeth's policy was to pursue economy and increase the customs
revenues to create a surplus on her ordinary account. In this
situation, there was no pressing need to undertake the slow, painful
revaluation of the Crown lands which would have been necessary to
push up their income. In the period when spending on war was
relatively low, the Elizabethan regime could survive without administratively difficult and possibly unpopular policies towards its

---

[65] Table 2.2 above and for fuller details, Thomas, 'Administration of crown lands', pp.
94–100.

[66] The figure for sales is from BL, Lansd. MS 165, no. 27 (fol. 137); the total for exchanges
includes exchanges with the bishops (see Heal, 'The bishops', p. 239). I have calculated the
figure for exchanges with the laity from an examination of the Patent Rolls, State Papers
and the Receiver-Generals' accounts.

tenants. In the war years, there was no question of revaluing the lands; they had to be sold quickly in order to generate cash.[67] The financial situation was quite different under her successors; faced with a chronic deficit on the ordinary account, Salisbury had to begin the process of surveying estates, improving the value of manors and woods and pushing up the yield of lands.

It may reasonably be argued that raising the yield of the estates was incompatible with their other, non-fiscal uses for patronage and pleasure. Elizabeth's use of her lands as a source of patronage stemmed from the Crown's shortage of cash and from her own desire for economy; feeling unable and unwilling to increase her servants' incomes in a time of inflation, she chose instead to reward them with licences to collect parts of her own income. Thus, senior officials were allowed to share in the Crown's right to profit from wardship or to lease the lands of recusants, while lesser members of the household could profit by selling surplus food.[68] On the Crown lands, servants could be rewarded with offices, leases and exchanges.

We have already seen how the Crown lands were a source of many part-time jobs which were used to supplement the incomes of courtiers. And, it has been shown how this handicapped the successful administration of the estates. The granting of favourable leases, whether in reversion or of the right to hunt for concealed lands, will be described in chapter 7 but these too were incompatible with the administration of the Crown lands as a source of revenue. Salisbury attempted to restrict their use in the Book of Bounty.

The use of exchanges of land as a form of patronage was less harmful to the Crown's interest. Elizabeth took part in forty exchanges, usually with members of the nobility, but diplomats, secret agents and clients of the Cecils also benefited. As a result of these exchanges, she acquired land worth about £5,700 a year, equivalent to about 8 per cent of the annual value of the Exchequer's lands at the start of her reign.[69] The mechanism of an exchange was quite simple: the Crown would receive a large estate or a number of estates, usually let at rack-rents. In return, it would grant a large number of small parcels which in many cases would not have had

---

[67] I have followed the analysis of government finance given in Scott, *Joint-Stock Companies*, III, pp. 493–509.

[68] On patronage, see R. C. Braddock, 'The rewards of office-holding in Tudor England', *JBS* 14 (1975).

[69] The figure excludes exchanges with the bishops which were not a form of patronage.

their rents increased since the dissolution of the monasteries. The advantages to the beneficiary are obvious: he would be getting a large number of small parcels of land which would be easier to sell than one manor and he would be exchanging land let at rack-rent for undervalued Crown property.[70] In 1595, George Margitts told Robert Cecil that he knew of a parcel of Crown land in the West of England which was valued at £60 a year. If Cecil could obtain it in an exchange, Margitts knew somebody who would pay £6,000 for it; Cecil could then use the money to buy other land worth £300 a year.[71] In 1551, lord Clinton received the manors of Epworth and Crowle in an exchange with the Crown. He immediately took steps to increase their value, removing superfluous officers, converting parkland to farmland and pushing up rents. As a result, their value increased from £254 in 1551 to £439 in 1566. He then persuaded the Crown to accept these manors in exchange for other property.[72]

From the Crown's point of view, exchanges had real disadvantages. They involved the sacrifice of potential income through granting away undervalued property and the loss of future entry fines. Thus, no fine could be levied on a lease of Epworth manor which the Crown had acquired from lord Clinton because, as the auditor reported, the rent at which it had been accepted was very high.[73] Robert Johnson reported that exchanges had cost Elizabeth £20,000–£30,000, 'disguised for all that with some show of good husbandry'.[74] Moreover, there was a real danger of fraud; in 1566, Clinton gave the Crown a wood worth £14 a year in an exchange. Two years later, the auditor reported that the wood was valueless because it had been cut down just before it had been passed to the Crown.[75]

Exchanges, however, had a few major advantages. First, they were a way of increasing the Crown's net income; in a number of cases, Elizabeth imposed a fee-farm rent on the land she granted and managed to increase her rental income by £1,100 a year in this way. Secondly, all large manors which were granted in exchange were held in chief by knight service and this increased the Crown's potential income from fiscal feudalism. Finally, they were a mech-

---

[70] M. C. Cross, 'An exchange of lands with the Crown, 1587–88', *BIHR* 34 (1961).
[71] HMC, *Salisbury*, v, p. 113.
[72] E318/27/1515, mm. 40–1; E318/43/2319, m. 12; SC11/857.
[73] E310/17/78, m. 49.
[74] Johnson, *Letter*, BL, Add. MS 41613, fol. 98 (Bodl., MS Perrot 7, fol. 6ov).
[75] E310/17/75, m. 8.

anism for improving the quality of the royal estate. They permitted the Crown to replace a large number of scattered properties (which were expensive to administer) with a few large, coherent manors which were comparatively cheap and simple to run. Exchanges were one of the few mechanisms for improving the quality of its landed estate which the Crown used in this period. The benefits arising from exchanges should not be underrated. When in 1609, Salisbury decided to entail the most valuable parcels of Crown land to prevent their alienation, over a third of the properties in Lincolnshire and Huntingdonshire that he selected had been acquired by the Crown as a result of exchanges.[76]

A similar policy had been pursued by Henry VIII who made aggressive use of exchanges as way of consolidating major royal estates. Lord Windsor, for example, surrendered the manor of Stanwell which had belonged to his family since Domesday as Henry wanted to add it to his Windsor estate. Family tradition was that Henry, having dined at Stanwell, told his host that he liked it so much that he must have it at once and lord Windsor was forced to leave, despite having laid in his provisions for Christmas. Dr Miller's careful examination of the chronology of the exchange has disproved this story, but she has shown how Henry used exchanges to expand the royal honours of Grafton, Hunsdon and Petworth, as well as Enfield Chase and other properties.[77]

There was one aspect of the Crown's administration of its lands which was totally non-economic: Henry, Elizabeth and James all acquired enormous houses and parks for hunting. Because these properties were used for pleasure, not farming, they did not contribute to the Crown's rental income, while their maintenance added considerably to its expenses. All three rulers were passionate hunters: in the sixteenth and seventeenth centuries, this sport took place in enclosed deer parks for which much potentially valuable agricultural land had to be sacrificed.

Henry VIII was avaricious in his pursuit of houses; by the end of his reign he owned over fifty – more than any other monarch before or since. Thirty-one of these were acquired between 1535 and 1545, eleven from the dissolution of the monasteries, seven by exchange with the bishops, two by forfeiture and the rest by purchase and

---

[76] SP14/46, fols. 22r–v, 46r–8r.
[77] H. Miller, *Henry VIII and the English Nobility* (Oxford, 1986), pp. 218–19, 229, 244, 248–9.

exchange with lay landowners.[78] When, towards the end of his life, Henry 'waxed heavy with sickness, age and corpulence of body, and might not travel so readily abroad, but was constrained to seek to have his game and pleasure ready and at hand', he established a game preserve – Hampton Court Chase – along the Surrey side of the Thames. This soon proved a very expensive undertaking, a lot of land was taken out of agricultural use and rents were lost, there was the cost of maintaining the fencing and of providing hay for the deer. Worse, the deer damaged woods and copses and did not confine themselves to the King's lands, but ate the crops of his neighbours. The chase was returned to farmland early in the reign of Edward VI.[79]

Henry's successors were much less enthusiastic house owners and disposed of many of his properties, while others were allowed to fall into decay. In 1561 a commission was issued to the senior officials of the Exchequer to identify superfluous castles, houses and other buildings and to sell, lease or demolish them; the proceeds of the sale of the building materials were to be used to restore those felt worthy of preservation. Care was to be taken not to interfere with churches which were still in use or to damage funeral monuments which had an antiquarian interest and a practical value for family history or determining rights of inheritance. A concern for antiquity was also evident in the Crown's treatment of castles belonging to the Duchy of Lancaster. These were surveyed in 1562 and it was decided to preserve those which had either a military or an historic value. Tickhill achieved the distinction of being the first building in England to be declared an ancient monument. However, the Crown's desire for economy soon overcame its interest in conservation. Most of the castles were not repaired and allowed to decay. Tickhill was ruined by the farmer of its demesnes who stripped the lead from the roof and burned the masonry to make lime. After a further survey in 1609, the only castles to be maintained were ones with a continuing use: Dover, Windsor, the Tower, Pontefract, Tutbury, Chester and Ludlow.[80]

Elizabeth shared her father's love of sport and she acquired some estates for hunting, as well as one major residence. In 1566, she

---

[78] H. M. Colvin and John Summerson, 'The King's Houses, 1485–1660', in H. M. Colvin (ed.), *The History of the King's Works*, IV (London, 1982), p. 2.

[79] *APC 1547–50*, pp. 190–2.

[80] H. M. Colvin, 'Castles and government in Tudor England', *EHR* 83 (1968), pp. 231–4, and see above, pp. 42–3.

obtained lord Clinton's property on the Isle of Axholme in north Lincolnshire. Her motives in doing this appear to have been concerned with sport and prestige. The report of the commissioners who surveyed the estate for the Queen emphasised that its acquisition would provide a splendid opportunity to extend Hatfield Chase and create one of the stateliest manors within Her Grace's realm.[81] Quite who would hunt in this obscure corner of a brute and beastly county was not discussed.

In 1592, Elizabeth acquired the great palace of Nonsuch in Surrey which had been built by her father but which her sister Mary had granted to the earl of Arundel. In 1580, it passed to Arundel's son-in-law, lord Lumley, who also acquired responsibility for Arundel's enormous debts. The Queen was a frequent visitor to Nonsuch and in 1591 agreed to accept the palace in return for cancelling Lumley's debts. The terms of the agreement were beneficial to both parties. The Queen acquired a desirable property, valued at £534 a year, Lumley was enabled to pay off his debts and acquired royal lands to the value of £500 a year (for which he had to pay rent for the rest of the Queen's reign). He was also allowed to continue to live at Nonsuch and to lease the Great Park for £222 a year. In 1599, he was forgiven the rent of the park and promptly let half of it for £130 a year. James bought out Lumley's interest in the park, added other lands to it and then spent £1,076 fencing it.[82]

James acquired two major houses, Theobalds and Holdenby as well as hunting lodges at Newmarket, Royston and Thetford. James was attracted to Theobalds with its parks for red and fallow deer as 'most convenient for his princely sport and recreation, and commodious for His Highness's residence'. The property was acquired in an exchange with the earl of Salisbury, but it is clear that the earl benefited more from the exchange than the Crown. In return for lands worth about £500 a year, plus some woods and the house itself, Salisbury was given Crown lands worth £780 a year which were burdened with a fee-farm rent of £571. The rent was never paid and Salisbury's heir had a pardon for all arrears and future rent. Salisbury and his heirs were able to raise £25,000 by selling some of these lands and by 1640 had increased the rental value of the remainder to £1,500. James was not content with the size of the park he had acquired from Salisbury and spent £11,070 on extending it.

[81] SC11/857.
[82] J. Dent, *The Quest for Nonsuch* (London, 1962), pp. 165–74, 183–5.

He built a wall 9 miles long to enclose it in 1620–2; this was done in a fairly casual fashion, cutting across the holdings of individual Crown tenants, and a survey had to be made to discover what lands had been included in the park and what rents needed to be adjusted in consequence. In one case a tenant's rent had to be abated because a stable for camels had been built on his property.[83]

The terms of the Theobalds exchange may have been disadvantageous to the Crown because Salisbury was both the King's senior adviser and his partner in the exchange. When the Crown acquired Holdenby for the duke of York in 1608, it tried harder to ensure that it profited from the deal. Holdenby was an enormous house – bigger even than Theobalds – which had been built by Sir Christopher Hatton, Elizabeth's Lord Chancellor. Hatton had died heavily in debt, his lands had been seized by the Crown and so, in 1608, his descendant, also Sir Christopher Hatton, was anxious to come to some financial settlement. He gave Holdenby to James and received in return a parcel of fee-farm rents of roughly equivalent value. His trustees were also allowed to lease those of his lands which had been seized for debt by the Crown. This was apparently a good deal for James who was acquiring a valuable property, whose rents could be improved, in return for a number of fixed rents. Events proved otherwise.

First, James was mainly interested in the sporting aspects of the estate and one third of the land was devoted to unproductive parkland. Secondly, the farmland did not prove capable of improvement. A very optimistic survey of 1610 listed the rents when Holdenby had been acquired, showed that they had been increased by about 12 per cent and that they could be increased by a further 14 per cent when the price of wool rose. By 1625, the tenants were complaining that the 1610 rents were much too high and the Exchequer was considering reducing them to about the levels paid when the property was owned by Hatton.[84]

Even Charles, who might have been thought to have had other financial concerns in the 1630s, spent £27,000 on enlarging Richmond Park. A further £8,600 was spent on surrounding it with a wall and £700 on making ponds and fencing coppices. As at Theobalds,

---

[83] L. Stone, *Family and Fortune. Studies in Aristocratic Finance in the Sixteenth and Seventeenth Centuries* (Oxford, 1973), pp. 40–2; VCH, *Hertford*, III, p. 448; LR2/216, fols. 14–37.

[84] Colvin and Summerson, 'The King's Houses', p. 153; SP38/9, 18 March 1607; SP14/57, no. 37; E178/4036; SC12/38/36; *CSPD 1603–10*, p. 453.

the construction of the wall was started before the consent of all the relevant property holders had been obtained and there was considerable local opposition.[85]

Acquiring houses and parks inevitably increased the cost of maintenance and building works. Under Elizabeth, the Office of Works had undertaken a few major projects, but had mainly functioned as a palace maintenance department. James and Charles spent much more on building, and expenditure under James rose to be four times the level reached under Elizabeth. Some of this was to maintain and improve the parks; Woodstock was expanded and enclosed with an eight-foot-high wall in 1635. In 1637–8, considerable sums were spent at Theobalds, including the construction of eighty-seven buttresses to prop up the famous park wall.[86]

The other use which was made of the Crown lands was as a source of capital. All three monarchs sold land to meet pressing shortfalls in revenue. Elizabeth's sales were confined to the early years of her reign and to three large sales in 1589–90, 1599 and 1601–2. In all, she raised £816,000 by selling land with an annual value of £28,000. The government tried to maximise its income from these sales, setting minimum prices which corresponded to the current market price for land (taking into account the very low level of rents) and requiring larger properties to be held by military tenure. The long-term value of the Crown estate was protected by a ban on sales of Duchy property, houses reserved for the Queen's access, parts of the ancient demesne or lands in strategic areas, such as the Isle of Wight, while manors worth more than £30 a year were excluded from the 1599 sales. The Crown's desperate need for money at the end of the reign caused it to modify its position; halfway through the 1599 sale it cut its prices, relaxed the restriction on holding property by military tenure and allowed manors worth up to £40 a year to be sold. In 1601, prices were cut even further and the upper limit on the size of manors which could be sold was lifted entirely. The Elizabethan sales inevitably reduced the quality of the remaining estate; in Lincolnshire, 74 per cent of the property sold consisted of manors and lands which were leased or held at will; the very types of holdings whose rents could easily be increased.[87]

[85] VCH, *Surrey*, III, p. 535.

[86] Colvin and Summerson, 'The King's Houses', pp. 32, 278, 349.

[87] The Elizabethan sales are discussed above, pp. 15–21; Thomas, 'Administration of crown lands', p. 99.

James was also forced to sell lands to meet a deficit on the ordinary account. Salisbury appears to have tried to dispose of the least attractive properties: mills, chantry lands, parsonages, tithes and lands which were already subject to long leases. Attempts were made in 1604 and 1609 to prevent the alienation of the best lands by the creation of an entail. Dorset and Northampton, too, were keen to dispose of the least attractive properties; Dorset sold mills, while Northampton was commissioned to sell ruinous houses, woods and timber. Lands worth about £27,000 were sold between 1603 and 1613 and £682,000 was raised. Charles sold a similar quantity of land between 1625 and 1635 and raised about £642,000. He also conveyed land worth £12,496 a year to the City of London to satisfy his debts to them.[88]

The failure of Elizabethan government to push up rents on its lands led ultimately to the destruction of the royal estate as a major source of revenue. Because Elizabeth had not increased rents, the capital value of the lands had increased dramatically. Land was normally sold at a price which would yield the purchaser an income of 5 per cent, so property which was let at its true annual value would be sold for twenty years' purchase. The Crown lands were let at far below their true value and consequently were sold at much higher rates. In 1599, the Crown was able to sell a good deal of property at forty years' purchase or more.[89] A sale at forty years' purchase of a property worth, say, £5 would have earned the Crown £200; the income it was sacrificing was only 2.5 per cent of this capital sum. Charles was able to convey lands worth £12,496 a year to the City of London at twenty-eight years' purchase to cover debts of £349,897 and was able to do so without any major loss of income for the lands were granted in fee-farm.[90] If they had been sold in fee simple, the income he would have sacrificed would have been equivalent to only 3.57 per cent of the capital. Alternatively, had he used the capital sum to buy a twenty-year annuity of £12,496, the interest rate would have been 3.4 per cent.

In these circumstances, it was almost inevitable that the Crown would sell land. Faced with a shortage of money, it had two choices. It could borrow (if lenders could be found) and attempt to push up

---

[88] Dietz, *English Public Finance*, pp. 124–5, 147–8, 157, 238, 247, 299; the figures from table 1.2 above.

[89] See above, pp. 18–20 and table 1.3.

[90] R. Ashton, *The Crown and the Money Market, 1603–40* (Oxford, 1960), pp. 69, 135

the yield on the Crown lands. Alternatively, it could sell land. Given that the prospects for improving the yield from the Crown lands were at best uncertain, and that James could borrow at 10 per cent and Charles at 8 per cent, the cost of selling land to cover short- or medium-term financial crises was far less than the cost of borrowing. The long-term effect was described by Robert Johnson, who compared the Crown to a vintner who draws a gallon of wine out of a tun and replaces it by water; 'how often might he thus do before the tun be left full of water only and no wine at all?'[91]

[91] Johnson, *Letter*, SP12/283A, no. 80, fol. 167v (Bodl., MS Perrot 7, fol. 68r–v).

CHAPTER 3

The Elizabethan Duchy of Cornwall, an estate in stasis

Graham Haslam

The Duchy of Cornwall existed primarily to provide an income and territorial base for the monarch's eldest son and heir-apparent.[1] Between the accession of Edward VI and James I, there was no heir and so no duke, and during this period the lands reverted to the Crown. The void created by this lack was not filled by an executive council and judicial apparatus comparable to that which supervised the Duchy of Lancaster, which served both to govern the Duchy and advocate its interests. The Queen had no particular concern for the Duchy's fortunes; she was a perpetual absentee from its estates. By 1558, it no longer possessed any great houses which could provide a focal point and serve as a resting place for a peripatetic monarch. Berkhamsted, Byfleet and Kennington Palace had either been relinquished or had fallen into disrepair (the fabric of Kennington had been robbed in the 1530s to build the new palace at Whitehall). Throughout Elizabeth's lifetime the Duchy was, *de facto*, a department of the Exchequer, but one distinguished from the estates as a whole by the guarantee of the charter of 1337 and its statutory confirmation. The lands were, in law, inalienable, and yet, in contravention of this special status, they were largely sold in the last years of the reign.

As there was no one to impart any special managerial dynamic to the estates, an examination of the Duchy's lands can serve to reveal not only what was individual about the Duchy but also problems of

---

[1] The two best works on the Duchy are John Hatcher, *Rural Economy and Society in the Duchy of Cornwall, 1300–1500* (Cambridge, 1970), and Mary Coate, 'The Duchy of Cornwall: its history and administration, 1640–1660,' *TRHS* fourth ser., 10 (1927), pp. 135–69. Hatcher studied the tenurial, social and economic condition of the seventeen assessionary or conventionary manors owned by the Duchy in Cornwall. Within these manors tenants took their lands for a seven-year term, paying a fixed rent for seven years and a fine determined in open court for the first six years of the term. The movement of fines was studied to determine how a major landowner deployed the resources of his estate. For the other royal Duchy, with which the Duchy of Cornwall bears similarities, see Somerville, *Duchy of Lancaster*, 1.

management which were general to the Crown lands as a whole. The capacity of its administrators to alter circumstances on the estates was limited by the strength of local custom. The estates were hardly static but were actively responding to the generalised impact of a doubling of the national population between 1500 and 1650 (from 2.5m to 5.2m) and a substantial growth in the money supply under Elizabeth. The elaborate social hierarchy which had persisted throughout the middle ages within the confines of each manor had wholly collapsed by the end of the sixteenth century. The distinctions which had marked men as free and unfree were transferred from people to the forms of tenure by which they held. Elizabethan land law, itself evolving, especially in relation to leasing arrangements, may still be described as hierarchical and influenced by local legal tradition. The changes taking place on the land, at paces varying from manor to manor in response to both environmental and legal factors, meant that the nature of the whole estate was undergoing complex restructuring.

The Duchy was both the endowment of a duke, or in his absence, the monarch, but a rich source of patronage, having at its disposal offices, which were always actively sought, as well as leases of lands, mills, advowsons, hunting, fishing and mineral rights and other regalities. These prizes, judiciously bestowed, could help secure allegiance by involving the nobility and gentry in the affairs of the Duchy, provide important local status and control and sometimes indirectly bestow valuable economic concessions. The shrievalty for Cornwall was (and is) a Duchy nomination. It was also the case that the most modest tenant-at-will within the Duchy, as all tenants upon the estate, was directly responsible, at least in theory, to the Queen as lord of the manor in even the most mundane of actions within the manorial court. The problems faced by those charged with day-to-day responsibility for the administration of the Duchy was to mix these possibilities in such a way as best to achieve the current needs of the Crown and polity. The frequently cumbersome nature of the royal administration, the entrenched interests of Crown servants and tenants all combined with the nature of Elizabethan land law to make this a difficult, sometimes impossible task.

I

The advent of Queen Elizabeth brought no immediate change either
to the structure or fortunes of the Duchy of Cornwall. In 1558, it was
a part of the Exchequer because it was administered through the
Augmentations office, the vestigial rump of the once financially
pervasive Court of Augmentations. The initial step, leisurely taken,
by the new regime to deal with this ancient patrimony was to reestablish a direct link with the Crown. The Lord Treasurer,
Winchester, and the barons of the Exchequer, by warrant dated 13
February 1560, authorised payment of Duchy net receipts directly to
the Treasurer of the Chamber.[2] This connection with the monarchy,
which had existed for the first three decades of the sixteenth century,
made the Duchy a ready source of income which successive monarchs
could utilise at any time without recourse to the vagaries of the
Exchequer.

The estate which generated this income for Elizabeth was much
changed by 1558. When the first Tudor came to the throne, it was a
great barony with lands in nineteen counties scattered across England
south of the Trent. In 1515, it was the most lucrative of all the
Crown's great estates: in that year, the earldom of Richmond yielded
£2,406, the Warwick and Spencer lands £1,740, North Wales, £970
and the earldom of Chester and Flint £933, but the Duchy of
Cornwall generated a net income of £5,540.[3] At the beginning of the
sixteenth century, the Duchy provided approximately 12 per cent of
all revenues derived from Crown lands and 5 per cent of the royal
income.[4] The pattern of landholding had been significantly changed
by 1558. In 1540, Henry VIII severed the honour of Wallingford
from the Duchy in order to establish the honour of Newelme. By way
of compensation, he annexed to it twenty-eight manors, all but one of
which was located in Cornwall.[5] The addition of many more Cornish
estates reflected the Henrician estate practice of consolidating
holdings into more rational geographical units. Six of the new
manors were derived from the former Priory of Tywardreth, nine
other manors came from the dissolved Priory of Launceston and

---

[2] DCO, Rolls Series, Receiver-Generals' Accounts, Roll 234. The warrant is quoted on m. 6.
[3] SC6/345.
[4] The percentages are derived by comparison of net Duchy receipts with aggregate figures for
Crown lands given in B. P. Wolffe, *The Royal Demesne in English History. The Crown Estate in
the Governance of the Realm from the Conquest to 1509* (London, 1971), p. 217.
[5] 32 Hen. VIII c. 53 (not printed in *SR*, III). See also *Letters and Papers of the Reign of Henry VIII*,
XV, p. 213.

another thirteen manors were from the former possessions of the attainted marquis of Exeter. Though individually small, these manors added over 7,549 acres in leasehold, copyhold and conventionary lands within the single county of Cornwall.[6] The aggregate income derived from these lands was actually slightly greater than the receipts from Wallingford, but the exchange served to concentrate more than ever the holdings of the Duchy in the South-West and made it a landlord without parallel in Cornwall itself. Even so, before 1558 receipts from estates outside the South-West (described with consummate inverted snobbery in the Duchy's accounts as 'foreign') produced a greater net income than lands in the South-West.

Because the Duchy and its possessions had been established by charter confirmed by Parliament, it was more difficult and complicated to add, subtract or exchange Duchy property and so there was a greater continuity of possession than upon the Crown estate as a whole. The honour of Castle Rysing was severed from the Duchy in an exchange of lands by act of Parliament in 1543–4 with the duke of Norfolk. However, though the Crown may have received property in compensation for the honour of Rysing, the Duchy did not.[7] Another Duchy manor, Byfleet in Surrey, was added to the honour of Hampton in exchange for Shippon in Berkshire in 1541–2. But there were no exchanges involving the Duchy for the whole of Elizabeth's reign.

Despite additions to and deletions from the Duchy's landed estate, its other major source of income, revenue derived from the mining and smelting of tin, remained an intact part of its jurisdiction in 1558. The income from this source often equalled, sometimes surpassed, manorial receipts. Money from the tin-mining industry was derived from two sources. First, toll tin was paid as a royalty for mining activities upon Duchy land. This was a relatively negligible

---

[6] This acreage figure is collated from a compendium of surveys now in the DCO, 'Abreviat or compendius abstracte of the surveis of all suche manors as have bene surveid by John Nordon aswell by virtue of a commission of the late most worthy P[rince] Henrie, d[uke] of Cornwall as of the moste admired Prince Charles, now eldest sonn of the moste puisant James, King of Great Britaine, France and Irelande and now duke of Cornwall within the counties of Somerset, Wiltshire, Dorset, Devon and Cornwall, abstracted by the said Norden in November, December and Jannarie, anno Christi, 1615', (hereafter Norden, 'Abreviat'), fols. 35–55. This compendium of surveys taken between 1610 and 1615, although made considerably after the beginning of Elizabeth's reign and nearly three-quarters of a century after the manors were actually annexed to the Duchy, represents the first comprehensive attempt to survey the lands.

[7] The act is not included in *SR*, but is cited in both ministers' accounts and Receiver-Generals' rolls. See, for instance, DCO, Rolls Series, Receiver-Generals' Accounts, Roll 125.

source of income. Second, a tax was paid to Duchy officers for the weighing and assaying of tin in coinage centres in both Devon and Cornwall. A duty was levied for each pound of tin presented for coinage. Production of tin, which by 1558 had shifted decisively to Cornwall, was in gradual decline from the middle of the 1530s, but remained a crucial source of income for the Crown, miners in Cornwall and, at the end of Elizabeth's reign, those involved in overseas trade.

In the absence of a Council, the Duchy possessed three officers each charged with different aspects of the Duchy's management. The premier officer, the Lord Warden of the Stannaries, was charged with overall responsibility for these operations and supervised the Duchy's stannary courts.[8] There were only three holders of the office during Elizabeth's reign. Edward Hastings, Lord Loughborough (d. 1572) was a Marian appointee who suffered imprisonment in 1561 for his refusal to take the oath of supremacy. Thereafter he retired to his Leicestershire home and ceased to be of any importance in Duchy affairs.[9] Elizabeth's own appointees were both courtiers, Francis, earl of Bedford, in 1572 and his successor, Sir Walter Raleigh in 1585. Both possessed West Country connections; Bedford was influential as an important landlord in the South-West while Raleigh possessed that most dangerous, tenuous form of influence, popularity.

The Duchy Receiver-General occupied a central administrative position. Comparable to the receiver of Crown lands for a county or number of counties, this officer was responsible for collection of all monies due, 'the charge', which included both landed revenues and receipts from the coinage of tin. He held the money until called upon by the Treasurer of the Chamber to account. Receivers employed their own deputies and had subordinate particular receivers who were responsible for the collection of revenues from groups of estates which were more or less defined by geographical convenience. The composite account of the Receiver-General was passed by a baron of the Exchequer for the whole of Elizabeth's reign.

Sir Edward Waldegrave, Mary's trusted councillor and head of her wardrobe, continued to hold the Duchy receivership until his

---

[8] See Robert R. Pennington, *Stannary Law, a History of the Mining Law of Cornwall and Devon* (Newton Abbot, 1973), and George Randall Lewis, *The Stannaries, a Study of the English Tin Miner* (Cambridge, MA, 1924). This should be read with John Hatcher, *English Tin Production and Trade before 1550* (Oxford, 1973), and John Hatcher and T. C. Barker, *A History of British Pewter* (London, 1974).   [9] *DNB*.

death as a prisoner in the Tower in 1561. He had sold a partial interest in the office to John Cosoworth in 1553.[10] The Cosoworths, a Cornish family from the parish of St Columb Minor, flourished as London merchants trading in cloth and silks. John's son Thomas succeeded him in the office in 1574. The receivership passed to Sir Francis Godolphin in 1586. The Godolphins, who had long held important local offices connected with the tin-mining industry in Cornish coinage halls, were the most important tin-mining family in sixteenth-century Cornwall, and certainly the richest. The acquisition of this office was the culmination of their career in the Duchy and another step on their way to national office at the end of the seventeenth century. They built a fine manor house in the Italian style near Helston in the west of Cornwall not far from their important tin-mining interests. Granted a lease of the Isles of Scilly in 1571, Sir Francis fortified them with a castle and ruled the islands much as a Crown colony. (The Scillies remained in Godolphin hands until the end of the eighteenth century.) For all of Elizabeth's reign, the office of receiver was dominated by Cornish families with strong City connections, and often a link, business or otherwise, with the court.

The Duchy retained the services of an auditor who, from about 1570, was one of the auditors of the land revenue.[11] It was through this office that the Elizabethan Exchequer exercised financial control over the Duchy. This post, in or out of the Exchequer, required legal and accounting expertise as well as a wealth of practical knowledge concerning the administration of a landed estate. The Duchy auditor reviewed all the disparate manorial court accounts and from this information, which he distilled into two accounts, the ministers' account for Devon and Cornwall and that for the 'foreign manors', he prepared the charge for the receiver. This latter was the net sum owed from each property for which the receiver became responsible. Information from the stannaries and coinage halls came to the receiver from local stannary officers, not the auditors. At the beginning of Elizabeth's reign the office of auditor was held by Walter Mildmay. It passed to John Conyers in 1567 and to William Neale in about 1574. Robert Paddon received the appointment in about 1590 and was finally succeeded by Nathaniel Fulwer in 1602.

---

[10] For Cosoworth, *HP 1558–1603*, I, pp. 661–2. *CSPD 1547–80*, p. 55; *CPR Philip and Mary*, I, p. 235. [11] For the Exchequer auditors, see above pp. 45–7.

The Duchy employed other officers, including an Attorney-
General, a feodary and escheator, a woodward, a havenor for its West
Country customs rights, an assay master and controller of the coinage
and each manor or honour had an array of local officers. The Lord
Warden of the Stannaries was also the chief steward of all Duchy
manors so the appointment of deputy stewards was in his gift.

II

Two important characteristics of the Duchy in the Elizabethan
period continually influenced its management. The first was the
Queen's remoteness from Duchy affairs. It is hardly likely that she
would have taken a great interest in an estate dedicated to the honour
and maintenance of a male heir. That neglect, initially benign, was
eventually transformed into hostility in the last years of her reign by
an administration pressed for money. The second, shared equally
with all the Crown lands, was the diversity of tenures which subsisted
upon Duchy lands. Each manor, honour, liberty or soke was a legal
entity with its own variations of tenure and custom. Here it is
necessary to mention that on the seventeen assessionary or conventionary manors in Cornwall, the customary tenants held for
seven-year terms paying fines at the beginning of each new assession.
The leasing by the Exchequer to individuals of demesne lands, rights
and other prerogatives associated with the estate was, of course,
extra-manorial. The Elizabethan regime also inherited a network of
subsisting leases which for its own reasons it did not choose to disrupt.
This meant that it could only deal with them individually as they fell
in or as lessees sought renewals. Within the legal system of the manor
(which stretched back to the middle ages without interruption), or
the system of Exchequer leasing (which had acquired a new
importance during the dissolution), it was difficult in the extreme to
impose changes. They could be implemented neither uniformly
across the entire estate in the case of tenures emanating from a
manorial court nor simultaneously in the case of leases issued at
different times for varying terms. The overwhelming characteristic of
management was its piecemeal nature, by individual estate and
particular tenement. Nor does this appear to be in any great contrast
with private landlords.[12]

---

[12] E. Kerridge, *Agrarian Problems in the Sixteenth Century and After* (London, 1969), pp. 42 and
following. It may be that those private landlords who owned single estates and wished to

Just as with the Crown lands, manorial demesnes and whole manors were leased. The whole of the honour of Berkhamsted in Hertfordshire was leased from 1577 until 1611. Curry Mallet in Somerset was in lease to the Paulet family from 1546 until 1610. Kennington, near London on the Surrey side of the Thames, was farmed for the whole sixteenth century. The great deer parks of Lanteglos and Helsbury, once part of the manor of Helston in Trigg, had been disparked by Henry VIII and the combined 426 acres leased. Another considerable park, Kerrybullock, at Stoke Climsland, Cornwall, was also let for the whole of the reign. By the 1590s it was in the hands of Thomas Cornwallis. A legal dispute of 1595 revealed it to be valuable for more than its grazing; Cornwallis maintained two knocking mills, two blowing mills and a crazing mill (all for the processing of tin ore) as well as a grist mill within the park.[13]

The policy towards leaseholds on the Duchy estates may best be seen through an examination of the particulars of leases of which 124 have survived for the estates in Cornwall (including the new annexations) from between 1560 and 1601.[14] They are not, of course, a genuine legal instrument but embody details of the conditions upon which the Exchequer was willing to let individual parcels of property. Each particular produced by an auditor or his deputy noted the rent, fine, name of the prospective lessee, proposed duration of the lease, names of guarantors and often information concerning terms of the former lease. A few are incomplete, either in terms of location, financial details or in other ways. A number of grants of small parcels of land could be inserted into a single particular so that an auditor could only charge a fee for property with an aggregate rental value of 40s.[15]

introduce change in order to promote better agricultural practice or higher financial returns were in a far stronger position to do so than those owning scattered estates, especially large estates run by absentee landlords.

13 Richard Carew, *The Survey of Cornwall* (London, 1603), p. 23. See also SC6/Eliz. 1/5964, 5984. Helsbury and Lanteglos were taken by Sir John Arundel and the park at Restormel leased by the Russell family. LR1/8, fol. 75.

14 For the particulars for leases, see also Dr Thomas's chapter below, pp. 169–90. The particulars drawn on here are E310/10/15 (forty-one items), 16 (fifty-three items), 17 (twenty-four items), 18 (seventy-five items), 19 (fifty-two items), and 20 (forty-four items). These files relate to Crown, Duchy and ex-monastic lands in Cornwall. The ex-monastic property belonged to religious houses in Somerset, Devon and Gloucestershire as well as Cornwall. There are thirty particulars from the 1560s, forty-one for the 1570s, thirty-one for the 1580s and twenty-two from the last decade of the century.   15 LR1/12, fol. 86.

Auditors became familiar with the properties and rights described in the particulars from their visits to Duchy manors when amassing information for the ministers' account. However, some of the particulars betray an ignorance of the property by the auditor involved. When in 1567 John Arundel sought a lease of the borough of Bossiney and site of Tintagel Castle upon the north coast of Cornwall, the auditor noted the castle was in utter decay and 'what number of acres the said island and meadows do contain or the goodness thereof, the auditor knoweth not'.[16] Even a property which was sought by more than a single individual could be unknown; in 1560, Nicholas Kendall applied for a twenty-one year lease of ex-monastic property, but the auditor admitted that he 'doth not know what the land is that appertaineth to the farm, but it is sued for by diverse ways. And there will be given for a fine £40.'[17] Particulars were usually countersigned by the Treasurer and Chancellor.

Particulars were issued for grants related to land, woods, mills, tithes and advowsons, toll of tin and fishery. In a few cases, especially with regard to mills and woods, land and other rights were granted simultaneously. An analysis of the particulars by type produces a slightly different total because an individual particular may include several of these categories. Of all those for Cornwall, including Duchy and Crown lands, leases of lands were by far the most common, representing eighty-two instances, leases of tithes and advowsons were sought in twenty-three cases. Particulars for grants of woodland occur sixteen times, mills, ten times and fisheries only twice, though those Duchy manors located upon the Cornish shoreline or in its river valleys often possessed either a several or a particular fishery. On at least one Duchy manor, Helston in Trigg, the tenants possessed an hereditary several fishery.

The terms under which leases were sought and granted by the Exchequer are directly reflected in the particulars. In fact, conclusions derived from this material may be applied to the period between 1536 and 1600. This is because arrangements in the preceding lease were frequently recited within the particular so that a composite history of a property can be established for two or sometimes three generations of lessees. It is clear, for instance, that in the case of former monastic lands, which had often been leased for terms of thirty, forty, fifty or even sixty years, the first lease issued by the Crown was normally for either twenty-one years or three lives. In

---

[16] E310/10/19, m. 27.   [17] E310/10/18, m. 20.

seventy particulars the nominated lessee sought a lease of three lives, while in forty-six particulars a term of twenty-one years was proposed. A lease for three lives was clearly more favoured, and, presumably, more attractive to the lease in actuarial terms. As with copyhold tenure, which they resembled, the three nominated lives had to be alive at the time of the grant, but a lessee for three lives was not obliged to attend the manorial court and such a lease conferred the advantage that it could be sold without the purchaser paying a new fine. A very few particulars, however, with the usual Tudor disregard for historical categories, indicated that the lessee would owe suit and service to the manorial court. Three particulars proposed leases of forty, forty-one and thirty years duration respectively. In the case of the particular proposing a term of forty years, the property was reported as decayed. Only a single particular was for a lease held during pleasure.[18] The remainder of the particulars do not include a term of years.

The financial details derived from these documents are further suggestive of the Crown's policy towards the Duchy estate. Rents, of course, remained fixed in an overwhelming number of cases. The assessment of fines followed a discernible pattern. In forty-seven cases, the fine was levied at four years' rent; this was normally the amount charged for the first lease by an individual seeking the usual term of three lives or twenty-one years. In twenty-five particulars the fine was set at two years' rent and in twenty others at only one year's rent. Of those fines assessed at two years' rent, ten were renewals by the lessee before the term of the lease had actually expired or were leases in reversion. Those granted at one year's fine also often involved renewals, adding a name shortly after the grant of the lease, and, in one case, taking a lease of premises from which only a decayed rent had formerly been derived. Some fifteen particulars indicated no fine at all. These included four granted by direct warrant from the Queen as patronage, one as a reward for discovering concealed lands, three in which the prospective lessee pledged to act as a rent collector while two were for lands which had been in conventionary tenure before the application for a lease. In two particulars, a fine of five years' rent and in three cases six years' rent was proposed. There was virtually no change in the pattern of imposition of fines from decade to decade throughout the period. The situation on Duchy lands conformed closely to that on other Crown estates and the Exchequer

---

[18] *Ibid.*

figures for monies collected from fines remained conspicuously stable after 1574.

This evidence, which, after all, is restricted to Cornwall alone, indicates that the Exchequer between 1560 and 1600 did not seek to increase fines, but this needs to be read with a qualification. As noted, the terms in the particulars were reduced to twenty-one years or three lives from the much longer fixed terms granted before the lands were first taken into royal control. This was weighted towards the first decade of the reign; naturally, as leases came up for renewal in later decades the term was compared with the previous grant. This served effectively to increase fines by forcing lessees to seek renewals more frequently. However, 60 per cent of leases were for terms of three lives, and here it is difficult to judge whether landlord or tenant gained from this arrangement. Even if the Crown achieved greater frequency of renewal, as in the case of leases for twenty-one years, it certainly lost the ability to predict with any certainty when leases for lives could terminate and from the point of view of financial management alone it was impossible to know definitely when additional income would become available. This only exacerbated the Crown's disinclination to impose any general policy which might lead to a general improvement in landed revenue.[19]

It must also be recognised that certain categories of leases were inherently protective of Crown prerogative. Fines derived from these leases were of secondary importance. Farms of fishing, fowling and hunting rights in particular, manorial mills or mineral rights less so, may be seen as attempts to maintain an absentee landlord's land-related prerogatives. Richard Carew and his sons, Richard and Hobby, gained a reversionary lease of the site of Trematon Castle, woods at Liskeard, Climsland, Calstock and elsewhere in Cornwall, the fishing of Trematon in the Tamar valley and the right to quarry stone at Shippon in the Thames valley in 1590. These rights had not produced an income for the Duchy and the new lessees pledged to 'try Her Majesty's title therein' at their own cost whenever necessary.[20] This was a shrewd amalgam of the exercise of patronage

---

[19] Compare pp. 172–4 below. The argument by G. R. Elton that Crown leases were always conceded upon terms below market levels must be approached with considerable caution. It is important to compare them not only with other contemporary leasing arrangements, but also with the previous terms of letting when the property had been in church hands. G. R. Elton, *The Parliament of England, 1559–1581* (Cambridge, 1986), p. 196.

[20] E306/10/18, m. 59.

and practical economic management. In 1583, a Mr Lichfield offered to take a lease of former monastic land for which a rent of £5 3s 0d had been paid. He offered a new rent of £6 13s 4d if he could recover Her Majesty's title to the property.[21] Hugh Tregarthen was rewarded in 1564 for his travail and great expense with a lease of five holdings within the borough of Liskeard at an annual rent of 75s for recovering these concealed lands.[22] Though not common, these are not isolated examples.

Where these leases served to protect and maintain the Crown's interests, the farming of Duchy woodland, clearly an appreciating asset throughout the latter half of the sixteenth century, led to its unremitting disafforestation under the regime of lessees.[23] In 1558, the Duchy possessed 1,121 acres of woodland overall which had diminished to only 443 acres by 1615.[24] In 1559, the manor of Liskeard, Cornwall, contained 235 acres of woodland, but by 1615 only 95 acres remained. At Calstock, over 200 acres of trees existed in the first year of Elizabeth, but by 1615 this had been reduced to 61 acres.[25] There were two abiding problems which impeded effective management. Of all Duchy offices, the woodward was amongst the least efficient; returns by the office were almost always partial, incomplete and sometimes non-existent. The situation was not improved when in 1568 the woodward apparently won a long struggle with the Exchequer auditor and assumed control of woodland in former parks belonging to the Duchy.[26] An attempt at conservation occurred in 1576 when the Exchequer auditor, Mr Neale, attempted to define under what conditions tenants could generally take timber for ploughing, housing, carts, fencing or firewood.[27] This attempt at a general remedy did nothing to curtail the felling of timber. Tenants could usually find an obfuscating variety of local custom to immunise them from general dicta.

The terms upon which woodland was leased made it far from easy for Exchequer and Duchy officers to enforce them. Trees were sometimes reserved when leases were granted, leaving the herbage, but this was probably in practice a virtually unenforceable covenant. An acreage was usually allowed to tenants for fencing and more for firewood, hedging and cartage for manorial tenants or lessees of the

---

[21] E310/10/16, m. 20.   [22] *Ibid.*, m. 34.

[23] The problem of woodland is considered further by Dr Thomas, above, pp. 67–9.

[24] E306/13/4 and 5.   [25] *Ibid.*

[26] DCO, Rolls Series, Receiver-Generals' Accounts, Roll 237.   [27] *Ibid.*, Roll 252.

demesne. This probably led to abuses as well. Occasionally, the nature of the lease could present obvious difficulties for the woodward and auditor. In 1582, over 264 acres of woodland contained in some fifteen manors, encompassing twenty-nine sites, were leased to Charles Paget and John Maynard at a fine of only two years' rent.[28] Sir Francis Walsingham secured a grant of Duchy woodland in 1588 for twenty-one years without any fine.[29] One Thomas Hancock leased 162 acres of woods which were described as much destroyed and paid a fine of only 20s on an annual rent of £4 19s 4d.[30] In 1574, the woods of Calstock, a Duchy manor in the Tamar valley, extending to 178 acres, were combined with 32 acres of wood in Ramsey, Essex, in a lease to Roger Taverner.[31] The latter was not a part of the Duchy and it is unlikely that Duchy officers would have visited the site.

The Crown's discretion in the granting of leases and setting of fines served as a form of patronage to courtiers and other Crown servants. Restormel Park, perhaps then as now one of the most beautiful inland river valleys in Cornwall, had been leased to the Russells since 1540. When the lease was renewed by the earl of Bedford in 1562, the fine of £112, equal to four years' rent, was given as a 'gift and liberality' from the Queen to Bertrand Cranishe, a German mining engineer who had been commissioned to prospect for gold and silver in Cornwall.[32] This, indeed, is a creative example of Crown patronage. More mundane, the tithes of the rectory of Wendron in the far west of Cornwall were first granted to the Godolphins in 1578, but renewed by them in 1592 at the traditional rent of £22 with a fine of only £5 because it was only 'altering names' upon the lease.[33] In 1566, Robert Beaumont, one of the Queen's musicians, was granted a lease of five tenements in the manor of Bonyalvey, Cornwall, for twenty-one years without any fine.[34] In 1567, a lease in reversion of the toll tin for the manor of Tewington, Cornwall, was granted to two members of the Queen's guard.

The leases of Duchy land issued from the Exchequer throughout the Elizabethan period indicate efforts to achieve several objectives. The granting of leases generated revenue through the imposition of fines. The Crown was interested in maintaining its title to its various properties within the Duchy and issued leases on a concessionary basis

---

[28] E310/10/15, m. 39.   [29] *Ibid.*, m. 3.   [30] E310/10/18, m. 38.
[31] E310/10/20, m. 31. Taverner was surveyor of woods; see above, p. 54.
[32] E310/10/15, m. 23.   [33] *Ibid.*, m. 8.   [34] E310/10/19, m. 23.

to those willing to defend it. It also used leases, of course, as a reward for those within the court circle or to Duchy and Exchequer officers.

The attempt to satisfy several gods brought the Duchy and its lessees into conflict with those who held lands from the Duchy's manorial courts. Lessees who accepted farms upon financially favourable terms with the pledge of legal action to protect or recover title were often defending that putative title against the Crown's own tenants. When in 1580 Thomas Earle sought a renewal of his lease of Wareham and Greenscombe woods, extending to 183 acres, the auditor reported that the lessee requested that no fine be imposed because

The farmer of the said woods hath answered Her Majesty [for] the said rent yearly since the commencement of the said lease and hath not enjoyed the same nor taken any commodity thereby for that it hath depended in suit between the said farmer and the tenants of the said manor who claimed the same as parcel of their tenures.[35]

The request was granted.

The lease held by Thomas Cornwallis of Kerrybullock Park was challenged, apparently by tenants of the manor, because it was argued that the mills included were actually conventionary and not a part of the demesne. Again, at Stoke Climsland the auditor in 1570 refused to renew the toll of tin by conventionary tenure, even though it was shown that it had been granted on the same terms since 1527, because he thought it his 'bounden duty' to defer the application until the Chancellor and Lord Treasurer had an opportunity to consider the matter and decide if the Queen had a right to the fine which a lease would allow. Indeed, the Lord Treasurer and Chancellor did sanction a lease and a fine was taken.[36] When John Arundel leased Bossiney on the northern coast of Cornwall in 1567, it was noted that the previous tenant had held the land as conventionary from the manorial court.[37]

Duchy tenants reacted strongly to these attacks. On Bodmin Moor, tenants defensively sought a lease of eight tenements, fourteen houses, seven cottages, four messuages and two pieces of ground in 1567. The rents for these properties were reported as decayed and in arrears amounting to £165 6s 8d, which 'charge the tenants will bear so as they may have leases of the same'.[38] The lessee, Anthony Will, was to

[35] E310/10/16, m. 9.   [36] *Ibid.*, m. 1.   [37] E310/10/19, m. 27.
[38] E310/10/20, m. 19.

hold the properties to the use of the existing tenants. Another such defensive lease was requested in the same year by the tenants of two tenements at Climsland Prior and a tenant of Carnedon Prior, both formerly monastic lands. Each sought a twenty-one-year lease, but the auditor noted that these tenements had previously been held for eighty and seventy years respectively.[39] Attached to this particular is an important memorandum by the auditor:

that at Michaelmas term last, 1566, one John Harris of the county of Cornwall gent made supplication unto the Lord Treasurer and Sir Walter Mildmay, Chancellor of the court of the Exchequer on the behalf of the Queen's majesty's tenants of the new annexed land in Cornwall, humbly beseeching their honours that it would please them to stay the granting of any lease of the said new annexed lands until such time as the same were surveyed. Whereby the Queen's majesty might be better served and the poor tenants in more assurance of their farms and livings for diverse of the said tenants having convent seals [i.e. monastic leases] of their several farms for many years yet to come by persuasions of the surveyors and stewards of the same county gave up their said indentures and took copies of the same officers and paid their fines for the same and yet their estates are void in law. So as if their farms should be granted from them, they were utterly undone, as the said Master Harris affirmeth.

The doubts suggested by this supplication extended not only to the Duchy's recently acquired ex-monastic lands, but also to its ancient possessions in Cornwall. In 1587, John Champneys applied for a lease of five tenements, a grain and stamping mill at Helston in Kerrier, one of the conventionary manors. The auditor noted that the premises previously had been let for a term of seven years according to the custom of the manor, but the tenants, fearing an imperfection of title, sought a lease.[40] These serious charges may have led to the retirement of the Duchy auditor, John Conyers, who was granted a pension in lieu of office. He was replaced by an Exchequer man, William Neale. There is no direct evidence that Conyers was forced to retire, but Duchy auditors generally left office feet first.

If there was a general concern amongst the Duchy's conventionary tenants for the title to their lands, so too the Exchequer auditors found it difficult to maintain the received legal title. In 1570, an auditor complained that the inhabitants of Lydford, on the western edge of Dartmoor in Devon, claimed to hold two mills, one in the town and one within the Forest of Dartmoor, as a fee-farm, in order

[39] E310/10/19, m. 29.   [40] E310/10/16, m. 39.

to allow the mills to decay, presumably so they could avoid their obligation to grind their corn at the manorial mill.[41] Trematon Castle, Cornwall, centre of a conventionary manor and honour overlooking the Tamar, was utterly decayed and the manorial constables occupied the site by entering their names in the conventionary roll. The recommendation was to allow the premises to pass under Exchequer seal as a lease.[42]

Occasionally, Duchy tenants scored a victory against their lord. At the end of the 1570s, the Crown sued the customary tenants of Fordington, an open-field manor lying to the south of Dorchester, Dorset, for intruding upon the demesne land. The case was heard at the assizes in Dorchester and the claims of the tenants vindicated. The Exchequer then resorted to its standard device, granting a lease of the supposed demesne to Maurice Brown who again took the case to law. This time Burghley, Mildmay and the Chief Baron of the Exchequer heard the case. With a rather dizzying consistency, they also found for the tenants.[43]

III

Agricultural historians, only interested in seeds and breeds, have paid scant attention to the possibility of great organisational change because they have overwhelmingly concentrated upon the productivity of farmers and the land. Indeed, through the whole of Elizabeth's reign, there is only one clear example of agricultural improvement upon Duchy land. In 1602, Christopher Bill applied for a renewal of his lease for three lives of the tithes of Lanracke in Cornwall. Bill stated that in 1583 when he initially took a lease,

at the time of the date of the said letters patent and for divers years after, there were neither beans nor *peason* used to be sown upon the soil whence the said tithe is gathered. But that now and for some years past those pulse are and have been sown there.[44]

He offered an increased rent if the tithes of peas and beans could be included in his lease, but he was rewarded with a lease for his desired term with an unchanged rent and no imposition of a fine.

Change on the estates took a number of forms, all of which were, in a memorandum of 1577 by Auditor Neale, considered to be

[41] *Ibid.*, m. 37.   [42] *Ibid.*

[43] Norden, 'Abreviat', fol. 27. For a further discussion of this case, see below, pp. 193–4.

[44] E310/10/17 m. 1.

detrimental to the Crown's position as landlord. Neale enumerated seven major difficulties which threatened the Crown's title to its lands.[45] The gentry who owned land abutting Duchy manors obtained surrenders of tenements and waste in order to annex the property to their own. Conventionary tenants claimed the right to cut timber upon their own tenements without delivery and further asserted an hereditary right to take timber from the 'Prince's wood' so long as it was declared before the manorial steward. Neale claimed that tenants abused the imposition of heriots in two ways. First, those who held more than a single tenement within a manor claimed that they owed only one heriot for all their holdings, and secondly, the value of the heriot was determined by two tenants, which meant that the true worth of the best beast was 'not answered'. He also criticised the manorial stewards for failing to record all the surrenders of lands which took place.

In his report, these complaints were preceded by two far more serious charges of abuse. Neale reported that many of the tenements were dismembered as parcels of land were surrendered to others until the house was left without land. This caused a 'great intricateness and confusion' of the payment of entry fines, known as New Knowledge upon some Cornish manors, so that the tenant alone could estimate the amount of the fines. This was complicated by another abuse of the tenurial system. When the land of a tenement had been surrendered to others, the ancient rent was attached to the house which meant that the lands formerly associated with it could be claimed as an estate of inheritance.[46]

Neale's report is significant. It suggests that the manorial rent roll, including the roll produced at the assession every seven years, was primarily a legal record which noted those who owed responsibilities to and enjoyed privileges from the Duchy. It had ceased to be a wholly accurate reflection of the organisation of farms and messuages by the mid-Elizabethan period. Of course, the records of the auditors

---

[45] DCO, Bound MSS, C/M/4, Assessionable Manors: Miscellaneous Papers, fol. 48. For very similar complaints, see the writings of Sir Robert Johnson of 1602–3, described below, pp. 205, 228.

[46] Neale's report, in the middle of the Elizabethan period, and the far more exhaustive work of Norden, encompassing the first two decades of the seventeenth century, collectively suggests that both Tudor and early Stuart monarchy opposed depopulation upon Duchy lands and attempted to enforce the medieval structure of landholding whenever it could. This contradicts the oblique conclusion of Lawrence Stone, 'The bourgeois revolution of seventeenth-century England', *Past and Present* 109 (1985), pp. 44–54.

were not the only class of documents which reported title. Manorial court rolls continued to act as a record for virtually all legal transactions concerning customary land within a manor. They were the bedrock of title to which surveyors referred in disputed cases, an accurate historical record of the services, liabilities and privileges of tenure, but they were a record between the legal tenant and the lord and not the legal tenant and the occupiers of the land.

There can be no doubt that important changes were occurring in the pattern of landholding amongst 'unfree' tenants, that is, those who were obliged to act through the manorial court. Some chose to sublet their holdings in part or entirely. It is likely that on some Duchy manors at least, a group of kulaks emerged in Elizabeth's reign who possessed the capital to acquire control of considerable acreages with the intention of subletting on a rack-rent basis or amalgamating holdings to create a larger farm for their own use. The Crown's legal relationship was with these tenants. The manor of Calstock is coterminous with the parish of the same name. A seating plan exists for the church which can be dated to 1586. On the assession roll of 1584, 112 tenants for the manor are listed. Of these, 44 are not listed on the seating plan. However, 21 of the 44 have the same surnames as persons named on the plan. If it is assumed that these latter are tenants on behalf of family, it suggests that only 19 per cent of tenants were absentees. If all names not found on the church seating plan are included, the absentee rate would be 39 per cent. This meant that in many cases the Crown as landlord had no legal relationship with those actually farming.

It is clear that leasing, while it may have served to maintain the immediate legal title of the Crown, frequently damaged its long-term interests as landlord. Equally, changes could be wrought to the face of the land by lessees without the Crown discovering matters for some time. In 1581, George Keckwich leased lands within the manor of Bonyalvey, a small manor along Cornwall's south coast. He held three tenements extending to more than 145 acres. Additionally, he held the two mills of the manor. When the manor was surveyed by Norden in 1608, he found 'notorious waste' so extreme that it was 'punishable by statute'. Keckwich had depopulated the manor, turning tenements from 'habitations to desolations', had not manured the land and of the four original tenements, only one was inhabited at the time of the survey. Norden noted that Keckwich's own land ran with the Duchy manor and his Duchy holdings were simply absorbed into his own for the lessee's own purpose.[47] Within the manor of Curry Mallet, Somerset, leased by Sir Hugh Paulet under Elizabeth, Norden reported that Paulet was long since deceased 'as also infinite goodlie oaks' which had been cut by the lessee.[48]

Auditor Neale's report of the abuses current on the estates may be seen to mark a boundary between the earlier and later Elizabethan administration of Duchy lands. Nowhere does Neale indicate how long the abuses had been taking place. There is evidence to suggest that this process antedates the Elizabethan regime. A much less general report, probably dating from the Marian period, complains that conventionary tenants were 'decaying the houses', taking timber without licence and not living upon their tenements. This report concerned only six tenements, all apparently in the same manor, but it noted that none of the half-dozen tenants actually lived on their land and one charged a sub-tenant a heriot equal to the value of ten oxen.[49] Even if these abuses had been taking place for a lengthy period before 1577, the fact that Neale noted them as a widespread phenomenon suggests that they were becoming prevalent enough to be a source of anxiety to those charged with land administration. Quite clearly, the changes which may be inferred from the evidence do not reflect a difference in attitude between earlier and later Exchequer administration. On the contrary, changes occurred despite the continuity of administrative practice. What took place was not as a result of imposed authority, but rather because circumstances, seemingly widespread over areas without great geographical uniformity, were changing on the land.

Of the seventeen conventionary manors, seven may be described as dynamic in that they showed marked increases in the number of tenants between 1570 and the first two decades of the seventeenth century. By 1617, the number of tenements at Tintagel had increased from fifty recorded in the second quarter of the fourteenth century to eighty. At Moresk, the number had grown from fifty to sixty. The manor of Stoke Climsland, consisting of 100 tenements in the fourteenth century, had increased to 159. Tywarnhaile grew from twenty-five to fifty-five, Tibesta from fifty to sixty-three, Liskeard

---

[47] Norden, 'Abreviat', fol. 56v, and DCO, John Norden, John Connock, Surveys of Cornwall, Bound MSS, T/M/3, fols. 90–1.

[48] Norden, 'Abreviat', fol. 2, and he also roundly condemns the customary tenants for taking timber.   [49] E315/472, fol. 80r.

from eighty to 104 and Calstock from eighty to 144.[50] Within the latter manor, sixty-nine of the tenements were held by two or more individuals in partnership.

Growth of manorial receipts is also indicative of change. At Mere, Wiltshire, net receipts remained low between 1530 and 1562. From then to 1570 they increased by 22 per cent, followed by a decline until 1578 after which they recovered to virtually the level of 1570 for the remainder of the century. This manor possessed a preponderance of tenants-at-will and changes in their numbers seem to have been the greater influence on receipts. With the conventionary manors in Cornwall, Moresk, Trematon, Helston in Trigg, Helston in Kerrier, Calstock, Liskeard and Stoke Climsland, there were significant increases in receipts between 1570 and the end of the century.[51] Liskeard, for instance, yielded a 99 per cent increase in net income between 1547–1553 and 1596–1602. The other conventionary manors did not produce notable differences in receipts. It is evidence perhaps of a mixture of circumstances from place to place. If all seventeen conventionary manors are considered together, receipts rose by 72 per cent when 1547–53 is compared with 1589–95.

The significance of these increased receipts is not to be found in the amounts, but rather in the indication of changed circumstances to which they point. Conventionary tenure was especially sensitive to local conditions and served to reflect changes wherever it did not become merely stereotyped and moribund. Upon other Duchy manors which remained under the direct control of the Exchequer for the Elizabethan period, receipts reflect stability rather than increase. At Kirton in Lindsey, Lincolnshire, socage tenure effectively precluded any increase from non-demesne lands, though there, the diminution of revenue occasioned by the mid-sixteenth-century agricultural slump simply carried forward as a new norm. On manors where copyhold for lives was the usual tenure, such as Bradninch in Devon, the pattern was one of stability. A similar situation existed at Fordington, Dorset, and Shippon, Berkshire.

---

[50] Hatcher, *Rural Economy and Society*, pp. 17–29. The implication of increased numbers of tenements is that waste was being enclosed to accommodate an increasing population since, if nothing else, the Duchy auditors ensured the survival of established holdings by reference to the previous assession roll. The figures for 1617 are derived from the assession roll, E306/4/4, 5.

[51] All data for the assessionary manors between 1570 and 1610 are derived from the net receipts noted in the Receiver-Generals' accounts. These are within SC6 and DCO, Rolls Series. There is data for all years.

But if income on these manors remained static, changes in the actual possession of land continued apace. A few copyholders were able to concentrate holdings within manors. At Bradninch, six copyholders possessed 688 acres between them out of a total of some 2,377 acres of copyhold land in the manor in 1615. At Fordington, an open-field manor where 1,900 of the 2,000 acres were copyhold, John Gould held an estate totalling 159 acres. At Midsomer Norton, Somerset, three individuals held 275 acres of copyhold between them.[52] Just as Auditor Neale had complained of demolished tenements, so too did John Norden. It is clear that the trends of extensive subletting and amalgamation of traditional farms continued and increased. At Old Shoreham, Sussex, which consisted of 228 acres, he found all tenants 'non-resident thereupon' who only let their lands to 'poor under tenants upon the rack, wreaking the land and ruining the houses'.[53]

Significant agricultural changes also took place in the townships which grazed within the Forest of Dartmoor. The manor of Lydford, of which the forest was manorial waste, extended to more than 60,000 acres. Dartmoor was effectively a common for the parishes which surrounded it. The forest was divided into four quarters, in each of which drifts were held to bring together the grazing animals so that small fines, known as venville rents, resembling but slightly different from levancy and couchancy, could be collected from the owners of the animals. Many of the surrounding parishes held very small populations. Nevertheless, the numbers of grazing cattle were high. In 1502, the four bailiffs counted 6,031 head. By 1556, the herd had declined to 4,166, and by 1567, only 3,738 cattle were drifted. Numbers had recovered to 5,778 by 1574 and remained at this approximate level until the end of the century. Several factors may have influenced fluctuations in the numbers of cattle grazing in any one year: weather affected available grass, disease, too, could have killed large numbers more or less at random.

Sheep were also pastured on Dartmoor. In 1502, only 244 were drifted by the bailiffs, in 1550, 324 and at the beginning of Elizabeth's reign the sheep flock numbered 606. By 1574, it had grown to 1,400. There are no reliable figures after that date until 1617 when the flock

[52] Norden, 'Abreviat', fols. 31, 25 and 8v. These surveys were taken in the first and second decades of the seventeenth century. Nevertheless, Norden provides the ages of copyholders and it is clear that most had at least begun to acquire their lands while Elizabeth reigned.

[53] Norden, 'Abreviat', fol. 177. See also, DCO, Norden, 'Surveys: Surrey, Dorset, Devon, Berkshire and Sussex'.

represented 1,203 sheep. The most significant increases in the sheep population occurred in the north and south quarters and there may have been an attempt by the bailiffs to provide separate ranges for sheep and cattle.[54]

The increase in the sheep flock, an important change in upland Dartmoor husbandry, suggests change for the whole of the highland region for which Dartmoor served as a common. The implications of the changes there affect many manors. This example of change is local, circumstantial and clearly not stimulated or imposed by the Duchy authorities. In fact, it illustrates how the Crown chose to maintain a policy of continuity in a period of significant change in population or, as in the case of Dartmoor, the local farming economy.

IV

Exchequer policy towards the Duchy may be described as benign neglect in the period between Elizabeth's accession and 1570. Sir Nicholas Bacon, speaking for the Crown as Lord Keeper in 1563, alluded to the perilous state of the realm and the Queen's need to sell her own land, and again in the Parliament of 1571 he extolled her self-sacrifice in disposing of her landed patrimony. Elizabeth's ministers finally grew disinclined to this policy of sacrifice. In 1575, Sir Walter Mildmay in his speech for supply indicated that Crown revenues had diminished because of land sales and the policy would no longer be pursued.[55]

Perhaps Mildmay could see the problems arising from the continued eroding of the Crown's ancient patrimony, a source of income free from political interference, or perhaps he was merely scoring a point in a political debate. The difficulty with advocating the good husbandry of Crown lands was that as a financial resource they performed quite unspectacularly. Between 1560 and 1590 Duchy net receipts never exceeded £4,100 and often were less than £3,500. Unlike Crown lands, the Duchy was protected by statute; selling its lands required an act of Parliament and this would have looked unattractively cumbersome to ministers when in need of immediate financial assistance. The Duchy's connection with the Chamber, though rather easily exaggerated, was an important

---

[54] DCO, Rolls Series, Ministers' Accounts, Rolls 84, 116, 127, 129, 169 and 181.

[55] T. E. Hartley (ed.), *Proceedings in the Parliament of Elizabeth I*, I, *1558–1581* (Leicester, 1981), pp. 84, 185 and 443.

connection with the court. Equally, so long as a powerful courtier such as the earl of Bedford held the offices of Lord Warden of the Stannaries and Chief Steward, he could act to ensure that the Exchequer did not encroach too far upon the ancient Duchy prerogative.

Sir Walter Raleigh was appointed Lord Warden in 1585. Whilst he enjoyed enormous popularity amongst the tin miners, Raleigh did not possess a personal fortune nor did he command a political base. Even if he desired to resist the blandishments of the Cecils and later Buckhurst, he was unable to do so. In 1595, he allowed the Duchy to slide into the hands of the Exchequer by sanctioning payment of Duchy revenues to it rather than the Chamber.[56] Benign neglect was transformed to active dismemberment in the crises of the 1590s, especially when the need to raise money for war led the government once again to the sale of Crown lands.[57] By 1601, some eighteen Cornish manors, all from the group of ex-monastic and former marquis of Exeter lands, had been sold. The Exchequer ignored the legal niceties of the Duchy's constitutional position, the auditors simply endorsing the particular for sale with the observation that the land was not part of the ancient Duchy.[58] Cecil, Buckhurst, perhaps even the Exchequer auditors, may not have realised the legal position, but Raleigh, as Lord Warden, either knew or should have known. Cecil, a commissioner for the sales, acquired the fee-farms of five manors and the earl of Essex bought three others.[59]

The attractions of selling Duchy lands were several. Sales could be accomplished swiftly and yield large sums of ready money. Since the disposal of land did not affect any but the Crown and the purchaser, it was likely to be a popular expedient at any time for raising funds. Especially where sales were made in fee-farm, they were now merely a further stage in the inability or unwillingness of the late Tudor and early Stuart monarchs to reclaim their prerogative rights in the demesne lands within their landed inheritance. This failure is crucial to the history of the estates. It is probably related to developments

---

[56] DCO, Rolls Series, Receiver-Generals' Accounts, Roll 263. This was accomplished by levying a tallia on virtually the whole of the disposable income.

[57] For the Crown's response to crisis, see R. B. Outhwaite, 'Studies in Elizabethan government finance: royal borrowing and the sale of crown lands, 1572–1603' (University of Nottingham, PhD thesis, 1964), p. 299.

[58] DCO, Bound MSS, T/M/3, 'Sale of Duchy Lands by Queen Elizabeth, Anno 1601, Particulars and Warrants'.

[59] DCO, Bound MSS, T/M/3, 'Sale of Duchy Lands by Queen Elizabeth, Anno 1601, Particulars and Warrants'.

within individual manors. By the end of the sixteenth century, unfree tenure continued to exist, but the status of individuals as free or unfree disappeared on most Duchy manors in the last two decades of the sixteenth century. The hierarchical distinctions which existed within a manor passed from individuals to the parcels of land they possessed. Even though economic circumstances may have favoured a return to demesne farming or at least direct Crown control of its demesne by the end of the sixteenth century, the intricate network of leases, the lack of legal gradation of the population, precluded any attempt to alter fundamentally the received system of administration in favour of former practices.

The Duchy had plumbed the depths of its fortunes by the end of 1601. It existed as an administrative backwater, surviving only because it had been in part forgotten. As a Queen without an heir, vague until the end about the succession, Elizabeth had no use for the Duchy of Cornwall. From this inauspicious Tudor end, it would be transformed by the Jacobean polity.

CHAPTER 4

Exchequer officials and the market in Crown property, 1558–1640

Madeleine Gray

In the summer of 1604, John Wynn of Gwydir in Caernarfonshire, the future baronet, commissioned Richard Budd (who was at that time clerk to Thomas Hanbury, the Exchequer auditor for Wales, and an experienced agent and dealer on the property market) to act on his behalf in leasing land from the Crown.[1] Enraged by this, Wynn's usual agent Thomas Martin wrote that

> I could have passed the thing as well to your good as Mr Budd and better cheap, for Auditor Hanbury is in no grace with my L[ord] Treas[urer], I have seen him crouching and creeping pitifully unto my L[ord], I know the cause he was fain to make good means else to hazard of his place

adding for good measure

> if I did complain that the Auditor his man did pass anything for any other I think barely he should have had passage and be well checked, but I will forbear for your sake and not for his.[2]

Four years later, Richard Gwynn, Budd's colleague and Thomas Hanbury's deputy, was indignantly denying the charge levied against him in the Exchequer court of being 'a common dealer in leases'.[3] From these two instances it might appear that dabbling in the market for Crown property was an activity forbidden not only to officials but even to their privately appointed clerks. However, if it was disapproved of, the prohibition seems to have been largely ignored.

---

[1] The research for this chapter was funded by a grant from the British Academy. I am also grateful to Sir John Sainty for his help and advice: his book, *Officers of the Exchequer* (List and Index Soc. special ser., 18, 1983) is the obvious starting-point for a study of this kind, and provided most of the biographical information not otherwise attributed.

[2] NLW, Add. MS 465E, no. 293. The Wynn letters are calendared in J. Ballinger (ed.), *Calendar of Wynn (of Gwydir) Papers, 1515–1690* (Aberystwyth, 1926).

[3] T. I. Jeffreys Jones (ed.), *Exchequer Proceedings Concerning Wales in tempore James I* (Board of Celtic Studies, History and Law ser., 15, Cardiff, 1955), p. 58.

Budd's other fellow-clerks Thomas Odingzelles and George Sallus both dealt in Crown land, though not as extensively as Budd, as did William Cave, one of the clerks to Thomas Hanbury's successor William Hill. Meanwhile, Francis Phillips, clerk to another of the auditors, was receiving a series of massive grants of Crown land as a nominee on behalf of several groups of London businessmen. Edmund Sawyer may have been active as a nominee and dealer before he entered the service of the Exchequer but he did not allow his clerkship to interfere with his other activities. Budd and some of his contemporaries scaled down their dealings on becoming auditors, but Sawyer (who succeeded to office in 1621) continued to deal in Crown property at second hand until the 1630s while Budd's former clerk Thomas Brinley, auditor for north-east England from 1626, appears on the Patent Rolls in 1636 as a grantee of reclaimed land on behalf of some of Cornelius Vermuyden's partners.

Crown officials had in fact played an active part in the market for Crown land since at least the great dispersal of monastic property in the 1540s. Many of the agents and dealers who flourished at that time can be identified with officials or their private clerks. The purchase of land from the Crown was an expensive, complicated and time-consuming business and presented particular problems for land-owners from Wales and the remoter counties of England who had no London residence. However, the fact that dealers like James Gunter could make massive profits selling land to well-connected gentry and officials suggests that even a busy administrator might find it to his advantage to employ an agent.[4] At this period, the commonest practice seems to have been for the aspiring purchaser to come to London, secure a 'particular' or description of the property from the relevant Exchequer auditor, then hand it over to an agent to negotiate the valuation. The agent would receive a grant of the properties ordered by a number of clients, thus economising on the time and expense taken to secure a patent; the properties would then be resold to the clients.[5] Many of these agents are described in their patents only as 'of London, gentleman' but it is sometimes possible to find more specific descriptions on the particulars for grants. From

---

[4] For Gunter's profits, see M. Gray, 'Mr Auditor's man: the career of Richard Budd, estate agent and Exchequer official', *WHR* 12 (1985), pp. 307–23.

[5] For details of this process, see, for instance, Joyce Youings, *The Dissolution of the Monasteries* (London, 1971), pp. 117–31.

these it appears that some were London tradesmen but many were described as the servants (which in this context may well mean privately appointed clerks) of courtiers and officials.[6]

Senior officials also acted as agents and dealers. Many were prepared to buy on behalf of local connections but some also dealt in land as a commercial proposition. In most cases, it was the client who took the initiative, but even in the 1540s, there were agents prepared to advertise their services. John Bellow, a Court of Augmentations surveyor, went about the East Riding proclaiming publicly that 'if any would buy any land, the king was disposed to sell lands and he [Bellow] would help them to it'.[7] From this, it seems possible that Bellow saw it as part of his duties to foster the market for Crown property, and he may well have received official encouragement to do so. These advertising activities would have been to the Crown's advantage generally: the market for land was never so active that it could not do with a little encouragement. There would, however, be a more immediate reason to advertise the availability of Crown land since its sale was not a continuous process. A commission would be empowered to sell land to a certain annual value, and sometimes of a specific type: once the limit had been reached, no more sales were made until the next commission. At times when the Crown's need for money was most pressing, there might be a commission more or less continually in session and the inevitable delay in processing applications can give the impression that sales were continuous. By the same token, there were sometimes lengthy periods, such as that from 1564 to 1590, when no commissions for sales were issued and those who wished to acquire Crown land had to resort to means other than outright purchase. In the absence of evidence, it is generally difficult to say how the news that a commission had been issued was spread through the provinces. Only three proclamations have been found, all in the seventeenth century and two of them dealing only with land enclosed out of the Crown's wastes and forests; the third announces Charles I's intention of granting copyhold and leasehold properties in fee-farm to save administrative costs. This is perplexing, since it was obviously in the Crown's best interests that commissions should be as

---

[6] E.g. George Cotton and Thomas Reve, servants of Richard Duke, clerk to the Court of Augmentations; Thomas Marshe, servant of the Lord Chancellor; Jerome Halley, servant of Sir Robert Bowes, Master of the Rolls; John Middleton, servant of Sir John Thynne.

[7] C. J. Kitching, 'Studies in the redistribution of collegiate and chantry property in the diocese and county of York at the dissolution' (University of Durham, PhD thesis, 1970), p. 114.

widely publicised as possible. John Bellow's statement indicates the role played by Augmentations and Exchequer officials in this; there were other, local, officials who were in fairly regular contact with London, including sheriffs, receivers and other administrators of Crown property. There were also more informal means of notifying possible purchasers: when Parliament was in session, Members could expect to hear of government decisions, and most landed families had at least a cousin working somewhere in the administrative system who could be trusted to pass on such news.[8]

Privately employed agents and lawyers who were frequently about the Exchequer could also have access to information: later in his letter, Thomas Martin assured Sir John Wynn that 'I think leases will hardly pass until Michaelmas, if any do you shall hear of it.' In an earlier letter he had warned Wynn 'touching taking of a lease in reversion...I think verily things that shall pass will be dearly rated, as yet they be in sale and no lease passeth, very shortly leases shall pass, I will do all I can to pass it for you but you must send money.'[9] It must have been obvious, however, that Budd, who was actually employed in the Exchequer and required as part of his duties to draw up particulars of land for sale or lease, was a more reliable source of information. In 1614, another of Sir John's agents, Maurice Owen, wrote to him from London that

Your letter to Mr Richard Wynn & your letter to Mr Budd I delivered yesterday and I understand by them that the last commission for sale is filled but they tell me that there is a new commission in making for the sale of two thousand pounds more of the King's rent, but when the same shall be [?signed] or when the commissioners will first sit it is not known. But Mr Budd promised that he will sue forth a particular as soon as the commission shall be signed.[10]

The annual tour of the provinces which the auditors of land revenue or their deputies made to check the accounts of Crown bailiffs and receivers was a more regular channel of communications and ideally suited for matters relating to Crown land.

With the exception of a few individuals like Bellow and Gunter, those who dealt on the property market in the 1540s and 1550s were not in

---

[8] *Stuart Royal Procs.*, I, nos. 49, 52; II, no. 50. The matter is considered further in the introduction, p. 48.　　　[9] NLW, MS 9052E, no. 289.

[10] NLW, MS 9055E, no. 649. Richard Wynn is probably the Richard Gwynn, Budd's colleague, mentioned previously (the 'G' is frequently dropped in Welsh).

any sense full-time estate agents. Few of the 'London gentlemen' received more than one or two composite grants, while for the officials these activities were obviously very much a sideline. By the end of the century, however, students of the market in Crown land have noticed the emergence of a group of agents and dealers whose names recur in the records over a period of some years. This development may be the result of a change in the methods used by agents or in the available documentation: the easiest agents to identify are those who dealt by bargain and sale endorsed on the Close Rolls, and the indexes to vendors on the Close Rolls only run from 1574.[11] However, the fact that most detailed local studies of the market in Crown property concentrate on the period before 1575 suggests that dealers from that period should if anything be better known than their successors.

By the last quarter of the century, structural changes in the nature of the Crown's estate and the methods by which it was sold or otherwise alienated had altered the nature and scope of the agents' activities. For various reasons, the early purchasers had concentrated on larger properties – monastic sites and demesnes, manors and whole estates and, in Wales, the Crown's marcher lordships – leaving the Crown with smaller properties, single tenements and scraps of land which were both difficult to administer and less attractive to the wealthier purchasers. Elizabeth's reversionary leases, fee-farm grants and exchanges were often made not to the courtiers she wished to reward but to nominees who would act for them in selling the property.[12] Many resales took place so quickly that the buyer must have been found before the Crown grant was made, and in some cases the second buyer can also be identified as an agent or dealer using contacts at court to buy Crown land at a time when official policy made a straightforward purchase impossible.

Outright sales began again in 1590 as a consequence of financial pressure resulting from war with Spain and Ireland. James I & VI's

---

[11] As a fortuitous result of legislation on the law of real property in 1536 it became possible to convey land without the cumbersome ritual of livery of seisin if the conveyance was subsequently enrolled in a court of record. The Close Rolls were already being used for the enrolment of private deeds and became the most popular place to register the new conveyances, known as bargains and sales. The Close Rolls thus provide a useful though incomplete register of private conveyances from 1536. (For further details see M. Gray, 'The Close Rolls as a source for sixteenth-century history', *Archives* 17 (1986), pp. 131–7.) This method was, for obvious reasons, popular among London-based agents, and conveyances endorsed on the Close Rolls thus form the basis for this article. They are too numerous for individual references but can be traced through the contemporary indexes.

[12] On exchanges, see above, pp. 79–81.

policies of peace and conciliation reduced foreign expenditure but his court was far more expensive than Elizabeth's. He, too, rewarded courtiers with gifts of land for resale through nominees and in 1609 resumed the practice of issuing commissions to sell land, ostensibly to diminish the burden of administering small and fragmented properties. A determined attempt was made to confine the sales to the fragments of former chantry property which had proved so difficult to administer, and to other unpopular types of property like mills and the extensive spiritual revenues which the Crown had acquired at the dissolution of the monasteries. These properties were not immediately attractive to wealthy purchasers, though they might offer the possibility of consolidating an estate or of acquiring the tithes of land already held. An increasing number of purchasers, therefore, were very minor gentry, townspeople or lesser landholders, some of them investing in their first piece of freehold land. Even for the more experienced purchaser, however, the small properties now available scarcely justified the expense of a direct purchase from the Crown.

Meanwhile, the Crown desperately needed ready cash and had no time to negotiate over small sums of money. Thus, the Exchequer failed to regain control of the process of sale. Consortia of London merchants headed by men like Sir Arthur Ingram and Sir Baptist Hicks, many of whom had already loaned substantial sums of money to the Crown, contracted to pay in advance for the right to sell land to a given annual valuation. Commissioners still sat to check the value of property, calculate the purchase price and decide when the predetermined annual value had been reached but the contractors ostensibly took over the time-consuming and unpredictable business of selling the land, offering the Crown a guaranteed price in return for the opportunity of profit.[13] The Crown was thus selling not only the land but also the process of sale and much of the potential profit. Since groups of ten or twelve purchasers could not conveniently act together to resell land, grants were customarily made to two nominees acting on behalf of the consortium. The intending purchasers negotiated with the Exchequer over the price of individual properties and the nominees arranged for resale to the genuine purchasers or their agents. The contractors made up the total by buying further properties on their own account for subsequent resale and these were managed and eventually disposed of on their behalf by their nominees.

---

[13] For a discussion of the contractors' sales, see above, pp. 21–6.

Both nominees and agents can often be identified as lesser officials
or their clerks. We can almost certainly assume that these clerks had
no financial interest in the sales they arranged: they would have been
moving far out of their own league in associating with some of the
wealthiest merchants and financiers in the kingdom. They were
presumably paid for their services but, as with so many aspects of
their activities, no evidence of payments has as yet come to light.
Attempts to reform Crown finance led to a cessation in sales after
1616 but they were resumed in 1625, as were grants to courtiers and
the Crown's creditors. The market was inevitably not as brisk as it
had been earlier in the century – in spite of the inroads which were
being made into the Duchy of Lancaster, there was less to sell, less
choice and therefore less to tempt investors – but sales and other
grants continued to fund the government in the absence of parliamentary finance until the late 1630s.

There were, therefore, a number of ways in which officials and
clerks could become involved in the market for Crown property. For
some it was the reward for their services: even a lowly household
servant might at some time expect to be granted a lease in reversion,
though it is seldom possible to find out whether the Exchequer
granted a reversion knowing that the tenant would be prepared to
pay for its assignment or whether the tenant or another interested
party had already approached the Crown's grantee.[14] Most of the
senior officials and courtiers who received fee-farm grants or
exchanges employed agents to handle the disposal of the land but
some, including (perhaps unexpectedly) Sir Christopher Hatton,
chose to deal with the business themselves. Other officials used their
own servants or the servants of their subordinates as nominees or
partners. Charles Harbord, the future Surveyor-General, was himself
still a servant (albeit one of the most senior estate officials of the earl
of Pembroke) when in 1630 he took advantage of a grant of land in
lieu of £2,350 owed to him by the King to pay a further £4,250 and
receive lands worth a nominal total of £300 a year.[15] The grant, to
Harbord himself, his own personal clerk Thomas Young and
Christopher Favell, a London jeweller, was dated 4 October. The
first resale took place on 16 November and several parcels had been
sold by the end of the year, suggesting that Harbord may have had

[14] For leases in reversion, see below, pp. 184–90.
[15] This was in fact a generous valuation, being twenty-two times the nominal rental and
probably about seven times the true annual value, though Harbord would, of course, have
had the expense of resale.

some tentative purchasers lined up. Many of the grants of this period, particularly those in which an element of Crown favour was involved, contained a clause allowing for the reexchange of property which could not be sold. The earliest reference on the Close Rolls to Harbord, Favell and Young's grant is in fact a reexchange of part of the property on 14 October, which may indicate that a planned sale had fallen through.[16] Harbord also stood as a nominee for grants to the earl of Berkshire in 1629 and for at least one of a series of grants to Sir John Eden, Lieutenant of Ordnance, in the 1630s. But for these men, as for the officials who dealt in Crown land in the 1540s, the property market could hardly be more than a sideline. This chapter proposes to concentrate on the increasing number of officials and clerks who bought and sold Crown land as a regular activity over a number of years.

Such officials could be found in all the lower ranks of the government and household. The Mr Merry, whose unsuccessful negotiations for the township of Mostyn in Flintshire during 1614 were retailed with such glee by the young Richard Wynn to his father, was clerk of the kitchen;[17] Ellis Wynn, Sir John's younger brother and one of Richard Budd's early partners, was gentleman harbinger in the royal household and a clerk of the petty bag in Chancery.[18] As well as acting in partnership with his master Charles Harbord, Thomas Young received several other grants in partnership with Thomas Sara of London, gentleman, Edmund Toller of St Martin in the Fields and Richard Long of Winterbourn Monks in Wiltshire, reselling in some cases within weeks of the grant and disposing of all the property fairly rapidly, suggesting that he was always in touch with a possible purchaser before arranging to buy.[19]

Employment in the Exchequer or in one of the other departments dealing with the Crown's landed estate obviously offered the best facilities for an agent. One of the earliest agents and dealers, Edmund Downing, active from 1553, was for over thirty years an Exchequer official as well as acting as Sir Walter Mildmay's man of business.[20] Another of Sir John Heydon's nominees, William Scriven, was a clerk in the office of the Lord Treasurer's Remembrancer and also dealt in

[16] C54/2862, no. 5, 14 Oct.; C54/2828, no. 2; C54/2845, no. 6; C54/2847, no. 30, etc.
[17] NLW, MS 9055E, no. 662; cf. Ballinger (ed.), *Wynn Papers*, nos. 661, 662, 665; for an extract from the latter, see below, p. 120.
[18] For his career, see *HP 1558–1603*, III, pp. 670–1.
[19] E.g. C54/2622, no. 5; C54/2629, no. 1; C54/2647, nos. 29 and 32, Thomas Young and Thomas Sara, 10–22 Feb. 1626.   [20] *HP 1558–1603*, II, p. 52.

land on his own behalf. While working his way up through the
hierarchy in the Pipe Office, Christopher Vernon made himself such
an expert in ferreting out concealed land revenues and recovering
lost titles for the Crown that by 1623 he was acting as the Prince of
Wales's solicitor in such matters.[21] But by far the most important as
well as the most numerous of these agents were to be found in the
offices of the auditors of land revenue.

With the benefit of hindsight, this is what we might expect. The
auditors were of all the London-based officials of the Exchequer the
closest to the local communities and the most involved with the
preparations for selling land. That such inside information was
valuable to an agent is evident from the letter of Richard Wynn
already referred to. Richard Budd was again acting on Sir John
Wynn's behalf and had promised 'I for my part will provide kind
weapons for Mr Richard Wynne to fight withal for he must deal for
it [Mostyn township] with the lords.'[22] The nature of these weapons
is made plain by Richard Wynn, who reported that 'Mr Deccam[23]
was there (who informs the lords of the value of all things) but Morris
by my advice gave him five pounds which did stop his mouth, and did
us very much good.' The entire letter is a fascinating and detailed
account of the rating of several pieces of property. In the case of
Mostyn township, rival bidders were left while the commissioners
were called away. The other bidder was Mr Merry, who wearied of
waiting, and when the lords returned Richard Wynn secured the
property at fifty-three years' purchase. Mr Merry returned too late
with an offer of seventy years' purchase. Richard Budd claimed the
credit for this, as it was he who, knowing from his work in the
auditor's office that another particular of the property had been
drawn up, warned Wynn of the competition. Another piece of
property was rated for Wynn in the absence of the Master of the
Rolls, who on his return informed the commissioners of the true value
of the property, but the former rating was allowed to stand.[24] It
appears from these episodes that an offer of property at a particular
valuation was regarded as binding on the Crown, which made the use

---

[21] G. E. Aylmer, *The King's Servants, the Civil Service of Charles I, 1625–42* (London, 1961), p. 315.
[22] NLW, MS 9055E, no. 656.
[23] 'Mr Deccam' was presumably John, later Sir John Dackombe, who was granted the
reversion of an auditorship of imprests in 1610 but died in 1618 before succeeding to office.
He was briefly Chancellor of the Duchy of Lancaster in 1616–18. Sainty, *Officers of the
Exchequer*, p. 136; Sir John Somerville, *Office-holders in the Duchy and County Palatine of
Lancaster from 1603* (Chichester, 1972), pp. 1, 7.
[24] NLW, MS 9055E, nos. 656, 661–2, 665.

of guile and inside information even more important. Budd could also promise to protect his clients from similar competition by drawing up particulars in secret, 'whereby none shall know of it'.[25]

That the auditors and their clerks do not become prominent in the market for Crown property until the late sixteenth century (Budd, one of the earliest to be identified, first appears in the records in 1586) may be the result of changes in the nature of the market or may simply be an illusion arising out of improvements in the available documentary sources. However, it may also reflect changes in the personnel of the Exchequer. It was preeminently the auditors' clerks who were involved in the property market: those auditors who functioned as agents were almost always those who are known to have worked as clerks and deputies, and their activity while auditors was often confined to managing and selling property they had bought earlier. The work of an auditor required specialised financial skills which could only be learnt by practice, as there was no formal training available. By the late sixteenth century, an unofficial but well-established career structure had developed whereby privately appointed clerks progressed to deputising for older auditors, secured the grant of a reversion to office and eventually became auditors themselves. This control of admission and training makes the auditors less of a bureaucracy than a proto-professional group, exhibiting at least some of the criteria of professionalisation listed by modern sociologists. New entrants were thus not merely clerks: they were ambitious younger sons and members of the minor gentry or of urban families, anxious to better themselves. Unfortunately, we have so little information about the auditors and their clerks before the late sixteenth century that we cannot say whether this progression was in fact a new development.[26]

The traditional role of the agent was to buy land from the Crown on behalf of, and at the initiative of, a client or a group of clients. This was still being done at the end of the century, though it was far from being the exclusive preserve of Exchequer clerks. Many of the grants under late sixteenth-century commissions for sale went to scriveners

---

[25] *Ibid.*, no. 649.

[26] For a discussion of career structures and professionalisation in the sixteenth- and seventeenth-century Exchequer, see M. Gray, 'An early professional group? The auditors of land revenue in the late sixteenth and early seventeenth centuries', *Archives* (forthcoming, 1992); on sixteenth-century clerical bureaucracies in general, see J. D. Alsop, 'Government, finance and the community of the Exchequer', in C. Haigh (ed.), *The Reign of Elizabeth I* (Basingstoke, 1984).

like Henry Best[27] or to London tradesmen. The clerks were more strongly represented as nominees in the fee-farm grants to Crown servants and favourites, but they really came into their own when the near-bankruptcy of the Crown in 1608 forced James's advisers to recommend the sale of land. The nominees of the great land-buying consortia might well be chosen from the group of investors: John Eldred, William Whitmore and Martin Freeman each received several grants on behalf of their partners. However, the representative of the investors was frequently accompanied by another nominee who did not appear in the list of investors and who can often be identified as an auditor's clerk. In some cases, the second nominee is not known to have been a clerk at the time of his first grant: evidence as to the names of clerks is scanty, but the career pattern of employment as a clerk, activity as an agent and eventual appointment as an auditor is so well established by 1640 that we may even feel justified in reversing the model and arguing that agents who became auditors had probably begun as clerks.

Fortunately, the most active of the early seventeenth-century nominees, Francis Phillips, who in partnership with various contractors and others between 1608 and 1613 received twenty-one grants of land worth about £4,000 a year, is known to have been a clerk to one of the auditors since the 1590s.[28] He became auditor for the north Midlands in 1619. Edmund Sawyer received his first grants in 1607 but our first evidence as to his other occupation is in 1613 when he was described as clerk to his cousin William Hill, the auditor for Wales.[29] Between 1607 and 1616 he received a further fourteen grants from the Crown, as well as dealing extensively at second hand. Thomas Brinley, who was Sawyer's junior partner in 1612[30], is known to have been Richard Budd's clerk by 1620.[31] Among other auditors' clerks who were acting as nominees in this decade was Justinian Povey, the future auditor for London and the South-East. He had worked in the office of the auditor of north-east England since about 1590. In 1609, Nathaniel Fulwer, auditor for south-west

---

[27] For the scale of Best's activities, see R. B. Outhwaite, 'Studies in Elizabethan government finance; royal borrowing and the sale of crown lands, 1572–1603' (University of Nottingham, PhD thesis, 1964), pp. 364–5.

[28] In 1638 he described himself as having served in the audit for over forty years; *CSPD 1638–9*, pp. 254–5.   [29] E112/90/135.

[30] The relative standing of the partners can be deduced from the order in which they appear in the grant and from the way in which they are listed in the contemporary indexes to the Patent and Close Rolls. Clerks appear as junior partners to contractors and officials; the senior partner of the two clerks is presumably the more experienced.

[31] Jeffreys Jones (ed.), *Exchequer Proceedings*, p. 111.

England, offered to appoint Povey as his assistant, and in 1611, he achieved official rank as auditor of the Queen's estates, a post he held under both Anne and Henrietta Maria.[32]

Francis Phillips was unusual not only in the amount of land granted to him as a nominee but in that he never dealt in Crown land at second hand. Some agents limited themselves solely to that part of the market. Perhaps the best example – certainly the easiest to trace – is Richard Budd, who between 1588 and 1629 dominated the market in Crown property in Wales, buying and selling land with a yearly value of about £250, most of it in small fragments.[33] Budd was also unusual in confining himself to dealing in land within the audit circuit for which he worked: the very few purchases which he made outside Wales were almost certainly for himself and were all retained until his death. He may well have found the remote and comparatively undeveloped land market in Wales a large enough sphere for his activities and his specialisation contributed to his dominant position. Other clerks spread their activities more widely, encouraged perhaps by their experience as nominees. The scale of Budd's activities seems small in comparison with Phillips, but the work of an intermediate agent and dealer was more complex and probably more lucrative than that of a nominee. Other clerks dabbled in the second-hand market: Philip Darell, who was Brinley's clerk and deputy in the 1620s and became an auditor during the Civil War, made occasional purchases from 1609 to 1639. Edward Bateman, a clerk who Phillips inherited from his predecessor Alexander King and who served as Phillips's deputy from at least 1621, bought land in Lancashire (the area in which he worked) for £165 in 1631 and sold it the following year for £170: he also bought the lease of a rectory in Cheshire but its resale has not been traced. This seems to have exhausted his enthusiasm. He may have had other resources: he never became an auditor but by 1631 he had a residence in New Windsor, and the property in Frogmore for which he paid £200 in 1638 was probably for himself.

Some agents even specialised in leaseholds, particularly in reversionary leases. These were yet another method of granting away

---

[32] *CSPD 1603–10*, p. 574; *CSPD Add. 1580–1625*, pp. 476–7.
[33] Gray, 'Mr Auditor's man'. Thanks to the Board of Celtic Studies, the Exchequer proceedings relating to Wales up to 1625 have been calendared (E. G. Jones (ed.), *Exchequer Proceedings (Equity) Concerning Wales, Henry VIII–Elizabeth* (Board of Celtic Studies, History and Law ser., 4, Cardiff, 1939), and Jeffreys Jones (ed.) *Exchequer Proceedings*) so that agents active in Wales are always easier to study.

the right to exploit the difference between nominal and actual values on the Crown's estate. By the late sixteenth century, such leases were designed not for eventual tenancy by the grantee but for assignment at a profit, often through an agent or nominee.[34] In order to prevent the tenancy from being granted away over their heads, however, existing tenants were also forced to take out new leases well before the old had expired, and in this they might well require the services of an agent. It is particularly difficult to trace the activities of these agents. Small leases were granted under the Exchequer seal and do not even appear on the Patent Rolls. Particulars for leases do not survive after the end of the sixteenth century; there was no need for assignments to be enrolled, and because they did not confer permanent title they are seldom preserved in estate muniments.

Evidence of dealing in leases does, however, appear in Exchequer proceedings: again, the most readily available examples are from Wales. Richard Budd began his career negotiating a reversionary lease in Carmarthenshire for Sir John Perrot, but the evidence suggests that by 1600 the majority of his transactions were in property in fee. Richard Gwynn bought land in partnership with Budd and others but it appears from the Exchequer proceedings referring to him that he concentrated more than Budd did on leasehold property, for all his denials that he was 'a common dealer in leases'. Gwynn, like Bateman, never progressed beyond a deputy auditorship but seems to have made a comfortable living from that and his land dealings, and was sufficiently influential to be able to secure the reversion to an auditorship for his son William. He had inherited his family's estate at Frogmore near Windsor by 1608; he had apparently retired from Hanbury's service by 1611 but was still active in 1621, by which time he had moved a few miles west to Clewer.[35] Thomas Odingzelles, another of Hanbury's clerks, also bought some land outright in partnership with Budd and others but dealt far more extensively in leases and on his own. So widespread were his acquisitions in Pembrokeshire that G. Dyfnallt Owen believed he was building up an estate for himself there, but in most cases he can be shown to have been dealing on behalf of others.[36]

---

[34] See below, pp. 184–90.

[35] Jeffreys Jones (ed.), *Exchequer Proceedings*, pp. 48, 262; Ballinger (ed.), *Wynn Papers*, no. 619; C66/1906.

[36] G. Dyfnallt Owen, 'Agrarian conditions and changes in West Wales during the sixteenth century with special reference to monastic and chantry land' (University of Wales, PhD thesis, 1935). For Odingzelles's dealings, see also Jones (ed.) and Jeffreys Jones (ed.),

Most agents, however, threw themselves with equal gusto into all aspects of the market. Edmund Sawyer, perhaps the greatest of the early seventeenth-century agents and certainly the most successful financially, began in March 1607 with a lease (most of it of Welsh property) and a grant on behalf of Sir Thomas Smith, the clerk to the Privy Council. In May of that year he bought, apparently on his own behalf, a lease of some land in Yorkshire which he assigned within a fortnight at a considerable profit. In July, he and Edmund Cooke, his partner in the grant on behalf of Smith, bought the manor of Appleton in Yorkshire through the nominees Richard Lydall and Edmund Bostock. From 1609, he made regular purchases through and from most of the recognised nominees, buying both for himself and on behalf of clients, alone and in partnership with other 'London gentlemen' including Peter Page, Peter Phillips and Thomas Brinley. His next grant from the Crown was in March 1612 when he was the junior partner of a London businessman, Martin Freeman, in a grant of land in Lincolnshire, Derbyshire, London and Durham. By this time, he had been granted the reversion to an auditorship. In May 1612, he and William Whitmore, another businessman, received a grant in twenty English and Welsh counties on behalf of Freeman and the leading contractor Sir Arthur Ingram. His earlier grant with Freeman gives no indication of how much money was paid or of how it was raised; the grant to him and Thomas Brinley in July 1612 of land in Cardiganshire, Carmarthenshire and six English counties was again made in conjunction with Sir Arthur Ingram but Sawyer and Brinley were subsequently able to buy him out.[37] From 1613 to 1616, Sawyer appears as junior or senior partner in a further nine grants covering virtually the whole of England and Wales, in partnership with Francis Morice, Francis Phillips, William Whitmore and several other businessmen and 'London gentlemen'.

During the lull in Crown sales after 1616, Sawyer and his partners continued to offload their purchases while diversifying into the private land market. Sawyer bought a small estate for himself at Heywood in Berkshire in 1623 and added to it by several later purchases. He eventually became an auditor in 1621 and was one of the few holders of that office to be knighted and to sit in Parliament, where he represented Windsor in 1624 and Berwick in 1628 until the

Exchequer Proceedings, passim, and E. A. Lewis and J. C. Davies (eds.), *Records of the Court of Augmentations Relating to Wales and Monmouthshire* (Board of Celtic Studies, History and Law ser., 13, Cardiff, 1954), *passim.* [37] Jeffreys Jones (ed.), *Exchequer Proceedings,* p. 107.

House of Commons expelled him for complicity in a scheme for unparliamentary taxation.[38] He had already offered a critique of the traditional proceedings of the Pipe Office in the Exchequer in 1616, and in 1633 he was asked to present an official report on the subject.[39] He was one of the trustees of the earl of Suffolk's debt-encumbered estate and in 1630 entered into partnership with the earl of Banbury for the disposal of a grant of land from the Crown. When Charles I recommenced selling land he resumed his role as an agent and dealer, confining himself to dealing at second hand. This may have been dictated by necessary caution, as he was now an official, but it may also indicate that the status of an intermediary was regarded as being higher than that of a grantee.

Exchequer officials did stand as nominees or partners but only for senior courtiers, aristocrats and others whom the Crown wished to favour. The Surveyor-General, Charles Harbord, received grants on behalf of Sir John Heydon, Lieutenant of Ordnance, in lieu of Crown debts to Heydon; both Harbord and Sawyer acted as trustees of the earl of Berkshire; and Thomas Brinley received a massive grant of reclaimed land in Yorkshire for the partners of Cornelius Vermuyden. In all these cases, we can assume that the services of an official to manage and dispose of the property was an additional favour from the Crown to the beneficiary of the grant. What had changed since the earlier years of the century was that under Charles I the auditors themselves, as well as their clerks, were expected as part of their duties to work for private individuals at the Crown's command.[40]

Edmund Sawyer had begun his career as a nominee and rapidly graduated to working as an agent and buying on his own behalf. Justinian Povey began by buying on his own account through nominees and subsequently became both agent and nominee. In August 1599, he and Edward Bee, the future gentleman usher, bought land in Yorkshire which had been granted so recently by the Crown to Thomas Wagstaff and John Awdesley that they must have been buying on behalf of Povey and Bee. That the latter were buying on their own account is suggested by the fact that it took them nearly two years to resell the property, even though some of it went to the

[38] See the biography of his son in B. D. Henning (ed.), *The History of Parliament. The Commons, 1660–1690* (3 vols., London, 1983), III, pp. 399–400.

[39] *CSPD 1611–18*, p. 388; *CSPD 1633–4*, p. 362.

[40] See *CSPD 1635–6*, pp. 298–9, 457–8; *CSPD 1639–40*, pp. 133, 168, for instructions to auditors to examine private accounts.

tenant's son. By this time, they had bought some more Yorkshire land which they sold in 1604, again to a relative of some of the tenants. Thereafter, Povey dealt on the property market almost continuously until the early 1630s, on his own and in partnership. His partners were a pretty heterogeneous bunch: a list of them provides us with a cross-section of most of the groups who were engaged in this area of the property market during his lifetime. As well as Bee, he teamed up with William Court, his rival for the auditorship of the Queen's estates; the lawyers John Parkinson and Henry Stanley (who may himself have been connected with the Exchequer if he was the Henry son of Auditor (John) Stanley referred to by Thomas Posthumous Hoby in 1609[41]); John Halsey, a London citizen and fishmonger; the future auditor Philip Darell; two London gentlemen, Robert Morgan and George Ward; and in the 1620s, when he had himself become an auditor, a Richard Kinsman who may have been his own clerk.

It is typical of the tangle of interlocking partnerships operating on the land market that Povey should have bought from several nominees who had also been his partners in other deals. Like Sawyer, he continued to dispose of land during the 1620s and moved into the private property market as a dealer and mortgagee, though he bought no more land from the Crown after taking office in the Exchequer. He was not as successful a social climber as Sawyer but by 1635 he was a justice of the peace for Middlesex and his will mentions land in Cambridgeshire, Norfolk and London as well as his manor of Houndslow.

Many of the other agents whose names appear on the Close Rolls can be identified, conjecturally or certainly, as auditors' clerks. William Court had been deputy to Ralph Ewens, auditor of Queen Anne's estates, since Ewens was appointed in 1603; he was also clerk to the auditor of north-east England, Robert Paddon, who thought sufficiently highly of him to recommend him as Ewens's successor.[42] He had been dealing in Crown land since before 1600, and in 1607 he was one of Lord Hay's nominees for a grant of land in Yorkshire. Between then and his death in 1612 he made several small purchases in partnership with other London agents including Robert Crompton, Philip Darell, Justinian Povey and George Ward. William Cave,

---

[41] *CSPD 1603–10*, p. 502. Povey and John Stanley may have been colleagues: Nathaniel Fulwer offered to appoint them as his deputies in 1609 (above, n. 32); for references to Stanley as an auditor, *CSPD 1603–10*, p. 564; *CSPD 1610–18*, p. 458, though he does not appear in Sainty, *Officers of the Exchequer*.   [42] *CSPD 1610–18*, p. 72.

a clerk to the auditor for Wales, William Hill, made at least two purchases of land in Wales from his fellow-clerk Edmund Sawyer in 1615 and 1618.[43] William Collins, who was one of Charles Harbord's fellow-nominees for the earl of Berkshire in 1629 and received grants on behalf of Sir William Russell, Treasurer to the Navy in the 1630s, as well as dealing extensively at second hand, may have been the Mr Collins who was Edmund Sawyer's clerk in 1630 and who arranged the purchase of land in Llanddwywe, Merionethshire, for Robert Lloyd: no other Collins is known to have been active as an agent at that time. William Collins was deputy successively to Sir Francis Crane and Harbord as auditor of the King's lands as Prince of Wales and was certainly an auditor by 1643.[44] Richard Kinsman (auditor for the West Country, 1635–43) and James Symes (auditor for the same circuit during the Civil War and Commonwealth) had both dealt in Crown land in the 1620s and 1630s in partnership with each other and with Justinian Povey, whose clerks they may have been.[45]

The advantages which Exchequer officials – and particularly auditors – enjoyed in dealing in Crown land were considerable. The principal duty of the auditors was to examine the accounts of local officials, and to this end they and their clerks toured their circuits annually for the Michaelmas audit. This gave them a detailed and comprehensive knowledge of local economies and property values and of the potential markets for Crown land. In London, their main activity was the preparation of particulars for the sale or lease of that land, which again gave them an unrivalled insight into the state of the market.

In cases where dealers sold land within a few months but not immediately, they may have bought with a particular purchaser in mind, and some grants made provision for the reexchange of land which had proved difficult to sell. In many cases, however, property remained in hand for a number of years: it took Richard Budd twenty-two years to dispose of the land in Flintshire which he had bought through William Birch and William Blake in 1607. The income from a number of scattered properties cannot have been great and would normally have been difficult to collect, but the auditors and their clerks were well placed to gather rents and other profits

[43] Jeffreys Jones (ed.), *Exchequer Proceedings*, pp. 112, 136.
[44] NLW, MS 9062E, no. 1546; SC6/Chas. I/1639, 1640; *CSPD Add. 1625–49*, p. 656; LR9/10/1465.
[45] Symes was acting as an auditor in 1645 and his appointment was official by 1646; LR9/123; LR9/71, fols. 21, 35.

from land within their circuits or to negotiate with colleagues for the administration of property in other areas. Income was further reduced by the costs of the inevitable lawsuits over title and management of land, many of them arising out of the confused history of fragments of monastic and chantry property. In Wales alone, between 1603 and 1625, auditors and their clerks were party to at least eleven suits in the Court of Exchequer concerning property they had bought as agents or dealers. However, the fact that cases touching former Crown land were normally tried in the Exchequer was a further advantage to officials who already worked elsewhere in the same establishment and had the necessary contacts in the court.

Those who employed auditors and their clerks as agents could expect to share in these benefits. Richard Gwynn was described by Sir John Wynn as being 'so perfect in the office and of so great a memory that upon the gift of xls unto him he will unfold unto you all the secrets of that matter',[46] but all the servants of the audit office could put inside information at the disposal of their clients. An agent could advise on the availability of land and its likely price, check the Crown's title and find out whether it had been burdened with a number of reversionary leases. The Exchequer dealt with the effects of inflation on land values not by adjusting the valuations but by increasing the number of times the nominal rent was multiplied to arrive at a purchase price. As the rate increased it became more variable, so that there was more scope for bargaining and more need for good advice. Even when a straightforward purchase was being made from the nominees of a group of contractors, it was important to know when to attend the court and who to bribe, while purchases through the nominees of a courtier or official were even more tricky.

Thomas Martin's boasts that 'Mr Suckling my L[ord] Treas[urer] his secretary will tell me anything that passeth in that country… Peradventure my good L[ord] Treas[urer] would have abated me some year or two of the common rates'[47] may well have been exaggeration, though taken in conjunction with his argument that Budd could not expect to buy cheaply because his employer was out of favour is testimony to a belief that even a lowly clerk could use indirect influence to reduce prices. Senior officials certainly expected lower prices as an indication of their status and prestige. For Sir Francis Crane, Harbord's deputy as Surveyor-General, the ap-

---

[46] NLW, MS 9055E, no. 652. [47] NLW, Add. MS 465E, no. 293.

pearance of concession was more important than the reality. Writing to Harbord in 1634, he begged: 'If my offer be accepted of for Ashton, I desire then that my L[ord] Treas[urer] will do it so much for my reputation, as I may not seem to have it because I give more for it, but that his Majesty will reserve it out of the compositions to accommodate me with it.'[48]

For the clients of lesser officials, however, the savings they could make by their skills and inside knowledge probably outweighed any concessions they might expect to receive. As for the clerks who were employed as nominees by courtiers and financiers, their knowledge of prospective purchasers may have enabled them to advise on suitable property to buy, while their local contacts and those of their fellow-clerks in other circuits certainly assisted them in reselling at a profit. An officer of the audit could also administer property on behalf of a client as well as on his own behalf, and could act in the client's interests at law; it was for this reason, as much as for their skill in disposing of property, that audit clerks were so popular as nominees.

Clients came mainly from the middle ranks of society. Noblemen might employ a clerk as nominee or trustee but would seldom have to buy for themselves through an agent. The upper gentry might also approach the Crown directly with requests for land, especially when they were also courtiers or Crown servants and could expect grants in reward for services,[49] but used agents to handle small or difficult negotiations. Budd bought on behalf of Sir John Carne of Ewenny and Sir Henry Jones of Abermarlais as well as Sir John Wynn. However, the main contribution which the audit clerks made to the market for Crown land was to widen its range. Lesser landholders, yeomen and artisans had always appeared among the purchasers but it was not until the end of the sixteenth century that they became numerous, thanks partly to the efforts which the Crown was making at that time to sell smaller properties and partly to the activities of agents and dealers who were in a position to identify and encourage likely purchasers, explain the necessary procedures to them and offer them easier financial terms than the Crown could afford. This had, of course, to be paid for: when Leonard Meyrick, the rector of Llandegfedd in Gwent, bought chantry land in and near his parish from Budd, he paid at the rate of £20 every six months for five years. This amounted to over 200 times the annual rent of the property at

[48] LR17/1.
[49] E.g. Sir John Perrot's request for a grant of 80 acres near Whitland Abbey in Carmarthenshire in 1585–6, *Analectica Hibernica* 12 (1943), p. 41.

a time when the normal price would have been about a quarter of that.[50]

Clients and prospective purchasers could be contacted in the course of a clerk's official duties, on circuit or in London. Budd also used personal contacts. In 1614, he wrote to Sir John Wynn asking for recommendations to the latter's sons-in-law Sir Roger Mostyn ('for though I say it, I have done him good service') and John Bodfel.[51] Official contacts could also be used to facilitate the mechanics of disposing of the property. As far as we can see, agents preferred to buy and sell by bargain and sale endorsed on the Close Rolls, but this would normally require that the purchaser visit London to see the deed enrolled. Budd tried to assure Leonard Meyrick that 'the d[eed]s may be as well past unto you in your [absen]ce as in your presence'[52] but this required considerable faith on the part of the purchaser, since failure to register a bargain and sale rendered the conveyance invalid and left the dealer free to sell again.[53] The alternative was the traditional method of enfeoffment validated by livery of seisin, which also required the presence of both vendor and purchaser, in person or by attorney. This again gave an advantage to the audit official who could convey property while on circuit and who knew a number of local officials capable of acting as attorneys. If the client could not come to London to sign his counterpart of the conveyance, it was possible to convey the property to another to his use, though this still had to be confirmed by livery of seisin.[54] It was not even necessary for the agent's name to appear on the deeds at all. We know from their correspondence that it was Budd who arranged Sir John Wynn's purchase of Fach rectory in 1606 but the conveyance was made from the Crown's grantees direct to Sir John.[55]

It is seldom possible to identify the means by which these clerks raised the initial finance necessary to begin trading in land on their own account. The auditors did not normally handle the Crown's cash balances themselves and as their clerks were not Crown officials it is even less likely that they had access to such resources. Some may have been investing the profits of work as agents or nominees; others may have used money provided by their partners. Most of the clerks whose family circumstances have been identified came from comparatively

---

[50] NLW, Llangybi Castle A. 941.   [51] NLW, MS 9055E, no. 662.
[52] NLW, MS 17102D (formerly Llangybi Castle 1270).
[53] See E112/29/2 for a complaint that James Gunter had done just that.
[54] E.g. Glamorgan RO, D/D C/19.   [55] NLW, MS 9053E; C54/1845.

obscure backgrounds or were younger sons but it is possible that some
had small inheritances to invest. It is equally difficult to estimate the
profits which these agents made from their dealings. The purchase
price is normally omitted from their deeds, and even when a figure is
given we have no way of knowing whether it included fees and
expenses or whether these were paid for separately. In only one case
do we have a detailed account. When Budd arranged Sir John
Wynn's purchase of Fach rectory he claimed a total of £25 in
expenses, £1 10s for messengers and £26 13s 4d for his own fee. The
fee was exactly double the annual rent, suggesting that this may have
been the basis on which it was calculated.

If the few figures we have are typical, a dealer could expect an
average profit of about twenty times the nominal annual value of
property bought on his own account for resale after the deduction of
expenses. The higher profit from dealing on one's own account was,
of course, counterbalanced by the risk that property would not be
sold. The picture is further complicated by the need to apportion
profits between partners, the difficulty of ascertaining whether a
buyer was acting as nominee, agent or dealer in any given transaction
and the fact that we have no idea what nominees were paid for their
services. Richard Budd confined himself to one sector of the market
and his gains are thus slightly easier to calculate. He bought property
nominally valued at £250 a year, of which about £50 was in hand at
his death. About three-quarters of this he seems to have bought on his
own account as a dealer; more than half of his purchases involved a
partner, so we must deduct a further third for the share given to his
partners. This leaves an income of about £2,000 as a dealer. To this
we can add about £100 for fees as an agent. His income from the
assignment of leases, interest on payments by instalment and fees in
purchases where his involvement has not been recorded cannot be
estimated, but in all he would have been lucky to make more than
£2,500 from his dealings over about forty years. His annual earnings
were probably higher in the years from 1590 to 1616 when he was still
a clerk and when the sale of Crown land was at its height, but his most
diligent activities could hardly have earned him more than £100 in
any year.[56]

For those agents who were also employed as nominees, virtually
our only means of estimating their profits is to look at the estates they
left. Sir Edmund Sawyer was deprived of his office as an auditor

---

[56] For details of these calculations, see Gray, 'Mr Auditor's man'.

between 1643 and 1660; his estate was sequestered for a time and he was stated in 1648 to be a delinquent who had not compounded for his offence, for all that he had previously contributed to parliamentary funds. In spite of this, his will, proved in 1676, made cash bequests of over £4,000 in addition to the landed estate which had already been settled. His income as an auditor before 1643 and from 1660 to 1676 undoubtedly contributed to his eventual prosperity, but he had bought the nucleus of his Berkshire estate in 1623, only two years after his appointment: much of the money must therefore have come from his work as a dealer and nominee.[57]

Like Sawyer, Justinian Povey was deprived of office during the Civil War; he was assessed at £500 for the contribution to parliamentary funds in 1643 but discharged on payment of £210. As well as his manor of Houndslow, not valued but implied in his will to be worth over £1,000, he left land and rents worth over £400 a year and about £300 in cash.[58] As with Sawyer, however, it is impossible to assess how much of his money was made by dealing in property. One audit clerk, William Court, died after several years as an agent and dealer but without having graduated to the rank of auditor. He left money amounting to nearly £1,150, though some of this was not due to be paid until his children came of age and could have been raised by the sale of property in hand.[59] Even in Court's case we have to bear in mind that he had been for some years deputy to the auditor of the Queen's jointure as well as clerk to the auditor of north-east England. Edward Bateman never progressed beyond a deputyship and made only a few pounds on the property market but was able to buy a small estate near Windsor; Thomas Hanbury and Hugh Sexey, whose dealings in Crown land were minimal, both left extensive estates, Hanbury's in Wiltshire and Hampshire and Sexey's in London and Somerset.[60]

It seems that it was those who acted as dealers and middlemen who made the profits: for all his work as a nominee, Francis Phillips appears to have acquired little or no land for himself. He had an

[57] M. A. E. Green (ed.), *Calendar of the Proceedings of the Committee for the Advance of Money, 1642–1656* (3 vols., London, 1888), I, p. 181, II, p. 968; Henning (ed.), *Commons 1660–1690*, III, pp. 399–400; PROB11/352, fols. 70–1.

[58] Green (ed.), *Calendar of the Committee for the Advance of Money*, I, p. 170; PROB11/220, fol. 1.

[59] PROB11/120, fol. 48.

[60] C142/332/167; C142/384/133; C142/784/36. Sexey placed a part of his estate in the hands of feoffees with the intention of devoting it to charitable ends but died before the arrangements could be made; his feoffees finally decided on a hospital at Sexey's birthplace, Bruton, Somerset. J. Collinson, *The History and Antiquities of the County of Somerset* (3 vols., 1791), I, pp. 211–12.

address in Teddington, Middlesex, in 1623 but was still living in
London at the time of his death and no probate or grant of
administration has been found for him in the records of the
Prerogative Court of Canterbury, suggesting he had no extensive
estate to leave.[61] There is, however, little to suggest that even the
more active dealers were much more prosperous than their colleagues, though without more detailed research into their family
backgrounds it is impossible to be certain of the source of their
prosperity. The most we can say is that the combination of office and
property dealing enabled them to raise their social class by a couple
of points, but there is no evidence of the spectacular fortunes that
could be made elsewhere in the Crown's service.

The role of the estate agent changed from the late sixteenth century
to the 1630s, partly as a result of internal developments but largely in
response to changes in the type of land the Crown was selling and the
way in which it was sold. Perhaps the most important development
was the way in which clerks, and later officials, were directed to
receive grants in partnership with or on behalf of Crown favourites
and creditors. This eventually spread to other areas of the auditors'
duties: the State Papers for the 1630s contain several instructions to
auditors to investigate the private accounts of individuals and
organisations favoured by the Crown.[62] As efforts were made to sell
off smaller properties, and as the social class of the purchasers
declined, the power of the agent and middle-man rose. The increasing
involvement of officials (as opposed to private clerks) as agents and
dealers may also have raised the prestige of this occupation, but it
inevitably increased the danger that officials would prefer their own
interests and those of their clients to those of the Crown.
    Even when they were ostensibly acting under directions from the
government, however, the auditors must have experienced some
degree of conflict of interest. The sale of Crown land was a short-
sighted and ultimately self-defeating response to the problems of
national finance, while both Elizabeth's fee-farm grants to courtiers
and James's sales to London businessmen reduced the function of the
Exchequer to the processing of applications for land which was
intended for resale for private profit. A conscientious financial expert
might have advised against this; instead, the auditors and their clerks

---

[61] Record of admission of his elder son Francis to the Inner Temple, Nov. 1623: W. H. Cooke,
    Students Admitted to the Inner Temple, 1547–1660 (London, 1877), p. 239.
[62] *CSPD 1635–6*, pp. 298–9, 457–8; *CSPD 1637*, p. 99; *CSPD 1639*, pp. 133, 168; etc.

became part of the process of exploitation. When they acted as intermediate agents and dealers the conflict became more acute. Richard Budd was prepared to offer a bribe to his employer to reduce a valuation: reporting his negotiations for Sir John Wynn's purchase of sheepwalks in Dolwyddelan, he spoke of persuading Hanbury not to certify them as having been worth £16 in Edward III's time, 'promising him etc. which you are to perform otherwise it would have hindered these proceedings'.[63] It was probably on his advice, too, that Richard Wynn bribed John Dackombe to secure his silence for a similar purpose.

The government did benefit in some ways from the activities of these agents. Underpaid officials were able to earn more money by the use of privileged information; the market for Crown property was widened, and buyers were found for fragments of land which would be difficult to sell in any other way. The long-term effect which this dispersal had on the political complexion of the nation is difficult to assess and beyond the scope of this chapter. It is equally difficult to judge whether the advantages to the Crown of the sale of its smaller properties outweighed the diversion of profits necessarily resulting from the activities of its own employees as agents.

In general, the clients seem to have gained from their dealings with these intermediaries. Sir John Wynn's lengthy association with Richard Budd, even after the latter had tried to cheat him in 1607, suggests that he valued Budd's advice and efforts on his behalf.[64] Wynn may have felt that he had the power to control and outwit a mere clerk, but very minor families of local gentry such as the Aldeys of Hardwick and Chepstow in Gwent also returned to Budd time and again to purchase the single farms and urban tenements from which they were slowly constructing their estates. By the 1620s, however, perceptions of corruption in public life were changing; what had been acceptable in the sixteenth century, when patronage and the activities of agents and dealers in the Crown's service combined to spread the rewards of investment in Crown land, became unacceptable when the Crown had so obviously lost control of the process and the main profits were going to favourites and 'new men'. The ensuing crisis in government finance led Parliament to attack the taking of bribes by officials and to demand that they be responsible to

---

[63] NLW, MS 9053E, nos. 416, 437. Wynn had agreed to buy Fach rectory for twenty-five times the nominal rent; Budd managed to secure it for twenty-four years' purchase and tried to pocket the difference but was caught out by John Wynn jun.

[64] NLW, MS 9055E, no. 656.

the public. Corruption thus became a political issue and even after the death of the duke of Buckingham the reforms of Charles I were not enough to restore confidence. There was, after all, a considerable difference between John Bellow's offers of easy access to the land market and the use of the auditor Thomas Brinley to sell reclaimed land in the fens on behalf of the heirs and associates of Cornelius Vermuyden.[65]

The 1630s saw the last great sales of Crown land in an attempt to raise money. After the Restoration, fee-farm rents were sold and the financial importance of the audit diminished. The office of auditor became a political rather than a professional appointment, with the actual work performed by clerks who were now officially appointed but could never aspire to becoming auditors. These changes seem to have ended the function of audit clerks as estate agents, leaving the field open for their rivals, the scriveners and attorneys.

[65] For a discussion of changing interpretations of and attitudes towards government corruption in the early seventeenth century, see Linda Levy Peck, 'Corruption at the court of James I', in B. C. Malament (ed.), *After the Reformation* (Manchester, 1980), pp. 75–93.

CHAPTER 5

Power, patronage and politics: office-holding and administration on the Crown's estates in Wales

Madeleine Gray

Viewed in purely financial terms, the Welsh estates never made any significant contribution to the Crown's landed wealth.[1] The calculation of exact profits from land is a virtually impossible exercise – how far, for example, does one allow fees paid to officials as a necessary expense and how far does one consider them as money available for the purposes of patronage – and it is possible to criticise any available estimate without necessarily being able to improve it. The most recent figures suggested, those for 1609 by Geraint Dyfnallt Owen in *Wales in the Reign of James I*, are probably as open to detailed criticism as any others, but do at least offer the possibility of a broad comparison with England. He calculates that Wales provided only £4,600 out of a total of £66,870 for the whole Crown estate.[2] The figure would have been higher in 1540, before the great dispersal of monastic land and the alienation of some marcher lordships under Edward VI, but the percentage was probably about the same.

Paradoxically, however, the Crown in its capacity as a private landowner held a higher proportion of land in Wales, particularly in the north and west, than anywhere in England. The two principalities of North Wales (Caernarfonshire, Anglesey and Meirionydd) and South Wales (Cardiganshire and Carmarthenshire) had from the time of their conquest in the thirteenth century been treated as Crown marcher lordships, and in the course of the fourteenth and fifteenth centuries a number of other marcher lordships, notably those of the Duchy of Lancaster and the earldom of March, had come into Crown hands. These marcher lordships were in some ways virtually independent kingdoms, being based on the numerous (and

---

[1] The research for this chapter was partly funded by a grant from the British Academy.

[2] G. Dyfnallt Owen, *Wales in the Reign of James I* (Royal Historical Soc., Studies in History, 53, Woodbridge, 1988), p. 174, based on SP14/46, May 1609.

often very small) kingdoms of pre-conquest Wales.[3] Private marcher lords claimed regalian jurisdiction over their lordships and argued with varying degrees of success that the King's writ did not run there. The larger marcher lordships had a fully developed administrative structure, each with its own chancery, exchequer and judicial system; sheriffs and bailiffs administered local justice and accounted for local revenue including the rents of assize of those tenants who held directly of the lord. The principalities of North and South Wales were similarly organised, with a central administration based at Caernarfon and at Carmarthen and Cardigan respectively, sheriffs and escheators in each county, and bailiffs or beadles in the commotes, which were themselves based on petty kingdoms but now functioned in a similar way to English hundreds.

All these independent jurisdictions were ostensibly swept away by the Acts of Union of 1536 and 1543. The principalities already had some of the organisational structure of an English shire. By the Acts of Union, the Welsh march was also divided into shires – or, more accurately, the marcher lordships were amalgamated into shires more or less on the English model.[4] This did not, however, bring Wales under the same administrative structure as England. What in fact happened was that many aspects of the private and decentralised character of marcher administration were extended to cover the whole of Wales but were now exercised by the Crown in its capacity as a private landlord. In all the Welsh counties except Monmouthshire, sheriffs as well as escheators, customers and lesser officials accounted locally before the auditors of land revenue and their accounts were enrolled not on the Pipe Rolls but with those of the other accountants from the Crown's landed estate on the rolls of ministers' accounts.

Monmouthshire was, and long remained, an anomaly. It was counted as English for the purposes of judicial administration: it was placed under the Oxford assize circuit and the King's courts at Westminster. Financially, it was regarded as Welsh in that it came

---

[3] For a discussion of the constitutional position see J. Goronwy Edwards, 'The Normans and the Welsh March', *Proceedings of the British Academy* 42 (1956), pp. 155–77; R. R. Davies, *Lordship and Society in the March of Wales, 1282–1400* (Oxford, 1978), esp. pp. 1–9, 249–73.

[4] For a fuller discussion of the Acts of Union, see P. R. Roberts, 'The Acts of Union of England and Wales', *Transactions of the Honourable Society of Cymmrodorian*, 1974, pp. 49–72; *idem*, 'A breviat of the effectes devised for Wales', *Camden Miscellany* 26 (Camden fourth ser., 14, 1975), pp. 31–48; *idem*, 'The union with England and the identity of "Anglican" Wales', *TRHS* fifth ser., 22 (1972), pp. 49–70.

under the supervision of the Exchequer auditor for Wales, but the sheriffs and their subordinates did not account before the auditor. Elsewhere, in effect, the administrative structure of the great lordships which the Crown held, such as Denbigh, Pembroke and Glamorgan, had been extended to cover the whole of the counties of which they were the core. In the counties of the two former principalities, bailiffs accounted for substantial sums for assize rents and the farms of individual townships, mills, fisheries and other leasehold properties as well as the profits of the hundred court. Bailiffs and sheriffs still accounted for the traditional renders for the maintenance of the royal household, *pultura stallonum* and *staurum domini*, the Welsh *dawn bwyd*, though in many cases a nil return was made for these. The sheriff also accounted for the profits of his tourn, a monthly freeholders' court which like the hundred court dealt with minor civil cases, mainly petty debt and trespass, and for the profits of Quarter Sessions. Outside the principalities, the bailiffs do not appear on the ministers' accounts and the sheriffs' accounts are more perfunctory but they still account for profits of court and rents, some of which must have been collected by the bailiffs.

The judicial functions of the central courts at Westminster as well as the assizes were performed in Wales by the itinerant Courts of Great Sessions, which took their name from the central courts held regularly in the principality and occasionally by many marcher lordships. Great Sessions were partly funded out of the Crown's land revenue accounts and their profits were accounted for by the sheriffs. The structure was topped by the Council in the Marches of Wales, whose prerogative jurisdiction was similarly funded out of the landed revenue: a crisis in funding in the early seventeenth century, when much of the Crown's Welsh estates were reorganised as an endowment, first for Prince Henry then for Prince Charles as successive Princes of Wales, could only be met by diverting more of the revenue from what remained.[5]

Legal business from Wales did reach the London courts, particularly those of the Exchequer and Star Chamber, but was always subject to the complaint that the case could have been tried locally or before the Council in the Marches, and had to be justified by the argument that the defendants were too powerful or too well protected to permit of a fair trial in Wales. It would obviously be going too far

[5] Owen, *Wales in the Reign of James I*, pp. 35–6.

to say that the whole of Wales after 1536 was run as the private estate of the English Crown, but the devolved nature of financial administration in post-1536 Wales and the blurring (whether deliberate or coincidental) of the distinction between governmental revenue and the Crown's private income as a landowner reinforce John Goronwy Edwards's thesis that the Act of Union in its administrative and constitutional aspects did not so much integrate Wales with England as integrate Wales within itself by extending the judicial machinery and constitutional position of the three shires of the principality of North Wales to cover the whole.[6] This in turn made the Crown's landed estate a vital link in the system of communication between the central government in London and provincial and local government in Wales.

OFFICE-HOLDING AND WELSH SOCIETY

While status in England ultimately depended on the ownership of land, far more emphasis was placed in Wales on service to the King or greater lords. Many of the leading county gentry of the sixteenth century were descended – as were the Tudors themselves – not from native monarchs or aristocrats but from their officials.[7] The reasons for this are probably to be found in the agricultural poverty of much of Wales and the peculiarities of its land law. Under the strictest interpretation, land was owned not by the individual but by the agnatic kin group and was therefore in theory inalienable; even when this was circumvented, the practice of partible inheritance militated against the accumulation of large hereditary holdings. For Welsh landowners after the Conquest, office was one way out of the straitjacket of small estates, partible inheritance and the colonial status of Wales which prevented them from exercising real power in government.

---

[6] J. Goronwy Edwards, *The Principality of Wales, 1267–1967. A Study in Constitutional History* (Caernarfonshire Historical Soc., 1967).

[7] R. R. Davies, *Conquest, Co-Existence and Change. Wales, 1063–1415* (Oxford, 1987), p. 263; A. D. Carr; 'An aristocracy in decline: the native Welsh lords after the Edwardian conquest', *WHR* 5 (1970), pp. 103–29. On local families of office-holders see, for instance, A. D. Carr, 'The making of the Mostyns: the genesis of a landed family', *Transactions of the Honourable Society of Cymmrodorion*, 1979, pp. 137–57; for the Morgans of Tredegar Park and the Kemeyses of Cefn Mabli, A. C. Reeves, *Newport Lordship, 1317–1536* (Ann Arbor, MI, 1979); Bryn R. Parry, 'Hugh Nanney Hên (c. 1546–1623), Squire of Nanney', *Journal of the Merioneth Historical and Record Society* 5 (1967), pp. 185–206.

Although landholding in Wales was not as crucial a determinant of social status as in England, it was, of course, important, and became more important during the later middle ages as respect for the traditional Welsh forms of landholding declined and ways were found to circumvent partible inheritance and the inalienability of land. The construction of a consolidated estate out of the morcellated fragments of traditional gavelkind holdings was, however, a painstaking and expensive process: it was far more common for an estate to be created or transformed by grants of land from the Crown. The population crisis of the fourteenth century was made more severe in its effects in Wales by the Glyndŵr rising and subsequent social and economic dislocation: much free land was left vacant and whole bond townships were deserted as the few remaining tenants were unable to meet the obligations of the whole township. Land which had escheated to the Crown in this way could be regranted free from traditional restrictions and became a marketable commodity. Bond townships became increasingly popular after the emancipation of bond tenants in the principality in 1507, but even before that date many free landowners were prepared to take on whole bond townships as well as *gwelyau* and *gafaelion*, the traditional units of free landholding. When Maredudd ab Ieuan ap Robert, ancestor of the Wynn family of Gwydir, moved from Eifionydd to Gwydir in the Conwy valley shortly after his marriage in 1480, he founded a new landed estate based on Crown leases of bond townships in Dolwyddelan. These leases had to be renewed regularly and the estate, though one of the wealthiest and most powerful in Gwynedd, was always vulnerable to grants of reversions as well as to pressure from its own tenants. One such dispute, in the early years of the seventeenth century, damaged Sir John Wynn's local power and prestige so severely as to contribute to his defeat in the parliamentary election of 1620.[8]

Similarly, on the Crown's marcher lordships, the quickest way to acquire or expand an estate was to take over free tenancies or lease demesne manors, but tenants were equally vulnerable to the loss of their tenancies by the granting of reversionary interests over their heads. Access to these properties for all but the most eminent

[8] J. Gwynfor Jones, 'The Wynn estate of Gwydir: aspects of its growth and development, *c.* 1500–1800', *National Library of Wales Journal* 22 (1981), pp. 141–69; *idem*, 'Sir John Wynn of Gwydir and his tenants: the Dolwyddelan and Llysfaen disputes', *WHR* 11 (1982–3), pp. 1–30.

applicants was through officials, the stewards of the lordships and the bailiffs of hundreds within the principality; the importance of Crown land in the calculations of virtually every ambitious landowner in Wales made office-holding correspondingly popular.

John Salcot, bishop of Bangor in the 1530s, was disparaging about this popularity. In a letter to his steward in 1537, he wrote:

> For the nature of a Welsh man is for to bear office & to be in authority. He will not let to run through the fire of hell & to sell & give all that he can make of his own & of his friends for the same, & also they be very tycle [?particular] of themselves.[9]

A more favourable attitude appears in the writings of the traditional poets, for whom the service of the Crown or of the great aristocratic landlords was an important part of the concept of gentility. While the offices which receive most emphasis in eulogy and elegy are inevitably those giving jurisdiction over people – the shrievalty, the commission of the peace, the deputy lieutenancy – there are also numerous references to financial and administrative offices. Eulogies and elegies to Sir John Puleston contain frequent references to his office of Chamberlain of North Wales. Huw Machno's elegy on Sir Evan Lloyd of Bodidris in Iâl, after mentioning the shrievalty and lieutenancy, describes him as 'steward of the country of Chirk, a golden spearhead to the wise':

> Bu siryf... Bu lifftenant...
> Bu stiwart eurddart iddoeth
> Swydd y Waun, dwys wiwddyn ddoeth

and Wiliam Cynwal, one of the best known of the Caernarfonshire bards of the late sixteenth century, speaks of the grief of the lordship at the loss of its steward: 'Swydd y Waun... sy dywyll am ystiwart'. Even constables and bailiffs of hundreds were commemorated; William Cynwal also wrote elegies to William Coetmor, bailiff of the hundred of Uchaf during most of Elizabeth's reign, and John ap Robert ap Llywelyn ab Ithel of Castellmarch. As bailiff of the hundred of Cafflogion and lessee of its rents of assize, John ap Robert was virtually the ruler of this part of the Llŷn. Wiliam Cynwal praises him in traditional terms as a just lord of his people, a man of integrity who did not oppress the poor or take their homesteads, one who

---

[9] BL, Harl. MS 283, fol. 153; also E. Owen, *A Catalogue of Manuscripts Relating to Wales in the British Museum* (4 vols., London, 1900–22), II, p. 125.

resisted oppression in his region and bore affection towards his people:

> Arwydd y sydd, yr oedd Siôn,
> Ordr enwog, ŵr dewr union.
> Ni threisiodd wan, odiddan ddyn,
> Un dyad, na dwyn ei dyddyn...
> Gŵr yddoed fu gariadol,
> Gwir sy wir, a gŵr sy i' w ôl

The importance of local office in conferring or reflecting status is also reflected in the changing geographical focus of this poetry. In the later middle ages, prestige was assessed in regional terms, based on the *gwlad* or *bro*; by the second half of the sixteenth century, however, the great man's sphere of influence was more likely to be described in terms of the new administrative unit of the shire or of a group of shires, suggesting the importance of the county offices mentioned above, all introduced or given wider powers by the Acts of Union, in the vocabulary of poetic praise. This restructuring of the traditional bardic landscape was further reinforced by the reorganisation of Crown land management on a county basis in 1547.[10]

The administrative and cultural traditions of Wales thus gave Crown office-holding an importance which it never possessed in England: the problems that this created form the main subject of this chapter. However, the enthusiasm of the Welsh for Crown office also has implications for the debate over Welsh loyalty to the English Crown both before and after the Acts of Union. For many lesser landowners, there was really no alternative, particularly by the

---

[10] I am grateful to Dr J. Gwynfor Jones of Cardiff for these references and for much of the information in the preceding paragraph: see his book, *Concepts of Order and Gentility in Wales, 1540–1640. Bardic Images and Interpretations* (Gwasg Gomer, 1991); his chapter 'Concepts of order and gentility', in J. G. Jones (ed.), *Class, Community and Culture in Tudor Wales* (Cardiff, 1989); and for further detail his articles 'The Welsh poets and their patrons, *c.* 1550–1640', *WHR* 9 (1979), pp. 245–77; 'Patrymau Bonheddig Uchelwrol yn Sir Ddinbych *c.* 1540–1640: Dehongiad y Beirdd', *Transactions of the Denbighshire Historical Society* 29 (1980), pp. 37–77; 'Reflections on concepts of nobility in Glamorgan, *c.* 1540–1640', *Morgannwg* 25 (1981), pp. 11–42; 'The Merioneth gentry in the social order: bardic evidence, *c.* 1540–1640', *Journal of the Merioneth Historical and Record Society* 9 (1981–4), pp. 278–307, 390–419; 'Governance, order and stability in Caernarfonshire, *c.* 1540–1640', *Transactions of the Caernarfonshire Historical Society* 44 (1983), pp. 7–52. The traditional poetry of this period is virtually untranslatable, depending as it does on the overtones of words rather than their specific meanings and on a complex web of alliteration and assonance (*cynghanedd*) to which the less accomplished poets were often obliged to subordinate the sense of what they said. I have not therefore attempted to translate these extracts but have given paraphrases of the relevant lines. I am grateful to Phyllis Brown and Ann Williams for help with these paraphrases.

fifteenth century when so many marcher lordships had come into Crown hands. Nor was their participation necessarily to the Crown's best advantage. The accounts for the lordship of Usk during the century when it was under Crown control suggest at first that the whole of central Gwent had suffered irreparable damage from the famines and plagues of the fourteenth century and the Glyndŵr rebellion in the early fifteenth. In fact, a more general study of the local economy indicates that slackness or deliberate concealment by officials, in their own interests and those of their families, may have obscured an economic revival.[11]

The real issue is that of what kind of loyalty was being offered, and from whom. The number of available offices was, after all, finite, even before 1536, when stewardships and other offices in the marcher lordships were of greater value, and the scarcity became worse when senior positions were monopolised by a few aristocrats. Even the use of deputies could not widen the scope of office-holding to include all the elite gentry of a lordship at a level they would consider suitable. The situation was alleviated after 1536 by the increasing of Welsh responsibility in local government, in particular by the introduction of justices of the peace. The commission of the peace was both prestigious and elastic; it could be made large enough to include all the upper gentry and gave them the real power which had for so long been denied them. The appointment of sheriffs for a year rather than for life also made possible a more generous distribution of prestige. For the lesser gentry, however, office on the Crown's estates remained a vital component of their local status. Here, too, the responsibility of the sheriff for appointing bailiffs and constables of royal hundreds made an annual changeover possible, but in some localities one family or group of families could still establish an effective monopoly, leading to possible disaffection among disappointed rivals.[12]

[11] For details see the present writer's thesis, 'The dispersal of crown property in Monmouthshire, 1500–1603' (University of Wales, PhD thesis, 1984), esp. ch. 2(i).

[12] W. R. B. Robinson discusses these issues, concentrating on gentry involvement in the administration of Glamorgan and the principality of South Wales before 1536, in 'The Tudor revolution in Welsh government, 1536–43: its effects on gentry participation', *EHR* 103 (1988), pp. 1–20.

APPOINTMENTS AND PATRONAGE

Discontent could also be created by the use of subordinate offices for family patronage or even for sale. Accusations of sale of offices were part of the general currency of sixteenth-century litigation and were particularly useful to discredit bailiffs who had distrained on the plaintiff's property. This appears to have lain behind some (though not all) of the complaints in Star Chamber against the notorious Edward Kemeys of Cefn Mabli, who served four times as sheriff of Glamorgan between 1575 and 1605 although he was accused of having 'abused every function which it was left to him as sheriff to commit'.[13]

In the course of a similar suit in which accusations of sales of offices were hauled into what was basically a dispute over the tithes of Haverfordwest, that acute observer of the Welsh social scene, George Owen of Henllys, deposed that

most that have been sheriffs of the counties of Pembroke and Carmarthen and other shires in Wales have and do usually bargain & sell the bailiwicks belonging to their office to several persons for divers sums of money...and that it is not by them accounted to be any offence against the laws and statutes of the realm so to do, but that they may lawfully take a reasonable consideration of them for bestowing the said offices being profitable & beneficial to them the said bailiffs.[14]

Further scope for dispute was created when the sheriff's undoubted powers of nomination were cut across by the Crown's exercise of its right to appoint bailiffs for life. These bailiwicks then became a commodity which could be bought and sold like land: another of the complaints against Edward Kemeys was brought by his neighbour Gabriel Lewis of Llanishen who had bought the bailiwicks of Dinas Powis and Miskin from the Crown's grantee Morgan Nicholas, a page of the Chamber, and was being hindered from collecting the profits of his office by Kemeys. As an afterthought, Lewis accused Kemeys of having leased out most of the other bailiwicks in the county as well as various legal offices and the post of deputy sheriff.[15]

Such appointments could also meet with opposition from the local tenants, particularly when the Crown's nominee was an outsider and

---

[13] Glanmor Williams (ed.), *Early Modern Glamorgan* (Glamorgan County History, 4, Cardiff, 1974), p. 107.

[14] STAC8/290/5.   [15] STAC8/197/29.

lacked the necessary local knowledge. William Herle, Burghley's
political agent, was granted the rhaglawry (or Welsh bailiwick) of
Cardiganshire in 1580 and considered it to be worth about £2,000
but sold it within a few months, complaining of the difficulty and
expense of Welsh business.[16] Crown grants of offices were originally
made for life or term of years and ostensibly as a favour or reward to
courtiers and Crown servants, but by the seventeenth century offices
were being sold openly and in perpetuity. The rhaglawry of Caeo,
Catheiniog, Maenordeilo and Mallaen in the principality of South
Wales was sold in 1614 to two London dealers and subsequently
passed through the hands of Wales's leading dealer in Crown land,
Richard Budd, before being bought by Thomas Alisbury of London
and Henry Vaughan of Derwydd in Llandybïe in 1618. Alisbury and
Vaughan subsequently sued the inhabitants of the rhaglawry in Star
Chamber for resisting them in the exercise of their office.[17]

The Crown's powers of direct appointment, therefore, whether
used for patronage or for profit, being inevitably more arbitrary and
irregular in their incidence, could cut across the more accustomed
hierarchies of local power exercised by the Crown's local representatives, the sheriffs. Even more disruption could result when the
Crown's rights were mediated through a single powerful nobleman.
The unrest arising out of the earl of Leicester's attempts to control
North Wales divided most counties into pro- and anti-Leicester
factions for many years after his death.[18] Similar tensions marked the
parliamentary elections of North-East and South-West Wales during
the ascendancy of the earl of Essex, though they were shorter-lived in
the north, where his influence was largely a matter of personal
allegiance, than in the south, where they were perpetuated by the
territorial interests of his family.[19] On a smaller scale, in Pembrokeshire, almost exactly the same factional conflicts marked the career of
Essex's relative by marriage and sometime ally Sir John Perrot.

Crown grants could also conflict with later aristocratic patronage:

[16] *CSPD 1547–80*, p. 692; *CSPD 1581–90*, pp. 14–5, 20; see also Herle's biography in *HP 1558–1603*, II, pp. 302–4.

[17] C66/2041, no. 9; C54/2259, no. 30; C54/2338, no. 12; STAC9/41/13.

[18] For details of appointments in the Denbighshire lordships controlled by Leicester and his brother the earl of Warwick, see S. L. Adams, 'Office-holders in the borough of Denbigh and the stewards of the lordship of Denbigh in the reign of Elizabeth I', *Transactions of the Denbighshire Historical Society* 25 (1976), pp. 92–113; see also below, pp. 151–2.

[19] J. E. Neale, 'Three Elizabethan elections', *EHR* 46 (1931), pp. 209–38; A. H. Dodd, 'North Wales in the Essex revolt of 1601', *EHR* 59 (1944), pp. 348–70.

when the royal favourite, Philip Herbert, earl of Montgomery, was appointed as Chancellor and Chamberlain of Caernarfon, Anglesey and Merioneth in 1605, he named as his deputy Rowland White of the Friars, Llanfaes. White was soon in dispute with the previous deputy, William Pennant, over the right to profit from the issues of seals, which Pennant claimed by a lease dating from 1595.[20] Part of the problem may have been that aristocrats and courtiers from outside the area did not realise the implications for local politics of their appointments; this almost certainly explains the earl of Dorset's controversial choice of Thomas Cheadle as his deputy constable in Beaumaris.[21]

OFFICE-HOLDING AND LOCAL POLITICS

The importance of high office in the Welsh march had been considerably diminished by the Acts of Union, but this does not seem to have had any immediate effect on the enthusiasm of the aristocracy for stewardships, constableships and other senior posts.[22] The military significance of these offices also declined during the second half of the sixteenth century, a reflection partly of Elizabeth's normally cautious foreign policies, partly of more settled conditions at home, partly of the alternative sources of military manpower offered by the county militia.[23] Crown generosity could be turned to military advantage, as when Robert, earl of Leicester, used his North Wales lands and official connections to raise troops for his expedition to the Netherlands in 1585–6.[24] The earl of Essex also used his Welsh offices and lands to gather support for his rebellion in 1601, though this was presumably not uppermost in his mind when he sought office there. Military ambitions had generally to be exercised through those who actually held the land, so that the official's powers only extended as far as his influence over the local gentry. Nevertheless, the pattern of

[20] T. I. Jeffreys Jones (ed.), *Exchequer Proceedings Concerning Wales* in tempore *James I* (Board of Celtic Studies, History and Law ser., 15, Cardiff, 1955), p. 46.
[21] B. Dew Roberts, 'Cheadles against Bulkeleys', *Transactions of the Anglesey Antiquarian Society* 1945, pp. 25–37.
[22] On the political implications of constableships, not strictly speaking an office on the Crown's landed estate but accounted for and paid through the land revenue accounts, see M. Gray, 'Castles and patronage in sixteenth-century Wales', *WHR* 15 (1990–1).
[23] For the effect which this had on the nobility in general, see H. Miller, *Henry VIII and the English Nobility* (Oxford, 1986), pp. 159–60.
[24] S. L. Adams, 'The gentry of North Wales and the earl of Leicester's expedition to the Netherlands, 1585–6', *WHR* 7 (1974–5), pp. 129–46.

office-holding continued to reflect and in some cases to create the power structure of Welsh society throughout our period.

The massive bloc of offices in South and East Wales held by Henry Somerset, second earl of Worcester, in the 1530s and 1540s was pruned but not completely broken up on his death in 1549.[25] Within the next decade, many of the south-eastern lordships of which he had been steward were granted to his kinsman William Herbert, earl of Pembroke, who also succeeded him in most of the more important offices, while his numerous lesser posts were divided among the local gentry. Pembroke's offices were in turn split up on his death; his son Henry succeeded him as steward of Dinas and Brecon but the stewardship of Montgomery, Ceri and Cydewain was granted to the idiosyncratic Sir James Croft of Croft Castle in Herefordshire. This appears to have been a personal decision by the Queen rather than a reflection of the local power structure: Elizabeth had never forgotten Croft's loyalty to her after the Wyatt rebellion and the grant of his stewardship was part of his rehabilitation after ten years of disgrace arising out of his responsibility for the failure of the siege of Leith in 1560. Croft succeeded in making enemies of both Pembroke and Leicester as well as of Sir Henry Sidney when the latter was President of the Council in the Marches but he was still followed in his stewardship by his grandson Herbert, a protégé of the earls of Essex and Shrewsbury and subsequently of Robert Cecil.[26]

The sphere of influence of the Herbert family had always been centred on the south-east; William Herbert, earl of Pembroke, was steward of Ruthin and Chirk but by the time he died the lordships had been granted to Leicester and his brother Warwick, and Pembroke was followed as steward by a series of local men. In South-West Wales the power of the Devereux family was reflected in their continuing tenure of the stewardship of St Dogmaels and of the Welsh courts in Cardiganshire. The Perrot family had long been established in South Pembrokeshire as tenants and officials of the lords of Pembroke, but it was the personal favour shown by successive monarchs to Sir John Perrot himself (a degree of favour which gave credence to the contemporary belief that he was the illegitimate son of Henry VIII) which made him the most powerful figure in Pembrokeshire. He was made steward of the Crown lordships and

[25] W. R. B. Robinson, 'Early Tudor policy towards Wales: the Welsh offices held by Henry, earl of Worcester (1526–49)', *Bulletin of the Board of Celtic Studies* 21 (1964–6), pp. 43–74.

[26] *HP 1558–1603*, I, pp. 671–5.

manors of Carew (subsequently granted to him outright), Coedraeth, Narberth and Cilgerran in Pembroke and of St Clears in the west of Carmarthenshire, constable of Narberth and Tenby Castles and gaoler of Haverfordwest. His position was further consolidated by a series of Crown leases, including land formerly of his kinsman Sir Rhys ap Gruffydd as well as the accumulation of land of Haverfordwest Priory which enabled him to become a power in the borough, serving as its mayor in 1560–1, 1570–1 and 1575–6, controlling the parliamentary representation and becoming MP himself in 1589. He was not challenged by the Devereux, who chose instead to concentrate on their interests in Cardigan and Carmarthen. The two families were eventually joined by the marriage of Sir John's elder son Thomas to Walter Devereux's daughter Dorothy in 1583, but Walter Devereux succeeded in remaining impartial in Sir John's political and territorial conflicts with his neighbours and was named as one of the overseers in the will of William Phillips of Picton, one of the leaders of the anti-Perrot faction.[27]

Mid-Wales was something of a political no-man's-land. The earls of Worcester held several lordships but, after 1549, no Crown offices. The earls of Pembroke controlled some Crown lordships in person or through clients. Three generations of the Devereux family served as stewards of Builth and the Talbot earls of Shrewsbury dominated Radnor as stewards of the lordship, constables and janitors of the castle, though both Walter Devereux and his son Robert, earl of Essex, served intermittently as clerks of the courts there. It was the earl of Essex, too, who had most impact on the parliamentary politics of the area, using his offices and the family connections of his steward Gelli Meurig to influence borough elections in Brecon and Radnor as well as in his home area of West Wales. The complex pattern of aristocratic interests in Mid-Wales made possible the emergence of two powerful local families, both cadet branches of the Herbert clan and both buttressed by Crown offices and lands, the Herberts of Montgomery Castle, later lords Herbert of Chirbury, and the Herberts of Powis Castle, later lords Powis.[28]

County elections in South and Mid-Wales were less susceptible to interference from Crown office-holders: the influence of the Herberts

[27] Brian Howells (ed.), *Early Modern Pembrokeshire, 1536–1815* (Pembrokeshire County History, 3, Haverfordwest, 1987), pp. 138–47; *HP 1558–1603*, III, pp. 205–7.

[28] W. J. Smith (ed.), *Herbert Correspondence* (Board of Celtic Studies, History and Law ser., 21, Cardiff, 1963), esp. pp. 4–7; biographies in *HP 1558–1603*, II, pp. 294–301; and W. R. Williams, *The Parliamentary History of the Principality of Wales* (Brecon, 1895).

and Somersets in the south-east and of the Devereux in the south-west probably owed more to landholding than to office, as did that of the Stanley earls of Derby in Flintshire. It is, however, worth remembering that most of these families owed their power if not their initial status to Crown influence, the earls of Worcester by the facilitation of Charles Somerset's marriage with Elizabeth Herbert, heiress to the Raglan estate, and the gift to his son of most of the lands of Tintern Abbey, the earls of Pembroke by a series of massive grants of lands in South-East Wales and elsewhere in the 1540s and 1550s and the Devereux family by office-holding and leasing of Crown manors.

North Wales, too, had no dominant aristocratic family in the mid-sixteenth century; as well as the principality, most of the marcher lordships were still under direct Crown control. While the absence of a single dominant family in Mid-Wales had led to the distribution of offices between several families, Elizabeth's use of her power in the north was broadly similar to her father's policy in the south-east: she used it to establish one dominant nobleman, in this case Robert Dudley, earl of Leicester. As well as outright grants of the lordships of Denbigh, Chirk, Arwystli and Cyfeiliog (and the grant of the adjoining lordship of Ruthin to his brother Ambrose, earl of Warwick), Leicester was appointed Chamberlain of the county palatine of Chester and Chancellor and Chamberlain of Caernarfon, Anglesey and Merioneth, which made him in effect steward of the principality. His supremacy in North Wales was further reinforced with several other offices including that of Chief Forester of Snowdon. This he elevated from a largely honorary title to one which enabled him to make a considerable nuisance of himself by enquiring into concealment and encroachment on the Crown's lands in most of mainland Gwynedd. His motives here seem to have been almost exclusively financial, and he was prepared to sacrifice political advantage by alienating some of the leading local landowners.

The result of his efforts was a series of massive grants of land which had been found to be encroached or concealed. The potential for local disturbance in his activities can be gauged by a survey of encroached lands in late sixteenth-century Merionethshire: this lists more than 400 encroachments amounting to over 10,000 acres, with the bulk of the land in the hands of leading gentry families – the Powises of Cymmer, the Nanneys of Nanney and the Vaughans of Corsygedol – though the greatest encroachers of all were the Price family of Rhiwlas, descended from Cadwaladr Price, younger brother of Leicester's chief local agent Dr Ellis Price. These families formed the political elite of the county and their alignments were largely shaped by opposition to Leicester and his agents. The county's only parliamentary seat was controlled until 1585 by Ellis Price and his allies the Owen family of Dolgellau and Cae'rberllan. A bitterly disputed election in 1572 led to the return of Leicester's protégé Hugh Owen of Cae'rberllan in spite of the efforts of John Salesbury of Rûg, but the campaign against encroachments eventually alienated Owen from his former patrons and may even have been responsible for bringing the longer-established local families into political activity. From 1586, it was they who dominated the county's representation: even Thomas Middleton of Chirk, MP in 1597, was a cousin of the Nanneys and the Lloyds and a creditor of the Salesburys and the Nanneys, while his defeated opponent John Vaughan of Caergai was the chosen candidate of John Lewis Owen and Cadwaladr Price.[29]

The earl of Leicester died in 1588 and the political influence of his agents crumbled, though the rifts he had created in local society persisted for another generation. He was succeeded as forester, after a lapse of some years, by Ellis Price's grandson Thomas Goodman, younger son of Gawen Goodman of Ruthin and nephew of Gabriel Goodman, dean of Westminster, and himself sacrist, auditor, searcher of the sanctuary, keeper of the chapel of Henry VII and bellringer at Westminster. Goodman was also janitor of Caernarfon Castle, constable of Conway and steward of Bardsey but was replaced in all but the janitorship by Sir Edward Herbert (later lord Herbert of Chirbury) and his son Richard in 1605. Neither Goodman nor the Herberts appear to have made any attempt to exploit the forestership, and there is no evidence to connect Herbert with the enquiry into encroachments in 1639. The other foresterships seem to have been purely honorary and most were used to reward comparatively minor Crown servants; by the 1590s, the Forest of Denbigh was in the custody of one of the county's leading landowning families, the

---

[29] Colin Gresham, 'The Forest of Snowdon in its relationship to Eifionydd', *Transactions of the Caernarfonshire Historical Society* 21 (1960), pp. 53–62; Colin Thomas, 'Patterns and processes of estate expansion in the fifteenth and sixteenth centuries', *Journal of the Merionethshire Historical and Record Society* 6 (1969–72), pp. 333–42; H. Gareth Owen, 'Family politics in Elizabethan Merionethshire', *Bulletin of the Board of Celtic Studies* 18 (1958–60), pp. 185–91; 'Merioneth', in S. T. Bindoff (ed.), *The History of Parliament. The Commons, 1509–58* (3 vols., London, 1981), I, pp. 278–9; *HP 1558–1603*, I, pp. 319–20; A. H. Dodd on Hugh Owen of Cae'rberllan in *HP 1558–1603*, III, p. 160; *CSPD 1547–80*, p. 586; *APC 1577–8*, pp. 99, 122.

Middletons of Chirk, who were also constables and magistrates of Denbigh, but the forestership of Ruthin was granted to Edward Shirburn, secretary successively to Robert Cecil, to the diplomat Sir Dudley Carleton and to Sir Francis Bacon, and the forestership of Bromfield and Yale formed part of the remuneration of Richard Budd, clerk to the Exchequer auditor for Wales and subsequently himself auditor for the West of England.

LEGAL OFFICE: STEWARDS AND RECORDERS

It is always difficult to be sure of the extent to which offices in the Crown's lordships were honorary, and equally difficult to say how far honorary offices were valued for the local power and prestige they offered rather than the annual fee. The role of the steward could be crucial in both the tenurial structure and the political complexion of a lordship. Stewards had the power to grant customary estates of inheritance as well as leases and were often suspected of complicity in encroachment, concealment and conversion of copyholds to freehold estates. These powers were, however, being eroded in the sixteenth century by the practice of obtaining leases direct from the Crown, by the reorganisation and formalisation of tenurial relationships in some of the lordships[30] and by the appointment of surveyors and other officials with the ability both to make leases and to investigate the steward's use of his powers.

The ending of regalian jurisdiction in marcher lordships by the Acts of Union had also done considerable damage to both the powers and the prestige of the stewards of these lordships. Nevertheless, the day-to-day work of a steward required some legal knowledge and by the seventeenth century lords of manors in lowland England were appointing increasing numbers of trained lawyers as stewards.[31] The steward's duties could also be time-consuming and in the case of aristocratic stewards of major lordships would naturally be performed by a deputy. We should, however, be careful in judging whether

---

[30] See, e.g., for Denbigh, S. L. Adams, 'The composition of 1564 and the earl of Leicester's tenurial reformation in the lordship of Denbigh', *Bulletin of the Board of Celtic Studies* 26 (1974–6), pp. 479–511. For an earlier petition against changes in tenures in Bromfield and Yale, LR17/1 (to be published by R. W. Hoyle); for a similar proposal, never in fact implemented, on the lands granted by the Crown to the earls of Pembroke, NLW, Bute box 93/163.

[31] C. W. Brooks, *Pettyfoggers and Vipers of the Commonwealth. The 'Lower Branch' of the Legal Profession in Early Modern England* (Cambridge, 1986), pp. 114–18.

appointments were functional or honorary on the basis of the office-holder's status: the earl of Bridgwater's stewardships of Denbigh and of Bromfield and Yale look at first sight to be purely honorary but were first granted to him in survivorship with his father Sir Thomas Egerton, later Lord Chancellor, who was well on his way to a distinguished legal career when he was first appointed to the stewardships in the 1590s.

Lesser stewardships on the Crown's Welsh estates were still more likely to go to the local gentry, though the John Thelwalls, father and son, who were stewards of Ruthin from 1604, came from a distinguished legal family even if they themselves had no formal legal training. The Owens of Frondeg, leaders of the conservative, crypto-Catholic, anti-Bulkeley faction among the Anglesey gentry, were stewards of the manor of Rhosfair (Rhosyr or Newborough) throughout our period, though this did not preserve them from a series of disputes over the land they leased within the manor. Lewis ab Owain ap Meurig of Frondeg, MP for the county in 1553 and 1572, was one of the three JPs who unsuccessfully attempted to remove Quarter Sessions from the Bulkeley capital of Beaumaris back to Newborough in 1556.[32]

The Mansells of Margam and Penrice, one of the most powerful families in Glamorgan, held a range of offices across South Wales, though their political influence does not appear to have extended much outside their own shire. A grant in survivorship to Sir Rhys Mansell and his son Edward in 1554 lists, as well as the chancellorship and chamberlainship of South Wales, Cardigan and Carmarthen, the offices of steward of all Crown land in Pembrokeshire, steward, chancellor and surveyor of Haverfordwest and Rhos in Pembroke-shire, steward of Cantrefselyf, Pencelli, Bronllys, Llangoed and Alexanderstone and gatekeeper of Bronllys and Hay Castles in Breconshire, most of which eventually passed in turn to Edward's son Thomas. This grant seems, however, to have been ignored in the grants of individual stewardships in Pembrokeshire to Sir John Perrot and after his execution to Robert, earl of Essex. Edward Mansell was educated at Lincolns Inn (to which his father had also been admitted late in life) but Thomas is not known to have received any formal education and it is highly unlikely that his father's training influenced

[32] Jeffreys Jones (ed.), *Exchequer Proceedings*, pp. 22–3, 82–3, 232; Philip S. Edwards, 'Cynrychiolaeth a chynnen', *WHR* 10 (1980–1), pp. 43–68 (with an abstract in English).

his appointments.[33] The popularity of the Inns of Court as a finishing school for the sons of gentlemen has always made it difficult to say whether local knowledge or local status dictated their appointments; after all, the training required to be a good steward was almost exactly the same as that which was advisable for the efficient management of one's own estate.

Recorderships were more likely to be given to lawyers, though even this may have been a matter of custom rather than necessity: the great Sir Eubule Thelwall, Master in Chancery and Principal of Jesus College, Oxford, can have had little time to devote to his recordership of Ruthin, and it is debatable whether his advice on legal matters was more valuable than the power and influence he could bring to bear on behalf of the town. The office did, however, consolidate his family's hold in the area, since he himself leased the lordship and was succeeded in the recordership by his nephews Edward and Simon Thelwall of Llanbedr. Simon was educated at Lincoln College, Oxford, and was a member of Gray's Inn; less is known of Edward, though he was the elder brother.[34]

Stewardships of monastic property had declined in value, particularly in the south and east where so much of the valuable land had been demised in fee-farm or sold by 1558, but were still capable of attracting the attention of the greatest landowners in the west.[35] The Devereux family retained the stewardship of St Dogmaels throughout our period and the stewardship of Bardsey was one of the offices granted to Edward Herbert, the future lord Herbert of Chirbury, in 1605. Henry VIII's readiness to confirm monastic grants left his successors with diminished control over these stewardships for much of the sixteenth century: William Phillips of Picton was made steward of St Dogmaels's daughter house at Pill in survivorship with his father in 1531 and retained the office until his

---

[33] *CPR Philip and Mary*, II, p. 61; Bindoff (ed.), *Commons, 1509–58*, II, pp. 565–6; *HP 1558–1603*, III, p. 12.

[34] *CSPD 1611–18*, p. 275; B. E. Howells, *A Calendar of Letters Relating to North Wales* (Board of Celtic Studies, History and Law ser., 23, Cardiff, 1967), pp. 22–3; Williams, *Parliamentary History*, pp. 73–4; J. E. Griffith, *Pedigrees of Caernarfonshire and Anglesey Families* (Horncastle, 1914), p. 369.

[35] For details of the rate of dispersal of monastic land, see Gray, 'Dispersal of crown property', pp. 152–94; Glanmor Williams, *Welsh Reformation Essays* (Cardiff, 1967), p. 100; H. A. Lloyd, *The Gentry of South-West Wales, 1540–1640* (Cardiff, 1968), pp. 31–40; G. Dyfnallt Owen, 'Agrarian conditions and changes in West Wales during the sixteenth century with special reference to monastic and chantry lands' (University of Wales, PhD thesis, 1935), pp. 366–88.

death in 1573. He was followed by Walter Jones, possibly a younger member of the Jones family of Abermarlais and hence an adherent of the Perrot faction. With the collapse of Perrot's power in the 1590s, Jones was succeeded by Phillips's son-in-law Alban Stepneth, a trained lawyer from St Albans who had moved to West Wales in the service of his relative Richard Davies, bishop of St Davids 1561–81, married two local heiresses (with both of whom he inherited family feuds with Perrot) and steadily accumulated an estate including numerous episcopal leases throughout West Wales. Stepneth was the anti-Perrot group's candidate for the constituency of Haverfordwest in 1571 but could hardly have hoped to succeed when all the borough officials had been appointed during the previous year while Perrot was mayor; he was, however, elected the following year with the aid of more favourable officials, and William Phillips, his chief promoter, took the county seat.[36]

FINANCIAL OFFICE: BAILIFFS AND RECEIVERS

Even the office of bailiff of a monastic estate could confer considerable local power, especially where there was no steward and the office-holder also leased or owned some former monastic land. The Powis family of Merionethshire leased much of the property of Cymmer Abbey and administered the rest as bailiffs for at least three generations. Simon Bracebridge, steward of Conwy Abbey, was an outsider, a servant of William Herbert, earl of Pembroke. In his absence, the abbey's upland holdings were ruled by Robert Wyn ap Cadwaladr of Foelas, son of the former monastic steward Cadwaladr ap Morris Gethin and member of a cadet branch of the Price family of Plas Iolyn and Rhiwlas. Robert succeeded his father as bailiff of Hiraethog, claimed some former monastic land by conventual lease and at least one holding by Crown grant to his father, and leased the upland grange of Hiraethog from the Crown. In a dispute over another holding, he was described as esquire and 'a man of great power in the county', in spite of the fact that he never appeared on the commission of the peace. In an elegy to him, the poet Siôn Tudur spoke of him as a patriot, 'like an oak tree to the commonwealth':

---

[36] Howells (ed.), *Early Modern Pembrokeshire*, pp. 137–43; *HP 1558–1603*, III, pp. 445–7.

Gwladwr oedd, a'r glod yr aeth,
Mal derwen am wladwriaeth[37]

Bailiffs of former monastic property were usually appointed for life, and the security this provided may have contributed to the enhanced prestige of the office. The bailiffs of Crown hundreds within the principality were (contrary to English practice) appointed by the sheriffs and were therefore in theory subject to replacement every year, though in fact some families succeeded in retaining the office for several generations. While the post did not normally attract the most eminent of the county gentry, the hundred bailiffs of Wales were frequently drawn from much higher social strata than those of England. The almost proverbial monotony of Welsh personal names, combined with the fact that, even in the south and east, patronymic forms had not yet settled into surnames in many families, makes it difficult to identify many of these officials and place them in a local and family context, even in counties like Anglesey and Caernarfon for which good biographical and genealogical sources exist.[38] One also has to bear in mind that the ones who can be traced are more likely to come from the more powerful families; nevertheless, there are enough of these to suggest that the office was popular among the gentry, particularly in the north-west.

Royston Stephens found that the bailiffs of Gwynedd in the 1540s and 1550s were mostly minor gentry, with a median assessment for the 1546 lay subsidy of £3 in lands or £12 in goods.[39] If anything, later lay subsidy rolls suggest their status declined slightly, and an increasing number cannot be found at all, possibly because they were younger sons, though this may also suggest they were using their local influence to reduce their assessments or to escape entirely. Even the unreliable evidence of the subsidy rolls, however, indicates that there were still some very wealthy (by local standards) men in office in the early seventeenth century. Richard Meurig of Bodorgan, bailiff of

[37] SC6/Ph. & M./400; SC6/Eliz./2989 *et seq.*; LR6/131/6 *et seq.*; E. A. Lewis and J. C. Davies (eds.), *Records of the Court of Augmentations Relating to Wales and Monmouthshire* (Board of Celtic Studies, History and Law ser., 13, Cardiff, 1954), pp. 65, 84–5; E. G. Jones (ed.), *Exchequer Proceedings (Equity) Concerning Wales, Henry VIII–Elizabeth* (Board of Celtic Studies, History and Law ser., 4, Cardiff, 1939), p. 155; Griffith, *Pedigrees*, p. 326; Gwynfor Jones, 'Patrymau Bonheddig Uchelwrol', p. 56.

[38] See for instance, Griffith, *Pedigrees*.

[39] Royston Stephens, 'Gwynedd, 1528–1547: economy and society in Tudor Wales' (University of California, PhD thesis, 1975, published by University Microfilms, Ann Arbor, MI, 1979), p. 184.

Malltraeth in Anglesey, was second in the list for his hundred on the 1613 roll, in spite of the losses his estate had suffered under his spendthrift father, another Richard Meurig; a cousin of the earl of Essex's agent Sir Gelli Meurig, he was regularly on the commission of the peace from 1594 but succeeded in surviving the disgrace of his cousin's family and was sheriff of Anglesey in 1614.[40] Lewis Owen of Frondeg, who combined the stewardship of the Crown manor of Rhosfair with the bailiwick of the neighbouring commote of Dindaethwy for much of Elizabeth's reign, was one of the wealthiest men in his own commote of Menai, represented Anglesey in the Parliaments of 1553 and 1572 and was twice sheriff of the county; he even went so far as to perform his duties as bailiff by a deputy, William ap Rees ab Ieuan.[41]

Bailiffs of hundreds within the principality had far wider powers than their English counterparts, being responsible for collecting rents and other dues from the Crown's extensive lands and presumably having at least some influence over new lettings. Like their English counterparts, they probably ran the hundred courts, which were still popular in Wales for settling minor civil disputes because of their speed and convenience in spite of the potential they offered for abuse. A bailiff could arrest without warrant and refuse to accept sureties for release, delay serving writs, empanel favourable juries and generally make life difficult, whether for his own enemies or for the adherents of his patron's opponents. The annual wage, usually £2, may also have been an incentive, particularly at the beginning of our period, in a region where £10 was a respectable annual income for a landed gentleman of considerable local power and prestige. In his study of Norfolk, A. Hassell Smith found that the hundred bailiffs there were normally drawn from the ranks immediately below the minor gentry – the more substantial yeomen and some attorneys – and even these were of higher status than the bailiffs of Somerset, who were dismissed as 'petty townsmen and husbandmen' in 1625.[42]

There is evidence that the Norfolk gentry were anxious to have

---

[40] E179/220/152; Griffith, *Pedigrees*, p. 126; E. G. Jones, 'Some notes on the principal county families of Anglesey in the sixteenth and early seventeenth centuries', *Transactions of the Anglesey Antiquarian Society*, 1939, pp. 74–5.

[41] *HP 1558–1603*, III, p. 162; Jones, 'Some notes', p. 63; LR6/132/4 describes William as deputy.

[42] Stephens, 'Gwynedd', pp. 185–6; A. Hassell Smith, *County and Court: Government and Politics in Norfolk, 1558–1603* (Oxford, 1974), pp. 141–52, quoting T. G. Barnes, *Somerset 1625–1640. A County's Government during the 'Personal Rule'* (London, 1961), pp. 137–8.

their servants appointed as bailiffs and Smith suggests that one reason for the revival in popularity of the office of sheriff was the control it offered over these appointments, though Owen Wynn of Gwydir claimed in the 1630s that the power lay at least partly with the receiver: 'The bailiffs for the quit rents in every hundred are but matters of pleasure to your friend's servants.'[43] The legal evidence suggests that in South Wales some sheriffs did sell offices or, when factional conflict was at its height, appoint their own clients or relatives or those of their allies, but in the principality of North Wales the higher status of many of the bailiffs presumably gave them more independence. Four generations of the Madryn family of Madryn in Llŷn served as bailiffs of the hundred of Dinllaen between 1560 and 1640 with only brief interruptions. The bailiff in 1610, Thomas Bodfel, was married to a Madryn widow, though the two families were members of opposing factions in county politics. The Madryn family normally headed the subsidy assessment for the commote, were almost continuously on the commission of the peace between 1558 and 1609 and provided the county with three sheriffs. Wiliam Cynwal spoke of Thomas Madryn, bailiff of Dinllaen in Llŷn in the 1570s and 1580s, as a person of authority and legal prowess, a wise practitioner of the law, fully equipped to deal with matters relating to law and order in his community:

> Doethder yw d'arfer yn d'oes...
> Y gyfraith, ŵr dewr gwiwfryd,
> Yn ddifost gwyddost i gyd

They were, however, vulnerable to political pressure: Thomas Madryn was imprisoned in Ludlow in 1578 for opposing the earl of Leicester's activities in the Forest of Snowdon, though this does not seem to have interrupted his tenure of office. One of his fellow-prisoners was Hugh Gwyn Bodfel, father of Thomas, but by the early seventeenth century the two families were divided over the question of the political aspirations of the Wynns of Gwydir.[44]

As with offices on former monastic estates, the office of hundred bailiff could be combined with leases of Crown property to give

---

[43] NLW, MS 9062E/1548.

[44] E179/220/111, 145 etc.; Griffith, *Pedigrees*, p. 242; Gwynfor Jones, Governance, order and stability', p. 25; *HP 1558–1603*, II, pp. 233–4; J. K. Gruenfelder, 'The Wynns of Gwydir and parliamentary elections in Wales, 1604–40', *WHR* 9 (1978–9), pp. 121–41.

almost complete control of a district. The hundred of Cafflogion in Llŷn was virtually the private estate of the Jones family of Castellmarch, the office of bailiff and the lease of its rents passing from John ap Robert ap Llewelyn ab Ithel to his younger sons Thomas and Robert Jones and his grandson William Gruffydd Jones. William's death in 1587 was followed by a break in the family's tenure when he was succeeded by his neighbour and sometime political enemy Gruffydd ap John Gruffydd of Cefnamwlch; in the same year, however, Gruffydd's daughter Margaret married William's son and heir William Jones, who soon resumed the family office of bailiff. This was the future Sir William Jones, the eminent lawyer and judge, thrice MP for Beaumaris and once for Caernarfonshire, and one of the few landowners in the west of the county to support the political aspirations of the Wynns of Gwydir, though in 1621 he gave his influence to his late wife's nephew John Griffith of Cefnamwlch, the leader of the anti-Wynn faction. Three years later, it was Jones who led the opposition to Sir Richard Wynn's proposal that the issues of the Greenwax in North Wales should be leased (to Wynn himself, naturally). Wynn had claimed that the profits from these issues had declined because of neglect and dishonesty by the bailiffs, 'against whose oppression the people complain', so Jones's response can be seen in part as a defence of his fellow-bailiffs.[45]

In spite of its hegemony in Cafflogion, the Jones family was still vulnerable outside its immediate locality. The family had long held a lease of the bond township of Bodfean or Buan in Dinllaen, where Robert Jones lived. In 1566, however, a reversionary lease of the township was granted to one of the gentleman pensioners, Henry Mackwilliam, and his wife. Robert Jones and his undertenants subsequently claimed that Mackwilliam had been prepared to assign the reversion to them, but that the Thomas Wynns, father and son, being at court at the time secured the reversion for themselves and threatened to evict the tenants. The dispute was still running in 1620: by that time the Madryns, bailiffs of the hundred, who had been accused of harassing the tenants and delaying arbitration in 1590, had acquired an interest in some of the ancient tenements and bought Bodfean Mill, which naturally led them to change sides.[46]

[45] Griffith, *Pedigrees*, p. 191; *HP 1558–1603*, II, p. 386; Gruenfelder, 'Wynns of Gwydir'; J. Ballinger (ed.), *Calendar of the Wynn (of Gwydir) Papers, 1515–1690* (Aberystwyth, 1926), nos. 1232–8.

[46] Jones (ed.), *Exchequer Proceedings*, pp. 54–5, 61, 71; Jeffreys Jones (ed.), *Exchequer Proceedings*, pp. 42, 65–6, 75–6. The two Thomas Wynns may have been from a junior branch of the

Bailiffs were in theory appointed by the sheriffs, and responsible to them in legal matters. However, as has been seen, the receivers, to whom they paid any money they collected in the course of their duties, also exercised some control over appointments. It was the receivers who undertook the local financial supervision of the Crown's estates: the auditors had an extensive advisory role but were based in London and seldom had any landholding connection with the regions they served. The rewards of a receivership could be considerable. In the letter already referred to, Owen Wynn of Gwydir valued the receivership of North Wales at £243 a year, of which £41 had to be spent on accommodation, transport and other expenses. A further £5 had been produced by loans to the drovers and the 'Shrewsbury men' under the old system, when money was paid over to the Exchequer in March, but since the creation of Charles as Prince of Wales the administration of the Welsh estates had been tightened up and money was now paid in June and November as well as in March. The then incumbent, Thomas Trafford of Wrexham, was said to have paid £1,100 to his predecessor, Sir Hugh Beeston, for the post.[47]

While receivers in England were normally local men, those for North and South Wales were usually drawn from the eastern and border counties or from even further away. Thus Sir John Salusbury of Lleweni, who as Chancellor and Chamberlain of the principality of North Wales was the chief financial officer there, also served as receiver of North Wales and Cheshire from 1547 to 1568, though in later years his duties were performed by his cousin and deputy Robert Puleston of Bersham. Salusbury was succeeded by Edward Hughes of Holt, on the Cheshire border, and Hugh Beeston of Plas Cadogan near Wrexham and Beeston in Cheshire. Thomas Trafford's appointment received official confirmation in 1603. Although all these were Denbigh men, only Salusbury came from the western part of the county: the others all originated in the royal lordship of Bromfield and Yale except for Beeston, whose family home was some 9 miles into Cheshire.

The situation in South Wales was more extreme. William Wightman of Coventry and London, a client of the earl of Pembroke,

Bodfean family of that name but cannot be fitted into the pedigree in Griffith, *Pedigrees*, p. 171.
[47] NLW, MS 9062E/1548; the figure c⁸ (for £5) is apparently misread in Ballinger's catalogue as cc (£200).

was succeeded as receiver by the deputy surveyor, Robert Davy. His name may suggest Welsh origins but he was in fact a typical member of the nascent professional class with a house in London and a country residence at Barnes in Surrey. He was followed by Herbert Croft of Croft Castle in Herefordshire and it was not until 1604 that a local man, Edward Carne of Nash in Glamorgan, was appointed to the office. He, too, had an administrative career, becoming a Teller of the Exchequer in 1623 and employing as his deputy in the receivership a John Thompson, identified by Jeffreys Jones as of Burford in Shropshire.[48] This perpetuation of the medieval practice of governing the principalities through senior officials drawn from Crown lordships in eastern Wales and the border counties and from the London official classes, a practice which is reflected in the choice of purely judicial personnel, may also help to explain the popularity of bailiffships of hundreds among the gentry of the principality.

CONCLUSION

Because office-holding was so important a determinant of status in medieval and early modern Welsh society, any history of Crown office inevitably involves the whole history of that society. Wales in the sixteenth century was undergoing radical change. In some ways, the patterns of appointment to Crown office remain remarkably stable. The greatest offices were still largely reserved for the aristocracy and outsiders; the gentry of the east were more likely to hold office, inside and outside their own areas, than those of the west, though in this aspect at least some change can be seen by the seventeenth century. Meanwhile, at the grass roots, the native gentry, the *bonheddwyr*, continued to rule the Crown's hundreds as well as taking up an increasing number of leases of Crown manors. The most important changes had taken effect before the beginning of our period. The population crisis of the fifteenth century, the resulting collapse of bond townships and the emancipation of bond tenures made the holding of Crown land of increasing importance in estate-building strategies. The Acts of Union created new judicial and administrative offices based on counties and regions and undermined those which were confined to the Crown's landed estates, though the effects of this were not really felt for over a century. Wales was at last given parliamentary representation, with single-member constitu-

---

[48] Jeffreys Jones (ed.), *Exchequer Proceedings*, pp. 29, 33.

encies, which sharpened political rivalries and made office-holding as well as land of crucial importance in the securing of political influence. The dissolution of the monasteries made a vast number of new offices available to the Crown, but by the time most of them were free the lands they administered had been sold.

Of course, all these events had an impact on the whole of Wales, which was forced in the sixteenth century to redefine itself as a part of a united kingdom of England and Wales rather than a colony. In this process, the holding of Crown office was a crucial part of the new image of the governing classes as well as providing a reassuring link with the past and confirmation of the local hierarchies of power and prestige on which the status of the Welsh gentry ultimately rested. It may not be entirely coincidental that as the Crown's landed estate declined in size, and Crown office thus lost importance while private estates grew, the Welsh concept of gentility changed from one based on pedigree and service to a more English interpretation of the gentleman as landowner.

CHAPTER 6

Tenure on the Elizabethan estates

Richard Hoyle

Although it may seem an appropriate subject for lawyers alone, a knowledge of the tenurial policies of the Crown is crucial to an understanding of the means and ends to which it sought to manage its estates. Tenure is the legal framework which regulated the relationship between lord and tenant and determined the financial obligations which the one owed the other. Two major categories of tenures can be identified in early modern England.[1] The first, customary tenures, mainly copyhold of inheritance but also in northern England tenant right, were systems of landholding in which precedent served to protect the tenants' right to inherit (and alienate) their land. Customary tenures were inflexible in that rents and sometimes fines, too, were fixed and incapable of being raised without overturning the relationship between lord and tenant. In this case, the lord's real income from his lands was progressively devalued by inflation and he had no means of maintaining the proportion of his tenants' income he expropriated at a time of rising demand for land and its produce. On some manors, the fines taken by the lord were 'arbitrary', but the equity courts instituted a test of 'reasonableness' in the later sixteenth century, placing the tenants' heirs' right of inheritance above the lords' financial interest. By the seventeenth century, customary tenure served as a break on lords' exploitation of their lands making the conversion of copyhold to leasehold a considerable desiderata, but by this date the only practicable way to rid a manor of its copyholders was by uniting the freehold interest with the customary, either through the tenants buying out the lord's freehold or vice versa.[2]

---

[1] For a full description of English tenures in the early modern period, E. Kerridge, *Agrarian Problems in the Sixteenth Century and After* (London, 1969) chs. 2, 3. The present chapter draws on the interpretative framework established by R. W. Hoyle in 'Tenure and the land market in early modern England: or a late contribution to the Brenner debate', *EcHR* 43 (1990), pp. 1–20.

[2] As argued by Hoyle, 'Tenure and the land market', pp. 13–18.

The second group of tenures were leaseholds of various types, all distinguished by the landlord's lack of any continuing obligation to his tenant outside the period of his lease. Tenants held for a fixed term, either of years or lives and the lord was entitled to make a new demise from the end of that term to whosoever would agree with him for an acceptable fine and rent. Copyhold for lives is strictly a customary tenure as its name would suggest, but it ought to be considered as a form of leasehold in that there was generally no legally enforceable obligation on the lord to favour the old tenant's heirs in making a new demise, nor was he restrained (except by his ability to find a tenant) in the fine he asked of a new tenant.[3] In leasehold tenures generally, tenants had to devise strategies to secure the succession of their family. This they did by surrendering unexpired terms for new leases or by securing a lease in reversion, but unscrupulous landlords could equally make leases in reversion to a stranger, dispossessing the sitting tenant when his term ended unless he could secure the reversioner's interest. As Dr Thomas shows in the next chapter, the Crown was such an unscrupulous landlord although it attempted to safeguard the sitting tenants by obliging the reversioners to sell on their interest.

On the Crown's estate, the procedures for a grant of a customary tenancy were quite different to those for the acquisition of a leasehold. Copyholds and tenant rights were granted by the manorial steward in the manorial court. Leaseholds, on the other hand, were granted by a standing commission of senior Exchequer officers sitting in London and were passed (according to the value of the property leased) under either the Great Seal or the Exchequer seal. The complicated procedures involved in the securing of a lease are described by Dr Thomas. The need to travel to London or to employ an agent with ready access to the central bureaucracy obviously made the renewal of a lease a costly undertaking,[4] but the lease conferred the advantage that its ownership could be transferred by sale or inheritance without incurring the payment of a further fine where one was due to the lord on the assignment of a copyhold. Logically, fines on leases needed to be larger than those on copyholds to allow for this, but in reality such considerations were not taken into

[3] On some manors the tenants maintained that their copyholds conferred an estate of inheritance where the lord argued that the copies entitled the tenants to hold for lives only. This was the case on the Crown manor of Brailes (Warws.), E123/26, fols. 42r–3v (1600). For the significance of such cases, Hoyle, 'Tenure and the land market', pp. 7–8.

[4] A point well illustrated by the 1602 commissions, described subsequently, p. 209.

account, and in any case the payment of fines when leases were prematurely surrendered perhaps served to level up the difference between the two.

The tenure by which a tenant held had serious implications for the rent he paid (and the way in which he paid it) and for his lord's profits. All lords were restrained by the need to demand no more than the market could bear. In the mid-sixteenth century, the possibilities for increasing the burden on the tenant were relatively small and in this situation it made little difference whether land was held by customary tenure or copyhold; the lord's income was overwhelmingly drawn from rent rather than fines (which tended to be set at nominal rates, often one or two years' rent).[5] By the end of the century, the demand for land was much greater. The new possibilities this offered were exploited by increasing the fine the tenant paid on the purchase of his term whilst maintaining the ancient rent. In time, the fine came to be calculated in years' value rather than years' (ancient) rent and as fines grew to be impossibly large, lessees came to pay a commercial rent.[6] At an extreme, a tenant might be rack-rented.

By the late sixteenth century, lords whose tenants held by copyhold of inheritance found that the legal security their tenants possessed prohibited them from exploiting the opportunities offered by the buoyancy in the land market. Those lords whose tenants held by lease found themselves in the happy position of being able to negotiate either higher rents or larger fines when leases were renewed, but it was only at a late date that the advantages of the lease became obvious to all. At the point that they did, tenants had every reason to resist attempts to convert their customary tenure into leasehold and the freedom of lords was correspondingly circumscribed.

Legal theory held that copyhold could never be created, for its customary status turned on it having existed from before 'memory of man'. The Crown, it will be shown below, took a more pragmatic line and created copyholds of inheritance as a matter of administrative convenience in the sixteenth century. But the customary status of copyhold could be terminated by making a lease of the lands. Seen from the standpoint of the seventeenth century, the conversion

---

[5] This is well illustrated by table 7.1 below (although it might be added that this compares income from leases with total rent income and makes no allowance for fines on copyholds).

[6] The transition from years' rent to years' value in calculating fines is poorly understood. For the relationship of the two, see below, pp. 228–9.

of copyhold and other customary tenures into leasehold was clearly
the correct thing for lords to do. It may be doubted whether this was
so obvious in the sixteenth century and certainly the Crown showed
no anxiety to change the tenancy by which its tenants held. In his
exhaustive analysis of the particulars for leases for Lincolnshire,
Thomas found only nine instances of copyhold tenements being
taken by lease and observed that when it occurred it was on the
initiative of the tenant.[7]

The notion that leasehold and customary tenures existed as two
distinct categories is complicated by the fact that the Crown made
leases of whole manors or groups of tenements to farmers who thereby
became the immediate lord of copyholders and lessees. One man's
copyhold could well be another man's leasehold. From the tenants'
point of view, the process of sub-contracting the seigniorial relationship was fraught with danger.[8] Where the occupiers held by
lease, they might be oppressed with extortionate demands for the
continuance of their tenancies. A group of cottagers in Rotherham
claimed in 1606 that the Crown's lessee was demanding fines of thirty
years' rent for the renewal of their leases.[9] One might recall the
trouble that the tenants of Dr Spufford's Orwell (Cambridgeshire)
had in their attempts to secure the manorial demesnes from the
Crown's lessees.[10] The Crown tried hard to avoid such profiteering at
the expense of the tenants through covenants and bonds which
obliged the lessee to assign his interest to the tenants in possession,
often for no more than their expenses. A lease of a moor in
Humbleton, Yorkshire, of 1564, contained entirely conventional
clauses voiding the lease if the lessee expelled any of the tenants or
failed to make subleases before the next Lady Day.[11] Where lessees
failed to keep their covenants, the tenants could seek an injunction
from the Exchequer court to compel compliance or ask that the lease
could be voided. As early as 1565, the farmer of the Cheshire manor
of Handbridge was forbidden to demand more than four years' old

---

[7] Thomas, 'Administration of crown lands', pp. 235–6.

[8] This may serve to explain why some tenant communities preferred to take leases of their
manors. It is hard to be certain how many did so, but for a clear case see Wellington, Som.,
CPR 1563–6, no. 2566, the character of which is made clear by E123/1B, fol. 48v. Pettit says
that the tenants of Brigstock, Northants., held a lease of their manor from the thirteenth
century onwards, *Royal Forests*, p. 167; they certainly did in 1650, having taken a contractors'
lease in March 1613. E317/Northants./17, m. 10.   [9] E112/134/934.

[10] M. Spufford, *Contrasting Communities. English Villagers in the Sixteenth and Seventeenth Centuries*
(Cambridge, 1974), pp. 97–8.

[11] *CPR 1563–6*, no. 781, also nos. 786, 1915, 2568. Cases could be multiplied almost infinitely.

rent for a fine on leases of twenty-one years.[12] Bills from tenants who were being expelled or paying excessive fines were a staple of the court's business.[13]

Much the same problems faced the copyhold tenants where the Crown leased the manor with its courts to a farmer. Especially on manors where the tenants held by copies for life, the possibilities for oppression were legion and tenants often sought the mediation of the Exchequer in disputes over the rate of fines, access to commons and in East Anglia, foldcourses. As early as 1564, Winchester, Mildmay and Sackville accepted a series of regulations to govern the relations between the farmer of the manor of Walton and Trimley in Suffolk and the tenants, which included transferring the responsibility for assessing fines from the farmer to the Queen's steward and surveyor.[14] Forty years later, the tenants of the manor of the Duchy of Lancaster's manor of Hinton Waldrist in Berkshire complained that their farmer would neither allow them their widows' estates nor grant them an extra life when two lives were living and generally demanded excessive fines. (Evidence was also offered that the farmer was interferring with the tenants' sale of their copyholds.)[15] An eighty-year-old tenant took the long view when he described how

before John Southby and Richard Southby became farmers, the copyhold tenants did usually pay very small fines for one life in possession, viz, in the time of Sir William Essex being farmer in the time of Henry VIII 6s 8d a yardland at the most and in the time of Mr Mathew being farmer a little after, for adding one life to a copy of two lives after 20s a yardland and about the beginning of the reign of Queen Elizabeth in the time of one John Chamberlain being farmer of the said manor, he the said farmer took but 5 marks for one life in possession of a hold of two yardlands and that the same farmer [Southby] took of one Thomas Dyer for a fine of two lives for $2\frac{1}{2}$ yardlands £30.

The Duchy court could see no wrong in its farmer's fines.

The court doth not find that any of the complainants ... have any just cause to complain against the defendant, yet this court doth think fit that His Majesty's tenants be well and conscionably dealt with in their fines in respect the present tenants may be the more encouraged to better and well husband their inheritance.

[12] E123/1A, fols. 88v–9r.
[13] This whole matter requires a fuller discussion than is possible here.
[14] E123/1A, fols. 123v–4v (articles of February 1563 decreed in May 1573).
[15] DL4/48/28 (depositions); DL5/23, p. 906 (decree), the quotations from the depositions and the decree respectively. See also DL5/24, p. 306.

This willingness to permit the farmer a relatively free hand stands in comparison with the restraint placed on the farmer of Walton. That the later years of the sixteenth century saw a change in attitudes to fining is further suggested by the case of Ombersley (Worcestershire). Here, Dr Large has shown how the tenants (who held by copies of inheritance) claimed to pay fines of two years' rent and had this arrangement confirmed by both their farmer and the Exchequer in 1571. In 1606, the then farmer, Samuel Sandys, abruptly demanded fines of one year's value from his tenants and when they declined, had the 1571 decree quashed by the Exchequer and obtained a ruling which admitted his right to take arbitrary fines. These he took at the rate of one year's value but by 1615 Sandys was negotiating for a further decree permitting him to take fines of up to three years' value.[16]

The Crown, as both Thomas and Hoyle show in the two following chapters, was satisfied to draw most of its income from rent during Elizabeth's reign with the result that by the early seventeenth century it had a great deal to catch up on more forward-looking (or simply fortunate) landlords. In his chapter Thomas describes the ways in which leases were used on the Elizabethan estates and shows how the Crown failed to take advantage of changing economic circumstances, seeing leases in reversion or of concealed lands as a means of rewarding courtiers and friends. Moreover, as Hoyle then shows, it pursued policies towards its customary tenants which appear to have been contrary to its economic interest *as seen from a later standpoint*. Customary tenures were confirmed, new copyholds created and in a few locations a policy of offering renewable forty-year leases was followed. This brought no immediate disadvantage to the revenue drawn from the estates in Elizabeth's reign but served to close the options open to the Jacobean administrators. The means by which they sought to exploit the technical weaknesses of the newly minted copyholders are explored later in this volume.

[16] P. Large, 'Rural society and agricultural change: Ombersley, 1580–1700', in J. Chartres and D. Hey (eds.), *English Rural Society, 1500–1800. Essays in Honour of Joan Thirsk* (Cambridge, 1990), pp. 114–18.

CHAPTER 7

Leases of Crown lands in the reign of Elizabeth I

David Thomas

The Elizabethan government's policy towards leasing its lands was based on its perception that the estate was both a source of income and the means by which its servants could be rewarded. In pursuing this policy, it did much to damage the financial prospects of its successors. This chapter will describe how leases of lands were normally made before turning to their use as the instrument by which concealed lands were recovered, courtiers and servants rewarded and revenue raised. The examples will primarily be drawn from the Exchequer lands in Lincolnshire.

I

Leases of Crown lands were issued by commissioners who were appointed by letters patent. They were the senior Exchequer officials; the Lord Treasurer, Chancellor and Under-Treasurer. For a brief period from 1567 to 1572 the Attorney-General and the Lord Treasurer's Remembrancer were commissioners while the 1599 commission included the Attorney-General and the Chief Justice of King's Bench. The terms of their warrant allowed them to make leases for twenty-one years or three lives at the accustomed rents or more. Decayed property or lands liable to flooding could be leased for longer periods at reduced rents. Entry fines or other payments could be charged. Farmers were to be bound to do all repairs except of sea banks or water works; timber was to be reserved to the Crown. Leases were to be void if rents were not paid within forty days of their being due. The commissions were very careful to specify which types of lease had to pass under the different royal seals, as this was a matter of considerable importance to the officials of the Exchequer and Chancery who received fees for issuing and sealing the leases. The simple rule was that the more valuable the lease, the more administrative stages it had to pass through and, consequently, the more the lessee had to pay in fees.[1]

The commissions gave no guidance as to the rents or fines to be charged. This was in sharp contrast to the very precise instructions which were issued when land was being sold. In 1601, for example, the commissioners for the sale of Crown lands were instructed to sell manors and lands for sixty years' purchase (i.e. the annual rent multiplied by sixty); parsonages impropriate and tithes for fifty and fee-farms for forty.[2]

To initiate the procedure for obtaining a lease, a potential lessee would approach the commissioners and secure a warrant instructing the relevant auditor of land revenue to draw up a particular of the property he wanted to rent. This gave brief details of the lands, buildings and rights as well as information about previous owners and any current leases. It was annotated by the auditor with relevant information about the property, whether, for instance, the buildings were decayed or lands liable to be flooded by the sea. The particular would then be taken to the commissioners who would determine the length, rent and entry fine of the new tenancy. A lease would then be drawn up and a formal instrument issued under one of the seals.[3]

This procedure relied on the auditor who supplied all the information on which the commissioners based their decisions; he was in a very powerful position as there was no independent check on his activities. Naturally, he would receive a fee from the lessee for his assistance. One anonymous, early Jacobean commentator said that when leases were renewed,

there hath been evermore usually given and paid by the tenant or purchaser upon such renovation either to the King's auditor, receiver, surveyor, steward, bailiff or some other of the King's officers, their clerks or servants a far greater sum of money for procuring than hath been usually given to the King and his predecessors for granting and renewing the same estate.[4]

There were some who believed that the auditors had abused their positions when drawing up particulars. Henry Russell claimed that

---

[1] *CPR 1558–60*, pp. 444–5; *CPR 1563–6*, pp. 493–4; *CPR 1566–9*, p. 14; *CPR 1569–72*, pp. 439–40; C66/1340, mm. 29d–31d; C66/1509, mm. 1d–4d.
[2] Henry E. Huntington Library, San Marino, California, Ellesmere MS 1574; R. B. Outhwaite, 'The price of crown land at the turn of the sixteenth century', *EcHR* 20 (1967), p. 238, and see above, pp. 19–21.
[3] M. S. Giuseppi, *Guide to the Contents of the Public Record Office* (3 vols., London, 1963–8), I, p. 74; rated particulars are in the class E310, transcripts of leases are in E311.
[4] BL, Cotton MS Titus B IV, fol. 267.

Thomas Neale had falsely described properties as being in decay or in danger of flooding to enable lessees to get leases on more favourable terms.[5] A bill introduced in the 1601 Parliament accused the auditors of falsely claiming that lands were charged with rents, pensions, annuities, etc., and that as a result the Crown had granted or leased various properties at far below their real values. The bill would have authorised the Lord Treasurer, Chancellor and barons of the Exchequer to hear and determine cases against offending auditors. It was moved late in the session and was not proceeded with because it had been badly drafted.[6]

The Crown had one potential protection against deliberate undervaluation of its properties. Each lease included a clause which stated that if someone were to offer a higher rent than the existing tenant, then the lessee would be bound to match the higher offer. Unfortunately, this requirement that the Crown lands should never be knowingly undersold seems to have been rarely used and only one case has been found for the whole of Elizabeth's reign. Sir Edward Hoby offered to pay £100 per annum more for the manors of Middleton and Marden in Kent which were leased to a Mr Bodley for £100. The Lord Treasurer told Bodley that he would have to offer as much or else lose his lease. Bodley said that he was willing to pay an additional fine of 500 marks if his tenancy could be extended from thirty-three to sixty years at the present rent. The matter ended inconclusively and no subsequent lease to Bodley or Hoby has yet been found.[7]

This raises the question of whether there was a competitive market for leases of individual Crown lands in this period. The evidence shows very clearly that most leases were granted to existing lessees or their assignees. Of 822 leases of land in Elizabethan Lincolnshire, 519 were granted on surrender, that is before the existing tenancy had expired, and of these, 357 went to people who can be identified as the current tenants. Probably most of the other early surrenders were also regranted to the relatives or assignees of the sitting tenants. Of the 370 cases in which the lease had expired or where there is no information about earlier leases, 100 were granted to the sitting tenants or their relatives.[8] There is also a remarkable shortage of

---

[5] BL, Lansd. MS 3, fols. 177–90.

[6] SP12/283, no. 28; *LJ*, II, pp. 242, 244, 254, 256, 257; Sir Simonds D'Ewes, *Journal of All the Parliaments during the Reign of Queen Elizabeth* (1682, repr. Shannon, 1973), p. 688.

[7] HMC, *Salisbury*, IV, p. 82.　　[8] Thomas, 'Administration of crown lands', pp. 202–7.

petitions for leases of Crown lands. A very few do survive; lord Willoughby d'Eresby, for example, asked Burghley for a lease of Edenham parsonage because he was concerned 'what trouble a stranger may bring unto me for wrangling for tithe wood, wool and lamb and for all other tithes appertaining to my manor of Edenham and demesnes of Grimsthorpe'; but examples such as this are comparatively rare.[9]

It is quite clear that there was a great continuity of tenancy on the Crown lands. Tenants would either obtain renewals of leases for themselves or else would assign their interests and the Crown would automatically grant leases to the assignees. This absence of competition should not have been an obstacle to increasing rents for most tenants had a long-term interest in retaining their holdings and would have been aware of the general increase in the level of interest and rents.

In fact, the commissioners for leases did not increase rents at all during this period and tenants continued to pay at the rates charged by the monasteries and other former owners of the lands. It may have been hard to push up rents because the Crown did not have sufficiently detailed information about its properties to make an up-to-date valuation. The Royal Commission of 1552 suggested that entry fines of twice the annual rent should be charged on new leases and from the early 1550s, the Crown began to use fines as a way of compensating itself for the low level of rents. The Duchy of Lancaster began charging fines for leases in 1551–2.[10]

By the start of Elizabeth's reign, a sophisticated system for assessing fines appears to have emerged. The commissioners would review the particulars and determine the level of the entry fine by assessing the real value of the property above the rent, taking into account any special features, for instance, the early surrender of a lease. Entry fines varied from four to eight times the annual rent and Habakkuk estimated that on a lease of twenty-one years, a fine of four years' rent corresponded to an annual value of 40 per cent in excess of the rent, a fine of five years' rent an excess of 50 per cent and a fine of six times the rent to an excess of 60 per cent. The Crown appears to have had a practical method of ensuring that its income from land kept up with inflation.[11]

---

[9] BL, Lansd. MS 45, fol. 69.
[10] Richardson, *1552 Report*, p. 183; H. J. Habakkuk, 'The market for monastic property, 1539–1603', *EcHR* 10 (1957–8), pp. 370–1; Somerville, *Duchy of Lancaster*, i, p. 306.
[11] Habakkuk, 'The market for monastic property', p. 371.

In 1563, for reasons which cannot now be explained, the Crown threw this system away. Between 1563 and the end of Elizabeth's reign, only two fines for leases of lands in Lincolnshire were assessed at more than four times the annual rent. A fine of four years' rent became standard.[12] In many cases, of course, lower fines were charged, either because the lease was being surrendered early or because the property was already let at a market rent. Land which the Crown acquired in exchanges was normally let at rack-rents and so no fines could be charged. In 1570, the auditor noted on a particular of Sempringham rectory that it had been bought from Henry VIII by lord Clinton and that the rent had then been £6 18s od; Clinton had managed to increase the rent to £30 and then gave it back to the Queen in exchange for other properties. The auditor said that the rent 'as is reported' was very great and consequently no fine was charged when the new lease was made.[13] Fines were generally lower if the property was in decay or burdened with other charges. In 1569, a particular was drawn up of a property called Dowsdale House, a fishery and several parcels of ground belonging to it. The auditor reported that the 'premises called Dowsdale house is a poor tenement where unto doth not belong one rood of land and the charge of the banks [the sea walls or river banks] there [is] so great as the commodity of the fishing many years doth not countervail the charges. The rest of the parcels fineable enough.' A fine of four years' rent was charged for the land; no charge was made for the house or the fishery.[14]

The gradual rise in the rates at which Crown land was sold, from thirty years' annual value in the 1560s to forty years' in the later 1590s (itself less than the Crown desired) shows how the Crown was fully aware that the rents did not reflect their true value.[15] Yet it made no effort to increase them and it abandoned the use of entry fines as a way of obtaining a share of rising property values. This is evidence that the Crown did not primarily manage its lands as a source of income.

Moreover, the yield of entry fines fell consistently through the reign. This was partly due to changes in leasing policy which will be discussed below. To some extent, it was also due to the Crown's policy of exchanging land; this meant that a higher proportion of the royal

---

[12] Thomas, 'Administration of crown lands', p. 210.   [13] E310/17/77, m. 9.

[14] E310/17/76, m. 42.

[15] For the rates at which Crown land was sold in Elizabeth's reign, see above, pp. 19–21.

Table 7.1. *Revenue from rents and fines in Lincolnshire, 1558–1602*

	Average income from rents £	Average income from fines £	Fines as % of rent
1558–62	4,646	262	6
1562–7	4,293	216	5
1567–72	4,964	371	7
1572–7	5,131	250	5
1577–82	5,463	356	7
1582–7	5,978	273	5
1587–92	6,073	197	3
1592–7	5,922	197	3
1597–1602	5,472	73	1

Sources: rental income drawn from SC6/Eliz./1306–50; income from fines compiled from E401/1794–871 with gaps filled by E401/2354–8, 2283, 2286, 1290.

estate was let at rents which fully reflected its value.[16] In addition, tenants seem to have become more enthusiastic about surrendering leases early. In the period 1560–75, 36 per cent of leases of land in Lincolnshire were surrendered early compared with 74 per cent in 1576–1602. The level of entry fines closely reflects this trend; 51 per cent of leases granted before 1576 had fines of four times the annual rent or more compared with only 9 per cent of those granted during the rest of the reign.[17]

The motive of tenants prematurely surrendering their leases can only be guessed at, but it may be that as they saw the value of their holdings rising and their rents remaining static, they thought it prudent to lock into their good fortune before the Crown became aware of economic realities. Another reason may have been that they were concerned about the Crown's increasing use of leases in reversion as a way of rewarding its subjects.[18] Tenants may have sought the early renewal of their leases in order to make their properties less attractive to courtiers seeking to profit from the Crown lands. The number of renewals increased towards the end of the reign in parallel with the growth of this method of rewarding Crown servants.

[16] See above, pp. 79–80.   [17] Thomas, 'Administration of crown lands', p. 211.
[18] See below, pp. 184–90.

The effect on the Crown's finances was predictable. In the period 1558–62, it received an average of £4,646 a year in rent from its Lincolnshire estates; an additional 6 per cent was earned from entry fines. In the last five years of the reign, the Crown's average revenue from fines was only equivalent to 1 per cent of its rental income. As table 7.1 shows, during Elizabeth's reign the Crown did not use fines as a way of compensating itself for static rents in a period of inflation.[19]

Lincolnshire is a coastal county and, in the sixteenth century, was much subject to flooding. One clear policy pursued by the Crown was to attempt to shift on to its tenants the cost of defending its lands against the sea. The previous policy had been for the Crown to accept this responsibility itself, but from about 1563, it began to slough off the burden.[20] The procedure was that when the leases were renewed, the tenants would become liable to pay for sea defences, but in recompense, would be excused from paying an entry fine. In 1565, a particular of lands in Hotofte and Mablethorpe was rated for John Purvey; no fine was charged because 'he shall be bound to the reparations of the seacharges and the channel which now the Queen's majesty by covenant of the leases doth bear'.[21] This was generally a once-and-for-all procedure; when the Crown had sacrificed an entry fine and compelled the tenant to accept responsibility for defending a property against the sea, it would impose the same conditions in future leases, but would not feel itself bound to make concessions over the fine. In 1566, some property in Hotofte was leased to Richard More. Previously, the Queen had spent a great deal to defend it against flooding, but More agreed to bear the costs himself. In 1582, the lease was renewed and the auditor reported 'the defence of the banks is chargeable sometimes in the year as the tenant sayeth, but the Queen's majesty [is] at no charge by reason of the covenant in the letters patent'.[22] A fine of two years' rent was charged. In all, 12 per cent of Lincolnshire leases had reduced fines because of the cost of sea defences.

The cost of repairing buildings was also shifted on to the tenants. Much of the Crown's property in Lincolnshire seems to have been in a poor state of repair. Fifty-six particulars mention buildings in

---

[19] Thomas, 'Administration of crown lands', p. 213.   [20] See also above, pp. 39–42.
[21] E310/17/77, m. 43.   [22] *Ibid.*, m. 28; E310/18/86, m. 36.

decay. Mills were a severe problem and seventeen of them were in need of maintenance. When leasing such property, the Crown normally granted a long lease with a low fine on condition that the tenant undertook the necessary repair work.

In return for the tenants' acceptance of these obligations, the Crown would sometimes grant longer leases of properties which were decayed or prone to be flooded. About 5 per cent of Elizabethan leases of lands in Lincolnshire were for longer than the standard period of twenty-one years or three lives.

The policy of transferring to its tenants the cost of maintaining property and protecting it against the sea was one of the Crown's few successes in the administration of its lands. One anonymous contemporary observer claimed that this had saved almost £5,000 per annum.[23] It is, however, easier to see this as an aspect of the overall Elizabethan policy of economy and reduction of expenditure than as part of a considered plan for maximising the income from its estates.

Turning to the terms of the leases, the second half of the reign saw a marked change in the periods for which leases were granted. From 1560 to 1580, there was only one lease for lives of lands in Lincolnshire; from 1581 onwards, 19 per cent of leases were for three lives. The reasons for this change are not at all clear. From the tenants' point of view, they were one way of creating a sort of family settlement and it appears that some people were prepared to pay heavily for the opportunity to provide security for their children; fear that the Crown may have been about to grant a lease in reversion over their heads may have been an additional motivating factor.[24] Edward Stanhope had a lease of Thornton rectory which still had fifty-one years to run but he was willing to surrender this in order to get a lease for the lives of his three sons.[25] At the same time, he was also seeking a lease of another property for the lives of three of his daughters.[26]

Leases for lives had some advantages for property owners. The contemporary agricultural writer Barnaby Googe believed that they provided continuity and ensured a close link between the tenant and

---

[23] BL, Lansd. MS 105, fol. 141v.
[24] On the complex legal status of leases for lives, see W. S. Holdsworth, *A History of English Law* (16 vols., 1903–64), VII, pp. 239–50; A. W. B. Simpson, *An Introduction to the History of the Land Law* (Oxford, 1961), pp. 229–33. On leases in reversion, see below, pp. 184–90.
[25] E310/17/78, m. 40   [26] E310/18/82, m. 42.

his land.[27] The lives of three living people were assumed to be equivalent to twenty-one years, although there was always a chance that the lease could be terminated much earlier. All three tenants of a lease for lives granted in 1584 were dead by 1595.[28]

The Crown was also entitled to a heriot, usually the best beast, on every change of tenant during a lease for lives. Unfortunately, the Exchequer did not have the administrative resources to enforce its rights. In 1586, a petitioner reported that there had been an increasing tendency during the previous few years for Crown tenants to exchange leases for years for leases for lives and that heriots were due but had not been collected. Burghley was sufficiently interested to ask all the auditors to make a return of the heriots they had collected; they replied that, although some had been collected from copyhold lands, none had been received from leasehold property. What seems to have happened is that the auditors were unaware of the specific terms of the leases for lives; they wrote the particulars for leases and kept them in their possession, but the requirement for a heriot was only added when the formal leases were drawn up and these were not seen by the auditors. In any event, Burghley does not seem to have pursued the matter. In 1611, his son, Salisbury, received a letter setting out the problem again. The writer claimed that leases were often not enrolled with the auditors and even when they were, the task of discovering when tenants had died was too time-consuming and difficult. These missing cattle are not significant in terms of the Crown's revenues for Burghley's petitioner only offered to pay £20 per annum for the right to collect all royal heriots, but they are illustrative of the Exchequer's inability to deal with the complexities of land administration and its failure to maximise the Crown's income.[29]

The Crown had two major options in the management of its manors. Manors could be kept in hand and administered through stewards, or put out to lease. The administration of manors kept in demesne posed a number of difficult problems. First, the rents received and the entry fines were too low. Secondly, the staff costs were too high; a Jacobean survey showed that the fees paid to officials were considerably more

---

[27] Barnaby Googe (trans.), *Foure Bookes of Husbandry...Conteyning the Whole Arte and Trade of Husbandry, Gardening, Graffing and Planting,* by Conrad Heresbach (1577), fol. 47v.

[28] E310/17/80, m. 64.

[29] BL, Lansd. MS 47, fols. 14–45; Add. MS 10038, fols 260–1.

than the revenue collected from fines and amercements.[30] Thirdly, there was a real problem of control; the stewards were responsible for making copyhold grants and because their actions were not closely supervised, they were in a strong position to demand bribes from tenants. In 1585, it was discovered that the deputy steward and understeward of the manor of Gedney had been engaging in systematic corruption. They would say to people wishing to take copyholds 'if you will consider me well, I will ease you of your fines'. They then took a large fee, but only recorded a small sum in the court rolls. The feoffees of Gedney paid a fine of £1 and a bribe of £5 13s 4d for some escheat lands 'otherwise they would not be admitted'.[31] In 1603, four officials on royal manors in Wiltshire and Gloucestershire were heavily fined by the Exchequer for similar abuses. In 1600, it was discovered that Carew Raleigh had been taking gratuities in return for charging low entry fines when he was steward of the manor of Mere.[32]

This systematic abuse of power to make copies was part of a wider corruption which threatened the Crown's manorial revenues. Sir Robert Johnson described how stewards had leased demesne lands as copyhold of inheritance and engrossed several separate tenements in one copy, thus depriving the Crown of heriots, and had failed to reserve rents on the copies they had granted.[33]

Opinion varied as to the best way of dealing with manors. Some writers favoured the idea that the Crown should move out of their management altogether. Copyhold should be converted to leasehold so that the Exchequer, rather than manorial stewards, would be responsible for granting leases. Sir Lawrence Tanfield argued in 1609 that 'by this means the abuses of stewards will be prevented, His Majesty's charge of many stewards and bailiffs eased and his yearly revenue much increased'.[34]

Alternatively, the Crown could let manors, either just the profits of the court, or the lands and manorial rights, to lords farmers. The Privy Council in Mary's reign appeared to favour this solution as it provided greater certainty of revenue, meant that no fees or

---

[30] BL, Add. MS 10038, fol. 9v (printed from another text in Spedding, *Bacon*, IV, p. 322).

[31] E178/1310.

[32] E123/28, fol. 358; E. Kerridge, 'The movement of rent, 1540–1640', *EcHR* 6 (1953), p. 32. See below, pp. 209–10.

[33] Johnson, *Letter*, BL, Add. MS 41613, fols. 95–6 (Bodl., MS Perrot 7, fols. 55r–9r).

[34] Quoted by G. R. Batho, 'Landlords in England: the crown', in *Agrarian History*, IV, p. 270.

maintenance costs would have to be paid, would cut down on corruption and would provide greater protection for the tenants.[35] The opponents of this approach believed that letting manors would be unprofitable and would break the link between the Crown and its tenants. Moreover, the farmers would not bother to preserve the customs and casual sources of profits. These writers tended to favour a continuation of the current system but with a greater emphasis on efficiency and supervision. The opponents of farming included men with real experience of managing the Crown lands, John Pym, Sir Robert Johnson and John Norden.[36]

The Elizabethan tendency was to farm whole manors. In Lincolnshire the Crown held seventy-two manors at the start of the reign and of these twenty-seven were leased to lords farmers. By 1603, another ten had been leased out. This was not always successful. In two cases, the Crown failed to make the lessee responsible for paying the fees of stewards and the costs of holding the courts and consequently there was no net financial benefit.

One major problem facing the Crown when granting leases was that it often simply did not have enough information about its lands to be able to provide its tenants with a satisfactory title.[37] The result was that when leases were made, tenants often found themselves in bitter and expensive litigation to resolve problems caused by the Crown's ignorance. In 1583, Richard Askue received a lease of lands in Great Paunton. Unfortunately, this land was claimed by Thomas Coney the elder and Thomas Coney the younger as their own. Askue took the matter to the Exchequer which found in his favour but this was only the start of his troubles, for the Crown's land was mixed with the Coneys' property and nobody could say which was which. Four separate commissions were issued from the Exchequer, all of which failed to identify the land Askue thought he had leased. Eventually, in 1597, the court forced the Coneys to give Askue 40 acres plus costs and compensation for lost rent. Askue's views on the incident are not recorded.[38]

In other cases, sloppy drafting deprived the Crown of much needed revenue. In a 1551 lease of the rectories of Sempringham and

---

[35] A report by the 'lords of the Council', quoted by Vernon, *Considerations*, pp. 69–70, and further considered above, pp. 34, 37–9.

[36] For Pym, BL, Add. MS 12504, fol. 168; Johnson, *Letter*, BL Add. MS 41613, fol. 120v (Bodl., MS Perrot 7, fol. 55r–v); Norden, Kerridge, 'Movement of rent', p. 32.

[37] On the Crown's lack of information about its lands, see above, pp. 47–8, 65–7.

[38] E123/22, fol. 233v; E123/23, fols. 133v–4v, 217, 259; E112/24/222.

Stow Green to lord Clinton, the Exchequer omitted to make provision
for the stipends of the vicars of the two churches. Clinton simply
refused to hand over half the rent of the rectories and claimed he was
using it to pay the vicars; the Exchequer initially tried to compel him
to pay but then backed down.[39]

II

Inevitably, the Crown's ignorance about its lands led to much
property being concealed. At the time of the dissolution of the
monasteries and chantries, the officials of the Court of Augmentations
failed to identify many lands and rights which should have passed to
the Crown. The occupiers wisely said nothing and continued to enjoy
the lands untroubled by royal bailiff or rent collector. This problem
was widely known and in the 1560s the government began to take
action with the issue of warrants to officials to hunt for concealed
lands. The method was comparatively simple; a special commission
was issued from the Exchequer or Duchy of Lancaster at the request
of a concealment hunter. The commissioners had to enquire in
specified parishes whether there was any concealed land; any
property which was discovered was granted to the concealment
hunter who would pay a fee-farm rent to the Crown. Later, people
were allowed to purchase any land they had discovered at a special
low rate to compensate them for the costs and hazards of their
investigations.

The activities of the hunters stirred up a great deal of opposition
and there was a series of half-hearted attempts by government to
restrict them. The problem was, however, that the Crown derived
income from rediscovered rents and from the revenue from sales. In
1581, the Crown licensed Edward Stafford to pursue concealments;
he was to have a lease for sixty years of any land he discovered.
Stafford's patent was taken over by Edward Dyer who, with his
partner William Tipper, did much to blacken the reputation of
concealment hunting. In 1583, Sir James Croft, Controller of the
household, adopted a different approach; he obtained a patent to
compound with alleged owners of concealed land. They would have
to pay a composition to Croft and obtain a lease of their property
from the Crown at full rent. In 1600, Elizabethan concealment

---

[39] E368/387, recorda, Hilary, m. 15.

hunting was stopped by the creation of a body of Commissioners to Compound for Defective Titles, but the game resumed with a vengeance under James I.[40]

Apart from grants of licences to courtiers and officials, concealed lands were also pursued at a local level. Here the mechanism was rather different; the Crown would grant speculative leases of allegedly concealed lands to opportunistic concealment hunters who undertook to recover the properties. Fifty-two such leases were granted in Lincolnshire in Elizabeth's reign. In a few cases, they were issued after the lessee had already proved the Queen's title. In 1566, Hugh Bands of Ropsley sued out a commission to enquire into concealed lands in Barston, Pickworth and other places. The commissioners met and found that the lands had been given for superstitious uses. The return to the commission was engrossed into a particular and Bands was given a lease of the property at the rents found by the commissioners.[41]

Most leases of this sort, however, were purely speculative, the grantee merely offering to disprove the title of the existing landholder. In 1584, Thomas Kirkham obtained a lease of a property called the Nuns in Grantham which belonged to one John Bellow and was already leased to a certain Sowcliff who was expecting to enjoy it for another forty years. Kirkham offered to go to law at his own expense to overthrow Bellow and Sowcliff's titles.[42]

The majority of grantees appear to have been local men although a few can be positively identified as officials on the royal estates; indeed, discovering a parcel of concealed land may have been one way in which people could bring themselves to the attention of the Exchequer. In five cases, men who had discovered such property were subsequently appointed as officials on the royal estate. The appointment of Richard More as Receiver-General in Lincolnshire followed his discovery of various concealed properties in the south-west of the country.[43]

In a few cases, existing tenants obtained leases to rectify anomalies with the titles to properties they already held. In 1575, the auditor

---

[40] C. J. Kitching, 'The quest for concealed lands in the reign of Elizabeth I', *TRHS*, fifth ser., 24 (1974), pp. 63–78; also H. H. Lockwood, 'Those greedy hunters after concealed lands', in K. Neale (ed.), *An Essex Tribute. Essays Presented to Frederick G. Emmison* (London, 1987). Joan Thirsk discusses the later history of concealment hunting in ch. 11 below.

[41] E310/17/76, m. 38; E178/2924.   [42] E310/18/82, m. 56.

[43] E310/18/83, m. 4; *CPR 1566–9*, p. 335.

reported that one third of the tithes of grain in Fleet had been concealed. A lease was granted to the rector of Fleet and his successors.[44]

Concealment hunting was deeply unpopular. It was widely regarded as a breach of faith with men who had given land for pious uses, it was a disincentive to spending on the service of God, it eroded the income of preachers and teachers and it led to expensive and tedious litigation. Some hunters were sufficiently unwise to attack the estates of powerful bodies: cathedrals, universities and city corporations. The activities of the concealment hunters often brought them into conflict with local communities and they must have caused deep resentment and ill-will. One example may illustrate this. In 1574, George Hothersall, an illiterate tailor from London, obtained a lease of some salt cotes in Gedney and Moulton. He had heard that they were concealed and later claimed to have spent £212 on recovering them for the Crown. There was no doubt about the validity of his claim; they had been built without licence on Crown property. However, the local inhabitants claimed that the salt cotes had been built for charitable purposes and the profits were used for maintaining the sea banks, repairing local churches and supporting the poor, as well as paying for soldiers to 'serve the progenitors of the Queen's majesty in their wars'. The Exchequer was not impressed and the locals were ordered to allow Hothersall to take possession of the salt cotes.[45]

The problems faced by the inhabitants of Gedney and Moulton brings us up against one of the characteristic weaknesses of the Elizabethan regime. Lacking the necessary administrative apparatus to manage its affairs effectively, it chose to hand over the problem to private enterprise, allowing courtiers and others to collect royal rights or enforce royal powers. The result was, inevitably, abuse of the delegated authority and resentment by the subject. The attack by the illiterate tailor on the Gedney salt cotes stemmed from the Crown's inability to survey and manage its lands. Exact parallels can be found in the use of professional informers to enforce penal statutes or purveyors to supply the royal household and patentees to enforce economic regulations.[46]

---

[44] E310/17/79, m. 18.

[45] E310/18/85, m. 34; E112/23/80; E112/23/82; E123/5, fols. 166, 219, 241.

[46] M. W. Beresford, 'The common informer, the penal statutes and economic regulation', *EcHR* 10 (1957–8), pp. 221–38; P. Williams, 'The crown and the counties', in C. Haigh (ed.), *The Reign of Elizabeth I* (Basingstoke, 1984), pp. 131–5.

III

One of the main uses which the Crown made of its lands in Lincolnshire in Elizabeth's reign was as a source of patronage. The Elizabethan government was faced with a deficit on its extraordinary account and with the ever-present problem of inflation. It tried to solve the first problem by maintaining a surplus on its ordinary account by pushing up the income from the customs and a rigid policy of economy.[47] However, inflation meant that that the wages of its servants rapidly lost value; moreover, it did not pay retirement pensions and had to find some way of allowing royal servants to make provision for their old age. Rather than increasing their salaries, the government chose to reward them in ways which would not cost it any money. Many were allowed 'to use royal authority to levy money on their own account from the consumer or the taxpayer'.[48] In this approach to paying its servants, it behaved similarly to other leading landowners; the Stanleys, earls of Derby, for example, rewarded their followers with grants of land, advowsons and offices. Writing in 1669, Dudley, lord North, said 'for not a full century of years past, masters gave small wages and their servants expected reward by a good pennyworth in some farm when they were aged'.[49]

The granting of land was an obvious way of rewarding royal servants. During the twenty years after the dissolution, when the Crown was well endowed with property, it could afford to give it away to reward loyal service or buy support. The heaviest concentration of giving occurred in the period 1536–40 and under Edward VI. About a quarter of the Devon monastic lands were given away to the Crown's clients before the accession of Elizabeth.[50]

By the 1550s, the Crown's landed estate had been much reduced and it moved from giving land away to granting leases on favourable

[47] W. R. Scott, *The Constitution and Finance of English, Scottish and Irish Joint-Stock Companies to 1720* (3 vols., Cambridge, 1912, repr. 1951), III, pp. 493–509.

[48] L. Stone, *The Crisis of the Aristocracy, 1558–1641* (Oxford, 1965), p. 425; R. C. Braddock, 'The rewards of office-holding in Tudor England', *JBS* 14 (1975), p. 37; W. T. MacCaffrey, 'Place and patronage in Elizabethan politics', in S. T. Bindoff, J. Hurstfield and C. H. Williams (eds.), *Elizabethan Government and Society. Essays Presented to Sir John Neale* (London, 1961), pp. 117–21.

[49] B. Coward, *The Stanleys, Lords Stanley and Earls of Derby, 1385–1672* (Chetham Soc. third ser., 30, 1983), pp. 87–9.

[50] K. H. S. Wyndham, 'Crown land and royal patronage in mid-sixteenth century England', *JBS* 19 (1979–80), pp. 23–5; J. A. Youings, 'The terms of the disposal of the Devon monastic lands 1536–58', *EHR* 69 (1954), p. 30.

terms. In the period 1550–3, about a third of leases of land in Somerset bore some mark of royal favour. In the reign of Elizabeth, the favourable lease and, specifically, the lease in reversion, became the standard method of rewarding members of the Queen's household. In Somerset, 37 per cent of leases of lands made in the period 1566–75 were on favourable terms.[51] In Lincolnshire, about a quarter of all Crown leases were granted in reversion.[52]

The grant of a lease in reversion was one of the more popular types of royal patronage to which a royal servant could aspire. In 1587, Julius Caesar, then a judge of the Admiralty Court, wrote to Walsingham asking for some financial help from the Crown. He wanted to be made either a Master of Requests, or Provost of Eton or master of a hospital, or to have a vacant deanery, or a lease in reversion of lands worth 100 marks.[53] In 1586, a list was compiled of petitions from members of the household in the hands of John Herbert, Master of Requests; it contains abstracts of twenty-seven petitions for rewards and of these, twenty were for leases in reversion.[54]

This form of patronage was uniquely a late Elizabethan phenomenon of which very few examples can be found from before 1588. It was entirely under the personal control of the Queen. The commissioners for leases were unable to grant leases in reversion without the Queen's specific instruction. The normal procedure was for a suitor to address a petition to Elizabeth who would then convey her assent to the commissioners either formally by means of a signet warrant or informally through a Master of Requests or a senior courtier. In many cases, the Queen kept the decision as to the fine and term of the lease in her own hands. In 1592, she agreed to grant a lease in reversion to Richard Coningsby 'reserving the number of years to her own princely limitation at the signing of the book'. In at least one case, it appears that she may have written the value of the lands to be granted on a signet warrant when she was signing it.[55]

[51] Wyndham, 'Crown land', pp. 29–30, and see also David Thomas, 'Leases in reversion on the Crown's lands, 1558–1603', *EcHR* 30 (1977), pp. 67–72.
[52] Thomas, 'Administration of crown lands', p. 283.
[53] L. M. Hill, *Bench and Bureaucracy. The Public Career of Sir Julius Caesar, 1580–1636* (Cambridge, 1988), p. 63.   [54] BL, Lansd. MS 51, fols. 69–74.
[55] The method of obtaining a lease in reversion can be inferred from an examination of the particulars for leases in the PRO. A representative example is E310/40/4, mm. 286–7; for the grant to Coningsby, Hatfield House, Salisbury MSS, Petition 2002; for the warrant signed by the Queen, E310/40/4, m. 382.

In a few cases, leases in reversion were granted to sitting tenants. Only 5 per cent of such leases in Lincolnshire were granted in this way and entry fines were charged on all of them. For a Crown tenant who wished to extend his lease, obtaining a lease in reversion to commence once his present interest had expired was a complex and elaborate process, involving a petition to the Queen and the drawing up of a signet warrant, which was presumably much more expensive than simply surrendering an existing lease and asking for it to be renewed. The main reason why tenants took this route was that they were afraid that a lease in reversion was about to be granted to someone else and that they would then risk losing their lands, or have to negotiate with the new grantee once their existing lease had expired. In 1591, Francis Colby petitioned for a lease of a Suffolk manor 'for that he is credibly informed that there is means made to procure a lease in reversion of the premises over his head'.[56]

The majority of such leases were granted as a form of patronage. A very few went to senior officials, including lord North, Sir Henry Cobham the diplomat and Sir Owen Hopton, Lieutenant of the Tower. Other grantees included a clerk of the signet and four gentlemen pensioners. The largest category of grantees (64 out of the 153 leases of land in Lincolnshire) were servants of the Queen's household. These ranged from senior figures such as Roger Manners, esquire for the body, down to comparatively humble people such as Anne Twist, laundress for the body and Arthur Ashby, yeoman of the woodyard, and musicians like John Bull, William Byrd and Thomas Tallis. Many such leases were clearly a form of retirement pension and were given for long service. Randolph Hatton received a lease in reversion because he had served the Crown for a long time 'and that he groweth into years and is become lame and impotent'.[57] Widows of royal servants were also beneficiaries. Elizabeth Aughton, widow of a yeoman of the scalding house, asked for a lease in reversion to be granted to John Lampen, the tenant of certain tithes in Cornwall, as he would then support her.[58]

In other cases, the Crown gave leases in reversion to people to whom it owed money. These included William Bence whose ship had been impressed by Sir John Hawkins for transporting soldiers and then lost, as well as Nicholas Hilliard who had been paid for

---

[56] Hatfield House, Salisbury MSS, Petition 723.   [57] E310/41/14, mm. 364–8.
[58] HMC, *Salisbury*, v, p. 146.

engraving the Great Seal.[59] Ironically, the Queen granted a lease to Sir James Croft in 1586 as compensation for the surrender of his patent for concealed lands; he was being deprived of one right to exploit the Crown lands for his own profit and being given another one in exchange.[60]

The essence of leases in reversion was the exploitation of the Crown lands for private grain. Most were granted without entry fines and were a delegation to the grantees of the Crown's right to levy this type of revenue. In a number of cases, the beneficiaries were required to enter bonds that they would assign their interest to the sitting tenants. Burghley noted on a particular of 1575 that a bond should be taken that the sitting tenants would not be expelled, but that they would be granted the interest in the premises 'upon reasonable fines'.[61] The letters patent granting a lease in reversion to Ellis Wynne at the suit of two yeomen of the Chamber contained the condition that the lessee was to make leases of the premises to the sitting tenants within a year for the rents at which they currently held the properties, or at rents to be determined by the Lord Treasurer and Chancellor of the Exchequer.[62]

The use of bonds to protect the sitting tenants appears to date from the early 1570s. About the same time, there was another change in the method of granting leases in reversion. The Crown began to grant leases which included property in more than one county. Of 133 leases of lands in Lincolnshire in the period 1569–1603, 105 also included land in at least one other county. A representative example is the 1588 lease to Thomas Thoroughgood and Freeman Young, two of the yeomen of the guard. This included land in five counties with a total annual value of £20 10s 0d of which the largest parcel was one in Northamptonshire valued at £8 per annum.[63]

Clearly, members of the royal household could not expect to enjoy such property themselves, nor could they have the time or expertise to negotiate with the sitting tenants. Instead, they used agents to act on their behalf. Twenty-seven leases in reversion of lands in Lincolnshire were granted to people who appear to have been acting as intermediaries. When the Queen wished to compensate William Bence for the loss of his ship, she granted a lease to Henry Best, scrivener. Of the people who obtained leases in reversion at the suit of royal clients, four, Best, John Wells, Robert Holland and John

[59] Ibid., vi, p. 34; E310/41/15, m. 511.   [60] E310/41/14, m. 393.
[61] E310/40/4, m. 390.   [62] C66/1446, m. 32.   [63] E310/41/16, mm. 588–95.

Thompson have been identified by Dr Outhwaite as agents involved in the sale of Crown lands.[64] Sometimes the whole process can be seen at work. In 1588, John Tailor, an 'ancient servant' of the Queen, had the lease in reversion of certain property in Ferriby which was in the tenure of John Kiddall. Tailor released his interest to Thomas Parke of London, who sold it to William Kiddall in 1595.[65]

It is not easy to discover what profits were made from leases in reversion as the evidence is scattered and difficult to interpret. The profit from an individual grant would be determined by the length of any unexpired leases on the property, the difference between the rent paid to the Crown and the real value of the lands and by the skill of the grantee in negotiating with the sitting tenants. There is some evidence that royal servants expected to make between seven and nine times the annual rent of the property. In 1574, William Herle told Burghley that Cocker of the Pantry had received seven years' fine for his lease in reversion.[66] In 1595, John Danyell offered Robert Cecil a bribe of £100 if he would arrange for the Crown to accept the surrender of Danyell's annuity of £40 per annum and grant him a lease in reversion of lands of equivalent value. Danyell indicated that he intended to sell or exchange his annuity for £280.[67] Clearly, Danyell expected to make at least £380 from his lease in reversion, i.e. the capital value of his annuity plus the bribe to Cecil. So he hoped to make a profit of at least nine and a half times the rent on his lease.

In two other cases, royal servants surrendered annuities in return for leases in reversion of lands of the same annual value as the annuities they were surrendering.[68] Like Danyell, they may have regarded the capital value of their annuities and thus the profits they hoped to make from their leases as about seven times their annual value.

It is also possible to point to reversioners making more spectacular profits. In 1599, three yeomen of the cellar got a lease of Luddington rectory which was to run for forty years from 1611 at an annual rent of £18. They sold their interest for an unknown sum to Sir Arthur Savage. In 1604, Savage assigned the lease to Thomas Lillingston for £634 10s 0d or eighteen years' rent. In 1614, Lillingston sold the

---

[64] R. B. Outhwaite, 'Who bought crown lands? The pattern of purchases, 1589–1603', *BIHR* 44 (1971), pp. 22, 30.   [65] E310/41/15, m. 467; LR1/156, fol. 55.
[66] BL, Lansd. MS 19, fol. 53v.   [67] HMC, *Salisbury*, v, p. 496.
[68] *Ibid.*, III, p. 362; E310/41/17, mm. 699–702.

residue of his lease for £1,200.[69] Robert Dalliston sold a lease in reversion of some property in Hotofte which was let at £10 for £220.[70]

Leases in reversion were not always so profitable and could sometimes be worthless. Courtiers were interested in obtaining ready money by persuading the sitting tenants to compound to have their leases extended. If the tenants refused to co-operate, there was little the grantees could do. George Lazonby was given a lease in reversion of lands in five counties in compensation for goods which had been spoiled in the war in the Low Countries. When he tried to compound with the tenants, they refused. Worse still, his lease included three parsonages which were in an appalling state of repair and were quite valueless. The Crown offered to let him surrender part of this lease in return for another one. Unfortunately, the second lease included some property in Wiltshire which had belonged to Sir Francis Englefield and the Crown's title to this was disproved in the Exchequer. Finally in 1595, five years after the first grant, this merchant who had lost his stock in trade was given a third lease in reversion.[71]

The peculiar mixture of venality and inefficiency which characterised much of the Exchequer's dealings with the Crown lands in this period did much to undermine the value of leases in reversion as a method of Crown patronage. Lazonby was by no means the only grantee to have been disappointed. John Bull, the organist, obtained a lease in reversion of some property in Radnor, only to find that Mr Merrick, the earl of Essex's man, had already compounded with the tenants meaning to obtain a lease in reversion for himself.[72]

The main problem appears to have been that once a grantee had obtained the Queen's assent to his suit for a lease in reversion, he had to deal with the auditors of land revenue to obtain particulars of suitable properties. The auditors, naturally, wanted a share of the action for themselves. The problem was explained in a letter from William Herle to Burghley in 1574; he had been granted a lease and tried to obtain suitable particulars but

My lack of skill how to deal in these matters made it the dearer and harder unto me and consequently to be so long about it, being crossed diverse ways

[69] Lincolnshire Archives Office, Foster Library MSS, F. L. Garthorpe and District, 2/28, 2/31.   [70] E112/25/316.
[71] E310/42/21, mm. 47–52; E310/42/26, mm. 556–7; BL, Lansd. MS 107, fol. 200.
[72] HMC, *Salisbury*, III, p. 393.

when I had gotten any good notes, either by caveats put in before or by the auditors and other clerks who lie in wait to buy up books good cheap, or else to hinder them that they may, which occupation defrauds the Queen's majesty's liberality many times and brings the profits thither, where it is less deserved and it hath made me pay 40 marks besides my former charges for particulars only; of the which, by their information to others and by the number of books that are now past and to pass, I have been prevented of many.[73]

For the Crown, leases in reversion probably appeared to be an efficient method of rewarding royal servants. They were a device for anticipating future revenue from entry fines while the yield to the grantee was far higher than the income that was being sacrificed by the Crown. They did have a number of disadvantages. They served to put an additional layer between the Crown and its tenants and may have disturbed their relationship and destroyed goodwill. In 1588, Henry Shorte complained that he and his ancestors had been tenants of the manor of Gillingham, Kent, for 100 years and that he had rebuilt the mansion house. A lease in reversion of the property had been granted to John Heyborne and Short had been expelled.[74] When tenants heard that a lease in reversion was about to be granted over their heads, they were often deeply anxious. John Savage wrote to Michael Hickes asking him about rumours that someone was trying to obtain a lease of lands held by his father and was planning 'secretly to defraud me of that which I intend, if it please God after my father, to procure for a longer term'.[75]

Moreover, leases in reversion cost the Crown income from entry fines. In both Lincolnshire and Somerset, the Crown was sacrificing a sum roughly equivalent to a quarter of its net annual revenue from entry fines in order to provide rewards for its servants. The average annual revenue from fines for leases received at the Exchequer was just over £4,000 a year. Had the Crown not used this method of patronage, then it could have earned annually an extra £1,000.[76]

The most deleterious consequence of this practice, however, was that it took the land out of the Crown's hands for a very long time. In 1569, Sir Christopher Hatton was granted a lease in reversion of some Glastonbury property; his lease would commence in 1589 and was

---

[73] BL, Lansd. MS 19, fol. 53.   [74] HMC, *Salisbury*, III, p. 310.
[75] BL, Lansd. MS 108, fol. 55.
[76] Calculated from F. C. Dietz, 'The Exchequer in Elizabeth's reign', *Smith College Studies in History*, 8 (2) (1923), pp. 80–9.

for thirty years. Thus in 1619, Hatton's assignees would still be enjoying a piece of property at a rent which was based on a valuation made in the 1530s.[77] Clearly, it would have been very difficult for the Crown to have increased the yield of its lands whilst so many of them were let at fixed rents for so long into the future.

Christopher Vernon described the practice of piling reversion on reversion of the 'best and most valuable and choicest parts of every manor' so that 'the Crown hath been by that means in a manner forestalled from making any benefit thereof, as if the same had been granted in fee-farm'.[78]

IV

Sometime before 1589, an anonymous observer described the activities of the Elizabethan commissioners for leases and reflected on their achievements. Unlike the Marian officials, they had restricted the length of leases to twenty-one years or three lives, except for decayed property or lands liable to flooding. They had saved the Queen almost £5,000 a year in the cost of repairs and had seen many damaged buildings rebuilt. Many decayed rents had been revived and the fines were greater than ever before, but the Queen had made more leases in reversion to her servants than had been granted since the Conquest.[79]

In a sense, this is a fair summary of the activities of the commissioners. Motivated by a desire for economy and a wish to recover concealed rights, they did much to reduce spending on repairs and pursued lost rights. However, they failed to manage the Crown lands as a source of income. Rents were allowed to remain static in a period of inflation and property was granted out on leases in reversion for enormously long periods. The Elizabethan administrators left their successors with the legacy of an estate whose administrative costs had been cut, but where rents were low and many properties had been let out on very long leases. The reforms of the land administration under James I were an attempt to rectify this situation. Ultimately, however, the effects of Elizabeth's policies could not be overcome and the royal demesne was abandoned as a significant source of Crown finance.

---

[77] Wyndham, 'Crown land', pp. 30–1.   [78] Vernon, *Considerations*, pp. 73–4.
[79] Quoted in Kerridge, 'Movement of rent', p. 31.

CHAPTER 8

Customary tenure on the Elizabethan estates

Richard Hoyle

How did the Crown treat its customary tenants in the reign of Elizabeth? In the previous chapter David Thomas shows how the Crown failed to extract the maximum advantage from its leasehold tenants. Rents remained unaltered, fines were informally fixed at a level which showed no regard for the economic or commercial value of any given parcel of land. It might be readily assumed that the Crown's failure to press forward with the abolition of customary tenancies was a further dimension of the undemanding management of its estates which Thomas delineates. Yet the tolerance of copyhold can be justified in simple financial terms. Customary land generated a larger income than leasehold land through the greater frequency of fines. The 1552 commissioners saw advantages in copyhold over leasehold. The income from the perquisites of courts in the North was small, they reported, because much land passed by lease and not copy. This hurt both the King's income and the tenants themselves and the commissioners recommended that all tenements rented at less than 60s (or 66s 8d depending on which version of the text is used) were to be let by copy with the tenants paying a year's rent on the change of tenant or alienation of the tenement.[1] A generation later, in 1585, the Duchy of Lancaster cancelled a lease of the demesne lands of Knaresborough saying that

if the premises should be let by lease and not by copy, it would be hurtful and prejudicial to Her Majesty, her heirs and successors by reason that the yearly revenues of the said castle and manor are more increased and augmented by the fines, reliefs and casualties yearly happening for the said premises than would go by the fines paid upon demises.[2]

---

[1] Richardson, *1552 Report*, p. 181.
[2] Decree in the customary tenants of the demesnes of Knaresborough v. Slingsby, DL6/34, mm. 227, 103–12. Likewise, when the Duchy of Lancaster reestablished customary tenure (in this case tenant right) on the manor of Newby in Yorkshire in 1572 having forced the

But the difference in income was surely marginal and a preference for customary tenure on these grounds may be condemned as a short-term view (although it would be unfair to blame Edwardian and Elizabethan administrators for their lack of prophetic vision). The contention of this chapter will be that customary tenancies were maintained, protected and even created in the later sixteenth century as a matter of deliberate policy for reasons, of which financial profit was one, which at the time were entirely rational (if less so as time progressed).

I

It is possible to point to instances where the Duchy of Lancaster acted to reinforce copyhold tenures which were under challenge or believed to be insecure by making confirmatory decrees. The honour of Knaresborough had one such decree in 1562 following a petition of the tenants and the investigation of the customs by special commission in 1559.[3] The Duchy also made confirmations in Furness (Lancashire) in the 1560s (which will be considered in the context of the Crown's policy towards its northern estates). Even late in the century the Duchy was willing to use its judicial discretion to strengthen customs which were challenged. In 1589, the Duchy confirmed the copyholds of the tenants of Glatton and Holme (Huntingdonshire) in acknowledgement of their investment in their tenements and the raising of their fines.[4] Five years later, the tenants of Over Whitley in Cheshire had both letters patent and a decree in the Duchy court confirming their customary tenancies which had been questioned by a Duchy lessee, whose lease was called in.[5]

The most striking respect in which the Crown declined to behave according to the preconceptions of later historians may be found in its readiness to create copyholds. Of course, the legal theory of the matter was quite certain; new copyholds which lacked the sanction of long customary usage could never be secure and might be withdrawn by the lord in changed circumstances. The creation of new copyhold estates had a long tradition on the estates. 'Demesne copyholds' were

---

tenants to take leases in 1562, it was acknowledged that the leases had proved less profitable than the customary tenancies they had replaced. R. W. Hoyle, 'Lords, tenants and tenant right in the sixteenth century: four studies', *Northern History* 20 (1984), pp. 58–9.

[3] B. Jennings (ed.), *A History of Knaresborough and Harrogate* (Huddersfield, 1970), pp. 128–30.
[4] DL5/19, fols. 40r–1r.
[5] *Ibid.*, fols. 107v–10v. The sealed bill suggests that the lease was made to draw a trial of the title. C82/1561 (unnumbered, 20 Nov., 36 Eliz.).

established by Henry VII when he disafforested the Forest of Pendle in eastern Lancashire in 1507. The tenants held estates of inheritance until their title was challenged after 1603 as a part of a scheme to cajole them into becoming fee-farmers.[6] A few years earlier, the tenants of the Duchy of Lancaster at Marshden in the honour of Pontefract had successfully petitioned the Duchy of Lancaster to extend to them the customs of the honour.[7] Statutes of the later years of Henry VIII's reign gave sanction to the establishment of copyholds in the demesne lands of Walsingham (Norfolk) and the wastes of Hounslow Heath.[8] In 1524, Catherine of Aragon authorised her officers to divide the demesnes of her jointure manor of Langley Marish (Buckinghamshire) amongst the tenants of the manor and make copies according to the custom. When in 1566 a lease was made of the demesnes, the Exchequer was persuaded by the tenants to call in the lease (with the tenants paying the appropriate compensation to the lessee) and in 1574, the court made a decree which effectively confirmed the tenants' possession by ordering that no further leases were to be granted.[9]

This is not the only instance of the Crown acting to protect demesne copyholds. Twenty years before, the Duchy of Lancaster had promulgated a series of decrees protecting demesne copies in Yorkshire. In 1554, it gave the possession of the demesne lands of Barwick in Elmet (Yorkshire) to an Edwardian lessee against the claims of a copyholder who held the demesnes by custom. In the following few years, it underwent a complete turnabout and made five decrees which favoured the copyholders. Obviously aware of the Barwick decision, the demesne tenants of Leeds, Rothwell and Scoles petitioned the Duchy to be permitted to exchange their copyholds for twenty-one-year leases. In 1556, the Duchy decreed (having weighed up the advantages of copyhold tenancies at some length) that no leases were to be made of any part of the demesnes held by copy of court roll. In 1557, the Duchy went so far as to cancel a lease of a part of the demesnes of Bradford.[10] A generation later, the Exchequer cancelled its own lease of the manor of Fordington (Dorset) where the

---

[6] G. H. Tupling, *The Economic History of Rossendale* (Chetham Soc., n.s., 86, 1927), pp. 145–7; see below pp. 235–6.   [7] DL42/21, fol. 71v.
[8] Statute 37 Hen. VIII c. 2, 35 Hen. VIII c. 13 (*SR*, III, pp. 986–7, 972).
[9] E123/5, fol. 155r.
[10] DL5/10, fols. 123r, 182v–3r, 201v–2r, 286, 315r–v, 320v. The decree for the demesnes of Knaresborough was restated in 1585, DL6/34, mm. 227, 103–12 (see n. 2 above).

demesnes had been divided amongst the tenants and held by them as copyholds.[11]

These cases reveal plainly enough the Crown's tolerance of arrangements which were invalid in law.[12] The Crown's policy was not only to support demesne copyholders if their possession came to be questioned, but also to create new copyhold tenancies when occasion required it. In 1561, Winchester advocated the granting of houses, gardens and wastes within towns by copy as a means of binding their occupants to attend the Queen's courts and do repairs. Something of this sort was done when the demesne or bury lands of the manor of Woodstock were granted to their occupants as copyholds in 1579.[13] On a number of occasions, the Duchy of Lancaster charged commissioners with the task of granting encroachments and improvements from the waste as copyholds according to the custom of the manor in which they lay. The last commission of this sort so far discovered dates from 1604.[14] A similar Exchequer commission was active in the Forest of Inglewood in Cumberland in 1578.[15] Copyhold estates were also created on manors in north-western England in the 1560s in circumstances we will have occasion to describe later in this chapter. In all these cases, the clear intention was to create an estate of inheritance.

In the eyes of seventeenth-century lawyers and administrators these grants were irredeemably flawed and of no legal worth. Norden encountered copyhold grants made by the Duchy clerk William Tusser in the honour of Pickering and recorded his opinion that they

[11] E123/1A, fols. 222v–4v. (This case is further discussed by Haslam, above p. 103.)

[12] The decrees in the Langley Marish case and in the Duchy cases from Yorkshire and Glatton do not confirm copyhold. They order that existing leases were to be cancelled and no further leases were to be issued. The Jacobean confirmations of customary tenure are just that; with the sanction of statute they declare that imperfect copyhold titles are made good. The difference is important.

[13] BL, Harl. MS 6850, fol. 103v; E123/1A, fol. 211r. For the suggestion that burgages in Richmond should be granted in this fashion, E163/15/29, fol. 1r (? of early Mary). In 1565, copies were granted by a commission out of the Exchequer of the fishermen's cottages which fringed the beach at North Shields, the innovation being justified in terms of transferring the costs of repairs to the tenants. E. Bateson et al. (eds.), A History of Northumberland (15 vols., Newcastle, 1893–1940), VIII, pp. 293–7.

[14] See for example DL42/98, fol. 72r–v (Ulverston, Lancs., 1590), 242v–4r (division of wastes in Colne and Marsden, Lancs., 1594), 264v–6r (similar for Padiham, Lancs., 1595); DL30/496/4, mm. 11d–13r (enrolled commission to William Yewart, 1604). The power to make copyhold demises of improvements was given to the lessee of Rochdale, Lancs., in 1586; DL5/19, fols. 1r–6r. For grants made by William Tusser, clerk of the Duchy court, in Leeds, J. W. Kirby (ed.), The Manor and Borough of Leeds, 1425–1662. An Edition of Documents (Thoresby Soc. pubs., 57, 1983), pp. 54–64.

[15] LR2/213, fols. 67r–74, copy LR1/134, fols. 66r–71v.

were voidable at the prince's will.[16] The lawyer Humphrey Davenport, when asked his opinion on the copies of the tenants of Ennerdale made in 1568, stated the conventional view that

the same grants by copies... are void in law, for copyhold land must have been of that name as copyhold land by all time of memory and therefore this being tenant right land until and at the granting of this copy, the same could not have been then made copyhold land which is to hold to the custom of the manor then in being.[17]

Against this strict application of legal principle might be weighed the comments of Burghley, Mildmay and the barons of the Exchequer in the Fordington demesne case of 1581. Finding for the tenants (and against their own lessee), they held that the fact that the lands were called bord or demesne lands was not proof that the lands had ever been demesnes; 'for the name of demesne lands is not any proof thereof because all customary and copyhold lands were sometime demesne lands and may retain that name of demesne lands and nevertheless be in truth customary and copyhold lands'.[18] Such a comment would have been greeted with incredulity amongst the generation which rose to prominence in the first years of the new century. The Elizabethan willingness to sanction copyhold was not indiscriminately applied. In 1586, the court squashed a grant by copy made two years previously of lands in the Forest of Feckenham, and whilst this was justified by the damage the grant threatened to do to the commoners in the forest, it was also held that the copy was void in law as the lands were part of the Queen's demesnes.[19] These apparently inconsistent instances can be understood if we appreciate that the strict law was tempered through the expedient need to grant or maintain customary tenancies as a means of protecting the Queen's tenants against predators who secured leases of demesnes with the intention of dispossessing the 'customary' tenants. The security of the tenants was therefore placed above the future economic interests of the Crown.

Copyhold was also an extremely convenient means by which tenants could hold land. It obviated the need for the central authorities to make leases of lands which were often small in both size and value. (In Inglewood 179 parcels were demised for a total rent of

---

[16] R. B. Turton (ed.), *The Honour and Forest of Pickering* (North Riding RS n.s., 1, 1894), pp. 31, 52. [17] LR9/83, Ennerdale file, opinion dated 29 Oct. 1609.
[18] E123/1A, fol. 224v. [19] *Ibid.*, fol. 323r–v.

69s; 93 of the parcels were of lands rated at 2d or less.) The concession
that the lands were to be held by inheritance was, of course, no
concession at all in early sixteenth-century circumstances when the
succession of tenants was both automatic and desirable. It was in the
early seventeenth century that such tenurial arrangements were
challenged, not out of any desire to recover the lands for the Crown
but as a means to raise revenue by having the tenants compound for
a secure title.[20]

II

The clearest example of new customary tenancies being created in
Elizabeth's reign comes from the north-western borders of England
in the 1560s.[21] Here we see the replacement of ill-defined customary
tenures with either copyhold or forty-year renewable leases, the
tenants apparently being permitted a degree of choice between the
two. Although the commissions which effected these changes justified
the substitution of tenures by arguing that the tenants' tenant right
was unrecorded in the court rolls and therefore invalid in law, the
tenurial reforms cannot be separated from the larger policy of
maintaining border service against the Scots.[22] A concern with the
security of the borders was exhibited as early as 1555 with the statute
'for the reedifying of castles and forts and the enclosing of grounds
from the borders towards and against Scotland'.[23] This aimed to
maintain the border population through rebuilding tenements, the
maintenance of tillage and enclosure. (Enclosures also served to
hinder the free passage of raiding parties and were desirable for that
end.[24]) The statute was to be implemented through a commission
issued out of Chancery. Whilst this anxiety remained throughout
Elizabeth's reign, conventional thinking on the matter came to
blame the tenurial exactions of private landlords for the decay of

---

[20] I describe this in ch. 9 below.
[21] There are various descriptions of circumstances on the Elizabethan borders including
R. Newton, 'The decay of the Borders: Tudor Northumberland in transition', in C. W.
Chalklin and M. A. Havinden (eds.), *Rural Change and Urban Growth, 1500–1800* (London,
1974), but the best account is the unpublished doctoral thesis of P. W. Dixon, 'Fortified
houses on the Anglo-Scottish border: a study of the domestic architecture of an upland area
in its social and economic context, 1485–1625' (University of Oxford, DPhil thesis, 2 vols.,
1976).
[22] This can be seen especially clearly in Winchester's remembrance of late 1561 which mixes
matters of land management with suggestions for the improvement of the defence of the
borders. BL, Harl. MS 6850, fols. 103r–5v.
[23] Statute 2 & 3 Ph. & M. c. 1 (*SR*, IV (i)), pp. 266–9).
[24] Dixon, 'Fortified houses', I, p. 157.

tillage and the conversion of arable into pasture which led to depopulation. A bill was drawn at some date after 1568 to confirm the tenants of tenant right lands in Cumberland in their tenancies and restrain lords from claiming fines of more than six years' rent.[25] A further statute of 1581 gave the commissioners appointed under the Marian statute powers to order the rebuilding of houses and enforce the residence of lessees on their lands. The act was never fully implemented, the government bowing to the opposition of Northumberland landowners expressed during its passage.[26]

After 1558, the Crown may be counted as the largest proprietor in the immediate border area, acquiring land here as a matter of policy.[27] This position was maintained by the customary prohibition on the sale of lands within 20 miles of the border (meaning most if not all of the four northern counties). The Crown was willing to use its position as a landowner to further its strategic aims. When the earl of Bedford, Sir Ralph Sadler, and Sir Walter Mildmay were sent to investigate the state of the defences of the middle and east marches in 1567, they saw nothing incongruous in including a recommendation that the Crown's tenants should be given interests for terms of years in their tenements in return for being bound to make enclosures, undertake repairs and border service.[28] From 1555, the Crown's leases specified that tenants should be resident on their lands or install able-bodied men in their place. Later leases obliged the lessee to enclose and in the 1560s, a few leases instructed the tenant to erect defended houses or bastles.[29]

The Duchy of Lancaster's eagerness to preserve border service may be seen in the prominence of clauses regulating the military obligations of its tenants in Furness in the decrees it made concerning quite unrelated matters. In a decree of 1564, the Duchy confirmed the tenant right of its tenants in Low Furness in return for their taking responsibility for the coastal sea defences. Before turning to the tenants' fines, the decree placed on the tenantry the collective responsibility to turn out sixty mounted and weaponed soldiers for service when the need required. When in the following year the Duchy issued a decree suppressing iron smithies in Hawkshead to

---

[25] *CSPD Add. 1566–79*, pp. 347–8.
[26] Statute 23 Eliz. c. 4 (*SR*, IV (i), pp. 663–7); S. J. Watts, *From Border to Middle Shire. Northumberland, 1586–1625* (Leicester, 1975), pp. 30–2.
[27] Dixon, 'Fortified houses', I, pp. 146–8; II, map 23.   [28] SP59/14, fols. 244r–5v.
[29] Dixon, 'Fortified houses', I, pp. 156–9.

protect the Crown's timber, a similar clause for the supply of forty
men was inserted along with a confirmation of tenant right itself. The
opportunity was taken in other Duchy decrees to confirm tenure and
spell out the military duties of the tenantry.[30]

The Duchy's campaign to confirm tenure on its manors in north-
western England proceeded side by side with the Exchequer's policy
of amendment. It is not clear why the Exchequer became interested
in tenurial conditions on these estates, nor why the campaign was
never carried over onto its Northumbrian manors. On all these
manors, the tenants claimed to possess customary estates of tenant
right. Whilst the new arrangements may have had the desirable by-
product of increasing revenue, this was a secondary matter to
regularising ill-defined arrangements on which the Exchequer
frowned. The Exchequer was keen to invoke the statute of 1555 and
to oblige the tenants to ditch and enclose, but the fact that the Welsh
lordships of Bromfield and Yale were concurrently undergoing a
similar experience (described below) suggests that military considerations were not paramount.

Shortly after the annexation of Augmentations to the Exchequer,
one James Fox brought to Winchester's notice the state of the
extensive lordship of Middleham in the North Riding where the
tenants held by custom but without the payment of fines (except in
the New Forest where a 'running gressom' was due). The tenants, he
reported, would be glad to take the lands by copyhold of inheritance
and pay at their first entry two years' rent, then two years' rent for a
fine at death or assignment and to stand the cost of repairs 'which
would be a great profit at the beginning besides a yearly profit and
the discharge of all manner of repairs'. This advice appears not to
have been acted on, but the idea reappeared as a general policy
towards all the Crown's northern estates in Winchester's remem-
brances of late 1561.[31]

Here may perhaps be found the origins of the special commission
which was issued to the Lord Treasurer, Under-Treasurer and
Chancellor of the Exchequer in July 1562 under the powers
conferred by the 1555 statute. They were empowered to issue

---

[30] Decree for the tenants of Low Furness, DL6/12, partly printed in T. West, *The Antiquities
of Furness* (1774 edn, repr. Beckermet, 1977), pp. 123–5, extended to other tenants by a
decree of 1573 and reaffirmed in 1589; DL6/21 (tenants of Low Furness v. Rawlinson) and
DL5/19 fols. 33r–4r. For the tenants of Hawkshead, DL5/13, fols. 704–9, printed in West,
Furness, App. ix (unpaginated); for Newby (1572), DL41/13/5; for Borrowdale, DL5/19,
fol. 36.   [31] E163/15/29, fol. 1r–v; BL, Harl. MS 6850, fol. 103r.

commissions out of the Exchequer for the survey of lands and negotiation with the tenants within the 20 mile zone for the making of leases for terms of up to forty years. In such leases the tenants were to pay fines as in tenant right rather than copyhold (on entry, the death or alienation of the tenant but also change of lord). Tenants were to be bound to enclose, hedge and ditch their lands and raise and repair buildings at their own expense. They were also to find either a horse and armour or armour alone for service on the borders according to the size of their tenement. The eldest son of the tenant was promised the preferment of the lands when a new lease came to be granted. And, in a final clause, the commissioners were empowered to make similar leases in the manors of Middleham and Richmond and Barnard Castle where the tenants also claimed to hold by tenant right.[32]

It must be appreciated that these terms were less advantageous to the tenants than might appear at first sight. Although a term of forty years might be thought liberal, the Crown sought to preserve its pecuniary interest by taking the full range of fines due from tenant right tenants whilst conceding the right of the tenants' heirs to the first refusal when leases were renewed. Nonetheless, the commission was never implemented. What may be the commissioners' report shows that where leases were offered to the tenants in Cumberland, they were declined and the tenants requested the confirmation of their tenant right.[33] In Richmond and Middleham, the tenants sought the aid of their steward, the earl of Northumberland, in seeking the confirmation of their customs and Northumberland was to receive the Queen's reprimand for his pains.[34] To meet this opposition, new commissions were issued in September 1564 and (with slightly altered terms) in June 1565.[35] The first conceded that the tenants of Middleham and Barnard Castle might take their tenements by copyhold if their rental value was 26s 8d or less; the second raised this ceiling to 40s. On the other hand, the 1564 commission did not extend this concession to the north-western manors. In a separate commission of June 1565, authority was given for the tenants of Holm Cultram, Ennerdale, Muchland and the

[32] *CPR 1560–3*, pp. 274–5.

[33] E315/409, fols. 53–64 (undated, but probably of 1562–3).

[34] BL, Lansd. MS 5, fols. 134–40; *CSPD Add. 1547–65*, p. 551.

[35] *CPR 1563–6*, nos. 930, 1082, 1083. SP15/12, fols. 176–9, is a description of the differences between the two commissions.

various manors of the honour of Penrith to be given copies in place of their tenant rights. The tenants' agreement to this was obtained at meetings between them and the Exchequer's commissioners held at Carlisle during August[36] but the actual granting of copies was a more protracted process. The manors around Penrith had copies during 1565, but it was January 1567 before the commissioners dealt with Muchland, April 1568 before they reached Ennerdale and October 1570 before they attended to the border manor of Holm Cultram. In all these cases, the procedures were much the same. Having satisfied themselves of the accuracy of existing surveys, the commissioners offered leases to the tenants which they declined, preferring to stand by their customary tenures. A jury was then impanelled which declared the existing custom. This done, the commissioners granted copies according to the custom of the manor.[37] It is impossible to be certain whether the customs declared by the tenants were a genuine record of previous practice. In none of these cases can an earlier declaration of custom be found, but the inclusion of a single rate of fining, a border service clause and perhaps most significantly the obligation to enclose their tenements with quicksets points to a degree of central direction.

The outcome on the other side of the Pennines was quite the reverse. The tenants of Middleham and Richmond and Barnard Castle came in August 1565 to accept leases for forty years. This may have been a close-run thing. There survives a roll of orders governing the possession of tenements in both manors agreed between the commissioners and the tenants which is headed by two exemplars of copyhold grants, one for life, the other for forty years.[38] Whether copies were granted that summer is unknown, but in the early 1570s the tenants all took leases for a term of forty years. The new arrangements applied only to those tenements where a customary right was claimed; elsewhere on the manors, normal twenty-one-year leases were to be made. The effect of the long leases was to preserve

---

[36] E178/7051. See *CSPD Add. 1547–65*, pp. 552–3, for a letter which may bear on this commission.

[37] In the manors around Penrith, the copies are said to have been granted in 7 Eliz., E164/47, fols. 94v–5r; Muchland, Cumbria RO, Carlisle, D/Lons/L/12/2/6, fols. 34r–40v (copy of an exemplification of the commissions and certificate); Ennerdale, R. P. Littledale, 'Ennerdale', *Transactions of the Cumberland and Westmorland Antiquarian and Archaeological Society*, second ser., 31 (1931), pp. 167–8; Holm Cultram, J. Nicholson and R. Burn, *The History and Antiquities of the Counties of Westmorland and Cumberland* (2 vols., 1777, repr. E. Ardsley, 1976), II, pp. 183–8.

[38] LR3/18/1. Cf. D. S. Reid, *The Durham Crown Lordships in the Sixteenth and Seventeenth Centuries and the Aftermath* (Durham, 1990), pp. 34–6.

the reality of customary tenure behind a contractual arrangement. Covenants were inserted in the leases which governed their inheritance. The steward and other manorial officers were given a role in overseeing the descent and alienation of the tenements, and the Crown gave an undertaking that on the expiry of the leases, the tenant in possession or his eldest son would have the preferment of a new lease on the same terms.[39] These were quite different covenants from those in an ordinary lease and when seen in this light, it may be appreciated that the substitution of leases for tenant right was an act of equal conservatism with the change to copyhold on the Cumbrian borders.

There is a case for arguing that the leasing of these manors might best be seen as an instance of changing the labels on tenants to clarify their status. In every case, though, the opportunity was also taken to bind the tenants to border service and increase their fines from God's Pennies (a nominal recognition of the commencement of a new term) to fines of one year's rent in Barnard Castle and two years' in Middleham. These were, however, alterations on the margin. In all the reforms of the 1560s the intention was to regulate rather than profit, to protect rather than oppress the tenants. The motivation might actually have been to prevent the Crown from making leases of tenant right lands to middlemen who, through their exactions, would serve to reduce the capacity of the tenants to defend the borders. As early as 1552, the tenants of Middleham had requested that no parts of the manor should be granted by lease and that the tenants should be allowed to retain their customs. The tenants of Newby had suffered from interlopers taking leases of their tenements in the 1550s. Lessees of tenant right lands in Ennerdale and Furness had their leases voided by decree in 1564 and 1573.[40] After the marquess of Northampton's lands in the barony of Kendal (Westmorland) escheated to the Crown in 1572, the Exchequer ordered that no leases of tenant right lands were to be made so long as the tenants continued to perform their border service. In 1580–1, the Exchequer was forced to intervene in the affairs of the manor of Barton, Martindale and Patterdale (the former lands of Leonard Dacre) where the tenants complained of the lessee's oppressions. The

[39] T. S. Willan and E. W. Crossley (eds.), *Three Seventeenth-Century Yorkshire Surveys* (Yorkshire Archaeological Soc. RS, 104, 1941), p. 147.
[40] *APC 1550–2*, p. 465; Hoyle, 'Lord, tenants and tenant right', pp. 53–4; Littledale, 'Ennerdale', p. 167 (citing E123/1A, fol. 58); DL6/21 (tenants of Low Furness v. Rawlinson).

decree which confirmed tenure was careful to spell out the border service obligations of the tenants.[41]

In these various ways, we find that the desire to maintain the security of the borders was bound up with and in some respects perhaps determined the Crown's policy towards its northern tenants. The predisposition to confirm customary tenancies was both a way of regulating practices which were prescriptive and undefined and maintaining border service by protecting the tenants from the oppressions of potential lessees. This instinct can be seen in practice as late as 1584 when the Exchequer confirmed the customary tenures of the tenants of Plumpton Park near Penrith, again emphasising their military duties.[42]

It needs to be stressed that the tolerance and confirmation of customary tenures was not limited to the strategically important northern borders. Confirmation could be seen as desirable in its own right (as at Knaresborough in 1563).[43] A close parallel to events in the North can be found in the Crown's treatment of the tenants of the Welsh marcher lordship of Bromfield and Yale.[44] Here, the tenants claimed to hold by a mixture of bond tenures and copyhold and themselves admitted in an Edwardian petition to the Council that their tenancies had not always been granted according to common law practice. In their petition, they complained of the granting of leases to strangers who oppressed the customary tenants and they looked for a promise that no more leases of this sort would be granted.[45] It was not until 1562 that the honour was surveyed. Using the sanction of a special leasing commission, an agreement (dated 1 August 1562) was struck between the commissioners on the Queen's behalf and the tenants whereby the tenants agreed to relinquish their existing tenancies, pay a fine of two years' rent and revive certain decayed rents in return for forty-year leases.[46] In these, the Crown covenanted to make further leases for the same rent, fine and term at

---

[41] E123/1A, fol. 150v, copy LR1/136, fol. 79; LR1/129, fols. 132–4v.

[42] E123/10, fols. 103r–4v. The tenants here were supposed to have been treated with by the earlier commissions but were apparently overlooked.   [43] DL5/13, fols. 399r–403v.

[44] For events here generally, A. N. Palmer and E. Owen, *A History of the Ancient Tenures of Lands in North Wales and the Marches* (second edn, n.p., 1910), pp. 204–11.

[45] The petition is in LR17/1 unsorted bundle; I hope to publish it later. For a petition to the Court of Augmentations complaining about such grants, E. A. Lewis and J. C. Davies (eds.), *Records of the Court of Augmentations Relating to Wales and Monmouthshire* (Board of Celtic Studies, History and Law ser., 13, Cardiff, 1954), p. 85.

[46] The commission is *CPR 1560–3*, pp. 278–9, the survey LR2/234. The composition itself appears not to survive but its general outline appears on many occasions, for instance E123/22, fol. 297r–v.

the end of each lease. An order of July 1563 instructed the tenants to take their leases by the following Michaelmas, the *habendum* to be from Michaelmas 1562. Such leases were granted from 1563 onwards, fifty-one being taken in the first three years but small numbers were still being taken each year at the end of the 1570s.[47] As with the leases taken in Middleham and Barnard Castle, these were not ordinary leases. By orders promulgated in 1564, the steward was ordered to enquire at each court for the deaths of lessees and for alienations and charge fines of one year's rent.[48] Moreover, it was held in James's reign by no less a figure than Lord Chancellor Ellesmere that the tenants' interest, being hereditary, was a real and not a chattel interest.

The granting of long leases or copyholds where the tenants held defective customary estates served many purposes, but amongst them was the establishment of a proper tenurial relationship between monarch and tenant. Questions of profit and military service were clearly involved with this but may finally be seen to be ancillary. Of course, the potential for increasing profits from tenants near the northern borders or in the Welsh marches was never very considerable. By establishing *de facto* estates of inheritance, the Crown gave little away. The willingness, both here and in the dealings over demesnes, to close the door on the option that fines could be increased in the future reflects the lack of importance attached to revenue from that source. Table 7.1 helps us understand why this should have been so. Such a policy seemed repugnant to later generations and by failing to accede to the tenants' requests for their estates to be confirmed by statute, the Elizabethans left open the possibility that in more prosperous times, their successors would attempt to overturn the arrangements of the 1560s for profit.[49]

---

[47] LR2/234, fol. 167v; LR17/1, abstract of leases.   [48] LR2/234, fols. 163v–4r.
[49] For requests for statutory confirmation, Cumbria RO, Carlisle, PR122/205 (Holm Cultram, 1570s); SC12/27/30 (Bromfield and Yale, after 1571).

CHAPTER 9

'Shearing the hog': the reform of the estates, c. 1598–1640

Richard Hoyle

The beginning of reform in the management of the Crown lands should be dated not to the death of Queen Elizabeth in 1603, nor (as is popularly the case) to the appointment of Salisbury to the Lord Treasureship in 1608, but to the death of Burghley in 1598 and the acceptance of the Treasurer's white staff by Buckhurst (created earl of Dorset in 1604). It is easy to demonstrate the inadequacies in the management of the Crown's estates in the last decade of the sixteenth century and the enormity of the task which awaited Burghley's successors. Contemporaries were in no doubt that the Elizabethan administration of the estates had failed to take advantage of rising land values and that lax management had permitted peculation. The history of the estates in the years immediately after 1598 is one of attempts to increase revenue through the exercise of a tighter control over officers, a determination to overturn the restraint which custom placed on income and a continuing search for concealments. From the middle years of the 1610s, strenuous attempts were made to raise additional income through the improvement of wastes and forests. But such constructive policies – whose success might be doubted – were finally undone by the imperative to raise large sums quickly through long leasing, fee-farming or sale to repay debts or fund war. By 1640, sale had reduced the Crown lands to a mere rump.

I

The specific criticisms made against the Elizabethan administration of the Crown lands in the 1590s and later by contemporaries such as Sir Robert Johnson, John Norden and many anonymous projectors need to be carefully weighed. There had been, it was generally acknowledged, a failure to raise rents and fines in line with the rising value of land. Rents remained fixed at customary levels. The surveys made in 1609 showed how large the gap between actual rents and potential value had become. In the West Riding of Yorkshire, tenants held leaseholds with an improved value of £2,012 2s 11½d for £609 6s 1¾d. Copyholds worth £273 4s 8½d were rented for £69 17s 10d. The disparity between value and income was greater still in Somerset. Leasehold lands worth £1,010 14s 0d were rented for £126 5s 9½d; copyholds worth £3,078 7s 6d were let for £165 12s 9¼d.[1] Nor was the Crown benefiting from the increased value of land by taking larger fines on leases and copies. David Thomas has shown in an earlier chapter how the rate of fines charged on leases remained at four years' ancient rent.[2] The situation with copies is more difficult to ascertain. Where the tenure was inheritable, fines recorded in the court rolls tended to remain fixed at low levels. On copyholds for lives, the fines actually demanded may have increased but to the benefit of the stewards and their underofficers rather than the Crown.

Ralph Agas, the East Anglian surveyor, was familiar with these failings. Writing for either Caesar or Dorset in 1606, he described his experience in surveying Crown manors after their sale. Rents were light, 2d or 2½d an acre where every acre could be let for 10s or 12s; fines (on copies), even where arbitrable, were charged at 6d or 12d the acre (and sometimes less) but once out of the King's hands the same land attracted fines of 10s or 13s 4d the acre.[3] That land was worth much more than the rents charged by the Crown is further evidenced by the much higher rents taken on sublettings.[4] Moreover, the Crown was disadvantaged by the natural process of the engrossment of holdings. Sir Robert Johnson, writing in 1602–3, described how copyhold tenements were being run together on manors where heriots were due so that the tenant paid a single heriot in place of several 'which custom I deem of as unreasonable against common right and directly prejudicial to Her Majesty'.[5]

A failure to keep up with rising rental values was only one of the Crown's problems. The Exchequer was also losing rents. Dr Thomas

---

[1] BL, Lansd. MS 169, fols. 107r–10v. For other instances drawn from these surveys, Dietz, *English Public Finance*, p. 298 n. 15. [2] See above, pp. 172–3.

[3] BL, Add. MS 12497, fol. 342r.

[4] J. T. Swain, *Industry before the Industrial Revolution. North-East Lancashire, c. 1500–1640* (Chetham Soc., third ser., 32, 1986), graph 5.2, offers evidence from the Lancashire manors of Colne and the Forests of Trawden and Pendle.

[5] Johnson, *Letter*, Bodl., MS Perrot 7, fol. 57r; for similar claims made by Auditor Neale in 1577, see above, pp. 103–4.

has already described how, through administrative failings, the rents of newly discovered concealed lands were not charged.[6] The surveyors were also used to discovering lands and tenements omitted from the rentals or claimed as freehold. Agas recalled surveying recently sold Crown manors in which both lands and tenements were found 'smothered up and concealed' and surrendered into his hands.[7] Norden took great pleasure in announcing his discovery of such tenements and demonstrating the tendentiousness of some of the claims of freehold with which he was confronted.

Such kind of freeholders are in most of His Majesty's manors, they do either pay rent and tender no service or pay rent and do suit to the court, but how they hold they will show no evidence, neither are their tenure known. By reason whereof strangers are entitled to His Majesty's rents, consequently to his tenants and lastly His Majesty loseth the rents for the time and their suits and the lands, escheats and reliefs for ever. For it is a common practice for men that list to revolt from His Majesty in this kind.[8]

The early Jacobean surveyors of the socage manor of Carlisle found that much of the demesne of the manor was claimed by its tenants as freehold and it was not until after protracted litigation by the Crown's lessee, the fourth earl of Cumberland, that it was recovered.[9] Sir Robert Johnson pointed to a variant problem: the conversion of demesne lands into copyhold. Such lands were undervalued when the manors were sold by the Crown, thus giving the new owners a healthy windfall when the copies were quashed.[10]

These problems were encouraged, it tended to be held, by the poor quality of supervision by stewards and other Crown officers. This was more than a matter of indifference towards their responsibilities. Johnson in particular was alarmed by the poor quality of the records kept by many stewards, but he and others identified peculation and calculated fraud against the Exchequer as the major problem. Johnson spoke darkly of pen clerks who climbed up to purchase £1,000 in lands; a decade before, a member of the Commons had

[6] See above, p. 70. This was not a problem peculiar to Elizabeth; arrears of assart rents accumulated under James because of a similar administrative failure. Pettit, *Royal Forests*, pp. 81–2. In 1623, Middlesex told the auditors to examine leases made in 1606–8 because increases in the reserved rents had never been collected. Bodl., Rawlinson MS C451, fol. 3r.

[7] BL, Add. MS 12497, fol. 342r.

[8] Dorset RO, D/WLC E190 'Observations tendered to honourable consideration...', 1613', in this case Keynsham, Som.

[9] R. T. Spence, 'The backward North modernized? The Cliffords, earls of Cumberland and the socage manor of Carlisle, 1611–1643', *Northern History* 20 (1984).

[10] Johnson, *Letter*, Bodl., MS Perrot 7, fol. 61v.

argued that the Crown could help itself by (amongst other things) making stewards account for the fines they received rather than rely on subsidies.[11] Johnson thought that only a tenth of the sums levied as fines reached the Queen. A memorialist writing after Burghley's death in 1598 claimed that stewards and tenants colluded to falsify the court rolls; having negotiated a fine of (say) 20s, steward and tenant would agree that only 10s should appear in the court rolls and so be estreated for the bailiff to collect. Heriots, too, were undervalued and sold for the profit of the steward. This writer put the cost of these frauds at £5,000 yearly. That the court rolls were deliberately falsified is confirmed by a book of such instances collected from manors in Hampshire and Wiltshire which showed the fines taken by stewards to be far in excess of those recorded in the rolls (if, indeed, any fine was recorded there).[12]

An early Jacobean projector petitioned for a seven-year licence to hold commissions to audit the accounts of stewards and identify just this sort of fraud. He, or another writer, conveniently identified the range of deceptions used. Tenants on manors where fines were arbitrable bribed the stewards or their deputies to take only a small fine for the Crown so that no precedent was set to the future disadvantage of the tenants. Where tenements were liable to be forfeited for waste, the tenants either paid a nominal fine for their readmission or bribed the stewards to overlook their offence. The projector was in no doubt of the scale of the problem; he offered £2,000 per annum or two-thirds of the sums raised for his patent.[13] It could not be argued that Burghley and his generation were ignorant of such peculation. As early as 1590 the copyhold tenants of the manors of Ford and Crimping in Sussex made highly specific allegations against their steward and his cronies which included receiving fines for their own use and granting the reversion of copyholds to their friends. A copy of the tenants' bill, with a breviate made for Burghley's use, survives amongst his papers.[14]

Stewards were not the only corrupt officers the Crown possessed. Woodwards were notoriously so, and in 1609–10 a major investi-

[11] *Ibid.*, fol. 65r–v; C. Russell, 'English Parliaments 1593–1606: one epoch or two?', in D. M. Dean and N. L. Jones (eds.), *The Parliaments of Elizabethan England* (Oxford, 1990), p. 198. Also 'The journal of Sir Roger Wilbraham', ed. H. S. Scott, *Camden Miscellany* 10 (Camden Soc., third ser. 4, 1902), pp. 25–6.
[12] BL, Lansd. MS 168, fols. 205–6; SC12/20/26 (cited in E. Kerridge, 'The movement of rent, 1540–1640', *EcHR* 6 (1953), p. 32n). For a further case, DL5/26, fol. 42 (Wighton, Norf., 1610). [13] SP14/5, nos. 40, 41. [14] BL, Lansd. MS 62, fols. 163r–90v.

gation revealed that John Banks, the deputy bailiff of the manor and Chase of Enfield and Robert Howe, the pound keeper at Enfield, had, amongst other misdemeanours, not accounted for the fines they had collected for strays on the chase (a sum of £87 being mentioned), nor for the strays they had sold on to butchers (or whose fleeces had been sheared whilst in their hands) said to have been worth £140 to them. If this was not enough, Howe was said to have been selling the Crown's wood as firewood at 3s 4d a load. The Master Forester of Enfield since 1587 had been, it might be noticed, the Lord Treasurer himself, Salisbury.[15]

All these problems were compounded in Johnson's eyes by the lack of adequate record-keeping. There was, experience had taught him, barely one manor in twenty with a perfect book of survey and practically none with adequate court rolls. Where manors were leased, he believed the lessees frequently failed to engross the court rolls but kept a record in rough paper books which were destined to be lost or embezzled, so making it harder for succeeding generations to take a grip on the dismal legacy of their predecessors. The answer, Johnson believed, was the establishment of a central muniment room for the Crown's court rolls.[16]

Better record-keeping was one of the ways in which the management of the estates could be improved, but it was to the closer regulation of officers that most attention was paid during Dorset's Lord Treasureship. Suggestions for instilling honesty and discipline abounded and many advocated the creation of new officers to regulate the first. Johnson wanted an act of Parliament to oblige every steward to return to the auditors at the end of each year a catalogue of fines, heriots and other casualties in the form of an indenture made between the steward and the tenants. One of the writers cited earlier suggested the appointment of one or two General Surveyors whose deputies would attend the granting of copyholds and the sales of woods to ensure that the Crown's profits were protected. Each year, they were to audit the stewards' and bailiffs' accounts.[17]

It is possible to see the influence of these commentators in Dorset's actions. From 1598, there was a small but significant flow of suits in the Exchequer brought by the Attorney-General against the Crown's officers, charging such men as Ralph Atkinson, the keeper of Middleham Castle (Yorkshire) with the sale of the very structure of

---

[15] D. O. Pam, *The Story of Enfield Chase* (Enfield, 1984), pp. 54–5.
[16] Johnson, *Letter*, Bodl., MS Perrot 7, fols. 70v–1v.   [17] SP14/5, no. 41.

the castle.[18] For the first time, there seems to have been an attempt to bring officers to book for straying over the bounds of permissible self-interest. In the summer of 1600, commissions to investigate peculation by officers were sent into at least thirteen counties in the South and West of England. The articles required reports on the copies granted in the previous twelve years and the sums of money paid for them to the Queen and to private individuals. The commissioners were to discover what heriots had been paid in the same period, establish the value of copyhold lands and certify whether any copyholds had been taken by Exchequer lease. The intention was clearly to provide an opportunity for the Crown tenants to declare the oppressions of their stewards.

In fact, the returns discovered relatively few clear instances of corruption.[19] In Devon, it is clear from the returns that the copyhold tenants often used intermediaries – sometimes Exchequer officials – to secure reversions to copyholds. The fees paid to these persons straddled the line between fee and bribe. At Heathfield, Auditor Neale's clerks were doing a nice line in procuring Exchequer leases for tenants, but the understeward was taking small sums (much smaller than the Queen's fines) on grants of copies. Richard Hake of Plympton Grange paid one Tobias Collins £15 in 1598 to secure a copy for three lives for his tenement, rent 17s 10d, for which he paid a fine of £10; but Collins, on being interviewed by the commissioners, testified that he had ridden to London twice to secure the grant. He had acted as a solicitor in the same fashion for other tenants.[20] At Mere in Wiltshire, the fines taken for the Queen on copies for three lives seem to have been realistic in scale; but here the steward was in the habit of demanding grain (typically a few quarters of oats) to ease the transaction through the court.[21]

The only evidence of major, systematic corruption came from the manor of Bisley in Gloucestershire. In the light of the commission's return, the Attorney-General moved a bill in the Exchequer against the steward of Bisley and other Gloucestershire manors, Thomas Neale.[22] He was accused of combining with his deputy, one Richard Bird, and the bailiff, Lawrence Keen, to make grants of copies to

[18] E112/55/699; for a similar case see E112/56/722 against Richard Pollard, the keeper of Sheriff Hutton Castle (who had been burning the fabric of the castle for lime amongst the usual embezzlements of ordnance and furnishings).
[19] The returns can be traced through the class list to E178, for instance E178/414 (Berks.), 460 (Beds.), etc.   [20] E178/681.   [21] E178/2457.
[22] Neale may be the retired auditor of that name. He was deprived of his stewardships from the day the commissions were issued in 1600.

friends and servants for little or no fine, making fraudulent compositions and assessing for the Queen's use small fines whilst taking much larger sums themselves. Neale was exonerated and Keen acquitted, but Bird was fined 200 marks and discharged from office.[23]

It might not be over complacent to suggest that the problem of corruption was less pressing than the literature of the projectors and commentators would suggest. The opportunities for fleecing tenants had only appeared later in Elizabeth's reign when the disparity between value and customary fine opened up; it might also be reasonable to suppose that they were limited for the most part to manors where the tenants held copies for lives. The need to secure reversions allowed the stewards in such manors an otherwise extraordinary discretion and opportunity for partiality and corruption. Dorset's answer to the general problem of corruption was to issue a circular letter in July 1607 which required stewards of manors with copyholds of inheritance to grant copies in open court in the company of a JP and the county surveyor.[24] In doing this, he more than accepted the advice of an anonymous projector who urged that copies should be granted jointly by the steward and surveyor.[25] The same injunction was repeated in Salisbury's printed directions to stewards of May 1608. Dorset's answer to the specific problem of the bribery and profiteering which copies for lives encouraged was, as we shall see, to secure their conversion into fee-farms.

In this way, stamping out corruption, raising profits and improving the quality of the Crown's record-keeping were intimately related. We have already seen how Johnson advocated the centralisation of court rolls, but the key to reform on the Crown estates lay not in this particular bureaucratic solution but in the wholesale utilisation of the survey. It has been recognised that the first decade of the seventeenth century saw a serious attempt to survey all the Crown lands, but neither the chronology nor the purpose of these surveys has ever been fully comprehended.

In doing this, we must first recognise that surveys were not neutral documents but were compiled by different methods to contain different types of information (at differing levels of accuracy) according to the purpose for which they were required. A four-fold typology may be identified (though in practice the distinctions

---

[23] E112/16/219; E123/28, fol. 358.
[24] SP14/32, fol. 160v; Essex RO, Q/SR/181/100.   [25] SP14/5, no. 41.

between them were never quite clear-cut). The lowest grade of record
was the rental. Here, the names of tenants were arranged by their
tenurial status (freeholder, copyholder, etc.) with a brief note of the
nature of their holding but always with a record of their rent. The
simplest manorial survey was an enlargement of the rental, made not
by the surveyor's inspection of each property but by the interrogation
of a specially assembled manorial jury. It contained a fuller
description of the tenant's property, often giving a rounded acreage
in customary acres and a note of the date and terms of the instrument
by which he held. In the early seventeenth century, it came to
contain an estimate, normally made by the surveyor rather than the
jurors, of the value of each holding.[26] In growing sophistication, the
third type of document was a survey in which each tenement was
broken down into parcels and measured. This type of survey can be
recognised by the use of acres, roods and perches. Detailed measuring
was obviously the key to a greater exactitude in valuation. This type
of survey might be accompanied with maps and this gives us a fourth
category of document.

In fact, there was no attempt to produce a general cartographic
survey of the Crown estates.[27] Mansfield's survey of Settrington in the
North Riding (1600) had three plans, of the manor house, the village
and a general view of the lordship, but this survey was seen by its
executant as a demonstration of his skills as a surveyor and
cartographer.[28] Norden's survey with plans of Windsor and Windsor
Forest (1607) was made for presentation to James and not for
ordinary administrative purposes.[29] The objection to making cartographic surveys of the estates was in essence one of expense. Norden,
consulted over this by Fulke Greville in 1616, thought that making
maps (except of demesnes and improvable wastes) was unnecessary
and that the cost would be twice that of preparing a written survey
and fieldbook with selective maps. This approach can be seen in
Norden's own surveys; these only contain plans of parks and other
locations (such as the environs of Exeter Castle) where the Crown's

---

[26] E. Kerridge, *Agrarian Problems in the Sixteenth Century and After* (London, 1969), pp. 26–8.

[27] The study of the maps made on the Crown estates was begun by the late Heather Lawrence
in a paper, 'John Norden and his colleagues: surveyors of Crown lands', a copy of which she
kindly sent me and which appeared posthumously in *Cartographic Journal* 22 (1985),
pp. 54–6.

[28] H. King and A. Harris (eds.), *A Survey of the Manor of Settrington* (Yorkshire Archaeological
Soc. RS, 126, 1962), pp. 1–8.

[29] S. Tyacke and J. Huddy, *Christopher Saxton and Tudor Map-Making* (London, 1980), p. 60.

title was in question.[30] The most notable end for which the Crown did commission maps was in its projects for the discovery and sale of assart and drowned lands and the enclosure of forests and woodlands although the plans themselves are almost entirely lost.[31]

It has been argued that because the Crown lands lacked surveys, the administration of the lands was in some fashion bad. This view is based on a misapprehension of the principles on which the Eliza-bethan Crown lands were run; there were no surveys, only rentals (and these often in the hands of local officials), because they were unnecessary for the collection of a fixed rental income and a fluctuating number of copyhold fines (charged on customary terms). Surveys were only useful when the rise in land values in Elizabeth's reign gave landlords the opportunity to secure higher fines, calculated in terms of value or, if tenurial relations allowed, higher rents. For this reason, the need for surveys was, like ministerial corruption in the matter of copyhold fines, a development of the later part of Elizabeth's reign. The premise, that lack of adequate documentation led to inadequate management was made by the early seventeenth-century surveyors, who, living in an age of new opportunities, failed to appreciate the logic of the lines on which the Elizabethan estates were run.

It was the existing Exchequer surveyors, of whom there was one for each county, who were the butt of their criticisms. Johnson, writing in 1602, drew the distinction between 'trusty and skilful men' (of whom he was doubtless one) and the fee-drawing 'idle and skilless surveyors'.[32] Another anonymous writer complained of the waste of fees paid to the Exchequer surveyors 'for it doth appear that amongst the 42 surveyors now present in fee, there are not many (I will say not one) who can execute the office of a surveyor'.[33] John Mansfield,

---

[30] SP14/84, no. 45; for such surveys BL, Add. MS 6027; BL, Harl. MS 6288. Interestingly, Norden also prepared copies of these surveys which lacked the maps; compare the BL MSS cited with E36/157 and Leeds Archives Dept, TN/SH/B4/1.

[31] Expenditure on plans for these projects between 1603 and 1612 can be found in table 9.1 below. *CJ*, XLIII (1788) (Third Report on Land Revenue, App. 12), p. 599, prints an inventory of 1621 listing twenty books of survey with plans of forests made in Nicholson's assart lands project. The only survivor of his plans appears to be of lands in Nottinghamshire, SP14/83, nos. 80, 81 (now MR 429 (1, 2), MPF 294).

[32] Johnson, *Letter*, Bodl., MS Perrot 7, fol. 60r. In his discourse on surveying of 1607, Johnson distinguished between the tasks which a 'sufficient man' could undertake and those 'of much greater skill [which] require an ability'. BL, Lansd. MS 169, fols. 117r–19v.

[33] SP14/28, no. 128. For more of the same, BL, Lansd. MS 171, fol. 395r–v (in the anonymous 'Discourse touching the survey of His Majesty's lands...').

himself an Exchequer surveyor (but one who measured and plotted), said of his rival for office in 1600:[34]

it grieveth me that his services should be in your lordship's conceit made equal with mine, he having done little that any ordinary writer could not have done. He hath only made a note of some tenants' leases and of some silly informations which have been given him and if I have any judgement there is little use for your lordship of this his service.

The hostility of the new surveyors to the old Exchequer surveyors was at heart a professional jealousy based on a search for fees. The Exchequer surveyors were not without a role any more than they were without skills.[35] They were responsible for making rentals of lands on their receipt by the Exchequer and, in theory if not in practice, charged with updating them, with supervising repairs and woodsales and valuing the woods on tenements on their sale by the Crown. They received a yearly fee and expenses for any work they were called upon to do.[36] But it remains true that their post was often a sinecure, exercised through deputies. No less a figure than Burghley secured a surveyorship for his nephew; Salisbury went one further and served as surveyor in Hertfordshire.[37] This, and their lack of modern surveying skills, exposed them to the criticism of a new professional group, the surveyors, who measured and valued land.

Measuring surveyors were very much an innovation of the late sixteenth century. It would be wrong to assume that there was a great demand for their services before 1600. That this was so can be seen clearly enough from the career of John Norden. Like Saxton (whose career displays a similar path), his early work was large-scale county cartography, but this completed, he was reduced in the 1590s to making a living by writing chorographies (county surveys) and religious tracts. When in Norden's *Surveyor's Dialogue* the surveyor admits that he has been and 'am sometimes employed in that kind of

---

[34] He then went on to list specific failings; King and Harris (eds.), *Settrington*, p. 1.

[35] The surveyors were an innovation of the Court of Augmentations adopted by the Exchequer when the two courts were merged. For an historical account of the office (which argues that a shortage of surveyors forced the appointment of gentry who were inadequate to the office), SP14/28, no. 128. The surveyors were not charged with surveying Crown properties before their sale. Given that sales were normally conducted at moments of desperate financial need in a buyers' market, to do so would have been much too time-consuming, expensive and of little benefit.

[36] See, for instance, the itemised account of Sir Richard Verney for making surveys in Warwickshire in 1604. LR9/121 (unnumbered piece).

[37] SP46/39, fol. 49; BL, Lansd. MS 171, fol. 397r.

service', we have an ironic reflection on his own early career and the prospects for the profession generally.[38] There is little reason to believe that the Crown lands were significantly behind the majority of lay estates in adopting measured surveys; on the contrary, a case might well be made for saying that they were in the vanguard.

In the eyes of its advocates, the survey would not only provide the Crown's officers with a wide range of information which they needed to have and mostly had not, but would also act as a universal panacea for all sorts of ills. The author of the 'discourse touching the survey of His Majesty's lands' of 1606 made the most moderate claims. Without adequate surveys, the administrators of the lands were ignorant when questions of profit arose. Lacking surveys, they were unable to check the particulars (for lease or sale) sent on by auditors who had themselves frequently never seen or trodden the lands of which they wrote but who depended on previous patents or information given them by suitors. Surveys would prevent the confusion between the Crown's lands and those of freeholders, especially in open fields. The surveys would serve as evidence in the settlement of disputes between lord and tenant and tenant and tenant.[39] Another anonymous author gave over a dozen itemised reasons for surveying lands, including recovering rents and conceal-ments, checking the actions of stewards and bailiffs, establishing a perpetual record of boundaries, preventing the alteration of tenures of holdings and the customs of manors, preventing suits between tenants, hindering the erection of cottages and establishing a control over decays. The survey would cover its costs by the additional income it raised and would serve to take away 'all future charges or troubles hereafter, so that a survey well and truly performed will satisfy most questions [which] may hereafter arise upon every occasion'.[40] The author of the discourse recognised that surveys would need to be repeated, but thought that if this was done every seven or ten years, the surveyor would replace the concealment hunter as the means by which lost profits were recovered to the Crown's use.[41]

Mansfield argued that the making of surveys was also a benefit to the tenants themselves. It allowed demises to be made without them

---

[38] For Norden's early career, W. Ravenhill, *John Norden's Manuscript Maps of Cornwall and its Nine Hundreds* (Exeter, 1972), chs. 1, 3; J. Norden, *The Surveyor's Dialogue* (London 1618, repr. Amsterdam 1979), p. 37. The additional point may be made that there was an oversupply of surveyors.   [39] BL, Lansd. MS 171, fols. 394v–6v.

[40] SP14/37, no. 37.   [41] BL, Lansd. MS 171, fol. 395v.

coming to London, it permitted just fines to be taken by value and not by multiplying the old rent. Acquiring up-to-date knowledge of the sitting tenants saved them from being displaced through leases being taken over their heads. The surveyor also fulfilled a useful function in settling disputes between tenants, so relieving the Lord Treasurer of the need to intervene.[42]

This literature must be read as not simply selling the virtues of the survey but also the professional status of surveyor. The discourse urged the replacement of the old county surveyors with surveyors of the new sort, each given charge of five or six counties in parallel with the auditors.[43] Another undated paper looked to the appointment of a Surveyor-General who would nominate a deputy in each county without whose sanction no grants of copyholds or sales of woods on copyholds would be made. These underofficers would also audit the accounts of stewards and bailiffs.[44]

Inevitably and unavoidably, such claims brought the advocates of surveying into conflict with the auditors. There are some clues to suggest that the auditors had, when need arose, made surveys of the old sort,[45] and it seems likely that such surveys and rentals as the central authorities possessed remained in their custody. (Their possession of these and other documents was itself the subject of a long-running dispute between the auditors and the officials of the old course of the Exchequer; in 1616, James I ordered that the auditors were to surrender virtually all their records into the hands of the Remembrancers and Clerk of the Pipe.)[46] Proposals that the surveyors should have a hand in auditing accounts obviously reduced the auditors' role and duties. But the most sustained attack on the auditors came in a paper circulating in Exchequer circles in late 1609 or 1610. This, in its fullest form, arranged in parallel the articles of a paper circulated by the surveyors' lobby, the auditors' response and a commentary on the auditors' position by the surveyors.[47] The temper of these exchanges was established in the response the

---

[42] King and Harris (eds.), *Settrington*, pp. 2–3, 7.

[43] BL, Lansd. MS 171, fol. 395v. One of the undated papers cited previously saw the appointment of a surveyor to work with each auditor as a way of preventing corruption by the latter. SP14/28, no. 128.   [44] SP14/5, no. 41.

[45] The survey of Leonard Dacre's attainted lands (1589) was made by Auditor King sitting with other commissioners. E164/42, fols. 1r, 46v.

[46] SP14/87, no. 43. Suffolk declined to enforce the order and it was reiterated after his fall, SP14/98, no. 70.

[47] BL, Lansd. MS 169, fols. 120r–1v; a copy of the surveyors' commentary only, LR9/1/130. The paper is unattributed.

auditors made to the surveyors' first proposition, that a surveyor should sit in person with the auditor at every audit and join with him in giving allowances to stewards, bailiffs and other officials. To this, the auditors replied that 'this article is altogether derogatory to the auditor's authority always heretofore used and established, neither is there any use or cause for such an overseer either in respect of His Majesty's benefit or good to the subject'. The surveyors came back

What derogation it may be to the auditor to have the surveyor sit with him at his audit is not suddenly understood when as it cannot be denied but that the surveyor is the ground and foundation of the auditor's office, unless happily they may fear somewhat may be thereby discovered whereof they desire none to take notice

with more of the same. The suggestion that the surveyors should sit with the stewards of manors at court barons and take responsibility for the assessment of fines on copyholds, the taking of heriots and ensure that all amercements were collected was referred to the stewards for consideration; but the suggestion that a general survey of manors be made was countered with the auditors' reminder that surveys had been made previously and should be examined before a new general survey be embarked upon. The surveyors wanted to view all buildings and authorise repairs; the auditors thought that the reporting of decays was already adequately covered. They made little comment on the surveyors' suggestion that they should share responsibility with the Surveyor-General of woods for the certification and punishment of spoils of woods. The auditors were unimpressed by the surveyors' request that they should have custody of the surveys, accounts and court rolls of their counties; they could, the auditors argued, always be consulted in the auditors' offices (although these were normally in their private houses). The surveyors counter-attacked by urging that such records be kept centrally in the Exchequer. And the surveyors claimed that it should be they and not the auditors who endorsed particulars of leases and sales with a note of the improved value. The auditors argued that once perfect surveys were made, they could do the task quite adequately, but in their response, the surveyors cast doubt on the auditors' ability to perform the task and blamed them for the sale of property at gross undervaluations in the past.

But the surveyors' lack of trust in the auditors and the latters' complacency can best be seen in the last article:

[The surveyors] And the said surveyors further to do all and every other thing necessary for the preservation of His Majesty's possessions and revenues to the uttermost of their power.

[The auditors]...the revenues are better ordered and answered than the surveyor can tell how to direct.

[The surveyors] If the revenues have been and are so well ordered, how cometh it to pass that there hath been of late so many abuses discovered, followed and many punished when the auditor knew not how to defend the same and many more would be etc. of several kinds, but modesty restraineth them to do hurt which have no power in themselves to salve the same again. But if it be now so good and perfect as it seemeth they avow, it must be concluded that necessity enforceth amendment of continued errors and yet if the beginning of order and instruction be respected it will be approved the surveyor the first in that service.

There is no evidence that the surveyors' lobby succeeded in increasing the centrality of the surveyors in the administration of the estates. By 1640 the office of county surveyor had disappeared.[48] Their dispensability was starkly revealed in February 1615 when Suffolk ordered the cancellation of their fees (with those of stewards and woodwards who held during pleasure), 'there being no use of their employment or service in the general work of survey intended by us'.[49] But the surveyors were still being given tasks to do in the early 1620s even though many of them had not been paid their fees for several years.[50]

The rise of the surveyor and the need to process the information they generated did prompt the establishment of a new office, that of Surveyor-General. The Exchequer already possessed the office of surveyor of woods south of the Trent, a position inherited from Augmentations.[51] In November 1610, after the death of John Taverner, the surveyor Robert Treswell was appointed Surveyor-General of woods.[52] The following March, Treswell and Norden were both given charge of circuits (Treswell's in the Midlands and East Anglia, Norden's in southern and western England) within

---

[48] They are not noticed by L. Squibb, 'A book of the several officers of the court of Exchequer... 1641[/2]', ed. W. H. Bryson, *Camden Miscellany* 26 (Camden Soc., fourth ser., 14, 1975).   [49] Lancashire RO, DDKe/5/31.

[50] Kent AO, U269/1, OE 7, 99, 260, 322, 361.

[51] W. C. Richardson, *History of the Court of Augmentations, 1536–1554* (Baton Rouge, LA, 1961), p. 308. (There was no corresponding office north of the Trent after its last holder was pensioned in 1554.)

[52] E403/2692, no. 40. One Thomas Morgan gent was granted the office in May 1603, to hold from the death or resignation of Taverner; Treswell was appointed on Morgan's resignation. Treswell was a herald; J. Schofield, *The London Surveys of Ralph Treswell* (London Topographical Soc., 135, 1987), p. 8.

which they were authorised to view all castles, lodges, forests and
chases and search for decays. The following month their circuits were
divided to make a third circuit for John Thorpe.[53] Their work chiefly
consisted of overseeing repairs to parks, lodges and pales and, to a
lesser extent, castles.[54]

A Surveyor-Generalship of lands was considered to be an essential
part of the administrative structure when the jointure and princely
estates were established after 1603; all, on their establishment,
appear to have commenced campaigns to survey their estates. Lord
Sidney (later Viscount Lisle) became Surveyor-General of the
jointure and surveyors were dispatched in 1604.[55] Prince Henry
employed Norden and Thorpe amongst others although his Surveyor-General, Sir William Fleetwood, made his own surveys of
Knaresborough and Macclesfield, perhaps to help launch a project to
make grants in fee-farm.[56] Norden successfully petitioned to become
surveyor (not Surveyor-General) to the Duchy of Cornwall in 1605,
but his relation to the Duchy after 1615 was as co-deputy to the
Surveyor-General with John Thorpe.[57]

The Exchequer failed to emulate this practice until the appointment of Sir Thomas Fanshawe in April 1625.[58] The survival in
Cranfield's papers of a proposal to create such an office suggests that
the idea had been current slightly earlier. This unsigned memorandum pointed to the inadequacy of the surveys available to the
Crown, many of which, it claimed, lay in paper books lodged with the
auditors or, if engrossed, with the Remembrancer of the Exchequer.
It advocated the creation of an office in which the records would be
kept. The Surveyor-General or his clerks would be responsible for
endorsing particulars with a note of the lands. The Surveyor-
General's fee ($£100$ was suggested) would be recovered by dismissing
the county surveyors whose patents could be readily termined as they
only held during pleasure.[59] The two surveyorships of woods and

---

[53] E403/2693, nos. 10, 28, 99, and cf. 2694 nos. 45, 77 (a surrender and regrant of Norden's
office to him jointly with one Alexander Nairne).

[54] This assessment is based on a reading of the order books, E403/2730-1.

[55] SP14/9, no. 64; papers re the surveying of the estates in Sidney's papers, Kent AO, De L'isle
MSS (U1475, U1500), passim.   [56] E351/2793; see below, p. 364.

[57] CSPD 1603-10, p. 191; HMC, Salisbury, xxiv, p. 46; DCO, Bound MSS, Warrant Book,
1615-19, fols. 5, 19, 74, 144.

[58] C66/2350, no. 9. Fanshawe was previously Surveyor-General to the Duchy of Cornwall; he
must be distinguished from his nephew Sir Thomas, King's Remembrancer 1619-41,
1661-5, cr. Viscount Fanshawe 1661. G. E. Aylmer, The King's Servants, the Civil Service of
Charles I, 1625-42 (London, 1961), p. 139.

[59] Kent AO, U269/1, OE 1,728. In fact Fanshawe had £200.

lands continued side by side despite a suggestion of 1692 for their amalgamation.[60]

As the minutes of the 1626–7 commission for sales makes clear, Fanshawe and Treswell were expected to appear and inform the members of the commission of the value of lands and their potential for improvement, and generally advise on policy. Where Fanshawe had no information, he was expected to engage surveyors (on a *per diem* rate) to view the lands in question.[61] His successor, Sir Charles Harbord, (appointed on Fanshawe's death in 1631) undertook work for all branches of government. Whilst he organised surveys of the King's interest in fenland drainage, he was also instructed to survey the navy's docks on the Thames and gunpowder mills in Surrey.[62] To all appearances, when information was required about the Crown's estates after 1625, recourse was made to the Surveyor-General's office and not to the auditors (although the Surveyor-General might seek information from them).[63] And it seems that it was he and not the auditors who had the custody of such surveys as existed.

If this diminished the position of the auditors, it also marked the end of the attempt by the surveyors to insinuate themselves into the central administration. Instead, like land surveyors everywhere, they became the purveyors of a technical skill, to be bought when required. Their predicament was crystallised in the experience of the two surveyors commissioned by Fanshawe to survey the Forest of Braydon in the winter of 1626–7. On their return to London, they petitioned the commissioners for sale asking for the payment of the balance of their fee of £210. With one of them present before the commissioners, Fanshawe offered to pay only as much as another surveyor would charge for the same work and when the surveyor persisted in withholding the plans, he was given two days grace to hand over their work or be committed to the Fleet.[64] Yet for all their lack of status, they were the informal memory of the Crown's projects. In about 1622 or 1623, one John Disney, the surveyor employed by the commissioners for surrounded lands in Lincolnshire, petitioned the Council and Cranfield urging that the commission be reactivated and offering to place his knowledge at its disposal. Disney

---

[60] Pettit, *Royal Forests*, p. 27.

[61] University of London Library, MS 195; Cheshire RO, DCH/X/15/5; SP16/69 *passim*.

[62] *CSPD 1633–4*, pp. 70, 271; *CSPD 1639–40*, p. 512. For Harbord, see B. D. Henning (ed.), *The History of Parliament. The House of Commons 1660–1690* (London, 1983), II, pp. 477–82.

[63] For instance, *CSPD 1635*, p. 535; *CSPD 1636–7*, p. 95.

[64] SP16/69, fol. 50v. Their rate was £10 per 1,000 acres plus an allowance for attendance.

knew the secrets of the commission; if it was to be finally abandoned, he asked for the settlement of his fees.[65]

In the event, the surveys which were made in the first decade of the seventeenth century were never a neutral description of the Crown's lands and rights but were designed to advance whichever policy was then being pursued by the Exchequer. The surveys themselves survive in large numbers in the Public Record Office and elsewhere, but there has been no previous attempt to distinguish the campaigns in which the surveys were made. The necessary understanding is best achieved through an analysis of the payments made to surveyors, recorded in the order books kept by the Tellers of the Exchequer.[66] These are only for surveyors employed casually by the Lord Treasurer and paid on his warrant. They do not include the salaries of county surveyors or those employed by the jointure or Princes' estates, but they do include payments to surveyors of surrounded and assart lands. Table 9.1 offers gross figures for payments in an attempt to reflect the cost to the Crown. This is quite different from the earnings of the surveyors.[67] Dorset's surveyor Hercy claimed for his subsistence and the expenses of the commissioners with whom he worked. Salisbury's surveyors were paid a *per diem* rate for surveying and supervising the engrossing of surveys and from this they were to pay their clerks and other expenses. Some favoured surveyors received occasional rewards; one had an *ex gratia* payment after he was robbed and assaulted near Uxbridge.[68] The normal practice was to make a payment to the surveyor on account ('imprest') when the survey was commissioned and then pay the balance when the survey had been received and approved. From these payments, it is possible to identify the surveyors, the nature of their tasks and the duration of their work.

During the year beginning Michaelmas 1602, the disbursement books record no payments to surveyors. In the following year (1603–4), £355 7s 0d was paid to one John Hercy for various pieces of surveying. Hercy was not a surveyor of the new sort.[69] His

[65] Kent AO, U269/1, OE 225, 1252.
[66] E403/2723 (starting Easter 1602) to 2730 (ending Michaelmas 1611) have been searched for this purpose.
[67] The surveyors had an additional income in that they charged for the enrolment of leases and copies. Some writers sought to regulate and limit these charges, e.g. BL, Lansd. MS 171, fol. 395v. For the fees taken by John Mansfield, see King and Harris (eds.), *Settrington*, p. 6.
[68] John Cowper of Woodstock. Cowper was a 'measurer', E403/2726, fols. 155r, 162r.
[69] His background was legal; in 1602 he received £96 for assisting the Queen's counsel in preparing books of evidence for an unspecified purpose; E403/2723, fol. 31v. There were in fact three men of the name, one his son; E403/2726, fol. 43v.

Table 9.1. *Payments to surveyors out of the Exchequer, 1602–11*

Year beginning	Lands	Woods	Assart lands	Surrounded lands	
Michaelmas 1602					[nil]
Michaelmas 1603	£395 7s 0d				£395 7s 0d
Michaelmas 1604	£1,238 4s 9d	£90 0s 0d			£1,328 4s 9d
Michaelmas 1605	£785 18s 5d				£785 18s 5d
Michaelmas 1606	£743 5s 1d	£268 11s 4d			£1,011 16s 5d
Michaelmas 1607	£1,676 11s 0d	£1,166 13s 4d	£568 11s 0d	£130 17s 8d	£3,542 13s 0d
Michaelmas 1608	£1,567 3s 0d	£2,993 9s 4d	£1,550 11s 8d		£6,111 4s 0d
Michaelmas 1609	£1,576 12s 2d	£622 12s 6d	£1,556 4s 4d		£3,755 9s 0d
Michaelmas 1610	£227 7s 8d	£46 13s 4d		£143 18s 5d	£417 19s 5d
Michaelmas 1611	£251 15s 10d		£295 10s 8d		£547 6s 6d
Totals	£8,462 4s 11d	£5,187 19s 10d	£3,970 17s 8d	£274 16s 1d	£17,895 18s 6d

Source: calculated from E403/2723–31.

surviving surveys were made by estimation, but this reflected their purpose and not necessarily Hercy's capabilities. On the other hand, on the one occasion when he was responsible for preparing measured surveys, he had the services of specialist surveyors.[70]. Hercy's task was to gather the necessary information to advance a programme of selling copyhold lands in fee-farm. On 13 December 1603, he had £40 imprest for a special service 'touching the survey and sale of certain copyhold lands of the King unto which on the King's behalf he is assigned by myself [Dorset] and diverse other of the lords'. On 24 February following he had £49 15s 4d for his expenses in surveying manors in Oxfordshire, Berkshire and Hampshire (including £10 for his clerks); on 28 February he had £60 imprest for the survey of manors in Wiltshire, Gloucestershire and elsewhere and payments in September for the survey of manors in Middlesex, in December for Surrey. In April 1605, he was given an advance to survey manors in Essex and was then engaged in surveying manors in the southern Midlands. In March 1606, he was sent to Somerset and Dorset, in May, Gloucestershire.[71] By the early summer of 1607, he had surveyed manors in most of the counties south-east of a line from the Tamar to the Wash. (It will be noticed that this is the area of copies for lives.) Having made the surveys, Hercy was instructed on 29 June 1607 to retrace his steps and assist commissioners in eight counties with the sale of copyholds in fee-farm.[72]

The original paper drafts of Hercy's surveys survive in large numbers in the Public Record Office. These are often annotated with the tenants' offers to buy their tenements.[73] Hercy was paid for engrossing his surveys on to parchment and the working sheets frequently bear notes to the engrossing clerks or of the number of sheets of parchment used. As will appear, the engrossments were ultimately sent to stewards and are correspondingly rare although the draft and engrossed surveys of Upper and Lower Slaughter (Gloucestershire) both survive.[74] Hercy appears to have made his surveys in the company of the county surveyor and a surveyor called William Blake; in form they were traditional presentments made by manorial jury with a note of tenurial status, a description of the buildings of the tenement and its lands parcel by parcel (with

---

[70] E403/2726, fol. 155r.
[71] The payments to Hercy referred to can be found as follows; E403/2723, fols. 197r, 227v, 233; E403/2724, fols. 82r, 157r; E403/2725, fols. 6r, 28v, 47v, 62v, 135v, 140r, 150v, 158r, 210v; E403/2726, fols. 15r, 22v.   [72] E403/2726, fol. 210v; SP14/32, fol. 160v.
[73] See below, p. 236.   [74] Gloucestershire RO, D45/M26.

acreages by estimation), the rents due and a valuation.[75] They fell far short of the ideal recommended by the new surveyors but their purpose was to provide the basis on which a sale could be made. This is not to say that Hercy's work was inexpensive. Between 1603 and 1610, he received in fees, expenses and rewards some £2,636.[76] Salisbury for one thought this expensive; Hercy blamed the high cost on the need to provide 'diet' for the gentle commissioners with whom he worked.[77]

The commissioners for assart and surrounded lands besides, four other groups of surveyors were active in these years. First of all, John Johnson and John Goodwin were engaged in the North of England. In the spring of 1604, they were surveying manors in Cumberland, Westmorland and the northern West Riding with a view to fee-farming. Later in that year, they surveyed the Anglo-Scottish border, the Debateable Lands and Bewcastledale in Cumberland, Wark, Redesdale and other border lands in Northumberland. For this, they received £471 18s 4d (of which £100 was reward) in February 1605.[78] In June 1605, they were commissioned to survey manors in Yorkshire, Cumberland, Durham and elsewhere although it is not clear if this was completed. Secondly, a decision was taken in July 1606 to survey the Crown's custody lands, and five circuits of surveyors were established for this purpose. The three John Hercys had one each, Hercy's assistant William Blake the fourth and the surveyor–architect John Thorpe the last.[79] Thirdly, much money and energy was invested in surveying Hatfield and Theobalds (which were being exchanged between the King and Salisbury) and Holdenby in Northamptonshire, acquired in 1608 as a house for Charles, duke of York. The Theobalds and Hatfield surveys were certainly measured; when Hercy was sent to Theobalds in 1607, he was accompanied by John Thorpe and John Cowper, both described as 'measurers'. Later in 1607, when John Thorpe, Henry Jenning and Israel Amyce were employed surveying woods incorporated into Theobalds Park, they had the assistance of five men paid to measure the land.[80] The final group of surveys made on Dorset's instructions were of the Crown's woods, ordered in December 1607, commenced in March 1608 and completed in the winter of 1608–9. The survey

[75] For Blake, see HMC, *Salisbury*, XXIV, pp. 143–4.
[76] Calculated from E403/2723–30 *passim*.   [77] SP14/32, fol. 158v.
[78] CRES40/19A, no. 6; SP14/9A, no. 97; SP14/10A, no. 60; BL, Lansd. MS 169, fols. 128–9; E403/2724, fol. 185r; SP14/12, no. 76.   [79] E403/2726, fols. 43v–4r.
[80] *Ibid.*, fol. 155r.

may well have been undertaken following the abandonment of the proposal to make a general lease of Crown woods, Sir Robert Johnson for one arguing that to make such a lease would be mistaken whilst the Crown remained ignorant of the extent and value of its woods.[81]

Salisbury deserves the fullest recognition as a patron of the new style surveying. In the way that his father appreciated the value of maps for strategic ends (although not, it would seem, estate management), Salisbury understood the possibilities of measured surveys so well that he could envisage making a national survey the basis of the recurrent taxation to be given James by the Great Contract.[82]

On his appointment to the Lord Treasureship in May 1608, Salisbury was made aware of Hercy's work and ordered that his surveys be lodged in the Lord Treasurer's Remembrancer's office where they were to be consulted by the auditors.[83] Sitting in the Treasury Chamber on 30 May, he reviewed the arguments for fee-farming with the chief officers of the Exchequer and decided to cancel the project. Hercy was paid off on 27 June (although he acted as one of the 1608 surveyors and in April 1609 was paid for preparing copies of his own surveys).[84] Salisbury then (on 27 June) ordered the surveying of the King's castles and houses. On 5 July, he instituted the survey of those manors (said by Caesar to number 306) not viewed by Hercy and dispatched sixteen surveyors to undertake this task. Some surveys were being engrossed in the month before Christmas and the payment of the surveyors began in the spring of 1609 as the surveys were accepted by the Exchequer.[85] Surveyors were still being dispatched in April 1609, possibly to fill gaps which had been discovered since the original commissions were issued. Some care was taken not to duplicate Hercy's work which was still in daily use in the 1620s.[86]

---

[81] E403/2727, fols. 130–3, 134v, 141v; E403/2728, fols. 56r–61v, 68v, 71r, 72v etc.; see below, p. 358.

[82] J. E. A. Dawson, 'William Cecil and the British dimension of early Elizabethan foreign policy', *History* 74 (1989), pp. 197–9, reviews the claims made for Cecil's cartophilia. E. N. Lindquist, 'The failure of the Great Contract', *Journal of Modern History* 57 (1985), pp. 641, 644–5.   [83] SP14/32, no. 85, 85I; LR9/9/1280/2 (order by Salisbury, 2 June 1608).

[84] L. M. Hill, 'Sir Julius Caesar's journal of Salisbury's first two months and twenty days as Lord Treasurer: 1608', *BIHR* 45 (1972), pp. 316, 317–18; E403/2727, fols. 215v, E403/2728, fols. 153r, 159r.

[85] Hill, 'Caesar's journal', pp. 320, 322, 325; E403/2727, fols. 230r–5v. Short certificates of a number of these surveys survive in BL, Lansd. MS 169.

[86] SP16/69, fols. 17r, 21v, 47r, 71v, etc.

The surveys made on Salisbury's instructions are on first sight more impressive than Hercy's; but where his survive as drafts, the 1608–9 surveys are generally engrossed copies on parchment. To all appearances, they were (more than Hercy's) based on the measurement of lands with valuations of the individual tenements. The speed with which they were made suggests strongly that the working methods used were not so dissimilar to Hercy's. Indeed, their reliability may be questioned. It was alleged that Aaron Rathbone relied upon the tenants' reports in surveying Kirkby Moorside in the North Riding and accepted 20 nobles for dealing with them favourably. His survey of Ayton was made in Stokesley some miles away.[87]

Inaccuracies notwithstanding, by the end of 1609, Salisbury had at his disposal a larger body of up-to-date information about the estates than had been possessed by any administrator since 1540. To what uses was it put? The surveys were deposited in the Lord Treasurer's Remembrancer's office where the auditors, having received a particular for lease or sale, were to send for an extract from the pertinent survey.[88] This would allow the commissioners for sales or leases to have before them, in detail, the nature and current value of whatever property was being solicited and so allowed a fine or purchase price to be settled on the basis of the real value rather than the application of a standard multiplier to the ancient rent. It was an answer to those critics who claimed that lands had been sold at gross undervaluations. On manors with copyholds, it was the intention to use the surveys as the basis on which copyhold fines were charged. The full consequences of this we leave to a discussion of the book of printed orders.[89] But it served to limit the possibilities for ministerial peculation for the steward was now charged with applying a fixed scale to a fixed assessment. Even more than in Dorset's scheme, he was reduced to the status of mere functionary.

Against this, we need to weigh the expense which, as table 9.1 shows, was quite considerable. In all, around £20,000 must have been spent by the various agencies of land management on surveys in the first decade of James's reign. No figures are available for the Duchy of Lancaster, but in the two years of its existence, the Duchy of Cornwall under Prince Henry expended £756 13s 4d on surveys and surveyors, about 1.8 per cent of the Prince's total receipts. Nor

---

[87] HMC, *Salisbury*, xxiv, pp. 191–2.   [88] LR9/1280/2.   [89] See below, pp. 237–9.

was this the end of expenditure. Haslam has calculated that Norden was paid £1,008 by the Duchy of Cornwall between 1615 and 1622.[90]

If the costs are treated as an investment, then it must be said that it was one that yielded a poor return for reasons which were not altogether foreseeable at the time. The improvement value given by the surveys was not, as some writers have assumed, an increment which could be translated into an immediate increase in rental.[91] In the case of copyholds, it could only be exploited by increasing fines when copies were renewed *if custom permitted* (which, as we shall see, it mostly did not). The new valuations could be used to rack-rent leaseholds when their leases fell in, if the will existed, which may be doubted. And the opportunity to implement these changes was lost in the contractors' sales of 1609–12 when land was leased or sold at bargain basement prices. (It is impossible to calculate what proportion of the investment in surveys was lost by selling newly surveyed manors.) Dorset's surveys, as has been shown, were directed to the practical end of selling copyholds in fee-farm. Salisbury's surveys were part and parcel of an attempt to modernise the estates through the acquisition of the rigorous and impartial valuation which contemporary ideas of estate management insisted he needed. The forced sales after 1609 terminated this heroic period and were a cruel end to an infatuation with a new and expensive technology of information gathering.

In the three decades which followed, there appears to have been little surveying on the Exchequer estates except as the preliminary to disafforestation and drainage. Norden was active in the West Country in 1613–14 although his surveys were a cover for selling copyholds in fee-farm.[92] In the second decade of the century, the estates receiving the most attention from surveyors were those of the Prince of Wales. The surveys which John Norden and John Thorpe made on the Prince's behalf are now scattered but deserve a study in their own right.[93] One Thomas Jenkins, who by 1633 was living at Calverton, Buckinghamshire, worked for Cranfield as the surveyor

---

[90] E351/2793; G. D. Haslam, 'John Norden's survey of the manor of Kennington, 1616', *London Topographical Record* 25 (1985), p. 61.

[91] D. L. Thomas, 'Financial and administrative developments', in H. Tomlinson (ed.), *Before the English Civil War* (Basingstoke, 1983) p. 107; A. G. R. Smith, *Servant of the Cecils. The Life of Sir Michael Hickes, 1543–1612* (London, 1977), p. 127.

[92] See below, p. 243. Dorset RO, D/WLC E190, dates from this period.

[93] They include E36/157 (manors in southern England, by Norden, 1617), DL42/124 (honour of Pickering, printed in bowdlerised form in R. B. Turton (ed.), *The Honour and Forest of Pickering* (North Riding RS, n.s. 1, 1894), pp. 13–63); BL, Harl. MS 6288 (Sheriff

attached to the disafforestation project, seeing service at Bernwood, Hatfield Chase and elsewhere in 1622; in one letter he expresses the hope of being employed at Whittlewood.[94] In the 1630s, the administrators of Henrietta-Maria's jointure were employing one John Hynd to prepare what was perhaps intended to be a general survey of the estates.[95] The work of Thorpe and Hynd was of a high standard but Norden should be particularly noticed for his habit of writing at length on the places he visited. His trademark was the keen application of a lawyer's antiquarianism to search out flaws in tenure. Only Norden would have used manuscripts of 1421 and 1551 to disprove the claims of the jury at Kennington (Surrey) or compared a custumal of Edward III with the conditions he found at Ottery St Mary (Devon) in 1617. It is far from clear that his findings were acted upon, but as a good self-publicist, he ensured that his findings circulated as separate readily digestible accounts.[96] In this, as in so much more, Norden was *sui generis*. With his death, the heroic age of the surveyor came to an end.

II

The making of surveys was the means by which criticism of the late Elizabethan management of the estates could be answered. They made it possible to stamp out peculation and detect concealments and formed the basis on which an accurate assessment of a property's value at sale could be calculated. But most crucially, they permitted the Crown to make the transition from taking fines in terms of years' rent to taking fines in years' value. The importance of this must not be underestimated. As ancient rent was fixed, it had increasingly ceased to represent the worth of the tenement. Sir Robert Johnson was aware of the effects of inflation on the Crown's fixed incomes, but he also describes a fraud in which tenants attached the rent of land to cottages or houses and so removed the burden from the land itself.[97]

Hutton); BL, Add. MS 6027 (Bromfield and Yale); and surveys surviving in the DCO and the Corporation of London RO, Royal Contract Papers.

[94] SP14/180, no. 82; Kent AO, U269/1, OE 217, 390, 1,129, 1,579. For the identification, E112/161/47. To my knowledge, none of his work survives.

[95] I have noticed E315/380 (1630); E315/390 (4) (1633); E315/419 (9–11) (1633–4). Hynd had previously been working at Feckenham, see below, p. 405.

[96] E36/157, fols. 52r–3r; Haslam, 'Survey of Kennington', p. 61; Dorset RO, D/WLC E190; SP14/111, no. 138.

[97] Johnson, *Letter*, Bodl., MS Perrot 7, fols. 58r–v, 61r–v. The same fraud was reported by Auditor Neale in 1577, above, p. 104.

Mansfield saw calculations of value as favouring the tenants: 'the old rent being a most unjust rule to have assessed fines by as the table [in his survey] will show, some poor men being loath to have been displaced from their tenements might have been undone by over-buying their farms and richer men might have had better farms for much less money'.[98]

From the landowner's point of view, calculations of value could be used to place a much greater burden on the tenant. A tenement's value was obviously much greater than its ancient rent, although the relationship between the two was variable. Hercy illustrated this in a memorandum on compounding with copyholders at two years' value which he prepared for Salisbury in late 1608. An acre of land worth 5s per annum with a rent of 4d had a value of 4s 8d, which doubled was 9s 4d or 28 years' rent. An acre of pasture worth 6s 8d with a rent of 4d had an annual value of 6s 4d which doubled was 38 years' rent. An acre of meadow worth 13s 4d per annum with a rent of 4d had an annual value of 13s, which doubled made 78 years' rent. But two years' value could also be less than one year's rent in an extreme case where the land was worth 2s 6d but highly rented at 1s 6d, the value doubled being only 2s.[99] Hercy's calculations show the way in which value allowed the Crown to maximise its income, to place high charges on the improving farmer and so to tax agricultural progress. Of course, estimates of value could be revised to take account of rising agricultural prosperity.[100] Increasing estate income in the early seventeenth century – and not merely on the Crown's estates – was a matter of persuading tenants to accept a different and (for them) highly disadvantageous method of assessing their obligations to their landlords.

The shift from ancient rent to value in the calculation of fines was a crucial moment in the reshaping of the lord–tenant relationship, and the survey was the means by which the appropriate information was supplied. But surveys, as we saw before, were also a costly investment which could only be recouped over a long period. The increase in income they generated was inadequate to satisfy the Crown's escalating requirements at a time when the estates had been reduced by both sale and the assignment of lands for the support of

[98] King and Harris (eds.), *Settrington*, p. 2.   [99] SP14/61, no. 66.

[100] This was a double-edged weapon; at Ombersley there were complaints in the difficult years of the 1620s that the valuations in a survey made in 1605 were too high. P. Large, 'Rural society and agricultural change: Ombersley, 1580–1700', in J. Chartres and D. Hey (eds.), *English Rural Society, 1500–1800. Essays in Honour of Joan Thirsk* (Cambridge, 1990), p. 118.

the Queen and (after 1610) the Prince of Wales. The inadequacy of revenue and the rising level of the Crown's debt provided a tension in the management of the estates which was to persist until the catastrophic sales of the later 1620s.

Of course, the estates could only supply a partial solution to the Crown's financial needs. Dr Thomas's demonstration of how much of the Crown's land was held by forms of tenure which allowed it no freedom to increase its profits either in the long or short term needs to be recalled.[101] There was nothing to be done to increase the yield of leases before they expired unless Lord Treasurers were tempted (or forced) into the mistaken policy of selling premature renewals for ready cash. Increasing profits from copyholds might seem an easier option but many tenants of inheritable copyholds held by fixed fines. A return of the thirty-eight copyhold manors in the circuit of Auditor Neale in 1614 revealed that on six manors the tenants held for lives (so by implication their fines were arbitrary) but on thirty-two the tenants held by copies of inheritance, and of these nineteen paid certain fines.[102] The Crown's policy was to try to reduce the number of manors where fixed fines were due, but the small numbers involved shows how little additional income would result even if the project was implemented successfully.

The income from Crown lands was thus highly inflexible, and it is no surprise that successive Lord Treasurers turned to other ways of raising income in the attempt to solve the King's financial problems.[103] The early seventeenth-century administrator placed as much emphasis on retrenching spending as revenue raising. The court in particular was the subject of schemes, usually futile in execution, to trim expenditure.[104] Proposals for the Crown's estates ought properly be seen in the context of the larger history of Crown finance of which they are a part (and often a small part); but this is an ideal which cannot be achieved here. Much of the extant material on reforming the Crown's income and expenditure takes the form of lists of projects to be implemented or letters of advice of which those directed to Cecil by Sir Robert Johnson in 1602–3 were merely the first.[105] It is

---

[101] See above, pp. 61–3.
[102] E101/524/3 (unfoliated). The manors lay between Oxfordshire and Kent.
[103] See in this context the letter of the earl of Northampton of Feb. 1611, HMC, *Portland*, II, p. 22.
[104] See P. R. Seddon, 'Household reforms in the reign of James I', *BIHR* 53 (1980).
[105] See, for instance, the memorials by Cranfield and Ingram dated 1615 cited by Tawney, *Business and Politics*, pp. 148–51.

normally impossible to locate these in the context of the discussions from which they arose or prompted given that these debates tended to be informal affairs conducted within the Exchequer and Council.

More formal debates and investigations into the state of the King's finances took place on at least three occasions after Salisbury's death. In June 1612, Caesar was compelled to go to James to warn him of his dire financial situation. The Crown carried debts of £500,000, was running an annual deficit of £160,000 and was short of £60,000 to meet expected expenditure between mid-summer and Michaelmas. Immediate bankruptcy was staved off by another sale of Crown lands, but for the future Caesar offered the King four options. He could spend less; he could improve his income by disafforestation of forests, parks and by the improvement of commons; he could proceed with new projects (which Caesar feared would be open to parliamentary criticism) or he could seek parliamentary supply. James's response was to ask for a full exposition of his finances in Council before Henry, Prince of Wales, and subsequently he called on the Lord Chancellor and the Treasury Commissioners to produce recommendations for the increase of revenue and the abatement of his expenses. This was done in meetings in July 1612, where savings of £59,000 were identified and improvements in income of £85,700 suggested. Further projects were discussed during August and September by sub-commissioners appointed for that purpose, and towards the end of the year their conclusions were presented to the King. The range of projects considered in these months appears in Dr Thirsk's chapter; whether anything came of most of these efforts may be doubted.[106]

In September 1615, the Council met to consider what could be done to resolve the King's financial problems; uniquely we have a full report of the speeches made at the Council board by each member in turn. The clear preference was for a Parliament; but this was blocked by James. Instead, Sir Edward Coke's proposal for the establishment of conciliar sub-committees, each charged with worrying away at a particular area of income or expenditure, was adopted. Whether these committees made much impression on the problems before them may again be doubted. Nor can it be discovered when this

---

[106] BL, Lansd. MS 165, fols. 207r–10v, 223r–8v; Spedding, *Bacon*, IV, pp. 314–36, 358–62; Dietz, *English Public Finance*, pp. 150–3; see below, pp. 300–7.

experiment in conciliar supervision was abandoned or became defunct.[107]

The fullest attempt to secure a grip on the Crown's finances came in the panic following the failure of the 1626 Parliament.[108] At the end of June, it was decided (the Council having already forbidden suits for bounty) to establish a commission to consider 'all good ways and means as well for the augmenting of our said revenue as for the lessening of our charge'. This was formally instituted on 11 July and was still active in November 1627; it is not clear whether it was then wound up or continued a little longer. Its proceedings are, for once, well recorded and show how, with equal deftness, the commission attempted to restrain spending and enlarge income through estate improvements whilst the same men were concurrently (under the guise of a commission for land sales) liquidating the Crown's capital assets.[109]

Each of these commissions was faced with a choice between broadly similar options. Ellesmere's comment in 1615, that he had heard nothing moved that day at the board which had not been spoken of there before, reflects not as much any lack of imagination as the narrow range of possibilities open to the Crown.[110] First and most easily, it could release capital by the sale of lands to feed present income requirements or settle debts, but it diminished future revenues by doing so. Such a course was expedient and irresistible and it needs to be remembered that Salisbury's reforms, however favourably we might view them, had a counterpoint of heavy sales. Secondly, the Crown could engage in policies which would result in an increased recurrent income through raising fines (although by its nature estate revenue could never rise very quickly), by the exploitation of assart and surrounded lands (treated in chapter 11 by Dr Thirsk) or

---

[107] Spedding, *Bacon*, v, pp. 194–207. The list of sub-committees follows in the MS but is not printed. For the sub-committees, see also *APC 1616–17*, p. 215. Ellesmere's notes for the committee are printed by L. A. Knafla, *Law and Politics in Jacobean England. The Tracts of Lord Chancellor Ellesmere* (Cambridge, 1977), pp. 263–73, and see generally his ch. 4.

[108] See R. Cust, *The Forced Loan and English Politics, 1626–1628* (Oxford, 1987), ch. 1 (i), for 'the legacy of the 1626 parliament'.

[109] The commission has recently been discussed by G. E. Aylmer, 'Buckingham as an administrative reformer?', *EHR* 105 (1990). The chief source is University of London Library, MS 195, the commissioners' minute books. Cheshire RO, DCH/X/15/5, is the minute book of the commissioners for sales from 7 Nov. to 2 Dec. 1626, continued in SP16/69. (Earlier proceedings for these commissioners may be found in MS 195.) The commissioner's preliminary report is printed with minor omissions in HMC, *Cowper*, 1, pp. 291–5; the original is now BL, Add. MS 64890, fols. 63r–70v.

[110] Spedding, *Bacon*, v, p. 204.

increasing the landed area of the estates through disafforestation (considered in chapter 12).

Contemporaries were also aware of two additional options which allowed capital to be released without diminishing recurrent rental income. The first, fee-farming, has attracted little attention from English historians, although its use was by no means limited to the Crown; in Scotland, the process is familiar as feu-farming and was widely used by both lay and ecclesiastical landowners in the sixteenth century.[111] The distinction needs to be drawn between the sale of manors in fee-farm by the commissions for sale (which, as we saw, became increasingly popular after 1600) and projects to sell individual properties to their tenants with the reservation of the ancient rent. The fee-farming of all the Crown's manors and other lands was advocated on a number of occasions but only put into effect in 1626; attempts were made to convert copyholds into fee-farms by enfranchisement but as will appear later, these were rarely successful. Fee-farming, properly executed, promised to maintain the rental and, if the ideas of some of the wilder projectors could be implemented, perhaps increase it, but the Crown stood to lose the casual incidents of tenure, fines and heriots.[112] The other method for raising income in a (relatively) non-destructive fashion was by granting confirmations to those customary tenants whose titles could be claimed to be defective or who could be persuaded to pay for the fixing of arbitrary fines at certain rates.

The history of the Crown lands in the quarter-century after 1603 is one of projects taken up and put down, of administrative inconsistency and vacillation within these options, always under the pressure of an unbalanced budget and a considerable burden of debt. Lord Treasurers tired of trying to implement projects whose rewards, even if successfully pushed through to the maximum, would have made only a small contribution to the Crown's needs. Cranfield, who threw himself into both retrenchment and improvement with great enthusiasm, remarked after his dismissal from the Exchequer that projects proved 'like the shearing of hogs which make a great noise

---

[111] See most conveniently, M. H. B. Sanderson, *Scottish Rural Society in the Sixteenth Century* (Edinburgh, 1982), ch. 6.

[112] For fee-farming, see the introduction, pp. 28–9 above. For seventeenth-century proposals, see, for instance, the paper attributed to Bacon (1612), printed in Spedding, *Bacon*, IV, pp. 327–36, which envisaged fee-farming at around treble the ancient rent and the (?derivative) comments in Sir Robert Cotton, 'The manner and means how the kings of England have from time to time repaired their estates, 1609', in J. Howell (ed.), *Cotton Posthuma* (London, 1651), pp. 179–81.

but yield no wool'.[113] We will explore this verdict in relation to copyhold before turning, in section III, to leasehold policy.

Earlier, it was shown how Dorset was taking steps to stamp out ministerial corruption and peculation whilst at the same time John Hercy was employed to prepare surveys which were the essential preliminary to a fee-farming project.[114] This policy may be traced back to a meeting held in the dark days of the summer of 1599 between Sir Francis Bacon, William Gerrard, clerk of the Duchy of Lancaster and Sir Roger Wilbraham, lawyer and Solicitor-General in Ireland. At this conference, the peculations of stewards were discussed, but their main business concerned the advantage that would come to the Queen if her copyhold tenants could be required to double their rents in return for having their fines made certain. This, it was thought, they would be willing to do although it would be at the cost of a loss of patronage for those royal officers who had the appointment of stewards.[115] Although the *sale* of copyholds is nowhere mentioned, the brief notice we have appears to outline a fee-farming project; why else should stewards lose their places? But the idea appears to have been put to one side until after the accession of James I. Wilbraham reports that in the summer of 1603, Dorset propounded four 'propositions' for the increase of the King's revenues. One, a proposal which repeatedly appears in the parliamentary history of the following seven years, was for the conversion of the Crown's prerogative right of wardship into an annual rent. Another was for a composition for respite of homage, an idea still looking for its moment in 1626.[116] It is the other two which especially concern us here: that all copyholders should be sold their freeholds, and that all the King's lands should either be leased for sixty years or sold in fee-farm in return for a doubling or trebling of their rents.[117] It was a policy with potentially large rewards; in 1606, Dorset was confident of raising £40,000 in this way.[118]

Dorset's 'propositions' established the policies which were applied to the estates in the following quarter-century. Their implementation

---

[113] Quoted by Prestwich, *Cranfield*, p. 465.

[114] See above, pp. 208–10, 222–3. Some of what follows first appeared in my paper '"Vain projects": the crown and its copyholders in the reign of James I', in Chartres and Hey (eds.), *English Rural Society, 1500–1800*.

[115] 'Journal of Sir Roger Wilbraham', ed. Scott, pp. 25–6.

[116] Composition for respite of homage were still being considered in 1626, University of London Library, MS 195, pt i, fol. 38r, ii, fols. 37r, 45r etc.

[117] 'Journal of Sir Roger Wilbraham', ed. Scott, pp. 62–3.

[118] Dietz, *English Public Finance*, p. 145.

started more or less immediately. In February 1604, Dorset announced a temporary cessation of grants of copyholds until surveys of the Crown's estates had been completed and a full understanding of the worth of its estates acquired.[119] A commission to Dorset and others empowering them to fee-farm copyhold lands was issued on 26 October 1603. Both the commission and the accompanying instructions were closely modelled on the commissions and standing orders issued to commissions for the sale of lands. The commission was to grant fee-farms at a purchase price (if it could be obtained) of 100 years' ancient rent. This, it might be noticed, was considerably in advance of the rate prevailing in the sale of whole manors. As in the commissions for sales, a prohibition was placed on the fee-farming of lands which belonged to royal houses, on manors which belonged to the ancient inheritance of the Crown, the Duchy of Cornwall, earldom of Chester and principality of Wales, nor were they to sell lands in the Isles of Wight, Scilly or Sheppey or at Portsmouth. As in other sales of lands, the tenants were to enter into bonds for the purchase of standing timber on their lands.[120]

So armed, the sale of fee-farms proceeded on three fronts. By June 1604, John Johnson and John Goodwin had surveyed twenty manors in northern England (all in Cumberland and Westmorland except for Baston, Lincolnshire, and Sutton in Galtres and Newby, both Yorkshire) as a preliminary to their sale. (They argued that the intention behind their surveys had to be kept secret or else the tenants would not co-operate with them.) These had an annual yearly rent of £1,490 but might raise £52,800 if sold in fee-farm. When their surveys were finished, they thought that £200,000 could be raised in this way in the North.[121] Later in the year, they surveyed various manors in Northumberland.[122] But the opportunity for making grants in fee-farm in the North was diminished by the alienation during 1604 of much of the Crown's lands in Northumberland to the earl of Dunbar, grants made with the higher aim of bringing about the pacification of the region.[123] Only at Newby (in Yorkshire, near

[119] BL, Lansd. MS 89, fols. 6v–7v; another copy HMC, *Towneshend*, pp. 12–13.
[120] C66/1611, dorse; SP14/4, no. 31.   [121] CRES40/19A, no. 6.
[122] BL, Add. 14048, printed in R. P. Sanderson (ed.), *Survey of the Debateable and Border Lands ... taken in AD 1604* (Alnwick, 1891). Their short certificates are BL, Cotton MS, Titus B IV, fols. 281r–2v; BL, Lansd. MS 169, fols. 128r–9v, a later copy SP14/9A, no. 97. This survey makes no reference to grants in fee-farm.
[123] S. J. Watts, *From Border to Middle Shire. Northumberland, 1586–1625* (Leicester, 1975), pp. 134, 165; R. T. Spence, 'The pacification of the Cumberland borders, 1593–1628', *Northern History* 13 (1977), p. 125.

Ingleton) can it be shown that an offer to make grants in fee-farm was made. Johnson and Goodwin rated Newby as one of the most promising manors they surveyed and in February 1607, Dorset offered the tenants the opportunity to compound for the purchase of their tenements in fee-farm. The tenants were divided in their response, some visiting Dorset to plead the validity of their customary tenant right while others petitioned him expressing their willingness to buy. But Salisbury chose not to proceed and in general the attempt to sell fee-farms in the North appears to have been abortive.[124]

The commission was empowered to treat with the tenants of the Duchy of Lancaster. By April 1604, an approach had been made to Richard Molyneux, the Duchy's steward of the honour of Clitheroe in Lancashire proposing the enfranchisement of the tenants in the honour, an idea which Molyneux sought to discourage on the grounds that the tenants were so poor that fewer than ten could be expected to take advantage of the offer.[125] Why the hope of selling fee-farms on the Duchy's northern estates was abandoned is nowhere recorded; but the signs are that it was precipitately cancelled. In its place, the Duchy commenced a campaign of selling fee-farms to selected copyholders whose customary titles were technically impeachable at law. In the case of the Forest of Clitheroe, the Crown approached the tenants of the Newhold (who held by copies originally granted in 1507) in April 1607, arguing that they had neither a customary nor a prescriptive claim to their lands and had never been freed from their subjugation to forest law. The cure for their legal insecurity was the purchase of their copyholds in fee-farm; to encourage them to do this, the admittance of tenants was suspended in 1607. The arrangement arrived at the following year between Salisbury, Caesar, the Chancellor of the Duchy (Parry) and a delegation of tenants was not the conversion of copyholds into freeholds but a confirmatory decree backed by statute. It is unclear whether this outcome arose from a change of heart on the Crown's part or the realisation that the tenants could afford twelve years' rent for a confirmation (where the Crown initially demanded twenty) but were unable to raise sufficient to pay a reasonable price for their freeholds.[126] But the fact that something similar happened at Wakefield argues for a deliberate

[124] Leeds Archives Dept, Acc. 1448, nos. 214, 217, 222.
[125] Swain, *Industry before the Industrial Revolution*, p. 73.
[126] G. H. Tupling, *The Economic History of Rossendale* (Chetham Soc., n.s., 86, 1927), ch. 5; Swain, *Industry before the Industrial Revolution*, p. 61; Hoyle, '"Vain projects"', pp. 85–6.

policy reversal. Here, an undertaking on the part of many tenants in the spring of 1607 that they would buy their fee-farms was transmuted by late 1608 into an agreement to confirm copyholds, albeit with an increase in fines.[127] It is hard not to see the decisive change of the period as being the appointment of Salisbury to the Lord Treasurership.

The greatest investment of time and energy in fee-farming was in the project in southern England managed by the surveyor John Hercy. The payment of £40 imprest to him on 13 December 1603 towards 'a special service touching the survey of certain copyhold lands of the king's' to which he had been appointed by Dorset and other privy councillors on 30 November marks the beginning of this effort.[128] It has already been shown how, by the time of Dorset's death, Hercy had made surveys of 300 or so of the Crown's manors in southern England. These obviously served to fulfil all the usual purposes of surveys – to increase revenue by detecting concealments, to permit the Crown to know the value of what it was leasing or selling – [129] but they were also intended to be the preliminary to the sale of fee-farms, and some of the draft surveys contain notes of the tenants' interest or disinterest in purchase. There is a puzzle as to why this project took so long to come to fruition. Whilst the surveys show that Hercy was actively gathering offers to purchase as early as 1604, these seem to have been put to one side. In June 1607, commissions were issued to gentry in Oxfordshire, Berkshire, Wiltshire, Gloucestershire, Somerset, Dorset and Devon to view the Crown's copyholds in those counties and negotiate their sale with the tenants. Hercy was to act as their assistant.[130] In February 1608, Hercy had a further commission to negotiate the sale of customary tenements in fee-farm in Hampshire, Wiltshire, Somerset, Dorset and Devon and these offers still lay on the table at Dorset's death. It was Salisbury's decision not to proceed with the option of fee-farming, 'proving by reasons incontrovertible that the former granting of copyhold estates would be more gainful and advantageous to His Majesty's coffers and far better to his posterity'.[131]

Dorset, it would seem, had proposed to fee-farm copyholds for lives whilst tightening up on the fines paid on copyholds of inheritance. Salisbury abandoned the fee-farming project and applied the initiative to increase fines on both types of copyhold tenancy. The

---

[127] DL28/33/32; Hoyle, '"Vain projects"', pp. 85–6.   [128] E403/2723, fol. 197r.
[129] SP14/32, no. 85(i).   [130] E403/2726, fol. 210v; BL, Add. MS 11,402, fol. 128v.
[131] SP14/32, no. 85(i), Hill, 'Caesar's journal', pp. 317–18.

chosen instrument for this was a book of printed orders, the *Directions for commissioners with the steward of each manor to assess fines of copyholds*..., issued in the names of Salisbury, Caesar and the barons of the Exchequer at the end of May 1608.[132] This contained two sets of orders within the same covers, the first applying to the fines charged on copyholds for lives, the other to copies of inheritance. In the former case, the commissioners, who were to be the steward of the manor, the county surveyor and a JP (or in the absence of the surveyor two JPs), were to satisfy themselves of the value of the tenement and then make admissions for fines of nine years' value for three lives, seven years' for two lives and five years' for one life. Where no heriot was paid, an extra year's value was to be added. Similar rules of thumb were laid down for other circumstances. The instruction that the children and kin of tenants were always to be favoured (if they would pay the appropriate fine) served to restrain the stewards from favouring their own servants or taking bribes to favour suitors.

In the case of copyholds of inheritance, the commissioners were again to gauge the value of the tenement and where the copyhold paid a heriot, they were to take fines at a rate of 1.5 years' value, and, where not, 2 years' value.[133] Where the tenants claimed a certain custom of fining, it was to be accepted by the commissioners only if it was evidenced by the court rolls of Henry VII and earlier. If the tenants maintained their custom in the absence of such proof, the tenants were to be admitted but the fines respited until the King's counsel was satisfied by the tenants' claims. In every case, the stewards were to send estreats to the Exchequer.[134] In fact, one feature of the directions was quietly abandoned. Instead of the value of each tenement being assessed by commissioners, instructions were sent to stewards in March 1609 telling them to take each tenement's value from the surveys made in 1608 and earlier. Stewards who had

---

[132] SP14/32, no. 76 (*Short Title Catalogue*, no. 7705); the book was issued for the Duchy of Lancaster on 6 June, *Short Title Catalogue*, no. 7705.4. (I was ignorant of this when I wrote '"Vain projects"', cf. p. 80 n. 26.) The same instructions appear to have been issued in a different form in 1620, SP14/116, no. 94. For similar instructions issued by the Prince's Council in 1623, SP14/155, no. 33.

[133] Subsequently, Salisbury claimed that these values were adopted as the rates accepted by the equity courts in disputes over fining; BL, Lansd. MS 90, fol. 129r.

[134] The letter sent to stewards then instructs them to warn all tenants to prepare to attend on Salisbury in Michaelmas term where, on the surrender of their leases, they would be invited to compound for new leases of twenty-one years or three lives. The letter is unclear whether this referred to tenants generally or simply lessees; but the plan was never carried through. BL, Lansd. MS 90, fols. 122r–3v.

not received a copy of their survey were to have one on request and in November 1609, the auditors were told to ensure that this was being done.[135] The same procedure – using values taken from surveys – was established in the instructions given to the Prince of Wales's stewards in 1623.[136]

Whether the book of printed orders may be claimed as Salisbury's is to be doubted. In one of its features – the use of the surveyor and a JP to regulate the steward's actions – the book certainly copies Dorset's order of 1607. In a circular letter sent out in December 1608 under the signatures of Salisbury, Caesar and Chief Baron Tanfield, it was recalled how Dorset had issued a general prohibition to the stewards of all Crown manors restraining them from granting copies (for either lives or inheritance) until surveys of the Crown's manors had been made. (This may refer to an order of 1604 which survives in the same archive.) This prohibition was lifted by Salisbury, in the case of Barking (Essex) at least (but we may assume generally), when the printed instructions were sent out in June 1608. But the letter of December says quite clearly that the printed orders were drawn up by Dorset in the light of the surveys, and claims for Salisbury only the initiative in sending out the instructions when he became Lord Treasurer.[137] It is possible that the instructions left by Dorset only covered copyholds of inheritance and that the orders were extended to copyholds for lives with the cancellation of the fee-farming project, but this cannot be proved. Certainly, it seems that less can be claimed for Salisbury and more for Dorset than Salisbury's hagiographers would have us believe.

The book of printed directions simply declared all fines on copyholds of inheritance to be arbitrary and liable to be taken at a market rate unless proved otherwise by a stringent test. This may be thought a bold stroke, but the outcry which the orders provoked revealed the author (whoever he was) to be naively innocent of the realities of the situation. Tenants would not willingly accept the arbitrary alteration of the fines they paid. We may envisage that at the Michaelmas courts many groups of tenants decided to resist the

---

[135] SP14/44, no. 4 (another copy E163/15/33, fol. 11); SP14/51, no. 19 (another copy LR1/12, fol. 40v).   [136] SP14/155, no. 33.

[137] The letters cited are BL, Lansd. MS 89, fols. 6r–7v (15 Feb. 1604); 90, fols. 122r–3v (13 June 1608), 129r–30v (20 Dec. 1608). All come from the papers of Sir Michael Hicks as steward of Barking (Essex) and my attention was drawn to them by Dr Smith's biography of Hicks.

implemention of the directions, some claiming a customary practice of fining and others confirmatory decrees made under Elizabeth. At Rowington (Warwickshire), the steward in the company of two JPs searched the court rolls back to 25 Henry VI, satisfied himself that a custom of fixed fines existed and returned a certificate to that effect. At Knowle (Warwickshire), where the steward was Hercy himself, the tenants sued the Attorney-General rather than pay fines at Hercy's valuation. The fines were finally discounted. In the honour of Clitheroe, the tenants refused to pay fines according to the printed instructions until they had a confirmation of their customs in 1618.[138] These and other difficulties in implementing the instructions prompted a change of tactics, announced in letters sent to stewards in December 1608 and outlined at greater length in an undated memorandum directed to the King.[139]

James was told by Salisbury that where fines were acknowledged to be uncertain by custom, or where uncertainty could be proved, he intended to make them certain by decree in the Exchequer. Given that most tenants claimed their fines to be certain, Salisbury wrote that he foresaw great difficulties in discovering whose claims were genuine and whose not; he had therefore given instructions for all court rolls to be brought down to the Exchequer where they were to be searched for evidence of variations in fining.[140] Where the fines could be justified, they would be allowed, but where any deviation from the alleged custom could be found, even, in the case of monastic lands, from before the dissolution, the fines were to be declared arbitrary. The memorandum continued by explaining that Salisbury had sent letters to those manors where copyholders of inheritance held by uncertain fines inviting the tenants to appear before Salisbury, Caesar and the barons of the Exchequer to negotiate compositions for the payment of their fines at a lower rate than was stipulated by the book of directions. The resulting agreements were to be decreed by the Exchequer.[141] The tenants called to the Exchequer had been

---

[138] For these and other cases see my '"Vain projects"', pp. 94–5. SP14/37, nos. 21, 80, are abstracts of the certificates returned by stewards. DL41/15/3 is a bundle of original certificates from which DL30/80/1088 has strayed.

[139] BL, Lansd. MS 90, fol. 129r–v (20 Dec. 1608); SP14/43, no. 113.

[140] For this order, LR1/12, fol. 1r (undated, of late 1608).

[141] A draft decree was being circulated in March 1609; SP14/44, no. 4. To encourage confirmations to be made, the Parliament of 1610 enacted a bill to give statutory confirmation to decrees made in the Duchy or Exchequer courts in the following three years; statute 7–8 Jac. c. 21 (SR, IV (ii), pp. 1180–2).

charged by the printed book with fines of two years' value, but had accepted the invitation to compound for fines of one year's value in perpetuity with a down payment of two years' value as the price of the Exchequer's concession. Hence, in Salisbury's example, a copyhold worth £10 'upon the rack' (that is, at a market rent, but not including the Crown's rent) and which was not liable to pay a heriot, whose tenant was by the directions to pay £20 for his fine, would pay £20 for the privilege of paying fines of £10.[142]

It proved to be a highly resistible offer. In the letter of 20 December 1608, the stewards were ordered to call courts and present the offer of a composition for their fines to the tenants. The tenants were then to nominate a delegation to meet with Salisbury in late January. On one of the Essex manors of which Sir Michael Hicks was steward, the tenants failed to proceed even as far as electing their representatives.[143] Whether such extreme hostility was general it is hard to say; but persevering with the project throughout 1609 produced a thin haul of compositions. In November 1609, Hercy was acknowledging the 'unexpected slowness' of copyholders to compound and was offering Salisbury advice as to how to persuade more to come forward.[144] In fact, less than £3,500 was received from this source before Michaelmas 1612, a pitiful total, drawn from a mere handful of manors.[145]

Rather more was received from compositions made on the estates of the Duchy of Lancaster. We have already seen how in the months between the spring of 1607 and the later part of 1608 the project to make enfranchisements was abandoned and a plan to raise capital by confirming the copyhold customs of the same manors (where the custom was in someway defective) was adopted in its place. The tenants of the Newhold in the Forest of Pendle paid £3,763 for the confirmation of Henry VII's copies.[146] Sir Richard Molyneux paid twelve years' rent (£192) for the confirmation of his copyhold title to lands in Croxteth and Symondswood.[147] At Wakefield, the tenants agreed with the Privy Council in November 1608 for the confirmation of their copyhold fines (at double the traditional rate) and their

[142] SP14/61, no. 66, a memorandum by Hercy (drawn on above, pp. 228–9) which clearly bears on this project with Hercy advocating two years' value for a fine rather than a fixed number of years' rent.   [143] BL, Lansd. MS 91, fols. 2r–12v.

[144] SP14/49, no. 60. The advice appears not to survive.

[145] Hoyle, '"Vain projects"', pp. 83–4, table 1, p. 102.

[146] Tupling, *Rossendale*, p. 149.   [147] Lancashire RO, DDM 17/105.

copyhold estates (including those made of waste grounds) for a payment of thirty-five years' ancient rent. The receipts from Wakefield between Michaelmas 1608 and Michaelmas 1613 totalled £6,171 13s 1d.[148] Other Yorkshire manors of the Duchy received similar offers of confirmation but only here was the negotiation seen through to its conclusion. Nonetheless, the project brought into the Exchequer somewhere over £10,000, a great deal more than Salisbury's confirmatory project.[149]

It was the failure of the Parliament of 1610 which produced a further reversal in policy. In September 1610, Caesar had before him a project for copyholds, subscription to which was to be enjoined on the Chancellor of the Duchy, which did little more than develop the principles of the printed instructions of 1608. Where fines were acknowledged to be arbitrary, no action was to be taken. Where the tenants claimed to possess fixed fines, the steward, auditor and surveyor were all to search for evidence of their past variability; but where certainty was proved, the tenants were to be offered a composition.[150]

But the failure of the Great Contract forced a return to fee-farming. Sir Robert Johnson was advocating fee-farming in a paper circulating in January 1611.[151] A commission to enfranchise copyholds was issued to Salisbury in November 1611, surely suggesting that financial pressures had forced him to pick up afresh the policy he had rejected in 1608; but there is no sign of it being put into effect until after his death.[152] Earlier in 1611, the decision was taken to proceed to a general enfranchisement of the Duchy of Lancaster's northern estates. On 12 March, Thomas Fanshawe, the Duchy's general auditor, was given instructions for a general survey of the Duchy's copyholds during which he was to establish the details of the tenants' customs. His 'private instructions' authorised him to treat with the copyholders for the purchase of their estates in fee-farm with the reservation of ancient rents, suit of court, the enfranchised lands to be held in socage. But while this was the preferred course, if the tenants wished to remain copyholders, then he was to offer confirmations backed by the provisions of the statute of 1610,

---

[148] Calculated from E401/2411–20.   [149] Hoyle, '"Vain projects"', p. 87, table 1.

[150] BL, Lansd. MS 166, fols. 276r–7v, docketed by Caesar to 1 Sept. 1610. The propositions made by Mr Auditor Fanshawe on 23 Aug. fols. 278r–9v (another copy of which is SP14/61, no. 67), follow the same conservative lines.

[151] BL, Lansd. MS 165, fols. 146r–7v.   [152] C66/1915.

confirming or reducing fines to certainty. Irregular copies of demesne and waste lands were to be confirmed. Where the tenants had commons by the explicit grant in their copies or by prescription, Fanshawe was to offer either enclosure, with the reservation of a share to the King or the sale of the commons to their tenants. He was to use the threat of the sale of their lands to strangers 'from whom they cannot expect any such offer of favour and security as is now offered' as a threat to cajole them into submission.[153]

Neither the surveys Fanshawe was to make nor the books of proceedings he was to keep can be found. However, his accounts show him travelling about the north of England from 27 May to 26 August (during which time he returned to London to confer with Salisbury) and about the north Midlands from 24 September to 11 October. It appears he first made surveys, moving from Duffield Frith and other Derbyshire manors to Clitheroe (Lancashire), Bradford, Pontefract and Tickhill (Yorkshire) and Long Bennington (Lincolnshire), then Tutbury (Staffordshire) and Halton (Cheshire). He then repeated this circuit to take answers to the King's propositions. Hence, he impanelled juries to make surveys at Wirksworth on 6 June and returned there on 19 July. In the autumn, he travelled about to bring the tenants of the honours of Bolingbroke, Tutbury and Leicester and the manor of Long Bennington to composition.[154]

The Duchy's tenants were generally hostile to these proposals. The reports of the local commissioners appointed for Clitheroe and Pontefract suggest that Fanshawe's bringing of 'His Majesty's great grace and favour' and his willingness to raise sums by confirmation rather than by 'questioning their estates and customs' which he would have to do if he were 'not pleased graciously to deal with them' was received with little enthusiasm. The Clitheroe tenants made 'a great show of unwillingness to deal with us at this time', asked for further time to consider his propositions and thought that their customs and commons were as secure as could be made by any decree. In the end, a grudging consent to proceed with a composition was obtained. The Pontefract commissioners wrote that they 'did not find at first any great desire the tenants had to deal with us'. After much persuasion, the tenants made an offer of thirty years' rent for the purchase of their freeholds. At the end of the year, a request was

---

153 BL, Lansd. MS 166, fols. 280r–3v; the quotation from fol. 282v.
154 DL41/33/14A. Somerville, *Duchy of Lancaster*, II, pp. 17–19, offers additional information from the same source.

made that the tenants of Westerby (Lancashire) should have further time to send a delegation to Salisbury. None of these hopes came to pass. A search of the Duchy receiver's accounts and the Exchequer receipt books reveals no income from confirmations and only one case of Duchy tenants, those of Whitley and Cogeshall in the honour of Halton in Cheshire, taking their fee-farms.[155]

These grants doubtless revealed the two sides of fee-farming; that whilst it could yield useful sums to the Exchequer, it was also an extraordinarily laborious and painful way of raising revenue. It was against this discouraging background that Caesar regarded fee-farming as a project 'not likely to prove well' in 1613, but it had its supporters, including Sir Francis Bacon and Sir Robert Cotton, both of whom offered papers advocating it in 1612.[156] The commission for granting fee-farms was renewed in June 1612 but remained un-activated until the spring of 1614 when John Norden and other Exchequer officials sold copyholds to the value of £11,928 in manors in Hampshire, Wiltshire and Devon.[157]

Side by side with the campaign to implement the book of printed orders and its metamorphosis into a project to sell confirmations to copyholders was Salisbury's campaign against tenant right tenants, many of whom were the successors of the tenants whose fortunes under Elizabeth were considered in chapter 8 above. There, it was shown how in the sixteenth century the association between tenant right and border service had worked to the tenants' advantage. After the unification of the Crowns, this link acted very much to their detriment, for the assumption was readily made that the redundancy of border service had rendered tenant right void. This belief is seen most clearly in the King's proclamation against tenant right of 1620; it was not until 1625 that a judicial tribunal found that the two did not in fact proceed in tandem.[158]

[155] SP14/64, no. 37; SP14/65, no. 75; SP14/67, no. 6; DL28/11/6 (unfoliated, recording payments from the tenants); DL44/903; SP14/104, no. 73. W. Beamont, *A History of the Castle of Halton and Abbey of Norton* (Warrington, 1873), p. 105.

[156] Caesar, BL, Lansd. MS 165, fol. 225v; Bacon, Spedding, *Bacon*, IV, pp. 327–37, possibly of 18 Sept. 1612 (see pp. 311–12); Cotton, in his 'Means to repair the King's estate, 1612', BL, Cotton MS Cleo F. VI, fol. 44v.

[157] C66/1953, no. 27; their report is CRES40/18, fols. 187–93, and their book of agreements with tenants LR2/203, fols. 39r–71v. Receipts from these sales can be found in E401/2421.

[158] The history of tenant right after 1603 remains to be written. For the 1620 proclamation, see *Stuart Royal Procs.*, I, pp. 488–90. For the judicial decision of 1625, J. Nicholson and R. Burn, *The History and Antiquities of the Counties of Westmorland and Cumberland* (2 vols., 1777, repr. E. Ardsley, 1976), I, pp. 57–8.

As early as 1606, the Privy Council wrote to the tenants of the Duchy's manor of Newby advising them that their tenancies had lost their validity in law on unification; whilst some of the tenants opened negotiations with Lord Treasurer Dorset for the purchase of their fee-farms, nothing appears to have resulted from this and the matter was not immediately pursued.[159] It was left to Salisbury to exploit the potential in the situation. It appears that the tenants of the manor of Tynemouth (Northumberland) were called down to compound for leases during the summer of 1609, but the campaign against tenant right began in earnest with an order issued by Salisbury on 4 December 1609.[160] This instructed the tenants on manors where they held by tenant right to appoint representatives to attend on Salisbury in the following Easter term to take leases. The concession was made that where the tenants held by copy or had an earlier decree of the court favouring their custom, they should present such evidence to be scrutinised.

Some tenants made to demonstrate that they were entitled to the continuation of their tenant right. Those of Langwathby, Gamblesby and Scotby in the honour of Penrith (all manors where the tenants had taken copies in 1565) petitioned Salisbury asking that they should not be made to enter into any composition, and this he seems to have accepted.[161] The tenants of Holm Cultram (who had also taken Elizabethan copies) paid £300 to have an Exchequer decree confirming their customs.[162] Those of some townships in Tynemouth successfully defended their customary estates of inheritance and were allowed to have a confirmatory decree for £789 13s 4d or about six years' rent. The tenants of North Shields, whose copies had first been granted by commission in 1565, were allowed to take twenty-one-year leases for a payment of about ten years' rent.[163] On the manors in North Cumberland which had come to the Crown on the attainder of Leonard Dacre, the tenants appeared and admitted that they had no confirmation or ancient records with which to prove their customary estate of inheritance. This not withstanding, they were allowed to compound for forty-year leases of their lands which were broadly similar in character to those granted in Middleham and

[159] Leeds Archives Dept, Acc. 1448, nos. 214, 217.
[160] A petition of the North Shields tenants of February 1610 refers to them having received an order to attend on Salisbury during the previous summer. LR9/61, pt 2, Yorkshire auditor's entry book, fol. 1v. For the order of 4 December 1609, LR1/195, fols. 228v–9r.
[161] Cumbria RO, Carlisle, PR/90/15.   [162] Ibid., PR/122/252.
[163] LR1/195, fols. 95r–7r; petition of the tenants cited in n. 160 above; E. Bateson et al. (eds.), A History of Northumberland (15 vols., Newcastle, 1893–1940), VIII, pp. 293–7.

Bromfield and Yale in the 1560s. The tenants had covenants inserted in their demises which reproduced the features of their inheritance and other customs. For this concession, they were to pay a fine of six years' rent on the granting of the lease and four years' fine on the death of the lord of the manor and each tenant.[164] At much the same time, Salisbury permitted the tenants of Middleham and Richmond to renew the leases granted them in the late 1560s for a further forty-year term.[165]

The attempt to capitalise on the perceived weaknesses of tenant right produced differing conclusions from manor to manor and it might be suggested that each outcome was largely determined by the tenants' notion of what they might rescue from their predicament. But it also appears most clearly how Salisbury's ambitions extended only so far as taking cash payments for the continuance of existing arrangements, albeit that in some cases the alteration of tenure served to suggest that more substantial changes were being made. The result of this rather half-hearted approach was that there remained opportunities for exploitation which the Prince of Wales's Council seized in the following decade when some of the same manors were granted to the Prince in augmentation of his ducal revenues.[166]

Under the direction of Suffolk (Lord Treasurer 1614–18) and Sir Fulke Greville (Chancellor 1614–21), the Exchequer attempted to enforce the provisions of the printed instructions whilst working towards (in the first instance) a further enfranchisement. Suffolk's device to obtain conformity was a letter sent to stewards in August 1615 which became known, because it prohibited the holding of courts, as the Great Restraint. This described how some stewards had wrongly taken credence of customs pretended by tenants and others had allowed a backlog of fines to develop. In future, all stewards were to apply the book of printed directions rigorously to any unassessed fines and seize the lands of any tenants who refused to pay the fines laid down by the book. To assist the execution of the commission for enfranchising copyholds, all stewards were forbidden to hold court barons or make admittances. A letter to the auditors, informing them of the policy they were to follow on their autumn circuits, insisted that they were not to permit stewards to assess fines at less than the

---

[164] E124/11, fols. 131v–8r. There is a hint that an attempt was made to sell forty-year leases in Ennerdale in 1609; R. P. Littledale, 'Ennerdale', *Transactions of the Cumberland and Westmorland Antiquarian and Archaeological Society*, second ser., 31 (1931), p. 174.

[165] LR1/195, fols. 65r–6r. [166] Considered below, pp. 249–50.

values set down in the book, custom or prescription notwithstanding. Where the court rolls supported claims of a customary rate, the matter was to be referred to Suffolk and Greville.[167]

The immediate result was to revive old grievances over fines as at Holm Cultram (Cumberland) where the tenants had recently bought of Salisbury a confirmation of an already certain custom and would not (in the words of their steward) 'condescend to the printed instructions'.[168]

But as in the prohibition to stewards of 1604, the suspension of court barons was intended to pressure the tenants into taking fee-farms of their lands. The letter to stewards instructed them to inform their tenants of the royal intention and the auditors were commanded to spread the word further as they went about their circuits in the autumn of 1615; but the project was for some unknown reason aborted. A letter rescinding the Great Restraint was sent out at some point in the next two years, but this instructed stewards either to apply the book of orders where fines were arbitrary or, if the tenants claimed a certain custom, to refer them to the Exchequer where their customs would be judicially decreed. In April 1618, this order had to be reiterated as some stewards had simply ceased to hold courts, a state of affairs which continued on some manors into the 1620s.[169] Moves were afoot to examine the customs of a number of manors and in 1618, a handful demonstrated their claim to possess certain fines and were exonerated.[170] The instruction to take fines at the rates set down in the book of printed instructions was circulated afresh in July 1621, the stewards being instructed to take fines as if they were arbitrary if the customary rate had not been accepted by the court.[171]

The Great Restraint created muddle not profit. It was perhaps an admission of the Exchequer's inability to cope administratively with the fines that prompted the idea of making a general farm of copyhold fines and receipts of courts in 1619.[172] The Duchy was more successful; throughout the middle years of the decade, it was working

---

[167] Copies of the Great Restraint can be found in HMC, *Rutland*, i, p. 445, *Towneshend*, p. 19, and Cumbria RO, Carlisle, PR122/254f. The letter to auditors (of 23 Sept. 1615) is in E306/12, pt 2 (unsorted).

[168] The tenants of Ennerdale, also in Cumberland, took the same line. LR9/107, file of letters to Suffolk as Lord Treasurer, 1614–15.

[169] LR9/9/1309; LR9/1/46.   [170] Hoyle, '"Vain projects"', p. 91.

[171] LR1/140, fol. 39, another copy LR9/102 (book of general warrants 1619–28), fol. 23r–v.

[172] *CSPD 1611–18*, p. 139; *CSPD 1619–23*, p. 61 (Grant Book, p. 281); BL, Add. MS 12504, fols. 170–5 (papers opposing the idea).

towards the granting of confirmations on many of its manors. Somerville has shown how information about tenure was being gathered as early as the autumn of 1614, but it was not until 1617 that the work of selling confirmations really began. In September the Chancellor of the Duchy in the company of the Duchy's Attorney-General, the auditor and receiver were touring Lancashire explaining their proposals. Roger Kenyon was busy preparing surveys of the Duchy's Lancashire manors in the late spring and summer of 1618, and in June 1619 he was instructed to extend this work to the Derbyshire, Staffordshire and Leicestershire manors.[173] The decrees themselves (of which there were seventeen for manors in Derbyshire, Lancashire, Leicestershire, Lincolnshire, Northamptonshire, Staffordshire and Yorkshire) were made in 1618–20, normally at a rate of forty years' ancient rent. In one or two cases, forty-five years' rent was accepted for the settlement of the tenant's title in commons. Whilst the decrees dwelt on the imperfections of the tenants' copies and in some cases confirmed the possession of demesnes or former waste (roodland), it must be acknowledged that the Duchy never envisaged using these flaws as a means of recovering the lands in question. Their role was to conceal the larger truth that the confirmations were designed to raise money.[174] As such, it could not be said that the project was entirely successful. Whilst the decrees show that the total raised was a little short of £18,000, only half of the composition money was paid on the making of the decree, the other half being reserved until the statutory confirmation of the decrees which, as things turned out, had to wait until the Commonwealth. On some manors, of which the honour of Clitheroe was one, confirmation did bring to an end the impasse between the tenants and the Duchy produced by the attempt to impose the 1608 printed orders.[175] Not that tenants readily accepted a composition. It appears that a majority in favour of proceeding to a decree could not be found amongst the tenants of West Derby and Wavertree and no decree resulted. The alternative the Duchy offered those who rejected the

[173] Lancashire RO, DDKe 5/45, 46, 70.

[174] Somerville, *Duchy of Lancaster*, II, p. 19; Hoyle, '"Vain projects"', pp. 91–2, App. 2. R. B. Manning, *Village Revolts. Social Protest and Popular Disturbances in England, 1509–1640* (Oxford, 1988), pp. 121–4, describes the experience of Raunds in Northamptonshire but takes the claim of legal imperfections in the tenants' estates at its face value and never realised the degree to which this confirmation was part of a larger movement.

[175] Somerville, *Duchy of Lancaster*, II, p. 20; Swain, *Industry before the Industrial Revolution*, p. 62.

option of confirmation was the enforcement of the book of printed instructions.[176]

This appears to have been the last attempt to raise extraordinary profits from the Duchy estates; indeed, by granting the tenants an unimpeachable security of tenure, it may be seen as having made impossible any future attempt to do so. On the Exchequer estates, two further attempts were made to raise revenue by confirmation or fee-farming. Cranfield had been an advocate of fee-farming the Crown lands as early as 1616.[177] Once Lord Treasurer, he empowered a commission of Exchequer officials to sell customary tenancies in fee-farm or confirm customs. Whilst the commission sat throughout the summer of 1623 (and in the autumn called the tenants of a number of northern manors to appear before them), it made neither sale nor confirmation. Business appears to have been thin, but the few who did trouble to offer for their lands generally offered derisory sums. 'We grew to composition and agreement with none of the tenants for that the most... offered far short of what was thought fit.' A few individuals did offer reasonable sums for single properties, but the commission was unwilling to condone the dismemberment of the King's manors and finally found itself unwilling to recommend any of the offers it received to Cranfield.[178] Perhaps ignorant of this sorry debacle, the commissioners for retrenchment of 1626 sought the advice of Christopher Vernon of the Pipe Office as to the plausibility of fee-farming. He advised that the tenants of both leaseholds and copyholds should be invited to take the fee-farms of their tenements before a certain date, after which His Majesty would be free to dispose of them as he wished. A proclamation inviting all royal tenants to purchase their fee-farms was published on 13 August. And it must be admitted that some tenants took advantage of this, taking their tenements at a rent double that customarily paid. By the end of the year, the commissioners for sales had sold lands with a rental value of £845 per annum for £30,000 and an increase in rent of £876.[179]

[176] Lancashire RO, DDKe/5/66; Leeds Archives Dept, Acc. 1448, no. 233. Additional refs. can be found in Hoyle, '"Vain projects"', p. 92 n. 68.

[177] Tawney, *Business and Politics*, pp. 150–1.

[178] Hoyle, '"Vain projects"', p. 99, citing the commission's working papers in LR9/6/712/1–9. Subsequently, I discovered that the commissioners had their working notes engrossed on parchment for presentation to Cranfield with their report; Kent AO, U269/1, OE 1518.

[179] University of London Library, MS 195, pt i, fols. 11v, 37v–42v, etc., pt ii, fol. 34r; *Stuart Royal Procs.*, II, pp. 102–5. The project suggesting a further enfranchisement placed in the State Papers under 1640 (SP16/451, no. 123) and accepted by some authorities (e.g. S. J.

The policy of confirming copyholds for large cash compositions was also pursued on the jointure estates of Anne of Denmark and the lands granted to Charles Prince of Wales in augmentation of his ducal estates. Little can be discovered of the Queen's confirmations; in 1611, the tenants of her manors in the honour of Pontefract (Yorkshire) paid £393 6s 8d for compositions, but these were agreements for her life only.[180] The compositions made with the Prince of Wales can be enumerated and the negotiations leading to their formulation examined more fully thanks to the copious materials in the Duchy of Cornwall Office. Four confirmations were made: at Kendal (1619), Penrith (1620), Macclesfield (1621) and Cheltenham (1625). In other places, the Duchy can be seen to have investigated the possibilities and then drawn back.[181] In every case, the Duchy found some cause to question the customary tenure of the tenants. At Kendal, the Duchy disliked the tenant right custom of the honour and the tenants' possession of enclosures made from the wastes.[182] A survey of Macclesfield made in the summer of 1619 found that the tenants had made large-scale encroachments on the commons, cut timber and made coal pits on their customary lands.[183] A number of the Penrith tenants held copies first granted in 1565; the Duchy seized on the invalidity of these and forced the copyholders into a composition to validate their titles.[184] In the case of Cheltenham, it was claimed that the tenants used all manner of unreasonable customs and owed arbitrary fines; the steward was ordered only to make admittances to tenants who conceded the Duchy's claims.[185] The result in every case was that the tenants were persuaded into paying lump sums for the confirmation of their tenures and received the Prince's consent to them having a decree in equity or a private statute to confirm their possession and customs. An agreement was struck with the Kendal tenants on 21 June 1619,

Madge, *The Domesday of Crown Lands* (London, 1938, repr. 1968), p. 60) as belonging to that year may, on internal evidence, be just as easily of 1626. It is not clear how many of the grants were of copyholds. The commission also revived the idea of selling copyholds and established commissions in five counties to test the water; but as the matter never reappears in the minute books, it was doubtless found to be of little profit (University of London Library, MS 195, pt i, fols. 6v, 12r).   [180] SP14/67, no. 27; SP14/68, no. 58.

[181] For instance at Leeds, DCO, Bound MSS, T/M/1, Order Book II (1621–5), fols. 92r, 129r, 134v.   [182] DCO, Bound MSS, T/M/2, Warrants and Letters, 1615–19, fol. 99r.

[183] DCO, Bound MSS, T/M/2, Warrants and Letters 2, fols. 17r–18r; 3, fol. 113v.

[184] DCO, Bound MSS, T/M/2, Warrants and Letters 2, fols. 65r–6v, Order Book A, fols. 42r–6r; PRO E36/47, fols. 93r, 94r–v. 95r.

[185] DCO, Bound MSS, T/M/2, Warrants and Letters, 1621–3, fol. 106r–v; 1623–6 fol. 46v.

the Prince's consent to a degree in equity given on 18 October, a bill introduced in Chancery on 28 October and a decree made on 4 November.[186] The decree was to be confirmed by statute.[187]

The quarter-century or so after 1603 saw the partial implementation of two distinct policies towards copyholds. The first was the progressive policy of modernising custom so that tenants paid fines which bore a relation to the market value of land. The second was to release capital from customary tenancies by selling them to their tenants or, as a second best, selling confirmations, both of which served to close the door irrevocably on the possibility of increasing fines from these lands in the future. At the risk of being judgemental, the first course was in the long-term interest of the Crown; the second could only be justified as an emergency measure when the pressure to reduce debts was greater than the need to raise income (although paradoxically reducing debts did raise disposable income if the debt was interest-bearing). The two policies are interconnected; we have already seen how the threat of the implementation of the book of directions was used as a means to cajole tenants into purchasing fee-farms or confirmations.

Yet neither course was followed through to its end; rather, policy can be seen as a series of switches from one option to another to suit immediate needs. This reflected both the frequency with which the higher executive personnel of the Exchequer changed (and the lack of administrative continuity) but also the inability of the Exchequer to master a gradually deteriorating financial state of affairs. The damage done to the Crown's reputation and interests amongst its tenants by this tacking between raising fines and selling confirmations was acknowledged by an anonymous writer of Salisbury's time:

This business hath often time been set in hand by the lords, and by themselves upon solemn debate with the barons of the Exchequer laid down again when many tenants were ready to have gone that course which had made the tenants conceive that either good assurance cannot be made to them, or that the state affecteth it not further than as a business which necessity enforceth and thereupon many tenants who did once desire it are now afraid therein.[188]

---

[186] DCO, Bound MSS, J/M/3, Acts of the Council, 1618, fols. 204, 221–3; T/M/3, Warrants and Letters, 1619–20, fols. 19v–21; PRO C78/504, no. 8.
[187] W. Notestein, F. H. Relf and H. Simpson (eds.) *Commons Debates 1621* (7 vols., New Haven, CT, 1935), VII, pp. 65–70.   [188] SP14/59, no. 44.

In this way, the tenants of Pontefract in 1611 remembered the cavalier treatment of the tenants of neighbouring Wakefield four years earlier.[189]

If executive and administrative inadequacies handicapped the implementation of both policies, how successful had either been by 1625 or 1640? It is exceptionally difficult to come to any considered account, not least because successive Lord Treasurers had charge of an estate which was rapidly diminishing. The book of printed directions was almost certainly applied without difficulty to copyholds for lives, where the fines demanded had reached very substantial levels by 1640. Tenants holding copies for lives had no means by which they could resist the terms laid down there; it was inherent in the very basis of such a copyhold custom that there was no restraint on fining, nor any test of reasonableness. The only restraint on the lord was his ability to find a tenant willing to pay his fine. In fact the printed directions, in that they instructed stewards to favour the kin of previous tenants over strangers in granting copies, might well have been welcomed by them.[190]

Whether the implementation of the book significantly increased the profits the Crown received from copyholds of inheritance might be doubted. Where the fines were acknowledged to be arbitrary, as at Barking (where fines were reported to have been taken at about one year's value in 1608), it may well have increased the rate. But on those manors where fines were fixed by custom or prescription, it brought nothing but trouble and strife (and in the short term a refusal to pay fines) as successive Lord Treasurers ordered stewards to disregard customary practices.[191] There was, one senses, a persistent refusal to appreciate the difficulties of increasing fines in these circumstances, and for all the talk of court rolls being sent up for scrutiny, there are no cases of the Crown proving its right to take arbitrary fines where the tenants contended otherwise. On the contrary, the policy adopted was to shout loudly about the Crown's rights and then confirm the tenants' custom.

The superb evidence of the Duchy of Cornwall reveals just how

---

[189] SP14/65, no. 75.
[190] Individual fines were very large at Mere (Wilts.) in the decade before the Civil War which suggests that the tables in the printed instructions or the order of the Prince's Council of 1623 were being enforced. But the way in which fines for copyholds were calculated makes it impossible to estimate the rate of fines unless the term conceded is known. E317/Wilts./40.
[191] When the steward of Warton (Lancs.) wrote to Suffolk for instructions in 1617, he stressed the loss of fines which the restraint produced. Bodl., Rawlinson MS D908, no. 2.

hard it was to secure a satisfactory composition for the confirmation of the tenants' customs. When the tenants of Leeds attended in July 1623, they offered 200 marks for the confirmation of their custom. This was refused and the tenants excused.[192] The Kendal tenants, despite the aggressive legalism of the Duchy's attempt to pick holes in their titles, stood firm in their claim to hold by a customary tenure with fixed fines. A commission of February 1619 to compound with the tenants proved abortive, the tenants showing themselves 'obstinate and refractory'. The Duchy then demanded that the tenants should pay ten years' rent for their fines, pointing out that neighbouring tenants paid fifteen or sixteen years' rent. But in an accompanying private letter to the commissioners, the Council permitted its agents to accept six years' rent if that was all that could be obtained. When negotiations reopened in June 1619, the tenants offered £1,000 for the confirmation of their customs and the figure of £2,700 (including arrears of fines) was finally agreed upon. As this gave the tenants the rates of fines they had claimed all along, it did nothing to increase the Duchy's recurrent revenue and must be viewed as a defeat.[193]

It could not be claimed that the Kendal debacle was in someway the result of the Duchy's inability to deal with northern truculence. The negotiations later in 1619 over Macclesfield opened with the Duchy demanding £2,000 or 40 years' rent for a confirmation of the tenants' fines and the overlooking of their various infringements of the lord's rights. The tenants countered with an offer of fifteen or sixteen years' old rent or a year's improved rent. After consultations, the tenants' counsel offered 2,000 marks (although many tenants, he reported, thought this too much) and this was accepted.[194] The detailed Duchy minute books leave the clear impression that the Duchy's claims were so much bluster, that the demand for arbitrary fines was merely a stratagem and that the Duchy was more concerned to obtain a token payment, no matter how modest, rather than risk a prolonged dispute over relatively small increases in casual income.

The Crown's inability to make much progress with its copyholders makes its flirtation with fee-farming all the more understandable. For successive Lord Treasurers, fee-farming was a philosopher's stone,

[192] DCO, Bound MSS, T/M/1 Order Books, 1621–5, fols. 92r, 129r, 134v. This was the sum accepted by Anne of Denmark in 1611 (SP14/67, no. 27) and was about three years' rent.
[193] DCO, Bound MSS, T/M/2, Warrants and Letters, 1615–19, fols. 244v–5r; J/M/3, Acts of the Council, 1618, pp. 162, 179, 184, 204, 221–3.
[194] DCO, Bound MSS, J/M/3, Acts of the Council, 1619–20, fols. 20r–1v, 100r, 104r.

the means by which debt could be reduced to manageable levels. The prospect it offered doubtless explains why it raised otherwise sober-headed advisors to the most over optimistic excitation. Johnson acknowledged that the tenants might not be over eager to fee-farm, but once they realised that it would make an end to fines, they would praise it 'as the greatest favour that ever did proceed from a King to a people'.[195]

Other commentators had their feet placed more firmly on the ground.[196] Not all tenants would wish, or be able, to enfranchise. There would be a need to maintain officers and courts, and problems were envisaged in the collection of rents. The interest of any Crown lessees would have to be bought out. Tenants would require time to pay their compositions. Provison would have to be made for the transfer of commons and other customary perquisites. There were procedural and conveyancing problems. Moreover, one of these writers was sceptical that the tenants would be willing to pay a respectable sum for their fee simples. Tenants, he explained, would never pay forty or fifty years' rent when the contractors for the sale of Crown lands had bought the fee simple of copyhold lands for twenty-five years' rental value or less for chantry lands.[197]

This was doubtless true. The most efficient way for a tenant body to acquire the fee simple of their tenements was to buy the whole manor, tenements, commons, the right to hold courts and all, as a syndicate, and then make assignments to each tenant of his tenement and share of the manorial rights. As the last writer indicates, in the early seventeenth century this could be done relatively cheaply and without the penalties which fee-farming could bring with it. That said, many tenants preferred to remain tenants. The obligations placed on freeholders, notably that of jury service, were not, as a later tradition might have it, the valued freedoms of politically active men but expensive and time-consuming chores.

There was also a striking disparity between the valuation put on the fee simple of copyhold land by tenants and Crown. Even in the case of copyhold for lives, where fines and tenant insecurity were greatest, Hercy's contracts show that tenants were generally willing to offer only small sums for the fee simple. At Frodingham

---

[195] BL, Lansd. MS 165, fol. 146v.
[196] SP14/59, no. 44, placed in the State Papers under 1610 for no obvious reason. SP14/104, no. 74, is based on this text. SP14/104, no. 73, is incomplete. Its references to the Lord Commissioners probably makes it of 1612–14.   [197] SP14/59, no. 44.

(Dorset) in 1607, some tenants offered over fifty years' rent, but others placed a very small valuation on their lands. Henry Ridge would give only £30 for the fee simple of the copyhold he rented at £3 4s 10d or £20 for the fee-farm, but was outbid by a gentleman who offered £100 for the fee-farm.[198] In 1606, at Bulford (Wiltshire) tenants by copy for lives offered paltry sums, for instance 20 marks and double the rent for a tenement valued at £10 or £20 per annum and a double rent for 60 acres valued at £26 and rented for 33s 6d. Other tenants expressed themselves content for another man to buy the fee-farm.[199]

The 1614 commission in the West Country was able to make sales at between forty and fifty years' old rent or between six and ten years' value, but this was no more than the renewal of a copy would cost under the book of printed directions. Nonetheless, it proved impossible to liquidate entire manors. At Frodingham, only six tenants accepted in 1614 (including a leaseholder). At Bovey Tracey, nineteen tenants contracted to buy their tenements, but seventeen refused and their freeholds were sold to a neighbouring gentleman. The commissioners themselves thought that they could have sold a third more tenements but for doubts over title and if longer days of payment could have been offered.[200]

Copyholds of inheritance were an even less attractive prospect for purchase, whether by the outsider or tenant. For the tenant, there was little advantage in buying the fee simple when the right of alienation and inheritance was admitted and (as was normal on the northern manors of both Exchequer and Duchy) fines were fixed. There was no interest in fee-farming copyholds in the honour of Clitheroe, although some handsome rates of composition were offered in Wakefield before enfranchisement was abandoned. Copyholders of inheritance lacked that element of insecurity that made copyholders for lives amenable to persuasion.

Just how little the Crown's tenants valued their security is revealed by the dismal response drawn by the 1623 commissioners for enfranchisement. The tenants of Ditton and Datchet (Buckinghamshire) appeared and offered five years' old rent for their fines to be made certain and ten years' to be enfranchised. The commissioners demanded sixty years. The tenants of Hampton offered forty years',

[198] LR2/203, fol. 20.   [199] Ibid., fols. 369–71.
[200] CRES40/18, fols. 187–93 passim; LR2/203, fols. 20–31.

those of Twickenham thirty years'; again sixty years' was demanded.
A tenant of Shitlington (Bedfordshire) offered ten, twelve or at most
fifteen years' on behalf of his fellow-tenants. He was turned away.
The Duchy of Cornwall's Council cannot be credited with any
greater success. When the decision was taken to fee-farm the lordships
of Bromfield and Yale in 1624, the tenants' spokesman opened the
bidding at ten years' old rent. The Council asked for fifty years' or
forty at the least. The tenants offered twenty years', the Council
asked for thirty and accepted twenty-five years' (although there were
then difficulties in agreeing days of payment).[201]

The persistent diversion of policy towards copyholds from raising
fines to selling freeholds makes plain the subordination of improvement to asset stripping. It is ironic that the latter could only be
successfully pursued through the sales of copyholds for lives, where
the possibilities for improvement were greatest. Fee-farming must
have brought nothing but disappointment to successive Lord
Treasurers. For all the labour invested, the sale of freeholds to an
ungrateful tenantry simply failed to realise sums of a size to make a
significant impact on the Crown's finances, for the total raised during
King James's reign was probably less than £20,000. Confirmations of
copyholds brought in more, perhaps £3,500 on the Exchequer estates
in 1607–12, £10,000 on the Duchy of Lancaster's estates in the same
period and an additional £18,000 promised from them in 1618–21,
but against this needs to be weighed the diet of commissioners in the
field, the cost of surveying and the rewards which the Crown
habitually gave its servants for their endeavours. But the failure of the
Crown to raise the sorts of sums it desired from enfranchisement or
confirmation reveals its impotence in the face of tenant discontent
and intransigence.

III

A simple lack of readily assimilated sources makes it difficult for any
discussion of the Crown's leasing policy under James I and Charles I
to be more than cursory. The particulars for leases, used to such effect
by Drs Haslam and Thomas in earlier chapters, are not extant after

[201] DCO, Bound MSS, J/M/3, Acts of the Council, 1624–5, fols. 56r–v, 92r–v, 107r, etc.;
Warrants, 1623–6, fols. 123v–4r. The fee-farming of the lordships was confirmed by statute
in 1627, statute 3 Chas. I, c.6 (SR, v, pp. 31–3).

1603. Moreover, the series of entry books of leases which cover much of Elizabeth's reign all peter out in the early years of the new century for reasons which will become apparent.[202] Of course, leases passing the Great Seal continued to be enrolled on the Patent Rolls but the extraction of an adequate number for analysis was a larger task than could be contemplated on this occasion.

All landowners recognised that the profits of leases could be manipulated. At moments of financial need, tenants could be invited to take new leases, so extending their interest in their tenement before their existing lease had expired, and the fines taken on a new lease could be increased by lengthening the term offered to the tenant. Premature leasing or long leasing was a way of anticipating income at the cost of tying the landowner's hands long into the future. The Crown used both these methods as a means to increase receipts with the result that its income from leases was liable to wild fluctuations.

In fact, the fines paid on leases became unimportant as a source of revenue after Salisbury's death. The reasons for this are two-fold; in part, it naturally follows from the diminution of the estates by sale but it also reflects how in 1609 Salisbury anticipated the expiry of many leases with a great bonfire of leasing. Consequently, in the 1630s only a little over £5,400 was received at the Exchequer from fines on leases and of this 70 per cent came in two exceptional years; in four other years the receipts totalled less than £100.[203]

There is evidence that Dorset abandoned the Elizabethan rules for leasing identified by Dr Thomas. When the estates of the late countess of Lennox were leased in c. 1603, the fines taken amounted to about fifteen years' rent.[204] During 1604 or 1605, Dorset introduced the practice of making leases for forty-year terms with each lessee paying an increased rent. Of a sample of twenty-four leases from late 1606, rents of £34 were added to ancient rents of £83, but these leases attracted fines of a little short of £600. The small number of leases in reversion made at the same moment were for twenty-one years, but whilst these had increments in their rental, they paid very considerable fines; old rents of £42 attracted

[202] Corporation of London RO, RCE 114C, contains five entry books of leases passed under the Great and Exchequer seals of Elizabethan and early Jacobean dates. RCE Papers 155, is a similar volume of leases under the Exchequer seal for Devon, Wiltshire and Somerset for 24–41 Eliz.   [203] Dietz, *Receipts and Issues*, pp. 148–9, 152–3.
[204] CRES40/19A, unnumbered.

increments of only £10 but fines of £228.²⁰⁵ A later source refers to these increments as being for the provision of the royal household so their origins might be located in the contemporary debate over purveyance.²⁰⁶ The appearance is that Dorset was trying to raise the Crown's rental but in doing so was conceding a longer term to the tenant than contemporaries would have thought wise.

It is to his considerable credit that Salisbury prohibited the granting of leases in reversion to strangers which, as Dr Thomas has shown, had such a debilitating effect on the lands.²⁰⁷ But Salisbury saw leases and timber as the means to relieve the pressing problem of debt which he inherited and which he never managed to master. One of his first steps on becoming Lord Treasurer was to arrange for the redemption of manors mortgaged to the City of London by Elizabeth in 1599. He then secured a commission (on 14 June 1608) to lease these lands with the deliberate purpose of raising large sums. Caesar's journal records that Salisbury made leases of mortgaged lands for fines of £5,185 in his first weeks in office and called on additional tenants to compound in Michaelmas term.²⁰⁸ On this occasion, his method was to have the tenants compound to have their existing leases extended to forty years (conversely, it might be said that he made forty-year leases against which the tenants had the value of their existing leases credited). In the case of the manor house of Blewbury (Berkshire), rented for £43 16s 8d but worth £100 per annum, twenty-six years of a lease were left to run but it was felt that two years' value of the premises would be an adequate fine to enlarge the term to forty years; the fine demanded was therefore £200 or a little over four years' ancient rent. In the case of the manor of Greens Norton (Northamptonshire), the basic price for a forty-year lease was eleven years' value. Leases with thirty years' or more to run (so needing an additional concession of only ten years) were granted for one year's value, leases with ten years to run five and a half years' value, eight years seven years' value and three years nine and a half years' value. In all, the topping up of leases at Greens Norton was

²⁰⁵ E401/2407 (unpaginated), the sample taken from the first three pages of Cary, *Fines Dimissionum*. The new practice is not seen in the spring of 1604 (when all leases were for twenty-one-year terms) but had been introduced by Michaelmas 1605; E401/2403, 2405.

²⁰⁶ Bodl., Rawlinson MS C451, fol. 3r.

²⁰⁷ See above, pp. 184–90. 'The Book of Bounty' is printed by Notestein, Relf and Simpson (eds.), *Commons Debates 1621*, VII, pp. 491–6.

²⁰⁸ Dietz, *English Public Finance*, pp. 86–7; SP14/50, fol. 106v–10v; Hill, 'Caesar's journal', p. 326.

worth £3,883 16s 6d or a little under three year's value, but about eleven years' ancient rent. The releasing of the mortgaged estates was calculated to be worth £23,372 19s 2d or just over three years' value or seventeen and three-quarter years' rent.[209]

The use of long leases to raise large sums of ready money was extended to the estates as a whole in 1609. A commission for sales of 10 May (two days after the signing of the deed of annexation) authorised the leasing of annexed lands for the maximum permissible term (including the lease in hand) of sixty years. The concession of granting these leases of lands with a rental value of £2,000 on these terms was sold to the first of the contractors' syndicates for a gross fine of twenty-two years' ancient rent.[210] The leases were made as letters patent to John Eldred and others who then assigned particular parcels to members of the syndicate. They in turn assigned their interest to the tenants of the lands. In the case of a contractors' lease of lands in the honour of Pickering, Eldred and others assigned their demise to George and Thomas Whitmore on 1 November 1609; they sold it on to the tenants' agent the following day and he made conveyances to each tenant.[211] The consideration for these leases was, by the standards applying on the Crown lands, more than adequate, but it had the effect of short-circuiting the normal process of lease renewal in exactly the same way as Elizabeth's leases in reversion had done. For this reason, relatively few leases were granted in the years immediately following (excluding such special occasions as the leasing of the estates of Prince Henry which followed his death) and this doubtless explains why the entry books and other registers of leases tend to have been abandoned in the following few years.

The consequences of the contractors' leases are not merely archival. Being of such great length, the possibility of raising capital in the future by selling reversions was hardly an attractive prospect until well towards mid-century; and so, while the 1609 leases not only froze the Crown's rental income from these lands at their sixteenth-century level, they also ensured that any future crisis in Crown finance would have to be met by sale rather than leasing. It is in this

[209] SP14/36, no. 53. It might be added that these are calculations of potential profit rather than actual receipts. Dietz gives £8,612 as receipts for fines on mortgaged lands in 1609.

[210] SP14/50, fols. 110v–15v; SP14/45 no. 159. The agreement between the commissioners for sale and the contractors was for leases in reversion of a length which added to the existing lease would form a term of sixty years, but the leases granted were all for sixty years.

[211] Turton (ed.), *The Honour and Forest of Pickering*, pp. 89–90.

light that Dietz's figures for the value of fines on leases made in the years of financial crisis in the mid-1620s must be read; only in 1624 did they exceed £1,000, and in 1627 fell below £100. Likewise, the fines on leases played practically no part in financing the Anglo-Scottish war after 1637.[212] That said, the lands leased to Charles Prince of Wales (extra to the Duchy) in County Durham were leased in 1626 for characteristically long terms, eighty years being standard.[213]

One of the few subsequent occasions on which leases were made in large numbers was in the redemption of the honour of Grafton from Sir Francis Crane.[214] Here again, we see financial need placed before judicious estate management. The honour was mortgaged to Crane in March 1628 for £7,500 with a covenant making the mortgage absolute if Crane had not been repaid the principal within two years. By 1634, reports were circulating within the Exchequer that Crane had begun to treat the manor as his own freehold, having appointed his own officers, held courts in his name and made leases. He also demolished much of Henry VIII's house at Grafton and used the stone to build his own house.

Sir Miles Fleetwood secured a warrant to make additional leases to the Grafton tenants with the purpose of raising enough in fines to repay Crane. His chosen method was to make leases of thirty-one years in reversion and he succeeded in making contracts with the tenants worth £15,614. Fleetwood justified this by arguing that the lands were in lease for long periods because of the existing contractors' leases and he weighed the eventual possibility of raising rents when the leases expired with the obvious disadvantage of the existing arrangements. Crane objected to the procedure and alleged that Fleetwood's renewals were made too cheaply. This was partially confirmed by a commission of enquiry which travelled to the estates in July 1635. This body was of the mind that where the tenants already had long unexpired terms the fine expected on the grant of a reversion was too small to be worth taking given the considerable

---

[212] Dietz, *Receipts and Issues*, excluding those sums in his figures for leases of customs farms. Russell has noticed the making of leases for long terms in these years, 'Charles I's financial estimates for 1642', *BIHR* 58 (1985), p. 119.

[213] The commission is C66/2385, dorse, no. 1. LR1/200, fols. 254v, 271–7, 285–93, 313. The receipts for these fines were paid to the Receiver-General of these incomes and are additional to the receipts in the Exchequer.

[214] For Grafton, see R. Ashton, *The Crown and the Money Market, 1603–40* (Oxford, 1960), pp. 62–4.

benefit it conferred on the tenant.[215] Fleetwood's actions were finally approved by the Exchequer court in 1636.[216]

It would be wrong to read the preceding account as indicating that the Crown was blessed with opportunities of which it quite failed to take advantage, trading, as it were, the promise of the future for its immediate needs. Increasing the profits from leases turned as much on finding tenants who were willing to co-operate as did fee-farming. On one well documented occasion, the Duchy of Cornwall attempted to implement a rigorous policy of improving the income from some of its lessees in County Durham.[217] When leases in the lordships of Brancepath, Raby and Barnard Castle expired *c.* 1620, the Duchy's steward, one Ralph Emerson (perhaps significantly a Londoner who had moved to Durham as the earl of Somerset's steward) proposed to increase income by doubling the ancient rent and taking a fine of up to eighty years' rent for leases for forty years. Where the tenants were willing to negotiate, the fines were treated flexibly but the rent was invariably doubled. Those tenants who declined to take new leases on these lines (and at Long Newton, all rejected the Duchy's overtures) had their rent increased six-fold. By 1623, the rental of the three lordships came to £2,156 where before it had been £892.

So far, this seems a perfect example of aggressive, modernising landlordism. In retrospect it was ill-timed; 1622 was marked by harvest failure and a general disruption of the economy. But the tenants were already engaged in passive resistance. By the end of 1622, arrears, mostly of unpaid fines, had reached nearly £5,000 and continued to rise until 1628 when they stood at £6,770. In 1624, the Duchy admitted defeat and negotiated a new composition with the tenants along less severe lines, still doubling the rent but asking fines of only twenty-five to thirty years' rent for terms of thirty-one years. To ease the tenants' acceptance, the arrears arising from the earlier composition were cancelled. This was still an honourable outcome and perhaps a satisfactory compromise after the Duchy had so severely overstretched itself. But by the time the new compositions had been agreed, the Crown had sold the lordships to the City of

---

[215] SP16/286, no. 19; SP16/291, no. 41, LR17/1 (letter of Crane to Harbord, 1634), C205/14/10; also SP16/260, nos. 104–5; SP16/307, nos. 17–18; SP16/342, no. 3; *CSPD 1625–49*, p. 579.   [216] E126/4, fol. 248r–v.

[217] These estates were 'annexed' to the Duchy in 1616; they had previously belonged to the earl of Somerset who had them of the grant of James I. The account which follows is based on D. S. Reid, *The Durham Crown Lordships in the Sixteenth and Seventeenth Centuries and the Aftermath* (Durham, 1990), pp. 46–8, 76–8; it could certainly be filled out by materials in the Duchy Office.

London as a part of the Royal Contract. It was the City (and its purchasers) who were to benefit from the Crown's protracted struggle.

From the landowner's point of view, leases were rather like timber. In times of need, both could be rapidly sold to realise large sums, but thereafter it took a generation for a process of renewal to take place before the resource could be exploited again. Whilst Dorset's policy of raising rents and fines was surely right, the extension of the tenants' terms in the leases he made suggests that his estate management was a compromise between immediate needs and the longer-term interest of the estate. After the contractors' leases, there was practically nothing left to lease. The estates were still heavily committed in 1650. At Greens Norton (a part of the honour of Grafton), the average length of unexpired terms in 1650 (of the twenty-four cases where it can be calculated) was forty-one and a quarter years. The longest terms in hand were a lease of eighty years granted in 1626 in reversion of a lease for three lives granted in 1608, the last life of which was aged sixty and a lease for thirty-one years granted in 1637 in reversion of a lease of forty years granted in 1610, itself in reversion of a lease for two lives granted in 1608, both lives of which were still living and aged only forty-two and forty-seven.[218] In this way, the only possible policy towards the Crown's leaseholds was simply that of waiting.

IV

For all its good intentions, the Crown's policy towards its tenants proved to be so much bluster. It took all the appropriate steps to modernise the estates. It regulated its local officers ever more closely, engaged surveyors of the modern kind and attempted to raise fines on copyholds and leases. Persistently, it underestimated the practical difficulties of implementing the printed directions of 1608. What the estates could not do was assuage the Crown's continuing demand for ready money. The various steps it took to improve income were being imposed on an estate which was progressively shrinking. It was this hunger for revenue which led the Crown into fee-farming and confirmations, both devices designed to release capital from the estates whilst stopping short of sale in fee simple, but methods which in common with long leasing fixed the income from the estates at much less than its market rate. The same pressures appear in the

[218] E317/Northants./30.

accounts of concealment hunting and disafforestation offered subsequently. Improvement, it might justly be said, was hard. Sale was easier. Cranfield's hogs were never destined to grow wool.[219]

---

[219] Readers still puzzled by this simile may welcome knowing that hogs are sheep before their first shearing.

CHAPTER 10

Jacobean Phoenix: the Duchy of Cornwall in the principates of Henry Frederick and Charles

Graham Haslam

Raleigh's dismissal from the Wardenship of the Stannaries and his replacement by the earl of Pembroke coincided with the change of dynasty and a reversal in the Duchy's fortunes. The new monarch not only negated the spectre of a dynastic war, he was welcomed as head of a family, with two sons and a daughter to ensure the succession, through whom the virtues of a Christian society devoted to family prosperity were mirrored. But a royal family, rather than a solitary monarch, also promised to create a new, more complicated political milieu where the relatively simple lines of power and prestige which had existed for almost the whole of the latter half of the sixteenth century would become more differentiated as individual members of the royal family assumed independent social and political roles.

To have not one but five members of the royal family promised to add new burdens to the King's advisers' tasks. Clearly, it was going to cost more money. But whilst the early Tudor precedents were consulted, the settlement of estates on the Prince of Wales could never be simply a revival of the earlier practice, for that was itself inconsistent. Henry VII, who initiated an elaborate political construct to allow his eldest son, Arthur, to assume political control of the West, did not attempt to repeat the experiment after the Prince's death in 1502. His second son, Prince Henry, was given no role of political consequence and was made duke of Cornwall in name only. After Prince Arthur, no English monarch attempted to create a royal apanage and the power and prestige of the royal family was never again defined in strictly territorial terms. Members of the Stuart dynasty gathered a circle not as a dimension of their landholding but through patronage of the arts, by building, and by placing themselves at the head of a glittering entourage which indulged the fashions of the day.

To contemporaries, office-holding in a revived Duchy appeared to offer the promise of great rewards. It was the institution the King's eldest son, Henry Frederick, would inherit for his honour and maintenance. The careers of the early Stuart princes have been neglected or completely ignored by modern historians. Even their biographers have assumed that they, like the children of Zeus, sprang fully grown on to the political stage.[1] In fact, Prince Henry had a brief, but important principate in which he fashioned norms of style and method. More importantly, Prince Charles spent a crucial nine years of early manhood governing the Duchy of Cornwall, overseeing the development of policies which sometimes emerged as departures, occasionally innovative methods of government, and which look forward to the techniques the King employed to govern the country during the personal rule. Of the senior advisers who gathered around Charles, several were promoted to high national office and three figured prominently in the political controversies of the decade prior to the Civil War.

I

The opportunities that office-holding in a revived Duchy might bring were not lost upon either the important or unimportant in 1603 and the struggle for position began almost as soon as James arrived. The attraction of Duchy offices which had been only minor sinecures was greatly enhanced because they possessed the promise of close association with a prince. Obtaining a position within the Duchy was complicated because it was an unknown, arcane institution. After its Elizabethan neglect, there were difficulties in determining just what offices and duties existed. As late as 1612, one hapless seeker wrote that he was unable to pursue his quest for the office of clerk of the Prince's Council Chamber because when he attempted to discover its responsibilities, he found that,

being all that I can any way gather, either of the practice of this place, or of the allowances that have anciently gone with it, I would more willingly have left it to the consideration and judgment of his Highness' Council, than to have said anything of it, but being they have pleased to command me to

---

[1] See, for instance, Pauline Gregg, *King Charles I* (London, 1981), p. 38 and *passim*. Contemporaries could be explicit and pragmatic concerning the power and financial resources available to the Princes, as Sir John Dodderidge, *The History of the Ancient and Moderne Estate of the Principality of Wales, Dutchy of Cornwall, and Earldome of Chester* (London, 1630). The paucity of material on the principate is reflected by G. E. Aylmer, *The Personal Rule of Charles I, 1629–40* (London, 1989). His comprehensive summary of recent scholarship begins only at the accession in 1625.

deliver them in writing what rights I suppose to have belonged unto it, I will be bold to offer unto them by way of information those observations that I have made.[2]

As the attraction of place grew, the Exchequer saw its role in Duchy administration threatened and only grudgingly allowed its separation. The auditor's office, separated from the Exchequer in 1603, went to Sir Francis Godolphin before coming to rest with Richard Connock. It was a sought-after position; Walter Cope, an unsuccessful rival, paid £200 to a courtier for the expedition of his suit.[3] Scion of a Cornish family from Calstock, Connock's father had been deputy to the Duchy feodary, William Killigrew. Richard had been useful to Raleigh, Buckhurst and Sir Robert Cecil in 1600 when they carried out delicate negotiations with Cornish tin miners concerning the monopoly of tin. A companion of Inigo Jones and John Donne and a lawyer with a growing reputation, he advised Prince Henry on a range of issues concerning the Duchy and produced papers concerning its legal history.[4]

The Exchequer auditor responsible for the Duchy's affairs, Nathaniel Fulwer, refused to surrender the records. He and Connock could not amicably resolve their differences and the Lord Treasurer and Chief Baron were called upon to adjudicate. A meeting was arranged at which Fulwer did not turn up; later he claimed he had not received notice. The fact that Connock's letter to him explaining the reasons for the meeting survives amongst Fulwer's papers rather suggests that this was not so. For the next seven years, Fulwer continued to fight a rearguard action, claiming that the loss of office cost him more than 1,000 marks annually.[5]

Far more important for the Duchy's future direction under the Stuart princes was the appointment of John Norden as a surveyor of Duchy lands in 1605.[6] Norden slipped into the Duchy; he seems to have pursued an appointment through Exchequer connections, perhaps Salisbury, for whom he had worked privately. In his petition

[2] Inner Temple Library, London, MS 538/17, fol. 417.   [3] SP14/5, no. 30.

[4] HMC, *Sackville*, I, p. 271. Raleigh said of Connock to Buckhurst and Cecil, that 'you could not have reported any man, as I think, both for diligence and knowledge, of more sufficiency'. HMC, *Salisbury*, x, pp. 374–5.

[5] SP46/162, pt I. The calendar indicates this undated letter to be Edwardian, but it probably originated sometime in late 1603 and is addressed from Connock to Fulwer.

[6] Salisbury had employed Norden to survey his own property. See Lawrence Stone, *Family and Fortune. Studies in Aristocratic Finance in the Sixteenth and Seventeenth Centuries* (Oxford, 1973), p. 131.

for office, he claimed that he had spent £1,000 on surveying Duchy lands. As at that date he had not carried out a single survey of a Duchy manor, he could only be referring to his county atlas, which naturally included maps of counties where the Duchy held estates. His influence within the Duchy grew only after 1608, and became pervasive between 1615 and 1622.

Another development which was crucial to the Duchy's immediate fortunes and the formulation of its policies was the debate within the Exchequer circle concerning the revenues of the Crown.[7] The participants included Salisbury and Sir Julius Caesar, and discussions were started early enough for Dorset to have been aware of the problems and suggestions.[8] It was apparent that Crown lands and other revenue sources did not yield realistic sums. The choices for the Crown estate were either to continue to sell, piecemeal or more deliberately, or to seek improved rents and fines. If income from estates could be increased, not only would it provide greater certain revenues year in and year out, but help to alleviate the political pressures inherent in attempting to raise money from sources which required parliamentary consent. Characteristic of Norden's Duchy surveys was an orientation towards providing realistic land values so that genuine capital values could be determined. In the case of Kirton in Lindsey, a Lincolnshire soke of 21,000 acres which Norden surveyed for the Duchy in 1616, he estimated that its true value was no less than £45,378, at sixteen years' purchase, provided improvements in management could be introduced.[9]

It was clear that not only had rents been rendered obsolete by price rises, but that there was also an active market for land and its produce. Dorset and Salisbury, major estate owners in their own right, could hardly have been ignorant of the changes which were taking place upon the land as population increased and tenants adopted *ad hoc* methods to deal with tenurial matters. By participating in crisis selling, the Crown had effectively been unable to take advantage of the premiums available to a vendor during a sellers' market. Initially, surveying was perhaps nothing more than an effort to introduce a little honesty into transactions which were sometimes

[7] L. M. Hill, *Bench and Bureaucracy. The Public Career of Sir Julius Caesar, 1580–1636* (Cambridge, 1988), pp. 122–3.

[8] P. Croft (ed.), 'A collection of several speeches and treatises of the late Lord Treasurer Cecil...', *Camden Miscellany* 29 (Camden, fourth ser., 34, 1987), pp. 273–318.

[9] DCO, Bound MSS, T/M/3, Courts of Survey Minutes, Cornwall, Devon, Dorset, Somerset, Wiltshire, Norden's Observations on his Surveys, fol. 178v.

characterised by fraud and corruption on a scale which may even
have embarrassed late Elizabethan and early Stuart administrators.
All these factors militated for change. However, there were formidable obstacles. The entrenched bureaucracy, dependent upon fees,
resisted any reforms which affected its position. Tenure was still
overwhelmingly local in character. Tenants could resist an absentee
landlord such as the Crown by claiming benefit of local custom or
rights which could exclude them from any general policy. Even leases
of demesne, over which the Crown theoretically possessed greater
control, also presented problems. Leases passed under Crown seal
whenever the property became available, a reversion was sought or
when the lessee wished to renew. The process as a whole was
hopelessly piecemeal. It was impossible to introduce changes which
could affect the whole royal estate simultaneously.

In 1607, the Duchy's officers failed to renew tenancies on most of the
seventeen conventionary manors. It may be that the idea of selling or
fee-farming the Crown lands had advanced so far towards implementation that it was decided to await a decision; perhaps the
newly emerging Duchy administration, unaided by an Exchequer
cadre sulking in its tent at the loss of fees, simply did not realise the
nature of the tenures and failed to carry out the proper legal
procedure. Duchy administration was much more assiduous in
pursuit of defective titles. In 1606, Chief Justice Coke held in the
'Prince's Case' that lands which had been annexed to the Duchy by
parliamentary statute could not be severed except by a subsequent
act.[10] This judgement meant that all those Duchy lands which had
been sold hastily at the end of Elizabeth's reign could be recovered.
After this decision, the Duchy's Attorney-General threatened to issue
writs of *scire facias* and normally the unfortunate grantee agreed to
surrender his title rather than face hopeless and expensive litigation.
This process took time; it was not before the reign of Charles I that
all the alienated lands were recovered. Robert Cecil made a
conspicuous show of loyalty to the new dynasty by surrendering to
the Crown those Cornish manors which he had purchased from the
Duchy in 1601.[11]

Those who had bought the lands from the Crown commission in
innocence were offered leases of the manors for terms of years.

---

[10] Sir Edward Coke, *The Reports* (7 vols., London, 1776–7 edn), IV, pp. 1–31.
[11] Thomas Birch, *The Life of Henry Prince of Wales* (London, 1760), pp. 58–9.

Between 1607 and 1615, some thirty-two actions were either threatened or actually initiated in Chancery on behalf of the Prince. To one of the unfortunate landholders the Prince's Council wrote,

Whereas you hold the manor of Ryme Extrensis in the county of Dorset which is parcel of the possessions of the Duchy of Cornwall and belongeth to our Master the Prince's Highness. Although the usual course heretofore hath been in like cases to sue out a *scire facias* without any other warning, which hath been a great charge and trouble to the persons which held such lands in their possessions, we being desirous to prevent such charge and trouble if it may be...you shall this next term repair unto us and acknowledge the defect and weaknesses of your Estate and submit yourself to his Highness.[12]

Many similar offers were made. Thomas Randall, pursued from 1613 by first the Exchequer and then the Prince's Council, finally surrendered the manor of Trelugan in 1619. In return, he was granted by warrant the benefit of the copyhold of the whole estate as well as a tenement of his own choosing for two lives in reversion without paying any fines.[13] Chamberlain reported to Carleton that Sir Edward Cary was forced to surrender Berkhamsted to Prince Henry in 1611, and 'your cousin Pawlet hath lost 400 marks a year of demesnes about his house, wherein his grandfather had a long term, and getting the fee simple in recompense of his service, drowned his lease and thereby hath lost both lease and land'.[14] Occasionally, those who surrendered land received financial compensation. In 1618, John Molles, who lost the manor of Tregamere, received £100.[15] Lord Stanhope, represented by counsel before the Prince's Council, was awarded £300 for surrendering Eastway in Cornwall. Paulet actually compounded for Curry Mallet in 1615 and received a lease for three lives at a fine of £500. Some families seemingly had no nose for the prevailing political winds. William Long took a long lease of Stratton-on-the-Fosse (Somerset), only to have it recovered by the Prince's Council. His son, Lisleborne Long, purchased the same manor in the Commonwealth sales of Crown lands and lost it again at the Restoration.[16]

---

[12] DCO, Bound MSS, T/M/1, Letters and Warrants, 1615–19, 29 Dec. 1615.
[13] DCO, Bound MSS, T/M/1, Letters and Warrants, 1619–20, 17 Nov. 1619.
[14] SP14/67, no. 67, 27 Nov. 1611.
[15] DCO, Bound MSS, T/M/1, Letters and Warrants, 1615–19, 12 June 1618.
[16] DCO, Bound MSS, K/B/2, *Liber Irrotuli*, 1615–25, vol. II, fol. 57, and Surveyor-General's reports, 1695–97, fol. 201.

In addition to lands in Cornwall, the Duchy also recovered ten manors in Somerset which had been leased and out of its control for the whole of the sixteenth century. By 1613, nine had been returned to direct management and the tenth, Stoke under Hambden, was recovered in 1635. These manors formed two broad bands stretching from the Mendip Hills to the eastern border of Somerset and west from Yeovil to within 5 miles of Taunton. Over 10,000 acres were recovered, but much of the traditional manorial structure had disappeared. John Norden, who surveyed most of them, could identify few freeholders, and in only one of the ten was he able to establish the traditional right of the lord to fish, hunt and fowl. There were efforts by the Prince's Council to ensure that fiefs, especially manors associated with Duchy honours, were recorded, but those attempting to amass the information constantly complained that the lack of adequate records and reliable information from local juries prevented a genuinely realistic compilation of data. Nevertheless, Stuart administrators produced long lists of manors which owed obligations to Duchy honours.[17]

On 1 September 1610, at the traditional age of sixteen, the Prince was granted livery of his lands, which included the Duchy of Cornwall, principality of Wales and earldom of Chester. The value of these lands and the other sources from which Prince Henry drew his income are shown in table 10.1. Salisbury reckoned the Prince received not less than £51,000 a year from all sources.[18] In fact, the Prince's income equalled about 10 per cent of all Crown revenues. Connock's revenue and expenditure account for the last year of the Prince's life shows receipts of £49,315 from certain income, £2,353 from an Exchequer grant, £5,550 from casual receipts, £1,099 from surveys with £22,437 of arrears. Of this, £30,589 had been paid to the Prince's Cofferer and £15,992 turned over to Sir George Moore, the Prince's Receiver-General.[19] Nonetheless, the costs of maintaining Prince Henry rose more or less steadily. In 1610, Salisbury estimated that Henry's diets alone cost £10,000 annually. By that year, £18,000 was being expended upon Henry's house, £3,000 for his wardrobe and another £4,000 on his privy purse expenditure.[20] His investiture as Prince of Wales cost a staggering amount: £1,300 went on fireworks, robes cost £7,001 and the clothes worn on the day

---

[17] For example, DCO, Bound MSS, T/M/3, Knights Fees, Ancient Tenures, Extents.
[18] HMC, *Salisbury*, XXI, pp. 270–1.   [19] Inner Temple Library MS 538/17, fols. 425–6.
[20] Inner Temple Library MS 538 fol. 417; SP14/57, no. 80.

Table 10.1. *Revenue of Henry, Prince of Wales, 1611–12*

Fineable lands:	
Principality of Wales	£1,804
Earldom of Chester	£154
Duchy of Cornwall	£1,152
Manors annexed from Crown lands	£7,627
Total	£10,737
Fee-farms and certain rents:	
Principality of Wales	£2,233
Earldom of Chester	£185
Duchy of Cornwall	£598
Manors annexed from Crown lands	£43
Total	£3,059
Coinage and tin fines:	
Coinage	£2,168
Casual fines	£91
Total	£2,259
Money granted for the Prince's livery:	
Principality of Wales	£4,268
Earldom of Chester	£78
Duchy of Cornwall	£4,002
Manors annexed from Crown lands	£7,048
Total	£15,396
Total of received income	£31,451

Source: DCO, Rolls Series, Brief Declaration, Box 127.

alone cost £1,311. From Easter 1610 until 20 May 1611, his household expenses ran to £11,200 and total payments for the period amounted to £31,849.[21]

The Prince created an administration to deal with his complex financial affairs. A commission dated 8 December 1610 established a Council of Revenue consisting of Sir Edward Phelips, Adam Newton, Sir Thomas Moore, Sir Oliver Cromwell, Sir William Fleetwood, Augustine Nicolls, Thomas Stephens and Richard Connock. All were appointed during pleasure and a quorum of four, the Chancellor, Secretary, Receiver-General and Surveyor-General, established. The quorum could be reduced to only two if the Prince consented. The members of the Council represented both Duchy servants and

---

[21] HMC, *Salisbury*, XXI, p. 800.

members of his entourage. The Prince's tutor and secretary, Adam Newton, received all correspondence directed to the Prince from his tenants, but Richard Connock was appointed to audit both the Duchy's revenues and the monies spent by the household.[22]

The use of the Council as an administrative device cannot be seen as an innovation. Medieval princes since Edward of Woodstock had governed the Duchy in the same manner. However, because over a century had elapsed since the last appointment of a Council, there was some latitude in how and for what the Council would become directly responsible as the collective manager of the estate. Prince Henry's selection of Council members and, in particular, the omission from its membership of the Lord Warden of the Stannaries, Pembroke, represents a significant departure in methods of governing the Duchy. The Lord Warden, who had always been the pivotal figure in the Tudor administration of the Duchy, was eclipsed by the Council which took direct responsibility for all administrative matters until their positions were again reversed after the Restoration.

The most important councillor was the Chancellor and custodian of the Prince's Great Seal, Sir Edward Phelips, who was appointed during pleasure with fees of £200 a year. When he received an order from the Prince's Secretary requesting a lease or grant, the Chancellor issued a warrant to the auditor for a particular and then asked the Attorney-General to prepare the document for the Prince's signature. Once returned under the Prince's privy seal, he could engross it and allow it to pass under the Prince's Great Seal. He was also responsible for taking bonds or recognisances against default for any office of receipt.[23] Sir George Moore displaced Lord Knollys as

---

[22] Besides retaining the auditorship of the Duchy with the much enhanced fee of £240 a year, Connock also received the offices of Solicitor-General at £30 per annum and Auditor-General for the whole of the Prince's revenues with fees of £100; he also had leases for forty years of the Duchy parks of Liskeard and Restormel with the fishing of the Lyner and Fowey rivers. DCO, Prince Henry's Patent Roll, 539. The land grants were given 'in consideration of the good and faithful service heretofore done to his highness ... and of great sums of money heretofore laid out and disbursed in and about the causes and affairs and business of the said Prince'. He was also granted the bailiwicks of Glaston and Sherbourne at £10 17s 0d a year. *Ibid.*, 540. As auditor, he examined the accounts of the receivers and escheator and prepared an account of expenditure in the household, the wardrobe and on building works which he submitted to the Council for approval. He also was responsible for ensuring that all grants, patents and leases were properly enrolled to provide an accurate record. DCO, 'Instructions, orders and directions'. In 1611, he relinquished the auditorship to William Hockmore, appointed 9 Aug. 1611.

[23] DCO, Bound MSS, D/B/2, 'Certain Instructions, Orders and Directions allowed and approved by Prince Henry, Prince of Wales, Duke of Cornwall and Earl of Chester concerning the rule, ordering and direction for the true collecting and disposing of his

Treasurer of the household and Receiver-General of all the Prince's income in 1611. He was charged with preparing exact accounts so that 'we may always understand the estate of the Treasure'.[24] Moore was also Chancellor of the Order of the Garter and in 1615 made Lieutenant of the Tower. He was eventually deprived of office in March 1611, but the reasons are unclear. The Prince seems to have attempted economies in his household and decided to dispense with his Treasurer and have only a Receiver-General.

The Prince's former tutor, Adam Newton, took the office of Secretary to His Highness at 100 marks a year with emoluments. His duties included that of keeper of the privy seal, presenting and answering petitions submitted to Henry, marshalling correspondence which was to be directed to the Council and providing copies of answers, preparing warrants for leases or money for the Chancellor's attention and also acting as head of the secretariat for the acts, letters, mandates and certificates passed by the Council.[25] In administration, past or present, the individual who acts as postman always has a powerful role to play. Newton received correspondence and bore it to the Prince who would then refer it to his Council either with or without specific instructions. Newton is typical of the new men who gathered first around Henry and later Prince Charles. A learned adventurer, active as a teacher in France between 1580 and 1590, he eventually made his way to Scotland where he came to the King's attention.[26] By 1614, he had amassed a modest fortune, and then owned land in Kent worth £500. He purchased a baronetcy in 1620.[27] Finally, the Council included Sir Oliver Cromwell, uncle of the future Lord Protector, who received the relatively minor office of Master of the Prince's Game.

Prince Henry revived an office which had not been employed in Duchy management since the demise of the Court of General Surveyors in 1547. Sir William Fleetwood was appointed Surveyor-General of the Duchy at £50 a year. This office added a new dimension to its management, not because it was a new administrative technique, but because it was the conjunction of a formerly disused office with new surveying techniques, which allowed a

revenues and treasure for his highness greatest honor and best profit', fols. 37–44 (hereafter cited as 'Instructions, Orders and Directions'). This is an eighteenth-century copy of a lost original.   [24] Ibid.   [25] Ibid.

[26] For Newton, see his entry in D.NB. The biography of Prince Henry by Thomas Birch published in 1760 was largely based upon Newton's correspondence.

[27] HMC, Salisbury, xxii, pp. 13–14.

departure from administrative practice. The increasingly sophisticated methods of surveyors, using scientific instruments such as the theodolite to create accurate, scaled maps, had been almost completely avoided by those responsible for the Crown estate because the continuum of administration simply did not make a place for new practices. The recreation of the Duchy allowed new men and ideas to augment traditional methods and offices. The work of the Surveyor-General was carried out by deputies. A commission dated 9 July 1611, addressed to all Council members and also John Norden as deputy surveyor, made provision for surveys of various Duchy manors.[28] Other surveyors were included in this and later commissions, but Norden, amongst the most advanced cartographers of early seventeenth-century Europe, best illustrates how the Prince and his new administrative creature were able to seize the advantages offered by new techniques. For the next twelve years, Norden worked for the Duchy. Always as a deputy, paid on a *per diem* basis, he laboured frequently with his son, John Norden, junior. The administrators of Duchy lands, though essentially London bound, were able to extend their influence and authority in ways which were previously simply not possible by employing local servants. Norden, John Thorpe and others were commissioned to search for decays and defects of rents, titles and revenues and were empowered to call before them manorial juries, stewards, bailiffs and reeves. The initial intention may have been to establish values of lands in order to sell them, but even the earliest commission suggests that the new Council was interested in far more than capital values.

The Council was enlarged on 6 July 1611 by the appointment of Francis Crane as clerk of the Council. This gave the body its own secretariat. Crane, though not a voting member, was given charge of all books and presumably would have organised petitions, reports and general correspondence directed to and from the Council. Though not Cornish, he was connected by marriage with the Arundels and other important Cornish gentry.

Prince Henry and his advisors created a small, dynamic, omnipotent institution which could manipulate the resources of the Duchy of Cornwall and other estates assigned to the Prince. The members of the Council were neither young nor inexperienced. Moore was fifty-seven years old, Fleetwood and Phelips about forty-

---

[28] DCO, Prince Henry's Patent Roll, 539.

seven and Newton probably in his forties. Connock may have been the youngest member. He and Newton were totally dependent upon the goodwill of the Prince for preferment. Though mature and with developed careers in law or Crown service, the Prince's councillors (with the single exception of Phelips) were on the fringes of the political scene and by the standards of the day most were too young to hold high office. Connock, of course, was Cornish and Phelips could advise upon any matters concerning Somerset. The Council dealt with all aspects of business and every tenant directly. Grants of leases and renewals of copyholds, petitions and all decisions concerning the Stannaries were taken at the board. Manorial courts merely existed to record its decisions; the Council communicated either in person with tenants or by representation of counsel. Just as it had created a secretariat to sustain its administrative needs, so it developed a modus for conducting its business which included a provision for green cloth for the board.

II

This elaborate construct, pregnant with new possibilities, collapsed abruptly when Prince Henry contracted a sudden fatal illness and died on 6 November 1612. At his death, the Council automatically ceased to function, the charter of livery was abrogated and the estates again merged with those of the Crown. Very quickly, Henry's household servants were paid off and Connock produced a final account of the balance of his revenues.[29] Immediately, rumours began circulating concerning the possible disposition of the Duchy to James's younger son, Charles, duke of York. The inimitable gossip, Chamberlain, notifying Carleton of the Prince's sudden death, repeated the story that Charles was excluded from the succession to the Duchy by a 'quirk' of the entail.[30] The founding charter of 1337 simply referred to the right of succession of the eldest son. Henry VII, after the death of Prince Arthur, created Prince Henry duke of Cornwall by act in the Parliament of 1503–4, but he did not grant livery of the estate to Prince Henry. Five months after Chamberlain reported the dilemma to Carleton, Sir Edward Phelips wrote to him stating that the question of the reversion of the Duchy had been settled in favour of the Prince.[31] By definition, whoever is duke of Cornwall is heir-

[29] SP14/71, nos. 47, 48. Henry had ninety-six servants in his household and another thirty-six in his chamber.   [30] *Ibid.*, no. 32. Chamberlain to Carleton, 12 Nov. 1612.
[31] SP14/72, no. 46.

apparent. Despite the considerable drain on royal finance, James was anxious to bestow the titles and privileges reserved for the heir to the throne. In 1613, the Crown sought and published a legal opinion by Sir John Davies.[32] This constructed a broad view of the succession and argued that the charter of 1337 might be construed to mean the eldest, surviving son. James did not make recourse to Parliament for confirmation of this opinion. Prince Charles, only fourteen, was still too young to receive livery so that Davies's opinion simply suggested the King could confirm the titles upon the Prince if he wished.

On 21 June 1615, when the Prince was still only fourteen, the King issued a charter of livery granting the Duchy of Cornwall to Prince Charles. It was another eight months before the King bestowed the other titles and lands which Prince Henry had held to augment his revenue and only in November 1616 did the King install Charles as Prince of Wales. The Prince issued a temporary commission to deal with specific problems.[33] On 1 March 1617, Sir Francis Bacon took the oaths of supremacy, allegiance, councillor and Chancellor before the Prince at St James's Palace. On the same day, Bacon administered oaths to Sir James Fullerton, Thomas Murray and Thomas Trevor. Three days later at Gray's Inn, three more councillors, Sir Thomas Howard, Sir Robert Cary and Sir John Dackombe, were sworn. Within a month, Bacon surrendered his office, having concluded his task of creating a structure to administer the Prince's lands. Sir Henry Hobart replaced him as Chancellor on 3 April and five days later Murray, Adam Newton, John Walter, Sir Richard Smyth and Sir Oliver Cromwell were also sworn to the Council.[34] A further warrant was issued on 20 July when Hobart, Howard, Cary, Dackombe, Murray, Fullerton, Newton, Walter and Trevor were charged with governing all the Prince's rights, lands and revenues.[35] Between 7 October 1616 and 8 October 1622, Charles reorganised his Council eight times; the dates on which this was done and the names of the Prince's councillors may be found in table 10.2. On average it numbered between nine and ten members. Each new commission

---

[32] For Davies, see *DNB*. His authorship was confirmed by George Moore, *Essay on the Rights of the Prince of Wales Relative to the Dutchy of Cornwall* (London, 1795), p. 23. Though the Irish Attorney-General from 1606 to 1619, he was in England during 1612–13 and later received a small reward from Charles. See also SP14/72, no. 47.

[33] DCO, Bound MSS, T/M/1, *Liber Irrotuli*, vols. 1 and 11. By December 1615, Suffolk and Greville were trying to arrange for extraordinary payments of arrears so that the accounts could be settled when Charles took full control.

[34] DCO, Bound MSS, K/B/1, Acts of the Council, 1615–18, vol. 11, fols. 1–3d.

[35] DCO, Bound MSS, T/M/1, Enrolments of Patents, Prince Charles, 1615–18, fols. 126v–7v.

Table 10.2. *Councillors and the dates of their appointment*

	7 Oct. 1616	20 July 1617	4 Feb. 1618	20 Jan. 1619	1 Nov. 1619	29 Dec. 1619	13 Jan. 1622	8 Oct. 1622
Sir Francis Bacon (#)	*							
Robert Cary		*	*	*	*	*	*	*
Charles Chiborne				*	*			
Francis Cottington								*
Sir Oliver Cromwell			*	*	*	*	*	*
John Dackombe(#)	*	*						
Robert Douglas								*
Henry Fane							*	*
James Fullerton(#)	*	*	*	*	*		*	*
Henry Hobart(#)		*	*	*	*	*	*	*
Thomas Howard		*	*	*	*	*	*	*
James Ley (#)						*	*	*
Thomas Murray	*	*	*	*	*	*		
Adam Newton		*	*	*	*	*	*	*
Thomas Savage							*	*
Richard Smyth (#)			*	*	*	*	*	*
Thomas Trevor (#)	*	*	*	*	*	*	*	*
John Villiers					*	*		
John Walter (#)	*	*	*	*	*	*	*	*

(#) indicates Duchy officers

brought a change of personnel, but the broad powers of the Council remained the same throughout the Caroline principate.

The members of the Caroline Council, like that of Prince Henry, were Duchy servants, household officers or lawyers. Hobart, a distinguished lawyer who succeeded Coke as Chief Justice of the Common Pleas, had been Attorney-General of the Court of Wards and Liveries since 1605.[36] Both John Walter and Thomas Trevor were lawyers and possibly clients of the earl of Pembroke. Trevor became the Prince's Solicitor-General and Walter received the office of Attorney-General. Though they advised the Prince upon all legal business, their fees were paid by the Duchy. Both Trevor and Walter were able to use the Prince's Council as a springboard for their careers. Walter became Chief Baron of the Exchequer in 1625 and Trevor was one of the twelve judges who gave a favourable verdict for

---

[36] For Herbert, see *DNB*. See also DCO, Bound MSS, T/M/1, Enrolments of Patents, Prince Charles, 1615–18, fol. 58.

the Crown in the ship money trial of 1637. Sir Richard Smyth, fourth son of the famous Customer Smyth, had been Receiver-General of the Duchy since 1604. Besides the many business connections his brothers provided, he was personally active as a member of the East India, Virginia, Levant, North-West Passage, Moscovy and Bermuda Companies.[37] His own family had long been interested in mining and the metal trade.[38] It was Smyth who organised the Crown's brief, but successful, monopoly of the tin trade in the first decade of the seventeenth century. Servants of the Prince's household included Sir Robert Cary, a man of fashion whose ship came in when his wife was appointed Charles's governess. He received the offices of Chamberlain of the household and Gentleman of the bed chamber.[39] In 1625, he was rewarded with an earldom. Sir Thomas Howard, also an household officer, was made Master of the Horse. The second son of Lord Treasurer Suffolk, he remained close to Charles throughout the principate.[40] The office of Groom of the Stool was given to Sir James Fullerton who also served briefly as Surveyor-General. Thomas Murray, Prince Charles's tutor, a man with a reputation for honesty and of a puritan disposition, succeeded to the Secretaryship. Eventually he fell into disfavour when in 1621 he opposed the Spanish match and was confined to his house.[41]

During the course of the principate, the Council grew from its original six to fourteen. Nevertheless, five remained the quorum and the numbers are more analogous to Elizabeth's Privy Council in the 1570s than the contemporary Jacobean Council.[42] With one or two significant exceptions, Charles's councillors were not established figures and most of them anticipated important office rather than having already attained it. A sample of five members appointed between 1616 and 1622 yields an average age of 48.6. The oldest of

---

[37] T. K. Rabb, *Enterprise and Empire, Merchant and Gentry Investment in the Expansion of England, 1575–1630* (Cambridge, MA, 1967), p. 378.

[38] M. B. Donald, *Elizabethan Copper. The History of the Company of Mines Royal, 1568–1605* (London, 1955), pp. 66–72.

[39] DCO, Bound MSS, K/B/1, Acts of the Council, 1615–18, vol. II, fol. 1.

[40] *Ibid.*, fol. 1. Also, Enrolments of Patents, Prince Charles, 1615–18, fols. 45–6.

[41] For Murray, see *DNB*. For his patent, see DCO, Bound MSS, T/M/1, Enrolments of Patents, Prince Charles, 1615–18, fol. 44. On 9 June 1616, he was granted the site of Berkhamsted for life. *Ibid.*, fols. 20–1v. Deprived of his office in 1621, he was replaced by Francis Cottington, later Chancellor of the Exchequer. See *DNB sub nomine*. Also, DCO, Bound MSS, T/M/1, Enrolments of Patents, Prince Charles, 1620–5, fol. 143 (dated 5 Oct. 1622).

[42] Michael B. Pulman, *The Elizabethan Privy Council in the Fifteen-Seventies* (Berkeley, CA, 1971), pp. 17–51.

the sample was Cary, fifty-six at the date of his first appointment, and
the youngest, Thomas Trevor, who was only thirty. Six of the
nineteen councillors owed their reputations more or less exclusively
to their legal abilities. Only two, Howard and Cromwell, may be
described as the possessors of significant landed wealth, but the latter
only in the sense of a country gentleman. It may be that country
gentlemen dominated the House of Commons, but lawyers predomi-
nated in the affairs of the Prince. Relative youth, an important bias
towards the law and a comparatively small group capable of working
rapidly and cohesively were the three outstanding characteristics of
the Prince's Council in this period.

If lawyers dominated, City men and courtiers were also influential
at Council meetings. It was genuinely a ministry of all the talents. It
is difficult to judge the amount of work carried out by individual
members of Council and impossible to gauge the varying influence of
each. Signatures on letters, orders and warrants are not necessarily
an indication that an individual actually participated in creating
policy; correspondence, then as now, could easily be shunted around
to garner the requisite number of signatures for a particular item
once a response had been collectively determined. Nevertheless, a
signature assumes a measure of responsibility and the incidence of
signatures is at least suggestive of attention to the business of the
Prince's Council. In 1621, Thomas Trevor's name appears most
often: he signed 142 items; Fullerton signed 141. Sir Richard Smyth
attested 114 documents and John Walter, 94. The Chancellor,
Hobart, signed 87 items; Newton, 73; Cromwell, 50; and Thomas
Murray, only 65, but he fell from office in that year. Neither Howard
nor Cary appear after March and they were probably in personal
attendance. James Ley, who was not appointed to the Council until
1619, signed 110 items. In 1622, the incidence changed markedly.
Henry Fane and James Fullerton each signed 201 documents,
Savage, 186, Smyth, 168, Trevor, 141, Newton, 100, Cromwell, 79,
Hobart, 74, Walter, 70, Howard, 67, and Cary, 45. Robert Douglas
and Francis Cottington, not appointed until October, each signed
only eight items. Some correspondence was endorsed collectively 'by
advice of the Council' and letters of the same date occasionally bore
different signatures.

Meetings of the Prince's Council were frequent and regular.
Mondays, Fridays and sometimes Wednesdays were the usual
meeting days. Occasionally, additional meetings were arranged and

more than once, the Council met on a Saturday. The usual pattern
was to meet in the mornings, but these sessions could be extended into
a full day of work when required. In 1620, the Council sat seventy-
six times. The pattern of meetings for that year averages 6.3 sittings
each month. August and September were reserved for the long
vacation and no business was transacted at Christmastide. Attendance varied: Fullerton appeared at all but a single sitting,
Thomas Trevor, the Solicitor-General, was present for sixty-eight
meetings and Sir Richard Smyth, the Duchy Receiver-General,
attended sixty-five sittings. Sir James Ley, Lord Hobart and John
Walter all made a significant number of appearances. Members of
the Prince's household were least in attendance. Thomas Howard
attended only eight times, Cary, seven and even the Treasurer of the
household only came to eleven meetings. Despite the quorum
indicated in the commission, a number of sittings had only three
councillors in attendance. These meetings, however, were always to
answer petitions and never to decide policy.[43] Throughout Charles's
principate, a secretariat headed by the clerk of the Council,
Hieronimus Cocke, was responsible for maintaining an extensive
array of records including enrolments of leases, copies of all letters
and warrants and also copies of all patents issued by the Prince. From
1619, a series of books of orders was established which served as an
important precedent for administrative forms employed in the 1630s
by the King.[44]

The Council was positioned mid-way between the assets held by the
Prince on the one hand and his immediate financial needs upon the
other. Through the whole decade of the principate, the Council never
developed what today would be described as an investment strategy.
It did not risk capital or deploy resources in the hope of securing a
greater return. In that sense, it was a purely reactive governing body
in the medieval tradition. Those managing the Prince's estate saw

---

[43] DCO, Bound MSS, K/B/1, Acts of the Council, 1619–20.
[44] None of the work done on the books of orders has recognised the administrative precedents
created while Charles was duke. See B. W. Quintrell, 'The making of Charles I's book of
orders', *EHR* 95 (1980), pp. 553–72. He could not find the influence of a 'minister of
outstanding influence' in the creation of the form which was designed in part to keep the
gentry in the country. See also Paul Slack, 'Books of orders: the making of English social
policy, 1577–1634', *TRHS* fifth ser., 30 (1980), pp. 1–22. The important differences
between the books of orders of 1631 are noted and he argued that it was not a sudden or
eccentric innovation. Quintrell suggests that the work could have been in part inspired by
Bacon.

their role as nurturing or 'husbanding' its inherent wealth to ensure that all obligations and privileges between tenant and lord were satisfied. Despite the constant application of the Council over a decade, its collective view never departed from the principles employed previously in estate management. However, it did consistently insist upon each and every right of title and prerogative. With a vigour which endured for the whole of the principate, the Prince's advisers investigated every possible avenue of title, privilege and regality in order to achieve a maximum income. Since no duke had been in direct control of the estate for over a century, it was often difficult for the Prince's advisers to discover what actions they could legitimately undertake. The mounting controversy which this single-minded pursuit engendered eventually spilled over into a political struggle capable only of parliamentary resolution.[45] Tenants perceived attempts by the Prince's Council to manage local affairs from the centre as a threat to custom and right. It was in the complexities of local custom that tenants often sought refuge.

Rigorous attempts to raise income from the Prince's estate were sometimes tempered by a measured paternalism towards the less fortunate or those who had felt the force of the Council's actions. When an individual compounded for a fine of £90 which he was to pay in three quarterly instalments of £30 and then defaulted, the Council allowed him additional time to raise the cash and arrange sufficient security for the payments.[46] In Cornwall, the Duchy possessed the right of escheat and its feodary was instructed to seize the goods of convicted felons. However, the Council merely exercised the right and normally returned the bulk of the estate to the hands of the immediate family of a convicted felon if he had left a widow and children.[47] When the lands of Francis Buckland at Westharptree, Widcombe and Milton Falconbridge in Somerset were seized and fines of £1,290 exacted, he was left completely impecunious. In 1617, he petitioned for aid for himself and seven children. Dackombe and Trevor recommended that he be allowed a small tenement for his keep and Prince Charles assented to this suggestion.[48]

The Council defended the Prince's prerogatives against attempted incursions. In 1618, the Council wrote to the farmer of tithes at

[45] See below, p. 295.
[46] DCO, Bound MSS, K/B/1, Acts of the Council, 1615–18. The item is dated 15 May 1618.
[47] DCO, Bound MSS, T/M/2, Book of Orders, 1619–21, 20 June 1621. See also, DCO, Bound MSS, T/M/1, Letters and Warrants, 1626–32, 16 Feb. 1626.
[48] DCO, Bound MSS, K/B/1, Acts of the Council, 1615–18, 3 Nov. 1617.

Stratton Sanctuary in Cornwall requiring him to cease exacting payments from Duchy tenants in the parish by suing them in church courts. Many were too poor to afford a proper defence and the Council argued that tithes might have been discharged at the dissolution of the former monastery and should be discontinued until they were completely satisfied of his title.[49] In 1620, a complaint was directed to the sheriff of Hertfordshire that the denizens of Berkhamsted, another Duchy manor, did not owe him suit or service and he must desist from summoning them to his court.[50]

The Prince's prerogative was also defended against Crown officers. On 28 January 1619, Sir James Fullerton was made Master of the Prince's Wards with instructions to follow the precedents established by the Master of the King's Wards to ensure the Prince's 'reasonable profit' and provide for the proper education of the wards in 'religion and good breeding'.[51] Three months later, Murray, Chiborne and Walter received a commission to aid Sir James Fullerton to carry out his duties.[52] On 12 June, Chiborne, Walter, Hobart, Trevor and Fullerton reached agreement with Sir Benjamin Rudyard, Sir James Ley and Sir Miles Fleetwood, respectively Surveyor, Attorney and Receiver-General of the Court of Wards and Liveries, concerning the extent of Duchy jurisdiction over wards. It was agreed that the Prince would possess wardship in the whole of Cornwall, Chester and Flint on all Crown, Duchy and earldom lands. In exchange, the Prince surrendered any rights he might possess over manors outside these counties where he possessed lands which were not part of the Duchy. When individuals who died within the counties to be administered by the Prince's officers possessed lands *in capite* elsewhere, the Prince was given complete right of wardship. The Prince was granted the right to sue in the court in the Crown's name or his own in order to recover his prerogative rights. Finally, if disputes arose between Crown officers and the Prince's Council, provision was made for informal discussions so that the issues could be resolved without 'suit or law'.[53] These arrangements remained in place until 1625, when the Council surrendered the former Prince's prerogative for an annuity of £3,000.[54] Occasionally, the Council ceded the Prince's prerogative to

---

[49] DCO, Bound MSS, T/M/1, Letters and Warrants, 1615–19, 5 July 1618.
[50] DCO, Bound MSS, T/M/1, Letters and Warrants, 1619–20, 16 May 1620.
[51] DCO, Bound MSS, T/M/1, Enrolments of Patents, Prince Charles, 1618–20, fols. 9–12.
[52] *Ibid.*, fols. 21v–2v.　　　[53] Cornwall RO, A.D. 403 (Accession 1648).
[54] DCO, Bound MSS, T/M/1, Letters and Warrants, 1623–6, letter to Fleetwood, 29 March 1626.

the Crown, but only if an economic price could be negotiated. In 1624, the Council met to consider the sale of the right of Greenwax, a fine for sealing legal documents, to the Exchequer. Cottington suggested a price of £1,400, but argued that the right for Cornwall should be reserved. Cromwell felt that the whole prerogative right should be sold for the price suggested by Cottington. Crane argued for a sale price of £2,000. No consensus could be reached and the matter was again considered by the Council on the following day when it accepted Hobart's recommendation of a sale price of £1,300, but with the reservation of Cornwall, Chester and Wales.[55]

The Prince's Council directly controlled manorial affairs and jurisdiction from London. This was accomplished in a number of ways. Patronage of manorial stewardships was divided amongst councillors. Hobart, for example, apparently at the expense of the local magnate, the earl of Lincoln, appointed the steward of the soke of Kirton in Lindsey. Additionally, he nominated the steward for Curry Mallet in Somerset. Sir Richard Smyth was awarded the stewardships of Shepton Mallet and Stratton-on-the-Fosse, also in Somerset. The Council allowed the Lord Warden to appoint the steward of Mere, Wiltshire.[56] Smyth was asked to recommend a bailiff for the manor of Shippon in Berkshire and he and Fullerton were consulted for the appointment of a bailiff at Berkhamsted.[57] This was not merely self-interest; Norden, in his acerbic and direct manner, had counselled, 'It is a dangerous thing for His Highness to make great men stewards of his lands, I can give instances to approve it.'[58]

All tenants, whether leaseholders, copyholders or tenants-at-will, seeking renewals of their terms did so by petitioning the Prince. Their petitions were then referred to the Council which recommended action and, in the case of copyholds, instructed the relevant steward to have an entry made in the court rolls and admit the tenant. In this way, the legal forms were observed, though all decisions concerning the estate were taken centrally in London. In 1622, the Prince ordered that any petition for the lease of lands or tenements under 20 marks in value should be automatically directed to the Chancellor

[55] DCO, Bound MSS, K/B/1, Acts of the Council, 1622–3, fols. 362–5.
[56] DCO, Bound MSS, K/B/1, Acts of the Council, 1615–18, 10 Feb. 1617 and May 1617.
[57] DCO, Bound MSS, K/B/1, ibid., May 1616 and 15 Oct. 1616.
[58] DCO, Bound MSS, T/M/1, Courts of Survey Minutes, Cornwall, Devon, Dorset, Somerset, Wiltshire, 1611 & 1615, 1617 & 1619, fol. 185.

and Council. In addition, any benefice of the same value was to be dealt with by the Council without reference to the Prince.[59]

Despite the presumption of the powers of the manorial court, the Council constantly attempted to maintain manorial discipline. It was no easy task. Rights of common, heriots, the nature of copyhold, suit and service at court all varied from one manor to the next and depended upon local usage hallowed by immemorial custom. In 1620, the Council dispatched an open letter to the tenants of Mere ordering them to cease grinding corn at a mill owned by William Chafyn. The customary mill formerly produced £100 a year for its miller when it could operate in an exclusive environment.[60] This was a constant problem. A year before, the Council complained of two new grist mills within the confines of the manor and others 'near adjoining' which were successfully competing with the manorial mills.[61] The steward of Carnedon Prior, Cornwall, was told to take action against a new mill there.[62] In 1616, the mayor and burgesses of Bradninch in Devon were cautioned to hold their market only on the prescribed days and to ensure that an accurate account of the profits was prepared so that the Duchy would receive the correct royalties.[63]

The Council assumed the powers of a quasi-court. Though never a court of record, all legal instruments were enrolled in the manner of a law court. Disputes which could not be resolved by local manorial officials were referred to it for arbitration. Parties in these cases could be represented by counsel, who would be heard (as in a controversy concerning tithes at Ledbury in Herefordshire) by councillors before they adjudicated.[64] The Prince's Council also assumed powers of arbitration between its own officers and tenants. In 1634, the steward of the manor of Fordington, Dorset, Sir John Strangeways, was ordered to grant a tenement to John Gardner after a disputed claim could not be settled in the manorial court.[65]

The power exercised from London by the Council was not merely financial. It equally endeavoured to establish political and social control. This was not only 'fiscal feudalism'. The Council sought first

---

[59] DCO, Bound MSS, T/M/1, Enrolments of Patents, Prince Charles, 1620–5, fols. 120r–v, 202v–3v.   [60] DCO, Bound MSS, T/M/2, Book of Orders, 1619–21, 17 Nov. 1620.

[61] DCO, Bound MSS, T/M/1, Letters and Warrants, 1615–19, 11 Feb. 1619.

[62] DCO, Bound MSS, T/M/1, Letters and Warrants, 1623–6, 29 Nov. 1624.

[63] DCO, Bound MSS, T/M/1, Letters and Warrants, 1615–19, 16 Feb. 1616.

[64] DCO, Bound MSS, T/M/1, Book of Orders, 1621–5, 20 April 1624.

[65] *Ibid.*, 28 Nov. 1634.

to raise money, but also to establish the hegemony of a perpetually absentee landlord over estates which had not experienced the direct authority of a manorial lord since the high middle ages.

III

When Charles became King, he ceased to be duke of Cornwall, but departed from previous constitutional practice by not merging the Duchy with the Exchequer. On 28 May 1625, he issued a new Council commission, increasing its membership to eighteen, and adding to those previously named Richard Weston, Chancellor of the Exchequer, Humphrey May, Chancellor of the Duchy of Lancaster, Sir Edward Bromley, Sir John Denham, both barons of the Exchequer, Sir Francis Crane, Sir Walter Pye, attorney of the Court of Wards and Liveries, and Sir Thomas Fanshawe, Surveyor-General. The commission gave them full authority to make leases and agreements, audit accounts and supervise all Duchy officers. As in previous commissions, five constituted a quorum.[66] The volume of business considered by the Duchy Council – it cannot be described as the Prince's Council – declined markedly. Of the eighteen nominees, only those active in affairs prior to Charles's accession regularly dealt with business. The office of Chancellor lapsed in 1625 since there was no separate seal.

This maintained the estates of the Duchy as a distinct entity within the Crown lands and ensured that their unique purpose would be preserved. As before the principate, net revenues could be called upon by tally from the Exchequer or by warrant from the King's Receiver-General for his household. With its powers intact, the Council continued to function until London was abandoned in 1643. Charles's heir did not receive livery of his lands before the breakdown of royal administration. Though the Duchy's Council continued to pursue policies which provided a much improved revenue, by the 1630s, it was eclipsed by a Crown administration which had adopted many of the same techniques for application to the whole realm.

IV

The various sources of Prince Charles's revenues at the beginning of his principate are shown in table 10.3. In table 10.4 the income from the Duchy is broken down more fully. Overall, it may be seen that the

---

[66] DCO, Bound MSS, 'Instructions, Orders and Directions'.

Table 10.3. *Total revenues of Prince Charles, 1617–19*[a]

	1617	1618	1619
Rents received from:			
Manors annexed from Crown lands	£8,151	£9,487	£10,321
Principality of Wales	£4,968	£4,922	£5,508
Earldom of Chester	£685	£703	£785
Bishopric of Durham	£903	£1,348	£4,278
Duchy of Cornwall	£16,521	£17,583[b]	£15,612
Total income	£31,228	£34,043	£36,504

[a] These amounts are 'ready money' and exclude arrears. The receipts for the Duchy are slightly understated in that certain privy seal warrants for household pensions and items such as woodsales are impossible to extrude from the aggregate totals given. The Duchy receiver normally paid net sums directly to the cofferer in instalments.
[b] This figure differs from that in the Receiver-Generals' accounts because a large benevolence was paid directly to the Prince's cofferer, Sir Henry Vane.
Sources: these figures are derived by collating DCO, Rolls Series, Receiver-Generals' accounts, box 105, nos. 284–6, and DCO, Household Accounts of Prince Charles, 1617, 1618, 1619, box 127, Z4. All accounts are from Michaelmas to Michaelmas.

Duchy provided about a half of the Prince's total income but, in turn, around a half of that was drawn from the Duchy's involvement in the mining and sale of tin. The Duchy endeavoured to increase its income from all these assets but in the long term, managed its mineral income with the greater success. For that reason it is considered here first.

The Duchy's mineral wealth consisted largely of the receipts from tin mining. As a property owner, the Duchy had the right to collect dues from minerals taken from its lands. These were not of much significance and were expensive to collect; the Caroline Council continued to farm this right, as had its Elizabethan predecessors. More importantly, the Duchy also possessed the coinage of tin. This regality represented a tax paid on every pound of tin which was assayed, weighed and stamped or 'coined'; this consistently provided significant income for the Duchy as well as an important means of control over the tin-mining industry. Throughout the sixteenth century, revenues from the coinage roughly equalled and sometimes surpassed receipts from landed income. England remained the major supplier of tin to the world throughout the early modern period. It was a commodity which could be easily traded in the Levant and

Table 10.4. *Net revenues of the Duchy of Cornwall, 1617–19*[a]

	1617	1618	1619
Certain receipts:			
Rents	£1,909	£1,922	£1,922
Coinage of tin	£2,000	£2,000	£2,000
Monopoly of tin	£9,000	£9,000	£9,000
Total	£12,909	£12,922	£12,922
Casual receipts:			
Fines	£1,755	£971	£1,058
Perquisites of courts	£218	£220	£205
Improved rents	£1,024	£792	£777
Wardship	£177	£820	£0
Havenor	£215	£177	£197
Feodary	£94	£54	£49
Greenwax	£129	£363	£404
Total	£3,612	£3,397	£2,690
Total receipts	£16,521	£16,319	£15,612

[a] These figures include 'ready money' and exclude arrears. Some items, such as woodsales, were carried in other accounts. All figures are Michaelmas to Michaelmas.
Source: as table 10.3.

other centres opening to the newly emerging long-distance trade. It was sought not only by English merchants trading to these markets, but also by the Dutch. There also existed a significant internal market largely represented by the Pewterers' Company.

Associated with the coinage was the right of preemption, the Crown's prerogative monopoly of the trade in tin which had been presented for coinage. Grants of monopolies are a well-known late Elizabethan and early Stuart fiscal device. The grant of the preemption differed from other government schemes in that it was relatively successful and because the Crown briefly chose to exploit the prerogative directly using its own resources. The preemption of tin was exercised in 1601, when a rent of £3,000 annually was exacted and a guaranteed wholesale price of £27 per thousandweight (MWT) agreed for tin.[67] The scheme failed because rival factions amongst City merchants refused to purchase tin stocks from the monopolists. A determined Crown servant with some City ex-

[67] C54/1690. See also SP14/78, no. 9.

perience, Sir Richard Smyth, stepped in during the summer of 1605, and aided by members of the Pewterers' Company and officials of the Exchequer, embarked upon an attempt to sustain the monopoly with the Crown's own resources. Though a financial success, the project was abandoned because the Crown simply could not afford the very large amounts of capital it continually demanded.

In 1607, the government once again looked to City men to take over the monopoly, and after renegotiation by Salisbury in 1608, the monopoly was granted by patent for £2,000 per annum.[68] When Prince Henry received livery, he immediately voided the existing grant, since it had not passed under his seal, and accepted a rival offer of £9,000 which included a guaranteed wholesale price of £30 per MWT for the miners.[69] The patent had not been sealed before Prince Henry's death, but the monopoly was subsequently granted by the Crown on the terms arranged by his advisers. This patent granted the monopolists the right to inspect smelters and administer oaths to ensure tin was not smelted surreptitiously for sale to other merchants. In 1614, it made an additional grant which conceded to the Pewterers' Company the right to purchase 500,000 pounds of tin annually and export the pewter they produced for a rent of £4,000 each year.[70] The total revenue collected annually from the pre-emption of tin had risen to £15,000.

In fact, the Crown found it increasingly difficult to sustain the rents for the preemption negotiated for Prince Henry and the monopoly passed to another consortium led by Clement, John and Thomas Harvey and Robert Charleton in May 1615. They contracted for the tin not taken by the Pewterers' Company for £4,500 annually. They also paid £2,000 a year for coinage rights. This was a reduction in the rent paid to the Prince. In this instance, the Crown appointed an 'assay-master' who would be responsible for determining the quality of tin though the patentees continued to control the weighing beam. They also acquired the right to appoint their own customs agents

---

[68] DCO, Rolls Series, Receiver-Generals' Accounts, Roll 282.   [69] SP14/78, no. 1.

[70] DCO, Rolls Series, Receiver-Generals' Accounts, Roll 280; PRO, C66/2032; *CSPD 1611–18*, pp. 197, 270. The group included the most important members of the Pewterers' Company: Thomas Dunning, Master in 1605 and again in 1610, Roger Glover, Master in 1615, Peter Brokelesby, one of the two wardens in 1616, Thomas Wickerley, warden in 1622, Thomas Smyth, warden in 1629, Master in 1631 and 1632 and eventually Receiver-General of the Duchy, as well as seven others. See Charles Welch, *History of the Worshipful Company of Pewterers of the City of London* (2 vols., London, 1902), II, app. 2, and also John Hatcher and T. C. Barker, *A History of British Pewter* (London, 1974), p. 131.

who could take sworn statements and search for cargoes of illegally exported tin. Should any tin for illegal export be discovered, its owner was to be fined double its value. The patentees, as previously, had the right to send representatives into smelters to ensure the purity of tin.[71] The patent was issued for five years; it was guaranteed by the Crown that if Prince Charles was granted livery of the Duchy, he would issue a new patent to them upon the same terms.

For this reason, it was not until May 1621 that the Prince's Council was able to renegotiate the terms. The preemption was sold to another group of City men for an annual rent of £16,000. In return for this significantly increased payment, the Council allowed the new consortium recourse to the Exchequer court if they wished to bring suits against anyone who infringed their monopoly.[72] They assumed the whole administration of the coinage, including the right to appoint bailiffs to search the innumerable creeks and 'suspected places' in Cornwall so that they could prevent smuggling which would 'enable them to pay their rent and not prove prejudicial to his Highness'.[73] The Prince also occasionally borrowed money from members of the consortium using future revenues from the grant as collateral.[74] After Charles became King, a new patent was granted in 1628 to another ad hoc group of merchants for only £12,000 a year. However, by 1635, when pressures on Crown finances were mounting, the patent was again sold for £16,000.

In the thirty-four years between the initial grant of the preemption and that made in 1635, the efforts of the Stuarts to achieve the maximum financial return from a Duchy right had met with marked success. The annual rent paid for the monopoly, with fluctuations, had increased by just over 533 per cent. But the management of this asset must not be seen only in monetary terms. The Stuarts balanced their financial requirements against the needs of tin miners, the ambitions of City merchants and the officers traditionally employed to regulate the tin-mining industry. The introduction of London merchants into the Crown's relationship with the industry distanced the King from the miners. Whilst the Duchy (or the Crown when the Duchy had lapsed) manipulated the preemption to secure greater

[71] C66/2060; *CSPD 1611-18*, p. 287; and DCO, Rolls Series, Receiver-Generals' Accounts, Roll 283.   [72] C66/2257; SP14/141, no. 338.
[73] DCO, Bound MSS, Book of Orders, 1621-5, 17 March 1624. Earlier, the Lord Warden had been requested by the Prince's Council to help the preemptors. DCO Bound MSS, Letters and Warrants, 1623-6, 28 May 1623. Later the Privy Council was also solicited for its aid. *Ibid.*, 1 July 1624.
[74] DCO, Bound MSS, Book of Orders, 1621-5, 17 April 1623, 18 Sept. 1623 and 7 Nov. 1623.

revenues, it also tried to protect (or at least be seen to be protecting) the interests of the miners. This latter objective became extremely difficult because the monopolists were also granted the right to supervise the assaying and weighing of the metal at the coinage halls. A Jacobean report indicated extensive malfeasance by the monopolists,

the farmers having the whole do wrong the tinners in their weight by falsehoods in the beams and weights, their own officers being those that weigh it. Also their [as]saymaster being their own officer doth find faults in much tin to be hard or faulty tin whereas in truth much of that which they find, and tax to be faulty, is good and perfect tin and yet by the wrong of their own officers they charge the tinners with rebates without just cause.[75]

The Duchy also needed to act as arbiter amongst the monopolists and between differing sections of the trade. In January 1624, Sir John Catcher, a principal member of the consortium since 1621, owed £8,536 to his partners. They complained to the Prince's Council which adjudicated in the matter. He was ordered to find a new partner to take his share of one sixth. When this failed, the Council declared him in default and allowed the sale of his share.[76] In May 1624, the Council adjudicated between the rival City interests represented by the consortium which had taken the preemption and the Pewterers' Company. The monopolists secured a decision favourable to their interests, but agreed to pay 1,000 marks 'so long the said fore mentioned order...do stand and remain in force'.[77] Decisions of the Council were not wholly venal. In 1621, a petition from the Plumbers' Company requested additional supplies of tin which would go entirely to solder, but this was rejected because it would have violated the terms of the patent.[78]

Most of those involved in the preemption were also engaged in other financial dealings with the Crown. First as Prince and then as sovereign, Charles gradually, and with some success, attempted to integrate the groups of merchants active in the monopoly into royal service. By the 1630s they had assumed an almost semi-official role as Crown servants. A merchant such as Job Harby slowly but surely entered the Prince's and then the King's orbit. Involved in the monopoly of the preemption since 1615, he was by 1636 a creditor to

[75] SP14/118, no. 83.
[76] DCO, Bound MSS, Book of Orders, 1621–5, 1 Dec. 1621, 30 Jan. 1624 and 26 Dec. 1624.
[77] DCO, Bound MSS, Prince Charles in Spain, Bond Debts and Burgesses in Parliament, 1623–4, pp. 43–4.   [78] DCO, Bound MSS, Book of Orders, 1619–21, 1 June 1621.

the Crown and in 1640, he acted as an agent for the monarchy in the purchase of arms abroad.[79] Those involved in the monopoly used their credit facilities to aid the Crown in the collection of ship money. The cost of transporting cash was high, and to avoid this the preemptors were asked to pay into the Exchequer an amount equivalent to that due in Cornwall from ship money, and in turn the Crown agents engaged in its collection in the county were instructed to turn their receipts over to the patentees' factors there. In this way, the money actually collected from the Cornish in 1637 never left the county, but was simply employed by the factors in the purchase of tin. Incidentally, it forced the patentees to absorb any loss which might occur between expected and realised revenues. This same technique was employed in Devon a few months later and Peter Taylor, their Devon factor, complained to the Privy Council that he was unable to recover the total sum.[80]

In all of this, the position of the tinners was much more problematical. Production remained flat, hovering at about one million pounds a year both before and during the exercise of the preemption, but in the latter half of the 1630s, it was apparent that miners found it much more difficult to sustain output levels because the wholesale price was too low. The price of pewter increased by just over 43 per cent between 1600 and 1640.[81] In May 1636, the Crown appointed Lord Cottington (whose knowledge of tin-mining affairs dated from 1622 when he first joined the Prince's Council), the archbishop of Canterbury, the Lord Treasurer, the Secretaries of State and the Lord Warden of the Stannaries to examine the causes of the difficulties. The Lord Warden was charged with ascertaining the views of the tinners who pointed out that as mines deepened, it became difficult to reopen them should they be abandoned because of the accumulation of water.[82] The tinners argued for an increase in the wholesale price paid to miners. The initial grant of the preemption in 1601 fixed a wholesale price of £27 per MWT.[83] In the grant to the Harbys in 1628 the guaranteed floor price was £30, which subsisted into 1636. This represented an increase of only 11·1 per cent over thirty-five years and contrasts markedly with the increases in rent paid by the farmers.

---

[79] SP38/16, 31 Dec. 1636 (when the King had pawned 'certain jewels and precious stones' to an unstipulated value); SP16/451, no. 80.

[80] SP16/303, no. 19, SP16/314, no. 65 and for Devon, SP16/351, no. 2.

[81] Hatcher and Barker, *History of British Pewter*, p. 276.   [82] SP16/322, nos. 1, 2.

[83] C54/1690. See also SP14/78, no. 9.

On 12 June 1636, the commission met in plenary session with the King in attendance to consider the tinners' requests. It was suggested that the miners meet the monopolists to arrive at a new and acceptable price which could be sustained by an increase in the price of tin 'vented in foreign parts' and would 'scarce be discernible' to the huge trade. They were also free to suggest any other means so long as they would not incur loss to the Crown.[84] The King favoured a price increase, but nothing could be done for two years until the patent expired.[85] The miners sought a 'penny in the pound' increase, which would have provided a guaranteed floor price of £34 3s 4d per MWT, but the monopolists argued that this was impossible because tin from new mines in Barbary was already reaching Italy, France and Holland. It is likely that these claims were grossly exaggerated or wholly false.[86] After two years of hesitation, the King ordered an increase of £2,000 a year in the total wholesale price on 19 December 1638. This was far less than the miners had requested, bringing the price to only £31 10s 0d per MWT. The increase was paid half by the Crown and half by the patentees. The King, perhaps suspicious that the increase might only find its way into the pockets of mine owners, rather than the miners, required that 'the poor labourer and worker belonging to the said tin-works shall feel and receive the good benefit'.[87]

A pamphlet, written not later than 1652, but probably after the execution of the King in 1649, argued the tinners' case against the preemption, especially in the 1620s and 1630s, when the revenues received by the Prince and then the sovereign 'grew higher and higher as the times grew worse, with some petty increase of price to the tinner'.[88] The pamphlet argued that the position of tin miners had declined so that they were like the 'Indians that dig for the Spaniard'. An argument for the abolition of the preemption and the subsequent increase in wholesale prices which a return to a free market could bring was obviously pitched to win support among the Cornish for the parliamentary cause.[89]

The sale of the monopoly of tin was not solely an act of financial expediency by the Crown. Certainly, ministers hoped to find more money for monarch or Prince, and this they accomplished with

---

[84] SP16/322, no. 8. [85] *Ibid.*, no. 60, and SP16/322, no. 61.
[86] SP16/451, no. 80. [87] SP16/404, no. 102.
[88] *The Case of the Stannaries Stated: With the Ground and Reasons of their Petition to the Honourable House of Parliament, together with the Answers to Several Objections that May be Made Them in Law or Policy Humbly Proposed* (Goldsmith's Library copy, University of London, n.d.), p. 5.
[89] *Ibid.*, pp. 6–8.

spectacular success, but the initial patents were for modest rents, and even allowing for the possibility of bribery or the favouritism of the Crown officers involved, it is clear that the Crown repeatedly considered the position of miners. However, within a decade of the first grant, income became the most important objective for those in the Prince's service. The complicated matrix of relationships between miners, mine owners, merchants and Prince was steadily simplified as the duke mortgaged ever more of his prerogative rights to the mercantile interest alone. Those who purchased the preemption were London men, removed from the areas of production, and they sought to manipulate the industry for gains in trade rather than the immediate welfare of those who produced tin.

In the late Tudor period, the tin-mining industry was dominated from extraction and smelting to the point of sale by large producers, such as the Godolphins, who held significant offices in the Duchy. The Stuart Princes superintended a fundamental change in the Duchy which allowed control of the whole extractive process to pass from Cornwall and Devon to London.

V

The second asset controlled by the Prince's Council was represented by all receipts of land, such as rents, fines and incidents. It was shown earlier that there exists good evidence that as population increased in the last half of Elizabeth's reign, pressure on the land forced rents to increase on manors where tenurial forms could readily reflect such changes.[90] This occurred despite, not because, of the neglect of late Tudor government. The early Stuart period marked a significant change. Crown lands generally received far greater consideration; there was a growing awareness of the possibility that the Crown lands could yield greater returns. In the first seven years of James's reign, Duchy officers shadowed sentiment within the Exchequer and surveys were carried out with a view to sale. Whether or not a way around the statutory prohibition of alienation of Duchy real property could have been found was an issue which was not confronted. The failure of the Great Contract concluded the debate. However, the surveys taken for the purpose of sale, as well as those commissioned by Prince Henry, indicated the contemporary market value of the land

[90] See above, pp. 106–7.

and excited the interest of those around the Prince to find a way of increasing revenue from them.

In common with the Crown, Prince Henry's Council encouraged Norden and other surveyors to recover concealed lands. Norden had particular success in this endeavour; in Dorset alone he was able to recover two manors in which the Duchy had a moiety interest.[91] The Prince's Council also acted upon the information provided by surveys to grant leases at realistic values. At Mere in Wiltshire, it was reported that there were 300 acres of arable in common of which 280 acres were sown every two years. Additionally, there existed considerable hill pasture for over 1,200 sheep and small amounts of meadow and pasture for oxen. In 1617, the Council estimated that the real annual value amounted to £262. A lease of the demesne for three lives was granted that year and a fine of £700 exacted as well as the traditional rent.[92]

The revenue devices adopted by Prince Charles were based in large part upon his position as duke of Cornwall. Once livery of his lands was bestowed by his father, the Prince then could operate as an independent landowner. Grants of leases and offices or any privilege which required his consent, expressed by the application of his seal or sign manual, became as legitimate as a royal grant. Both Princes, Henry and Charles, claimed the right to void all legal instruments made by their predecessors. At a stroke, this meant that all who held from the Duchy were liable to renew their leases. Between Michaelmas 1615 and Trinity 1617, over £14,499 was raised from compositions for the confirmations of existing contracts.[93]

The use of the grant of livery as a device to oblige all Duchy tenants to renew their estates was described by Prince Henry's Receiver-General, Sir Charles Cornwallis.[94] In his memoir of the Prince's life, published posthumously in 1641 (and pointedly dedicated to the young Prince Charles), Cornwallis described how the Prince sought to live within his means and did not seek to improve fines, nor take advantage of forfeitures or reap the 'benefit that both law and right afforded unto him'.[95] It seems most likely that this account was

---

[91] DCO, Bound MSS, T/M/3, Surveys by Norden: Surrey, Dorset, Devon, Berkshire and Sussex, fols. 165–80. Also, Courts of Survey Minutes: Cornwall, Devon, Dorset, Somerset, Wiltshire, Norden's Observations on his Surveys, 1611 & 1615, 1617 & 1619, fols. 165–78.
[92] E306/13/21.   [93] DCO, Bound MSS, T/M/3, Compositions, fol. 164r.
[94] Birch, *Life of Henry Prince of Wales*, pp. 229–30.
[95] Sir Charles Cornwallis, *A Discourse of the Most Illustrious Prince, Henry, Late Prince of Wales* (London, 1641), p. 10.

intended as an oblique criticism of Charles I. When a further edition of his work appeared over a century later the sense was completely reversed; when Henry,

at last, bethinking himself that Wales and Cornwall, etc., his principality, had a long time been without a Prince of their own, he thought he might the rather show his authority in renewing and avoiding leases; wherefore having first by a writ, called *scire facias*, avoided and annihilated all the former rights and leases, he brought them under a general submission to compound, take and hold new of him...Whereupon surveyors and commissioners were appointed, and dispatched to survey all his lands, and to return a true certificate of the whole value.[96]

If this represents Cornwallis's genuine view of events, stripped of mid-seventeenth-century propaganda, it suggests that Prince Henry's Council originated the idea of compounding with all Duchy tenants, not just from those who held lands recovered by action of *scire facias*. His death meant that this policy could not be implemented until Prince Charles was granted seisin of the Duchy.

From those who held by customary tenure, Prince Charles exacted a benevolence. For instance, the total of fines collected from the assessionable manors for 1617 amounted to £2,103 14s 6d. In the same year, tenants on these manors after negotiating with John Dackombe, agreed to offer a benevolence of £2,588 19s 0d which they could pay over two years.[97] On a number of manors, the compositions were the occasion for rent increases. The tenants of Fordington, where manorial receipts had averaged just over £80 a year, paid £346 in 1622, and those at Mere paid £849 in 1624 after an average of less than £100 before 1610. A Cornish gentleman complained that a visit from the Duchy rent collector 'was like that of the gospel that when one devil was cast out seven worst came instead of him. But seriously: I pray put him in mind thereof carefully, for it must either be redressed or the Prince's profit of that kind must not be collected'.[98] Unlike the Crown estate, the Prince's Council could insist that all tenants apply for renewals of leases or pay benevolences simultaneously. It was the positive advantage which the duke possessed. On some estates where improved rents were imposed, they were resisted, as at Fentrigen, where tenants simply refused to pay for several years.

[96] Sir Charles Cornwallis, *An Account of the Baptism, Life, Death and Funeral of the Most Incomparable Prince Frederick Henry, Prince of Wales* (London, 1751), p. 25.
[97] E306/12, File 24, Items 9 and 3. These figures are included in a breviat dated 22 Nov. 1617.
[98] SP14/117, no. 21 (1620).

The revenue devices employed by the Prince were unpopular, perhaps profoundly so. In the Parliament of 1623–4, the Crown agreed a statute which outlawed this behaviour in future. The act stipulated that leases could be made for Duchy lands for three lives or thirty-one years, but could not be abrogated by grant of seisin to a new Prince. The act also went further than merely protecting the terms of existing Duchy leases, stipulating that, where known, only the ancient rents were to be charged or, if unknown, a rent of a twentieth of the net annual value of the land.[99] This statute became a precedent and was reenacted no less than nineteen times in the following 169 years.

The unpopularity of Charles's policy may be assumed. But why he accepted such legislation is impossible to discover. There is nothing to suggest that he was coerced by the King's advisers. On the contrary, there is everything to suggest that the early Stuarts were always careful to present a united front so that political opposition, unlike the eighteenth century, could not coalesce around a disaffected member of the royal family. Under considerable fire for the proposed Spanish match, the Prince may have been glad to grant a concession in an effort to divert criticism.

Once Charles ascended the throne, the receipts of the Duchy remained upon a plateau until the financial difficulties of the 1630s again forced the Duchy Council to adopt revenue-increasing devices. However, in relative terms Duchy income remained high, over 300 per cent above the levels of 1600 to 1610. In the years 1607 to 1608, from Michaelmas to Michaelmas, the Duchy produced a net income of £5,256; by 1610, it had doubled to £11,000. By 1616, it had again increased to £18,345. In 1630, net revenues were only £10,999, but by the middle of that decade, they had climbed to £15,498, at which level they hovered until the beginning of the Civil War.[100]

The Duchy, though, was not merely a successful land-managing agency. It was also a political machine. The Council consistently supported the political aims of the early Stuarts. Throughout the 1620s, it placed nominees into the fourteen seats which the Duchy controlled in Cornwall and also encouraged other boroughs where it possessed some kind of landed interest to accept its recommended candidate. This successful manipulation of the political assets of the

---

[99] Statute 21 Jac. I, c. 29 (*SR*, IV (ii), p. 1240).

[100] DCO, Rolls Series, Receiver-Generals' Accounts, Rolls 275, 277, 285, 286 and 293. See also, Receivers' Accounts, 1634–49, for 1635–6 and 1639–40.

Duchy and other lands provided the government with reliable political allies which it often sorely needed in the Commons and demonstrated to the Prince how his political power as a landlord could be wielded for the benefit of his dynasty.[101] In this, as in other matters, the Prince's Council went to extraordinary lengths. In April 1626, the Council encouraged the borough of Hertford to accept a restored franchise, pledging the Prince's support. The Council then sent another letter nominating a member for the town. Though politically inexperienced, the burgesses accepted the franchise, but rejected the Council's nominee.

In this, and the other endeavours, the Prince may have become the victim of his own successes, believing he could govern the realm as he had the Duchy. The Duchy of Cornwall served as an important nursery of experience for methods of finance and government which remained with the King and shaped his views and suggested alternatives in the face of uncooperative Parliaments. The increased financial yields, the 'fiscal feudalism', which were achieved during the Caroline principate were no less important than the kinds of social control which the Prince's Council attempted to enforce upon often remote areas of England. The removal of local control first to London, eventually even to the Prince's palace, Denmark House, is a remarkable indication of just how extensively and how closely local affairs were directed from a distance by Prince Charles and his circle.

---

[101] Graham Haslam, 'The duchy and parliamentary representation, 1547–1640', *Journal of the Royal Institution of Cornwall*, n.s., 8 (1980), pp. 224–42.

CHAPTER II

The Crown as projector on its own estates, from Elizabeth I to Charles I

Joan Thirsk

Plans for reforming the management of the Crown's estates were regularly deemed 'projects' in the reign of Elizabeth, and under James I the term became a veritable catchword.[1] In an industrial and trading context, it had already acquired a wealth of meaning. At first, a project implied entrepreneurial boldness, and adventurous innovation, and conveyed a sense of exhilaration and optimism. By the end of the sixteenth century, however, reference to a project was likely to elicit a more mixed response: while enthusiasm continued unquenched among the originators of projects, it could stir apprehension, if not sour suspicion, among others who had been victims, or even mere onlookers.[2] Projects for improving the management of Crown lands, therefore, were introduced by government against a background of preconceptions, wild rumours and innuendoes. At the same time, Exchequer officials did their best to inspire the loyalty of loving subjects towards King James, by constantly stressing the great expenses of his family and by underlining with every new demand the generosity of the monarch in devising such moderate and reasonable measures for raising money from his people.

The purpose of the following chapter is to survey the whole programme of projects from Elizabeth's accession, through the reigns of James and Charles, to gauge their novelty, their procedures, their impact on tenants and on the larger political scene. The financial consequences can be gauged only roughly, for they would require much more thorough investigation to arrive at an accurate final score.[3] By 1640, exactitude on the financial score was, perhaps, less

---

[1] BL, Cotton MS Titus B IV, no. 12, fol. 11v, no. 98, fol. 289v; BL, Add. MS 38445, fol. 15v and *passim*.

[2] Joan Thirsk, *Economic Policy and Projects. The Development of a Consumer Society in Early Modern England* (Oxford, 1978), *passim*.   [3] See further below, pp. 347–8.

important than public perceptions of what had, or had not, been achieved. In any case, the financial benefits fell short of the original hopes.

Surveying the whole programme of projects involves examining a steadily changing scene on a very wide canvas. Its full dimensions have not yet been properly measured, for scholars hitherto have either focussed on one geographical area, and failed to appreciate the magnitude of the picture covering the whole kingdom, or, alternatively, they have focussed on the reign of one monarch, and not seen the steadily developing policy over three reigns and more. In fact, a recognisable outline of Stuart policy had been formulated under Elizabeth. This was expanded under James, at first cautiously, and then carelessly; when curtailed in one direction, it was propelled more energetically in another. Under Charles the whole programme is much less well documented, for it was less publicly proclaimed. Nevertheless, it continued in the same direction, and in the thirties was audaciously expanded, leaving a trail of grievances, which plainly lurked at, or near, the surface when Parliament and people assembled their many complaints in the Grand Remonstrance in December 1641. The Crown's reform of its estates was one of many factors shaping prejudices and diluting loyalties when the Civil War broke out.

When the Age of Projects began under the first Tudors, it had involved private inventors and investors, taking risks to build up new and profitable business enterprises in manufacture and trade. The same spirit of enterprise duly infected noble and gentlemanly landowners, and when projects for reforming the Crown's estates were initiated, they were obviously driven by the same sense of exhilaration. A certain will to improve the efficiency of Crown management is discernible in the reigns of Henry VIII, Edward VI and Mary, but it was Elizabeth who took more radical initiatives that paved the way for the Stuarts.[4] Much of the evidence of Elizabeth's measures, however, is indirect, and some of it does not emerge until James's reign when Exchequer officials looked back to see what had gone before. Elizabeth's role in the development of Crown projects, therefore, is best judged from a backward-looking vantage point. In James's reign, in contrast, a wealth of new discussion documents was

---

[4] The search for concealments in Henry VIII's reign is seen in 1525–6 in BL, Cotton MS Vesp. C xiv, no. 105, fol. 243v.

generated, the whole problem was fully discussed, the plans elaborately laid and justified, and Exchequer officials took a long view of their tasks. The first decade of James's reign is the best time at which to take stock of the whole list of projects for reforming the administration of Crown lands.

Remarkably soon after James I arrived in England, Exchequer officials showed unprecedented zeal to adopt new, or more effective old, measures in order to increase the revenue from the Crown's estates. As much of this paperwork has survived, we can watch the proposals in these early days being advanced and debated cautiously, until finally the best suggestions were distilled and a realistic plan of advance was drawn up. The proposals ranged widely, and some were so radical that senior government officers could not stomach them all.[5]

The papers of the Chancellor of the Exchequer, Sir Julius Caesar, one of the most influential figures in this cleansing movement, contain plentiful evidence of endeavours in the Exchequer to start a new chapter in managing the Crown's estate. (We should not forget that Caesar himself has been described as a successful manager of his own estates, and had shown a liking for varied projects to better his own fortunes.)[6] Revenues had to be increased, and so, as the heading of one of his papers showed, 'projects to raise money' were the order of the day.[7] At the outset, reforms focussed on administrative procedures of a routine kind. But Caesar's papers also contain many documents constructed in a debating style that give an inkling of the detailed planning that produced the larger programme of reform. As the tabulated objections on some of these papers show, consultation accompanied every new proposal. Moreover, independent figures like Sir Robert Johnson proffered advice. He considered the lack of good surveys and court rolls to be 'the chief foundation of mischiefs', hence his paper on the duties of a surveyor, and the rational use of surveying manpower. Thorough-going surveys took pride of place on Johnson's agenda. But he also noted ruefully that his suggestions had 'effected more mischiefs and frowns to myself than all the other

---

[5] For example, Henry Hobart, the Attorney-General in LR2/194, fol. 155r–v (quoted at length below, p. 320).

[6] L. M. Hill, 'Sir Julius Caesar's journal of Salisbury's first two months and twenty days as Lord Treasurer: 1608', *BIHR* 45 (1972), p. 312; Alan Haynes, 'Dr Julius Caesar. A stately measure of advancement', *History Today* 21 (1971) p. 789.

[7] BL, Lansd. MS 165, no. 43.

businesses of my life' – a remark that presaged the storms that might lie ahead.[8]

Lists of schemes for raising revenue from projects survive from 1606, 1609 and 1612.[9] In the light of fresh experience, the list of reforming projects was revised and rephrased; but the most thorough examination of the options and possibilities comes from the Commissioners 'touching Projects and Improvement of the King's Revenue' who were appointed in the summer of 1612 and who duly appointed sub-Commissioners. A paper prepared by them for the King in September 1612, coming after nine years of cogitation, experimentation and experience, was most systematic in its arrangement, and is chosen here as a convenient platform from which to survey earlier, current and subsequent action. Its status as a working programme is confirmed in the fact that an undated paper (but of a later date, i.e. after 1613) in the Cotton manuscripts, which reported on the results of efforts to increase the King's revenues, plainly followed the headings in this document of 1612.[10]

The first of the four headings under which Exchequer officials expected to overhaul the management of Crown lands concerned what it called 'the disinherison' (i.e. losses) of the King through 'concealments'. Items for investigation under this heading looked back to past abuses which had gone unchecked through negligence. Although both Mary and Elizabeth had pursued 'concealments' with some determination, many still continued undiscovered. The other three main headings looked forward to future improvements. The first of these schemes concerned the King's revenues, actually received, but capable of improvement; next came tenurial incidents and casual revenues such as perquisites of courts, which might be more efficiently collected under a different system; and finally came new projects, which need not concern us here for they were ideas for raising money from sources other than Crown lands, for example, busses, usury, apprentices, starch, etc. Nevertheless, they serve to

---

[8] Johnson, *Letter*, Bodl., MS Perrot 7, fols. 49r–86v, esp. fols. 66v–71r; BL, Lansd. MS 169, fol. 119r. For the policy of reform pursued in these years, see above p. 000.

[9] BL, Add MS 10038, fols. 327, 29r–30v, 6r–11v.

[10] *Ibid.*, fols. 6r–11v. A further copy of this document is BL, Cotton MS Cleo. F vi, fols. 82–8, from which it was printed in Spedding, *Bacon*, iv, pp. 314–27. Some headings in this text appear earlier in a list of Dorset's 'means to raise money', evidently circulating at his death in 1608. BL, Lansd. MS 165, fols. 111v–12v. The subsequent state of progress (by October 1613) is described in BL, Lansd. MS 165, fols. 240r–241v, another copy BL, Titus B iv, fols. 258v–9r.

illuminate the background to the exercise by showing how imagination was being stirred to work on any fertile idea for solving the King's financial problems. The so-called apprentices project matured into a scheme for enrolling apprentices, which was given to a patentee and was bitterly denounced in the Commons debates in 1621 as a grievance.[11] Two ideas which appeared in another document, and which evidently did not find favour were 'that the king may have the profit of pepper as the king of Spain doth', and 'a reservation upon interest given for loans'.[12] This last may be the same notion as that entitled 'usury' in our programme of 1612.

Each of the main headings of the 1612 document was broken down into single projects, and each was explained and analysed. Undoubtedly, the best and richest source of fresh revenue was anticipated under the first heading, by pursuing the search for concealed lands. These embraced land of four kinds. First were assarts in forests, that is, lands already cleared and improved by individuals who quietly enjoyed them but offered small or no rent to the Crown. The royal forests numbered eighty, and to find improvements the Crown had a large task on its hands. Public spokesmen since Henry VIII's reign had urged the settlement of poor landless people in wastes, forests and parks. Thomas Starkey in his *Dialogue* in Henry VIII's reign had urged this as a means of increasing the population 'of which there is a great lack at present'.[13] The poor had readily taken this advice, and now all the evidence of the surveyors pointed to a veritable flood of landless people pouring into the forests, generally deemed by the surveyors to be a disorderly, idle rabble. For decades ahead, the assarts both of small men and great were likely to prove a happy hunting ground for 'concealments'.

The second category of 'concealments' were more precisely defined as 'defective' titles. Crown tenants, high and low, often held more or different land from that which their deeds acknowledged, or

---

[11] *Stuart Royal Procs.*, I, no. 217.

[12] BL, Add. MS 10038, fol. 29. For other ideas, *CSPD 1611–18*, p. 27, nos. 61, 64.

[13] The novelty of this argument in Henry VIII's reign needs to be stressed. Thomas Starkey's *Dialogue* showed concern for underpopulation, and wished to encourage the poor to marry and have children by giving them land in waste grounds, forests and parks. In this way, barren land would be cultivated, and the population increased. Thomas Starkey, *A Dialogue between Pole and Lupset*, ed. T. F. Mayer (Camden Soc., fourth ser., 37, 1989) p. 49. The Statute of Improvement of 3 & 4 Edw. VI may have accelerated this movement. See below, n. 64.

else they claimed to hold by a tenure which was not authenticated in their documents. Alternatively, they held deeds which did not sufficiently specify acreages, boundaries and appurtenant rights. The Exchequer was currently receiving £1,000 p.a. from tenants remedying defective titles, but expected to treble that sum for the next five years; this was the judgement of one of the Exchequer agents, Mr Tipper, which he expressed in a paper calling for more support in his search.[14] One of his proposals for improving its effectiveness was that local gentlemen should act as informants on defective titles. Every wapentake and lathe, he maintained, should have its informers. This gives some inkling of the ugly nature of the task that lay ahead.[15]

The third source of income to come from concealments was expected from 'surrounded grounds'. These were grounds, formerly subject to flooding by the sea, which had been made more or less safe and dry, and were quietly being put to productive use by local inhabitants. Attention at this time was focussed especially on Lincolnshire where commissioners of survey, 'by the assent of the inhabitants', it was stressed, had found 55,000 acres of surrounded grounds, though it was recognised that not all these lands would prove to belong to the King. The favoured procedure, as in other counties where the same matter was at issue, was to invite townships to petition to compound for the lands. They would pay a lump sum for past omissions, and agree to pay a new annual charge in the future. Local people were to be encouraged to respond speedily by emphasis on the King's generosity in admitting them to composition. In cloaked language, however, they were warned that the opportunity might not last for ever. For this project, Exchequer officials insisted that only the clearest cases should be chosen as examples to the rest.

The fourth possibility of revenue was to be sought from 'tithes out of parishes'. The scale of this opportunity was not clear to the commissioners, and so they could not estimate what gains it might bring. Land out of parishes meant extra-parochial land, which was likely to be found in forests and fens, particularly in places where 'borderers', as they were called, living in adjoining parishes, claimed common rights. A report from Gloucestershire showed a surveyor guessing that Kingswood Forest was likely not to be a parcel of a parish.[16] He was not certain, and, plainly, in many other such areas,

[14] BL, Add. MS 10038, fols. 7v–8r.   [15] BL, Lansd. MS 169, fol. 15.
[16] HMC, *Salisbury*, xxiv, p. 170.

it was not going to be easy to find the exact extent of extra-parochial land. To enquire into this, and then to call for tithe payments on such land, was going to raise a hornet's nest; either tithes were not being paid at all, or they had been appropriated by private men. Even the Exchequer officials murmured among themselves at this project, pointing out that tithes 'by the intention of the law' were intended 'to the use of the church'. However, they seemed to arrive at an agreement that if these tithes had been appropriated by private men, then, indeed, the Crown was entitled to divert them to its own use.[17] Another controversial project was allowed to proceed.

The fifth form of concealments were entitled 'encroachments'. These were found in great wastes (such as moorlands), and in and near towns, and were deemed likely to prove of great value. In fact, they were hardly different from assarts in forests. As with other suggestions, the sub-commissioners knew they were treading on dangerous ground in broaching this matter, and so, 'considering the case is of a tender nature,' they wrote, 'we dare not advise for the present any proceeding to raise benefit'. A commission had, in fact, been granted to enquire into one manor only, and they preferred to await the outcome of that before proceeding further.[18] Mr Otto Nicholson (who had been investigating assarts) was urged to take an interest in encroachments as he went about his other business, but only if he were sought by the tenants to do so. A distinctly cautious approach was deemed essential here, and since it was thought that the Duchy (of Lancaster) had taken some action, the Exchequer plainly expected to benefit by its experience. At the time of compiling their report for the King, however, the sub-commissioners had not discovered any certain information. Here concluded the Exchequer plan for investigating different classes of concealments. It represented a large programme, but it was only part of the total project for reforming the management of Crown lands.

Under the second main heading were considered revenues already being received which might be improved. The sub-commissioners considered first the Crown's entitlement, in the long term, to reversions and remainders on estates in tail. The sale of such

---

[17] W. Notestein, F. H. Relf and H. Simpson (eds.) *Commons Debates 1621* (7 vols., New Haven, CT, 1935), VII, pp. 344–5.

[18] This may be a reference to an Exchequer Special Commission in Kent in 1610 (E178/3943) in Otford, Penshurst and Chevening or perhaps Middleham (Yorks.), described below, pp. 329–30.

remainders was not a new project; instructions for the sale of manors at the end of Elizabeth's reign (1600) allowed these to be disposed of, but the scheme had lapsed and was now being resurrected.[19] A computation by the auditors of the Exchequer of the ancient value of such lands as were known to them had arrived at a figure of £6,081 p.a., and since it had been past practice to sell these remainders at fifteen years' purchase, the Crown could reasonably expect a sum of about £91,000, if it sold the rest outright. However, various alternative courses of action were now offered for consideration, either the outright sale of the remainders, or the imposition of an improved rent, or a mixture of sale with a rent reserved. Peering deeper into this pond, the sub-commissioners saw even more golden fish. The reversions sold hitherto had been confined to entails made since 27 Henry VIII (1535). They now suggested selling lands with entails of more ancient creation, and persuading the Duchy of Lancaster to do likewise. But they urged that only cases where seven lives and more were in being should be considered.[20] Another undated document recognised the onerous investigation, which this proposal called for, into the records of grants in the Tower. It also acknowledged the possibilities of corrupt reporting by the searchers: they might well claim that twenty lives were in being on an estate, when there were only two, in order to have the chance to pursue lucrative-looking cases.[21]

Wastes and commons were next considered for improvement. Concealed behind these three innocent words was a much denser undergrowth of debate that will be further considered below. Suffice it to say here that the Crown knew, from the surveys already conducted, that its manors encompassed thousands of acres of wastes and commons that were capable of improvement, and could yield far greater benefit both to the Crown and the kingdom if improved. The sub-commissioners also recognised that this project would require extended surveys. They therefore drew back. This was something 'which we dare not for the present advise'. They suggested proceeding instead by means of surveys that were not avowedly of commons and wastes but rather of whole manors. These should be chosen one by one, and the question of improving the commons should only be raised where tenants themselves 'either out of their

---

[19] J. P. Collier (ed.), The Egerton Papers (Camden Soc., 12, 1840), pp. 285–6.
[20] Spedding, Bacon, iv, pp. 318–19. BL, Lansd. MS 165, fols. 43r–4v, is a list of remainders and reversions belonging to the Crown, doubtless prepared for the launching of this project.
[21] BL, Cotton MS Titus B iv fol. 139.

own motion or by some discreet preparation shall be petitioners for it'. Repeatedly we see in the discussion of reforms that would lead to enclosures of land apprehension and wariness, caused by the Midland Revolt of 1607. It cast a dark shadow of foreboding over all attempts to promote the improvement of commons.

Next on the list were coppices and underwoods in forests, bringing revenues to the Crown which could be much increased by better supervision. One surveyor alone had already found in certain forests 26,000 acres out of a total of 47,232 acres on which leases had expired and not been renewed. It was recommended that new leases for thirty-one years or three lives be issued (thus allowing the lessee two cuttings of coppice), in return for a fine and a rent, and that certain conditions be imposed for preserving the spring. Surveyor Robert Treswell offered for £400 to view all the woods south of the Trent within a year, and so complete a thorough survey.

Finally, suggestions had been made from time to time that old houses and castles which the sovereign never visited, and which were falling into disrepair, should be sold in order to save expense. It was, therefore, proposed that the Lord Admiral and the Master of the Ordnance should decide which should be sold and which kept. Those suitable as gaols were to be offered for sale to the appropriate counties or towns.[22]

The third of the main headings in the 1612 discussion document was concerned with 'tenures and other incidents with casualties'. The first of these consisted of corn rents, dayworks, etc., which were due under now mostly obsolete forms of tenure, and which brought in an annual revenue of £17. The obvious decision here was to lease their collection to private men. Second were revenues from perquisites of courts, which in the year ending March 1609 brought in £4,213. Since it was estimated that fees and allowances to stewards and bailiffs exceeded that figure by £16, the recommendation in this case was to put their collection out to lease for a short time, 'whereby charge will cease and profit is like to be improved by private industry, which may afterwards be used for a precedent by the king for improvement when the leases should expire'. Next were outlawries, which the sub-commissioners had not had time to 'cast into such a frame as we dare advise to be safe and convenient'. Next came

---

[22] BL Lansd. MS 172, no. 43; E178/2031 (27 Eliz.). A survey of all the castles and King's houses was ordered by Robert Cecil on his taking office as Lord Treasurer in 1608, in preparation for their repair or a decision on their future. Hill, 'Caesar's journal', p. 320. BL, Lansd. MS 165, fols. 45–6, is a list of castles, county by county, prepared for this project.

alienations, meaning fees due to the Crown when tenants-in-chief sold their land. The Crown's officers had already in the previous year raised £1,500 more than the year before under this heading, and it was hoped that again without clamour (written in Latin this time, *sine strepite*) and 'with reasonable using of the subject' further improvements could be achieved. The publicity recommended by the Officers of Alienations for achieving this reform was by proclamation 'like unto some proclamations that came forth some two years since'. But as these were not thought to have had much effect, and some improved phraseology was being prepared for the next proclamation, the sub-commissioners did not wish any immediate action to be taken.[23] Finally, issues royal were listed, namely fees for privileges enjoyed by chartered towns, and fees for silver brought to the mint, neither of which projects concern us here since they did not touch on Crown estates.

Here was a mammoth programme for raising more revenue, prying into every nook and cranny, and involving an unprecedented search for documentary proofs of title, both in the Exchequer and locally. It presaged unending argument, bargaining and dispute on every single Crown manor in the kingdom. But even this list does not run the full gamut of the projects under way. Another scheme, to which the Crown was already committed, was the enfranchising of copyholds on its estates. A commission for this purpose was issued as early as October 1603 (James's reign had begun on 24 March), and some offers by tenants were already noted in 1604. By 1608, it was being described by Salisbury as a 'vain project' of the previous Lord Treasurer, Dorset. But in the late spring of 1611, the policy was being actively pursued again. The commission to enfranchise was renewed in June 1612, and in one case in Cheshire the negotiations came to fruition.[24] The explanation for its omission from the 1612 document is uncertain, but it may simply be that it was the responsibility of a different set of sub-commissioners.

At all events, the bundle of projects on which the Exchequer was embarked by 1612 represented a daunting task, and required a veritable army of lawyers, clerks, surveyors, assistants, searchers and negotiators to carry it out. Occasional asides in official documents make it clear that word of these opportunities soon passed among gentlemen's younger sons and other footloose young men. They

---

[23] The only known proclamation on alienations at this period is that of 1 Oct. 1608, *Stuart Royal Procs.*, I, no. 90. It was not, in fact, followed by another.

[24] See above, pp. 233–43.

thronged Westminster in search of appointment, and showed some originality in selling themselves. Ralph Agas, the surveyor from Suffolk, printed an advertisement of his services, adding the gratuitous information that more abuses by way of concealments and encroachments had been perpetrated in the last hundred years than in the previous five hundred.[25] For tasks which gave payment by results, others tendered a variety of competitive financial terms for their labours.[26] Since the work called for individual initiative, and few or no rules of procedure were laid down, it promised rich pickings to the Crown's chosen agents. Crown tenants, on the other hand, were ill prepared for the bout of fresh energy infused into these projects of a new reign.

The 1612 list of proposed reforms mirrored a refining process by which Exchequer officials had broken down three main headings concerning Crown lands into thirteen separate projects (or fourteen with the enfranchisement of copyholds).[27] But how many of them were entirely new to James's reign? To answer this question we have to look for earlier signs of them, either under way, or in gestation, under Elizabeth. The search for some concealments was certainly not new in James's reign. Under Mary, upwards of 100 informations were filed on concealments in Yorkshire alone, and 700 in the same county under Elizabeth.[28] In a survey of the search for concealments under Elizabeth, Dr Kitching identified them as being 'almost totally attributable to the dissolutions of the monasteries, chantries, and kindred institutions'.[29] From our vantage point in James's reign we can see that two changes had now occurred. First, the term 'concealments' had been much enlarged, and then subdivided. It now accommodated assarts in forests, surrounded grounds, tithes out of parishes and encroachments in great wastes – all now classed as concealments – leaving concealments of dissolved monastic and chantry land to be termed 'defective titles'. Secondly, the search for defective titles under James was cast wider than before since titles going back well before the sixteenth century were called into

---

[25] BL, Lansd. MS 165, fol. 91, printed in H. C. Darby, 'The agrarian contribution to surveying in England', *Geographical Journal* 82 (1933), pp. 531–2.

[26] See further below, pp. 322–3.

[27] The total would be fifteen projects if 'issues royal' (not concerning Crown lands) were included.

[28] Stuart Moore, *A History of the Foreshore* (third edn, London, 1888), p. 170.

[29] C. J. Kitching, 'The quest for concealed lands in the reign of Elizabeth I', *TRHS* fifth ser., 24 (1974), p. 63.

question. In short, the search for concealments under Elizabeth was nominally followed under James, but the definition of 'concealments' was radically, but silently, enlarged to set the programmes on a far more ambitious course.

As for the agents of the search, James took his cue from Elizabeth, and employed much the same kind of people, even though they had many times been found unsatisfactory. Under Elizabeth, the task had been given by patents to courtiers, who were usually (and perhaps always) either creditors of the Crown, or debtors who hoped by this means to repay their debts. The first patent had been awarded between 1559 and 1561 to Sir George Howard, Master of the Royal Armoury, who had also been a pioneering searcher under Mary.[30] A groom of the privy chamber and a gentleman pensioner were two more of Elizabeth's first patentees. Early in the 1570s, however, Elizabeth became aware of abuses by searchers, and intervened to modify, but not end, the policy of search. A fresh offer to search by a different procedure, or for different kinds of payment, procured another patent, but more public discontent prompted further reappraisal. A list of the worst grievances against concealment hunting was drawn up in 1592, without working any noticeable change. Finally, in 1600, Commissioners to Compound for Defective Titles were appointed.[31] Now landowners could compound for, in other words, insure against, defects in their titles, but since searchers were still needed to seek them out, such agents, formerly employed by the patentees, were taken more directly under the commissioners' own supervision.[32] Apart from this change, at James's accession the commissioners continued their work without a break. As a 'Commission granted for amendment of Defective Titles', they used the same manuscript volume as that used to record compositions under Elizabeth.[33]

[30] Ralph M. Sargent, *At the Court of Queen Elizabeth. The Life and Lyrics of Sir Edward Dyer* (Oxford, 1935), pp. 132–9; Kitching, 'Concealed lands', p. 66; *CSPD 1603–10*, p. 450.

[31] Kitching, 'Concealed lands', pp. 68, 70, 73, 77.

[32] Hence the many offers by freelance agents to do this work on various terms. The arrangement for supervising agents directly was vitiated by the return to Elizabethan procedures *c.* 1617, allowing some courtiers to receive patents and employ their own agents. This is made clear in the Commons debates of 1621.

[33] E315/87B records grants from 1599 through to 1606. The continuance of the searchers is shown in BL, Lands. MS 165, fol. 322, where William Tipper's account of expenses and moneys received runs from 1585 to 1607. Moreover, Tipper was working under some kind of agreement with Sir Edward Dyer and Sir Edward Stafford. Dyer owed money to the Crown (see Sargent, *At the Court of Queen Elizabeth*, pp. 132–9). Stafford was Remembrancer of First Fruits and Tenths (see PRO, *Lists and Indexes*, xxxvii, List of special commissions and returns in the Exchequer, 1963 repr., p. 61).

Even so, it is clear from the later uproar that the meaning of a
'defective title' in subtle ways was enlarged; the spirit in which the
project was conducted changed. If a deed did not butt and bound
every piece of land, did not explain precisely what the appurtenances
comprised, or omitted one vital word defining the tenure, it could be
deemed defective. The landholder could then be threatened with the
loss of his land unless he paid composition. In understanding the
dilemma of landowners who hastened to compound without knowing
whether their titles were defective or not, it should be noted that this
was now an age of land hunger, whereas many deeds had been drawn
up in a more carefree age when competition for land was far less
intense, and the legal verbiage more casual. So while the new King
James might appear to be following Elizabethan precedents, the
meaning of a 'defective title' had now been pushed to a point where
no one holding Crown land (or, indeed, former Crown land) could
feel safe.

Another category of concealment, namely, tithes out of parishes,
was evidently not a fresh idea, since it was described in another
document of 1612 as a project 'long discontinued'.[34] When it
originally started is not yet clear; under Elizabeth Special Commissions of enquiry concerned concealed tithes, but they were not
described as being 'out of parishes'. The documentary clues will
probably be best searched for in places where non-parochial land is
most likely to be found. At all events, it was probably a reform that
had begun piecemeal, and then petered out.

Yet another category of concealments were encroachments in
great wastes, and enquiry into these was also not an entirely new
suggestion. In the north of England, where so many extensive wastes
awaited improvement, the Duchy of Lancaster had shown itself alert
to unlawful encroachments from the beginnings of Tudor rule, and
Dr Tupling, in his careful study of the Forest of Rossendale, listed
such presentments in one of the manorial courts (Accrington)
between 1495 and 1551.[35] Encroachments were taken up more
seriously by the court of the Duchy, particularly when commissions
of enquiry were issued. The honour of Clitheroe underwent such a
commission in 1546 and again in 1553, and all Duchy lands in
Lancashire underwent scrutiny in 1561. No further grand enquiry
occurred, but less systematically, on individual manors, encroachments on wastes were pursued under Elizabeth as opportunity

---

[34] BL, Lansd. MS 169, fol. 15.
[35] G. H. Tupling, *The Economic History of Rossendale* (Chetham Soc., n.s., 86, 1927), pp. 57–8.

offered. Hence, on the manor of Colne, in Lancashire, tenants reached an agreement to compound for encroachments in 1594, and Exchequer commissions of enquiry, which covered the whole of the two counties of Berkshire and Cheshire in 1573 and 1577, and Romney Marsh in 1589, may have produced more settlements.[36]

Two categories of concealment remain to be considered as possible fresh initiatives undertaken in James's reign. New patents to search for assarts (in forests) were issued by James in 1605.[37] But Elizabeth had enquired into assarted lands in the Forest of Dean in 1580, assarts were being recovered in Sherwood in 1586–7, and in a careful study of the Northamptonshire forests, Dr Pettit shows Otto Nicholson being granted a lease in 1600 of the right to hunt for concealed assart lands in the counties of Northamptonshire, Buckinghamshire and Huntingdonshire. Nicholson then continued with the same task in James's reign.[38] In short, this project was under way in certain forests before James ascended the throne. The other concealment of 'surrounded grounds', i.e. lands recovered from the sea, for which the Crown now claimed payment, was a long-drawn-out saga of Elizabeth's reign, which she left without a conclusion at her death. The story of this project before the accession of James needs to be more fully recounted, since it savoured of arbitrary use of the prerogative by the Crown. It pushed the Crown's legal claims to land beyond the limits of reason and credibility. But whereas Elizabeth proceeded slowly and tentatively, perhaps restrained by positive opposition from some of her advisers, that caution was gradually abandoned under James, and was wholly disregarded by Charles. The search for surrounded grounds in Elizabeth's reign set a dangerous example to the Stuarts, offering emphatic warning lessons to which they paid no heed.

Surrounded grounds were lands once overflowed by the sea, but now inned and made sufficiently dry for the local inhabitants to use them. The Queen undoubtedly had a right to claim inned grounds adjoining her own manors, and this was how she took the first step to claim ownership. But she was subsequently persuaded to lay claim to the whole foreshore around the kingdom. On this score, she had a thoroughly dubious legal title, and thus overstepped the line between

---

[36] *Ibid.*, pp. 59–68; John Swain, *Industry before the Industrial Revolution. North-East Lancashire c. 1500–1640* (Chetham Soc., third ser., 32, 1986), pp. 61–2. For Berkshire, Cheshire and Kent, see E178/2847, 496 and 2966.   [37] C66/1684.

[38] E178/880; SP46/34, fols. 109, 140; Pettit, *Royal Forests*, pp. 72 *et seq.*

defensible measures to improve revenues from the Crown estate and unscrupulous, indefensible measures, verging on the fraudulent. The judges themselves were not willing to aid and abet this last claim, and matters were left inconclusively at her death.

We are left to guess how attention was first directed towards the large areas of formerly flooded land, now being used productively by local inhabitants. But in any search for concealed land, marshland along the coast which had been recovered from the sea, and was now being used as good pasture or arable, was bound eventually to attract notice. It may have happened inadvertently, when the silting of old watercourses posed problems of drainage, and upon enquiry it was discovered that silting had created new grazing grounds. Early in Elizabeth's reign, in 1561, a lawsuit was brought against certain inhabitants of the Crown's manor at New Romney, when witnesses to a commission of enquiry in 1562 spoke of the silting of old channels and described the consequent enclosure of newly reclaimed marsh.[39] Another investigation followed in 1562, again surveying lands in Romney Marsh. Neither case raised new principles; the manor belonged to the Crown and its right to concealed land was not in dispute.[40] Then in 1564 on the Crown's manor of Tetney, Lincolnshire, 163 acres of regained marsh were discovered. This time, the Duchy of Lancaster's Chancellor and Council decided that it should remain as common of pasture for the inhabitants, doubtless after the payment of composition.[41] This set a precedent for the convention that local inhabitants should be given the chance to compound with the Crown for surrounded grounds. This was only reasonable since they were often already being used as common pasture by all commoners.

New developments in later decades, however, altered the scale of reclamation and attitudes towards it. In 1571, and again in 1598, severe storms shifted the currents on the east coast, and large areas of dry marshland accumulated with little help from human hands. At the same time, private landowners were becoming involved in schemes to drain wet lands along river banks and estuaries, and in the eastern fens. The possibility that such works could bring resounding success was made known to Englishmen by news from the Continent of Europe of reclamations in Italy and Holland,[42] and more emphatically still with the arrival of Dutch engineers offering their

[39] Moore, *Foreshore*, p. 177.   [40] *Ibid.*, pp. 178–9.   [41] DL44/130.
[42] B. H. Slicher Van Bath, *The Agrarian History of Western Europe, AD 500–1850* (London, 1963). pp. 200–1.

services to English engineers and landowners. War in their own
country gave the Dutch no chance at this time of obtaining
commissions at home, whereas in England silting around the English
coast was aggravating the decay of havens and harbours, and local
authorities were much exercised to find a solution. Surveys brought
more and more information to light about recovered land, and
nurtured fresh ideas. A multitude of converging circumstances thus
conspired to promote the advantageous notion that the Crown could
claim proprietary rights over all coastal land regained from the sea.

As the law was then understood and accepted, land on the
foreshore left dry by the sea belonged to the manors adjoining.
Doubtless, many reclamations had been made in the past; indeed, at
Sutton in Holland, Lincolnshire, traditional names for different
categories of reclaimed marsh proclaimed this fact: it was either
'conquest land', 'dearbought land' (i.e. land flooded after reclamation), or it was 'free increase land'.[43] But no official attention
had hitherto been paid to such reclamations, for it was assumed that
they were small, and of little consequence. Certainly, the Crown
showed no disposition before 1570 to contest the ownership rights of
adjoining manors.[44] Then a different theory was put forward by
Thomas Digges, a young projector in search of a livelihood. He was
an accomplished mathematician, the son of another celebrated
mathematician, Leonard Digges, and, moreover, a pupil of John
Dee.[45] Dee interested himself in marshland reclamation, and wrote a
paper on the great potential of such land for crop growing.[46] As a
gentleman's son, Thomas Digges made his way, like others of his
kind, with the support of Kentish kinsmen and useful contacts in
government and at court. He later became an MP, a surveyor of
Dover harbour, and muster master in the Netherlands. Any or all
of these experiences could have conferred knowledge of marsh
reclamation in progress. But already in a treatise, written by him
c. 1569–70, offering 'Proofs of the Queen's Interest in lands left by the
Sea and the Salt Shores thereof',[47] he showed familiarity with the
silting problems of harbours; he was convinced that the reclamation
of marsh was the cause of their decay,[48] and since he lived at Barham,

---

[43] DL42/119, fol. 379. SC12/30/33 precisely explains the meanings of these terms.
[44] Moore, *Foreshore*, pp. 28, 33, 45, 169.
[45] *DNB sub nomine*; Peter French, *John Dee. The World of an Elizabethan Magus* (London, 1987),
     p. 99.   [46] Bodl., Ashmole MS 242, no. 45.
[47] BL, Lansd. MS 105, the text of which is printed in Moore, *Foreshore*, pp. 185–211.
[48] Moore, *Foreshore*, p. 194.

between Canterbury and Dover, he doubtless based this statement on personal knowledge of the reclamations then in progress in the basin of the River Rother. Digges also showed an acquaintance with Flemish law relating to land engulfed by the sea; if drowned for one year, he alleged, and not recovered by the owner, it belonged to the Crown.[49] This may have been one of the considerations leading Digges on to argue for the rights of the Queen. The foreshore, he claimed, was part of the general waste land of the kingdom, and so belonged to the Crown. If the sea receded, then, as dry land, it still belonged to the Crown unless it was specifically granted away. Some foreshores had been so granted; a deed of grant to an ancestor of Sir Thomas Guildford surrendered Iham (Winchelsea) manor 'cum accrescentiis maris'.[50] But without such specific words, it was argued, no manorial lord could claim ownership. Digges's treatise also appended arguments against this view, but these were duly demolished one by one, presumably by the author himself.[51]

Digges's manuscript reached William Cecil, who read and endorsed it, and preserved it in his files. Digges's underlying purpose emerges in another of Cecil's papers, showing that he had petitioned for a grant to look for 'encroachments on sea wastes concealed'.[52] In other words, he was a hopeful projector, offering to look for concealed lands, and cleverly strengthening his case by urging that the Crown had a just legal right, not hitherto exercised. He showed knowledge of lawsuits relating to the Romney Marsh coast, though he was careless in interpreting their legal significance.[53] He was also fully aware that the gains of land made along the Kent and Essex coasts coincided with severe losses on the coasts of Zealand in Holland.[54] We can reasonably suppose that inned marshland, and corresponding losses elsewhere, were a topic of general discussion in official circles at this time.

On 25 July 1571, Thomas Digges obtained a patent, lasting for seven years, to look for concealed marshland. He had authority to commission surveys, and presumably had already used that authority, for three weeks earlier a commission had been issued by the Exchequer inquiring into lands in Kent left dry by the sea, and one of three commissioners appointed was a certain William Digges,

---

[49] *Ibid.*, p. 198.
[50] *Ibid.*, p. 206. I wish to thank Mrs Jill Eddison for identifying Iham.
[51] *Ibid.*, p. 182; BL, Lansd. MS 170, no. 7.   [52] Moore, *Foreshore*, p. 180.
[53] *Ibid.*, pp. 198–201.   [54] *Ibid.*, p. 210.

doubtless a kinsman. Their report was completed in 1572, and Thomas Digges started a number of lawsuits thereafter, some of which he lost, and none of which gave a clear verdict in his favour. Indeed, the judges in one case seem deliberately to have avoided acknowledging the Crown's right by referring to land that 'is but only averred to belong to the Queen's highness'. Elsewhere round the coast, especially in Suffolk, but even into Wales, further commissions of enquiry were issued under Elizabeth, but they do not seem to have led to proceedings, or, if they did, no clear judgement for the Crown emerged. One suit, on a related matter, a sea wreck on the shore of the manor of Holderness, East Yorkshire, confirmed the very opposite, that the foreshore was parcel of the manor adjoining.[55]

The legal position was left uncertain at the end of Elizabeth's reign, with some indications that the Crown's interest in pursuing the issue was fading. One man's ingenuity had been elevated into a Crown project, but the new legal principles that were being advanced had not overawed the judges. Nevertheless, the surveys all round the coasts of the kingdom doubtless stirred apprehension among occupiers of land, and these were greatest of all in Kent where most of the lawsuits had been prosecuted. Under James, our 1612 document showed some continuing doubts about the royal claim, pointing out that while 5,500 acres of surrounded land had been reported from Lincolnshire, it was uncertain how much of it would prove to belong to the King. Some petitions to compound had evidently been received from whole townships, which the Exchequer was disposed to concede, but uncertainty lingered in its advice that the matter be tested by suits brought against objectors in the clearest cases. Surrounded grounds, therefore, remained on the programme of projects, and a commission to search for them all round the coast was issued in 1613.[56]

The foregoing discussion of all the Exchequer's five projects for recovering lost revenues shows that none was an innovation under James, though they were innovations under Elizabeth. All that was new was the launching of a more thorough-going cleansing operation on all fronts at the same time. However, even that was tempered with

---

[55] *Ibid.*, pp. 212–24, 242.
[56] BL, Add. MS 10038, fol. 7; Moore, *Foreshore*, p. 243. The return of the Special Commission of 1613 is E178/4063. The legality of the claim to surrounded grounds was evidently taken for granted in 1608 when Salisbury took over the Treasurership from Dorset and within the first two-and-a-half months of office raised £70 (though a small sum) from 'drowned and regained lands'. Hill, 'Caesar's journal', p. 326.

some caution. The reforms were inaugurated piecemeal, by singling out individual manors, or single counties for attention.[57] Tenants were expected to acquiesce cheerfully in the new demands, and so encourage others elsewhere to follow their example. We shall have the opportunity below to observe the procedure on one manor in detail.

Meanwhile, it is necessary to pass judgement on the novelty of James's other projects. Four were placed under the second heading of 'revenues actually received but capable of improvement'. They concerned the sale of remainders, the improvement of wastes and commons, the leasing of coppices and underwoods and the sale of unused castles and old houses. The report of 1612 admitted that the sale of remainders was not a new idea, and, in fact, our records show that Elizabeth had allowed them into her commission for sale in 1600, and that James issued a patent to sell them in 1606.[58] Traces of a fresh campaign under Elizabeth to lease woods and coppices have not been found, but, again, as James's first commission came early in his reign – in 1606 – it is likely not to have been anything new.[59] As for the sale of superfluous castles, some interrogatories were drawn up under Elizabeth for a survey of Southampton Castle, and an Exchequer commission was appointed. One or two other castles were also the subject of Exchequer Special Commissions in random years, but it is impossible to say for certain whether any sale was under consideration.[60]

Under the third heading, covering small tenurial incidents and casual revenues, James's officials had named unpaid fines for the alienation of lands held in chief; no energetic search for these has been found under Elizabeth, but again the early date of James's first commission – in 1605 – suggests that it was regarded as a matter of course, carried over from the previous reign.[61]

Final judgement on whether *all* James's projects for raising money had been launched under Elizabeth must be suspended, until the documents are more thoroughly searched. The elusive ones, however,

---

[57] This is made clear in the county by county lists of Special Commissions in PRO, *Lists and Indexes*, xxxvii.

[58] Above, pp. 303–4, C66/1710.

[59] C66/1702.

[60] BL, Lansd. MS 172, no. 43. For the Southampton Castle commission of 27 Eliz., E178/2031; for Bamburgh Castle, Northumb., 17 Eliz., E178/1729.

[61] C66/1684.

are also the minor ones.[62] The main one of the four constructive projects for improving revenues was that to improve wastes and commons, and this had certainly been initiated long before James's reign. It was yet another minefield, into which James walked, at first with care, and then without.

To improve the revenue from wastes and commons meant enclosure, and although enclosure of arable land was anathema to Tudor monarchs, the improvement by enclosure of wastes and commons was seen as a separate issue.[63] Manorial lords were already allowed by the medieval statutes of Westminster and Merton to improve wastes so long as they left sufficient to maintain the stock of the commoners, and these two acts were reiterated in Edward VI's reign.[64] The statutes could not precisely define what was a sufficiency, but it was a convention to say that the commons must be adequate to serve the livestock needed to cultivate and manure tenants' holdings and maintain their households. In practice, the enclosure of wastes by private lords had proved to be a thoroughly controversial issue throughout the sixteenth century, and the Midland Revolt in 1607 made it a more tender matter still, understandably giving ministers pause when contemplating such a move on Crown land.[65] However, the Duchy of Lancaster had long had a policy of authorising enclosures for which tenants petitioned in advance. Thus, it allowed two in Rossendale, one in 1557 at Haslingden, and another in 1577 at Accrington. Further north, Elizabeth responded to a petition in 1587 from the steward and inhabitants of Slaidburn manor, granting them permission to enclose some of their wastes, and prescribing the rents to be paid per acre.[66] It is not impossible, of course, that the Duchy instigated all these petitions, in a deliberate effort to encourage the improvements of waste land, but in public it preferred

---

[62] They were dayworks, corn rents, perquisites of courts, and alienations. According to the Exchequer receipts, perquisites of courts were being sold in 1608 and 1609, and fines for alienations were farmed between 1603 and 1620. Dietz, *Receipts and Issues*, pp. 136–41.

[63] Discussed in Tupling, *Rossendale*, p. 60.

[64] *SR*, IV (i), pp. 102–3. The repetition of these two statutes was evidently intended to encourage lords to improve wastes, but it was also accompanied by a clause reassuring cottagers of their right to build houses with less than 3 acres of land, and orchard and garden ground of less than 2 acres, without fear of expropriation. This statute was referred to as the Statute of Improvement, and so appears in clause 32 of the Grand Remonstrance.

[65] BL, Add. MS 10038, fol. 7v.

[66] Tupling, *Rossendale*, pp. 52–7; R. H. Tawney and Eileen Power, *Tudor Economic Documents* (3 vols., London, 1924), I, pp. 81–4.

to maintain the appearance of having yielded graciously to the petitions of the inhabitants.

Concurrent developments brought another class of commons and waste into the arena of public debate, and here tipped the official argument heavily in favour of improvement. This was in the fenland where the Crown was only one of many private landowners with thousands of acres of wet waste land, known to lie under water for at least some months of the year. Private landowners were showing a willingness to employ foreign drainers, and the drainage lobby, led by foreign engineers circulating among courtiers in London, was building up the momentum of argument in favour of private projects. In the course of the 1580s, private gentlemen commissioned the Italian, Acontius, to drain Plumstead marshes, while other foreigners sought clients anywhere and everywhere, among landowners, courtiers and government officials. The Crown was swept along by these events, to consider its own position as the owner of many manors having undrained fenland, around the Wash, in Hatfield Chase and the Isle of Axholme. At the same time, Elizabethan surveyors drew attention on many occasions to land that was 'to a great quantity recoverable'. These words occurred in a survey of Fleet, Lincolnshire, and accompanied an estimate that the land when recovered would yield £100 in rent.[67] Furthermore, problems of floods and 'drownings' in the deteriorating climate of the 1590s strengthened the proposition that the improvement of fen wastes and commons would bring advantages to both commoners and the Crown.[68] Thus, ministers were inclined to hearken to drainage engineers who argued their ability to make this land dry, for the benefit of everyone. William Cecil's papers contain a proposal of 1584 from a Frenchman, called Latreille, to raise water and drain marsh and fen.[69] As Cecil lived on the edge of the fen, and possibly owned land there (certainly, others had urged him to buy fenland),[70] it is not difficult to guess where his thoughts strayed as he read and filed that scheme. Humphrey Bradley, the Dutch engineer from Brabant, wrote in Italian to Cecil in December 1589, proposing to drain the fens around the Wash and underlining the profit that would

---

[67] SC12/30/33.
[68] Deteriorating conditions in 1598 are made clear in HMC, *Salisbury*, VIII, p. 243; XIV p. 61; BL, Lansd. MS 87, no. 4.
[69] BL, Lansd. MS 42, no. 31.
[70] SP10/7, no. 43.

accrue to the Crown. In a subsequent appeal for an act of Parliament
to facilitate fen drainage (29 March 1593), which involved the
agreement of many different landowners, Bradley claimed that
'certain gentlemen of wealth' would undertake it.[71]

The Crown was carried along on a tide of enthusiasm, borne
forward by private landowners, and it is far from clear which
decisions and agreements in the fen were taken in the light of its
interest as a landowner, and which expressed a governmental desire
to promote the commonweal. A General Draining Act was secured in
1600, and in 1602 Captain Lovell was already at work in Deeping
and Spalding fens, where the Crown had much land of its own and
where it became a projector in partnership with a crowd of others.[72]

In two separate locations, then, Elizabeth as landowner encouraged the improvement of wastes and commons: in the fenlands
where she joined with other manorial lords in joint drainage
operations; and in moorland areas in northern England where she
gave permission when requested by the inhabitants. The latter case
is significant when taken in conjunction with the 1612 document,
which rehearsed the same policy. It envisaged the improvement of
more wastes and commons, but gave the advice to proceed 'seriatim,
one manor after another, and not by any more general commissions'.
The same document then added the further recommendation 'that it
were [should be] put in practice where tenants themselves, either out
of their own motion or by some discreet preparation, shall be
petitioners for it'.[73] The fact that importance was attached to
petitions coming from tenants of their own free will, and that this was
reiterated in a number of discussion documents in the early years of
James's reign, upheld a principle from the previous reign.

A framework of projects and certain important rules of procedure
were clearly inherited by James from Elizabeth. Indeed, we may
suspect that the inherited framework was a more complete edifice
than our documents show, even though this cannot as yet be entirely
proved. Underlying attitudes, however, were different. The various
projects of Elizabeth were implemented with less concerted vigour
and confident assurance than under James. In operation, the policy
was hedged about with misgivings, and prudent apprehension, and

---

[71] BL, Lansd. MS 60, no. 34; *CSPD 1591–4*, p. 334; H. C. Darby, *The Draining of the Fens*
(Cambridge, 1956), p. 19.

[72] HMC, *Salisbury*, XII, pp. 177–80; Darby, *Draining*, p. 29.

[73] Spedding, *Bacon*, IV, p. 319.

its more modest scale made it less visible to the public eye. Some of that caution persisted in the early years of James's reign, but it gradually evaporated. A new spirit crept in, somewhere around 1617, and since we are given many insights into James's procedures for implementing his policy, we can actually watch it deteriorate. When compared with procedures under Elizabeth, it is best illustrated in the project for improving commons. When Elizabeth allowed enclosure of the commons at Slaidburn, for example, poor tenants and undertenants petitioned against their inadequate allotments, and were mollified by a revised, and more generous settlement. Under James, officials in 1610 debated the policy in principle, and considered whether they should grant all wastes and commons to tenants or reserve some for the Crown. In accord with the Elizabethan mode, they resolved to settle each case on its merits, but in practice such negotiations with tenants dragged on over many years, and the conciliatory gestures that were evident under Elizabeth disappeared from sight. With increasing vehemence, tenants protested at what they considered to be totally inadequate allotments, and with increasing frequency the Crown intruded its own grantees of improvable wastes, usually outsiders and courtiers, who ousted the commoners. No wonder that the 'improvement of commons' rankled and festered into a major grievance.[74] Our view of it all will now be taken from two sides, from the viewpoint of the Exchequer, and from the viewpoint of the Crown's tenants.

When the main discussions and operative decisions concerning the reform of estate management were completed in the Exchequer, all projects started with the appointment of commissions, which took responsibility and oversaw progress. The main commission in each case was headed by the Lord Treasurer, and included other principal ministers like the Lord Chancellor, privy councillors and finally lesser men who did the paper work in the Exchequer office. Chief ministers emphasised the care that was to be taken in the choice of its agents, to ensure that they were principled and moderate, and would command respect as impartial judges. They were not to be seen to have any interest in personal gain. Their task was to arrange for, and agree upon, the compositions that would be paid and recorded in the Exchequer to settle past offences. They would also set the seal of

---

[74] John Porter, 'Waste land reclamation in the sixteenth and seventeenth centuries: the case of south-eastern Bowland, 1550–1630', *Transactions of the Historical Society of Lancashire and Cheshire* 127 (1978 for 1977), p. 16; BL, Lansd. MS 166, fols. 282v, 279.

approval on any new fines and rents agreed for the future. They are
shadowy figures in the record; presumably they sat in Westminster,
received and analysed reports and surveys, and did not view with
their own eyes the lands with which they were dealing.

Senior ministers on the commissions, like Sir Julius Caesar and Sir
Henry Hobart, show in their surviving papers how seriously they
took their duties. Caesar's papers are voluminous, embracing
innumerable proposals, criticisms of them, reports by surveyors and
summaries of the financial information yielded by surveys. Quite
apart from their training in government, they were trained by their
experience of managing their own estates. Lionel Cranfield, who
became Lord Treasurer in 1621, showed notable precision and
originality in demanding a survey of one of his manors (at Broad
Campden, Gloucestershire) in 1607 which valued every yardland on
the basis of its yield of barley, wheat, pulses and hay, and the number
of livestock it could pasture.[75] Ministers studied their papers carefully.
When a more thorough-going investigation into concealed lands was
proposed in 1612, Sir Henry Hobart, Attorney-General, wrote a
vigorously hostile comment on it.

I do utterly mislike that this commission should give power (as is desired) to
enquire at large of all concealed titles or of the lands of the king's tenants free
and customary, or how much they have of one hold and how much of the
other or how, when and by whom their copyholds were granted ... for this is
almost infinite and will trench to the sifting and shaking of men's
estates ... there was never such a commission granted nor desired to my
knowledge, but the motions of this kind have been only to find out
encroachments upon the king's wastes and commons wherein there is (for
the most part) little question of title but of the fact only, for the waste or
common is agreed to be the king's and the question is only whether any
parcels have been enclosed or taken of it, which depends upon the view of
the place, and the memory and testimony of ancient men and other like
proofs.

The main purpose, as Hobart reminded, was to 'draw a composition
from him that hath made the encroachment', and the search was to
concentrate on cases 'where it is admitted clearly'.[76] Again and
again, ministers of the Crown, in planning projects, showed a desire
to pick and choose which cases they prosecuted, selecting those which
yielded both the strongest evidence, and tenants who were most
willing to admit their guilt.

[75] Kent AO, Sackville MSS 860.   [76] LR2/194, fol. 155r–v.

While Lord Chancellors and Treasurers took the vital decisions on principles of policy, the role of the King should not be overlooked. James intervened very positively from time to time to make requests or to block decisions he did not like. He was, for instance, totally opposed for most of his reign to the sale or disafforestation of parks or forests.[77] He also gave emphatic orders when the New Forest was under survey with a view to reform *c.* 1613; he held an interview with the chief surveyor of the forest, John Norden, and ordered certain new coppices to be planted.[78] This proved an embarrassment to Norden when he found the woodwards equally emphatically opposed to the idea. James yet again gave stern orders against allowing lord Aubigny to become a searcher for concealed lands. Aubigny was one of James's favourites from his younger days in Scotland, who greedily laid hold on many patents and monopolies when James became King in England. For some reason, however, this particular grant offended James and he forbade it.[79] In short, in the first half of his reign, at least, James kept a close eye on policy relating to Crown lands; it is less certain that he maintained that vigilance later.[80]

Next in importance to the Exchequer commissioners in structuring the main elements of policy were the surveyors who sized up the present situation on the ground, measured the scale of the abuses on all Crown estates and advised on reform. The selection of the best surveyors – from 1604 onwards – was among the most successful achievements of the whole reforming programme, and contributed much to their enhanced professional status at this time. The zeal for reform of some of them was assiduous and exhilarating, and reflected considerable professionalism in the face of their formidable task.[81] It is they who were responsible for the large amount of information on which historians nowadays rely to show the increasing numbers of squatters on commons at this period. Their vociferous and repeated exclamations of dismay explain why so much attention was directed to the project for the improvement of wastes.

Last of all in the ranks of the royal servants were those who met the tenants face to face, to claim the Crown's due rights and payments.

---

[77] See below, p. 357.
[78] LR2/203, fol. 1.
[79] Notestein, Relf and Simpson (eds.), *Commons Debates 1621*, p. 352 n. 1. For the far from simple grounds on which this grant was withdrawn, see *CSPD 1603–10*, pp. 369, 328.
[80] R. Ashton (ed.), *James I by his Contemporaries* (London, 1969), pp. 230, 248, 252.
[81] See above, pp. 212–20.

We shall see something of the role played by local gentry, manorial stewards, forest officials and others when viewing the policy from the tenants' point of view. But the most visible and controversial were those who discovered, and then sought out, individuals allegedly holding encroached and concealed Crown lands, and compounded with them. These were the projectors with whom the general public came into most contact. Those who offered their services to the Crown at the outset of James's reforms were hardly different from adventurous industrial projectors, ready to tackle anything profitable that came their way. Indeed, some were frustrated industrial projectors. William Tipper, who had started under Elizabeth as an agent in the service of two courtiers holding patents for concealed lands (though he later served the Exchequer directly), presented a paper on the commercial and other advantages of cochineal.[82] Shotbolt and others who pressed for the improvement of Sedgemoor had sued for rights to transport seacoal.[83] One long-serving searcher, Otto Nicholson, was a Northamptonshire gentleman, who was alleged by his enemies to be a more competent measurer of silks and fustians than of land.[84]

Searchers needed no special qualifications. They first sent their humble petitions for a patent to influential patrons in court and government. They often presented their financial terms in some detail as well. They expected to negotiate with delinquent tenants for the payment of a composition, and appropriate for themselves a certain proportion of the cash. If tenants refused to pay composition, then the land was confiscated, and they claimed a part of that. The exact terms agreed with each searcher probably differed as much as did their first offers, and certainly show considerable variety over time. Thus, Thomas Fitzhughes and Roger Pennell asked in 1613 for

[82] BL, Lansd. MS 122, no. 1; Kitching, 'Concealed lands', pp. 72–5. Tipper was also a member of the Grocers' Company and of the Company of Merchants trading to Spain and Portugal. H. H. Lockwood, 'Those greedy hunters after concealed lands', in K. Neale (ed.), *An Essex Tribute. Essays Presented to Frederick G. Emmison* (London, 1987), p. 159.

[83] M. Williams, *The Draining of the Somerset Levels* (Cambridge, 1970), p. 98; see also below, p. 372.

[84] Pettit, *Royal Forests*, pp. 75, 79. Nicholson was in fact an Examiner in Chancery who died in 1622. His other claim to notice is that he financed the building of a conduit to carry drinking water to Oxford in 1616, the water being brought from springs on Hinksey Hill under the river to a cistern erected at Carfax. The wellhouse still stands; the cistern was removed in the late eighteenth century to the grounds of Nuneham Park where it remains, embellished with its donor's initials. See C. Cole, 'Carfax conduit', *Oxoniensia* 29–30 (1964–5), pp. 142–66, where illustrations of the cistern may be found.

half the money which they would raise on defective titles in the course of two years.[85] John Sparrow and his sons who searched for concealed tithes were actually promised the same terms of half the profits, but were given a grant for ten years.[86] Davyt Fowles, who offered (in an undated petition, early in James's reign) to search for defective titles, and was especially interested in contesting claims to freehold on land that was really copyhold, asked for a patent for forty years, and offered ten years' rent by way of a fine for the land which he expected to confiscate, or for which he would compound with the holder.[87] William Tipper, who searched for all kinds of defective titles in the course of his career, was receiving one quarter of all compositions in 1609, and to this was added in 1611 one fifth of the concealed lands which he discovered. In 1613, he was allowed one sixth of the profits on remainders of entailed lands.[88] A note from the commissioners (for concealed lands?) to the archbishop of Canterbury in 1618 ordering him to pass certain lands to the agent Robert Tipper (son of the above William) is doubtless an example of father Tipper's claim to one fifth of all concealed lands discovered.[89]

Later in James's reign, i.e. by 1617, searchers conducting a general search under the eye of the Exchequer were joined by others, usually agents of Crown creditors who were also generally courtiers. In other words, the old ways of Mary and Elizabeth's reigns returned, and patents were granted which lasted for a specified period, and allowed a search for concealed lands up to a specified sum. Sir Edward Coke differentiated these searchers when he inveighed against the whole system in the Commons debates in 1621; these were the men who were deemed most corrupt.[90]

None of the many documents of the Crown's servants discussed methods of implementing the policy, except through freelance agents. This was an age of projects and projectors, and the conventions of the time were unquestioningly accepted. No matter how cautiously matters were planned in the Exchequer, no matter how much diligent scheming went into ensuring that tenants were gently cajoled into paying composition to their gracious King, the whole edifice of

---

[85] *CSPD 1611–18*, p. 203.

[86] Notestein, Relf and Simpson (eds.), *Commons Debates 1621*, VII, p. 344.

[87] BL, Cotton MS Titus B IV, fol. 238.

[88] Notestein, Relf and Simpson (eds.), *Commons Debates 1621*, VII, pp. 351, 353–4; *CSPD 1611–18*, p. 181. See also Lockwood, 'Those greedy hunters', pp. 158–60.

[89] *CSPD 1611–18*, p. 590. [90] *CJ*, I, *1547–1628/9*, p. 533.

reform rested on individual projectors, who, when once they were let loose in the counties, were incapable of being restrained except by adverse reports from local dignitaries. Their livelihood depended on wringing as much cash as possible out of the King's tenants, and their earnings were inextricably tied with those of the Crown.

The energetic young men who appeared as projectors from nowhere were a band of hopeful adventurers swarming like bees around a honeypot. One guarded letter from the commission headed by lord Ellesmere warned King James against the importunities of suitors for these posts, for 'every private and needy person that hath wit to discern the scope of the commissions finds either one pretext or other to draw benefit from your Majesty'.[91] One qualification which helped suitors when at work, though it may not have been considered a condition for their receiving a patent, was local knowledge of the places where offences were most likely to yield worthwhile sums in composition. Searchers also had to find their way around the records in the Tower of London.[92] But here, they were given remarkable assistance by the Exchequer. They were not only entitled to see all records, but were authorised to carry out inquisitions locally in the name of the Exchequer. The innumerable Special Commissions in Class E178 of the Exchequer records in the Public Record Office bears witness to the scale of the effort, for a very high proportion of them arose out of the Crown's projects discussed here.[93] Such inquisitions involved the issuing of long lists of questions to local juries, and the holding of public meetings at which Crown agents cajoled, harangued or bullied their hearers. These meetings, of course, imposed great cost and inconvenience on local communities. Nor were landholders of high rank more secure than the lowest; the archbishop of Canterbury was subjected to an Exchequer commission of enquiry concerning defective titles in 1622.[94]

The Crown estate was so extensive and the projects so numerous that one might expect to find a whole army of projectors engaged on the task. In fact, the records reveal comparatively few names, and it has to be assumed that each patentee had a retinue of assistants, who

[91] BL, Cotton MS Titus B IV, fol. 233 (undated but before 1608).
[92] Pettit, *Royal Forests*, p. 74.
[93] PRO, *Lists and Indexes*, XXXVII, *passim*, though some of the descriptive titles given to the Special Commissions unintentionally disguise the connection.
[94] *CSPD 1619–23*, p. 420.

worked anonymously in collaboration.[95] Those who received the patents were licensed to search for one type of concealment or for several. But when the Exchequer found all projects overlapping with each other, it did not always maintain precise distinctions between the categories. Thus, a commission of 1611 on defective titles added tithes out of parishes in 1612. This must also explain why some Exchequer commissions investigated surrounded grounds, wastes and encroachments all in one enquiry, and agents also investigated a variety. Tipper is found seeking lands gained from the sea and encroachments.[96]

Searchers' instructions also changed in course of time. Thus, Otto Nicholson in 1600 received a licence to search for twenty-one years for assarts in the forests of Northamptonshire, Buckinghamshire and Huntingdonshire, and at that date he seems to have expected to confiscate the assarts without allowing the occupiers the chance to compound with the King. In 1603, his claim to proceed in this way was upheld against the opposing claim of tenants for the right to compound. But in 1604, the occupiers of assarts won their right to compound,[97] and proclamations later explained the conflict between the contending parties, i.e. the sitting tenants and the searchers, and tried to resolve it. This was an example of the way the Exchequer officials learned in the course of James's reign to moderate their more obdurate procedures and adopt alternatives that stirred less commotion. The new ruling obliged the Exchequer to make fresh financial arrangements with Nicholson, and to issue a new patent. Some at least of the subsequent revisions and reissues of patents to Nicholson are explained by further revisions of policy which continued throughout James's reign.[98] But patents also set a time limit, which meant that, in any case, they had to be renewed regularly.

From the searchers' viewpoint, changes of policy left them in a

---

[95] A small clue is vouchsafed by the Parliamentary enquiry into Mompesson's affairs. His agent was George Geldard, and Geldard had a man and a clerk as servants. Mompesson's abuses were judged by the enquiry to have arisen 'partly' because of Geldard's agreement with Mompesson; Geldard negotiated the composition with owners of concealed lands and 'had to make the best commodity' for himself. *LJ*, III, *1620–8*, pp. 62b, 63a. Similar agreements between the original patentees and their agents are shown in Elizabeth's reign in Lockwood, 'Those greedy hunters', pp. 157–8. Lockwood also uncovers more associates of searchers, pp. 156–61.

[96] Notestein, Relf and Simpson (eds.), *Commons Debates 1621*, VII, p. 354.

[97] Pettit, *Royal Forests*, p. 73.   [98] *Ibid.*, p. 73.

state of some insecurity and uncertainty from one year to the next. They also risked critical reports from local gentlemen to Westminster, which could unseat them. In 1608, Nicholson's patent to search for assarts was enlarged to allow him to search for encroachments, sales of common in forests and tithes. Since the offenders whom he found in the forests included influential gentry, he did not escape censure, and at one stage he was suspended. However, he was reinstated, with the judgement that he had performed his task 'with reasonable benefit and without clamour', and he seems to have continued at his post until his death in 1624.[99]

Nicholson's searches and inquisitions spanned a quarter of a century, and it takes little imagination to conjecture what the name of Otto Nicholson meant to the inhabitants of forest country. In the New Forest, imagination is assisted by a large batch of innocent-looking deeds involving Nicholson, which span the years from 1608 to 1613, and finish with one of 1631 in which Otto Nicholson's name is not mentioned, for he was now dead, but which show the policy continuing as before under Charles.[100] In each of six long deeds, many different properties, comprising messuages, cottages and varied pieces of land in the New Forest, were sold, following inquisitions held before Otto Nicholson and one other person, usually Sir Edward Greville.[101] Nowhere in the deeds appear any references to 'conceal-ments' or 'defective titles', and yet this is what they plainly are. Either the landholders had refused to compound (according to the proclamation of 1605 they should have been given a chance to do so), or possibly the ostensible purchasers were acting on behalf of a motley group of occupiers.[102] The first sale in December 1608 was made to George Merreil and Thomas Ely for £1,015 19s, following an inquest at Romsey on 20 July 1608.[103] The third grant to John Foyle of

---

[99] Ibid., pp. 73–5, 79; CSPD 1623–5, p. 312.
[100] D. J. Stagg (ed.), A Calendar of New Forest Documents. The Fifteenth to the Seventeenth Centuries (Hampshire Record Series, 5, 1983), pp. 242–79.
[101] Ibid., p. 120. Greville also worked alongside Nicholson in the Northamptonshire forests. Pettit, Royal Forests, pp. 75–80.
[102] Stuart Royal Procs., I, no. 52. A proclamation of 1609 allowed groups of landholders to compound in order to save them many separate lawyers' fees. It claimed to have 'suspended the rigour of a legal prosecution' and 'turned it into a gracious composition ... so that extremity of eviction may be avoided', ibid., no. 97. But the New Forest deeds start in 1608.
[103] It may be that this inquest was the one referred to in a note by John Norden to the Lord Treasurer in 1609, announcing that the commissioners and jury gave their attendance there and proceeded according to the articles of Sir Henry Fanshawe. The note added that their enquiry into wastes had had 'many oppositions and detractions by the perniciousness

Shaftesbury contained eight separately named properties, amounting to twenty-seven messuages, nineteen cottages, and 953 acres 1 rod 10 perches of land, and was sold for £228 8s, after an inquest at Hartley Row on 1 January 1609. The fourth grant in June 1609 to Edward Savage of Bradley, and Andrew Munday of Grove Place, both in Hampshire, followed an inquest at Romsey almost a year earlier, and disposed of the property of eighty occupiers, including Sir William Oglander, Richard Worsley, esquire, and humbler folk like Joan Hobs, widow, and Sibil Tutt. The fifth grant in 1613 consisted of assarts and purprestures, which had been presented at three separate inquests. The sixth was a tailpiece in 1631, indicating by its contents that the searcher was scraping the bottom of the barrel. For £200, forty-seven properties were sold to one John Chamberlain, esquire, having a total annual value of no more than £1 2s 6d. The individual parcels mostly comprised a single cottage with garden, a rod or two of land or scattered pieces of waste. We can only guess how the occupiers were affected by the sales of their property, if the purchasers were not, in fact, acting for them; at best they could expect to compound individually with the new owners. Details written into the deeds of each individual piece of land give an inkling of the toil of the searcher and his assistants before the concealments were discovered.

The most notorious projector of all was Sir Giles Mompesson, whose name became a byword for corrupt, greedy malpractice. He had offered a project to raise £100,000 in four years by selling decayed timber from the royal forests. This was accepted in 1617. He bought decayed timber in nine counties, and the only supervision he received to ensure that he did not commit waste or spoil in the forests was from the woodwards and JPs, men who had long since proved to be inadequate policemen.[104] He was an object of execration in 1621, when the House of Commons launched its bitter attack on patents and monopolies. How accurate were their accusations it is impossible to say, but they give some notion of the way agents – particularly those who served patentees, and who were not supervised by the Exchequer, when once they were roaming free in the counties – could manipulate matters to their advantage. In selling timber from the forests Mompesson was alleged to have collected a fee of £1,000 from the Exchequer at the outset, had made further profits of £10,000 by

of some that have estimated the power of the commission as being but a chequer commission'. SP14/48, no. 128.

[104] Pettit, *Royal Forests*, p. 62.

his sales, and was due to receive another £1,000 from the Exchequer at the end. He also had a patent to discover concealments, which allowed him to keep land worth £200 for himself.[105] So he undervalued each discovery in order to appropriate land worth £2,000 while claiming it was worth only £200.

Mompesson was the most notorious of the Crown agents in manipulating the financial agreement to his own advantage. Others were accused of harassing tenants and carrying out slipshod research when investigating titles. From their point of view, the work was finicky and laborious. Otto Nicholson in his searches at Oakley Parva, in the Northamptonshire forests in 1612, held an inquisition concerning 2 acres of one man, 10 rods 6 perches of another, and 30 acres in Whittlewood of a third man. His total discoveries listed in one book amounted to 255 acres, for which he collected just over £200 in fines, and set rents of £2 1s 5d to be paid for the future.[106] The short-term gain to the Crown was perhaps £100, the long-term gain was trifling. More revealing glimpses of the searchers at work are obtained by examining the policy as experienced by the tenants.

Frequently, tenants were first made aware of the investigations of their lands by the arrival of surveyors who made unusually thorough enquiries, assembled juries, interviewed individuals and inspected the ground. Surveyors were instructed to be circumspect, but they could not do their job single-handed. They were attended by clerks and measurers.[107] They had to be housed and fed. In the *Surveyor's Dialogue*, Norden admitted that surveyors had a bad reputation: 'oftentimes you are the cause that men lose their land and sometimes they are abridged of such liberties as they have long used in manors'.[108] Wherever they appeared, they created a stir.

After the surveys, when commissions had been appointed by letters patent to oversee the different projects, tactical decisions were taken to ensure good public relations. The Exchequer evidently chose to approach some individuals personally; that must be the reason why Salisbury, immediately on taking over the Lord Treasurership from Dorset in 1608 sent out 'at least 530 letters to private men to

---

[105] Notestein, Relf and Simpson (eds.), *Commons Debates 1621*, VII, pp. 483, 346; VI, pp. 12–13; II, pp. 188–94.

[106] SP14/194, no. 19.

[107] Heather Lawrence, 'John Norden and his colleagues: surveyors of Crown lands', *Cartographic Journal* 22 (1985), pp. 54–5.

[108] R. H. Tawney, *The Agrarian Problem of the Sixteenth Century* (London, 1912), p. 349.

compound, if they will, for the amendment of their defective titles'.[109] The Exchequer also chose the manors which were to be investigated first. In relation to concealments, the Exchequer picked on the most flagrant examples, where tenants could not but concede the justice of the King's cause, and where the authorities believed that publicity would do no harm. On the contrary, they argued, it would show how moderate were the compositions which the Crown was prepared to accept, and so would encourage other Crown tenants to come forward cheerfully to compound.

In one remarkable example, we are given an almost complete account of the 'discreet preparation' by which the Exchequer schemed to cajole tenants into compliance with its financial demands. The manor chosen was Middleham in North Yorkshire, and the date September 1611.[110] Three gentlemen, at least one of whom was already known to the inhabitants, had spent the winter in London, had learned of the King's financial needs and had seen projectors at Westminster casting eagerly around for the chance to earn profits by prosecuting tenants for concealments. These three gentlemen, calling themselves 'loving neighbours' of the Middleham tenants, summoned a meeting with them, with their 'learned steward' in attendance. The spokesman of the three, making the first speech, urged the tenants to compound for the extensive improvements they had already carried out on the waste, and warned them to seize their chance now and not imagine that it would always be available. The speech was written out carefully, and contained one cogent sentence which neatly paraphrased Shakespeare's speech in *Julius Caesar* about a tide in the affairs of men which taken at the flood leads on to fortune. 'There is a time for each thing upon earth', the tenants were told. 'Time once past cannot be had again. Opportunity is very precious. It is good setting the seal to the wax whilst it is soft.'[111] In response to this very frank speech, which contained an underlying threat, the steward replied confidently, assuring the three gentlemen that their titles were secure, having been granted by Elizabeth in

---

[109] Hill, 'Caesar's journal', p. 326.

[110] Procedure at Middleham followed closely the advice given in a report on enclosing wastes and levying rents from lands already enclosed. It recommended a start in Yorkshire. See Joan Thirsk and J. P. Cooper (eds.), *Seventeenth-Century Economic Documents* (Oxford, 1972), pp. 116–20, where the report is printed and dated 1612, but it must be of 1611 or earlier.

[111] LR2/194, fols. 164r–5v; *Julius Caesar*, IV, scene iii, lines 216–23. G. L. Kittredge, citing Cato, described the sentiment as 'a philosophical commonplace'. See T. S. Dorsch (ed.), *Julius Caesar* (The Arden Shakespeare, London, 1965), p. 108n.

1584–5. We may imagine the tenants' dismay when they were quickly disabused of the notion that their former agreement was unassailable. Because no Crown rent was reserved when the improvements were accepted, the agreement could be 'disannulled'. Also, it was plain to all that the tenants had abused their grant (by improving more land than was allowed to them). Finally, they were told that, whatever the form of words in the grant, by statute manorials lords could enclose any amount of waste land, so long as they left enough for the commoners. The Middleham tenants were then given fourteen days in which to signify their response. They did so promptly, for our three gentlemen returned their replies to the Exchequer.

The fact that the full text of the speech at Middleham was filed in Caesar's papers shows clearly that at least one government minister was privy to the occasion.[112] In fact, the meeting at Middleham exactly accorded with official policy to make 'discreet preparation' for agreements with Crown tenants. Those of Middleham were expected to compound for their concealments, and gratefully thank the King for his magnanimity. Seen from the tenants' point of view, however, we gain an inkling of their helplessness in the face of Crown messengers, who announced to them in legal language, and with a quite unwarranted assurance, the defects in their titles. In this case, The three gentlemen reported to London that the tenants were grateful, rather than aggrieved, at the peaceable demeanour of their visitors. They seem also to have been compliant. But this was in the early days, before the full consequences of the Crown's scrutiny of titles emerged. Other Crown agents were less peaceable and less scrupulous; and some were positively corrupt.

News of the Crown's reforms was doubtless spread abroad by tenants' gossip, but it was also spread abroad by many proclamations. They were much used by James, not only to publicise his endeavours, but to give a certain colour to his requests for compositions. Some were wordy essays on the geniality and charity of the King, and, indeed, in government circles the commissions were called Commis-

---

[112] In a posthumous tribute to Salisbury, Sir Walter Cope made a significant admission, illuminating the Middleham case. Salisbury, he claimed, was tender towards common rights, and 'he never durst offer to enclose nor to urge the tenants to any forcible compositions. But underhand set some to advise the tenants to become suitors themselves, with whom we have compounded for part and made a good precedent for the rest.' J. Gutch (ed.), *Collectanea Curiosa* (2 vols., Oxford, 1781), I, p. 124.

sions of Grace. The first proclamation was issued in February 1605, and dwelt on a small part of the programme, namely, the necessity for reviewing the leases and small rents being paid for assarts, wastes and purprestures in the forests. Tenants were invited to buy more secure titles. They did not respond promptly, however, for another proclamation in May expressed disappointment at the results. Tenants, this proclamation remarked, thought they could take their time, whereas the news of such opportunities had prompted speculators immediately to offer to compound in the place of tenants. If their offers had been accepted, they would have been able to dispossess the existing landholders, or bully them into paying higher rents than those the Crown was prepared to take. The King preferred to acknowledge the prior claim of the 'long and ancient possessors', and extended the time limit until 1 October 1605.[113]

From 1605 onwards, Crown tenants, whether they knew it or not, lived under the constant threat of being challenged for their lands. The patentees and their assistants combed the archives in London, and prowled around their chosen districts in the country. When interrogating individuals, they pounced upon any information yielded by one person which led to the discovery of others. Thus whole tracts of country were stirred into anxiety, and held in an unsettled state while agents lingered in the vicinity, endeavouring to uncover more and to persuade more people to compound.

Agents had the authority of their commissions and of the Exchequer to summon tenants for questioning. Complaints aired in the angry Commons debates of 1621 bring the enormity of the tenants' grievances to life. When the commissioners seeking concealed tithes arrived in a district, they summoned all adult male inhabitants to attend on them – doubtless in a nearby town. They chose inconvenient times, like harvest weeks, and they obliged the inhabitants to spend two or three days at their own charge away from home. If tenants wished to be heard quickly, they had to bribe the Exchequer officials, in order to jump the queue. The names of Sir John Wentworth, who was one principal commissioner, and his two most diligent agents, the Sparrows, father and son, were especially odious.[114]

In the course of years, the procedure for compounding was made clearer in yet more proclamations, which oiled the wheels in the light

---

[113] *Stuart Royal Procs.*, I, nos. 49, 52.
[114] Notestein, Relf and Simpson (eds.), *Commons Debates 1621*, v, p. 49; vi, p. 291.

of experience. The agent visited an estate and negotiated face to face with his victims, or alternatively he was visited by a willing compounder. He arrived at a financial agreement which he had to refer to senior commissioners, before concluding it. In one set of instructions, more candid than most, he was ordered quite explicitly to claim to have the authority to arrive at a composition, but in fact to temporise while he sought agreement from London. In the interval, he had to ensure that the compounder did not change his mind and attempt to bargain on different terms.[115]

In some cases, the demand for composition came from an agent in a more impersonal form. Such a summons was served by the Commissioners for Defective Titles on John Halliwell, owner of lands in Sillesworth(?), Northamptonshire. It ordered him on 20 March 1613 to compound with William Tipper before 1 April, in accordance with the proclamation, as 'otherwise the course of law against him cannot longer be stayed'. We have no way of knowing what forewarning Halliwell had received, but he was clearly marked out for individual attention, and was unable any longer to disappear into the crowd. He was given ten days' grace in which to reply; others were given a fortnight.[116]

Many gentry learned of the King's enquiries from within their own circle, for word quickly passed. The three gentlemen visiting Middleham had learnt both of the King's financial needs, and of the projectors casting around for patents, while spending the winter in London. They were expected to inform their tenants of the contents of proclamations; much later, in 1641, complaint was made against the ill-will of one manorial lord who did not inform his tenants of their chance to buy their freeholds.[117]

Crown tenants, who were summoned by commissioners but who refused to compound, were liable to be issued with a bill in the Court of Exchequer. The most graphic description of such a case was that given by John Smyth of Nibley, involving George lord Berkeley and other Gloucestershire gentry in a claim for ground recovered from tidal waters at Slimbridge, in other words 'surrounded grounds'. Smyth had bitter memories of 'great and tedious suits' which lasted for ten years from 1609 and were heard in King's Bench, Common Pleas, Chancery, the Court of Wards and Star Chamber.

---

[115] BL, Lansd. MS 166, fol. 278.
[116] *CSPD 1611–18*, p. 176; *CSPD 1619–23*, p. 457; *CSPD 1623–5*, p. 576.
[117] *Stuart Royal Procs.*, II, no. 50n.

But the account he wrote down concerned the last hearing in the Exchequer in Charles's reign in 1637, brought by the Attorney-General, Sir John Bankes, and prosecuted by a commission (presumably that for Surrounded Grounds) headed by Sir Sackville Crowe. Smyth was counsel for the defence, and so in the best position to see the case from the landholders' point of view. The dispute centred on 200 acres of land gained from the Severn at Slimbridge and another 300 acres elsewhere.[118] Charles claimed ownership of the foreshore, on the same basis as James and Elizabeth before him.

According to Smyth's account, Sackville Crowe and other commissioners were far from being impartial judges; on the contrary, they showed themselves openly to be interested parties. Smyth did not explain this allegation further, but doubtless meant that Crowe expected to take possession of the land for a project of his own. (He was much involved in projects to dig for iron ore and manufacture ordnance in the Forest of Dean.)[119] The total value of the land in dispute was £20,000 p.a. but the case had much wider implications, for if the Crown won, the decision threatened the tenure of other landowners on both sides of the river for 140 miles along the estuary. Smyth, the diligent and efficient manager and historian of the Berkeley estates, assembled a mass of documents in his master's defence, and prepared 'an invective speech which for some bitterness I had determined to have spoken in court at the end of my evidence... against Sir Sackville Crowe especially'. Crowe, he said, was the prime projector of the Severn business, and at his own charges had set himself at work suing out the commission, 'making himself and his fellows (interested with him) commissioners'. Crowe was alleged also to have bribed the undersheriff to choose, as some of the jurors, his own nominees.[120]

The vested interests of the commissioners were evidently undisguised; 'a number of the projectors', wrote Smyth, came to the hearing, and the long preparation of the case caused Smyth deep alarm and anxiety. To his gratification, it collapsed at the hearing before he had time to make his speech, since the documents showed

[118] Sir J. Maclean (ed.), *The Berkeley Manuscripts. The Lives of the Berkeleys by John Smyth of Nibley* (3 vols., Gloucester, 1883), III, pp. 330–1, 337–47. The Special Commission in this case is E178/6029 (1637), and names John Smyth as the occupier of two out of the three parcels of land discovered.

[119] Sharp, *In Contempt*, p. 202; *CSPD 1634–5*, pp. 487, 601.

[120] Maclean (ed.), *Berkeley Manuscripts*, III, p. 340.

clearly that lord Berkeley had a secure title. Smyth's bitterness was allowed expression in sardonic words: he hoped that Crowe's voyage to Constantinople, as factor for the Turkey merchants, would prove more prosperous.[121] Nevertheless, he rejoiced that the Exchequer case of 1637 had finally quietened all uncertainties concerning surrounded grounds in the Severn estuary.

More than twenty years before the Slimbridge case was tried, Lord Chancellor Ellesmere had shown keen awareness of the problem of selecting projectors. In 'Things to be considered of before a Parliament to be called' (1615), he had acknowledged that, while projectors ostensibly husbanded the King's treasure, they 'made their own gain thereby and so abused both the king and the suitors' (meaning, in this case, the compounders). His hope was to use projectors to increase the King's revenue 'so far forth as may stand with justice, honour, and conscience, and may be without inconvenience, grievance or offence to the people'. Debates in Parliament in 1614 had made Ellesmere sensitive to public complaints against the King's agents, but when he came to consider 'by whom the projects shall be executed' for selling forests, improving wastes, enfranchising copyholds, selling reversions and remainders, etc., he returned to platitudes about choosing ministers with integrity, benefiting by past experience and investigating the fraudsters so revealed. He placed reliance on good handling 'by faithful and industrious ministers', omitting to consider all the problems which loomed in face-to-face negotiations in the country at large.[122]

When John Smyth gave an insider's view of the tensions between local landowners and Crown commissioners, he omitted to remark on the fact that any of the Crown commissioners might be local landowners as well, thus engendering or intensifying local feuds. This, in fact, was a common occurrence, and one example must suffice. In an earlier case in Gloucestershire, when the Crown began an enquiry into the state of the Forest of Dean, with a view to reforming abuses, the commissioners appointed to hear the case in the Exchequer in 1611 were Sir Edward Winter, George Huntley, George Thorpe, and the King's Surveyor-General Treswell. But in the same year, when Norden, Treswell and Morgan reported on the saleable timber in the forest, they reported an offer from Winter for

---

[121] *Ibid.*, p. 347.
[122] L. A. Knafla, *Law and Politics in Jacobean England. The Tracts of Lord Chancellor Ellesmere* (Cambridge, 1977), pp. 263–4, 270–2.

six coppices, together with his answer to objections that had been raised against it. In other words, Winter was lying in wait for a bargain at the same time that he was a commissioner investigating abuses.[123]

In some of the claims made by informing agents it is clear that landholders believed themselves to have a perfectly valid and secure title until the agents alleged otherwise. The agents, however, started from the assumption that most tenants had defective titles, and they were encouraged in this belief by the surveyors. In a report on enquiries in Kingswood Forest, Gloucestershire, sent to Robert Cecil some time after May 1609, the writer, almost certainly a surveyor, referred disparagingly to tenants' claims to hold valid titles. 'Grants may peradventure be produced', he said, 'and the same may carry words to seeming good purpose to confirm their pretended right', but when examined they would show a great defect in not giving precise boundaries. Claimants would then produce 'a company of silly country partially affected inhabitants, ... who cannot speak of above sixty or seventy years, a weak proof'.[124] Tenure for sixty or seventy years was hardly weak proof; in fact, when the great quarrel broke out in the Commons in 1621 against patents and monopolies, James was obliged to accept the ruling that titles going back sixty years could not be questioned. Sir Edward Coke insisted upon this concession with great vehemence.[125] The earlier posture of the Crown's servants, however, showed their extreme bias against tenants. Modest landholders, with small financial resources and meagre advice, were no match for these men.

In the 1621 debates, an example was given of William Tipper's rough handling of one such case. The estates of Henry Courtenay, marquis of Exeter had been forfeited for treason in Henry VIII's reign (1538), and the Crown had dispersed the land into many hands. William Tipper searched for evidence of defective titles, and 'mislaid' it – either he did not find it, or he found it and forgot it. Judges pronounced the grants void if no record could be found, and Tipper proceeded to hound the tenants. Sir Edward Coke (or possibly someone else – two different accounts appear in the diaries) took an interest in the case, searched afresh for the record, and found it in an

<hr>

[123] E178/3837; BL, Lansd. MS 166, no. 94.   [124] HMC, *Salisbury*, XXIV, pp. 169–72.
[125] Notestein, Relf and Simpson (eds.), *Commons Debates 1621*, IV, pp. 180, 250; *CJ*, I, *1547–1628/9*, p. 532. Sir Nathaniel Rich wanted the time limit to be only twenty years, *ibid.*, p. 534.

Exchequer calendar.[126] Without this persistence, the tenants would
have been obliged to compound or be evicted. When single agents
had so much power, the fundamental question, *quis custodiet custos?*,
urgently called for answer.

The pressure placed on Exchequer commissioners and their agents
to make compositions was not exerted continuously throughout
James's reign. Energy waxed and waned. After the strenuous efforts
made between 1603 and 1605 to find compounders willing to pay
compositions, fresh surveys were put in hand and another campaign
followed between 1609 and 1610 to compound for defective titles,
concealed tithes and surrounded lands. In a proclamation of April
1609, tenants were reminded that the King was entitled to prosecute
and evict them for their defective titles, but instead offered 'a
gracious composition' which must be taken up before Michaelmas.
Some encouragement was offered in the shape of a clear statement of
the fine to be paid, namely five years of the old rent, and groups of
people, making offers amounting to £40 altogether (according to the
old rent), were now allowed to join in one patent in order to save legal
fees.[127] The time limit was short, however, and since the commissioners, who were mostly privy councillors, did not sit in the Long
Vacation and learned counsel also left London for the summer, the
time limit was extended in November until the following February;
in February it was extended until Easter.[128] Then the momentum of
this drive slackened, since no more extensions of time were granted.
Ten years later, in February 1619, new life was breathed into the
project in another proclamation, in which the King reminded his
loving subjects that he was entitled to seize lands held by defective
titles, but had decided instead to revive the commission for taking
compositions. The threat of eviction, if offenders failed to compound,
was now more earnestly emphasised. They should not expect another
chance. The same threatening posture was adopted towards those
who did not compound for surrounded grounds; they were to be
excluded from the King's grace.[129]

Such threats were far from idle. When Anthony Irby was ordered
in August 1620 to pay £125 to compound for his defective title to
marsh ground in Moulton, Lincolnshire, and Robert Adams was

---

[126] Notestein, Relf and Simpson (eds.), *Commons Debates 1621*, v, p. 61. For a different account,
IV, p. 180.

[127] See n. 102 above.   [128] *Stuart Royal Procs.*, I, nos. 106, 108.

[129] *Ibid.*, no. 185; BL, Lansd. MS 169, fol. 22.

required to pay £161 3s 6d for marshland in Tydd St Mary, Lincolnshire, they knew that if they did not do so, a certain William Smisby already held authority from the Exchequer to take possession of their land.[130] Irby's plight was singularly ironic, for in 1610, being a gentleman of a well-known Lincolnshire family, he had offered estimates of the revenue the King might expect from compositions for surrounded lands. He was then a younger man, perhaps hoping for advancement by his earnest endeavours on behalf of the King. Now he was the biter bit.[131]

Around 1619, the revived rigour of the Crown's campaign to secure compositions explains some of the bitterness in the parliamentary debates against patents and monopolies in 1621. The patent for discovering concealments was first on the list of grievances when the Grand Committee for Grievances held its afternoon session in the Commons on 2 March 1621,[132] and the names of, and anecdotes about, the most notorious Crown agents made a deep impression. Several diarists recorded them in some detail. It was on this occasion that Giles Mompesson's enormities in searching for all kinds of defective titles was held up for special execration. He had questioned the titles of Prince Henry (or Charles), great lords, hospitals, free schools and churches.[133] The likely truth of this last allegation is indicated in a Landsdowne manuscript, which is William Tipper's book of concealments of cathedrals and colleges.[134]

James's policy unsettled everyone occupying Crown land, and it is impossible to assess the numbers of small tenants so disturbed. It is less difficult to gauge the impact on the gentry. Indeed, in the Commons debate in 1621, Sir Thomas Edmonds named the Commission for Concealments as a grievance 'which extends to all gentlemen'. It may well have seemed so. Some notion of the scale of the demands mounted against them can be seen in the long lists of their names from any and every county, compounding for the sake of a peaceful life. One of William Tipper's lists of victims who heeded the proclamation of 22 April 1609, and had paid up by July 1610, ran to four pages, with another two pages of gentlemen waiting to pay. Alderman Cokayne had paid £162 16s 4d for Kent land, Sir Anthony Cope £50 for some Northamptonshire land, while Sir Henry

---

[130] *CSPD 1619–23*, p. 171. [131] BL, Lansd. MS, 169, fol. 9.
[132] Notestein, Relf and Simpson (eds.), *Commons Debates 1621*, VI, p. 24.
[133] *Ibid.*, p. 111; II, p. 191. [134] BL, Lansd. MS 59, no. 35.

Guildford was waiting to pay £20 in Sussex.[135] Whole volumes of
land revenue books in the Exchequer are filled with their compositions; and while some gentlemen may have paid up cheerfully,
others felt aggrieved, and suspected the workings of personal feuds in
discoveries made against them. One informer, for example, offered to
disclose information concerning a gentleman living abroad, who
relied for his support entirely on concealed Crown lands. William
Tipper in 1612 had wanted to erect a formal system of informers in
every wapentake and hundred, who would return their reports 'with
acreages'.[136] He was undoubtedly correct in expecting local gentry to
have the best knowledge of the vicinity, but what of the acrimony
their informing would engender among neighbours?

As a result of the great outcry in Parliament in 1621 against patents
(and monopolies), and the strong stand taken by Sir Edward Coke on
the matter, James complied with the demand not to pursue holders
of Crown lands who had enjoyed them for sixty years or more. It was
one gesture to quell the indignation. The third reading of the 'Act for
the general quiet of the subject against all pretences of concealments
whatsoever' was given in April 1621, and it passed into law in
1624.[137] But this was far from being the end to the Crown's use of
patents and private searchers to discover abuses on its lands. In 1623
– before the act was finally passed – Robert Tipper asked for the
renewal of his Commission to Compound for Defective Titles because
he had many applicants wishing to pay compositions, and did not
wish the lapse of his patent to hold them up. He promised never to
offer any disputable grants for signature, and perhaps in those words
indirectly expressed a more widely held view of the policy that would
be pursued in the future: it would continue on the same course as
before, but with slightly more circumspection.[138]

   Despite the storm of 1621 in the House of Commons, and despite
the statute of 1624 appeasing the protesters, the Crown's projects for
managing its estates were not brought to an end.[139] Titles more than
sixty years old were no longer challenged, it is true, but otherwise the

---

[135] Notestein, Relf and Simpson (eds.), *Commons Debates 1621*, II, p. 149; BL, Lansd. MS 169,
  no. 8.
[136] BL, Add. MS 10038, fol. 388; BL, Lansd. MS 169, fol. 15.
[137] Notestein, Relf and Simpson (eds.), *Commons Debates 1621*, IV, p. 250.
[138] *CSPD 1619–23*, p. 569.
[139] *SR*, IV (ii), p. 1210. It is often assumed that the 1624 legislation did end the use of private
  searchers. See, for example, Lockwood, 'Those greedy hunters', pp. 160, 165.

policy continued much as before, and in the mid-1630s, indeed, displayed signs of fresh ingenuities and even some bold innovations.

To some extent, the Crown's opportunities to make money in Charles's reign had been reduced by the many compositions for concealments already taken. So the impression given by the documents that the rigour of operations on the old lines was at first somewhat subdued may be correct. Nevertheless, public statements reiterated at an early date two of the main projects. A proclamation in 1626 announced the intention to sell fee-farms to all tenants willing to purchase, and this offer now included not only copyholders but leaseholders as well. So the enfranchisement of copyholders returned to the programme of projects, and leaseholders could also benefit. In 1628, another proclamation urged tenants of both the land administered by the Exchequer and by the Duchy of Lancaster to compound for defective titles as before, and Robert Tipper was again appointed the agent.[140] In 1630, the same opportunity was urged upon tenants of the Duchy of Cornwall and the county palatine of Chester, neither of which Crown estates had been mentioned in any earlier projects.[141]

Five years then elapsed without public pronouncements though compositions continued to be taken, and we may assume that Mr Tipper remained assiduous in his duties.[142] In 1635, the fire was kindled anew by the issue of a 'renewed and enlarged' Commission to Compound for Defective Titles.[143] Instructions to the commissioners named projects which had already featured in James I's list, but a few extras were added. Now tithes 'within' as well as 'without' parishes were included; castles featured as before; so did encroachments adjoining forests and parks; but the addition was made of 'enclosures upon the skirts of forests and parks'. It required a fine legal mind to determine how the different words now being used might be interpreted to embrace new classes of concealed lands.

Yet other changes may have been introduced in 1635 when commissioners were ordered to compound at the best value on record, or one tenth of the improved value, or, if the values were uncertain, then at a value decided by the commissioners themselves. It is unclear whether the precision of these instructions altered the

---

[140] *Stuart Royal Procs.*, II, nos. 50, 103.
[141] R. Steele, *Bibliotheca Lindesiana*, v. *A Bibliography of Royal Proclamations of the Tudor and Stuart Sovereigns... 1485–1714*, I, *England and Wales* (Oxford, 1910), pp. 189–90.
[142] *Stuart Royal Procs.*, II, nos. 103, 130, 203.   [143] *CSPD 1635*, p. 349.

conventions observed under 'gracious' King James. Those claiming
to be owners were still given the first chance to compound, as James
had long ago conceded, but a distinct change was introduced with
the ruling that surrounded grounds could now be granted to anyone.
This new principle was bound to cause bitterness, since many
surrounded grounds already had occupiers.[144]

Under Charles's personal rule, the documentary record of government decisions is more than usually meagre, and in the pursuit of
defective titles some of the measures taken produced documents that
do not announce their true nature clearly. One has to read between
the lines, and recognise the legacy from the past, using knowledge of
the old procedures. Certainly, patents to enquire into concealed
lands continued to be issued, and the Crown made the same kind of
deals with searchers who received a proportion of the profits. The
pursuit of occupiers of surrounded grounds was maintained, and
even extended, as we shall show below. Yet historians are inclined to
play down the strong feelings of the King's subjects against these
projects in Charles's reign, since so many other, new grievances came
to the fore during the same years.[145] In fact, the full measure has not
yet been taken of Charles's efforts to raise his revenues from Crown
land. Some of the scattered, yet positive, evidence is set out below,
showing both continuity with the past, and a determination to push
the Crown's projects beyond old frontiers.

One of the projectors in Charles's reign who had served his
apprenticeship as a patentee searching for concealed lands under
King James was James Hay, first earl of Carlisle, a Scotsman who
joined the court when James I acceded to the throne, served him
on many diplomatic missions abroad, and became Master of the
Wardrobe.[146] Carlisle had received a patent to search for concealed
lands to the value of £200 p.a. in 1617, when the high ideals that first
impelled reforms of the Crown estate were fading from sight, and
searchers were again being given patents to enable them to recover
debts due from, or to, the Crown. The terms of Carlisle's patent were
evidently the same as those on which the odious Sir Giles Mompesson
received his patent, but the arrangement was far from straightforward. According to Carlisle's biographer, two gentlemen, Sir John

---

[144] SP16/302, no. 21.
[145] G. E. Aylmer, *The Personal Rule of Charles I, 1629–40* (London, 1989).
[146] Roy E. Schreiber, *The First Carlisle. Sir James Hay, First Earl of Carlisle as Courtier, Diplomat
and Entrepreneur, 1580–1636* (Trans. Amer. Phil. Soc., 74, part 7, 1984), pp. 142ff.

Townsend and Sir Samuel Tryon, undertook to pay to Carlisle the sums owed to him in connection with wardrobe dealings, namely, £8,000 and £4,800 respectively, and in return they were to take either the lands which were discovered or the fines paid in composition.[147] Sir John Townsend seems to have been a patentee for concealed lands in his own right, or was commonly regarded as such, for he was vilified in the 1621 Commons debates for harassing seventeen hospitals, including one in Snape, Yorkshire, for land which it had occupied since the fifteenth century.[148] When Carlisle's patent was suppressed along with all others at the end of James's reign, Carlisle negotiated with Cranfield for another patent, for land worth £10,000, but in the course of renewed public protests in 1625–6, he announced his intention of giving up all interest in such searches.[149] In fact, all that happened was that he acted thereafter through agents. He received another patent in 1627, ostensibly granted to Daniel Lea and Richard Smith, to search for 'defective titles', i.e. the most ordinary type of concealed lands. Smith may have been the haberdasher of the same name who dealt with Carlisle at the Wardrobe. Sir John Townsend was also in some way still involved, or was keeping watch on Carlisle's interests.[150] The search for concealed lands was this time conducted along the Thames, in the Wapping, Stepney, Limehouse area, looking for encroachments in the River Thames where wharves and warehouses had been built. It aroused strong opposition from the occupants, and when the matter was nearing a judicial hearing in 1628–9, the King was persuaded by Carlisle's associates to intervene on their behalf; hence he wrote to the barons 'to take it into their better care'. The dispute festered for some three years, producing an angry petition from the 'poor inhabitants' of Stepney, Whitechapel and the neighbourhood who had constructed the wharves. They feared that they might not be given the chance to compound, but would see their properties sold over their heads by 'the pretended lords or some other rich men'.

---

[147] C66/2132. A similar arrangement whereby an agent shouldered the debts of a searcher for concealed lands in return for the rights of the patentee is shown in William Tipper's case. Lockwood, 'Those greedy hunters', p. 159.

[148] *CJ*, I, *1547–1628/9*, pp. 532, 573. Tryon was also mentioned in a Commons debate in a remark that searchers for concealed lands 'have always a moneyed man at hand', in this case, presumably, Carlisle.

[149] *CSPD 1623–5*, p. 266.

[150] *CSPD 1628–9*, p. 387.

Peter Pett, the naval architect, joined with thirty other signatories in this protest.[151]

The earl of Carlisle was engaged during Charles I's reign not only in the search for defective titles, however. He was also a grantee of surrounded grounds. These were allowed to him in 1635 in payment of a debt owed by the Crown of £32,000. The lands recovered from the sea lay in Suffolk, Norfolk, Flintshire and Cheshire, and may be among those investigated by an Exchequer commission of 1633, though the beneficiary in the case is not, of course, named in the order for the enquiry which Lord Cottington sent to twenty-six local lords and gentry.[152] Charles pursued these 'inned lands' from 1628 onwards, making a kingdom-wide search in 1637 which extended especially thoroughly round the Welsh coast. The lawsuits dragged on into 1641, and according to Stuart Moore, every bit of land on which the sea had ever flowed was granted by Charles to someone.[153] Carlisle proceeded to grant his lands away in 1635, and died in 1636. He was thus unaffected by an anxious petition in 1640, addressed to the justices of the Exchequer by the trustees of his estate and his purchasers, expressing fears at the insecurity of their titles. The petitioners believed that Charles by his prerogative claimed title to marshland between the ebb and flow tides in England, Wales, Scotland and Ireland, and 'in some cases', the document alleged, his right had 'been adjudged so in law'. Nevertheless, they recognised it to be 'the common outcry' that the King's title was 'not likely to prevail'. The petitioners therefore wanted a full debate of the matter between the Privy Council, the judges of the King's Bench, Common Pleas and Exchequer.[154] By 1640, legal doubts about Charles's prerogative rights extended over a very broad front, and the reference here to his claims to marshland around the Scottish and Irish, as well as the English and Welsh, coasts needs to be stressed, for this was a new claim, whose full consequences have yet to be investigated. The gravity of 'the common outcry' against the King's claim (on coasts

---

[151] *Ibid.*; Moore, *Foreshore*, pp. 260ff; *CSPD 1635–6*, pp. 21–2. According to Schreiber, Carlisle resumed control of the project in 1632 from Lea and Smith for a nominal fee, recorded on the Close Rolls (C54/2953, no. 41) when he knew that no Parliament was on the horizon. Schreiber, *Carlisle*, p. 143.

[152] E178/7310. This command did not, however, refer to lands in Cheshire.

[153] Moore, *Foreshore*, pp. 281–4, 258.

[154] *CSPD 1639–40*, pp. 479–80; Moore, *Foreshore*, pp. 274–6.

unspecified) is, however, clearly mirrored in the Grand Remonstrance in 1641.[155]

Dissatisfaction with the Crown's methods of searching for concealed lands almost certainly lies behind three bills on the subject, which were moved in the House of Commons early in Charles's reign, in 1625, 1626 and 1628, but their contents have not been discovered.[156] The absence of proclamations concerning concealed lands between 1630 and 1635 suggests a certain lull in the zeal of search (the Privy Council was preoccupied in these years with measures to relieve the poor and check enclosure), and the same lull is noticeable in the issue of Special Commissions from the Exchequer. But since action was resumed in 1634 in the forests, and this involved novel claims, strenuously pressed, the probable explanation for the earlier lull is that the Exchequer saw diminishing returns from its efforts in the old directions, and was pondering new ones.

Patents continued to be granted to individuals, in a random way, as the occasion arose. Sir Ralph Freeman petitioned in 1637 for encroached and concealed lands on the King's wastes in certain lordships in Denbighshire. He promised the King three halfpence an acre in annual rent 'as in like cases in Wales', suggesting that he was one of many searchers exploring further afield.[157] Charles cast his eye over a petition in 1637 from Katherine Elliot, wet nurse to the duke of York, who wished to claim concealed land on West Sedgemoor, Somerset, where the inhabitants had encroached. In return for a grant for sixty years, she was ready to pay 1s an acre and recover the land at her own costs; the King was willing to gratify her, but sought advice first.[158] Yet another petitioner, William Murray, groom of the King's Bedchamber, wanted to recover a concealed castle, the castle of Holderness, with rents and dues owing to the wapentake court of Holderness, in return for a payment of 100 marks a year. Without more ado, the King acceded to his request.[159] These cases undoubtedly represent a small proportion of all the grants to search for concealed land made by Charles I. But they suggest that courtiers, as ever, had the best chance of becoming patentees.

[155] S. R. Gardiner (ed.), *The Constitutional Documents of the Puritan Revolution, 1625–1660* (Oxford, 1979, pbk edn), p. 212.
[156] C. Russell, *Parliaments and English Politics, 1621–9* (Oxford, 1979), p. 66.
[157] SP16/323, p. 90.
[158] *Ibid.*, p. 109. This lady had earlier sought the right to seal silk stockings and waistcoats before export, in order to guarantee their quality, and to distinguish woven from 'knot' (?knitted) garments. SP16/323, p. 9.   [159] *Ibid.*, p. 100.

At the same time, grander schemes were being devised, and the fertile suggestions of great lords at court had a good chance of acceptance. In 1637, the search for waste lands awaiting improvement was revived, heralded by a revival of slogans that had inspired enthusiasm early in James's reign. James marquis of Hamilton, Edward earl of Dorset, Henry earl of Holland and Leonard Lee, gentleman, purporting to show concern for the high price of food, wanted to see the heaths and barren commons of the kingdom growing food. They sought to enquire by inquisition into areas of waste in order to agree with the commoners and owners on improvement. They promised the King one third of any profits that accrued to them. The King was agreeable if the proposal was thought by the Lord Treasurer and Solicitor-General to advance revenue.[160] Subsequently, in a commission of November 1637, seventy-one commissioners were appointed to accept compositions on grants of concealed lands in the counties of Middlesex, Surrey, Sussex, Kent, Essex and Hertfordshire, within 20 miles of London. Although the verbiage of this document was now somewhat different from the original proposition, it plainly represented the next step in the enquiry into areas of waste, for the marquis of Hamilton was to bear all the costs of the inquisitions in the Home Counties, which were to be initiated by these seventy-one commissioners, and he was now to receive half the revenue, rather than a third, from the *sales* of, or compositions paid on, encroached lands. The King was to receive the other half. We may reasonably guess that the original grant to four noblemen had been carved up between them into four separate operations, so that the earl of Dorset, the earl of Holland and Leonard Lee also had their separate circles of commissioners, investigating wastes in other groups of counties. The document enumerating Hamilton's commissioners was directed at all lands 'encroached upon the king's wastes, or otherwise concealed from the king'. In short, this was now an unadorned grant to search for concealed lands, which no longer made pretence, as in the original petition, at improving wastes in order to 'cause plenty of provision, enrich many thousands, supply the poor, raise a great benefit to Your Majesty, and be no prejudice to any'.[161]

---

[160] *Ibid.*, p. 89. (*CSPD 1637*, p. 189).

[161] SP16/372, no. 67 (= *CSPD 1637*, p. 571, where the significant reference to Hamilton is omitted). The grant referred to *sales* of encroached lands, but then in another paragraph allowed the commission to compound for land found in these inquisitions and any others

The attempt to dress up the search for wastes in the verbiage of the earlier search under James, as wastes awaiting improvement, shows how the Exchequer officials returned again and again to old slogans and old devices. But at the same time, they looked for slight variations of, or extensions to, the projects that would yield a little more cash, since the revenue-raising potential of these projects in their familiar form had been diminished by the results already achieved since 1603. Thus, the project for searching for surrounded grounds was much extended in Wales. If it was not already extended into Scotland, it had certainly been extended into Ireland.[162]

But it was in the forests that projects were most brazenly extended, by investigating breaches of forest law much more energetically than for decades past. Forest law was enforced with a new rigour from 1634 onwards, starting in Waltham Forest, Essex and the Northamptonshire forests, and moving out to the Hampshire forests in 1635, and the Oxfordshire forests in 1636. Courts of enquiry were still under way in 1639.[163]

Perhaps more conspicuously than in the search for waste lands, the fines for breaches of forest law fell on influential nobility and gentry, who were considerable owners under the Crown, and who directly exploited and enjoyed their hunting and other rights. Fines of £19,000 imposed on the earl of Westmorland's family, and £20,000 on the heir of Robert Cecil, both for offences in the Northamptonshire forests, were not likely to be forgotten, even though these families subsequently disputed the claims and managed to settle for less.[164] As Clarendon later shrewdly remarked, this device for raising revenues 'lighted most upon persons of quality and honour, who thought themselves above ordinary oppressions, and were therefore like to remember it with more sharpness'.[165] The overbearing methods used to claim fines for offences against forest law rankled in Waltham Forest especially, while in the Forest of Dean owners also had good reason for bitterness at the way the Stuarts handled fines, and gave grants for improvement.[166]

The second forest project, also launched by Charles in 1634, involved extending the bounds of the forests to their medieval limits,

---

within 20 miles of London. It would be helpful to identify all the seventy-one commissioners who included many gentry. Were they JPs in their respective counties?

[162] See below, p. 348.   [163] Pettit, *Royal Forests*, pp. 83–5.

[164] The composition for the earl of Salisbury's £20,000 fine was finally fixed at £3,000. Pettit, *Royal Forests*, pp. 87–8, 92.

[165] *Ibid.*, p. 83.   [166] *Ibid.*, pp. 84, 91.

so that compositions could be levied from many more landowners, to procure their freedom from forest law. In Salcey Forest, Northamptonshire, for example, forty-two villages were now claimed to lie within the forest, compared with six formerly.[167] Again, it was landowners in the Forests of Dean and Waltham who paid the most in fines, £16,647 in Waltham and £15,460 in Dean, compared with £6,560 in the Northamptonshire forests. In Waltham, moreover, order was even given to imprison those who did not pay.[168] Charles I thus commenced two different assaults on the tenures of forest landowners in 1634, and since instalments of the fines were still being paid in 1640, and suits at law were still pending in 1641, it is not surprising that the angry memory of Charles's unprincipled manipulation of forest laws and customs burned in 1641, when a bill was presented in the Long Parliament 'for the Certainty of the Forests', and 'the enlargement of forests, contrary to *Carta de Foresta*, and the composition thereupon' was itemised as a grievance in the Grand Remonstrance.[169]

The fourteen projects of James I for reforming the Crown estates underwent many modifications and transformations between 1603 and 1641. Their local impact was doubtless equally varied, although the full story awaits deeper investigation. What is certain is that none of the projects can be labelled an innovation at James's accession. The innovator was Elizabeth, if any monarch can be so described when judging the work of an ancient institution like the Exchequer, whose officials continued in office from one reign to the next. Elizabeth's enquiries into concealments were unprecedentedly numerous, and continued throughout her reign. All but one or two of James's projects can be shown to have been on her list, while the elusive ones are likely to be found eventually in local, if not in central, records.

Elizabeth's projects gave rise to grievances, but she was sensitive to public opinion, and endeavoured to pacify her subjects. James took up the same projects, but in a more assertive, thrusting manner. His projects moved forward on all fronts at the same time, and from the outset showed an interest in ingenious, and then devious approaches.

---

[167] *Ibid.*, p. 88.   [168] *Ibid.*, pp. 89, 91.

[169] *Ibid.*, pp. 90–1; Gardiner (ed.), *Constitutional Documents*, p. 211. It was in this connection that a Special Commission was issued into the bounds of several forests in 1641. See C205/17/2.

In the first ten years, a readiness to discuss procedures before action was taken moderated excesses. But after about 1617, the initial caution was abandoned, and a different spirit infused the many grants of patents to courtiers and hangers-on.

In James's defence, it could be said that the abuses perpetrated by Crown tenants had grown giant-like in the later years of Elizabeth, partly under the stress of land hunger, partly because of the opportunities given by an indulgent or lax administration. But Exchequer officials in the early years of James's reign constantly advised the same caution that Elizabeth had heeded, so that it was James's responsibility when it was abandoned. It is true that many gentlemen and lesser tenants during both reigns paid fines and compositions, seemingly without shrill complaint, but when these proved not to be once-for-all settlements, the undercurrent of seething discontent was dramatically revealed in 1621.[170] Judging by the evidence in Mompesson's case, some of the more recently granted patents, when examined line by line, did not have a standard form. Each patentee procured his own eccentric concessions and privileges which he exploited to the letter.[171] The persistence of Crown searchers returning again and again to the same scene became an outrage throughout the kingdom. Under Charles, the projects of James's reign were refurbished and equally resolutely pursued. From 1634 onwards, yet more ingenious, and ultimately preposterous, schemes were tacked on to the old ones. They were clothed in new verbiage, or the old verbiage was interpreted in a new way, and a thoroughly cavalier treatment was accorded customary legal processes. Finally, with the revival of medieval forest law, a device of the distant past was resurrected and summarily reimposed. Charles and his advisers had wholly lost touch with real life.

Were the financial benefits at any time worth a campaign engendering such hostility? The record of receipts in the Exchequer between 1603 and 1641 show so many changes in the basis of their estimates, leave so many gaps and present such great variations from year to year that it is difficult to pass a sound judgement on the financial rewards. Amid total Crown revenues which ranged

---

[170] Sir Arthur Throckmorton, for example, noted in a matter-of-fact entry in his diary on 31 Feb. (*sic*) 1594, payment to William Tipper of £20 for land in the Northamptonshire forests, clearly a composition for concealed land. Canterbury Cathedral Archives, Throckmorton diaries, II, fol. 123v, also fols. 125, 126v.

[171] *CJ*, I, *1547–1628/9*, p. 544.

annually between £300,000 and £800,000, they seem to have been
remarkably small. The most that the Crown received in compositions
for defective titles was £10,550 in 1616. Among the lowest sums
under this head was £203 in 1622, after the damning parliamentary
debates of 1621, while in 1638 and 1639, when financial pressures
under Charles were reaching their height, receipts were £1,200 and
£1,494. Assarts and marshgrounds brought in £3,789 in 1614, and
most of all – £6,252 – in 1619. But in 1620, this heading disappeared
from the summary accounts, and did not return, even though
marshlands were high on the agenda in the later 1630s. 'Spoil of
woods and forest offences' raised £9,000 in 1636 and £12,000 in
1638. But while offences in the Forest of Dean produced nearly
£9,000 in 1639, other forests went unmentioned in that year. In
short, the accuracy of these accounts cannot be trusted, although
they indicate orders of magnitude.[172]

Signs of a more oppresssive and more desperate set of Crown
expedients multiplied from 1634 onwards in the forests, and from
1637 elsewhere. New commissions of enquiry into surrounded
grounds were launched from the Exchequer in 1637. Charles became
a more than usually grand undertaker in the fens in 1638, with his
spectacular schemes for settlement in the Bedford Level.[173] Seeking
wastes for improvement, an army of commissioners was recruited in
1637: since 71 were needed in the Home Counties, then perhaps 250
and more were appointed to cover the whole kingdom.[174] The year
1637 is also the date when Sir James Barry claimed to speak on behalf
of 'all the judges of Ireland', and printed his argument justifying the
King's right to claim against owners of defective titles in Ireland,
dedicating his work to lord Wentworth.[175] This publication turns
attention to yet another campaign to raise money from defective
titles, first launched by James I, which had then lost momentum, and
was revived by Wentworth when he took charge in Ireland. At the
same time, a search for surrounded grounds in Ireland was evidently
put under way. It comes to light by chance in the career of Endymion
Porter. Porter had a hand in projects of many sorts. He had taken a
Crown grant of marshland (i.e. surrounded grounds) in North and
South Somercotes in Lincolnshire in 1632, and had a further grant in

---

[172] Dietz, *Receipts and Issues*, pp. 136–53.   [173] Darby, *Draining of the Fens*, pp. 58–61.
[174] See above, p. 344.
[175] James Barry, *The Case of Tenures upon the Commission of Defective Titles, Argued by All the Judges
of Ireland, with their Resolution and the Reasons of their Resolution* (Dublin, 1637).

the Forest of Exmoor upon disafforestation. About 1637, he took a grant of tidal marshland on the River Shannon in Ireland, thus revealing Charles's new interest in inned land in that country. In 1638, he entered into partnership with two others for a further project to improve marshes in Wales, in Carmarthen, Pembroke and Glamorgan. And having been allowed to enclose a common in Flintshire (presumably under the umbrella of the Crown's project for 'improving wasteland'), he was licensed to search for minerals in Flintshire in 1638.[176] Charles's many projects on Crown lands were being energetically pursued to the very end of 1639: William Polwheele, gentleman of the Privy Chamber, who accompanied Charles on his journey to meet the Covenanters in Scotland came home in December that year to find that he had been deprived in his absence of 49 acres of land in the Lincolnshire fens at Kirton, because they were deemed by the Commissioners for Surrounded Grounds to belong to the King; according to Polwheele he had held them for one hundred years.[177]

The full scale of the animosity stirred by the Crown's projects on its estates was exemplified in the Grand Remonstrance, which was submitted for acceptance by the Commons in December 1641. At that moment, MPs had many more immediate concerns on their minds than the King's projects on his estates. The war in Scotland and the insurrection in Ireland loomed largest, and after that Laud's church reforms, establishing 'an ecclesiastical tyranny', the continual wrangling over questions of the King's prerogative and men's liberty, and illegal taxation imposed to avoid the holding of Parliaments. These took precedence over grievances which had festered for a much longer period, but which had not recently provoked a sudden tumult of protest. Nevertheless, four clauses in the Remonstrance were clearly directed at the Crown's projects on its estates, while another six were not unconnected.[178]

Since John Pym is credited with responsibility for the final drafting of the Grand Remonstrance, it is worth noting that he was employed as a receiver of land revenue from 1607 onwards, and in 1621 had

---

[176] Gervas Huxley, *Endymion Porter. The Life of a Courtier, 1587–1649* (London, 1959), pp. 211–15, 203, 217. Huxley shows how diligently Porter used his friends and all influential connections to make the most of his grants. But he is entirely uncritical and incurious about the way the patents were implemented.

[177] *CSPD 1639–40*, p. 164.

[178] For the full text of the Grand Remonstrance, see Gardiner (ed.), *Constitutional Documents*, pp. 202–32.

been one of the three MPs deputed to investigate Giles Mompesson's abuses of his patent for concealments.[179] Over a long period, then, the presenter of the Grand Remonstrance had accumulated first-hand knowledge of the Crown's projects for reforming its estates. As for the individual clauses, these were assembled by MPs who were mostly country gentlemen drawing on their personal or local experience to air matters for concern. We can be confident that identifiable disputes lay behind every single clause, and that they embraced many a rancorous issue raised by the Crown's handling of its estates. Clarendon, in his later reflections, also stressed that Charles's abuses of forest rights and customs touched men of substance most nearly.[180] And by way of local illustration, Dr Pettit remarked in his study of the Northamptonshire forests that when the medieval boundaries were reimposed by Charles I, and fines were levied, the villages resisting most were not peasant villages but those dominated by the gentry or aristocracy.[181]

In short, the gentry in the Commons did not have to search far to substantiate their grievances at the Crown's handling of its estates. They were expressed in four clauses. (1) Clause 21 concerned 'the enlargement of forests, contrary to *Carta de Foresta* and the composition thereupon'. (2) Clause 25 concerned 'the general destruction of the King's timber, especially that in the Forest of Dean, sold to the Papists, which was the best store-house of this kingdom for the maintenance of our shipping'. This despoliation had followed upon the decision to disafforest the forests, and allow improvements. (3) Clause 26 concerned 'the taking away of men's right, under the colour of the King's title to land, between high and low water marks', and was an unmistakable reference to the King's claim to surrounded grounds. (4) Clause 32 complained that 'large quantities of common

---

[179] On Pym's Receivership, see E. Gore and C. Russell, 'John Pym and the queen's receivership', *BIHR* 46 (1973), pp. 106–7; for his role in disafforestation, see below, p. 372. *CJ*, I, *1547–1628/9*, p. 540. His role in the Mompesson impeachment is considered by C. Russell, 'The parliamentary career of John Pym, 1621–9', in P. Clark, A. G. R. Smith and N. Tyacke (eds.), *The English Commonwealth, 1547–1640* (Leicester, 1979), pp. 152–3.

[180] See above, p. 345. Some historians credit Pym with writing the whole Remonstrance (see Anthony Fletcher, *The Outbreak of the English Civil War* (London, 1981), p. 82). But considering the many months of its preparation, the changing membership of the committees responsible, and the varied knowledge and experience that plainly underlay each clause, it is more likely that Pym polished the final text. See H. L. Schoolcraft, *The Genesis of the Grand Remonstrance from Parliament to King Charles I* (University of Illinois Studies I (4), 1902), pp. 7–45.

[181] Pettit, *Royal Forests*, p. 88.

and several grounds hath been taken from the subject by colour of the Statute of Improvement, and by abuse of the Commission of Sewers, without their consent, and against it'. This was a clear reference to the Crown's project to improve wastes. It may have risen to the surface partly because of Charles's most recent commissions to the marquis of Hamilton and others in 1637.[182] But the reference, in the same clause, to abuses by the Commission of Sewers focussed special attention on the fenland commons, of which large areas, when drained, had been appropriated by the Crown, with other landowners and the drainers themselves. In the history of fen drainage generally, a heightened phase of unrest is noticeable in the years 1636–8, and if any single dispute lay behind this reference, the most likely one was that in the Bedford Level. In 1638, it brought Charles himself into the ring as a projector, allegedly dissatisfied with 'all the cheats of the undertakers', and prepared to consider building 'an eminent town' in the Great Level to be called Charlemont, 'the design whereof he drew himself'. Charles's allotment of fen, in return for his participation, was to be 57,000 acres, and was agreed by the Sewer Commissioners.[183] Everywhere in the fens, of course, the inhabitants' bitterest complaints centred on their losses of common grazing rights, and the butt of their criticisms were the Commissioners of Sewers, accused of taking arbitrary decisions that ran totally against local opinion. MPs who had a hand in preparing the Grand Remonstrance can have had no trouble in assembling a multitude of instances under this head.[184]

Thus, dealings by the Crown on three of its most important projects – concerning forests, surrounded grounds and the improvement of wastes – were explicit grievances in the Grand Remonstrance. Five other clauses remonstrated at the Crown's legal procedures, prompted no doubt by a larger body of complaints, but representing abuses which had also come within the experience of Crown tenants.[185]

---

[182] See above, pp. 343–4. [183] Darby, *Draining of the Fens*, pp. 58–62.
[184] *Ibid.*, p. 62.
[185] They were Clause 37, concerning extravagant censures in the Court of Star Chamber; Clause 41, referring to new judicatories having been erected without law; Clause 43, alleging that the Chancery, Exchequer Chamber, Court of Wards and other English courts 'had been grievous in exceeding their jurisdiction'; Clause 47, charging the common law courts with frequently forsaking 'the rules of the common law, and straying beyond their bounds, under pretence of equity, to do injustice'; Clause 48, complaining that titles of honour and judicial offices had been sold to corrupt and corruptible men; and, finally, Clause 49, complaining that commissions investigating excessive fees punished offenders,

When in 1641 gentlemen in the Commons listed their complaints at the abuse of royal authority, they were acutely aware of the unflagging energy and, indeed, renewed ingenuity and enthusiasm being shown in the Exchequer to wring more revenue from Crown lands. The programme of projects showed no signs of entering a quiet phase. On the contrary, projects under way in 1637, 1638 and 1639 were more preposterous and wide-ranging than ever, and to those MPs whose memories went back to 1621, the brazen enormity of the Crown's claims seemed to continue without end. Those who lived to hear Clarendon's later condemnation of the whole policy must have deemed it a just verdict: 'Unjust projects of all kinds, many ridiculous, many scandalous, all very grievous, were set on foot; the envy and reproach of which came to the King, the profit to other men.'[186]

but never recompensed those who had originally suffered the abuse. Examples of those offences deserve a systematic search. In the fens the levying of drainage rates, especially for new work, was one cause of complaint at the abuse of power by Commissioners of Sewers. For other abuses of authority by government in the fens, see Clive Holmes, *Seventeenth-Century Lincolnshire* (History of Lincolnshire, VII, Lincoln, 1980), pp. 126–30; Mark E. Kennedy, 'Charles I and local government: the draining of the East and West Fens', *Albion*, 15 (1983), pp. 28–31.

[186] E. Hyde, earl of Clarendon, *A History of the Rebellion and Civil Wars in England* (8 vols., Oxford, 1826 edn), I, pp. 119–20, cited in Pettit, *Royal Forests*, p. 94.

CHAPTER 12

Disafforestation and drainage: the Crown as entrepreneur?

Richard Hoyle

The financial rewards of improving copyhold fines, selling fee-farms and seeking out an ever-widening range of concealments were neither large nor sufficient to satisfy the Crown's appetite for money. It was perhaps inevitable that it should become interested in ventures to improve its forests through disafforestation, and fens and other lands liable to flooding through drainage. It has long been known that the Crown was involved in projects to this end throughout the 1620s and 1630s although little has been written to reveal their scale or success. The most recent writers on the subject, Buchanan Sharp on the West Country forests and Keith Lindley on the fens, have been concerned not so much with the process of improvement as the popular disorder that it provoked.[1] The matter of resistance to the Crown's improvements is not our central concern on this occasion (although it might be noticed that practically all the projects discussed subsequently met with either passive footdragging or open disorder which greatly hindered the execution of the projects and delayed the receipt of income). The questions to be posed here – what the Crown was trying to achieve, what its financial stake in improvement was and whether its achievements were commensurate with its ambitions – have been neglected. Yet John Morrill has recently been moved to make the large claim that the Crown's involvement in projects to improve its forests and fens was a component of one of three changes which 'transformed England in the seventeenth century'.[2] The first item on Morrill's checklist would secure general subscription, that 'the demographic turnaround in mid-century... changed the whole economic, social and political context'. His third factor was the

---

[1] Keith Lindley, *Fenland Riots and the English Revolution* (London, 1982); Sharp, *In Contempt*. See also the slighter account by J. H. Betty, 'The revolts over enclosure of the royal forest at Gillingham, 1626–1630', *Proceedings of the Dorset Natural History and Antiquarian Society* 97 (1976). [2] J. Morrill, 'Christopher Hill's Revolution', *History* 74 (1989), pp. 251–2.

creation of a 'new cultural climate, rationalistic, empirical, pragmatic'. It is the second which concerns us here and is in effect another
change in mentalities:

> the recognition by governors that they could solve their financial problems
> by encouraging and then taxing progress rather than by inhibiting it. The
> early Stuarts were halfway there (realizing that there was money to be made
> from encouraging progressive economic activity and rationalization such as
> fen drainage, woodland clearance, new draperies etc. as well as from
> propping up vested interests and from the inhibitory aspects of feudal
> fiscalism).

Readers of Thirsk's *Economic Policy and Projects* might be tempted to
antedate the moment of realisation to the middle years of Elizabeth's
reign rather than the early seventeenth century.[3] It must also be
recognised that to speak of drainage and clearance as 'progressive
economic activities' is to share the early modern prejudice against the
pastoral economies of forests and fens. We are not talking here of
waste ground in the sense of vacant land, rather, land which might on
first sight appear to be used unintensively, but which in fact supported
a whole range of pastoral and semi-industrial activities to which
migrants were drawn. A petition against the disafforestation of
Leicester Forest spoke of 'a great confluence of poor people [which]
hath been made to this place by reason of the benefit which the chace
hath afforded them, who being still to inhabit there will be destitute
of means to live if it be disafforested, the ancient towns not being able
to relieve them'. Every forest or fen had its role in the local and
regional economy. Delaware Forest in Cheshire supplied the poor of
the neighbouring villages with peat fuel; when disafforestation was
mooted, the fear was expressed that the poor would be obliged to
compete for wood with the nearby salt wicks. At Leicester, the
borderers and commoners stressed how taking away the right of
common would leave cottagers reliant on poor relief, make small
freeholdings unviable, prevent the inhabitants of the bordering towns
from paying taxes and produce a shortage of fuel.[4] Of course, much
of this may be dismissed as scaremongering. But there is no escaping
the fact that disafforestation and drainage meant dispossession and
the destruction of local economies.[5] The question is whether one

---

[3] J. Thirsk, *Economic Policy and Projects. The Development of a Consumer Society in Early Modern
England* (Oxford, 1978).

[4] Cheshire RO, DAR A/6; University of London Library, MS 195, pt ii, fols. 53v–4v.

[5] In this respect, disafforestation as it is discussed here differs from the 'disafforestation'
undertaken after the extension of forest boundaries in the 1630s when landholders were
invited to be relieved of forest law by composition.

believes that this was desirable for some greater good or whether it should be seen as the cynical means by which ill-defined customary rights were abolished (with, of course, some compensation) to produce a marketable asset held absolutely for the benefit of private men.[6] Historians should be familiar enough with discussions of this dilemma in the contemporary Third World to feel some ambivalence over this. Contemporaries, too, were not all of a mind about the advantage to be gained from improvement. The petition against the disafforestation of Delaware Forest came from the Cheshire gentry. The impending disafforestation of Bernwood Forest (Buckinghamshire) drew a petition from a number of Oxford colleges asking that it should be preserved.[7] Disafforestation and drainage as practised on the Crown's lands are but part of an age-old and continuing conflict between communal rights and private property, arable and pastoral agriculture. It would be wrong to suppose that the only defenders of the pastoral and unimproved were the inhabitants of these countries.

Forests and woodlands posed particular problems for the Crown.[8] Forests, it must be recalled, were not necessarily wooded. A forest was a jurisdiction over a territorial area rather than a wooded game reserve. Some forests might be entirely open, others heavily coppiced. The Crown did not need to own all or, indeed, any of the soil within a forest; where it did own the freehold, its possession might be compromised by the acknowledged right of commoners to graze.[9] The forest could have been eaten away by assarts, illegal encroachments and the grant of parks and coppices. Trees, as much as game, were difficult, indeed impossible, to defend from the attentions of poachers and thieves. In his study of Feckenham which follows, Peter Large shows how the gentry officers of the forest took the lead in cutting timber for their own use and how ineffectual the Crown's supervision of their activities might be. Of all the Crown's officers, it was the woodwards and the keepers of the King's parks and forests who probably had the lowest reputation. A correspondent of Laud's

---

[6] It might be said that the evidence of this chapter tends towards the latter position.

[7] F. W. Bateson, *Brill, A Short History* (Brill, 1966), pp. 6–7.

[8] See above, pp. 67–9, 99–100.

[9] The proportion of land which the Crown owned in its forests was declining as a consequence of the sale of assart lands; this cannot but have compounded existing problems of maintaining discipline. As an example, in 1616 the Attorney-General sued one Augustine Belson for felling timber in Bernwood Forest, Bucks. Belson admitted taking the timber, but only from the lands of his freehold in the forest, an assart which had been sold in 1611. E112/70/61.

informed him that the keepers of Shotover Forest in Oxfordshire each had more benefit from the forest in one year than the King had in five. Three years later, the forest's lieutenant, Sir Timothy Tyrell, sought to defend the destruction they wrought by asking how the keepers could live on fees of 26s 8d per annum, then ten years in arrear.[10]

Such dishonesty was one obvious weakness in administration, but the major flaw in the way in which the forests were supervised lay in the dislocation of the lines of command from the Exchequer to the local officers. Although the Exchequer secured its control over the Queen's forests and woods by stripping the earl of Sussex as Justice in Eyre of his authority over woodsales in 1567,[11] the Surveyor-General of Woods proved incapable of maintaining order. Although he could bring suits in equity against woodstealers and corrupt officials, no procedure was ever devised whereby the Exchequer took over the prosecution of thefts and abuses found by the forest courts, the swanimotes.[12] The responsibility for the prosecution of their present-ments lay with the Forest Eyre, an institution which was effectively defunct until its Caroline revival. (No Northamptonshire Eyre was held between 1556 and 1635.) Johnson in 1610 suggested a system whereby the proceedings of the swanimotes were transmitted to the Exchequer for prosecution and something like this was put into effect in 1616, but it may be doubted if this innovation was successfully implemented in practice.[13]

The exclusion of forests, woods and parks from the sale commissions resulted, inevitably enough, in their coming to form an ever-larger proportion of the estates. The schedule of lands annexed to the Crown in 1609 included 68 forests, 117 parks and 9 chases. A census of the King's deer in Yorkshire in 1615 showed that they were scattered between sixteen forests, parks and chases. No monarch had hunted in any of them in the previous half-century or more.[14] In revenue terms, forests and woods were dead space. The capital value of the standing timber and coppice could be considerable – £285,000

[10] See below, pp. 404–6; *CSPD 1626–9*, pp. 522–3; *CSPD 1631–3*, pp. 331–2.

[11] E123/1A, fols. 95v–6r. The responsibilities of the Exchequer and Chief Justice were further defined by judicial resolution during Dorset's Treasureship (probably of *c.* 1606) which clearly turned on the Chief Justice's attempts to regulate woodsales. Sir Edward Coke, *The Fourth Part of the Institutes of the Laws of England* (London, 1797), pp. 298–300.

[12] For what may be corruption in the prosecution of offenders by John Taverner, see above, p. 55. In some forests the swanimote may quickly have fallen into disuse; see the complaint from Bernwood, *CPR 1575–8*, no. 2191. [13] Pettit, *Royal Forests*, pp. 41–2.

[14] York City Archives, Acc. 104 0/2a–b.

in a survey of woods in eighteen counties in 1608 – but timber needed a long period to mature and yearly revenue from woods was small.[15] Hammersley showed many years ago how the profits from sales of wood in the first years of the seventeenth century averaged only £650 per annum. Against this, needs to be weighed the costs of officers and fences to protect the woods. Even when leased, coppice was much less valuable than other forms of agricultural land.[16]

Any attempt to improve the profitability of forests was inevitably hindered by the desire to protect their huntable inhabitants. James certainly invested substantial sums in the refurbishment of park pales and lodges. The enlargement of Theobalds was merely the extravagance which capped many smaller improvements.[17] But the investment of resources was basically *ad hoc* according to whim. After the King hunted in Leicester Forest in 1612, the earl of Huntingdon devoted a great deal of time and energy to creating a laund and coppices at his request to improve the quality of the hunting at the cost of stirring up a storm amongst the commoners.[18] The special status of forests clearly made local initiatives for their improvement impossible and James was notoriously opposed to disafforestation, Johnson, for instance, taking care to withhold his proposals for improvement from the King. When the Council considered the means to reform the polity in 1615, the improvement of forests and parks was the only one of their proposals to which James would not assent.[19] This was more than a matter of maintaining the royal sport. Bacon, speaking in Star Chamber when sentencing poachers in the royal forest of Gillingham in 1614, explained how forests, parks and chases were a noble part of the King's prerogative, 'the first marks of honour and nobility and the ornament of a flourishing kingdom. *You never hear Switzerland or Netherland troubled with forests.*'[20] This doubtless explains why the disafforestation of even *remote* forests, although suggested as early as 1552,[21] taken up by Johnson in 1602, widely

---

[15] Pettit, *Royal Forests*, p. 59, table 2.

[16] G. Hammersley, 'The crown woods and their exploitation in the sixteenth and seventeenth centuries', *BIHR* 30 (1957), pp. 143–4, 147.

[17] The tables in Dietz, *Receipts and Issues*, seem to suggest that expenditure lay mostly in the years 1608–15, pp. 158–61.

[18] *The Aristocracy, the State and the Local Community* (microfilm edition of manuscripts of the Hastings family in the Huntington Library, California), reel 3, HA 5439, 2158, 9869, 5441–4.

[19] Johnson excluded his comments on improvement made to Cecil from the copy of the same letter which he sent to the King. Spedding, *Bacon*, v, p. 206.   [20] *Ibid.*, p. 88.

[21] Richardson, *1552 Report*, p. 227.

advocated in the following decade and a part of the general currency of debate thereafter, had barely commenced on the King's death in 1625.

In the same way as Dorset attempted to raise revenue from copyholds, he also looked anew at forests and woods.[22] Dorset appears to have favoured a general farm (or lease) of woods, but proposals laid before him by a syndicate in 1607 were severely criticised by Johnson, not least on the grounds that no contract could be entered into before the woods were surveyed.[23] The decision to survey was taken in December 1607 and the surveyors sent into the field in March 1608.[24] The surveys formed the basis of Salisbury's heavy sales of timber in 1609; whilst these served to pay the surveyors' fees, they immediately made the surveys outdated. Salisbury's sales, which raised about £40,000, were surrounded with allegations of fraud, and suggestions that they should be investigated were made after his death. Eschewing a general farm, Salisbury sought to negotiate the farm of individual tracts of coppice. The indications are that this policy was largely unsuccessful. Despite his best endeavours, two-thirds of the Crown's coppices remained unleased at his death in 1612.[25] The few leases which were taken were either surrendered as unprofitable or cancelled in 1620 on the pretence that the farmers' requirements were damaging to the game.[26] As late as 1626, Treswell put the annual profits at only £2,200 but thought that this could be raised to £10,000 by letting 100,000 acres of coppice to farmers.[27]

Salisbury also instituted the making of enclosures in a number of forests and took steps to increase revenue from the Forest of Dean where the proprietors of the iron works were permitted to take greatly enlarged areas of coppice for their furnaces.[28]

Salisbury's memorialist, Sir Walter Cope, wrote that when Salisbury became Lord Treasurer he found that no one knew the area, number or worth of the Crown's coppices, 'so as his lordship, at his first looking into them thought himself in a wood indeed'.[29] But

---

[22] A more detailed account of policy in these years can be found in Pettit, *Royal Forests*, pp. 54–61.   [23] E101/151/29.   [24] E403/2727, fols. 130r–3r, 134v.

[25] Hammersley, 'Crown woods', p. 143; Pettit, *Royal Forests*, pp. 54–61.

[26] Pettit, *Royal Forests*, p. 61; Kent AO, U269/1, OE 813, 1326.

[27] University of London Library, MS 195, pt i, fol. 25r.

[28] Sharp, *In Contempt*, pp. 91–2, 191 (and see SP46/70, fol. 22); C. E. Hart, *Royal Forest. A History of Dean's Woods as Producers of Timber* (Oxford, 1966), pp. 86–93.

[29] Sir Walter Cope, 'An apology for the late Lord Treasurer, Sir Robert Cecil, earl of Salisbury', in J. Gutch (ed.), *Collectanea Curiosa* (2 vols., Oxford, 1781), I, p. 123.

these were all approaches to the problem of increasing revenue
without damaging forests as game reserves. Moreover, improving the
rent from coppices did nothing to raise the income from those of the
Crown's forests which were forests only in name or which possessed
only decayed or dotard trees. Typical of these were Blackmoor and
Pewsham in Wiltshire, said to be of no use for hunting because they
were too small and open ('so that the deer fly all over the country');
their only wood was old 'firewood' trees.[30] Salisbury was in possession
of more radical proposals for increasing income through disafforesting remote or decayed forests. Johnson had suggested to him
the improvement of forests, parks, chases and other waste grounds in
1602 and worked out his ideas at greater length in a paper addressed
to the earl of Devonshire.[31] The first project from the period of
Salisbury's ascendancy is by Sir Roger Manwood and was dated by
Caesar to April 1609. John Norden submitted his own paper, but the
longest and fullest proposal from the same general period is unhappily
both anonymous and undated.[32] The whole issue received a public
airing in the tract on surveying and woodland management
published in 1612 by Rock Church, where a didactic four-handed
discussion (in which the surveyor plays a prominent role) served to
press home the advantages of this policy.[33]

As might be expected, the projects varied greatly in emphasis. The
projectors were generally unspecific as to how much the improvement
of forests would bring the King, Church barely mentioning the
Crown's interest in improvement, preferring with the others to
concentrate on the benefits to the commonwealth.[34] The anonymous

---

[30] CRES 40/5, fol. 33r.

[31] Johnson's observations on improvement are omitted from the letter sent to James I and may
be found at SP12/283A, fol. 173v. His proposal addressed to the earl of Devonshire
(Mountjoy) is undated but falls between Mountjoy's creation as Devonshire in July 1603
and death in April 1606. BL, Harl. MS 3796, fols. 41r–4v.

[32] The projects can be found printed in St John, *Observations*, Apps. i–iii (independently
paginated). The original of Manwood's proposal is LR2/194, fols. 274r–5v and Norden's
ibid., fols. 304–7v. I have been unable to trace the original of the anonymous project. Dr
Thirsk has shown me how this project is closely connected with a dialogue advocating the
improvement of forests and wastes, BL, Add. MS 38445, with which it shares both order,
argument and illustration. A further undated but much less sophisticated project, probably
of the same date, is BL, Cotton MS Titus B IV, fols. 295–6.

[33] R[ock] C[hurch] *An Olde Thrift Newly Revived*... (London, 1612) pt 2. (The author is
sometimes identified as R. C[hurton].) Church had been employed as a surveyor of woods
by Dorset and Salisbury and in his preface speaks of his discourse being prompted by the
observations he made in their service. The preface also praises Northampton at length,
suggesting that it was published after Salisbury's death in May 1612.

[34] There is no sign that any of them worked with the evidence of the surveys before them.

writer offered a throw-away figure; 'the spacious forests, chaces and wastes in England, if royal consent and the vulgar whom it concerns were conformable, might be improved to upwards of £2 million per annum'.[35] Only Manwood offered a worked-out estimate. His Majesty, he believed, could lease to 5,000 yeomen 100 acres apiece. These industrious people would enclose the land and build on each 100 acre parcel a house and other buildings and give the King a rent of £20 per annum, making an annual revenue of £100,000. (Another proposal of these years offers £200,000 in entry fines and a rent of £30,000 per annum.)[36] All the authors took care to say that they did not envisage a general disafforestation, but the improvement of selected forests remote from the King's houses. Manwood went so far as to argue that the game would be improved by enclosure and envisaged his 5,000 yeomen living alongside the deer and the hare, pheasant and partridge.[37]

In discussing the advantages which enclosure would bring the commonwealth, general themes emerged. For one, there was a general assumption that there was a demand for land and tenancies which enclosure would serve to satisfy. Manwood, in common with Norden and the anonymous commentator, was aware of the strains caused by population growth; 'the commonwealth [would be] greatly enriched and bettered by providing of so many dwelling houses for so many desolate people which do now want places of habitation'. Manwood and the anonymous commentator also saw the enclosure as a way of reducing food prices by increasing supply, Manwood seeing this as a precondition to setting idle people to work.[38] The anonymous commentator saw enclosure as way of improving the quality of animals, arguing that 'one cow well kept in grounds enclosed is worth in profit two pasturing in common'; an ox brought up in an enclosure could do the work of two kept in a common.[39]

But there was also a particular interest in enclosure as a means of improving the human stock. So, in Norden's words,

The good of the commonwealth shall undoubtedly grow abundantly by reducing the former unprofitable inhabitants to a civil and religious course of life and to bring this to pass they must either be removed from their obscure dwellings and be replanted where they may first learn and so live according to laws or else bring the places wherein they live to civility which

[35] St John, *Observations*, p. 8.   [36] Pettit, *Royal Forests*, pp. 65–6.
[37] St John, *Observations*, pp. 1–2.   [38] *Ibid.*, p. 2.   [39] *Ibid.*, p. 6.

cannot be done as they now stand. Therefore the best and most likely is to make a more full plantation in those parts and to turn some of those unprofitable places into farms and dwellings for men of more worth.[40]

The anonymous author also took a dim view of the present occupants of the forests:

It will be objected that the poor, who have built houses upon these wastes will suffer [the] greatest wrong because they have no right in the places where they have settled, but whereas they now dwell in woods and deserts as abandoned and forlorn men, deprived of the means to know God or their duties to magistrates and live like drones, devoted to thievery, among whom are bred the very spawn of vagabonds and rogues, they shall be instructed, civilized and better maintained. The civilizing of these unhappy persons and instructing them in moral and religious duties is one strong argument in favour of enclosing the wastes and commons.[41]

Here we see an instinct to human engineering on an Irish scale (notice Norden's use of 'plantation'). The same themes were taken up by the Crown's surveyor in South Wales in 1619. The writer, one Thomas Canon, advocated the settlement of wastes with nucleated groups of houses, never more than ten in number, each with a court leet. But his aim was not so much to raise profits as to drive out the thieves and outlaws who inhabited such waste grounds.[42]

It was also argued that enclosure would be in the best interest of the poor. The anonymous commentator believed it would increase their profits, avoid the dangers of being crowded off the wastes by overgrazing by rich men but, moreover, 'the poorest that dwell upon wastes that now stand in nature of trespass against all lawful commoners, not having right to a foot, shall have a portion secured them to enclose about their cottages to raise herbs and roots, keep a cow and sow some corn for their better relief'.[43] Church thought along similar lines; extending the cultivated area would produce work for the poor allowing them to live more plentifully than they could possibly do upon a bare common, able with more ease, profit and pleasure to husband 5 or 6 acres by sowing it with some profitable grain, grazing, planting fruit trees, hops and roots.[44]

But Church also had his yeoman argue that the costs of surveying, ditching, quicksetting and planting their new enclosures would be

---

[40] *Ibid.*, p. 3–4. [41] *Ibid.*, p. 14.
[42] SP14/109, fols. 192v–3r, described by G. Dyfnallt Owen, *Wales in the Reign of James I* (Royal Historical Soc., Studies in History, 53, Woodbridge, 1988), pp. 181–2.
[43] St John, *Observations*, p. 10. [44] C[hurch], *An Olde Thrifte*, pp. 36–7.

beyond the means of the poorer commoners; freeholders would benefit but copyholders, farmers and cottagers would lose all the advantage of their commons in paying rack-rents for what they had previously taken for free. Church's surveyor went so far as to claim that the poor would be better off paying the rack-rent.[45] Church put into the mouth of his woodward another reason why forests should not be enclosed: fear of disorders. Both Church's surveyor and the anonymous commentator countered the argument that enclosure would produce another Northamptonshire rising by arguing that this enclosure was intended to increase tillage where the 1607 revolt had been concerned about its conversion to pasture.[46] Only the anonymous writer conceded that the commoners might offer violent resistance. He complacently thought that the law as it stood made ample provision for their suppression.[47] Sir Robert Cotton showed an acute understanding of the dangers of stimulating an agitation against the Crown and its servants.

But in the carriage of this business there must be much caution to prevent commotion, for in them [forests] there are many that have right of common *sans* number. And the resolution in agreement with them must be sudden and confident, for multitudes are jealous and inconsistent. And the instruments to effect this must be such as are neighbours, interested and popular, not strangers and the first demise to the inhabitants at under and easy values.[48]

For the generality of writers, the self-evident logic and advantage in their proposals were sufficient to persuade the commoners to accede to enclosure.

The assumption that the co-operation of the commoners could be relied upon proved to be excessively optimistic. In every case, the enclosure of forests (and drainage of fens) was marred by acts of violence against not only the new fences and drains but also, on occasion, the improvers' workmen. In part, this reflects not only an appreciation by the commoners of what they stood to lose, but also the Crown's failure to follow Cotton's sage advice and the casting to

---

[45] *Ibid.*, pp. 34–6.   [46] *Ibid.*, pp. 35–7.   [47] St John, *Observations*, pp. 10–11.
[48] Sir Robert Cotton, 'The manner and means how the kings of England have from time to time supported and repaired their estates, 1609', in J. Howell (ed.), *Cottoni Posthuma* (London, 1651), p. 183. The argument that the project needed to be managed through neighbours can be compared with Cope's comments on Salisbury's practice, see above, p. 330 n. 112.

one side of the hopes of Church and the anonymous commentator that the poor would be favoured over the interests of the larger commoners and the Crown. It is the case that parcels of common land were often reserved for the poor. At Hatfield Chase (Yorkshire) a stock of hemp was provided to employ the poor in the making of sackcloth and cordage as some compensation for the loss of their fishing and fowling. These may be read as humane concessions, although the truth is that they were overdue attempts to buy peace from crowds who prevented the Crown's patentees from exploiting their assets.[49]

It is one thing to show that the idea of raising revenue through disafforestation was in circulation and even had its publicist in the form of Rock Church, another to show that it determined policy within the Exchequer. There are clues to suggest that steps were afoot to disafforest a number of Crown woods in the last two years of Salisbury's life. Cotton gave the idea his cautious approval in his paper on the improvement of royal revenues of 1610–11.[50] Surveys of forests were certainly made in 1611 although none appear to survive except as a series of general descriptions in Sir Julius Caesar's papers.[51] Word of a proposed disafforestation was circulating by the autumn of 1611 when Salisbury received a letter pleading that the Forest of Galtres (Yorkshire) should be spared.[52] By mid-1612, Caesar was able to draw up a list of forests to be improved and the income that might be expected from them.[53] These estimates appeared to confirm the projector's claims that very substantial sums could be raised through selective disafforestation. Morsse Forest in Shropshire, extending to 3,675 acres, would raise £7,000 in fines and a rent of £200. The open grounds of Needwood Forest in Stafford-shire (13,000 acres) and Duffield Frith in Derbyshire (14,000 acres) were worth 13s 4d and 6s 8d respectively. Their parks were worth

---

[49] Buchanan Sharp, 'Common rights, charities and the disorderly poor', in G. Hely and W. Hunt (eds.), *Reviving the English Revolution* (London, 1988), pp. 128–31; J. Tomlinson, *The Level of Hatfield Chace and the Parts Adjacent* (Doncaster, 1882), pp. 90, 100.

[50] Cotton, 'The manner and means how the kings of England', pp. 182–3; for the date of this, K. Sharpe, *Sir Robert Cotton, 1586–1631. History and Politics in Early Modern England* (Oxford, 1979), p. 122 n. 49 (It might be noticed that a cut-down version of this tract containing the same suggestion was published in 1715 as *A Treatise of the Rights of the Crown* under the name of William Noy, Attorney-General 1631–4).

[51] LR2/194, fols. 16–31. These are undated, but a draft of the return for the Forest of Bowland in the Northamptonshire RO, FH 3524, is dated to 17 Aug. 1611.

[52] *CSPD 1611–18*, p. 78.   [53] Bodl., MS North a.2, fols. 158–9.

£100 each. Bernwood Forest in Buckinghamshire would produce £800 per annum. But, for whatever reason, disafforestation was not recommended by the commissioners who sat after Salisbury's death in 1612.[54]

In fact, the only place where it appears any attempt was made to tap the potential of disafforestation was in the Forest of Knaresborough.[55] Here, several attempts, all apparently abortive, were made to enclose lands from the open waste of the forest. As early as the winter of 1610–11, a surveyor called John Moore was making a measured (and planned) survey of the forest. This remained incomplete – he complained of his advanced years and abandoned his task when snow came and the River Nidd froze – but he left an opinionated 'discourse' of his activities. Much of his work seems to have been to identify the bounds of the forest, but in those parts of the forest he surveyed, Moore identified considerable acreages fit to be enclosed.[56] Who commissioned Moore's survey is unclear. When Knaresborough was granted to Henry Prince of Wales in July 1611, he sent in his own Surveyor-General, Sir William Fleetwood,[57] and in the spring of 1612 the Prince made leases of all the wastes of the forest for forty years to nominees of the tenants. These would have produced a rent of £750 but took effect for only a short period. They were surrendered after the death of Prince Henry to the Treasury Commissioners who elected to fee-farm rather than lease the wastes.[58]

During May 1613, Caesar received an estimate drawn up by the late Prince's auditor, Richard Connock, of the expected profits of improving the wastes by granting parcels in fee-farm. Connock clearly had before him a survey of some sophistication; he reckoned the size of the forest at about 20,000 acres falling into three categories. Fee-farmed, the best land would attract a rent in perpetuity of 12d and a fine of 20s, the worst 4d in rent and 3s 4d in fine. Overall, the forest would yield a windfall of £10,333 6s 8d in fines (to which could be added £1,550 as the profit of selling woods) and a recurrent

---

[54] Spedding, *Bacon*, IV, pp. 314–27.
[55] B. Jennings (ed.), *A History of Knaresborough and Harrogate* (Huddersfield, 1970), pp. 130–2, gives an outline of events. (Knaresborough was of the Duchy of Lancaster but was used to augment the estates of both Prince Henry and Prince Charles.)
[56] Moore's 'discourse' survives in a copy in a commonplace book of a member of the Fairfax family, University of Leeds, MS Brotherton 20, fols. 198r–201v. Much of the discourse is a commentary to Moore's maps and correspondingly unintelligible without them.
[57] The original of Fleetwood's survey can be found in Leeds Archives Dept, Ingleby MS 3101, and a copy in University of Leeds, MS Brotherton 20, fols. 202r–4v.
[58] E317/Yorks./32, fol. 22; BL, Add. MS 15235, fol. 109v (11 Dec. 1613); E112/139/1417.

revenue of £583 6s 8d in rent.[59] A commission to sell the wastes in fee-farm was issued in August 1613. In October and November, the inhabitants of Knaresborough and the forest townships agreed to the enclosure and appointed delegates to travel to Westminster to confer with the Treasury Commissioners. In December, the Treasury Commissioners instructed the tenants' nominees to join with the surveyors Robert Wray and Samuel Swale to break the waste into allotments for the townships.[60]

What happened in the following two years is unclear but may be surmised. On 1 August 1615, a new commission for making grants in fee-farm was issued. This, unusually, conferred on the commissioners the authority to punish persons hindering them or who in the previous two years had cut turves on the waste. They were given authority to instruct malefactors to appear before the Privy Council. And, to underline the fact that the previous commission had encountered local opposition, the new commissioners were ordered to place the interest of the poorer sort of commoners before that of the richer, particularly favouring those who had previously shown their willingness to accept allotments of the waste.[61] Resistance to the allotment followed. By November 1615, the commissioners had been reduced to sending the vicar of Knaresborough a proclamation to read at divine service in which the richer sort of Knaresborough, Bilton and Harrogate were denounced as 'men not respecting neither the King's profit nor their own'. The commissioners believed that the rich had acted to prevent the poor from coming to them to compound; they therefore invited the poor to approach them directly. The townships of Tentergate and Scriven had boycotted the commissioners completely; here again, the poor were told to approach the commissioners directly. Their failure to do so, the commissioners warned, would force them to sell lands to outsiders.[62] This threat seems to have been partially successful. In January 1616, the commissioners were able to compile a list of nearly 150 individuals

---

[59] LR2/194, fols. 34r–6v. Connock was named to the commissions of both August 1613 and 1615.

[60] C66/1993, dorse, unnumbered. The dating of the Treasury Commissioners' order is uncertain, the three copies known to me giving dates of 11 December 1613 (Yorkshire Archaeological Society, Leeds, DD56/A6/14, the only contemporary copy), 11 December 1612 (Yorkshire Archaeological Society, Leeds, DD146/12/2/15, pp. 29–32) and 6 December 1612 (Leeds Archives Dept, Ingleby MS 3105, unpaginated). The date in December 1613 seems to favour the narrative best.

[61] C66/2038, dorse, unnumbered.

[62] Yorkshire Archaeological Society, Leeds, DD56/A6/14.

(including some outsiders) who had contracted for parcels, some clearly working as groups joined together to secure land. A proclamation was issued instructing them to appear before the Chancellor of the Duchy of Lancaster to seal their purchases.[63] In all, the commissioners received offers for the fee-farm of 2,000 acres (at a rent of £255 9s 10d) and the sale of 3,268 acres at a yearly rent of £309.[64] Yet by May 1616, the opponents of the enclosure had secured a hearing before the Privy Council to complain of the commissioners' partiality and the allotment of land to strangers. The Council found the commissioners to have been faultless in their work, but they were still told to reconsider.[65] This may have spelt the end of the project; there is no sign of activity in the remainder of 1616 or thereafter and in the following spring the honour and forest were granted to the new Prince of Wales.

The Crown's first foray into disafforestation appears to have brought little income to James. The potential in improving forests was too great to be neglected and it appears repeatedly in the next few years as a means by which the income of the Crown could be increased. Lord Chancellor Ellesmere included in his proposals for the increase of revenue of September 1615 the idea of selling in fee-farm 'some of His Majesty's forests, chases [and] parks, lying far off and remote from any of His Highness royal houses of access and of which His Majesty has neither pleasure nor profit' and 'to enclose and improve some of his great wastes and common grounds and to grant the same in fee-farm'. These proposals were adopted by Council in its recommendations for reform devised that same month.[66]

Despite James's declared opposition, these ideas were put into effect during Suffolk's term as Lord Treasurer. A commission to disafforest the Forests of Pewsham and Blackmoor in Wiltshire was issued in April 1617 and one for Hatfield Chase (Yorkshire) in July 1618.[67] Letter of June and July 1617 show that work at Pewsham was

---

[63] DL44/1084.

[64] Notes by the commissioners grossly misdated and placed under 1640–1; SP16/474, no. 20.

[65] APC 1615–16, pp. 532–5.

[66] L. A. Knafla, Law and Politics in Jacobean England. The Tracts of Lord Chancellor Ellesmere (Cambridge, 1977), p. 269; Tawney, Business and Politics, pp. 142–3 (citing Spedding, Bacon, v, pp. 206–7).

[67] C231/4, fols. 61v, 66v. The Pewsham and Blackmoor commission was reissued in the name of the Treasury Commissioners in September 1618, ibid., fol. 71v. See also the enrolments, respectively C66/2176 (Hatfield), 2180 (second Pewsham commission).

proceeding under the direction of Robert Treswell who was charged not only with disafforestation but creating a new park for the King. Progress at Hatfield Chase was hindered by the lack of adequate surveys but it was, the letters make clear, the work for the following year.[68] The first steps towards the enclosure of King's Sedgemoor (Somerset) were taken in the summer of 1618 when a commission was issued to declare the King's plans to the commoners and seek their consent to the waste's division.[69] But it is Cranfield with whom the implementation of this policy should be particularly associated. Within a month of his appointment as Lord Treasurer in September 1621, a commission was issued for the survey and enclosure of Leighfield and Beaumont Forests in Rutland and Northamptonshire. This was followed by commissions for Bernwood in February 1622 and a whole portfolio of forests and wastes (Bernwood, Feckenham, Hatfield Chase, Broile (Sussex), King's Sedgemoor (Somerset) and Frome Selwood (Wiltshire)) in April.[70] The following year, moves were afoot to improve Tiptree Heath in Essex although there is no sign that anything came of this.[71]

From this time onwards, disafforestation and the improvement of wastes for profit was a major plank in all attempts to solve the Crown's financial problems. Sir Edward Coke incorporated the improvement of forests into his speech to the 1625 Oxford Parliament on the means to revitalise the Crown's finances.[72] Sir Robert Heath, in an undated paper (but probably of 1625–6), thought that the improvement of remote and decayed forests would yield £20,000 per annum, a significant sum but small compared with the £60,000 per annum he proposed to raise by squeezing recusants.[73]

It was therefore inevitable that the possibility of raising revenue through the improvement of forests, parks and chases would be reexamined when the Caroline government was forced to look to its own resources after the failure of the 1626 Parliament. Discussions in the Privy Council in late June over the means to raise and save revenue were continued with the establishment of a commission to consider 'all good ways and means as well for the augmenting of our

---

[68] SP14/92, nos. 58, 90.   [69] See below, p. 378.

[70] C231/4, fols. 129v, 134r, 137v (the second and third enrolled as C66/2258 and 2282, dorse, no. 1).

[71] *CSPD 1623–5*, p. 41. The Essex RO tell me they have a petition of that date asking for the preservation of common rights, D/B 3/3/217/12.

[72] C. Russell, *Parliaments and English Politics, 1621–9* (Oxford, 1979), pp. 244–6.

[73] SP16/44, no. 1.

said revenues as for the lessening of our charge'.[74] The survival of the commission's minute books allows us to follow the decision-making process which lay behind disafforestation in greater detail than before.

One of the commission's first acts was to call on Fanshawe, the Surveyor-General and Treswell, the Surveyor-General of woods to prepare a certificate of all the King's forests, chases and parks and of the quantities of land they contained. With this before them, the commission resolved to improve such forests and parks as lay in remote parts of the kingdom and distant from the King's principal houses or landholdings. On 17 August, Buckingham brought to the commission a list of parks and forests of which the King had approved the disafforestation; two days later, he suggested that the royal studs should be moved from Tutbury and Malmesbury to near Dover, partly for the benefit of the horses but also to permit the disparking of the grounds they occupied. Later that month, Fanshawe presented the board with another list of parks in the charge of the Exchequer and Duchy of Lancaster which the King was happy to see improved by leasing or granting in fee-farm. (The King had not yet, Fanshawe reported, decided on the forests to surrender up to stringency.) Fanshawe then reappeared on 11 September bearing the King's decision over his forests. Charles would keep eighteen and have forty-eight improved; unfortunately the minute book fails to list them. The surveying of the parks and forests was then put in hand.[75]

It was at this moment that Sir Miles Fleetwood, the Receiver-General of the Court of Wards and Liveries, makes his first appearance as the commission's agent. How he became the driving force behind the disafforestation of selected forests is not clear; when he first appears in the minutes we find the commission seeking his advice as to the most promising forests with which to begin. Fleetwood suggested the Forest of Bere (Hampshire) and when told that the King would not countenance its improvement, recommended Leicester and Roche Forests.[76] Fleetwood subsequently busied himself at Leicester. On 7 November, he appeared before the

---

[74] See in general, G. E. Aylmer, 'Buckingham as an administrative reformer?', *EHR* 105 (1990); in addition, HMC, *Cowper*, I, pp. 272–3. For the commissioners' draft report, *ibid.*, pp. 291–5 (the original of which is now BL, Add. MS 64890, fols. 63r–70v).

[75] University of London Library, MS 195, pt i, fols. 2v, 4v, 17r–v, 19r, 22v–23r, 28r–v, 31r–v. The list of parks of 28 August is also SP16/34 no. 43; for a further list of 6 October, SP16/525 no. 4.   [76] University of London Library, MS 195, pt i, fols. 37v, 38v (20–1 Sept).

commissioners and reported that he had already reached an agreement with many of the commoners, but now needed a commission to adjudicate on the claims of 'pretended commoners'; he was confident of reserving 1,200 or 1,400 acres for the King when all other claims had been satisfied.[77] Having concluded the Leicester disafforestation, he negotiated the settlement at the other Midland Forest of Feckenham, always regularly reporting his progress to the commission and accepting their line on policy matters. At one moment he was intending to go on to Roche Forest but seems finally to have had no share in the work there.[78] At the same time, Treswell undertook the disafforestation of Gillingham (Dorset) and Braydon (Wiltshire).[79]

In fact, the implementation of the decisions taken in 1626 was far from complete on the eve of the Civil War; disafforestation proved to be a far from expeditious way of raising money unless the process was 'privatised' through the sale of the Crown's interest to private entrepreneurs. The general policy was actively pursued on both the Exchequer and Duchy of Lancaster's estates throughout the 1630s. The Duchy decreed the enclosure of Duffield Frith in Derbyshire in Michaelmas term 1633 although it is not clear if the Duchy's patentee ever gained possession of the third of the commons allotted him; in any case the enclosures were thrown down in 1643. The disafforestation of the High Peak was commenced in 1635 and was still incomplete in 1640.[80] Plans for the disafforestation of the Forest of Dean were drawn up in 1639 and proceeded as far as an agreement to allot the commoners 4,000 acres before the forest was abruptly sold to Sir John Wintour in 1640.[81]

It may be helpful to rehearse what a disafforestation entailed and the procedures followed to bring it about. The whole process was delegated to commissioners who arranged for the measurement of the forest or waste and heard the claims of commoners and landowners. They then began a process of negotiation in which a proportion of the ground, normally a third, was secured for the Crown's private use in return for the surrender of its claim to own the soil of the whole forest

---

[77] Cheshire RO, DCH/X/15/5, fol. 1r–v.
[78] SP16/74, no. 21; for Fleetwood's work at Feckenham, see below, pp. 407–15.
[79] University of London Library, MS 195, pt ii, esp. fol. 27v; SP16/69, fol. 14v.
[80] J. C. Cox, *The Royal Forests of England* (London, 1905), chs. 14, 15; Somerville, *Duchy of Lancaster*, II, pp. 22–4.   [81] Hart, *Royal Forest*, pp. 122–7.

and for the abolition of forest law. Where private landowners held
land within the forest, this too was liable to forest law and subject to
the common rights of forest townships. The Crown claimed a third of
such land for the abolition of its forest jurisdiction and a further third
was surrendered for the use of the commoners in lieu of their common
rights. In the case of Roche Forest in Somerset, Sir John Wyndham
surrendered one third of his land in the forest to the Crown; he then
bought it back for £400.[82] Once the allotments of the Crown and any
private landowners had been secured, the balance was divided
between the townships and landowners who possessed common
rights. In most disafforestations, land was specifically assigned for the
maintenance or support of the poor. The 40 acres assigned to the poor
of Leicester in the disafforestation of Leicester Forest was amongst the
smaller parcels; the tenants of the forest townships within Bernwood
had 231 acres, albeit in an unprepossessing situation, together with
the right to exploit the brickclay pits around Brill village. The
commissioners for the disafforestation of Bernwood also charged the
Crown with the payment of £6 per annum for the employment of a
preacher at Brill, 'being very populous'.[83]

The negotiation and physical division of the land was most
certainly a process of considerable complexity. More than a dozen
townships claimed the right to graze in the Forest of Galtres and over
twenty-five in King's Sedgemoor. The danger existed – and came to
pass in the enclosure of both Galtres and Braydon in Somerset – of
landowners making a late claim of common rights or refusing to
accept an allotment of the size offered them. The commissioners were
also charged with laying out roads and in the case of Galtres made
arrangements for the building of a bridge on the York–Thirsk road,
the arterial route northwards.[84] At Gillingham Forest, the commissioners amended their proposals in the light of objections that the
allotments were inaccessible and the rights of way through the forest
inadequate. It was when these revisions were not implemented that
the first disorders broke out.[85]

The commissioners' certificate of their arrangements then formed

---

[82] E159/479, Hilary, ro. 56. This, with the previous rotulets, are agreements between the
commissioners for disafforestation of Roche and landowners within the forest of 1634.

[83] L. Fox and P. Russell, *Leicester Forest* (Leicester, 1948), p. 137; E126/4, fols. 84v–7. For the
provision of allotments for the poor in the enclosure of the West Country forests, see Sharp,
'Common rights, charities and the disorderly poor', esp. pp. 128–9.

[84] E125/9, fol. 155r.   [85] Betty, 'Revolts over enclosure', p. 22.

the basis of a decree in the Exchequer or Duchy court in what was probably (although not certainly) a collusive action initiated by the Attorney-General against the commoners. The decree formally announced the abolition of forest rights, established a title for the new parcels and granted the commoners licence to enclose and improve their allotments. Several decrees might finally be needed, with the court modifying or confirming its earlier orders. It needs to be added that with rare exceptions, this was not achieved in a day; five or six years between first commission and final decree was not unusual.

What remains unclear is how the Exchequer administered individual disafforestations. There are clues to suggest that in most instances, one commissioner, either an Exchequer official or entrepreneur, was appointed to 'undertake' the project. In some cases, it can be shown that the Exchequer set financial targets for the projector to meet.[86] These individuals might have a financial interest in the outcome, either in the expectation of a reward or the promise of a share of the Crown's allotment when the process was complete. At an extreme, Sir James Fullerton was granted both the lease and stewardship of Gillingham Forest with a licence to undertake its disafforestation.[87] The Dutch drainage engineer Cornelius Vermuyden had a formal contract to drain Hatfield Chase. In return for raising the investment required for the drainage works, he was to have a third share of the lands recovered.[88] With other contractors, no formal arrangement is known to have been entered into. At Sedgemoor, one Adam Moore was named as the King's agent in 1618 or 1619, although it is unclear how he related to John Shotbolt alias Battalion who claimed to be the originator of the project.[89] In the King's initial letter to the gentry of the area around Sedgemoor, Shotbolt was amongst those who were to declare the King's intentions to the commoners. When the division appeared to have been achieved in 1623, he was doubtless one of the 'inferior actors' who was asking for their reward, seeking 500 acres where the Crown thought 300 more reasonable.[90] But Moore's and Shotbolt's position as undertaker

---

[86] The targets for Leicester and Roche are discussed below, pp. 374–5.

[87] Betty, 'Revolts over enclosure', p. 21.

[88] Printed in Tomlinson, *Hatfield Chace*, pp. 237–9.

[89] BL, Add. MS 48111, fol. 2r; on one occasion, Shotbolt claimed that the discovery of Sedgemoor was his and that it was he who brought it to James's notice. BL, Royal MS 17A xxxvii, fols. 2v–3r.

[90] Dorset RO, D.124 box 18, copy signet letter of 20 Aug. 1618; E112/119/285; SP14/139, no. 6; SP14/140, no. 16.

was challenged by Humphrey Walrond and Sir Giles Mompesson who tried to persuade the King that Shotbolt was inadequate to the task. The Walrond–Mompesson undertaking was then challenged by a third syndicate, possibly that led by Sir Richard Strode (who owned a manor bordering on Sedgemoor) but by some means, Shotbolt regained the management of the enterprise.[91] In 1626, Shotbolt and Moore were seeking the support of Buckingham and the commissioners for retrenchment for a project to drain moors in Somerset and Devon (apparently including Sedgemoor), raising for the King £200,000 in fines, with the projectors having a 20 per cent share of rents or fines generated. In 1627, Moore was named as the Exchequer's agent.[92] When in 1631 Kings Sedgemoor was abruptly sold to Vermuyden, Shotbolt ferociously attacked Vermuyden and denounced the transaction as corrupt in any theatre open to him. The reasons for this are more readily understood if we appreciate the long and uncompensated investment Shotbolt had made in the project.[93] Shotbolt appears to have had a mercantile background; in 1619, he had a patent for a monopoly of repairing roads with a machine of his own design; in 1628–9, he was one of a syndicate that tried to secure a monopoly over the London coal trade.[94]

Other undertakers can be identified. John Pym and Robert Treswell were clearly the central figures in the disafforestation of Pewsham and Melksham, the former so much so that Cranfield secured Pym's release from custody in 1621 to permit him to carry on the work.[95] Sir Sackville Crowe appears to have had the oversight of the improvement of Roche and Selwood Forests and in 1637 was seeking either £2,800 or £1,806 (the figure varies between manuscripts) in out-of-pocket expenses.[96] But the undertaker whose work is best documented is Sir Miles Fleetwood. His reports to the commissioners for retrenchment and the few extant pieces of his correspondence show that he spent much of late 1626 and 1627 organising the disafforestation of Leicester Forest and overseeing the

---

[91] BL, Add. MS 34712, fol. 192 (undated but c. 1620); Strode's project SP16/44, no. 53 (which I take to be of c. 1622).

[92] University of London Library, MS 195, pt i, fol. 23r–v; pt ii, fol. 28r; SP16/524, no. 104; SP16/71, no. 12.

[93] See below, pp. 377–8. In 1626 they told Buckingham that they had 'run ourselves to wreak therein', having never received any fee for their labour. SP16/524, no. 104.

[94] CSPD 1619–23, p. 46; BL, Stowe MS 326, fols. 1–20.

[95] See especially Kent AO, U269/1, OE 591 (Pym to Cranfield, 23 May, 20 Aug. 1622), 786 (Willis to Cranfield, 14 Aug. 1622).   [96] Bodl., Bankes MS 47/24 i–v.

allotment of its lands. When a petition opposing the disafforestation was presented to the commissioners in March 1627, he was able to reassure the board that he had already satisfied many of the criticisms it contained and that its prosecution was in any case the work of an unimportant fringe. In November, Fleetwood was able to appear and announce that a general agreement had been reached and the commission authorised him to have the arrangement entered as a decree in the Exchequer. By this time, he was already at work on the disafforestation of Feckenham which he brought to a conclusion in 1630–1.[97]

What changed between the early and mid-1620s was the end to which the project was devoted; improvement began as a means to increase revenue in the long term but with the passage of time a greater emphasis was placed on the immediate objective of releasing capital. The first disafforestation brought to fruition, of the small Wiltshire Forests of Pewsham (sometimes called Chippenham) and Melksham (Blackmore) commenced in 1619 and completed in 1622–3, shows what might have been. At Pewsham, the commissioners' task was aided by their refusal to acknowledge the common rights of local landowners. After a new park had been carved out of the forest and allowance made for highways and fences, the commissioners had at their disposal 1,040 acres. This they divided into twenty-six parcels of a wide range of sizes; eleven of less than 20 acres, but five of more than 100 acres. All were let at a market rent for twenty-one years, paying a fine of a year's rent.[98] In addition, they leased eighteen cottages (and odd parcels), mostly for 2s each, at a fine of a year's rent. The total rents came to £674 9s 8d.

The same commissioners were at this time also disafforesting Melksham. This was the larger forest – 2,036 acres, but 554 acres were granted out in satisfaction of common rights. The balance was broken down into twenty parcels and let on the same terms as at Pewsham for a total rent of £238 14s 10d. In both forests, the tenants were allowed timber for the construction of their houses and buildings, but most of the standing timber was felled and sold by the

---

[97] SP16/69, fols. 9v, 33v–4r, 39r; University of London Library, MS 195, pt ii, fols. 53, 68r–v; SP16/66, no. 84; SP16/80 nos. 40, 75.

[98] The indications are that the rents were very competitive. Some tenants claimed that the lands were always too poor to answer the rents, but they were certainly beyond the means of the tenants in the distressed years which followed. From late 1622, Cranfield was receiving letters and petitions asking for reductions, for instance, Kent AO, U269/1, OE 70, 565, 629 (and 906), 821 (i, ii) and his rejection of this petition, 1357A.

commissioners in 1618–21 for about £4,200 (exclusive of the costs of labour). This income was used to fund the commissioners' expenses and the costs of purchasing land enclosed in the new park made in Pewsham Forest. The sale of timber made the project self-financing; in addition, £900 in fines was raised and £900 in recurrent rental income. Here, we see the implementation of Manwood's project of 1608; the creation of a community of leasehold tenants ranging from cottagers to substantial farmers carved out from a derelict woodland.[99]

Bernwood Forest in Buckinghamshire, some 10 miles east of Oxford, was another of the first forests to be identified as an asset with the potential for improvement.[100] But here, the existence of common rights and the fact that the Crown owned only a part of the forest made the situation more complicated than in the Wiltshire forests. Bernwood contained within its bounds three villages, Boarstall, Brill and Oakley, each of which possessed common rights within the forest. Several neighbouring villages also claimed grazing. The forest itself contained extensive areas of coppice, some of which belonged to the Crown but was leased out, some of which was in private hands. The first commission for disafforestation was issued in February 1622; the work of the commissioners was decreed in February 1627 after a new commission was issued to settle irreconcilable differences between the commissioners and Sir John Dynham of Boarstall, the major landowner in the forest. The result was the allotment of $577\frac{1}{2}$ acres to the freeholders and inhabitants of the forest towns as compensation for the loss of their common rights. As these rights extended over Dynham's lands in the forest, he contributed about half the lands taken to form the commoners' allotments. This land was charged with a small quit rent to the Crown. After riots in September 1629, adjustments and further concessions were made and a new decree issued in 1632. The Bernwood disafforestation served to divide the Crown's lands in the forest from Sir John Dynham's. It abolished the commoners' grazing rights and compensated them with closes held in severalty; almost incidentally, the forest officers were paid off. But there was no attempt to plant the Crown's newly won lands with tenants to increase rental income; in May and September 1627, the whole of the Crown's lands acquired under the disafforestation, some

---

[99] Bodl., Rawlinson MS B 443; Sharp, *In Contempt*, p. 92.
[100] I hope to write further on Bernwood in association with Dr John Broad.

1,296 acres, was sold for £12,052 with the reservation of a fee-farm rent of £17 9s 7½d.[101]

The disafforestation of Leicester may be seen as spanning this change in ends. A commission to survey was issued late in 1626; a commission to disafforest in March 1627. The arrangements were completed by November of that year and a decree made in February 1628 by which the commoners and manorial lords of adjacent townships received 2,784 acres and the Crown 1,034 acres. The survival of the minute books of the commissioners for retrenchment shows Fleetwood offering them in February 1627 the alternatives of having an annual rent of £800, or £366 in rent and £4–5,000 in fines on leases. After consideration, the commission declared that they preferred an improvement in revenue to fines in hand. When Fleetwood returned to the commission in November to announce the conclusion of his negotiations, he said that his work had been worth £5,000 or £6,000 in ready money and £200 or £250 in rents for ever. The disparity between intention and outcome strongly suggests that the appetite for cash had increased substantially during 1627 and Fleetwood's agreement had been tailored to meet this need. In fact, the agreement was yet further remodelled; in June 1628, the King sold all his interest in the forest for about £7,500, reserving a rent of £80.[102] The arrangements for Roche, disafforested in 1628–31, also placed a premium on the release of ready money. Crowe was told to raise £20,000 by the sale of lands. By 1638, all had been sold for £18,099 save for a small residue of 200 acres, worth £3,165; but against this needed to be weighed unspecified charges and compensation totalling £7,850.[103] The Crown's continuing interest in the forest was clearly very small but typical of the later disafforestations.

The pressures of war finance effectively made disafforestation not a means of improving revenue but a device for rearranging the landscape to make an underrented and underutilised asset immediately saleable. The disafforestation of Roche, for instance, was expressly linked to the need to pay off the Fleet on its return in 1627.[104] The only further way to expedite the release of money was to sell the asset before the process of transforming it from common

---

[101] C66/2437, no. 12; C66/2431, nos. 13 and 14.
[102] C231/4, pp. 430, 444; SP16/69, fols. 33v–4r; University of London Library MS 195, pt ii, fol. 68r–v. BL, Add. MS 18795, fols. 13v–14r, conveniently lists the purchasers, the acreages purchased and the considerations (which I total at 1,251 acres and £7,348 16s 2d respectively, where Sharp, *In Contempt*, p. 89, has 1,598 acres and £7,760).
[103] SP16/154, no. 92; SP16/404, no. 129.   [104] SP16/70, no. 23.

resource into private property had been completed – or even begun. This we can see happening in the later 1620s and 1630s and nowhere more clearly than in the case of Malvern Chase. Malvern was one of the areas identified by the commissioners for retrenchment in 1626 as being worthy of improvement even though the Crown's interest consisted only of the forest jurisdiction. In the summer of 1628, orders were given to clear the chase of deer, the chase was surveyed and in late 1630 it was sold for £5,000 to the Dutch draining engineer and speculator Sir Cornelius Vermuyden. It was not until February 1631 that a commission was appointed to oversee the disafforestation and the allotment of the lands (in which the King's nominees took a third) was decreed in March 1632.[105] The Forests of Mocktree, Bringwood or Prestwood in Herefordshire were sold to the earl of Lindsey in 1631 and a decree setting out the commoners' share was made seven years later. Likewise, the Forests of Gillingham in Dorset, Galtres in Yorkshire and the waste of King's Sedgemoor in Somerset were sold in advance of the final decree.[106]

Mention of King's Sedgemoor in the Somerset levels raises the whole question of the Crown's involvement in fen drainage. The improvement of forest or moorland was a simple matter compared with the drainage of marshland. There was little expertise required for the former, but more importantly, the enclosure of forest could be self-financing through the cutting of timber, and responsibility for fencing could be assigned to the Crown's tenants and the commoners. Drainage was obviously different, not least in that it required technical skills of a high order to plan and execute the drainage works, and so a substantial capital input. The result was that drainage projects attracted undertakers who volunteered to pilot the project at their own expense (and risk) in return for a grant out of the lands reserved for the monarch in the apportionment of the marsh.

Amongst these were Robert Tipper and John Gascon who petitioned for (and were granted) a patent for draining both fresh and salt marshes in 1626. Their request was for a general patent for fourteen years to undertake drainage works wherever they wished and according to their own methods. In return, they required that when they drained fresh water marshes belonging to the King, they would receive a quarter of the land and the King three-quarters.

---

[105] B. S. Smith, *A History of Malvern* (Leicester, 1964), ch. 9 *passim*.
[106] Gillingham, Sharp, *In Contempt*, p. 87; Galtres and Sedgemoor, see below, pp. 380, 386; Mocktree, E126/4, fols. 321r–5v.

When they drained fresh water marshes belonging to private lords, they would grant the King a third of such lands as were allotted to them. With coastal marshes, the costs were higher so they wished the King to grant them three-quarters of his salt marshes and offered him a quarter of the lands allotted by private lords. On top of this, they offered the King an additional 10,000 acres of drained marsh as a gift for their patent. Undaunted by the scale of their task, they promised to drain 20,000 acres in their first year.

Rather surprisingly, this proposal was accepted by the commissioners. Tipper and Gascon were unable to avoid the problem that the Crown could not easily force its patentees on private landlords. Whilst they suggested commencing in the East Anglian fens, in early 1627, the Privy Council was writing to expedite their activities on the south coast. Given that their contribution to the history of drainage has gone unremarked, we may infer that they were largely unsuccessful.[107]

But drainage could not be viewed in isolation; patterns of drainage did not follow lines of property ownership. It involved not only the compensation of commoners but equally required interfering with the freehold of other landowners, either to include their lands in the scheme or for easements for drains. In a few locations, the Crown could act without reference to other landlords; in the majority of cases, drainage was only possible using the powers of the Commissioners of Sewers to coerce recalcitrant lords and finance the construction of drains and banks through local rates.

King's Sedgemoor in Somerset was an obvious subject for improvement. Located between Glastonbury and Bridgwater, Sedgemoor had been the property of Glastonbury Abbey before the dissolution and whilst the bordering manors had been sold, the Crown claimed to own the soil of Sedgemoor itself. The Crown's surveyors measured it at about 14,000 acres; it was used as common by the inhabitants of twenty-five neighbouring manors. Steps to enclose and drain the moor began in 1618 but, after early progress, little had been achieved by 1640.[108] Yet as with other projects, overwrought claims were made for the value of the land and profits that the Crown could expect to receive. In 1626, John Shotbolt (alias

---

[107] SP16/32, no. 45 (another copy, HMC, *Cowper*, I, p. 277, now BL, Add. MS 64889, fols. 83r–4v); University of London Library, MS 195, pt i, fols. 6v, 9v; *APC Jan.–Aug. 1627*, pp. 207–8.

[108] For general accounts of the drainage activity of these years, T. G. Barnes, *Somerset 1625–1640. A County's Government during the 'Personal Rule'* (London, 1961), pp. 150–5; M. Williams, *The Draining of the Somerset Levels* (Cambridge, 1970), pp. 86–110.

John Battalion) and Adam Moore, who were eager to restart the stalled undertaking, offered Buckingham a tract explaining how the moor could be made to yield £200,000.[109] A few years previously, a rival group of undertakers had claimed that the Crown's third would be worth 2s an acre on a lease of thirty years or £400 per annum; after that period, the rent could be increased to £2,000 per annum; another project spoke of an income of £20,000. It was later claimed that James rejected an offer of £80,000 for the land.[110] King's Sedgemoor completely failed to answer these expectations.

On 20 August 1618, James I directed a signet letter to commissioners (including Shotbolt) announcing the proposed enclosure and justifying it in a mixture of commonwealth and financial terms

[F]or many weighty reasons, the improvement and enclosure of it [King's Sedgemoor] ought greatly to tend to the good of our commonwealth, the relief and right of the borderers and lawful commoners thereof who are much wronged by foreigners that dwell far remote and the just increase of the revenue of our Crown.

It would additionally be to the advantage of those of the King's subjects who 'by reason of the abuse and ill husbandry of this and much land of like nature' were forced to buy their food from abroad.[111] The commissioners were to call before them the lords of the manors bordering the moor and persuade them to accept the enclosure and distribution of the land. The share of each lord was to be granted to him in free socage.[112] It appears that the bordering lords declined to accept the Crown's claim to own the soil of the moor and the King was forced to commence litigation in the Exchequer to demonstrate his title. At much the same time, the story started circulating that the project was designed not to advance the King's revenues but those of some private man, a rumour which the commissioners were instructed to deny.[113] What happened next is unclear. By September 1619, Walrond and Mompesson seem to have been running the project and secured a letter from one of the

[109] SP16/524, no. 104.
[110] Bodl., MS North b. 26, fols. 50–1; SP16/44, no. 53 (by Sir Richard Strode) SP16/339, no. 22.
[111] Dorset RO, D.124 box 18, copy signet letter, 20 Aug. 1618. These themes were enlarged upon in the (doubtless official) 'Reasons for the enclosure of King's Sedgemoor to be urged to the borderers by the gentlemen at the time of their meeting'. Somerset RO, DD/PH 225/35; another (fragmentary) copy, Dorset RO, D.124 box 18.
[112] Dorset RO, D.124 box 18, letter, 17 Sept. 1618. The lord of Compton Dundon, Sir John Strangways, was told to present himself at Bridgwater on 25 September.
[113] E112/119/385 (Attorney-General v. Peter van Lore and others); SP14/118, no. 116.

bordering lords giving his conditional support to the project.[114] A single undated letter from the commissioners to the Lord Treasurer describes the willingness of the bordering lords to make a partial division of the waste between themselves, but their reluctance to consent to a full enclosure or to concede a share to the King. There had also been some hostility expressed to the commission's surveyors by 'idle persons'.[115] It seems that the endeavour was becalmed until January 1623 when the bordering lords petitioned the King to accept 4,000 acres of the moor in return for granting the remainder of the moor to the lords in fee simple. The offer was graciously accepted.[116]

Whilst this agreement might seem to open the way to the enclosure of Sedgemoor (and matters progressed as far as surveying the bordering lordships and dividing the moor between them in proportion to their inland grounds), it proved to be a hollow victory. In July 1623, Cranfield wrote to Lord Brooke in despairing terms, saying he saw no way to advance the project and the moor remained undivided when it was sold in 1631.[117] There was certainly a great deal of local footdragging. Shotbolt and Moore were quite convinced that they were being hindered and produced for royal approval a long and detailed discourse which described no fewer than seven categories of opponents ranging through the 'rich oppressors', the 'simply ignorant' to the wilfully obstructive and beyond.[118] The Lord Treasurer, Marlborough, was so impressed by the evidence of local hostility to the project that in November 1626 he advised the commissioners for retrenchment to proceed with it no further:

that he had understood, touching the common of Sedgemoor in the county of Somerset, that divers gentlemen in the county adjoining, though they seemed willing to further the improving of it, yet they had underhand opposed it; that the commoners be generally against it, and the preachers do also speak much against it because they conceive it will tend to the diminution of their profit, and that there hath been ill carriage in the going about it, the second proceeding in it having crossed the former and that therefore it cannot be but a dangerous thing to proceed in, the popularity being so opposite to it.[119]

[114] Dorset RO, D.124 box 18, letter, 2 Sept. 1619.
[115] Somerset RO, DD/PH 225/36.
[116] Dorset RO, D.124 box 18, copy petition, 10 Jan. 1622/3. The idea of doing this was current in the previous autumn, Kent AO, U269/1, OE 651.
[117] Kent AO, U269/1, OE 1,058.
[118] BL, Royal MS 17A xxxvii (undated but on internal evidence addressed to James I). Dr Thirsk points out to me that this tract is drawn upon in Adam Moore's *Bread for the Poor* (London, 1653). [119] Cheshire RO, DCH/X/15/5, fols. 2v–3r.

But other counsels must have prevailed for in July 1627 Marlborough and the Chancellor, Weston, wrote to the bordering lords in an attempt to revitalise the project. Here, the tenants were blamed for resisting the King's proceedings, but the resolutions sent with this letter show how far the Crown's plans had been reformulated to meet the commoners' anxieties. It was promised that the King's allotment would be let to the inhabitants of the bordering manors and that the cottagers of each village should have land assigned them.[120]

It may also be that the longer proceedings dragged on, the less likely it became that anything could be rescued from them. After attempts to fire the enthusiasm of the commissioners in 1629, the Crown sold its interest in the moor to Sir Cornelius Vermuyden and one Geoffrey Kirby of London.[121] Vermuyden appears to have been acting for himself, but Kirby was acting as executor to Paul, Viscount Bayning (d. 1629). Each party paid half of the purchase price of £12,000 but in Kirby's case the consideration was the release to the Crown of £6,000 of debts owing to Bayning's estate. Vermuyden undertook to pay Kirby £6,000 from the profits of the undertaking and so buy out his interest. It might be suggested (although it cannot be proved) that Kirby was not a willing investor in an uncertain project but received a part share in an unsaleable and unimproved Crown asset in settlement of bad debts. His share was later bought by Vermuyden. The grant reserved a fee-farm of £100 to the Crown, the payment of which was to commence when the division of the moor was completed.

So far the conveyance appears to have been above board and may best be read as the Crown acting to clear a debt by liquidating its interest in an otherwise unsaleable property. It served to close the door on Battalion's and Moore's interest in the improvement of the moor; as late as May 1630, Shotbolt had been seeking an audience with Charles I to explain the business and his part in it. By 1635, he was seeking to overturn the transaction by arguing before the Lord Commissioners of the Treasury that the consideration failed to represent the real value of Sedgemoor and that the sale had been

---

[120] SP16/71, no. 12; the resolutions, Dorset RO, D.124 box 18 ('The division and allotments of King's Sedgemoor...', undated), a copy, Somerset RO, DD/MKG 22.

[121] C66/2566, no. 6; C54/2889, no. 36. Kirby was lending to Charles in 1629; R. Ashton, *The Crown and the Money Market, 1603–40* (Oxford, 1960), p. 169. The transaction has been the subject of some confusion, Williams, *Somerset Levels*, p. 100, but cf. L. E. Harris, *Vermuyden and the Fens* (London, 1953), p. 120, for allegations of fraud made against him in 1656.

brought about through the corrupt dealing of Sir Robert Heath, the fallen Chief Justice of Common Pleas and, at the time of the sale, Attorney-General. James, he claimed, had turned down an offer of £80,000 for the royal allotment of 4,000 acres. Heath and Vermuyden, it was suggested, had accepted £30,000 from a third party for the purchase of the land and purloined the balance. These allegations were later spiced with the additional claim that Laud had intended to investigate the fraud but his plans had been curtailed by the appointment of Juxon as Lord Treasurer in March 1636.[122] There is no sign that any of this troubled Vermuyden, but he was unable to bring the enclosure of the moor to fruition. In 1639, a further commission was issued to lay out the 4,000 acres conceded to James I by the manorial lords, but this, like other commissions issued in Charles's reign, appears to have been inoperative. In 1653, he petitioned Cromwell for a new commission and in 1655, failed to get the partition of the moor sanctioned by statute.[123] After that, he sold his interest and the moor remained unenclosed until the end of the eighteenth century.

Yet if King's Sedgemoor remained in its native condition, Hatfield Chase in Yorkshire was successfully drained by Vermuyden (albeit at the cost of drowning the lands of neighbouring lords).[124] Compared to the forests considered previously, Hatfield Chase was an extremely large tract of land of which the improvable part was variously estimated at between 40,000 acres and 70,000 acres lying between the Rivers Don and Trent.[125] It was identified as having a potential for improvement as early as 1617; the first commission to drain Hatfield was granted in 1618 but appears to have been inactive.[126] Cranfield, though, appears to have been determined to make a success of the project. A new commission, which included Hatfield within its remit, was granted in April 1622 and a commission established to view the lands and negotiate with the tenants. The surveyor, Thomas Jenkins, prepared a plan of the chase. The tenants submitted to the King's will provided that their rights in the commons were protected, that the

---

[122] SP16/339, no. 22.   [123] SP18/100, no. 50.

[124] All the existing accounts of the draining of Hatfield are to a greater or lesser degree confused and unsatisfactory. For a general account of the financing of drainage in the 1630s which clarifies many matters, M. Albright, 'The entrepreneurs of fen draining in England under James I and Charles I', *Explorations in Entrepreneurial History* 8 (1955).

[125] SP14/180, no. 82 (40,500 acres); Tomlinson, *Hatfield Chace*, pp. 84 (at least 60,000 acres), 99 (about 70,000 acres).

[126] SP14/92, nos. 58, 92; C231/4, fol. 66v (30 June 1618).

poorer commoners had some provision made for them and that the works were carried through at the King's expense. They also offered their opinion that the drainage was impossible to achieve. It would appear that the tenants were divided amongst themselves. A petition from the better sort of commoners to Cranfield of 1623, whilst favouring the enclosure, again expressed scepticism at its plausibility and cost and conceded that the petitioners were unable to sway 'the multitude' from their opposition to the programme.[127]

Cranfield's ace was to employ Vermuyden to undertake the drainage. A memorial by Jenkins is quite clear that the introduction of Vermuyden to Hatfield was made by Cranfield and so took place before his fall in May 1624; but the project was then neglected for a time. It was not until May 1626 that a formal contract was made with Vermuyden in which he undertook, at his own risk, to make the ground fit for tillage or pasture in return for a grant of a third of the drained area. Vermuyden's commitment was considerable. When it was proposed in the commission for retrenchment in December 1626 that the improvement of Hatfield might be taken up again, the commission was informed that an agreement had already been reached with 'a Dutchman' and that it would cost him £30,000 or £40,000.[128]

The Crown risked nothing but stood to gain a great deal. It needs to be conceded that Vermuyden came close to success within two years using Dutch labour and apparently financing the operation by selling shares in his third in the Low Countries.[129] Many of the subsequent difficulties arose from basic flaws in the design of the drainage scheme and the work was concluded with money raised by a rate amongst the Vermuyden's backers and neighbouring land-owners. As the Crown ventured nothing but stood to gain 15,000 or 20,000 acres of newly drained marsh, it was perhaps just that its final benefit was minuscule. Hatfield manor together with the other adjacent Crown manors were mortgaged to Vermuyden for £10,000 in July 1628 and when the Crown defaulted on the repayment of the principal, the sale was made absolute for the payment of an additional £6,800 (less the interest on the mortgage principal). With this came the Crown's share of the chase. Of course, the Crown retained the

---

[127] SP14/180, no. 82; Kent AO, U269/1, OE 332 (undated but notice the signature of Robert Foster); Tomlinson, *Hatfield Chace*, p. 84.

[128] SP14/180, no. 32; the contract is printed by Tomlinson, *Hatfield Chace*, pp. 237–9; University of London Library, MS 195, pt ii, fols. 25v–6r; SP16/69, fol. 9v.

[129] Everything to do with Vermuyden's business affairs is obscure but see C2/Chas. I/U3/42.

interest of the fee-farm rents reserved in the manor and in its third share, but these were subsequently granted to the second duke of Buckingham.[130] Within ten years, it was being argued in royal circles that this had formed a poor bargain for the King and that the real worth of the lands (at a moderate fifteen years' purchase) was nearer £30,000.[131]

Disafforestation and drainage was brought about with the minimum of investment and financial cost to the Crown. Manwood supposed that the demand for land was so great that his yeomen, offered the opportunity to assart in the Crown's forests, would erect houses and buildings at their own expense.[132] At Pewsham and Blackmoor, the commissioners assigned the new tenants wood and gave them a rent break. Elsewhere, rents were deferred for a period, but no more. Similar concessions were offered to Vermuyden at Sedgemoor and Hatfield. The expense of fencing the Crown's allotments was passed on to the commoners. Evidence as to the costs the tenants had to bear is rarely recorded. The traffic in petitions from the tenants of Pewsham and Blackmoor asking for rent abatements offers a handful of figures. Sir Thomas Sackville contracted to take 220 acres at £144 per annum, giving as much again for his fine; he claimed to have expended £300 in building, grubbing up trees and fencing. Nicholas Wythers, gent. (whom Treswell identified as a notable malcontent), took 510 acres in Blackmoor at 7s per acre (£178 10s per annum) with a year's rent for his fine. He then purchased trees on the lands for £437 9s 1½d. He put his costs in clearing and fencing the land at £203; besides this, he had spent over £100 in travelling to London, lost 600 sheep, endured attacks on his fences, suffered the commoners' cattle on his land and had been indicted at Quarter Sessions for closing a highway over his lands. When Cranfield refused him a reduction in rent, he gave up the lands, but still claimed to have lost £148 18s 4d besides the arrears of rent and the unpaid balance of his purchase money for trees.[133] Even allowing for some exaggeration,

---

[130] The letters patent granting the manor are printed by Tomlinson, *Hatfield Chace*, pp. 240–52. They committed Vermuyden to the payment of £196 3s 5d as the ancient rents of the manors and from Michaelmas 1631 an additional rent of £425 for the improved grounds; for grounds at Wroot in Epworth manor he paid a fee-farm of £8 6s 6d and an improved rent of £60, again from 1631.　　[131] *CSPD 1638–9*, p. 499 (SP16/413, no. 78).

[132] St John, *Observations*, p. 1.

[133] Kent AO, U269/1, OE 629 (Sackville), 821 (petitions by Wythers), 734 (Treswell to Cranfield, Aug. 1622), 1357A and 1448 (detailed account of Wythers's income and expenditure, 1620–2).

and conceding the fact that these were both substantial lessees of the newly enclosed lands, the figures make clear the scale of the investment needed to bring forest land to a fruitful state.

There were costs which the Crown could not evade. The interests of lessees might need to be bought out to remove an impediment to improvement. A forest office was a position of profit which could be bought or sold; as such, compensation needed to be paid when the office – or its duties – were extinguished. The earl of Pembroke was promised £3,000 for the stewardship of Gillingham Forest. Sir Robert Hyde had £200 for the abolition of his rangership of Braydon.[134] It was suggested that the three keepers of Leicester Forest should be compensated with annuities of £100 (for two of them) and £66 13s 4d for the third. The earl of Huntingdon valued the profits of his lieutenancy of the forest at £336 9s 1d per annum and claimed (ten or so years after the event) that he had been promised 400 acres of the forest as compensation for his loss. This and other promises had never been honoured; he now asked for the grant of a Star Chamber fine of £5,000.[135] The keepers and woodwards of Roche demanded £450.[136] Compensation was therefore a sizeable charge, but so too were the costs and rewards of the commissioners: Fleetwood, for instance, having £950 for his expenses at Leicester; the commissioners for Roche looked for £2,750.[137]

Selling forests and flooded wastes before the work of disafforestation was complete – or even begun – might be seen as the means by which profit might be maximised. The Crown received cash in hand for an asset whose realisation would probably be both expensive and long-delayed whilst retaining some financial interest in the land through the reservation of a fee-farm rent. Indeed, on first acquaintance it seems that such assets were eagerly sought by both predatory courtiers and private purchasers. It is salutary to realise that practically none of the forests or fens whose disafforestation was carried through in the 1620s remained in the Crown's hands in 1640. The Villiers circle did especially well. Buckingham secured Leighfield Forest in Rutland in 1622 and undertook the disafforestation himself. An undated note to Buckingham urged him to seek the grant of an unnamed forest in Somerset with a view to undertaking the disafforestation. It was alleged in the Exchequer in 1633 that the disafforestation of Bernwood was undertaken for the duke's profit.

[134] *CSPD 1638–9*, pp. 144–5; *CSPD 1628–9*, p. 11.
[135] SP16/329, no. 20 (of late 1626 or 1627); SP16/375, nos. 36, 36i.
[136] SP16/154, no. 92.   [137] *CSPD 1628–9*, p. 223; SP16/154, no. 92.

The proceedings were conducted in the King's name to ease their completion, but the sale of timber was overseen by the duke's officers and the profits paid to his executors.[138] After Buckingham's assassination, Charles I honoured his father's intention to grant him the benefit of the improvement of Hatfield Chase by presenting the fee-farm rents to his son. Buckingham's brother, the earl of Anglesey, had a grant of the fee-farm of Blackmore in 1623. Sir James Fullerton, groom of the stool, was first lessee and steward of Gillingham Forest (whose disafforestation he oversaw) and finally its fee-farmer.[139] The driving force behind the disafforestation of Braydon was the earl of Berkshire who had been promised £15,000 out of the profits.[140] And some individuals sought the grant of forests to secure lands which they had traditionally controlled. When the report circulated in 1628 that the Forest of Delaware (Cheshire) would be disafforested, Lord Strange petitioned the King to be allowed to purchase it.[141]

If these individuals sought newly disafforested or drained lands, the reverse is probably true in other cases. Much of this land formed a highly unsatisfactory investment entered into only as a way of recovering money owed by the King. It has already been shown how King's Sedgemoor was sold in part to recover debts owing to the lately deceased viscount Bayning and the sale of Hatfield followed on the mortgage of the manor to Vermuyden.[142] When Braydon Forest in Wiltshire was disposed of in 1627 (unusually by lease) it went to Philip Jacobson and Edward Sewster for a fine of £21,000 (which included the purchase of game and woods and licence to erect an iron works), £10,000 of which was credited to Jacobson for debts owed to him.[143] In just the same way, Sir Thomas Roe petitioned in 1636 for a lease of 1,200 acres in the Eight Hundred Fen at a rent of 8d per acre, Roe bearing the costs of fencing and ditching, in recompense for a debt of £3,760.[144] But the clearest instance of a forest sold for the settlement of debt, and which illustrates how disadvantageous this could be, is that of the Forest of Galtres in Yorkshire which lay between York and Thirsk.

---

[138] *CSPD 1619–23*, p. 442; *CSPD 1625–49*, p. 187; E112/161/47, answer of George Danvers.
[139] Sharp, *In Contempt*, pp. 87, 92–3.
[140] University of London Library, MS 195, pt ii, esp. fols. 12r, 27v; SP16/69, fol. 3.
[141] SP16/91, no. 99.
[142] Ashton regarded the mortgage as little more than 'a form of indirect sale in which the purchaser made an advance payment of the purchase money before it was due' (*Crown and the Money Market*, p. 61), but I remain unconvinced that the Crown intended to dispose of Hatfield in mid-1628. [143] Sharp, *In Contempt*, p. 90.
[144] *CSPD 1635–6*, pp. 202–3.

The Crown's creditor in this case was Sir Allen Apsley, a client of Buckingham's who rose to be Lieutenant of the Tower and served as one of the surveyors of naval victuals in the wars of the mid-1620s.[145] Apsley's enthusiasm and efficiency in the office led him to borrow money for provisions on his own security; by 1629, the Crown owed him £100,000. In August 1629, Charles agreed to grant him lands to the value of £20,000 in settlement of debts and Apsley elected to take the Forest of Galtres.[146]

Galtres was one of the forests identified by the commissioners for retrenchment of 1626 as being worthy of improvement. The forest was surveyed during 1627 but negotiations with the commoners of adjoining townships for the compensation of their rights dragged on until a final decree of May 1634.[147] What is more, Apsley bought a diminishing resource; his contract was for the purchase of lands which together totalled 8,550 acres (out of a total forest acreage of 14,178 acres) but as claims for compensation came in, the Crown's share of the common was reduced by slightly over 1,000 acres. As the contract had promised that the Crown would refund 40s for every acre its share fell short of 8,550 acres, the cost was carried by the Crown itself.[148]

It was Apsley's choice to have the grant of the forest made out to Peter Lenarts, Thomas Austen and John Daling, to whom Apsley owed £15,000. It appears he intended to redeem the forest but he died in May 1630 leaving his creditors in involuntary possession of a large tract of unimproved north-country real estate. Moreover, in February 1632, the Court of the Exchequer was petitioned by two more of Apsley's creditors who sought to be relieved out of the forest. The court held that the forest should be sold and after the satisfaction of the debt owing to Lenarts, Austen and Daling the surplus was to be distributed amongst Apsley's other creditors.[149] In fact, the patentees found themselves unable to sell the forest and it remained in their hands until 1636.[150] But to our considerable advantage the court required the patentees to bring into court for audit their accounts for

---

[145] See his brief biography in *DNB*.

[146] Ashton, *Crown and the Money Market*, pp. 165–6, gives his debts as £41,000, but the contract with the King shows that this was only part of a larger whole. *CSPD 1628–9*, p. 139; C54/2767, no. 4; C54/2816, no. 18.

[147] LR1/201, fols. 64r–5r (survey of timber, 1627); E125/9, fols. 151r–8r (19 Nov. 1630); E126/4, fols. 155v–8v.   [148] C54/2816, no. 18; SP16/317, no. 93 (i).

[149] For the patent, see the copy in LR1/201, fol. 445. The patentees' title and the other litigation is conveniently summarised in SP16/317, no. 93 (ii).

[150] *CSPD 1641–3*, pp. 33–4.

the forest over the five and a half years since their purchase in September 1629.[151] The patentees acknowledged receipts of £1,570 3s 10d, but claimed disbursements totalling £2,407 10s 2d including £240 to the Crown in fee-farm rent and £1,217 2s 7d in legal and surveying fees. Not only had income fallen short of expenditure, the patentees also wished to be credited for accumulated interest on the principal lent totalling a little under £5,000. It needs to be conceded that no receipts were shown for 1630 and only small sums for leases of grazing in 1631–2 (£39 2s 4d), a rather larger sum in 1633 (£231 13s 1d) and considerably more in 1634 (£993 8s 8d). No money at all had been received for fines on leases but even an income of £1,000 per annum would barely have serviced Apsley's debts.

It may be that Galtres was mismanaged and others would have made more of the forest's resources; but this is perhaps unfair. The newly disafforested land was subject to disturbances by the former commoners as late as 1633. Four years later, the then owners petitioned for permission to establish a community of French tenants (with their own church) because the locals would not pay rent for that which they had until recently possessed in common.[152] The evident hostility the patentees faced was felt elsewhere. Sir James Fullerton lost heavily on the Forest of Gillingham if only because of the burden of legal costs incurred in defending his title against the commoners and in the expense of rebuilding the fences they cast down. The lessee of Braydon, Philip Jacobson, suffered a major riot in May 1631 and repeated attacks on his fences. He finally secured damages in Star Chamber but by 1636 his rent was four years in arrears and it may be doubted whether he drew much profit from the forest in these years.[153] It is hard to see that Vermuyden – whose personal finances are largely mysterious – ever made a profit out of his enterprises (or received any income at all from King's Sedgemoor). Sir Robert Heath at Malvern appears to have found it difficult to either sell or lease the disafforested lands of the chase and in 1637 sold his interests to clear debts.[154] In general, the acquisition of newly improved waste was not an easy way to make money and perhaps a certain way to lose it.

---

[151] The audited accounts are LR9/13/358. SP16/202, no. 30, is the auditor's report on the accounts.   [152] SP16/178, no. 17 (ii); *CSPD 1637*, pp. 195–6.
[153] Sharp, *In Contempt*, ch. 4, *passim*.
[154] Smith, *Malvern*, pp. 154–5; P. E. Kopperman, *Sir Robert Heath, 1575–1649. Window on an Age* (Royal Historical Soc. Studies in History, 56, Woodbridge, 1989), pp. 274–5.

In the first two decades of the century, a degree of idealism was attached to the improvement of forests and wastes. Of course, the stimulus was in large measure that of improving the royal finances; but this was just one of several arguments which might be deployed in favour of disafforestation and drainage. The enclosure and renting of wastes, by offering tenancies to the landless, civilising the rootless and improving the nation's food supply, served the greater good of the Commonwealth. The moves to disafforest King's Sedgemoor in 1618 were perhaps the last occasion on which such arguments were deployed; a decade later, they would have appeared wholly threadbare. The improvement of royal wastes was transmuted from a public good to a private gain. One might see 1627 as the year in which improvement became the means of raising capital by making unsaleable assets saleable through abolishing forest law, clearing away the deer and compensating common rights with the creation of allotments in severalty. Where the Crown had possessed the freehold of the soil of a forest or chase (which had been little short of a legal fiction), it now possessed the most tangible commodity. In the years which followed, it even ceased to be a projector in its own right and came to sell to private men the right to exhume its interest for individual profit.

Can this be viewed as evidence of a new approach to the estates, a more entrepreneurial style of management? The haste to sell meant that the Crown itself could barely be called an entrepreneur if such a person is one who takes risk. But even in the more leisured age of James I, the Crown was never an investor, merely a facilitator, licensing an alteration in land use which others could exploit at their own risk. Overall, the Crown's disafforestation and drainage ought to be seen in the tradition of concealment hunting, as a cynical manipulation of the law, a squeezing of a last advantage from a residue of unprofitable assets and jurisdictions rather than evidence of some new spirit afoot in the Exchequer. It was, finally, a form of sale in which all whom it touched, Crown, purchaser and commoners, were losers.

CHAPTER 13

From swanimote to disafforestation: Feckenham Forest in the early seventeenth century

Peter Large

The neglect of the Crown lands as a source of improved revenue in the second half of the sixteenth century was nowhere more in evidence than in the desultory administration of the royal forests. In the early seventeenth century, as the Crown sought to restore the value of its landed revenue, many commentators and projectors argued for the improvement of the royal forests. These proposed improvements were wide-ranging and the most frequently advocated schemes were the leasing of Crown coppices, the discovery of assarts, the systematic sale of timber and the disafforestation of distant forests.[1]

Despite the many possible sources of revenue identified by contemporaries, the nature of the forests and their administration rendered the improvement of revenue a complex and often frustrating enterprise. The forests were not merely areas of woodland and waste inhabited by royal game. They were tracts of land subject to forest law, embracing coppices, villages and agricultural land, and the Crown was only one of numerous landowners. Moreover, the progressive weakening of the Crown's administrative hold during the sixteenth century had effectively handed over the control of many royal forests to their inhabitants.[2]

During the first decade of the seventeenth century, the Crown began to reassert a proprietorial interest in the forests. For the Crown, the forests were both game reserves and a potentially valuable source of timber and coppice wood. The dual nature of the forests made it difficult for the Crown to follow a consistent and thorough

---

[1] G. R. Batho, 'Landlords in England: the crown', in *Agrarian History* IV, pp. 271–2; Pettit, *Royal Forests*, pp. 50–95; G. Hammersley, 'The crown woods and their exploitation in the sixteenth and seventeenth centuries', *BIHR* 30 (1957), pp. 144–6.

[2] Pettit, *Royal Forests*, pp. 40–67; G. Hammersley, 'The revival of forest laws under Charles I', *History* 45 (1960), pp. 86–7.

financial strategy. Both Dorset and Salisbury, as successive Lord Treasurers, and Sir Julius Caesar, as Chancellor of the Exchequer, were assiduous in their search for schemes to raise revenue from the forests.[3] But James I placed a high value on the royal forests as hunting grounds and he was only prepared to exploit the financial potential of the forests provided the game was preserved. In 1604, he rejected the sale or disafforestation of any forest as a method of raising revenue and similarly in 1609, disafforestation was deleted from Sir Julius Caesar's list of New Projects of Gain.[4]

Between 1604 and 1622, various attempts were made to improve revenue and exploit the forests and woodland whilst protecting the game. In 1604, a commission was appointed under the aegis of Otto Nicholson to compound with occupiers of assart lands.[5] Most assarts were of medieval origin and by the late sixteenth century many had been concealed; the rent receipts from the remainder were paltry. Through surveys and by local inquisition, a vast number of assarts were revealed and between 1604 and its termination in 1616, the Commission of Assarts raised in excess of £38,500 in fines.[6]

The discovery of assarts was at least a modest success in raising revenue, particularly in the early years of the commission. But the major potential revenue source was the direct sale of surplus wood and timber and the leasing of Crown coppices. In 1606 and 1607, a number of schemes for increasing revenue from Crown woodlands were considered. A national farm of the Crown woods was given serious consideration by Dorset, but rejected as detrimental to the game, whilst a proposal favoured by Salisbury for the survey and sale of all coppice woods and decaying trees was adopted only in part.[7] Surveys were conducted, but in order to protect the forest and game preserves, the national sale of timber trees in 1608 and 1609 was confined to decaying trees.[8] Similarly, in March 1617, a commission was issued to Sir Giles Mompesson for the sale of dotard and decaying timber trees in nine counties.[9]

James's insistence on retaining the forests as preserves for game under the forest laws and absence of a local administration in the forests on which the Crown could rely limited the scope for any improvement. Despite the determination of successive Lord

[3] Pettit, *Royal Forests*, pp. 54–82.
[4] *CSPD Add. 1580–1625*, p. 440; BL, Add. MS 10038, fol. 19.
[5] BL, Add. MS 36767, fol. 46.　　　　　[6] Pettit, *Royal Forests*, pp. 71–82.
[7] *Ibid.*, pp. 57–61; Hammersley, 'Crown woods', pp. 143–4.
[8] BL, Add. MS 38444, fol. 19.　　　　　[9] *APC 1616–17*, p. 137; Pettit, *Royal Forests*, p. 62.

Treasurers and the deployment of officers from the Exchequer, the forests remained a modest source of revenue in the first two decades of the seventeenth century. Against this background, disafforestation was increasingly advocated by both projectors and propagandists.

Disafforestation was the most radical solution to the problem of inadequate revenue from the royal forests. It constituted the freeing of land from forest law, the division of common land amongst those who held rights of common pasture in the forest and ultimately the enclosure and 'improvement' of the land. Between 1609 and 1612, a number of proposals were put before Sir Julius Caesar, but few contemporaries recognised the difficulties inherent in this comprehensive realignment of property rights. Most projectors characterised the forests as unproductive and desolate wastes. It was asserted that the disafforestation of remote forests, which had already decayed in timber and game, would augment Crown revenue and benefit the Commonwealth. The Crown would save the costs of administration and the forests, once converted to agricultural land, would accommodate the country's surplus population and increase corn production, so reducing the 'multiplicity of beggars'.[10] John Norden, the renowned surveyor, was particularly critical of the state of royal forests and described them as a diseased part of the Commonwealth, or:

desert forests... wherein infinite poor yet most idle inhabitants have thrust themselves, living covertly, without law or religion, *rudes et refractarii* by nature, among whom are nourished and bred infinite idle fry, that coming ripe grow vagabonds and infect the Commonwealth with most dangerous leprosies.[11]

Against a background of widespread and strident support for disafforestation, the Privy Council and Exchequer appear to have given increasing consideration to schemes which applied to the more remote and less well-preserved forests. In 1612, the Crown surveyors were instructed by Salisbury to view the royal forests and make recommendations for disafforestation. A strong case was made for disafforesting a number of distant forests including Feckenham in Worcestershire. Lying about 100 miles from London and remote from any royal house, the Forest of Feckenham was poorly situated

[10] BL, Add. MS 38444, fols. 7–9; J. Norden, 'Touching the Improvement of Parks, Forests and Chases' (1612), reprinted in St John, *Observations*, App. ii; Pettit, *Royal Forests*, pp. 67–9.
[11] St John, *Observations*, App., p. 3.

for hunting. Few deer could be found in the 2,000 acres of Berrow wood and Warkwood walks because they were forced to stray outside the heart of the forest by the 'great flock of sheep' kept by the inhabitants who claimed common without stint throughout all the forest walks. On the other hand, the soil and woodland owned by the Crown were considered valuable; Warkwood in particular had good timber trees. Thus the disafforestation of Feckenham, followed by enclosure and more systematic arboriculture, made good economic sense to the surveyors.[12]

This early enthusiasm for disafforestation was not followed through until the later years of the decade. It was not until 1622 that Cranfield was commissioned to survey and disafforest Feckenham among other forests.[13] In the event, Feckenham was one of several forests disafforested in the early years of Charles I. It represents, through its protracted and bitter process of disafforestation between 1627 and 1632, a good example of a difficult and often compromising method of improving Crown revenues in early Stuart England.

This chapter examines the background and process of disafforestation in Feckenham. It describes the operation of forest law in the early seventeenth century; its close association with the local manorial administration and the agrarian society it supported. Against this background, it examines the forces of change in the forest and finally the process of disafforestation, culminating in the litigation and rioting which was a feature of most of the early seventeenth-century attempts to replace the forest regime.

I

The medieval system of forest law was intended to reconcile the interests of the Crown and the commoners within the royal forests. From the Crown's point of view, the essence of forest law was the protection of *vert* and *venison*.[14] The deer required extensive feeding grounds and the covert of the forest was essential as a source of shelter and food. The destruction of covert by conversion to agricultural land, unlicensed encroachments by enclosure or building, and

---

[12] LR2/194, p. 19.

[13] SP14/70, no. 44; SP14/87, no. 75; SP14/123, no. 79; SP14/141, no. 359.

[14] *Vert* consists of the trees, underwood, bracken and grass of the forest. *Venison* was a collective term for all the beasts of the forest but by the sixteenth century it was applied exclusively to red and fallow deer. J. Manwood, *A Treatise of the Lawes of the Forest* (3rd edn, London, 1665), pp. 110–28.

unauthorised cutting of wood were all offences against vert. In the nomenclature of medieval forest law these infringements were 'assarts', 'perprestures' and 'wastes'. Such offences against vert could be committed anywhere within the bounds of the forest and even privately owned woods and coppices could not be cut without licence.[15] Legally, the deer were allowed to feed anywhere in the forests and each summer 'preserved grounds' were designated during 'fence month' to protect the deer when they fawned.[16] The inhabitants of 'ancient' houses and cottages in forest villages had common rights in recompense for the restrictions applied to vert and the privileges of the deer throughout the forest. Inhabitants could claim common-of-pasture in the forest wastes during summer for as many cows, bullocks and horses as they could maintain *levant* and *couchant* on their own lands in winter. The foresters also had rights of agistment and pannage; formal and controlled pasturage for cattle and pigs in the woodland.[17] In theory, the forest laws maintained a delicate balance of rights and restrictions for both the Crown and the inhabitants within the royal forests.

Until the early fifteenth century, forest law was administered through the local forest courts. A swanimote assembly was held three times a year to make arrangements for agistment, pannage and the fawning of deer. All offences against vert and venison were presented at the court of attachment held by four verderers every forty days. This court had jurisdiction over minor offences against vert, whilst larger infringements and all trespasses against venison were enrolled and heard in the court of the Chief Justice in Eyre. The verderers, who acted as judges in the court of attachment, were knights or esquires with substantial lands in or around the forest. A further twelve knights were sworn as regarders and they made a triennial search or 'regard' for infringements which were presented at the Eyre.[18] The execution of forest law depended upon the regular holding of an Eyre or 'Justice Seat' because legal proceedings against all but the most trivial offenders had to come before the Chief Justice. During the fourteenth century, the Justice in Eyre actively supervised

---

[15] *Ibid.*, pp. 136–80; G. J. Turner (ed.), *Select Pleas of the Forest* (Selden Soc., 13, 1901) pp. lix–lxii; Pettit, *Royal Forests*, pp. 37–9.

[16] Manwood, *Lawes of the Forest*, pp. 203–16.

[17] *Ibid.*, pp. 216–34; Pettit, *Royal Forests*, pp. 152–4.

[18] Manwood, *Lawes of the Forest*, pp. 400–526; W. S. Holdsworth, *A History of English Law* (16 vols., 1903–64), I (7th edn, 1956), pp. 95–101; Turner (ed.), *Select Pleas of the Forest*, pp. xxvii–lix, lxxv–lxxxvii.

the lower courts and punished offenders. However, from the early fifteenth century, the Eyres were seldom held and when Manwood wrote his treatise in 1598 he observed that the forest laws had 'grown into contempt with many inhabitants in Forests'.[19] Manwood pointed to the decline of the Eyre as the main cause of the decay of forest law, for 'if that Justices of the Forest would duly hold their Justice Seats...then the laws of the Forest would be better known, and also more regarded than they are now at this day'.[20]

An ebb in the Crown's interest in the forests as hunting grounds during the fifteenth century was largely responsible for the reduction in the incidence of Forest Eyres. The consequence of this failure to enforce the medieval forest laws was an increase in the scope of common rights. The entitlement to a restricted agistment in the Crown woods was replaced by a claim to common-of-pasture throughout the forest. This extended not only to the waste, but also to coppices which were thrown open after seven years of enclosure.[21] The case of Feckenham clearly shows that the ban on sheep pasturing was also ignored and Sir Edward Coke argued that forest inhabitants generally had the right to common their sheep within the forests by prescription.[22] The local forest courts were adapted by the inhabitants to regulate these more generous common rights. The disuse of the Justice Seat lead to a change of emphasis rather than a collapse of forest law. As the upper regions of the judicial system of the forest decayed, the swanimote extended its powers.

The swanimote of the sixteenth century differed markedly from the non-judicial meeting of the forest officers which made arrangements for pannage, agistment and fawning. From at least the late fifteenth century, the Feckenham swanimotes had developed into properly constituted forest courts.[23] Their jurisdiction emerged from a fusion of the swanimote assemblies, courts of attachment and regards which

---

[19] Holdsworth, *History of English Law*, I, pp. 101–5; Manwood, *Lawes of the Forest*, p. 71.

[20] Manwood, *Lawes of the Forest*, pp. 161–2.

[21] Pettit, *Royal Forests*, p. 153; W. Gould, *Letter to the Commoners in Rockingham Forrest* (Stamford, 1744), pp. 2–17.

[22] Sir Edward Coke, *The Fourth Part of the Institutes of the Laws of England* (London, 1644), p. 298. Extensive rights of common for cattle, horses and sheep were claimed in the Forest of Dean; C. E. Hart, *The Commoners of Dean Forest* (Gloucester, 1951), pp. 20–2.

[23] R. H. Hilton (ed.), 'The Swanimote Rolls of Feckenham Forest', *Miscellany* I (Worcestershire Historical Soc., n.s., I, 1960), pp. 37–40. The swanimote had a similar function in the Northamptonshire forests during the sixteenth century and in Windsor Forest during the late seventeenth and early eighteenth centuries. Pettit, *Royal Forests*, pp. 24–6; E. P. Thompson, *Whigs and Hunters. The Origin of the Black Act* (London, 1975) pp. 36–47.

were held in the forests of early fourteenth-century England.[24] The swanimote court retained one of the ministerial functions of the medieval assembly: the organisation of pannage. In its judicial capacity, the swanimote resembled the court of attachment in so far as the jurisdiction did not extend to amercing offenders against venison. But the new court functioned with a jury of twelve regarders drawn from the more substantial forest inhabitants. It had a much wider jurisdiction than the earlier courts of attachment and imposed heavier penalties than those placed on minor offenders against vert.[25] During the late fifteenth and early sixteenth centuries, the forest officers presented encroachments on forest land, unlicensed building, timber felling, overstocking of commons and the keeping of sheep in 'preserved grounds' during 'fence month'.[26] The introduction of a composition fine gave the Feckenham swanimote an authority previously only possessed by the Justice Seat, but the priorities of the regarders differed considerably from those of the Chief Justice. The regarders defended common grazing land against private appropriation, but asserted the right of the inhabitants to cut turf and 'surcharge' the forest wastes at the expense of the deer. In the late fifteenth century, the jurisdiction of the swanimote was extended further by the issue of by-laws. In this way, the court acquired the power to instruct landholders to pull down enclosures and mend hedges under the threat of heavy fines.[27]

In the issuing of by-laws and ordinances the swanimote resembled a manorial court, and it seems that the close association of the manor of Feckenham with the forest contributed to the development of the Feckenham swanimote. The forest was centred on the royal demesne manors of Feckenham and Hanbury and from the late thirteenth century, when the forest was reduced to 34 square miles, its jurisdiction was essentially confined to the manors of Feckenham and Hanbury. At most, the forest extended 5 or 6 miles from its headquarters at Feckenham.[28] From the early sixteenth century, the

---

[24] It seems rather inappropriate that this important local court should have adopted the name of the least powerful medieval assembly. This stemmed from a confusion of terminology. The General Inquisitions sanctioned by the *Ordinatio Forestae* of 1306 to enquire into all offences against vert and venison were known as swanimotes. In fact these medieval inquisitions and the swanimote courts of the sixteenth century were entirely different in their concerns and the swanimote had no jurisdiction over venison. However, even Manwood confused the original swanimote assemblies and the inquisitions. Manwood, *Lawes of the Forest*, pp. 461–85.

[25] E178/4781. [26] Hilton (ed.), 'Swanimote Rolls', pp. 39–40.

[27] *Ibid.*, p. 38. [28] *Ibid.*, p. 36.

business of the manor court and the swanimote increasingly
overlapped, and by 1591, the forest and manorial administration in
Feckenham had merged into a single body. The lord of the manors of
Feckenham and Hanbury was also the Master of the King's Game
within the forest whilst the manorial bailiff and woodwards also
served as the keepers within the forest walks. This was reflected in the
system of perquisites in the forest; according to 'ancient custom', the
bailiffs and woodwards of the manors of Feckenham and Hanbury
had a right to all the dead trees, 'windfall woods' and browsewood in
the forest.[29] Moreover, the swanimote assumed some of the functions
of a manorial court for the forest. It allowed claims for wood and
timber, stinted the forest for all animals and punished trespassers.

During the sixteenth century, the swanimote increasingly adopted
a more liberal attitude towards common rights and it presided over
a controlled surcharging of the forest commons. With the decline of
the Eyre and the absence of central control, the object of the forest
laws gradually changed. Farmers and cottagers were allowed to
assart the forest covert, and in the manor of Feckenham alone there
were 732 acres of assarts around Warkwood and Berrow wood by
1591.[30] By this time, immigration and perprestures were only
partially controlled and pannage regulations were abandoned. The
court only acted to prevent the deliberate spoiling of the trees,
destructive squatting and flagrant overstocking.[31] In this way, the
swanimote came to regulate the extension and exploitation of
traditional forest privileges. By the late sixteenth century, the
regarders who controlled presentments and punishments in the
swanimote were no longer knights and gentlemen, but local yeomen
intimately involved in the agrarian economy of the forest.[32] Thus, a
body of forest law which had been designed primarily to protect royal
privilege had been transformed to safeguard the interests of the

---

[29] E134, 15 Jac. I, Easter 3; Society of Antiquaries, London, Prattinton Coll., vol. xiv, survey
of the manor of Feckenham, 1591, pp. 91–2.

[30] BL, M.T.b.1. (12), a copy made in 1744 of a plan of the manor of Feckenham of 1591,
reproduced in Hilton (ed.), 'Swanimote Rolls', plate opp. p. 38. The acreage of assarts is
marked in red letters on the map.

[31] According to John Elvins, one of the most knowledgeable inhabitants of the forest, the
suppression of the swanimote during the early seventeenth century 'bred great spoils and
waste'. E178/4781. Likewise in Windsor Forest during the early eighteenth century, the 'ill
state and condition of the forest' was attributed to the disuse of the swanimote. Thompson,
Whigs and Hunters, pp. 40–4.

[32] E178/4781; E134, 6 Chas. I, Easter 18. Similarly in Windsor Forest the regarders
manipulated proceedings at the swanimote to reflect their conception of common rights,
Thompson, *Whigs and Hunters*, p. 47.

commoners and had lost its penal element. Those who lived under the forest law regarded it as beneficial and it was the Crown that found it restrictive. Whilst the forests were maintained as open commons or coppices over which common rights could be exercised, the Crown was precluded from a more rational arboriculture.

By the late sixteenth century, the merger of forest courts with the swanimote and the transformation of forest law seems to have occurred generally and in the more distant forests in particular; this was accompanied by a fundamental change in the operations of forest law.[33] The forests of Northamptonshire and the Forests of Braydon, Dean and Gillingham, like Feckenham, had been abandoned to their inhabitants.[34] These changes facilitated a significant expansion in the population of English forests between the 1570s and 1610s. Rapid population growth and, in some cases, enclosure in the Fielden areas caused many labourers and poor husbandmen to migrate in the hope of securing a livelihood in the royal forests and other unappropriated wastes. In Northamptonshire, the forests attracted immigrants from the open-field villages where common pasture was scarce and husbandmen evicted from enclosed villages.[35] In the north, the Forests of Galtres and Rossendale witnessed considerable expansion, whilst the West Midlands attracted migrants from the populous Fielden parishes in the east and from Wales. In 1615, John Norden commented on the 'very many cottages' built within the Forests of Dean and Kingswood which exceeded the needs of iron smelting and coal mining.[36] Even the disafforested Forest of Arden, which was already short of waste land, attracted settlers in the late 1600s and early 1610s, possibly from the area affected by the Midland Revolt of 1607.[37] Immigration was also important, but much more modest, in Feckenham Forest during the late sixteenth century and it is estimated that between 1563 and 1591 the population of the manor of Feckenham alone rose from about 510 to 840 inhabitants.[38]

[33] Hammersley, 'Revival of forest laws', pp. 86–7; *idem*, 'Crown woods', pp. 144–5.
[34] Pettit, *Royal Forests*, pp. 24–6; Hart, *Commoners of Dean Forest*, pp. 20–2; F. H. Manley, 'The disafforesting of Braydon', *Wiltshire Archaeological and Natural History Magazine* 45 (1930–2), pp. 552–6.   [35] Pettit, *Royal Forests*, pp. 24–6.
[36] A. Everitt, 'Farm labourers', in *Agrarian History*, IV, pp. 409–11; G. H. Tupling, *The Economic History of Rossendale* (Chetham Soc., n.s., 86, 1927), pp. 95–7; D. G. Hey, *An English Rural Community. Myddle under the Tudors and Stuarts* (Leicester, 1974), pp. 172–6; J. Thirsk, 'The farming regions of England', in *Agrarian History*, IV, pp. 37–8, 71, 95–6, 109–10.
[37] V. Skipp, *Crisis and Development. An Ecological case study of the Forest of Arden, 1570–1674* (Cambridge, 1978), pp. 17, 41–2, 99.
[38] BL, Harl. MS 595, fol. 210; Society of Antiquaries, Prattinton Coll., vol. xiv, p. 86.

In most forests, these waves of immigration led to the formation of
new forest communities in the form of scattered hamlets inhabited
by husbandmen and labourers. Such hamlets were a familiar sight
in the Forest of Dean and in the Staffordshire Forests of Kinver
and Needwood, but by contrast in Feckenham, the outlying and
expanding hamlets of Bearhall, Berrow, Home, Callow Hill, Hunt
End and Astwood all had resident gentry.[39] In Callow Hill, the
largest and most remote township, lived Joshua Hanbury, gent., and
Edward Morgan, esq., whilst John Millard, gent., resided in the
hamlet of Berrow on the edge of Berrow wood.[40] New settlers in
Feckenham were absorbed within the existing townships and the
swanimote prohibited unregulated cottage building within the
woods. However, on the northern edge of the forest, in the purlieus,
squatters' settlements did spring up. On Webheath and Bentley
common, in a remote corner of Tardebigge which bordered on the
forest commons, transient hamlets arose by attracting those who had
no right to common but looked towards the forest for a living. Such
were Thomas and Valentine Harrison who kept a 'peltering' ale-
house at Nether Bentley and maintained 'many disorderly persons'.
They were known to be 'great destroyers' of the deer and they
regularly stole horses, rode them to London and sold them in
Smithfield. Ultimately, Valentine was apprehended early one
summer morning in 1605 'trimming and marking' a horse in the
forest.[41] Other squatters were also a source of considerable crime
within the forest and they were involved in stealing sheep and poultry
as well as horses, and violating the Crown coppices.[42]

These squatters in the purlieus were quite distinct from the
immigrants who settled within the established townships and paid
small rents for their cottages. Those who settled within the forest were
integrated into the economy and society primarily through their
acknowledged right to common pasture. In Feckenham, according to
the survey of 1591, 'all the inhabitants' had common for cattle and
sheep throughout the year within 'divers great wastes, commons and
wood grounds' as well as in 'divers coppices & grounds with young

---

[39] Everitt, 'Farm labourers', ppl 410–12; J. Thirsk, 'Horn and thorn in Staffordshire: the
economy of a pastoral county', in J. Thirsk (ed.), *The Rural Economy of England. Collected
Essays* (London, 1984), pp. 165–8.

[40] Society of Antiquaries, Prattinton Coll., vol. xiv, p. 100.

[41] J. W. Willis Bund (ed.), *Worcester County Records. Calendar of the Quarter Sessions Papers of
Worcestershire, 1591–1643* (2 vols., Worcestershire Historical Soc., 1899, 1900), II, p. 78.

[42] *Ibid.*, pp. 219, 222, 289.

woods'.[43] This extensive common was a vital factor in the economic standing of the cottagers. It gave all a degree of economic independence and some the opportunity of becoming cottage farmers indistinguishable from the local husbandmen. But above all, through these common rights the cottagers held a close affinity with the rest of the farming population, since both found the forest invaluable as a source of grazing for sheep, cattle and horses. Close links were also forged by the process of assarting which was carried out at all levels of forest society. Assarts, like common rights, were recognised by the manorial court and many were granted by copy at small rents even though they had been made 'within the memory of man'.[44] In this way, the latitude of the swanimote towards common rights and assarts was vested with further authority through the manorial court.

At the turn of the sixteenth century, the Forest of Feckenham was administered by and for its inhabitants. The forest law of medieval England had been reshaped to the benefit of the local community. It was still capable of restricting the mass immigration of landless labourers which characterised certain forests, but it did little to protect the Crown's interests. The forest was exploited by its inhabitants through assarts and unstinted common rights throughout the forest walks, yet the timber and coppice woods were relatively well preserved. This was controlled exploitation by a farming population regulating the forest through the intertwined administration of the manorial and swanimote courts. In 1612, this regime was well observed by the Crown surveyor who found few deer but many sheep in Feckenham Forest.[45]

II

By 1612, however, the forest regime was already being threatened by the Crown's search for improved revenues. Feckenham had participated in both major Crown initiatives to raise revenue. The Commission for Assarts raised £821 from fines paid by the occupiers of 960 acres of assart lands in the forest whilst in 1609 the Crown woodsale included some 1,600 trees from Feckenham worth £1,100.[46] The fines for assarts, in particular, had financial implications for

[43] Society of Antiquaries, Prattinton Coll., vol. xiv, pp. 89–91.   [44] *Ibid.*, p. 105.
[45] LR2/194, p. 19.   [46] Pettit, *Royal Forests*, p. 80; E134, 15 Jac. I, Easter 3.

inhabitants in Feckenham and increased the pressures which were building up in the forest in the early years of the seventeenth century.

Sir Thomas Leighton, lord of the manor of Hanbury and Feckenham and Master of the King's Game was obliged to compound for coppices, lands and other assart lands granted to him by Elizabeth I. In 1604, the increasingly indebted Leighton was party to an attempt to thwart the Commission for Assarts by an act of Parliament. A bill to confirm assarts as private property almost reached a second reading when Henry Haynes, one of Leighton's servants, bribed the Speaker's servant for the purpose.[47] The composition fines left Leighton heavily indebted and he attempted to restore his financial position by exploiting his authority within the forest.[48]

As Master of the King's Game, Leighton could influence both the judicial and executive arms of forest government. It was his right to convene the swanimote court and to appoint the forest ranger, who, through six keepers, administered the four walks of the forest, for the protection of the game.[49] The ranger had considerable influence because technically he could subordinate the whole forest to the needs of the game. He controlled the granting of licences to cut timber on privately owned land within the forest and determined which parts of the Crown woods were to be enclosed as preserved grounds. The keepers enforced the ranger's regulations by impounding sheep and cattle and by reporting other infringements.[50] From 1585 until 1610 Humphrey Jennetts, a leading inhabitant of Feckenham, held the post of ranger. Jennetts accepted the swanimote's regulation of common pasture and adopted a lenient policy towards the 'surcharging' of the forest common by the inhabitants.[51] In 1591, he held 179 acres of land assarted from Warkwood and his administration represented the controlled exploitation of the forest writ large.[52]

In 1610, however, Leighton appointed one William Connard in place of Humphrey Jennetts and from this moment he suppressed the swanimote court and began exploiting the forest administration for his own gain. Henceforward, 'power and authority' within the forest was in the hands of the ranger and keepers.[53] Unlike Humphrey Jennetts, Connard was not one of the leading forest inhabitants but

[47] *CJ*, I, p. 197.   [48] E112/133/210.   [49] STAC8/25/9.
[50] C2 Jac. I/O6/68; E134, 15 Jac. I, Easter 3; STAC8/25/9.   [51] E178/4781.
[52] BL, M.T.b.1. (12); Society of Antiquities, Prattinton Coll., vol. xiv, pp. 103–4.
[53] E178/4781. This phrase was used frequently by the forest inhabitants to describe the position held by the ranger and keepers in the forest.

'a poor young man' from Droitwich. As well as the post of ranger, Connard also took on the less elevated job of bailiff of the manors of Feckenham and Hanbury.[54] His first act was to replace all six keepers within the forest walks. Men like Humphrey Smith, a Feckenham yeoman who was the keeper in Berrow wood walk for twenty years, and Edward Bunaker and John Turner, both Hanbury yeomen and keepers in the Cleeres walk were 'put out of office' by Connard. In their stead, men of lower standing and without any land in the forest were taken on.[55] Through Connard and his keepers, Leighton severed an important link between the forest administration and the farming and manorial inhabitants of Feckenham.

Under the guidance of Leighton, Connard began to enforce the ancient limits of sheep common within the forest more rigorously. But instead of presenting offenders at the swanimote, the keepers fined the owners of the sheep at the rate of 4d per score. Contemporaries estimated that there were approaching 4,000 sheep regularly grazed in the forest, so Connard had a significant financial motivation behind these moves. More serious offenders against vert were also presented by Leighton at the Quarter Sessions.[56] Thus the swanimote was by-passed, and its policy of controlled overstocking of the commons was reversed. The integrated forest society, based on extensive common rights, was threatened by the reimposition of an archaic element of forest law which cut across the manorial customs and the independent inclinations of the foresters.

The tension between the forest officers and the inhabitants was heightened by Connard's willingness to give the keepers considerable latitude in the execution of their duties. All keepers were accustomed to exploiting their perquisites of browsewood and windfallen trees to the full.[57] Under Connard, they had even more scope. For a fee, some keepers allowed outsiders, who had no right of common, to graze sheep in the forest at the same time as they were impounding the foresters' animals.[58] The protection of the forest from encroachment by outsiders had been one of the most important functions of the swanimote, but Connard's keepers did not share the inhabitants' proprietary attitude towards common within the forest.

The animosity of the inhabitants towards the ranger and keepers

---

[54] E134, 15 Jac. I, Easter 3; STAC8/25/9.   [55] E178/481; E134, 6 Chas. I, Easter 18.
[56] E134, 15 Jac. I, Easter 3.
[57] Pettit, *Royal Forests*, pp. 31–2; Society of Antiquities, Prattinton Coll., vol. xiv, p. 91.
[58] E134, 15 Jac. I, Easter 3.

was increased further by the enclosure of certain coppices in the
north-east of the forest around Warkwood. These coppices were
almost indistinguishable from the open woodland and thus the
regulated cutting of wood and enclosure to protect young growth in
the coppices was always a sensitive issue. More permanent enclosure
was regarded as an attack on the basis of the traditional forest
economy because the coppices accounted for a substantial proportion
of the common pasture. In the manor of Feckenham, the coppices
covered 457 acres representing some 27 per cent of the area over
which common rights could be exercised.[59] In 1610, however, Sir
Thomas Leighton resorted to felling certain coppices to augment his
income and he received £120 from the sale of wood from Brace
coppice in the Cleeres walk in Hanbury. This and other coppices
were subsequently enclosed, but instead of being protected so that the
'spring' could grow, they were mowed by the keepers and then
grazed by horses.[60]

The enclosure of coppices for private pasture reduced the common
within the forest. In the manor of Feckenham, at least 100 acres of
coppice common was lost and in 1613, a further 50 acres of woodland
was 'enrailed' for the use of Connard's friends. Like amercing
inhabitants for sheep grazing in the forest, the cutting and permanent
enclosure of coppices by Leighton was a financial expedient, but both
disturbed the economic balance of the forest and triggered opposition.
In March 1613, the foresters reacted to the restrictions and enclosure
by breaking into three coppices and depasturing their cattle in
them.[61] The timing of this action was probably in response to a
shortage of animal feed, since both the oat and barley harvests of the
summer of 1612 were deficient.[62] But it was also more deeply rooted
in the widely held belief that forest inhabitants had a right of
common throughout the forest and it was the prelude to a complex
series of lawsuits in which the forest population, both rich and poor,
joined in an effort to affirm the foresters' common.[63]

The opposition was led by William Cookes of Shiltwood and
intensified because of the long-standing enmity between the increasingly indebted Leightons and the improving Cookes. William Cookes
had enhanced his social standing and acquired considerable freehold

[59] BL, M.T.b.1. (12).   [60] E134, 15 Jac. I, Easter 3.   [61] Ibid.; STAC8/25/9.
[62] C. J. Harrison, 'Grain price analysis and harvest qualities, 1485–1634', Agricultural History
Review 19 (1971), pp. 150, 154.
[63] This term was generally used by the inhabitants of Feckenham Forest during the early
seventeenth century to describe the extensive rights of common practised within the forest.

interests in Feckenham through his marriage to Ann Jennetts, the daughter of Humphrey Jennetts. In consideration of the marriage, Jennetts conveyed Parkhill coppice in the manor of Feckenham to Cookes in 1589.[64] Jennetts gave William Cookes more of his Feckenham property in 1590, including his imposing house called Nargrove and its extensive freehold lands.[65] By 1610, William Cookes had become one of the most important landholders in the forest. He was in almost constant dispute with Leighton even before the latter began to disrupt the forest regime. In 1602, Leighton challenged Cookes's right to hold Parkhill coppice as copyhold and claimed it as an assart from the forest. In fact, it was an assart held by copy, and after a long lawsuit Cookes was obliged to compound with Leighton to secure the customary fee of the land.[66] In May 1606, Cookes was forced to compound yet again when Henry Haynes, one of Leighton's servants, claimed, before the jury impanelled to discover assart land in the forest, that the coppice was an assart of the Crown's woods.[67] In 1612, Cookes also became locked in a long and bitter dispute with Connard over the payment of the heriots for the coppices.[68] An intense feud between Cookes and Connard continued into the early 1620s.[69]

In October 1613, when William Cookes began to organise lawsuits to protect the common rights of the foresters, he also took the opportunity to settle old scores. Cookes found it easy to whip up support amongst the farmers and cottagers for a number of suits against the forest officers. Connard and three keepers were indicted at the Quarter Sessions for waste, on the evidence of William Steward who had been recently fined by Connard for killing deer. This indictment was followed by an action on the case for the diminution of common and by a series of warrants and writs for good behaviour taken out against the ranger and the keepers. These writs obliged two of the keepers to appear in London where they were arrested on various spurious charges of trespass and theft. All these causes and writs were solicited by William Cookes's brother Edward and financed by a 'general collection and common purse', held by

---

[64] C2 Jac. I/C9/24.   [65] E112/133/220.
[66] BL, M.T.b.1. (12); Society of Antiquaries, Prattinton Coll., vol. xiv, p. 39.
[67] C2 Jac. I/C9/24.   [68] E112/133/220.
[69] C2 Jac. I/D6/68. In 1615, Cookes was unable to approach the ranger directly for a licence to cut timber on his own land. A contemporary noted that Connard 'could do much in the granting of the said licence and would have done all the injury he could either for hindering the cutting of the said wood or anything else that lay in his power'.

William Cookes and Mr Vernon, the parson of Hanbury. Between 1613 and 1616, three collections were made amongst most of the foresters for actions against the 'enraylment' of coppices and the erection of the keepers' lodge and for the protection of the foresters' common. Cookes and his supporters prosecuted their cause to the full and some of them implied that they would not be willing to terminate the suits even if the immediate grievances over common land had been settled.[70]

In November 1617, the Attorney-General, who had been drawn into the disputes to represent both the forest officers in Star Chamber and the commoners in Exchequer, decided that the Crown could gain nothing by prosecution.[71] The dispute had been confused by the personal feud between Connard and Cookes, and the complaints about the keepers' zealous exploitation of their perquisites did not impress the Attorney-General. Keepers everywhere cut branches from trees and mowed coppices, and their activities were far more detrimental to the forest inhabitants than to the Crown. Furthermore, Connard had successfully limited the common of pasture within the forest, and even his most intransigent opponents, like John Turner of Hanbury, one of the keepers displaced by Connard, had to admit that Connard had increased the number of deer.[72]

Indeed, the tension was heightened still further by the introduction of more deer into the forest. Following Sir Thomas Leighton's death in 1613, the manorial and forest administration passed into the hands of several courtiers, including Sherrington Talbot, a local landowner, during the wardship of Edward Leighton. Presumably to ingratiate himself with James I, Talbot instructed Connard to augment the herd of deer in the forest by introducing deer from Feckenham Park and from Talbot's own park near Droitwich. Most of the deer had been driven out of the forest by the increasing number of sheep during the late sixteenth century, but now their extensive requirement for covert and feed again competed directly with the inhabitants' sheep and horses.[73]

Yet the failure of the Crown to intervene at this point and assert its authority in the forest proved to be most damaging to its interests. Since the prospect of disafforestation at Feckenham was raised and revived by the Crown on two occasions in the decade before 1628, there was almost an open invitation to its officers to abuse the forest.[74]

---

[70] E134/15 Jac. I, Easter 3; STAC8/25/9.   [71] E124/25, fol. 28v.
[72] E134, 15 Jac. I, Easter 3.   [73] E112/133/220; E134, 15 Jac. I, Easter 3.
[74] SP14/70, no. 44; SP14/87, no. 75; SP14/123, no. 79; SP14/141, no. 359.

With Edward Leighton installed as lord of the manors of Feckenham and Hanbury and as Master of the King's Game, Connard embarked on the destruction of the forest for their mutual gain. Part of this destruction was carried out under the commission issued in March 1617 for the sale of dotard and decaying timber trees which applied to Worcestershire amongst eight other counties. In Feckenham, however, this process went much further and continued longer at little profit to the Crown.[75]

From early 1617, Connard and Leighton systematically destroyed the wood and timber for their profit. By mutilating trees, more died and both Leighton and Connard were able to benefit from the subsequent felling. The Cleeres and Monkwood, two walks of the forest which constituted most of the waste of the manor of Hanbury, were ravaged. A Crown wood in the Cleeres called Benford Rough which covered about 40 acres of 'very ancient growth' was felled completely and sold by Connard to his brother-in-law. The Crown received a derisory 2s per tree and a substantial profit of at least £450 was shared by Connard and Leighton who sold the trees for an average of 10s each. In Warkwood walk between 1617 and 1624, numerous trees were lopped, 400 felled and four coppices cut down. Connard made use of some of this timber himself. In 1620, he built himself a lodge in Feckenham Park and in 1623 he 'inrailed' Feckenham pools for his dairy and constructed a wooden conduit to draw water to the ground. This destruction and tree felling continued unabated after 1617, and on Whitsuntide 1626, when John Hynd, a Crown surveyor, took 'a special note view and survey' of timber trees in the four walks of Feckenham Forest, he found nearly 3,000 trees 'headed, topped, lopped and dyvers girdled and cutt in ye middest'.[76]

Connard appointed more keepers to exercise his new policy. Once again, these were poor men drawn from outside the forest who were obliged to make their living by destroying woodland and game. Contemporaries described them as 'mean and shifting fellows living upon the waste and spoil of the King's woods'. Under Connard's direction, they converted parts of the forest waste and certain coppices into private pastures. Connard used the four coppices cut down in Warkwood for grazing and Benford Rough was enclosed and used as summer pasture for dairy cattle. The felling of trees and destruction of the spring of the coppices and woods also had disastrous

---

[75] Unless otherwise stated, the details of the destruction of woodland and game are taken from the extensive depositions taken by the Exchequer commissioners of enquiry on 30 April 1624 and 21 January 1627. E178/4781.   [76] E178/4781.

consequences for the deer. Benford Rough, for example, had consisted of oak, ash, maple, hazel and hawthorn and was considered 'the principal and best harbour for the deer' within the forest. As the covert was reduced, deer strayed into the purlieus and were destroyed. The keepers also seem to have been active in killing the deer and one Tardebigge glover admitted buying thirty dozen 'slaughter skins' from them. As a consequence of these actions, the deer population fell from about 1,200 to a mere 60 between 1617 and 1627.[77]

Whilst the keepers were devastating the forest, Connard persisted in his policy of restricting the foresters' common rights. Increasingly, sheep were impounded and fines extracted from their owners. Connard also assumed other aspects of the swanimote jurisdiction by limiting the building of houses, barns and cottages within the forest. On two occasions during the early 1620s, the forest inhabitants responded by throwing open the enclosures made by Connard in the Warkwood coppices. This destruction of enclosures was localised and directed at Connard. At this time, it proved to be the most effective form of retaliation because petitions to the Court of Exchequer received little attention as the probability of disafforestation increased. In 1625, for instance, the Attorney-General simply dropped the proceedings when Connard failed to appear in Exchequer to answer a bill of complaint.[78]

Between 1610 and 1627 the forest regime was persistently violated by the local forest administration. The usurpation of swanimote jurisdiction, the attempted enclosure of forest coppices and the interference with the established practice of foresters' common were an irritation but not a fundamental threat to the agrarian structure of the forest. Indeed, they were more damaging to the interests of the Crown than to those of the inhabitants. The Crown received nothing from the attempts to extract fines for sheep grazing and the barest return from the wanton destruction of woodlands. In the end, Leighton paid his composition fines for assarts, at least in part, by exploiting his position in the forest and destroying the Crown woodlands. The Crown's intermittent interest in the forest and its indecision over disafforestation allowed this exploitation to take place. Ultimately, the Crown had little financial alternative but to disafforest Feckenham.

---

[77] E134, 6 Chas. I, Easter 18.   [78] E124/34, fols. 321v, 346v; E124/36, fol. 48v.

III

In 1612, and again in 1616, the disafforestation of the forest was proposed and in 1622, Cranfield was commissioned to disafforest Feckenham. In April 1624, Exchequer commissioners began examining witnesses in Feckenham, but the commission was allowed to lapse and nothing further was done until 1626.[79] By this time, the cost of Buckingham's ambitious foreign policy combined with the opposition of the House of Commons to extra-parliamentary taxation necessitated large sales of Crown lands. Charles proved to be more willing than his father to contemplate the improvement of forests. During the late summer of 1626, a list of forests which could be dispensed with was drawn up and the commissioners for retrenchment began to put a policy of disafforestation into effect.[80] Sir Miles Fleetwood, the Receiver-General of the Court of Wards and Liveries, was commissioned in March 1627 to survey the forest, to establish its acreage and to whom it belonged. He was required to reconcile the claims of the Crown with those inhabitants who could 'justly claim' common rights in the forest. The fundamental problem was to decide how much of the forest woodland and waste should be ceded to the commoners in compensation for enclosure and the loss of common rights within the forest.[81] On the Crown's definition, these commoners included the manorial lords, freeholders, copyholders and the 'ancient' cottagers of the forest. It was necessary first of all to establish who had a genuine claim to common of pasture. Following the examination of witnesses in January 1628, a general meeting of all the inhabitants was held in April 1628 to begin the process of allotment.[82] Certain principal inhabitants in the three forest parishes of Hanbury, Feckenham and Bradley were chosen by Fleetwood as representatives of the commoners. Amongst the Feckenham and Hanbury representatives were Edward Leighton and William Connard.[83]

Whilst Fleetwood made an effort to recognise the many claims to common rights, it is clear that the Crown was especially generous to the manorial lords and quite arbitrary when considering the smaller claimants. In June 1629, it was decreed that Feckenham was 'freed from forest laws' and the partitioning of the 2,100 acres of Crown woods and wastes within the forest was announced.

---

[79] SP14/70, no. 44; SP14/87, no. 75; SP14/141, no. 359; E178/4781.
[80] *CSPD 1625–6*, pp. 521, 547; see above, p. oo. [81] E125/7, fol. 75r–v.
[82] E134, 6 Chas. I, Easter 18. [83] E125/7, fols. 75r–7v.

Table 13.1. *Allotment of forest waste and woodland, June 1629 (acres)*

	Crown	Manorial lords	Foresters[a]	Total
Feckenham	140	360	400	900
Hanbury	550	80	270	900
Bradley	100	60	140	300
Total	790	500	810	2,100

[a] Including allocation for cottagers and poor.
Source: calculated from E125/7, fols. 75v–8r.

In Feckenham, the Crown reserved 60 acres in Berrow wood and
80 acres in Warkwood, and a further 60 acres nearest to the woods
were set aside for the poor. Edward Leighton, as lord of the manor,
was offered four of the Crown coppices covering 360 acres in
exchange for consenting to the disafforestation and releasing any
claim on common rights in his manorial capacity. The remaining 340
acres of the woodland and forest waste was to be distributed amongst
the inhabitants who possessed common rights. In Hanbury, Leighton
was offered 80 acres in Monkwood whilst a further 120 acres of the
Cleeres were allocated to the freeholders and copyholders and 100
acres allotted to the inhabitants of ancient cottages. A further 50
acres was set aside for the inhabitants of Blickley and Holloway whilst
both Meere Green and Broughton Green were left out of the
assessment. The Crown claimed the remainder of the forest waste and
woodland, being 550 acres. In Bradley, the Crown had no woods but
reserved 100 acres of the soil of the waste freed from common rights.
A further 60 acres were allocated to Sir William Sandys as manorial
lord and the residue of 140 acres was distributed amongst the
freeholders and cottagers. Each 'ancient' cottage was to be allowed
one and a half acres and each new cottage one acre in lieu of an
allocation for the poor.[84]

Disafforestation removed 2,100 acres of woodland and waste from
the agrarian economy of Feckenham, and in its place proposed to
offer the foresters who could claim the common rights 810 acres, the
vast majority of which was to be enclosed at the commoners' expense
by 1 March 1630. The Crown laid claim to the majority of the
Cleeres and Monkwood in Hanbury and offered most of its coppices

[84] E125/7, fols. 75v–8r.

in Feckenham to Edward Leighton. Apart from the generally unsuccessful attempts to enclose parts of these woodlands by Connard, these areas of the forest had always been subject to the right of foresters' common which had been affirmed many times by the swanimote and manorial courts.

The substantial share of the waste land taken by the Crown in Hanbury and Connard's earlier destruction of woodland in the Cleeres and Monkwood ensured that the inhabitants of Hanbury were prominent in the opposition to disafforestation. This opposition manifested itself in numerous complaints about the specific allocation of land and the Crown's refusal to accept the claims to common rights made by particular landholders. But the widespread and prolonged nature of the opposition, across the entire forest community, was the consequence of a more fundamental grievance. Disafforestation represented a reimposition of Crown property rights rather than a confirmation of existing practice and boundaries. As far as the forest inhabitants were concerned, they enjoyed extensive common rights in the forest gained by prescription and enshrined in manorial custom.[85] These rights were denied by disafforestation, as the Crown reclaimed its property and granted a substantial part of it to the manorial lords within the forest.

The response to the allocation of land in June 1629 was immediate. A group of thirty-two leading inhabitants of Feckenham and Hanbury began the opposition to disafforestation by refusing to accept their allocations of common land.[86] They were dissatisfied with the procedures adopted and claimed that they had been forced to agree to them 'for fear and by terrible threats'. Of the principal inhabitants who had represented Hanbury in the negotiations, only Edward Leighton and William Connard were content. The remaining four representatives, including William Cookes, were opposed to the allotment. They claimed that the allowances made in Hanbury to compensate for the loss of common in the Crown lands were insufficient. Furthermore, certain inhabitants had been bribed to accept disafforestation with offers of additional allotments of waste land. Connard was at the centre of this and had offered at least two foresters, William Lacy and John Huntingdon alias Butler, 40 acres each in Warkwood to gain their consent. In the event, Connard had been the only beneficiary of these deals and had been allotted 40 acres

---

[85] These rights were claimed repeatedly by the foresters, E134, 6 Chas. I, Easter 18.
[86] E125/7, fols. 80v–1r.

in Berrow wood for his assistance to the commissioners. One of the most influential opponents of disafforestation was Gilbert Smith, a substantial Hanbury yeoman and representative of the inhabitants. At first he was persuaded by Fleetwood and Connard, but when the terms became clear he considered the Hanbury allowance far too small and blamed Connard for misleading the inhabitants.[87]

By October 1629, the foresters had moved to the offensive and a total of 155 of them complained to the Court of Exchequer and asserted rights of common which had not been recognised by the Fleetwood allotment. The Attorney-General described them as lesser inhabitants who had no right to allotments and were hindering disafforestation by making 'false claims' to common rights. He dismissed them as 'new pretenders', primarily assart holders, inhabitants of newly erected cottages and undertenants by lease or at will.[88] In fact, these protesters were a more varied group and represented the widespread and fundamental opposition to disafforestation amongst the farming and cottager population of the forest. Freeholders were almost as numerous as leaseholders and whilst about 70 per cent of those who can be identified held lands worth £10 per annum or less, there were some substantial farmers amongst them.[89] Henry Shayland of Berrow in Feckenham, for example, held land in fee simple with a reputed value of £60 and engaged in dairy farming on a commercial scale.[90] Another freeholder, Henry Leadbeter, held freehold land at Hanbury, Feckenham and Bradley.

Leadbeter had become accustomed to grazing sheep and cattle throughout the forest and he had served as a regarder at the swanimote of 1604.[91] Some inhabitants held land by lease in addition to freehold or copyhold properties. Foresters like George Butler, who rented lands worth £12 per annum as a supplement to his freehold lands of £10 per annum, were only entitled to an allotment of common for the land they held in fee. But many were cottagers who relied even more upon the common grazing, but had less claim to pasturage under forest law because they occupied cottages built

[87] E134, 6 Chas. I, Easter 18.
[88] E125/7, fol. 98r–v; E125/8, fols. 296v–7r.
[89] It is possible to identify 45 of the 155 'new pretenders' from E134, 15 Jac. I, Easter 3; E178/4781; E134, 6 Chas. I, Easter 18; E125/8, fol. 297r–v.
[90] Worcester RO, Probate Inventories, BA 3585, 1644/114.
[91] E134, 15 Jac. I, Easter 3.

Table 13.2. *The 'new pretenders' to common rights in 1629*

Yearly value of holding	< £2	< £5	< £10	> £10	Total
Leaseholders	4	5	4	4	17
Freeholders	6	2	3	5	16
Copyholders	1	3	1	2	7
Combined estates*a*		1	1	2	4
Tenants-at-will	1				1
Total	12	11	9	13	45

a Copyhold or freehold with leasehold.
Source: see n. 89.

within living memory. They included Francis Mogg, a labourer who kept a horse, a cow and seven sheep on the commons; Edward Weston, a carpenter, with a cottage but no land of his own; and William Bond, a shoemaker and carrier, who kept two nags, a mare and five sheep in the Cleeres.[92]

Although the majority of the 'new pretenders' were cottagers who supplemented their earnings as farm labourers, leatherworkers, woodcraftsmen and carriers, by grazing a few sheep in the forest waste, they were closely allied with the farming population in their opposition to disafforestation. Both cottagers and farmers placed a high value on unrestricted common rights within the forest. During 1629 and 1630 they argued relentlessly for rights of common 'throughout the waste and all unenclosed grounds' of the forest, which had been enjoyed from time immemorial and they feared that the forest would be 'straightened by inclosure'.[93] One of their strongest advocates was John Baylies, a Hanbury yeoman, who asserted that if disafforestation went ahead, many of the 'new pretenders' would be 'deprived of much of their means by a reduction of their common'. The Attorney-General saw things differently and considered their aim was to 'encroach unto themselves the whole benefits of the pasture and feeding of the said forest' once the Crown's privileges within the forest had been extinguished by disafforestation and the deer and much of the timber removed.[94]

The 'new pretenders' were successful in delaying enclosure. In

[92] Worcester RO, Probate Inventories, BA 3585, 1638/116; 1640/237; 1636/7.
[93] E134, 6 Chas. I, Easter 18.
[94] E125/8, fol. 297r.

November 1629, the barons of Exchequer yielded to the pressure of protest and decided to examine the multitude of claims to rights of common. Whilst the claims were examined, no enclosures could be made except on the land reserved for the Crown. On this land, gaps were left in the fences and hedges and the inhabitants continued to graze cattle and sheep throughout the forest.[95] In June 1630, however, the Exchequer ruled that none of the assart holders, undertenants or inhabitants of 'new' cottages were justified in objecting to the allocation of common land. Most of the 'new pretenders' had no right under forest law to common-of-pasture and according to Attorney-General Noy 'their pretence hath been by sufferance'.[96] The Court of Exchequer was able to exclude many inhabitants who had traditionally kept animals on the forest commons because forest law was interpreted as part of the Crown prerogative. No one could claim rights of usage or prescription as they could under manorial custom or the common law, and thus the common rights acknowledged by the swanimote and manorial courts were now denied.

In November 1630, a commission was granted for the final allotment of all common land within the forest and for the enclosure of the Crown land. Whilst not conceding to the pressure of the 'new pretenders', the Exchequer did increase the allocation of land in Hanbury by 90 acres and reduced the Crown's portion from 550 acres to 460 acres in recognition of the substantial imbalance created by the initial partition in June 1629.[97] This did little to appease the inhabitants of the forest. The landowners were ordered to enclose all lands by 1 March 1631 and the execution of this commission in the Crown lands sparked off the first forest riot on 28 March 1631.[98]

The riot was a direct response to the final enclosure of the Crown lands and no doubt exacerbated by the hardships resulting from the enclosure of common land at a time of grain shortage. In 1630, the harvests of oats and wheat were very poor and that of barley was disastrous.[99] The riot occurred at the end of winter when natural feed for stock as well as grain was in short supply and therefore when the impact of depleted common pasture was most apparent. Almost 3 miles of fencing around the Crown lands was thrown down by some

---

[95] E125/8, fols. 102v, 120v, 122v, 138r, 298r, 299r; E125/7, fol. 291v.
[96] *Ibid.*, fol. 349r.   [97] *Ibid.*, fols. 393v–4r.
[98] E125/9, fol. 249r–v.
[99] Harrison, 'Grain price analysis', pp. 151, 154.

300 rioters armed with spades, bills and pitchforks and by the end of April, cattle and sheep were depasturing throughout the forest as they did before enclosure.[100]

Both farmers and cottagers were involved in the riot and an examination of what the Privy Council called the most 'stirring offenders' establishes a clear connection between the rioters and the conflicts within the forest over the preceding two decades.[101] Six of the eight ringleaders were Hanbury yeomen and their role in the rioting was the culmination of an opposition to the restriction of common rights within the forest which they had sustained over almost twenty years. Two of the Hanbury rioters were amongst the most respected forest inhabitants. Gilbert Smith was chosen to represent Hanbury by the Exchequer commission for the allotment of land in 1628, whilst Henry Turner was one of the regarders at the swanimote courts in the first decade of the seventeenth century. William Steward was one of Connard's most determined opponents as early as 1616 and he was indicted for rioting in 1631 along with his son William. The other three Hanbury rioters, including John Baylies, had been amongst the inhabitants who first opposed disafforestation in 1629 and they were named as 'new pretenders' in 1630. One of these was John Elvins who was the son of John Elvins of Hanbury, an important figure in the swanimotes of the late sixteenth century. Another, Robert Boulton, had collected money to assist the poorer people called to London to defend their claims to common rights in 1630. He was a long-standing opponent of Connard and especially vocal in condemning the wanton destruction of the forest.[102]

The riot in Feckenham was not an isolated incident. During early 1631, riots against disafforestation also took place in the Forest of Dean and shortly afterwards in the Wiltshire Forests of Braydon, Chippenham and Melksham.[103] The fundamental importance of common rights in the forest economy and the limitation of these rights after enclosure were at the root of the riots. In all these forests, the inhabitants had traditionally surcharged the wastes but found

---

[100] J. Rushworth (ed.), *Historical Collections, The Second Part* (London, 1680), Appendix, Star Chamber reports, p. 48; E125/9, fol. 249r.

[101] SP16/461, fol. 95.

[102] STAC8/25/9; E178/4781; E134, 6 Chas. I, Easter 18; E125/7, fol. 80v; E125/8, fol. 297r-v.

[103] For a more detailed account of the western riots, see Sharp, *In Contempt*, esp. pp. 82–155; D. G. A. Allan, 'The rising in the west, 1628–1631', *EcHR* 5 (1952–3), pp. 76–85.

themselves excluded from prescriptive rights by the forest law.[104] The Braydon commoners echoed those of Feckenham in warning that enclosure would be 'the utter undoing of many thousands of poor people that now have right of common within the forest and do live thereby'. Braydon also experienced similar tensions to those described in Feckenham when the authority of the swanimote court was overruled by the executive branch of forest government in the early seventeenth century. As in Feckenham, the forest officers plundered the woodlands in a seventeenth-century form of 'asset stripping' as the Crown hesitated over disafforestation.[105]

The disturbances in Braydon and Dean were unified by a military style of rioting.[106] The uprisings were as much a vent for the anger and frustration felt by the forest inhabitants as they were a practical attempt to throw down enclosures. The second Feckenham riot of 17 March 1632 shared many features of the 'Rising in the West'. Most of the rioters were 'masked and disguised' and carried pikes and muskets. They appeared in the forest in a 'most daring manner' marching with a drum and other 'warlike ensigns'.[107] Some of them were substantial local farmers. Two of Connard's foremost opponents, Gilbert Smith and Henry Turner, were again prominent amongst the rioters, as was William Penn, a powerful advocate of the prescriptive right to forest common. But many of those who rioted in 1632 were poor people or 'foreigners' and this second riot appears to have been a final defiant, if rather futile, gesture in the face of the Crown prerogative.[108]

Whilst many rioters in Feckenham, particularly in 1632, were drawn from the poorer element of society, most dependent on the forest commons, there is overwhelming evidence of leadership by the more substantial inhabitants and the involvement of the entire forest population in the opposition to disafforesting.[109] In both the

---

[104] E. Kerridge, 'The revolts in Wiltshire against Charles I', *Wiltshire Archaeology and Natural History Magazine*, 57 (1957), pp. 66–9; Hart, *Commoners of Dean Forest*, pp. 20–5.

[105] Manley, 'Disafforesting of Braydon', pp. 556–8.

[106] Allan, 'Rising in the west', pp. 76–85; Sharp, *In Contempt*, pp. 94–107.

[107] *CSPD 1631–3*, p. 289; PC2/41, fol. 255r. By the early eighteenth century disguises had become a common feature in forest riots, immortalised by the 'Waltham Blacks', Thompson, *Whigs and Hunters*, *passim*.

[108] PC2/41, fols. 243r–v, 246v, 254r.

[109] The assertions made by Professor Sharp that the rioters in the western forests were overwhelmingly the poorest inhabitants is not supported by the evidence of Feckenham. Sharp, *In Contempt*, pp. 126–55. The class nature of the forest riots has been questioned more

Feckenham forest riots of 1631 and 1632 a clear descent can be discerned from the enfeebling of the swanimote courts of the late sixteenth century, through the corruption and damaging administration of Connard to the final surrender in disafforestation. The rioters placed a high value on the extensive and traditional common-of-pasture within the forest and were prepared to use force against a challenge from outside. They were aggrieved by the way these rights had been destroyed and were bewildered by the Crown's refusal to recognise prescriptive rights to common.

IV

Any assessment of the effectiveness of the attempts made by the Crown to improve the revenue of the royal forests must balance the local social and political costs against the purely financial benefits. The widespread and intense opposition to disafforestation was a reaction to the violation of deeply rooted values and the challenge to the validity of customary rights within the royal forests. This was especially apparent in Feckenham where the custom of foresters' common was unanimously upheld by the inhabitants and where the manorial and forest administration had become closely intertwined. This was unravelled by the Crown prerogative at a time when manorial customary rights were in the ascendant in the central courts.[110] Moreover, this prerogative was exercised through courtiers and collaborators and relied on Exchequer officers rather than the forest courts for its execution. It was interference from outside in the affairs of the forest and could not fail to evoke strong opposition.

The problem for the Crown had its origins in the progressive neglect of the distant forests from the late fifteenth century. By the early seventeenth century, the Crown was even uncertain about the extent or value of its royal forests.[111] More importantly, the collapse of the medieval forest law and its administration had allowed a new order to emerge. The forest courts administered an entirely different forest law based on prescriptive rights and favourable to the

---

generally by Professor Underdown. D. Underdown, *Revel, Riot and Rebellion. Popular Politics and Culture in England 1603–1660* (Oxford, 1985), pp. 108–12.

[110] P. Large, 'Rural society and agricultural change: Ombersley, 1580–1700', in J. Chartres and D. Hey (eds.), *English Rural Society, 1500–1800. Essays in Honour of Joan Thirsk* (Cambridge, 1990), pp. 120–3.

[111] Pettit, *Royal Forests*, pp. 42, 53, 55.

inhabitants rather than the Crown. Feckenham was typical of the distant forests in the manner in which it functioned.

It is only in the context of the Crown's neglect of the forests and the opposition in the localities that the financial assessment of the attempts to improve the revenue from the royal forests can be made. The survey of Feckenham in 1612 described the forest as 'well set with oaks for the most part good timber trees' and considered that 'this forest to be disafforested and severed into parts will be worth 20,000 marks to the King in fines'.[112] In the event, the Crown saw a derisory return from the sale of this timber and could command a fine of only £4,000, some 30 per cent of its original expectation, when alienating its remaining interest in the forest in 1631.[113]

The early attempt to prise more revenue from Feckenham Forest at the beginning of the seventeenth century proved to be destabilising. The imposition of fines for assarts created its own pressures and was directly responsible for the increased destruction of the Crown's woodland. The Crown's indecision over disafforestation served only to intensify destruction to the further detriment of the Crown. As in the case of other forests, the Crown had to reestablish its rights and even the boundaries of the forest in order to disafforest Feckenham. This required the acquiescence of the local manorial lords and the Crown had to pay for this support by permitting the partition of the forest rather than an orderly allotment of common land strictly according to common rights.[114] Inhabitants with rights of common under forest law received their allotments after the Crown had made generous grants to the manorial lords. Dissatisfaction with disafforestation was fired as much by the inadequacy of allocations to legitimate claimants as by the absence of allotments to 'new pretenders' who claimed a right of common by usage.

In Feckenham, the Crown ceded the majority of the forest waste in order to free its property from forest law. After a final concession in Hanbury, the Crown retained just 460 acres, under a fifth of the forest waste. It still had to grapple with local opposition, and was unable to enclose its land until 1632. The real beneficiaries of disafforestation were the principal forest officials and manorial lords on whose goodwill the Crown relied. William Connard, the forest ranger,

[112] LR2/194, p. 19.
[113] E125/7, fols. 85v–6r.
[114] It is difficult to accept that a partition of this kind represents enclosure by agreement as suggested by Professor Sharp. Sharp, *In Contempt*, p. 155.

made a handsome return through his ruthless exploitation of the forest and by his allotment of forest common. For Edward Leighton, lord of the manors of Feckenham and Hanbury, disafforestation was an outstanding success. He secured 440 acres of the forest common, including the most valuable Crown coppices in the forest. In 1631, he moved promptly to sell his improved interest in both manors and clear his debts.[115] Against this background, the reimposition of the forest laws must have appeared to be a rather attractive alternative to disafforestation for the Crown.

[115] VCH, *Worcestershire*, III, pp. 114, 375.

CHAPTER 14

Reflections on the history of the Crown lands, 1558–1640

Richard Hoyle

Our purpose has been to delineate and describe as much as to offer any novel interpretation of the place of the Crown's estates in early modern English history. In doing this, we have shown how wrong it is to assume that the estates were some quaint backwater of government finance, run indifferently on uneconomic lines or merely a vehicle through which patronage could be exercised. On the contrary, the Elizabethan estates were managed in ways which were indeed rational although the fiscal exploitation of the estates was compromised by the need to use them for patronage and recreation. The first decade of the new century certainly marked a turning point in the history of the estates; but for the moment let us consider certain aspects of the Elizabethan estates.

In the introduction to these essays, it was suggested that from the early 1550s a deliberate policy was pursued of stabilising net income at its maximum level by cutting the charges placed on it. The estate administration was reduced (although not as far as some intended); the burden of repairs was passed on to the tenants.[1] A low premium was placed on fines on leases or copies. Private individuals were invited to identify concealed lands at their own expense in return for a preferential grant. It can be argued that the fixed rental policy was in one respect the only policy possible. The scale of the enterprise and the scattered and unsystematic character of the estates, the lack of administrative staff, the unclear lines of responsibility established in the 1554 reorganisation, the need to devolve authority to local officers of uncertain reliability and the involvement of private individuals, lessees and tenants in the defence of the Crown's interests all contributed to the difficulty of making any positive improvement on the estates.

Nonetheless, it is hard to see either any or all of these restraints as

[1] See above, pp. 33–44.

being individually decisive in the determination of policy. There is a clear sense in which Burghley, as Lord Treasurer, failed to reform the estates, either in the sense of carrying through the incomplete reforms of the 1550s or pressing the Crown's claims as landlord. At the same time, he presided over their sale. It cannot be argued that he was uncommitted to the management of the estates. On the contrary, his work on the leasing and sale commissions, his role as the recipient of petitions from tenants and his application to his judicial duties in the Exchequer reveal an enormous expenditure of time and energy. Indeed, it would be unfair to characterise his management of the Elizabethan estates as being entirely without regard to business principles. The Crown may be praised for good housekeeping in its strenuous attempts to discover concealed lands and rents, but neither contemporaries nor historians have been impressed by these efforts, preferring to see them as a vexatious nuisance. And at the same time as it was trying to recover such scattered parcels, it was also disposing of much the same sort of lands through the mechanism of the exchange. It must be admitted that individual exchanges were often manipulated to the Crown's disadvantage. But this was not an exclusively Elizabethan problem, and the exchange (and even reexchange) was a means by which positive improvements could be effected.[2]

Moreover, the Elizabethan policy towards the estates possessed several virtues. The first was that it acknowledged the social obligations of lords and tenants. Queen Elizabeth's attitude to the issues which historians have identified as the 'agrarian problems of the sixteenth century', enclosure, depopulation, the conversion of arable to pasture and so on, is unknown, but requires examination. On at least one occasion, her intervention in a tenurial dispute was used for propaganda advantage. Mr Kershaw has shown the hostility of the Privy Council to the improvements which the earl of Shrewsbury was trying to effect in Glossopdale (Derbyshire) in the late 1570s and early 1580s. The Queen's councillors clearly subscribed to the view that disorder was caused by landlord rapacity and that disputes between the landlord and tenant should be resolved by the

---

[2] For exchanges, see above, pp. 79–81. Dr Thomas cites the cutting of timber by lord Clinton on land to be exchanged. Buckingham was accused of accepting manors in exchange from the Crown, cutting woods, making leases and enfranchising copyholders before surrendering the lands back at the same rent. It would be profitable to know with what justice these accusations were made and whether this practice had official connivance. C. Russell, 'The parliamentary career of John Pym, 1621–9', in P. Clark, A. G. R. Smith and N. Tyacke (eds.), *The English Commonwealth, 1547–1640* (Leicester, 1979), p. 153.

former's moderation or withdrawal of his claims. Hence Shrewsbury was told that he should make 'an end with them and rather to be a loser than to abide their clamour'.[3] It seems likely that the Queen and her elder councillors shared a distaste for agrarian modern-isation. At the individual level, both Burghley and Mildmay are known to have been conservative landlords. They were not alone; as late as 1601, lord Darcy could see it as a virtue that he had lived, as his father had before him, off the old rents of his lands.[4] The Queen herself was praised for this by Bacon; 'Pass on from the mint to the revenue and receipts. There you shall find no raising of rents, notwithstanding the alteration of prices and the usage of the times; but the overvalue, besides a reasonable fine, left for the relief of the tenants and reward of servants.'[5] The failure to 'modernise' tenurial arrangements was not merely an accident borne of ignorance of prevailing circumstances, but a commitment to an ideal of social organisation in which landlord and tenant lived in peace. Burghley's willingness to shoulder a heavy judicial burden may be seen as additional evidence of his subscription to this view of society.[6] The generation rising in the 1580s and later had little or no patience with such an ideal.

Secondly, the margin over and above the rental income could be used for purposes of patronage. As the Crown was generally disinterested in its receipts from fines, the fines could be granted to private individuals. This was in effect what happened in grants of leases in reversion: a lease was made without a fine as a form of patronage at the cost of losing a fine in the future. The grantee had an asset from which he could profit by either waiting until the existing lease expired or by selling the reversion on, normally, it would appear, to the sitting tenant. As Dr Thomas shows, the means

---

[3] S. E. Kershaw, 'Power and duty in the Elizabethan aristocracy: George, earl of Shrewsbury, the Glossopdale dispute and the council', in G. W. Bernard (ed.), *The English Nobility in the Sixteenth Century* (Manchester, 1992), the quotation from a letter of Secretary Wilson's; C. Haigh, *Elizabeth I* (Basingstoke, 1988), p. 151.

[4] Burghley's biographer says that 'He could never like or allow to put out any of the Queen's poor tenants.' 'He did never raise his rents, nor displace his [own] tenants. But as the rent went as he bought the lands, so the tenants still held them. And, as I know, some of his tenants paid him but £20 p.a. for a thing worth £200 which they enjoyed during his lordship's life.' This account, though, is written in ideal terms and needs to be checked against more impartial sources. F. Peck (ed.), *Desiderata Curiosa* (2 vols., London, 1732), I, pp. 42–3. For Mildmay, see his aphorism cited above, p. 44. Darcy, HMC, *Salisbury*, XI, p. 516. For similar attitudes, see L. Stone, *The Crisis of the Aristocracy, 1558–1641* (Oxford, 1965), p. 304.

[5] 'Mr Bacon's discourse in praise of his Sovereign' (?1592), printed in Spedding, *Bacon*, I, pp. 129–30.   [6] Peck (ed.), *Desiderata Curiosa*, I, pp. 18–19.

by which this was done and the profits which could be realised were understood and what at first seems like an oppression turns out to be less than that (although it cannot be denied that there were many individual injustices).[7] Of course, the consequence was that much of the Crown's estate was leased long into the future, delaying the moment at which the Crown could act as an improving landlord; but this is to view the policy with hindsight. A contemporary could equally well have argued that as the estates were gradually being dispersed by either grant or sale, the granting of a lease in reversion was the means by which an advantage could be drawn from the estates before their sale. At the time, it served the end of offering a cheap (and sought-after) form of patronage at a time when the Crown could afford neither gifts of money nor land. The leases of franchises and offices described for Wales by Dr Gray can be seen as both a dimension of the exercise of patronage as well as the means by which the Crown satisfied its obligation to offer its tenants government.

A further justification for not increasing the burden on the tenantry concerns its capacity to undertake military service, but this was progressively less important as time passed.[8] The crucial changes here are two-fold: the professionalism of fighting and the establishment of militias and county levies in place of 'feudal' means of raising men. Crown stewardships were sought in the early sixteenth century not merely because of their fiscal profits, but for the *manrede* and hence status which they offered. Even that most civilian of figures, Thomas Cromwell, was not immune from this way of thinking, for he secured appointment as the Chief Steward of suppressed monasteries north of the Trent.[9] There can be no reason for this other than the aim of making a credible showing in time of war. As the ethos of the court became less martial, the expectation of war diminished and the gentry ceased to expect to have to raise men for war, their interest in stewardships came to wane.[10] So long as the estates served this end, improvements which might reduce the capacity of the tenants to

---

[7] See above, pp. 183–90.

[8] J. J. Goring, 'Social change and military decline in mid-Tudor England', *History* 60 (1975), outlines this type of thinking.

[9] *Letters and Papers of the Reign of Henry VIII*, XIV (i), no. 135; also C. Haigh, *The Last Days of the Lancashire Monasteries and the Pilgrimage of Grace* (Chetham Soc., third ser., 17, 1969), p. 107.

[10] It is an illustration of the obsolescence of such thought that there was no attempt to revive the practice of making the Prince of Wales and duke of York into regional magnates when their estates were reestablished for Henry and Charles in 1609.

serve in war by transferring a share of their income to the monarch were impossible. Hence, the loss of the military aspect of the estates removed a restraint on their reformation.

By the death of the old Queen, the logic which had sustained the Elizabethan policy had ceased to carry conviction. There was no longer an anxiety about prompting social discontent: indeed, in some areas, progressive reform could be seen as a contribution towards the relief of social problems. Military reputation was no longer earned or displayed by the accumulation of stewardships; a reaction against profiteering and peculation at the Crown's expense (seen in both the enquiry of 1600 and the bill against auditors moved the following year) diminished the desirability of stewardships yet further. The decision recorded in the Book of Bounty of 1608 to withhold leases in reversion from suitors must have stopped the estates being the small change of patronage.

All of these factors allowed the Crown to view its estates in a more commercial manner. But these changed circumstances did not themselves *permit* the reform of the estates. What allowed the Crown (or any other landowner) to increase its profits from land was finally the demand for land. A great deal of our assessment of the success or failure of the Crown's management must turn on an understanding of the extent to which it turned its back on possibilities for improvement which were common to all landowners and this in turn requires some estimate of when a new range of possibilities arose. This is not a simple matter, for we need to distinguish between the moment when trends in the agricultural economy were reversed and the point at which estate incomes began to rise. The first probably came well before mid-century; the second followed some distance behind, delayed by cultural and legal impediments. If a decade can be isolated in which landlords' incomes began to increase significantly, it may be the 1580s (although any such suggestion needs to be treated with caution until properly evidenced).[11] If such a late date can be accepted, then the Crown was perhaps only a generation behind the most advanced English landowners in adopting a commercial attitude to its land. This may be seen in the way in which the estates

---

[11] Bowden plumped for the 1570s or 1580s (*Agrarian History*, IV, p. 690). Stone thought he saw little change in rents before 1590 although large increases thereafter (*Crisis of the Aristocracy*, p. 327). Aylmer suggests there 'was no general and sustained increase in [the] revenues [of Oxford Colleges] before the 1580s or 1590s' although their position was somewhat different (G. E. Aylmer, 'The economics and finances of the colleges and university, c. 1530–1640', in J. McConica (ed.), *The Collegiate University* (The History of the University of Oxford, III, Oxford, pp. 532, 536). The whole issue cries out for detailed study.

adopted surveying. If the measurement and valuation of land with a surveyor's exactitude is a key moment in the growing commercialisation of land management, then there was perhaps a lag of only fifteen or twenty years between the adoption of these techniques by the most advanced landowners and the Crown.

A relatively short delay, perhaps, but one which was to prove decisive in the future development of the estates. The consequence was that when the Crown finally grasped the nettle, the opportunity for tenurial reform had largely passed. There is every reason to believe that the Crown was slow to take up other forms of improvement on its estates. Enclosure, whether of open-field arable or common, was certainly being undertaken, but one suspects that the initiative came from the tenants (who carried the costs). When the Crown was involved, it was to offer the sanction of the Exchequer or Duchy courts to legitimise the claims of its tenants against their neighbours. The Crown then can be seen as an irrelevance to the processes of social and economic change on its estates; it was a distant, perhaps disinterested, *rentier*. It is easy to suppose that the Crown was unique in this, but such a view should be resisted. One can point to many instances of landlords pressing forwards with modernising improvements of the sort which historians are prone to applaud; it is harder to ascertain how many others failed to do so or (like the Crown) missed the bus.

It cannot be said that the Crown's lax approach to its estates arose from a confident financial position. Writing of Ulster landlords in the early nineteenth century, Dr Crawford has recently argued that

Landlords knew that although many of the farms on their estates were let much below their true value, their total rentals continued to rise: farming was becoming more commercialised, wasteland was being reclaimed and competition for holdings was intensifying. They did not wish to incur the animosity of their tenants by shortening the length of leases and enforcing covenants, as long as they could continue to manage [on] their own incomes.[12]

Crawford's description of circumstances in which these landlords failed to take advantage of changing economic conditions has broad similarities with the Crown's experience in the late sixteenth century. Where the analogy breaks down is in the needs of the lords. If the Ulster landlords were financially secure, it is beyond argument that

---

[12] W. H. Crawford, 'The significance of landed estates in Ulster, 1600–1820', *Irish Economic and Social History* 17 (1990), p. 56.

the last decade and a half of Elizabeth's reign was one of severe
financial difficulties for the English state. The estates were surprisingly little mobilised to assist in war finance. The Crown appears
to have adopted none of the options open to private lords for raising
money – selling timber, making leases in reversion or pressing
forwards with enclosure. Instead, there was a willingness to sell land.
This was a reversion to the practices of the 1540s and subsequent
periods of war. The exact calculations involved in adopting this
option are far from understood (although Dr Thomas's point that
selling was cheaper than borrowing needs to be borne in mind), but
the fate of the Crown lands needs to be considered in the context of
the government's inability to reverse the progressive deterioration in
the yield of the subsidy.[13] Bacon saw a clear connection between the
subsidy and the sale of land: 'you shall find moneys levied upon sales
of lands, alienations (though not of the ancient patrimony), yet of the
rich and commodious purchases and perquisites of the Crown, only
because she [the Queen] will not be grievous and burdensome to the
people'.[14] This brings us back to the view of society which we
suggested was shared by Burghley and the Queen, but in this light we
see moderation as less virtue than a calculation borne out of political
weakness and insecurity. The old Queen sold land rather than make
taxation work. The instinct to do this did not die with Elizabeth;
successive Jacobean Lord Treasurers played with fee-farming,
Salisbury was a heavy seller of land although he deserves credit for
the bold initiative of the Great Contract. The preservation of rents on
sales made them less damaging than might at first appear, but once
the option of financing war from capital was exhausted, the problem
of how war should be funded once more became a political issue in a
way it had rarely been since the 1520s.

The experience of the Crown lands between the accession of James I
and the convening of the Long Parliament illustrates how new
notions of management were not enough in themselves to reverse the
problems of the estate. The temptation to liquidate lands to raise
capital for the payment of debts or for furthering war continued to be
irresistible. The continued recourse to sales effectively undercut the
hopes of improvement. The tenants of some cottages in Rotherham
told the Exchequer court in 1605 that the Crown's lessee was asking

---

[13] See above, p. 86. I hope to discuss the relationship between the two on another occasion.
[14] Spedding, *Bacon*, I, p. 130. See also Mildmay's comment on this, above, p. 21.

thirty years' old rent as a fine from them; they objected that it was as much as the fee simple was worth. And so it was, and when the opportunity to buy the fee simple arose regularly, why should they pay a fine of that magnitude? Another commentator pointed out that the Crown was asking more of its tenants to enfranchise their copyholds than the contractors for the purchase of Crown lands had paid for fee simples.[15]

Despite the considerable literature advocating surveying, it has yet to be shown that the new techniques of land measurement made any appreciable difference to the Crown's income from land. Whilst the surveyor's valuation could be used as the basis on which a copyhold fine could be charged, this was only possible if the custom of the manor permitted arbitrary fines, which, as we have seen, it generally did not. Nor can it be shown that the possession of surveys made any difference to the procedures involved in selling or leasing lands although the commissioners for sale in 1626 certainly had copious (though dated) survey evidence before them. The adoption of surveying techniques was part and parcel of a tightening of accounting procedures within the Exchequer. The commissions of 1600 into officers' malpractices and peculations were clearly the first shot, the issue of the Book of Printed Orders in 1608 the second. The supervision of local officers was taken a stage further by the Council of the Duchy of Cornwall which, as Haslam shows, ran the estates in minute detail and made its local officers the mere executants of Council warrants. Nothing of this sort appears to have happened in the Exchequer and the records of the jointure estates are too poor for us to know much of the quality of estate management there.[16] But before the Duchy Council is held up as an example of what ought to have become the practice elsewhere, it must be recalled that its estates were largely in the West Country where the tenants held by copyhold for lives; it was therefore blessed with an unusual freedom to take arbitrary fines.

Two problems stood in the way of the improvement of the Crown lands. The first was the intermittently pressing need for sales which made improvement futile. The second was the range of institutional barriers which prevented improvement either in the short or medium

---

[15] E112/134/934; see above, p. 253.
[16] Somerville sees the development of special sittings of the Duchy (of Lancaster) court for revenue purposes from at least 1618, but this needs further working out. Somerville, *Duchy of Lancaster*, II, p. 6.

term (leases), or in perpetuity (copyhold of inheritance). The difficulty of scaling these impediments increased as more were erected over time as the result of pressing financial needs; the leases of 1609, the confirmation of copyhold customs and (had anything very much come of it) the fee-farming of the estates. The potential for reform was persistently sacrificed for short-term expediency. In this light, the most significant area of activity in the early seventeenth-century Crown lands lies not in the modernisation of tenurial arrangements or enclosure, but in the search for concealments or the revival of atrophied or extinct franchises.

Concealment hunting was not a seventeenth-century innovation. Dr Thomas shows it in use under Elizabeth and Dr Gray describes how Leicester's patent to search for concealments in the Forest of Snowdon poisoned relations there for a generation.[17] But as Dr Thirsk shows, concealment hunting became much more than the search for the detritus of monastic and chantry lands which had escaped the grasp of the Exchequer. It involved the investigation of anyone whose title arose from a Crown grant. Those Elizabethan bishops who held lands granted by the Crown in exchange or as part of the remodelling of episcopal estates were especially harassed; a technical fault in the patent which granted the main estates of the see of Norwich in 1536 had to be answered by a statute in 1597–8. Fighting off an attempt to claim the lands of Southwell Minster as concealments, Edwin Sandys remarked that 'nothing can stay these covetous cormorants which seek their gain by other men's losses', a sentiment which would have found widespread support.[18]

Thirsk reveals how though the history of concealment hunting runs continuously through our period, its character was being constantly transformed. The common feature of all the campaigns was the use of legal procedure (or the threat of its use) to demonstrate the Crown's title to land which it no longer possessed. The principle is essentially the same whether we talk of assart lands, foreshores, the recovery of lands alienated from the Duchy of Cornwall, disafforestation or the revival of forest law. In every case, we are talking of land which was 'owned' – never land which was empty or unused – by individuals whose titles were either customary or, on a strict reading, defective. This sort of legal terrorism is quite familiar in the Irish context. In the abortive plantation of Connacht commenced in 1635,

[17] See above, pp. 150–1.
[18] F. Heal, *Of Prelates and Princes. A Study of the Economic and Social Position of the Tudor Episcopate* (Cambridge, 1980), pp. 232; SP46/33, fol. 301 (1585).

three-quarters of the lands to which their owners could show no satisfactory title were to be offered back to them with a new regular title; the remaining quarter was to be the Crown's share and made available for plantation.[19] Here, a tradition of nationalist history writing has stressed the dispossession of 'Irish' landowners by the English state in its Irish guise; the idea that much the same techniques were used in England itself has tended to be overlooked in the subscription of many historians to the notion that the English state was law-abiding.

Whatever form of concealment hunting in England we speak of, the aim was generally not to enlarge the Crown's estate. The idea was to coerce the occupier of the land, once persuaded of the defects of his title, into compounding with the Crown for the grant of a new patent to regularise his title.[20] In those cases where the Crown became the possessor of land (as in foreshores or disafforestation), it was immediately sold for ready money, sometimes to the occupiers, often to courtiers or other private men wishing to make an investment (or clear the Crown's debts to them) with the reservation of only a small quit rent.

This points to the basic flaw in the Crown's policy towards its estates. To improve income from leasehold tenants, a landlord could wait to re-lease at a commercial rent. The Crown's pressing need for money never allowed it that patience, but always drove it into the premature renewal of leases on disadvantageous terms. Once the possibility of eradicating customary tenures by legal means had passed, what drove private landownership forwards was investment, not in buildings or improvements, but in the purchase of land and the buying out of the customary or leasehold interests of tenants.[21] A case of these policies being put into effect on a Durham manor has recently been offered: it is particularly apposite in that the manor in question, Long Newton in Barnard Castle lordship, was, until the Great Contract sales of 1628, a royal manor. The tenants held by thirty-one-year leases and a single eighty-year lease; after the manor was sold to Sir Henry Vane in 1635, Vane and his son Sir George set

---

[19] Nicholas Canny, *From Reformation to Restoration. Ireland, 1534–1660* (Dublin, 1987), p. 196. These were similar proportions to those suggested in disafforestation.

[20] The exception to this is the recovery of the alienated estates of the Duchy of Cornwall. In the Irish context, the surrender of lands to the Crown to be returned with a new title is of course known as 'surrender and regrant' and implies a change in tenurial status; in so far as both imply the replacement of a 'defective' title with a regular one, the processes are the same.

[21] R. W. Hoyle, 'Tenure and the land market in early modern England: or a late contribution to the Brenner debate', *EcHR* 43 (1990), pp. 12–18.

about buying up the leaseholds and secured the enclosure of the
manor in 1658–9. Some leases were allowed to run to their full term
and were then renewed at higher rents; others were bought out. Vane
purchased the manor for £1,600 but spent over £1,000 on the
purchase of leaseholds. This was a heavy investment and the rewards
were seen only in the next generation. By 1677, the manor had a book
rental of £700 against c. £35 before 1628, with the tenants paying
about 6s an acre against the 4d an acre their predecessors were
paying in 1607.[22]

Investing in its estates was precisely what the Crown did not do.
On one of the rare occasions when it acted to enlarge the estates, by
redeeming the honour of Grafton from Sir Francis Crane, the exercise
had to be self-financing, thus creating just the sort of impediment to
future improvement mentioned previously.[23] Unable to raise the
money to buy out tenants' customary rights, nor able to wait for the
expiry of leases (when higher rents might be introduced), the Crown
sought to profit from this position by strengthening the tenants' titles
by granting confirmations or fee-farms or (as in 1609) making leases
which extended long into the future.

In the special case of disafforestation, the Crown invested nothing
in its newly minted land. In the early West Country disafforestation,
where the intention was clearly to keep the new lands and populate
them with tenants, the tenants themselves were responsible for the
capital investment which was needed to bring forth fruit.[24] The same
applied in the Irish plantations; the Crown sold the freehold of
plantation lands to undertakers who made the necessary investment.
The Crown invested not even in the infrastructure of the new English
society which it erected in Munster; other than policing the patentees
to see that they maintained their covenants, the Crown's only interest
was that of rent collector.[25] The pressure was always to release money
which could be expended on current pressing concerns; investment
in the lands was an unthinkable luxury.

No amounts of concealment hunting could undo the damage of
sales. Moreover, the financial returns were normally disappointing
and rarely came near to justifying the claims for them made by their
advocates. In 1611, Tipper agreed to generate £100,000 in revenue

[22] D. S. Reid, *The Durham Crown Lordships in the Sixteenth and Seventeenth Centuries and the Aftermath* (Durham, 1990), ch. 4, *passim*.   [23] See above, pp. 259–60.
[24] See above, pp. 384–5.
[25] M. MacCarthy-Morrogh, *The Munster Plantation. English Migration to Southern Ireland, 1583–1641* (Oxford, 1987), *passim*.

for the Exchequer in the following five years. His actual contribution was in the order of £12,000.[26] Disafforestation persistently disappointed. In his detailed working out of the disafforestation of Feckenham, Peter Large shows how the Crown's profits were eaten up by the need to buy the support of all involved through generous allotments of land.[27] It is appropriate to quote in this context Sir Richard Weston, who writing to Secretary Conway in 1623 observed of proposals concerning soap and alum, that they would prove to be like most projects, 'glorious in show, difficult to effect and of little profit in the end'.[28]

This begs the question of why projects were difficult to put into effect. The answer is in part that projectors always outbid themselves to secure support for their proposal; much more was promised than could be delivered. But it would be too much to believe that the possessors of concealments were anxious to co-operate with the Crown's agents. We are familiar with the disturbances which accompanied the disafforestation of forests in the West Country and elsewhere in the early years of Charles I's reign, but there were more outrages against the Crown's patentees than has been appreciated. In the small Lancashire Forest of Fulwood, the Duchy of Lancaster made an improving lease in 1623 which came to be acquired by the borough of Preston. When an attempt was made to ditch and fence the waste, the commoners destroyed the ditches and did so again in 1639.[29] It is harder to be certain that delays in implementing enclosure were the result of footdragging. Yet it has been shown earlier that this was the case with King's Sedgemoor and that something similar occurred in the Forest of Galtres.[30] The tenants of Middleham in Yorkshire, whom Dr Thirsk has shown being offered the purchase of their commons in 1610, resisted all brandishments. The commons (in fact the tenants' stinted cattle pastures) were found to be concealed in 1619, and offered to the tenants by lease (which they rejected), before being granted in fee-farm to the earl of Peterborough and Sir Henry Compton in 1632. The Crown's patentees failed to secure possession or draw any rent from the tenants and in 1639 sought permission to surrender their interest back to the

---

[26] W. Notestein, F. H. Relf and H. Simpson (eds.), *Commons Debates 1621* (7 vols., New Haven, CT, 1935), VII, p. 354; Dietz, *Issues and Receipts*, pp. 140–1.
[27] See above, pp. 416–17.   [28] *CSPD 1623–5*, p. 54.
[29] R. C. Shaw, *The Royal Forest of Lancashire* (Preston, 1956), pp. 450–3. See also the account of the disafforestation of Bernwood, p. 374 above.   [30] See above, p. 387.

Crown.[31] But it would not be true to suppose that such a bloody-minded refusal to co-operate was characteristic of the inhabitants of Wensleydale alone. The Crown's attempt to claim the foreshore of the Thames downstream of the City of London was not attended by any greater anxiety on the part of the tenants to compound.[32] The truth is that property was property wherever it was found and the Crown, as an interloper, was invariably opposed.

In other circumstances, the Crown found it hard to stir up interest. The sale price of Crown lands failed to rise to the degree that contemporaries desired. It was plainly unable to persuade its customary tenants that it was in their interest to enfranchise or seek confirmations of their copyhold estates. Even the Duchy of Cornwall was unable to obtain from its tenants considerations of the size to which it believed it was entitled when trying to persuade them to compound for their defective titles. The tenants of its Durham manors appear to have simply withheld their co-operation from its attempts to increase their rents.[33]

The idea that tenants could and would hinder their lords' schemes for the improvement of their estates at this late date has been little considered by historians. And yet, in these cases, they evidently did, and with some success. The Crown was exposed, though, on two flanks. In the parliamentary forum, the search for concealments was the subject of hostile debate. In 1604, a private bill to grant a title to the occupiers of assart lands who could prove possession for a hundred years and a day successfully passed the Commons but was suffocated in the Lords. It was not until 1624 that a Statute of Limitations (giving title to occupiers with sixty years' possession) passed into law. In the same session, a further statute circumscribed the freedom of the Duchy of Cornwall by denying to future dukes the right to disown their predecessor's leases and forbidding them to put up rents.[34] The further reafforestation of the country through the use of medieval perambulations was forbidden by a statute in 1641 which made provision for the final determination of forest boundaries.[35]

It is thus easier to see why the Crown's estates developed in the way they did. Its freedom of manoeuvre was heavily restricted by

---

[31] See above, pp. 329–30; for the later history, *CSPD 1631–3*, p. 108; *CSPD, 1638–9*, pp. 575–7. I hope to write further about this matter in the future.

[32] See above, p. 341.   [33] See above, pp. 252–3, 260–1.

[34] See above, pp. 295, 338, 400; W. Notestein, *The House of Commons, 1604–1610* (New Haven, CT, 1971), pp. 34–5, 494; statutes 21 Jac. I c. 2, c. 29 (*SR*, IV (ii), pp. 1210–1, 1240).

[35] Statute 16 Chas. I c. 16 (*SR*, v, p. 119–20).

institutional limitations on its freedom – long leases, copyholds, the need to work through stewards and private undertakers – some of the Crown's own making, others forced on it by the logic of managing a scattered estate constantly undergoing a process of dissolution and regeneration as land entered and left its control. When the Crown did attempt to improve its position, it often met with the opposition of those who had a proprietorial interest in the estates as either tenant or commoner. In a simple conflict over competing property rights, it is not clear that the Crown, despite its legal and coercive powers, could ever win when its opponents showed so great a willingness to resort to violence or the boycotting of the Crown's projectors. On the other hand, the Crown, although the greatest single landowner in the century after 1540, never had the financial resources required to modernise the estates through the purchase of competing property rights. In fact, the demands of government could only be met through the sale of additional estates. The Crown was therefore imprisoned by the logic of its situation.

It needs to be stressed that the Crown was doing much more than selling land: it was progressively dismembering the whole legal superstructure which can broadly be characterised as feudal. In Elizabeth's reign, it was manumising serfs. In James's, it was selling whatever residual rights it possessed over copyholders. The Great Contract of 1610, had it succeeded, would have closed the door on concealment hunting and the assart lands project by extending the Statute of Limitations of 32 Henry VIII to the King.[36] In the later 1630s, the extension of the boundaries of forests was accompanied by the willingness to sell the Crown's newly discovered rights to the freeholder. Reafforestation was merely the occasion to invite a final disafforestation. Feudal tenures as a whole were effectively abolished in 1646 and finally wiped away by the Statute of Tenures of 1660.[37] But the Crown had shown itself willing to sell its prerogative rights a generation earlier, offering wardship for regular taxation in 1610 and debating the sale of the lesser incident of respite of homage in 1626–7.[38] Nothing came of either proposal; but it may be seen how the statute of 1660 merely concluded a process upon which the Crown itself had embarked. The willingness to turn any of the

---

[36] Notestein, *House of Commons*, pp. 265, 347.

[37] See most conveniently, A. W. B. Simpson, *A History of the Land Law* (second edn, Oxford, 1986), p. 23.

[38] On respite of homage, there is much unpublished material in the minute books of the commissioners for retrenchment, University of London Library, MS 195.

Crown's rights into a saleable commodity, culminating in the sale of its fee-farm rents in the 1650s and after, shows the estates slowly and progressively dissolving under the general insolvency of the state.[39] As this happens, we witness not only the propulsion of property from possession under a medieval, feudal system of land law to an absolute freehold, but also the collapse of the financial basis of medieval monarchy. What finally emerged was government supported by parliamentary taxation (especially the Excise), whose landholdings were essentially for recreation and status. The progressive decline of the Crown lands was a decisive factor in the emergence of the modern state.

[39] For the sale of fee-farm rents, S. J. Madge, *The Domesday of Crown Lands* (London, 1938, repr. 1968), pt ii, ch. 5; C. D. Chandaman, *The English Public Revenue, 1660–88* (Oxford, 1975), pp. 113–15.

Index

The counties named in this index are those existing before the reorganisation of 1 April 1972.

For EU product safety concerns, contact us at Calle de José Abascal, 56–1°,
28003 Madrid, Spain or eugpsr@cambridge.org.

www.ingramcontent.com/pod-product-compliance
Ingram Content Group UK Ltd.
Pitfield, Milton Keynes, MK11 3LW, UK
UKHW042316180425
457623UK00005B/15